Ius Gentium: Comparative Perspectives on Law and Justice

Volume 111

Ius Gentium is a book series which discusses the central questions of law and justice from a comparative perspective. The books in this series collect the contrasting and overlapping perspectives of lawyers, judges, philosophers and scholars of law from the world's many different jurisdictions for the purposes of comparison, harmonisation, and the progressive development of law and legal institutions. Each volume makes a new comparative study of an important area of law. This book series continues the work of the well-known journal of the same name and provides the basis for a better understanding of all areas of legal science.

The *Ius Gentium* series provides a valuable resource for lawyers, judges, legislators, scholars, and both graduate students and researchers in globalisation, comparative law, legal theory and legal practice. The series has a special focus on the development of international legal standards and transnational legal cooperation.

Vesna Rijavec • Wendy Kennett •
Tomaž Keresteš • Tjaša Ivanc
Editors

Diversity of Enforcement Titles in the EU

Springer

Editors
Vesna Rijavec
Faculty of Law
University of Maribor
Maribor, Slovenia

Wendy Kennett
Cardiff University
Cardiff, UK

Tomaž Keresteš
Faculty of Law
University of Maribor
Maribor, Slovenia

Tjaša Ivanc
Faculty of Law
University of Maribor
Maribor, Slovenia

ISSN 1534-6781 ISSN 2214-9902 (electronic)
Ius Gentium: Comparative Perspectives on Law and Justice
ISBN 978-3-031-47107-0 ISBN 978-3-031-47108-7 (eBook)
https://doi.org/10.1007/978-3-031-47108-7

This work was supported by Justice Programme of the European Union

This Springer imprint is published by the registered company Springer Nature Switzerland AG
The registered company address is: Gewerbestrasse 11, 6330 Cham, Switzerland

Paper in this product is recyclable.

Foreword

I was happy to accept an invitation to write a foreword to this book. Academics and practitioners owe the elaboration of this (further) work to Prof. Dr. h.c. dr Vesna Rijavec. For many decades, she has creatively initiated and implemented international projects thanks to her energy and perseverance. Voices from smaller EU Member States have obtained and continue to obtain a surprisingly significant hearing in these projects. These voices deserve to be heard. For it is especially in places where the distance to the border—and therefore to a neighboring country—is short that people gain experience of everyday cross-border issues that, although apparently minor, nevertheless prove quite complicated to resolve.

Such experience has a positive effect when there is trust between those involved and common solutions can be found. This is made easier by a willingness to get to know and to understand the procedural law and procedural reality of the "other" states. When it comes to questions of enforcement, this is both necessary and arduous: the enforcement laws of the individual states are extremely diverse (including in terms of the way that they are implemented in practice). And this means that the ways that EU civil procedural law interacts with the enforcement laws of the Member States are also diverse. It is important to foster a proper understanding of these interrelationships in order to resolve the problems that arise. These are the objectives that inspired the experts who contributed to this book: contributions for which they deserve thanks and appreciation.

Graz, Austria
December 2022

Wolfgang Jelinek

Preface

Due to a persisting lack of mutual trust, national authorities of EU Member States continue to treat enforcement titles from other Member States with reservations and mistrust. The diversity of national rules on the enforcement titles significantly contributes to this problem. Accordingly, the main objective of the book is to address judgments, court settlements, and authentic instruments, their types, structure, contents, and effects, from a comparative legal perspective, in interplay with the rules on recognition and enforcement under the Brussels I bis Regulation. We consider it as an important scientific contribution, that the chapters provide a general overview of enforcement titles with an attempt at their systemization. On the other hand, the book offers several chapters with a more in-depth legal analysis of the elements of the system. The authors approach the research topic from both a practical and theoretical angle, offering important insight for academia as well as practice. Special contribution to the theory of civil procedure is reflected in discussions on the effects of enforcement titles; these expert discussions reveal the existence of a universal character of the binding effects of enforcement titles, which can be understood by equal arguments. To ensure a holistic understanding of the research topic, select contributions focus on the *lis pendens* effect and the effect of related actions, which are innately linked to the effect of *res judicata* judgments. Namely, the rules on the rejection of recognition and enforcement of foreign titles in Brussels I bis also include the irreconcilability of two enforcement titles. It thus raises the question of the identity of two titles, which has to be systematically and coherently explained in the rules that the Brussels I bis includes for preventing the existence of multiple titles. Altogether these rules address the thorny question of the identity of claims, which the CJEU often must deal with.

The book draws heavily from a rich source of national reports, case-law, and theory and intertwines the domestic approaches with supranational (cross-border) considerations. In this respect, the research findings may be of particular importance for any further (non)legislative intervention at both domestic and EU level, since they identify existing problems and seldom attempt to provide solutions for a more effective free movement of judgments within the EU—the silent, yet paramount element for the proper functioning of the internal market and a cornerstone of effective judicial protection.

The research findings are based on the outputs of the "Diversity of enforcement titles in cross-border debt collection in the EU" project (831628—EU-En4s—JUST-JCOO-AG-2018). The content of this book represents the views of the authors only and is their sole responsibility. The European Commission does not accept any responsibility for the use that may be made of the information it contains. The project was coordinated by the University of Maribor and performed jointly by a large consortium of partner institutions, chiefly among them universities. The tried and tested methods employed in the project have provided a bedrock of information and accumulated knowledge that was used in the preparation of the present book.

Maribor, Slovenia
September 2023

Vesna Rijavec

Contents

Contributors

Philipp Anzenberger University of Innsbruck, Faculty of Law, Innsbruck, Austria

Denis Baghrizabehi University of Maribor, Faculty of Law, Maribor, Slovenia

Darius Bolzanas Mykolas Romeris University in Vilnius, Vilnius, Lithuania

Eric Bylander Uppsala University, Faculty of Law, Uppsala, Sweden

José Caramelo Gomes University Portucalense Faculty of Law, Porto, Portugal

Katja Drnovšek University of Maribor, Faculty of Law, Maribor, Slovenia

Maria Dymitruk University of Wroclaw, Faculty of Law, Administration and Economics, Wroclaw, Poland

Tjaša Ivanc University of Maribor, Faculty of Law, Maribor, Slovenia

Remigijus Jokubauskas Mykolas Romeris University in Vilnius, Vilnius, Lithuania

Maria Kaczorowska University of Wroclaw, Faculty of Law, Administration and Economics, Wroclaw, Poland

Wendy Kennett Cardiff University, Cardiff, UK

Tomaž Keresteš University of Maribor, Faculty of Law, Maribor, Slovenia

Mykolas Kirkutis Mykolas Romeris University in Vilnius, Vilnius, Lithuania

Flutura Kola Tafaj University of Tirana, Faculty of Law, Tirana, Albania

Marie Linton Uppsala University, Faculty of Law, Uppsala, Sweden

Bettina Nunner-Krautgasser Institute of Civil Procedure and Insolvency Law, University of Graz, Faculty of Law, Graz, Austria

Eugenio Pereira Lucas Politécnico de Leiria, Leiria - IJP, Porto, Portugal

Marta Pertegás Sender Maastricht University, Faculty of Law, Maastricht, The Netherlands

Neža Pogorelčnik Vogrinc University of Ljubljana, Faculty of Law, Ljubljana, Slovenia

Vesna Rijavec Faculty of Law, University of Maribor, Maribor, Slovenia

Piotr Rodziewicz University of Wroclaw, Faculty of Law, Administration and Economics, Wroclaw, Poland

Dalia Višinskytė Mykolas Romeris University in Vilnius, Vilnius, Lithuania

Marielène Wertenbroek Maastricht University, Faculty of Law, Maastricht, The Netherlands

Part I
General Considerations and Classification of Enforcement Titles

Enforcement Titles Under Brussels I bis Regulation from National to EU Frameworks

Vesna Rijavec

Abstract The ambition of this chapter is to provide a systematic generalised presentation of judgments and other enforcement titles in interplay with the rules on recognition and enforcement under Brussels I bis Regulation. It starts with the general concept and list of enforcement titles, falling within the scope of Brussels I bis Regulation, taking into account the definition of 'courts and tribunals' and due process requirement. The categorisation of the term judgment with regard to different aspects is foremost based on the distinction of judgment v. decision. Further, it is necessary to provide a categorisation by type of proceedings, by type of the decision in depence on parties' autonomy, categorisation of judgments by their positive or negative relief, and by the scope of decision. A crucial part is devoted to the variety regarding the structure of the enforcement titles in different legal circles, from specific issues with the operative part to the delineation between the operative part and reasoning, the content of the operative part including joinder of claims and parties, and the problem of precision of the content. In this context, it is important to explain the extended role of the certificates under Brussels I bis Regulation. Moreover, the chapter explores the effectiveness of the free movement of judgments through the theories on finality and *res judicata* as well as the binding effect of the operative part and reasoning. Special focus is devoted to the enforceability effect and to provisional enforceability. In this context, the chapter also observes the European dimension of the identity of many claims and pendency rules, related actions, the irreconcilability of judgments, and the criticism of Article 45(1)(c) and (d) Brussels I bis Regulation. The specifics of court settlements and authentic instruments are dealt with separately (concept, incompatible authentic instruments, different types of enforceable authentic instruments). For drawing conclusions on the issues of enforcement titles, it was decisive to mention the national problems of terminology. By applying comparative legal arguments, the author rendered a selection for their significance in the generalisation of the particular problem, since a detailed overview of all possible elements is naturally not possible.

V. Rijavec (✉)
University of Maribor, Faculty of Law, Maribor, Slovenia
e-mail: vesna.rijavec@um.si

V. Rijavec et al. (eds.), *Diversity of Enforcement Titles in the EU*, Ius Gentium: Comparative Perspectives on Law and Justice 111,
https://doi.org/10.1007/978-3-031-47108-7_1

1 Introduction

The efficiency of debt collection is one of the important goals established in order to promote better economic results in the EU. A better operating system of debt collection in cross-border cases in the EU however needs the further expedited import of foreign enforcement titles into the Member States addressed and ultimately needs to be followed by efficient enforcement systems.

Brussels I bis Regulation No 1215/2012 on jurisdiction and the recognition and enforcement of judgments in civil and commercial matters created a regime with the objective of the 'free movement of judgments'. To this end, it abolished exequatur and introduced the reversal of the procedural initiative to invoke grounds against foreign enforcement titles. However, problems still arise in applying Brussels I bis Regulation, which only provides a very general framework, while very heterogeneous national laws govern the specifics and details. Regarding enforcement titles, their concept, structure, content, and effects still significantly vary from one jurisdiction to another. Despite the upgraded certificate of enforceability introduced by Brussels I bis Regulation, which is meant to further facilitate the acceptance of foreign titles in the Member States where the enforcement is being sought in the enforcement phase, it is still not always easy to identify all the necessary elements of a foreign judgment from the certificate alone. Therefore, the fruits of this research will provide further helpful insights into national rules regarding judgments and other enforcement titles in interplay with the rules on recognition and enforcement under Brussels I bis Regulation. The research has also been focused on dogmatic and empirical concepts that in the end reveal themselves to be familiar to one another.

In general, academic and policy debates on harmonisation and the Europeanisation of civil procedures are indispensable. These debates are quite commonly focused on the EU and international level and less on the national level. Still, a better understanding of national particularities is essential for raising mutual trust, which underpins the Brussels I bis Regulation regime.

On the other hand, the ambition of this chapter is not to offer a complete comparative review but, a discussion on the most significant comparative legal arguments. They are taken from the different Member States considered in this research, selected for their significance in the generalisation of the particular problem. Despite all the variety of rules, the conclusion could be drawn that all the legal orders concerned are based on the same principles and have very similar objectives. It is just that they adopt different ways of reaching that objective. Nevertheless, all the states considered have developed interesting solutions and, in this paper, it may prove interesting to get further insight into the approaches of Slovenia, Croatia, and Austria, which are those best known to the author. The discussion also draws on the other national reports from the EU-En4s project and the knowledge collected during the research and from the results of previous EU-Justice projects. Put simply, things are compared because of some commonalities that they share.[1]

---

[1]Kennett (2021), p. 14.

Investigating the objectives of an enforcement title, will enable us to consider the accompanying requirements, classification, and effects. Attention will be paid to bridging the gap between the perspective of the State of origin and that of the State where enforcement is being sought with regard to Regulation's mechanisms.

This research has demonstrated that one of the significant problems is that, due to differences in national legal orders, the EU rules are more difficult to implement in some Member States than in others. The conceptual differences in procedures lead to different interpretations, and solutions that seem obvious in one jurisdiction and are much less obvious in another.

2 The General Concept of Enforcement Title

In all jurisdictions, enforcement procedure is exclusively based on the possession of an enforcement title. Within the enforcement procedure, the substantive legal situation is not considered or verified again. Moreover, the basis for enforcement is only the title and not the original claim on which the title is based.

Thus, an enforcement title is a document of special quality—an authorising instrument, on the basis of which it is possible to require coercive enforcement of a claim that is determined in this document.[2]

For instance, under Slovenian law, the enforcement title is appropriate for further enforcement if the creditor and debtor, subject, type, extent, and time for fulfilment of the obligation are stated in it. The Slovenian rules are similar to the Croatian ones. Certification of enforceability is required, but in addition the enforcement title document needs to be suitable for enforcement. Generally said for all countries, suitability derives from the content of the document. Essentially, it has to be explicit enough to identify the creditor, the debtor, as well as the type, extent, and time for performance of the obligation. This is also comparable to the other systems researched.

Moreover, legal systems are distinct with respect to the way that they impose enforceability effects on the judgment. In Slovenia, Austria, Croatia and the Czech Republic the operative part imposing liability meets the requirement for the certification of enforceability after the judgment has become legally binding and the term for voluntary performance expired. By contrast, in Germany, they consider the fact that the enforcement procedure is conducted by enforcement organs that are not familiar with the decision-making process, the benchmark for clarity of the title thus has to be the perspective of an uninvolved third party. Such a person must be able to reach a conclusion as to what the creditor is entitled to demand from the debtor

[2]Statement formed upon Art. 21 Civil Enforcement and Security Act - Zakon o izvršbi in zavarovanju - hereinafter ZIZ (Uradni list RS, št. 3/07, 93/07, 121/07, 45/08, 37/08, 28/09, 51/10, 26/11, 14/12, 17/13, 45/14, 58/14, 53/14, 50/15, 54/15, 76/15, 11/18, 53/19, 66/19, 23/20, 49/20, 61/20, 13/21, 36/21) and compared to national reports in the research.

through the enforcement title alone. Thus, in German law, it is the function of the enforcement clause to deliver and render transparent all the information that is necessary for the enforcement procedure (Klauselerteilungsverfahren).[3] A fully two-tier system can be observed in Lithuania. Their courts generally issue a separate enforcement note on the basis of the judgment. Enforcement without an enforcement note is prohibited, Article 586 of Code of the Civil Procedure of the Republic of Lithuania (hereinafter CPC of the Republic of Lithuania).

According to Article 1386 of the Belgian Judicial Code, at the request of the winning party, the court's clerk will stamp the enforcement formula on the judgment to transform it into an enforcement title. Nonetheless, for a judgment to be enforced a condemnation in the judgment itself is required. Generally, the Operative Part is located at the end of the judgment. Additionally, the Operative Part is often preceded by the phrase: for these reasons ('Om deze redenen'/'par ces motifs'). Nevertheless, this phrasing is not required by law. Even when courts utilise this formula, they may phrase it slightly different, for example: 'pour ces motifs'. However, 'par ces motifs' is the most common one.

Furthermore, the operative part may also be contained in the statement of reasons of the judgment. The position and form of the operative part of the judgment, which constitutes the decision of the court on the dispute, are not mandated by the Law. It is however necessary that the operative part, even if it is incorporated within the statement of reasons of the judgment, should have its effect.

Thus, we can distinguish between unique enforcement titles (e.g. a judgment including an order in the operative part) and double enforcement titles (e.g. a judgment with a separate order for its enforcement). The formers are equipped with a certificate of enforceability which only certifies when this effect occurs and doesn't include information on the claim to be enforced. The latter include a precise order to perform with further information necessary for the enforcement procedure.

A closer look shows that the difference between both approaches is not really substantial in cross-border cases. In systems where the judgment itself contains an order, a judge or a clerk certifies that a judgment became *res judicata* and enforceable. It is certification of the occurrence of these effects. In the two-tier system the court subsequently equips the judgment with the order to perform and so gives it the effect of enforceability. In both cases a document receives the status of enforcement title while obtaining the enforceability effect. For cross-border objectives it is relevant that the enforcement title satisfies the national requirements in the State of origin. But even if the clause implies permission to start execution in the state of origin (e.g. the 'Klausel' in Germany), this effect cannot produce any power regarding the use of coercive measures in another state. We can conclude that in Germany and other countries where the specification of liability is provided in an additional note the enforcement title has to be considered with both parts.

[3] Wolf and Volkhausen (2018), p. 85.

3 List of Enforcement Titles

In all countries a normative list of enforcement titles exists. For example, sections § 1 of the Austrian Act on the Enforcement of Judgments ('Exekutionsordnung') and § 274 of the Czech Civil Procedure Code set up comparable exhaustive lists of enforcement titles for judicial enforcement. Regarding the French enforcement system, a list of enforcement titles is established in Article L111-3 Code des procédures civiles d'exécution (hereinafter CPCE). Portugal also sets up a list of enforcement titles.

Comparable to § 794 German ZPO, Article 584 CPC of the Republic of Lithuania provides a list of documents that constitute enforcement titles.

Swedish enforcement titles are listed in Chapter 3§1 of the Swedish Enforcement Code. Comparable to the German system, private enforcement matters are mainly based on court judgments.

The Dutch Code of Civil Procedure[4] distinguishes three categories of enforcement titles: court judgments, authentic instruments, and other titles designated by law as enforceable.

Regarding the Belgian system, it sets up three categories of enforceable titles. The most common category contains an executable copy of judicial decisions and notarial deeds.

In contrast to the aforementioned Member States and as a typical approach of English law, the British enforcement system does not have a clear enumeration of enforcement titles. There is no formal recognition or clear distinction of a category of enforcement titles.

Nevertheless, enforcement titles can be in general be categorised by type of decision or another document into three groups:

1. Decisions (judgments, decisions/decrees)
2. Court settlements
3. Authentic instruments.

4 Civil and Commercial Matters: Enforcement Titles in the Scope of Brussels I bis Regulation

Definitions of civil and commercial rights and relationships have some common roots but there are differences of detail in different countries. Individual national laws cannot be decisive for the interpretation of civil and commercial matters under Brussels I bis Regulation. Rather, general legal principles and objectives that can be

[4] Dutch Civil code - Wetboek van Burgerlijke Rechtsvordering, Stb. 2016 288.

derived from the convention system and also from the fundamental principles of the legal order of each State are the primary starting point.[5]

The CJEU has contributed to the definition of civil and commercial matters in many cases already for the purposes of the BC and subsequent procedural regulations. The CJEU leading rulings on the interpretation of the concept of 'civil and commercial' have been issued in connection with the recognition and enforcement procedure. Although, the same issue is already relevant in determining international jurisdiction, the classification of the case is decided again in the process of recognition and enforcement.

Focusing on the division between civil and commercial matters, we find that the concept of commercial matters has never been explicitly defined but is considered as a sub-area of civil matters. Even in France, where the autonomy of commercial law is particularly emphasised, the view has been taken that commercial law is part of civil law. We can conclude that the strict division between civil and commercial matters remains irrelevant for the application of Brussels I bis Regulation as both categories are subject to the same rules.

Some areas of civil law areas are expressly excluded from the scope of Brussels I bis Regulation but for the purpose of this research, this issue is of no real importance. National overviews of the of the concept of enforcement titles in the research consider all civil and commercial area titles.

On the other hand, administrative decisions are not titles for the purposes of civil enforcement, therefore the complex delineation between civil and administrative matters deserves a short presentation. In distinguishing between civil and administrative matters, national theories have sought to establish a substantive definition of civil matters or administrative matters, but without definite success (e.g. Administrative Procedural Act ZUP,[6] Article 2). If there is no express provision, the administrative procedure shall apply if, for reasons of public interest protection, this arises from the nature of the matter. The ZUP defines an administrative matter as deciding on the right, obligation, or legal benefit of a natural or legal person or another party in the field of administrative law. Even this definition in the ZUP still does not exclude problems of overlap in national cases if the law has not yet determined the type of case. In Germany, issues concerning the distinction between administrative and judicial jurisdiction are addressed in discussions on the principle of separation of powers and the right to judicial protection.[7]

According to the case law of the CJEU, it is generally necessary to examine the subject matter at issue to distinguish between civil and public-law or administrative matters. The decisive factor is the exercise of public authority concerning the disputed subject or the fact that these are acts of specific authority subject to different

[5] Nagel and Gottwald (2007), p. 80.

[6] General Administrative Procedure Act - Zakon o splošnem upravnem postopku, ZUP (Uradni list RS, št. 24/06 - uradno prečiščeno besedilo, 105/06 - ZUS-1, 126/07, 65/08, 8/10, 82/13, 36/20 - ZZUSUDJZ, 61/20 - ZZUSUDJZ-A, 175/20 - ZIUOPDVE, 203/20 - ZIUPOPDVE, 3/22 - ZDeb).

[7] Geimer et al. (2005), p. 38.

rules from civil law.[8] The court might not take into account the nature of the powers of the authority, but the nature of the specific act, depending on whether the act falls within the exercise of public authority or not.[9]

From the recent case law, there continues to be an ongoing need for the CJEU to interpret borderline cases. In the case TOTO,[10] the court decided that an action for interim relief before a court of a Member State relating to penalties in respect of the performance of a contract for the construction of a public expressway concluded at the end of a procurement procedure where the contracting authority is a public authority falls within the concept of 'civil and commercial matters', because mere a fact that certain activities have a public purpose is not a sufficient element for the unequivocal treatment thereof as being carried out *iure imperii* if those activities do not involve the exercise of public authority. In the case, an action for interim relief was taken in order to ensure rights within a legal relationship (a contract) between the parties in which those parties have accepted the rights and obligations which they have freely agreed upon, regardless of the contract award procedure and public purpose of the object build under the contract.[11]

We still see some space for discussion on a possible upgrade in Brussels I bis Regulation for the more precise delimitation between civil and administrative matters.

5 Judgment

5.1 Concept

The most common general enforcement titles are judgments. A judgment is the conclusion or the result of court proceeding. In some countries, the form of a 'judgment' is reserved just for decisions on the substance of the matter, other decisions are named and formed differently. A judgment delivered in one State as a decision on a procedural issue may, in another state, be treated as a decision on a matter of substance. The same type of judgment may vary in scope and effects in different countries.

Nevertheless, Brussels I bis Regulation Article 2(a) tries to overcome national differences with a rather broad definition of the term 'judgment', to ensure that most court decisions issued in the EU will fall within its scope. In comparison to the

[8]Thus, expropriation proceedings do not fall under Article 1 of Brussels I Regulation, see Geimer et al. (2005), p. 134.

[9]Kaye (1999), p. 433.

[10]Case C-581/20, Skarb Państwa Rzeczypospolitej Polskiej reprezentowany przez Generalnego Dyrektora Dróg Krajowych i Autostrad v. TOTO SpA — Costruzioni Generali, Vianini Lavori SpA, 6.10.2021, ECLI:EU:C:2021:808.

[11]See also Case C-551/15, Pula Parking d.o.o. v Sven Klaus Tederahn, 09.03.2017, ECLI:EU: C:2017:193, paras 38-39.

national concepts of judgment, the concept in the Brussels I bis Regulation is far more inclusive. However, this definition is not very precise. Therefore, the definition of a 'judgment' has been elaborated by the CJEU. The question of whether a judgment is capable of recognition and enforcement must be interpreted autonomously, taking into account the overall scheme, the objectives, and the origin of the specific instruments of EU law.[12]

However, first of all a national law or an international treaty in the Member States of origin must provide the document with the effect of finality or the status of an enforceable title as this is the prerequisite for the decision to obtain its enforceability effect (e.g. Article 17 of the ZIZ). The category of that instrument in the Member States of enforcement might be different, so that without a guarantee from the state of origin, it might not provide the submitted document with the force of an enforcement title. Here the primacy of EU law implies that the term judgment in the Brussels I bis Regulation shall have an autonomous meaning that is detached from national procedural law.

At a high level, it may be suggested that a 'judgment' has four essential characteristics. First, it involves a decision, the formation of an opinion by the exercise of judgement in the wider (and differently spelled) sense of the word. Secondly, the decision is that of a judicial body exercising the judicial authority of the State. Thirdly, the decision involves the determination by the judicial body of particular matters which have been submitted to its judicial authority. Fourthly, the decision has some binding character.[13]

Judgments can be categorised in different ways according to:

- whether the decision determines the matters submitted by the parties (substantive), or merely some aspect of the decision-making process (procedural),
- the nature of the matters to which the decision relates (e.g. judgments in rem and in personam),
- the circumstances in which judgment was given (e.g. merits, default and consent judgments),
- identity of the court or tribunal (e.g. judgments of superior or inferior courts),
- the type of proceedings (e.g. civil and criminal judgments; ordinary and class action judgments),
- origin (domestic and foreign judgments),
- the relief granted by the decision (e.g. performance judgments, constitutive or declaratory judgments),
- whether the decision is final or partial.[14]

Some of the categories will be dealt with in more detail below.

---

[12]Case C-456/11, Gothaer Allgemeine Versicherung AG and Others v Samskip GmbH, 15.11.2012, ECLI:EU:C:2012:719.

[13]Dickinson (2007).

[14]Dickinson (2007).

5.2 *Bodies Conforming to the Definition of 'Courts and Tribunals' Under the Brussels I bis Regulation and Due Process Requirement*

Brussels I bis Regulation only applies to decisions issued by the courts or a tribunal but does not provide a definition of what constitutes a court or a tribunal.

The detail of the court systems in Member States are evident from the European legal atlas in civil matters.[15] On the other hand, discussions are found concerning certain bodies, and whether or not they are courts or tribunals. In Sweden two uncertain examples are the Rent and Tenancy Boards, and the Swedish Foreign Intelligence Court.

Bodies that do conform to the definition of courts in Sweden are the Labour Court, the Migration Courts and the Migration Court of Appeal, the Land and Environment Courts, the Land and Environment Court of Appeal, the Patent and Market Court, and the Patent and Market Court of Appeal, and the Maritime Court.

Other bodies, not just (*stricto sensu*) courts, may also decide on the issue of an enforcement title (e.g. notaries in abbreviated procedures in connection with payment orders in Hungary and Enforcement Authority ('Kronofogdemyndigheten') in abbreviated procedures relating to payment orders and assistance in recovery in Sweden).

Croatia also transferred judicial powers to notaries to undertake a summary procedure for issuing a so-called 'writ of execution'which contains two parts: (1) a payment order based on an 'authentic document' ('vjerodostojna isprava', more accurate translation would be 'credible document') and (2) grant of permission to enforce the said order. In the famous case of Pula Parking CJEU interpreted the relevance of such a notarial writ of execution as an enforcement title according to Brussels I bis Regulation,[16] the CJEU first approved that the case fits within Brussels I bis Regulation as a civil matter even though the procedure for the issue of a payment order was initiated for prohibited parking by a company owned by a local community against a natural person who was a resident in another Member State.

The decisive fact was that payment was claimed for the costs of removal of the car into a public car park, the management of which was conferred by the community on the creditor company. According to the CJEU, this claim was not punitive, but intended for the recovery of payment for the service rendered.

But at the same time, the CJEU ruled that the decision did not fall under the Brussels I bis Regulation because it was not issued by a court or other body which is equal to the court as required by the Regulation. The term 'court' should include institutions other than a court having jurisdiction over matters falling within the

[15] European Judicial Atlas in civil matters, European e-Justice Portal, https://e-justice.europa.eu/content_european_judicial_atlas_in_civil_matters-321-en.do.

[16] Case C-551/15, Pula Parking d.o.o. v. Sven Klaus Tederahn, 09.03.2017, ECLI:EU:C:2017:193.

scope of the Brussels I bis Regulation, but only if the Member State concerned communicated this exception to the Commission. Since Article 3 of the Brussels I bis Regulation refers only to bodies that are explicitly notified to the Commission as did Hungary and Sweden, notaries in Croatia are not covered by it, because Croatia did not give notification concerning the notary public's authority when issuing a payment order.

Additionally, an authority might be accepted as a court under Brussels I bis Regulation if the right to defence is guaranteed in a procedure which resulted in a judgment. The CJEU ruled that the legal remedy of opposition to the court against the writ of execution is not satisfactory. Although it is true that debtors have the opportunity to lodge oppositions against writs of execution issued by notaries and it appears that notaries exercise the responsibilities conferred on them in the context of enforcement proceedings based on an 'authentic document' subject to review by the courts, to which notaries must refer possible challenges, the fact remains that the examination, by notaries, in Croatia, of an application for a writ of execution on such a basis is not conducted on an *inter partes* basis.[17]

The relevance of notarial 'writ of execution' (summary proceedings concerning order to pay and consecutive authorisation of enforcement) was raised again in another case Zulfikarpašić not related to Brussels I bis Regulation but to EEO Regulation 805/2004.[18] The answer of the CJEU was very much the same as in the case Pula Parking. Notaries were not considered a court and writ of execution not a court decision. The test was also made if the document could be certified European enforcement order as an 'authentic instrument'. The answer was negative, because there was no obvious consent of the debtor with the claim and the uncontested nature was lacking. Again the CJEU stated: 'A national procedure whereby a writ of execution is adopted without service of the document instituting the proceedings or the equivalent document, and whereby information is provided, in that document, to the debtor about the claim, having the effect that a debtor is aware of the claim only when that writ is served on him, cannot be classified as *inter partes*.'

Later Croatia made notification of the transferred judicial powers to notaries to the Commission but the problem connected with the issue that the writ of execution based on an 'authentic document', is served on the debtor only after the writ has been adopted, without the application by which the matter is raised having been communicated to the debtor should be reconsidered.

The problem of this procedural standard is even broader than just in the context of notaries. It rases concerns of when summary proceedings for orders to pay at all may produce European enforcement orders under EEOR 805/2004. Since, summary

[17] See Case C-551/15, Pula Parking d.o.o. v. Sven Klaus Tederahn, 09.03.2017, ECLI:EU:C:2017:193, para 58.

[18] Case C-484/15, Ibrica Zulfikarpašić v Slaven Gajer, 09.03.2017, ECLI:EU:C:2017:199: Mr Zulfikarpašić brought an application for enforcement before a notary against Mr Gajer, domiciled in Germany, on the basis of an invoice, which was classified as an 'authentic document' under the Croatian Law on Enforcement. The notary issued a writ of execution based on that document which became definitive in the absence of any objection by the debtor.

procedures are particularly meant to issue *ex parte* payment orders with the aim they become enforceable if the debtor does not oppose them in time (e.g. Austrian Mahnverfahren, §§ 244 ff Austrian ZPO). We understand that according to EEOR 805/2004 some additional minimum standards to presume the silent debtor's consent with the claim have to be met and their disregard hinders certification. On the other hand, a payment order issued in the form of a court decision e.g. 'writ of execution' or another decree must according to Brussels I bis Regulation be subjected to recognition and enforcement with no limitations. A possible violation of a right to defence can be used later in a proceeding to invoke grounds against foreign judgment.

However, if we consider the Croatian legal remedy 'opposition' in the role of an appeal to the court, we cannot say that it does not sufficiently secure the protection of the rights of the debtor to satisfy the requirements of Article 6 ECHR. Despite being served with an *ex parte* issued decision together with the original application, the right to be heard is for the debtor established with the right of lodging opposition. Receiving the well-founded opposition, the court starts from the very beginning to adjudicate the case dealing with the application as with an ordinary action.

5.3 Judgment v. Decision

For the concept of 'judgment' within the meaning Brussels I bis Regulation, the form or the name given by the court of origin is not relevant. The definition in Article 2 (a) includes any judgment from Member States, whatever the judgment may be called, including a decree, order, decision or writ of execution, as well as a decision on the determination of costs or expenses by an officer of the court. It is a very broad definition that does not clearly distinguish between judgments in *stricto sensu* and other types of decisions. Therefore, replacement of the word 'judgment' with the general word 'decision' has been discussed *de lege ferenda*, as being a more neutral and generic term that should include judgments and other decisions.[19] However, the word judgment still has the strongest meaning with regard to the authoritarian decisions in all jurisdictions, and is the first to come to mind in adjudicating disputes. Therefore, Private International Law traditionally builds recognition and enforcement on the term judgment. The other documents for the purposes of recognition and enforcement by PIL are embraced using the clause 'judgments and the decisions equated with judgments'.

From a terminological point of view, another problem in discussions was the meaning of a term 'decision' which is used for the most general category of documents but also for the category of a group of decisions that are lower than judgments.

[19] See in this volume Bylander and Linton, Types of Judgments According to Different Criteria.

The majority of approaches in the EU Member States actually distinguish between decisions on the merits of the case—which are called judgments—and other decisions in proceedings—which are labelled differently. Germany and Austria differ between 'Urteil' and 'Beschluss' and most other countries too. The Slovenian ZPP for example, only authorises two types of court decisions, a judgment ('sodba') and a decision ('sklep'). The Swedish division is similar. A judgment ('dom') is a court's decision on the substance of the matter. A decision ('beslut') is a court's decision that does not concern the substantive matter but is usually a formal issue, for example, inadmissibility.

In order to omit the ambiguity, it would be possible to concretise the word decision with an additional explanation 'decision on procedure or other matters'. But this alone does not provide an adequate solution. To facilitate distinction between the two groups, the occasional usage of the word 'decree' seems more suitable. A decree/'Beschluss' is a separate type of decision regardless of its title as order or injunction. We stay aware that in the English language, translation of word 'Beschluss' with the word decree might sometimes be misleading.

5.3.1 Writ of Execution

This type of decision need separate attention as although the term is, used by non-English speakers it is hard to translate due to differences in national law concepts. It might be understood as a certificate of enforceability or an enforcement order. In any given case when this term is used, therefore, it is very difficult for the reader who does not already know the enforcement system of the Member State in question to understand what is meant.[20]

In Germany the decision 'Vollstreckungsbescheid' is the second decision in the summary procedure for a payment order and in the English version is designated by the term 'writ of execution'. The specific German summary payment order procedure is divided into two steps, where the writ of execution is the second step and is still a title issued in a 'Titelschaffendes Verfahren' (Art 688-703 German ZPO).[21] It is also different from a German enforcement clause ('Klausel'), which gives the creditor the power to execute, and is not subject to recognition and enforcement in other Member States.

Here one has to mention too that the Slovenian and Croatian decision/decree of enforcement based on an 'authentic document' ('sklep o izvršbi na podlagi verodostojne listine', 'rješenje o ovrsi na temelju vjerodostojne isprave') could be translated as a writ of execution as well.[22] In Slovenia this decree consists of two

[20]Kennett (2018), p. 328.

[21]Zivilprozessordnung, ZPO, BGBl. I S. 3202, ber. 2006 I S. 431, 2007 S. 1781, zuletzt geändert durch Gesetz vom 05.10.2021 (BGBl. I S. 4607) m.W.v. 01.01.2022.

[22]See English version of Case C-551/15, Pula Parking d.o.o. v. Sven Klaus Tederahn, 09.03.2017, ECLI:EU:C:2017:193.

parts: a payment order and at the same time a permit to enforce the claim with coercive means. Thus, this second part, as a judicial authorisation of enforcement, is not part of the enforcement title but is already the start of the coercive enforcement of the title. For this reason, this second part cannot be subject to recognition and enforcement. Furthermore an 'authentic document' itself is not an enforcement title but only a piece of evidence of special importance. It has just evidentiary value and does not develop any presumption of the truth, neither the reversal of the burden of proof. In Slovenia and Croatia, the creditor can start the summary procedure for payment only if he possesses an authentic document determined by law from which the required debt derives. The law determines the types of documents capable to serve as authentic/credible documents (e.g. invoices, cheques, bills of exchange etc.). Similar Austrian procedure 'Mandatsverfahren' became obsolete in the present time replaced by 'Mahnverfahren' which for the start does not require any authentic document.[23]

In this context it has to be pointed out that the very broad definition of 'judgment' in the Brussels I bis Regulation in the Article 2 (a) expressly listing a writ of execution, still does not mean that this includes foreign orders for the execution of a title applying coercive measures.

On the other hand, the term writ of execution has a specific notion in Anglo-American system that it does not correspond to the meaning of Brussels I bis Regulation. A writ of execution is a document issued by a court requiring or giving authority to put in force the judgment or decree of a court. These are typically given to a sheriff or other officer of the law, or directly to the person who is the subject of the judgment or decree.[24] Various different writs of execution exist. The most common type is a writ ordering the officer to seize tangible movables.

All of the above indicates that the writ of execution in common law follows a judgment and is just the authorisation for using coercive enforcement.

The fact that Brussels I bis Regulation in the Article 2(a) expressly lists a writ of execution, still does not mean that this includes foreign orders for the execution of a title applying coercive measures.

5.3.2 Decision/Decree in Merits of a Case

Legislators can intentionally introduce the form of a decision/decree instead of a judgment for a decision on the substance of a case to indicate that the decision is issued in a special civil procedure e.g. summary or non-contentious civil procedure. For example, the Slovenian ZPP determines the issue of a decision/decree in the summary procedure on payment orders (Article 431-441) and in disputes on disturbance of possession (Article 428) but not in small claims' disputes (Article 442).

[23] Rijavec (2018), p. 366.

[24] Kenton (2020).

Further in all Austrian non-contentious civil procedures (Ausserstreisverfahren) a decision is not a judgment but decision/decree/'Beschluss' (Article 36-44 AußStrG).

5.3.3 Decisions Besides the Main Claim: Decisions on Costs of Proceedings

Decisions on the assessment of costs for witnesses and experts are also enforceable, regardless of whether the decision on costs is included in a judgment or issued separately.[25]

5.3.4 Procedural Decisions

Decisions on Contempt of Court

Monetary penalties in the context of contempt of court (common law) as a means of enforcing injunctions, or enforcing performance via an astreinte (traditionally, France and the Benelux States) have two facets, being both an enforcement title and an order in the course of compulsion at the same time. Only a title can be recognised and enforced abroad (e.g. Slovenian provisional measures which can be divided into two parts: a title and authorisation of enforcement). If the two parts cannot be separated these are direct measures of enforcement. There is no provision for direct compulsion in the scope of the application of the Brussels I bis Regulation. However, we can find some signs of overcoming the general statement that it is strictly up to the states to decide on coercion on their territory. More attention should be paid to the reading of the case Realchemie Nederland[26] where the CJEU implicitly considers the application of Brussels I bis Regulation to an order imposing a fine for infringement of intellectual property rights. The fine was imposed on Realchimie pursuant to Paragraph 890 of the German ZPO (Erzwingung von Unterlassungen), by order of the Landgericht Düsseldorf, which is a coercion order but was anyway considered capable of recognition and enforcement in another Member State.[27] The cited decision was limited just to infringement of intellectual property, under Article 1 of Directive 2004/48 which concerns the measures, procedures and remedies necessary to ensure the enforcement of intellectual property rights.

[25] Schlosser (1979), the Schlosser Report.

[26] Case C-406/09, Realchemie Nederland BV v Bayer CropScience AG, 18.10.2011, ECLI:EU:C:2011:668, para 43.

[27] It has to be mentioned that the CJEU hasn't decided explicitly because the national court has not referred any questions on that point.

Decisions regarding contempt of court,[28] e.g. on fines imposed on witnesses, experts, and other participants for breaches of discipline at a hearing in any court proceeding shall be enforcement titles for civil enforcement.

According to the Schlosser report a court order appointing an expert and entrusting him to examine a building and report on its quality, however, affects the parties' position and rights. Before issuing such an order the court will indeed at the very least verify that the party requesting the appointment of an expert has a credible case to make. As such it should not be excluded from the scope of the regulation. On the other hand, priority must be given to the evidence regulation in order to obtain evidence located in another Member State. Hence a judgment ordering the hearing of witnesses, or the production of documents should be deemed to fall outside the Brussels I bis Regulation.[29]

5.3.5 Decisions for Inspection of a Document in Civil Proceedings

If there is a duty on a person other than one of the parties to hand over or permit inspection of the documents relevant for the litigation, the court may, in the evidentiary procedure, issue a decision on the delivery of documents, which is an enforcement title to be executed *ex officio* (Article 228 ZPP). This decision is capable of recognition and enforcement. On the other hand, a decision that a party must disclose and permit inspection of documents in Slovenian law is not an enforcement title. The court just has to evaluate the circumstance that the party refuses to comply with the court's order. It is the same in Croatia, Germany, and Austria. If in some countries orders to hand over documents are enforceable against parties too as a contempt of court, the question is if they fall under Article 2(a) Brussels I bis Regulation. However, the priority must be given to the Evidence Regulation.

5.3.6 Decisions on Admissibility of Procedure

The CJEU in the context of the old Brussels I Regulation interpreted procedural decisions on jurisdiction in the framework of Article 32 as being covered by a notion of judgment.[30]

If the court of a Member State declines jurisdiction on the basis of a jurisdiction clause, irrespective of how that judgment is categorised under the law of another Member State, such a decision is capable of recognition. Thus, the term 'judgment'

[28] Contempt of court is a legal violation committed by an individual who disobeys a judge or otherwise disrupts the legal process in the courtroom; Part 81 of the Civil Procedure Rules UK, which came into force on 1 October 2020, sets out the practices and procedures for contempt applications.

[29] Esplugues Mota (2016), Article 21, p. 543.

[30] Case C-456/11, Gothaer Allgemeine Versicherung and Others v Samskip GmbH, 15.11.2012, ECLI:EU:C:2012:719.

also covers those judgments that are restricted to a finding that the procedural requirements for admissibility are not satisfied (so-called procedural judgments).[31]

The CJEU in the Gothaer Allgemeine Versicherung case referred to the preamble to Brussels I Regulation and to 'the objective of free movement of judgments in civil and commercial matters'. That objective supports the position that the concept of 'judgment' for the purposes of Article 32 of Brussels I Regulation must be interpreted as encompassing judgments by which a court of a Member State declines jurisdiction on the basis of a jurisdiction clause. A failure to recognise such judgments could seriously undermine the free movement of judgments. The preamble also underlines the importance of the principle of mutual trust between the courts of the Member States in the recognition and enforcement of judgments, which also implies that that concept is not to be interpreted restrictively, in order to avoid, *inter alia*, disputes as to what constitutes a 'judgment'. That mutual trust would be undermined if a court of a Member State could refuse to recognise a judgment by which a court of another Member State declined jurisdiction on the basis of a jurisdiction clause. Nothing in the Brussels I bis Regulation has changed that broad meaning, even though the definition has been moved to Article 2(a).

One could however be more hesitant regarding a decision dismissing a claim for other procedural reasons. An example of dismissal for procedural reasons is a failure to comply with a time limit or to provide security for costs. It may be entitled to recognition. But, it is difficult to see how a party could benefit from the recognition of such a judgment.[32]

Nevertheless, completely procedural decisions (decisions on interim procedural conduct) do not attain a legally binding effect and are not capable of recognition.[33]

5.3.7 Decisions on the Course of Procedure

According to the Schlosser report, interlocutory decisions that are not intended to govern the legal relationships of the parties but to arrange the further conduct of the proceedings should be excluded from the benefit of the regulation. Orders made to set a hearing date or establish the order in which parties will present their evidence or submit their written pleading or to establish that certain evidence is admissible are therefore excluded from the scope of the regulation. In any case the relevance of such orders for the legal order of the state addressed is minimal if not non-existent as they relate to matters of procedural law of the state of origin.

[31] Kodek (2015), Articles 35–60 EuGVVO 2012, p. 476.

[32] Esplugues Mota (2016), Article 21, p. 544.

[33] Rijavec (2018), p. 365.

5.3.8 Judgments on Judgments

It has always been accepted that a judgment awarding a declaration of enforceability of a foreign judgment cannot in turn be the object of further recognition or enforcement proceedings. This is expressed in the French maxim 'exequatur sur exequatur ne vaut'.

5.3.9 'Merger Judgments'

To provide a more complete overview, the merger judgments shall be mentioned. These are judgments known in common law which incorporate a judgment from a third state with only a basic review. In H Limited,[34] the CJEU ruled that 'merger judgments' given by UK courts are decisions given within the meaning of Article 2 (a) of the Brussels I bis Regulation.

However, merger judgments are highly problematic as they allow judgments from third states—to which the principle of mutual trust does not extend—to circulate freely within the EU without any closer scrutiny. Recognition and enforcement can only be refused on the basis of Article 45(1)(a) of the Brussels I bis Regulation. However, the public policy clause only applies when the recognition and enforcement is manifestly contrary to the public policy of the Member State addressed. Usually, such violations must have already been raised before the court which has given the judgments for which recognition and enforcement is going to be refused.

The CJEU ruling might also encourage Member States to include merger judgments in their respective national laws in order to be attractive for foreign creditors.[35]

5.3.10 Procedural Decisions of Enforcement

Judicial acts adopted in enforcement proceedings are not capable of being recognised as judgments in other EU Member States.

5.4 Provisional, Including Protective, Measures

The Regulation explicitly refers to only a few exceptions which do not qualify as a judgment for its purposes. Article 2(a) does not include provisional, including protective, measures ordered by a court or tribunal which by virtue of this Regulation

[34] Case C-568/20, J v H Limited, 7.4.2022, ECLI:EU:C:2022:264.

[35] Hess et al. (2022), p. 18.

has no jurisdiction as to the substance of the matter.[36] Neither does it include *ex parte* provisional, including protective, measure although ordered by a court having jurisdiction under Brussels I bis Regulation on the substance of the matter, unless the measure is served on the defendant prior to enforcement.

Despite attempts in the Brussels I bis Regulation to build solid safeguards for creditors with an effective system of provisional measures, it remains the most problematic topic for cross-border enforcement, something which needs the further attention of legal scholars and practitioners.

When deciding which national measures fall under this provision of the Brussels I bis Regulation, the fact that the measure is a provisional or protective one in national law is not decisive, but rather the matter is judged in the light of the autonomous definition of the institution developed in the case law of the CJEU. The Brussels I bis Regulation also does not contain an explicit definition of the concept which would make it possible, in relation to an individual measure, easily to determine whether it falls within the scope of the Regulation or not. Therefore, the case law of the CJEU on the concept of a provisional measure is relevant.

The *lis pendens* rule of the Brussels I bis Regulation does not apply to provisional measures and enables multiple applications in the courts of different countries. [37] The court competent under national rules may, under Article 35 of that Regulation, also decide whether the main proceedings are pending in another Member State.[38] According to the Brussels I bis Regulation, it can no longer come to the conclusion that a measure issued in the State with jurisdiction to hear the substance of the dispute is contrary to a measure from another country, since the latter affects only the territory in which it is issued. On the other hand, an incompatible measure issued in the State having jurisdiction on the substance of the dispute is an impediment to issuing a measure in another Member State, since recognition and enforcement are automatic. The allegation that the decisions are incompatible, which is the reason for the refusal of recognition and enforcement, should be considered only in the case of measures taken in Member States that both had competence to adjudicate on the merits.[39]

Situations involving irreconcilable judgments can also arise if provisional measures have been granted by courts of country 'C', which do not have jurisdiction over the substance, on the basis of Article 35. Can the existence of such a measure be an obstacle to the recognition of provisional measures granted by courts of country 'A' which do have jurisdiction as to the substance?

[36] Relationship between the main proceedings and provisional measures, see Case C-581/20, karb Państwa Rzeczypospolitej Polskiej reprezentowany przez Generalnego Dyrektora Dróg Krajowych i Autostrad v TOTO SpA - Costruzioni Generali and Vianini Lavori SpA, 06.10.2021, ECLI:EU: C:2021:808.

[37] Hess (2010), p. 37.

[38] Schlosser (2009), p. 153.

[39] Rijavec (2018), p. 403.

All of these situations show the need for cooperation between the different courts. This type of cooperation could have indeed contributed to a better coordination of proceedings before the courts of different Member States. It was envisaged in the commission's proposal which expressly stated that 'if proceedings on the substance are pending in one court and another one is asked to issue a provisional measure, the proposal requires the two courts to cooperate in order to ensure that all circumstances of the case are taken into account when a provisional measure is granted'. Unfortunately, this idea is completely absent from the Brussels I bis Regulation, adopted in 2012. Finally, another different but related question may arise. One might wonder whether the existence of a decision granting provisional measures can be an obstacle to the recognition and enforcement of a foreign final judgment. In a 2006 decision, the French Cour de cassation[40] answered this question affirmatively. It held that a French provisional measure was an obstacle to the enforcement of a Greek final judgment. The reasoning was based on the concept of irreconcilability. The court held that this concept, within the meaning of the Regulation (then Convention), covers all judgments without distinguishing final and interim judgments. Even though the interim order is not *res judicata* as to the merits, that is enough as long as the two decisions have irreconcilable consequences. The solution was justified by the protection of the consistency of the forum's legal order. Commentators generally approved the solution.[41] Amongst other arguments, they invoked an important decision of the CJEU[42] about irreconcilable judgments which states that decisions on interim measures are subject to the rules concerning irreconcilability in the same way as other 'judgments'. Given the rationale, the solution would probably be the same in cases where French courts had theoretical jurisdiction over the substance and those where they did not.[43]

5.4.1 Intermediate Conclusion

Brussels I bis Regulation does not seem to address this question. It does not give priority to final judgments over provisional judgments. However, one can wonder whether the 2006 solution is compatible with the idea that a judgment from another Member State should be treated in the Member State of enforcement as if it had been given in that Member State. If this is the case, then surely a final decision should prevail over a provisional decision.

[40] Cour de cassation, civile, Chambre civile 1, 20 juin 2006, 03-14.553, Publié au bulletin.

[41] Ibid.

[42] Case C-80/00, Italian Leather SpA v WECO Polstermöbel GmbH & Co., 06.06.2002, ECLI:EU:C:2002:342.

[43] Boscovic (2018), p. 146.

6 Categorisation by Type of Proceedings

The case law has not set up any limitation regarding the type or stage of proceedings so that the term 'judgment' can cover non-contentious and contentious judgments, provisional or protective judgments and those which are final, and judgments that have become irrevocable and those against which an appeal may still be brought.

The following national decisions to perform an obligation issued in civil proceedings are enforceable but not all falling within the scope of Brussels I bis Regulation. These are:

- judgments and decisions issued in civil and commercial proceedings;
- decisions in non-contentious proceedings;
- a new enforcement title from enforcement proceedings, e.g., a special feature of the Slovenian enforcement law is also the decision on counter-enforcement. If the enforcement title has been later cancelled, the debtor can claim back the assets seized from the creditor within the enforcement procedure itself (Article 68 ZIZ);
- decisions in insolvency proceedings excluded from Brussels I bis Regulation;.
- decisions in proceedings before specialised courts; e.g. labour disputes and administrative disputes as well as arbitral awards do not fall in the scope of Brussels I bis Regulation.

On the other hand, criminal judgments and decisions shall be enforceable in respect of decisions in the adhesion procedure on a property claim.

7 Categorisation by Type of Decision Depending on Parties' Autonomy

7.1 Judgments by Default

The regulation applies likewise to judgments by default. Article 45 even provides a specific ground of refusal for this type of judgment. It may not always be easy to a certain whether a particular decision was rendered by default or must be considered to be contested. This is, in particular, the case with the various types of order for payment. The distinction is important since judgments issued *ex parte* do not benefit from the regulation's smooth mechanism of recognition and enforcement. The judgment issued by the CJEU in the Klomps case illustrates the difference within the framework of judgments in summary proceedings for the recovery of debts ('Mahnverfahren'). In that case a German creditor had issued an order for payment ('Zahlungsbefehl') against the Dutch company. After service of this order according to the rules prescribed by German law, the debtor failed to lodge an objection. The creditor then obtained an order for enforcement ('Vollstreckungsbefehl') which was later challenged by the debtor. It is clear that while the order for payment ('Zahlungbefehl') does not constitute a decision, an enforcement order must be considered to be a decision in the sense of the article. It will be a decision by default if the debtor has failed to lodge an objection. In order to characterise the decision, the court addressed must follow the rules of the state where the decision was rendered.

In the Netherlands before issuing a default judgment, the court first examines whether the document instituting the proceedings has been properly served on the defendant. In addition, the court examines whether the court fees have been paid by the claimant. Furthermore, the judge examines whether all formal requirements to issue a default judgment are met. If all the formal requirements are fulfilled the court grants the claim unless the claim appears to the court to be unlawful or unfounded. This examination is laid down in Article 139 Rv. This examination is not very extensive. It is a summary examination, so that the judge must prima facie be convinced that the claim is founded.[44]

7.2 Judgment on the Basis of Acknowledgment of the Claim

In the event of acknowledgment by the defendant, a judgment of acknowledgment or waiver (e.g. § 395 f Austrian ZPO) must be made at the request of the other party. In Slovenia, if the defendant has acknowledged the claim before the main hearing is over, the court shall pass, without further consideration, a judgment satisfying the claim (judgment on the basis of acknowledgment, Art 316 Slovenian ZPP). Notwithstanding that all the conditions have been fulfilled for handing down a judgment on the basis of acknowledgment, the court shall refuse to give such judgment if it establishes that the parties do not have over the right to settle the claim which is to be adjudicated (the third paragraph of Article 3).

This is a formal judgment on the claim, based on the defendant's explicit statement of acknowledgment of the claimant's request. Therefore, the court is not entitled to proceed with its own decision on the case.

Such a judgment is capable of becoming *res judicata* and enforceable and consequently of recognition and enforcement. It might be also certified as a European enforcement order under Regulation 805/2004.

7.3 Judgment on the Basis of the Plaintiff's Waiver

In some Member States, following the waiver of the claim by the plaintiff there is provision for issuing a judgment based on the waiver (e.g. Article 317 Slovenian ZPP) so that the principle of *res judicata* leads to preclusive effects. The claimant cannot start new litigation on the basis of the same claim.

[44] Sujecki (2020), p. 11.

If the plaintiff only withdraws the action without giving up the claim, the court rejects the action, but the defendant has to give his consent first. The decree on the rejection of the action becomes binding in relation to the end of the litigation at hand, but there is no preclusion regarding the claim. The plaintiff can submit another action with the same claim. The defendant might not consent to the withdrawal and might insist that the court renders a judgment with preclusive effects, which then protects the defendant from new litigation in the same case.[45]

8 Categorisation of Judgments by the Positive or Negative Relief Awarded with Respect to the Claim

8.1 Judgments Dismissing a Claim

Here we need to differentiate between national decisions on the merits of a case and decisions on the admissibility of the procedure.[46] In Slovenia, the ZPP makes a clear distinction between dismissal for entirely procedural reasons, which is not decided by a judgment but in the form of a decree, and dismissal of an unjustified claim using the form of a judgment.

Generally speaking, nothing prevents a party from applying to have such a judgment recognised. As there is no order to perform any obligation, enforcement is out of the question. However, Brussels I bis Regulation does not make any distinction with respect to the outcome of the foreign proceedings. There is no doubt that the regulation applies to a judgment holding that the plaintiff's claim could not be sustained on the merits as it is a determination of the parties' rights.[47]

The situation is different if the proceedings were dismissed for lack of procedural requirements. As aforementioned, such a decision is likely to be capable of recognition. In German civil procedure there is also a distinction in terminology. The words 'Zurückweisen/abweisen/verwerfen' are not synonymes. 'Zurückgewiesen' can also be translated as 'rejected' and is used when an application should not be granted for lack of formal procedural requirements. The term 'abgewiesen' (in English 'dismissed') is used when a claim is not upheld by a court.[48]

---

[45] Galič (2009), p. 86.

[46] See more, Decisions on admissibility of procedure of this Chapter.

[47] Esplugues Mota (2016), Article 21, p. 544.

[48] Mayr (2004).

9 Categorisation by the Scope of Decision (Final, Partial, or Interim Judgments)

If the judgment settles the legal dispute in full, one speaks of a final judgment (e.g. § 390 Austrian ZPO). If only part of the legal dispute is ready for a decision, the court can make a partial judgment (§§ 391 f Austrian ZPO). Both judgments are capable of recognition and enforcement.

If one of the parties has filed an interim application for a declaratory judgment or if the amount of the claim and the reason for the claim are disputed, the court can decide on the interim application in an interim judgment or determine the existence of the reason for the claim (§ 393 Austrian ZPO). This judgment becomes *res judicata* but due to its declaratory nature is only capable of recognition, not enforcement.

10 Factors Relating to the Structure of the Enforcement Title

10.1 Elements of a Judgment

In addition to the formal information about the court, the parties, and their representatives, it is common to all the jurisdictions studied that the judgment must contain, in particular, the decision on the claim (judgment) and the reasons for the decision. However, these elements are not always presented in the same manner and do not provide unified information.

It is critical for litigants to understand with complete certainty what a judgment does and does not encompass. Not least, a matter of substantial importance is what constitutes the actual entry of judgment, since the date of entry of judgment starts time running for making post-trial applications and lodging appeals and allows enforcement of judgments. Although the general approach to the elements of national judgments is obvious from the unified form in Annex I of Brussels I bis Regulation, the forms are not always filled accurately or in a unified way. Practice in relation to the short description of the subject-matter of the case is still developing.[49]

[49] See more on the role of a certificate in the para The Role of the Certificates under Brussels I bis Regulation in Identifying the Claim to be Enforced of this Chapter.

10.2 Introductory Part

Every judgment has to contain formal information about the court, the parties, and their representatives, the subject matter of the case, and the date of entry.

It is usual to incorporate the determination of the amount in dispute ('Streitwertfestsetzung').

10.3 Issues with the Operative Part

10.3.1 Delineation Between Operative Part and Reasoning of a Judgment

In several European legal orders (Germany, Austria, Slovenia, Croatia), the court must order the performance of the precise obligation in the operative part of the judgment.[50] Only the operative part can contain an order that acquires a *res judicata* effect. However, some legal systems—especially the French and Belgian legal systems—are less strict. In the latter the *res judicata* effect is, in principle, confined to the operative part. However, the '*motifs décisifs*', i.e., the parts of the statement of reasons forming the necessary support to the operative part, also acquire an effect of finality.[51] In Belgium, namely, there is no sharp separation between the statement of reasons and the operative part containing an order. According to the case-law of the Belgian courts, inspired by the Belgian Court of Cassation every decision on a litigated issue is an operative part even if contained in the statement of reasons (decisive reasons) regardless of the form in which it is expressed; in other words, the fact that the judge's decision is in the wrong place does not make it lose its character as a decision).[52] Therefore, lawyers from states east of France and Belgium are sometimes puzzled by the imprecision of Belgian and French enforcement titles. Traditionally, a foreign forum had to perform a title import of a Belgian decision in granting an exequatur. Nowadays, under the Brussels I bis Regulation, such a *modus operandi* is not feasible anymore.[53]

Problematic cases are those in which the operative part does not contain only the order to be enforced separately but other information as well.

When the claim is overlaid with text (the parties often state the legal basis, names, and addresses of the parties, various records such as 'pay', 'compensation' or 'rent' etc.), it should not be for this reason found erroneous to be dismissed. In most cases the judge omits such redundant parts of the text when formulating the operative part of the judgment.

[50] Fasching (1990), para 1044.

[51] Ferrand (2014), p. 149; Couchez and Lagarde (2014), para 400.

[52] de Leval (2021), para 156.

[53] Sladič (2018), p. 103.

10.3.2 Content of the Operative Part

In principle, the ruling/operative part of the judgment is supposed to include the decision on the claim (petitum)—whether it is one or more claims—and any counterclaim and decision on an objection by way of set off. For example, Article 319 of the Slovenian ZPP provides that a judgment that can no longer be challenged on appeal shall become *res judicata* in so far as it decides on the claim or counter-claim or on a claim which the defendant has asserted with an objection due to set-off.

The operative part of the judgment shall also include the following decisions ('Beschlüsse'): the decision on the costs of the proceedings (e.g. § 52 (1) Austrian ZPO), the rejection and dismissal of procedural claims ('Prozesseinreden') and a claim concerning the irregular formation of the court, if the main proceeding is continued (e.g. § 261 (1) Austrian ZPO), any other decisions reserved until the judgment or taken jointly with it (for example the approval of a change of claim). For the purposes of determining the exact scope of the *res judicata*, where a claim is dismissed, it must be clearly indicated what exactly has been dismissed. A judgment granting a claim corresponds, with regard to its content, entirely to the claimant's claim.[54]

10.3.3 Joinder

Joinder of parties ('Streitgenossenschaft') is usually specified in the header of the judgment along with the original parties to the dispute (e.g. § 59 et seq. German ZPO).

The joinder of claims, or the so-called objective accumulation of actions, is relevant to the statement of facts in the judgment, as well as to the operative part and the reasoning. For example, § 260 German ZPO regulates the so-called objective accumulation of actions. According to this provision, the claimant can combine several claims against the same defendant in one action, to therefore, not forced to assert several claims with several actions.[55] One form is the cumulative joinder of claims ('kumulative Klagenhäufung'). Usually, the claimant petitions a main and an alternative claim ('Haupt- und Hilfsantrag'), which take form of an 'eventuelle Klagenhäufung' ('potential joinder of claims'). The court can only decide upon the alternative claim if the main claim is dismissed. Otherwise, the alternative claim is disregarded. By contrast, an alternative joinder of claims ('alternative Klagenhäufung') 'liability with respect to [...] or [...]' is inadmissible due to the lack of certainty, § 253 II No. 2 German ZPO.[56]

To clarify the similar Slovenian rules on alternative joinder of claims some insight into substantive law is necessary. If the debtor is liable with respect to two

[54] Rechberger and Simotta (2009), pp. 214–215.

[55] Becker-Eberhard (2016–2017), para 260, margin 1.

[56] Wolf et al. (2020).

obligations in an alternative relationship (*duae res in obligatione una in solutione*—an obligation in which the debtor must perform one or the other), the debtor has a choice, unless otherwise agreed (Article 384 OZ). In such a case, the creditor must in the action claim for both things (one or the other). In Slovenia, the judgment condemns the debtor on both things but alternatively, and he is supposed to make a choice at the enforcement stage so that he is only obliged to perform one.

The position is otherwise, if, according to substantive law, the creditor has a choice which he can exercise immediately in a lawsuit requesting one thing only. But he can also sue alternatively (accumulating the claims for both things and preserving his final choice for the stage of enforcement).

In the case of alternative entitlement (*facultas alternativa, una res in obligatione, duae in solutione*), the plaintiff makes the offer in his action that he is prepared to accept alternative performance. If the court grants the claim, the debtor is left with the right to choose until the end of the enforcement proceedings. The creditor may demand from the debtor only the original object of the obligation, but it is up to the debtor to decide to fulfil his obligation with the other one.

10.3.4 Claim as the Subject Matter

The definition of an action to perform used in Article 84 of the modern Swiss Federal Code of Civil Procedure can be generally applied without any problem in the legal systems studied for this research. According to that definition, by filing an action to perform, the plaintiff demands that the defendant be ordered to do, refrain from doing, or tolerate something. These are obligations in substantive law. They may also be called liabilities.[57]

The focus of the research was monetary claims transferred into a performance action. Generally, a monetary/pecuniary claim must relate to the payment of a specific sum of money, and it must be due or its due date must be indicated in the title. The claim does not have to be expressed in numerical form in the enforcement title, but it must be possible to calculate the amount using a procedure sufficiently specified in the title. It is possible to specify the interest in percent at any time. On the other hand, it is not sufficient if the calculation requires further reference to national regulation.

The court may impose the performance of an obligation on a party only if such obligation has fallen due before the conclusion of the main hearing.

However, in a judgment recognising a claim for maintenance, the court may order the defendant to perform obligations that have not yet fallen due (Article 311 Slovenian ZPP).

In Germany, the legislator introduced the possibility of rewriting dynamic maintenance titles, which could not be confirmed due to a lack of certainty, into titles

[57] ZIZ defines a claim/liability as a right to a sum of money or to any other benefit, service, allowance or waiver (Article 16).

expressed numerically (Article 245 FamFG). The amount owed is quantified on request. The judicial authority that would be responsible for issuing an enforceable copy with an enforcement clause is responsible for this quantification.

In addition to the type of liability, the enforcement title must specify the scope of liabilities. Even a court settlement in which the amount of the claim is not stated is not an appropriate enforcement title.

The court in the enforcement proceedings in Slovenia as elsewhere is bound by the enforcement title. Therefore, the claim is enforced only to the extent specified in the enforcement title. However, an exception was stipulated by the ZIZ that where there has been a change in the amount of default interest after the enforcement title has arisen, the enforcement court has to decide on the obligation to pay default interest on the proposal of the creditor or debtor (Article 22).

10.3.5 Conditional, Reciprocal Obligations

Conditional obligations are dependent on the postponing or terminating condition. Substantive law distinguishes between conditional or time-limited claims and undue claims. In the case of an undue claim the legal relationship of from which the claim originates exists with full effect in the present, only its payment is deferred to a future specified date or is made dependent on the occurrence of a specific fact.

From a procedural point of view, both claims are conditional, even those which, according to the substantive law, are not considered to have fallen due yet. Enforcement depends on the occurrence of a certain time (deadline) or other facts (e.g. termination of the contract). The possibility of enforcement is therefore dependent on the fulfilment of the condition, which has to be verified in the state where the enforcement is being sought.

A claim recognised in a judgment cannot be conditional, because the non-occurrence of a condition prevents the claim from becoming due. As noted above, the court may decide only on claims that are due by the end of the main hearing (Article 311 of the ZPP). Exceptions include maintenance claims and claims for compensation for lost alimony and also life annuities awarded. In these cases, the relevant condition is not one on which enforcement would depend, and the court that issued the decision confirms enforceability, even though the deadline for voluntary fulfilment has not expired. For these periodic obligations, which fall due at certain intervals within one year from the date of the submission of the application, enforcement of the debtor's claim is then allowed in advance, despite not having fallen due yet.

Reciprocal obligations have to be proven at the stage of enforcement. Enforcement that depends on the previous fulfilment of a creditor's obligation or the occurrence of a condition, is allowed if, in the enforcement procedure, the creditor proves with a public document, or a document certified by law that he has fulfilled the obligation or that the condition has occurred. If he does not have a document, he must get a declaratory judgment (the first and second paragraphs of Article 26 ZIZ).

In the case of a claim with a terminating condition, the court will allow enforcement immediately because the claim exists in the present, and in the case of a suspensive condition, the claim is not due until the condition occurs.

10.3.6 Time of Fulfilment of Obligations

An integral part of the enforcement title's operative part under Slovenian law is also the indication of the deadline by which the obligation must be fulfilled ('paricijski rok'). If this element is missing it can be determined in the decision on authorisation of enforcement (the second paragraph of Article 21 ZIZ).

10.4 The Problem of Precision of Content

Difficulties with insufficiently well specified enforcement titles are still an urgent issue, although in all the jurisdictions studied the rules strive to achieve the position where the judgment handed down establishes a definite claim suitable for enforcement. The inconsistencies in the operative part are often the result of national approaches when adjudicating specific claims but also result from conflicting views of the necessary degree of certainty in the country of origin and the enforcement state. An important factor in this respect is the level of training of enforcement agents in each jurisdiction.

Where clarification is necessary, it can best be addressed in the state of origin. For example, in Germany, the decision on a final numerical amount in monetary judgments is supposed to be completed in the Klauselerteilungsverfahren (enforcement clause procedure). According to the provisions governing the enforcement clause procedure, the creditor can file an action if the calculation is wrong or calculated figures are too low (Section 731 German ZPO). The debtor can file an objection in accordance with § 732 German ZPO against the amount of the figures or bring an action in accordance with § 768 German ZPO.[58] On the other hand errors in the judgment are to be corrected by the court at any time, also *ex officio*. If it is the case, for example, that the decision on costs is only missing in the operative part but can be found in the reasoning, § 319 German ZPO is anyway applicable. The same applies to a claim that was dealt with in the reasoning but is missing in the operative part. Furthermore, a judgment that is incomplete as a result of an inadvertently omitted decision on the main or a subsidiary claim, or on costs, can be supplemented in accordance with § 321 Slovenian ZPP. Pursuant to § 716 German ZPO, § 321 German ZPO shall apply where a judgment has no decision on provisional enforceability. If the operative part is not in need of correction, it may nevertheless need to be interpreted.

[58] Rijavec (2012), p. 113.

The reasoning is used for interpretation.[59]

Another example can be found in Belgium. If the operative part is incomplete, incomprehensible, or inconsistent, recourse to Article 793 to 801 bis Judicial Code is needed. Three possible solutions are specified. The judgment may be explained, amended or supplemented.[60]

In Austria if an enforcement title is unsuitable for enforcement, there is provision for an action to supplement it ('Titelergänzungsklage', § 10 EO[61]). The aim of the action to supplement the enforcement title is therefore the closer specification of the adjudicated claim.[62]

If a foreign enforcement title is imprecise, the competent authority in the State of enforcement cannot simply refuse enforcement for this reason. The creditor is often not in a position to force the court of origin to correct the enforcement title to make it sufficiently well determined. The judgment can only be more precisely defined for enforcement purposes if the foreign court decision contains sufficiently specific data on the amount of (legal default) interest under the law of the country of origin, the costs of the procedure, the payment of tax, the time from which (default) interest begins to run or the currency of payment In the State of enforcement, a foreign court decision is enforceable if it is sufficiently well determined.

The closer specification of a foreign enforcement title is possible where any necessary calculation is done on the objective basis of foreign laws, judgments or statistical documents.[42] If foreign judgments cannot be rendered sufficiently specific, because it would be necessary to violate the prohibition on verifying the content of the judgment (Article 52 Brussels I bis Regulation), enforcement must be rejected.

Nevertheless, the Brussels I bis Regulation explicitly determines that a judgment given in a Member State which orders a payment by way of a penalty shall be enforceable in the Member State addressed only if the amount of the payment has been finally determined by the court of origin (Article 55).

A degree of certainty or at least determinability is required. The criteria according to which the obligation to provide payment is determined should be clearly identifiable from foreign regulations or similar circumstances that are equally accessible and reliably ascertainable in the state of enforcement. This means that the enforcement authority's decision must be designed in such a way that the claim can be enforced without a separate procedure. In German judicial practice, this problem is encountered in particular in connection with the declaration of enforceability of Italian and French judgments, in which interest and taxes are determined with reference to the laws that determine their amount.[63]

[59] Wolf et al. (2020), p. 55.

[60] Rys (2020).

[61] Austrian Civil Enforcement Act - Exekutionsordnung, RGBl. Nr. 79/1896.

[62] Brehm (2012), p. 220.

[63] Wolf et al (2020).

10.4.1 Interest

In general, there is often concern with respect to interest, in particular, if it has to be calculated during the enforcement process by a judicial officer who is unfamiliar with the calculations applied in the Member State of origin of the judgment. Still, the certificate in Annex I to the Brussels I bis Regulation does not contain a box showing the interest rate (statutory or contractual). It is not sufficient that in section 4.6.1.5.2, the box may be completed with regard to statutory default interest: 'statutory default interest (if applicable) is calculated in accordance with (specify the applicable law)'.

The problem can be illustrated by the following example. Unlike German and Austrian law, where the amount of default interest is, as a rule, fixed in the operative part of the judgment, judgments in some countries (e.g., France, Italy and the countries of the former Yugoslavia) often refer to the interest rate for statutory default interest in the calculation of interest. If a judgment creditor from Italy initiates enforcement in Slovenia, the Slovenian enforcement court has to calculate statutory default interest under Italian law in the process of authorising the execution. Under Italian law the judgment only refers to statutory default interest. Such a solution is better facilitated by the forms provided for in Regulations 805/2004 (EEOR), 1896/2006 and 861/2007. In the application of these regulations, the amount of statutory default interest in the certificate issued by the court of origin can be described in such a way that an application for interest can also be executed by a foreign enforcement institution. For example, the amount of statutory default interest in Slovenia is calculated on the basis of the Act on the prescribed interest rate for default interest, titled ZPOMZO-1 which is usually not known to the foreign enforcement institution. According to ZPOMZO-1, statutory default interest is calculated on the basis of the basic interest rate of the European Central Bank (ECB), plus 8% (Article 2 ZPOMZO-1).

The complexity of the legal solutions on the determination and calculation of interest adopted in European jurisdictions, as well as significant differences among them, mean that knowledge of the relevant national rules is of high relevance for effective enforcement. Specific regulations and practicalities regarding methods of interest calculation are frequently unclear from enforcement titles that originate in particular European countries. The same applies to certificates provided for under the Brussels I Recast Regulation.[64]

In this context, the contribution of the research undertaken as part of the EU-En4s project to improving the understanding of the legal and practical aspects of the payment of interest adjudicated in judgments issued in European Union Member States is crucial. The Interest Calculator software being developed by the project partners—the aim of which is to provide a simple user interface for interest calculation based on principal, date, and state information—is particularly worthy of attention.

[64] See in this volume Dymitruk and Kaczorowska, Comparative Issues Concerning the Determination of Interest.

10.4.2 Due Date

In the case of court decisions, it is not the due date that is a condition of enforceability, but only the date that a decision becomes *res judicata* and the expiry of the additional deadline for voluntary satisfaction of the claim (paricijski rok, delai de grâce). In fact, the issue of a court ruling on a liability that is not yet due is only possible in exceptional cases, e.g. if the court orders the defendant to pay alimony that is not yet due (Article 311 Slovenian ZPP). The same applies in Germany with a further extension: an action for future performance can be brought if the circumstances justify a concern that the debtor will evade timely performance (§§ 257-259 German ZPO).

If, however, an operative part is so contradictory and indeterminate in itself that its content cannot be determined even by way of interpretation, the judgment is ineffective and incapable of being a *res judicata*. An appeal may be lodged against such an ineffective judgment in the state of origin.[65]

10.5 Reasoning of a Judgment

The meaning of reasoning is multifaceted: the reasoning allows the party to become acquainted with the reasons for the decision (which is an integral part of a fair trial); it is only from the reasoning that it is clear whether the court has provided a fair trial; only comprehensive explanation guarantees the party a substantively effective right to a legal remedy; the explanation is a necessary element of uniform judicial practice (the latter is in Slovenia also constitutionally protected by Article 22 of the Constitution), and at the same time enables the development of the law.

In all the jurisdictions studied, decisions must incorporate reasoning/motivation. The requirement of reasoning differs in scope depending on the type of decision. It is only exceptional that decisions don't need reasoning, in situations that must be stipulated by law.Most of the countries studied have a specific order to be followed when drafting the reasoning. In Germany there is no separation between factual and legal grounds; these aspects do not follow a predetermined order, they can intertwine. Usually, the structure of the reasoning includesthe overall result ('Gesamtergebnis'), the interpretation of the prayers ('Auslegung des Klageantrages'), other preliminary inquiries ('Sonstige Vorfragen'), the admissibility of the action ('Zulässigkeit der Klage'), the merits of the case ('Begründetheit der Klage') and procedural rulings ('Prozessuale Nebenentscheidungen').

On the other hand, Belgian law does not provide a mandatory structure for the court's reasoning. The court must deal with all the claims of the parties that are correctly presented. Article 744 Judicial Code establishes a mandatory pattern to be used by counsel when drafting their respective statements of the case. If the structure

[65] Musielak (2016–2017), para 300 ZPO, margin 6.

provided by Article 744 Judicial Code is not followed by counsel, then the court does not need to answer any points of law presented in a different manner.[66]

Regarding the length of the reasoning, German law in § 313 III ZPO prescribes brief reasoning. But, if the decision does not set out the reasons for the judgment at all, an absolute ground for an appeal according to § 547 No. 6 ZPO is given. Furthermore, it is not sufficient to provide only keyword references in the sense of a 'reminder', which can only be understood by those who took part in the oral proceedings. The brevity of the reasons for the decision must not be at the expense of their comprehensibility.[67] A court decision is, legally speaking, an authoritative legal act. That being so, it must be placed on an abstract level in an imaginary pyramid, which expresses the hierarchical gradation of legal acts. In most countries, at the top of this pyramid is the constitution, followed by statues. Following the general theory of law, lower legal acts must be consistent with higher ones. If we look more closely at the normative framework, we can see that positive legal orders generally prevent the structure of the judgment from being arbitrary. The length of reasoning depends on the complexity of the case facts, on legal culture and tradition, on customs of style, on the framework of due process etc. The courts have to adjust their reasoning to the case they have at hand and its complexity, and no general statement can be made.

In cross-border cases, the length and transparency of judgments are not without significance. The enforcement authority has to deal with difficult foreign titles in translation, which can be rather confusing. Long translations significantly influence the rise of litigation costs.

Therefore, a discussion within the research also tackled the question of over-long judgments and ideas for improving the style of reasoning. There are some generally applicable tips for judges' orientation, such as: prioritise what is important, choose quality over quantity, choose words wisely. A thorough delimitation of the individual elements of the written material is the starting point. One part consists of rough (unprocessed) procedural material and the other is the judge's creation. The judge should give more focus on evidentiary conclusions and the creative part of the reasoning: the evidentiary assessment, the factual basis of the judgment and the interpretation of the law and the legal conclusion. The work is much easier and more transparent if we clearly distinguish these elements from each other. The question is what can be omitted from the court's reasoning without compromising legal correctness and legal certainty. The party's right to be heard will not be affected in any way if its statements are not completely transcribed into a judgment. This right will be violated only if the judge does not respond to it. Since the allegations made contribute to the introductory grounding of the dispute, a minimum statement of those allegations is required, which thus provides the parameters of the court proceedings. Careful legal diagnosis at the very beginning of the proceedings first helps the judge to analyse 'the issues in controversy' but also to ensure that the

---

[66] Rys (2020).

[67] Musielak (2016–2017), para 300 ZPO, margin 16.

proceedings run economically and quickly and that excess procedural material does not accumulate unnecessarily. The judge must never stop deliberating on the purpose of the judgment and the purpose of the reasoning and considering how to make the situation easier for the reader by maximising the messaging value and power of the judgment.[68]

11 The Role of the Certificates Under Brussels I bis Regulation in Identifying the Claim to be Enforced

11.1 Concept

Following the prescribed forms in Annexes, I and II the court or other competent authority of origin certifies the requirements for the direct enforcement of its own enforcement titles in other Member States. Brussels I bis Regulation names them: 'certificate concerning a judgment' and 'certificate concerning a court settlement or an authentic instrument'. Their nature and question of the scope of its binding effect are crucial.

Although the scope of the certificate is broader than it was before under Brussels I Regulation, the main point is still a determination of domestic enforceability effect. Therefore, the Brussels I bis Regulation certificate can be compared with the nature of national certificates of enforceability. A certificate concerning a judgment is a sort of a court's decision. Still, Brussels I bis Regulation doesn't contain provisions on remedies against the certificate, and they are a matter of national rules.

11.2 Effects

Further, there are some open questions regarding the scope of effects of the certificate, what is the binding effect of the entire certificate. Does the certificate establish the presumption of the cross-border case and the presumption of the truth of all the information in it? Is it necessary to challenge the certificate in the state of origin, or is it possible to invoke errors in enforcement procedures or in the procedure for refusal of enforcement? The procedural question is if the enforcement title should be immediately examined together with the certificate at the start of enforcement *ex officio*; or if the debtor may require the examination of the original judgment without submitting legal remedy (e.g., opposition); or if the debtor submits opposition in enforcement procedure (2 al 1. par. Article 55 SLO ZIZ); or if the debtor initiates the procedure for refusal of enforcement invoking grounds against recognition and enforcement (Article 46 and following Brussels I bis Regulation); are the issues

[68] Pavčnik (2015), p. 143.

bound to ET the matter of national remedy's procedure or the matter of procedure for refusal of enforcement (Article 46 and following Brussels I bis Regulation).

To these questions we can answer that Brussels I bis Regulation provides a legal presumption developed in the state of enforcement that the content of a certificate is true until proven otherwise in principle in the state of origin. By the fact of using the form (e.g., Annex I: certificate concerning a judgment in civil and commercial matters), the court of origin certifies that the judgment fits the scope of Brussels I bis Regulation as a civil or commercial matter (requirement '*rationae materiae*') and also affirms that the document fulfils the requirements of a judgment under the article 2 of Brussels I bis Regulation. On the other hand, this doesn't mean that the competent authority in the enforcement procedure has no right to prove if the judgment falls under the scope of Brussels I bis Regulation. Direct access to enforcement in another Member State is only guaranteed if Brussels I bis Regulation applies. The court or other enforcement authority may check this as well if the other prerequisites of a scope (territorial, timely, personal) are met. It is a matter of jurisdiction that remains in the addressed court sphere.[69] The court addressed, in other words, may decide that the dispute falls outside the scope of regulation even if the court of origin applied the regulation.

It has to be stressed that the certificate under Brussels I bis Regulation does not have the same effect as the certificate of EEO which is a transnational passport of the judgment. Therefore, legal presumptions bound to the certificate under Brussels I bis Regulation can be invoked in the Member States of enforcement (e.g., if the debtor proves that the enforcement title was later canceled, which removed the effect of enforceability).

De lege ferenda we can suggest the upgrade of the Brussels I bis Regulation with the binding force of the certificate as to the applicability of Regulation.

It has been also envisioned as a future legislative improvement in the Heidelberg Report, at paras 634-635.[70]

11.3 Accuracy of the Content of Certificate: Compatibility with Enforcement Title

The further question arises: what enforcement requirements the certificate is meant to certify? What elements benefit from this binding presumption until proven otherwise? How far can doubts about the certificate's accuracy arise concerning the content of the judgment? A judgment is an enforcement title but may contain a claim that is insufficiently determined. The answer to those questions is general that the certificate cannot replace the judgment.

[69] Esplugues Mota (2016), Article 21, p. 537; Kropholler (2005), Article 32, pp. 380–393; Briggs (2005), p. 432.

[70] Hess et al. (2007), in the literature known as the 'Heidelberg Report'.

Following the form in Annex I the certificate may include detailed answers to a wide range of questions concerning: the court of origin; the parties; the service of the judgment on the debtor; and the contents of the judgment (requiring the inclusion of an extract of the judgment and further detail as to whether or not it is presently enforceable in the Member State of origin, the identification of anyone against whom it is enforceable and the extent to which it is enforceable, and details concerning interest and the nature of any costs orders). An additional item to be certified under Article 42 is an extract of a judgment (Annex I—4.6.1.1.). The Regulation is not clear if the word extract is a synonym with the word summary, and what this extract should consist of. It does not mean anything specific in the legal orders of the German circle as the concept of extract of the judgment is not regulated. It neither has specific significance under French law. An 'extrait de judgment' will usually only reproduce what is in French, called 'le dispositive', as opposed to the 'motifs', in other words, the ruling as opposed to the motivation. However, a summary can be understood more broadly than just a 'dispositive' or Tenor, for it might include a short presentation of judgment's motivation as well.[71] It might be compared with the technique of drafting the German enforcement clause in which information on title is transformed. Annex I—4.6.1.1. actually requires a 'Short description of the subject-matter of the case'. To understand what is subject matter of the case we need to think on the decision in the operative part and the set of facts and rules on which the decision is based on. This information might be used to compare two irreconcilable judgments. It is though, confusing because in addition to the extrait of judgment the form in the field 4.6.1.2. extra foresees a compelling order too: 'The court has ordered ...(surname and given name(s)/name of company or organisation) to make a payment to: ...(surname and given name(s)/name of company or organisation)'. The information on payment from operative part is supposed to be filled in twice. It however makes sense to point out only the obligation adjudicated to be enforced.

A form for the certificate for an authentic instrument using the form set out in Annex II also contains a box for a summary, this time of the enforceable obligation recorded in the authentic instrument or of the agreement between the parties recorded in the court settlement (Article 60). The previous Brussels I Regulation does not contain any instructions regarding the content of the obligation recorded in an authentic instrument or settlement. In relation to making a summary, there is again a question as how to understand the scope of the summary: nevertheless, for enforcement to take place the exact obligation has to be made clear.

[71] Kennett (2018), p. 328.

11.4 The Primacy of the Enforcement Title

It has to be concluded, that the certificate has no self-standing effect. Preamble (32) Brussels I bis Regulation also gives an outline for the meaning of the certificate. It is meant merely to inform the person against whom enforcement is sought of the enforcement of a judgment given in another Member State. The primacy of a judgment is evident from the requirement that the certificate established under this Regulation should be served together with the judgment, if necessary.

In Germany it is clearly regulated that the certificate is issued together with the court decision including the enforcement clause, paragraphs 724 and 725 German ZPO). This also means one certificate of enforceability. Exceptions are only possible in the case of enforcement against joint and several debtors, to be conducted in different places, or in the case of enforcement against one debtor, which is carried out in different places. Each subsequent enforceable copy shall be indicated as a further (e.g., the second or third) copy of the judgment (paragraph 733 German ZPO).

We can conclude that the certificate under Brussels I bis Regulation should not be treated separately without a judgment.

In general, if the certificate is incomplete, the judgment can close possible gaps. The certificate alone is namely not a court decision that can change the legal status of the judgment but only declares whether the ruling has this attribute—it is the certification of facts. Although it is a court decision, it is not the enforcement's authorisation in the case at hand. So, there is no doubt that the certificate cannot diverge from the original enforcement title and cannot change or upgrade the enforcement title itself. In conflict, the content of a judgment is binding. If the certificate is uncomplete the creditor must not be forced to go back to the state of origin for the supplement.

From this research, it is obvious, that there are still many significant differences between national regulations and the ways of transposition of the short content of a judgment into the certificate. A still difficult issue is to transfer the claim of summary proceedings, ended by a simple approval of the claim in the claimant's document or the claim from a notarial act into the certificate form.

Consequently, the enforcement authority in the Member State of enforcement must have insight into the enforcement title itself. Thus, the translation is necessary even when the debtor understands the language of the title. The enforcement authority having trouble understanding certified contents can check the enforcement title on its own motion.

The Heidelberg Report noted that the issue of concretisation of enforcement titles in Brussels I bis Regulation can be alleviated by providing harmonised certificates, supplementing a fragmentary judgment with additional information. Some authors further develop that the need for judgment concretisation remained even though the harmonised certificate could be solved through judgment adaptation. The recast provides that unknown measures or orders be adapted to their closest equivalent.[72]

But it is not so simple. However, breaking down the operative part of a judgment into harmonised certificate segments does not entirely remove the need for judgment concretisation. The concretisation of the enforcement title is not only needed if the measure in it doesn't correspond to the domestic measures (the case meant by Article 54 Brussels I bis Regulation) but also in the case of unprecise or unclear enforcement title not capable for the enforcement. The conflict between the enforcement title and the certificate requires the competent authority to consider the enforcement title.

11.5 Rectification or Withdrawal of the Certificate

The courts often receive the wrong certificate from abroad (e.g. Brussels I instead of Brussels I bis certificate), or a certificate that is not filled in properly resulting in a difference of information between the certificate and the judgment. Interest may not be expressly indicated (e.g. interest according to the law), or some information may be missing (e.g. the name of the defendant or of the claimant, costs, the judgment, the amount that the court has ordered).

Issues of translation of the certificate also arise: there are some doubts about the language in which the certificate should be completed and issued. There are also questions concerning whether a certificate can be issued in relation to decisions concerning provisional and protective measures ordered by the court having jurisdiction on the merits and concerning the authority competent to draft the certificate (e.g. drafted by the court, drafted by the lawyer and submitted with the request to the court).[73]

The Brussels I bis Regulation does not provide rules for rectification or withdrawal of the certificate, or for the issue of a certificate of unenforceability or a restriction on enforceability, as provided in EEOR. Therefore, national rules apply which enable the way to request necessary extensions of the incomplete certificate. But as mentioned before, the creditor's position deteriorates significantly if he has to persuade the authority in the state of origin to issue different certificate.

However, when the judgment is later set aside, the central provision of the enforcement regime under Brussels I bis Regulation to consider is Article 39. It is focused on a judgment given in a Member State which is enforceable in that Member State. The loss of the quality of enforceability introduces the same situation as if a national title in the State addressed has lost it. The debtor can object to enforcement because the first prerequisite, the enforcement title, is missing. Enforceability ceases for all procedural and material reasons, which can no longer be claimed. These include the cancellation of a certificate of enforceability, which results in the loss of

[72] Hovaguimian (2015), p. 215.

[73] Kramer et al. (2018).

the enforceability of the decision. An incorrect certificate can be annulled by the authority that issued the decision on the request of the party or *ex officio*.

The CJEU, in the decided case Prism Investments[74] made it clear that the unenforceability of the judgment in the Member State of origin prevents enforcement in the Member State addressed. The enforceability of the judgment in question in the Member State of origin is a precondition for its enforcement in the Member State in which enforcement is sought.

Therefore, the absence of rules on rectification or withdrawal of the certificate is not a real problem. The situation may not be compared with the system of the EEOR. The difference between the EEOR and the Brussels I bis Regulation is the nature of the certificate. A European enforcement order certificate has a constitutive nature in forming a new type of transnational title. The certificate is a decision with its own effects. The certificate of enforceability under the Brussels I bis Regulation is on the one hand more than just certification of the mere fact of enforceability but on the other hand does not create a new type of enforcement title comparable to the transnational European enforcement order. However, it would be advisable to introduce in the future a unified approach to correction or annulment of the certificate of enforceability referred to in Article 53 of Brussels I bis Regulation, just as in EEOR (Article 10). It is possible that the court of origin might incorrectly enter some information in the certificate, resulting in a discrepancy between the judgment and the certificate (e.g., instead of the amount EUR 10,000.00, the amount in the certificate is EUR 100,000.00). It may also happen that the court of origin should not have issued the certificate referred to in Article 53 of Brussels I bis Regulation, but it did, nevertheless. For example, if the court issues a certificate of enforceability for a maintenance claim falling within the scope of Regulation 4/2009, or if the court accidentally confirms the enforceability of the judgment in a transient manner, but later it turns out that the delivery of the judgment to the defendant was invalid and should be repeated. For example, the defendant communicated the address of their new residence to the court, and the court delivered the judgment to the old residential address. Such issues are is subject to national legislation and regulated differently in each country.

11.6 Repeated Issue of Certificate of Enforceability

The possibility of multiple and parallel enforcement procedures significantly interferes with the interests of the debtor, which means they would have to defend themselves in several countries at the same time, which would enable the creditor to be paid twice for the same debt. On the other hand, the creditor has a legitimate interest in enforcing the judgment and enforcing it as soon as possible, in particular

[74] Case C-139/20, Prism Investments BV v Jaap Anne van der Meer, 13.10.2011, ECLI:EU:C:2011:653.

when the debtor's assets in one Member State are not sufficient for a full repayment of the claim. The Brussels I bis Regulation therefore does not contain restrictions for simultaneous enforcement in several countries, because debtors can defend themselves against the risk of double payment of the same debt by legal means within national enforcement procedures. There are numerous autonomous national laws of the Member States, which offer many different answers to this question. The German Regulation is restrictive, as in principle the court issues only one enforceable copy of the judgment (§724 and 725 German ZPO). This also means one certificate of enforceability. Exceptions are only possible in the case of enforcement against joint and several debtors, to be conducted in different places, or in the case of enforcement against one debtor, which is carried out in different places. Each subsequent enforceable copy shall be indicated as a further (e.g., the second or third) copy of the judgment (§ 733 German ZPO). The reason for the German rule is to prevent the creditor from receiving payment many times out of the same enforcement title. After complete payment, the creditor must hand over a copy of the judgment to the debtor.

12 Effects of Judgments

12.1 Introduction

Another fundamental problem that has to be addressed in order to facilitate cross-border enforcement of judgments is the proper extent of the judicial authority expressed in a judgment. It is still unclear whether the effects of a judgment may be based on a European principle of recognition. In a case on interpretation of the 1968 Brussels Convention, the CJEU ruled that a judgment falling within the scope of the Convention had preclusive effect.[75] Such a judgment precludes a plaintiff from starting new proceedings as to the substance of the matter in the Member State of enforcement, even though this new procedure is cheaper than the enforcement of the judgment rendered by a court of another Member State.

The Brussels I bis Regulation similarly does not operate with the term *res judicata*. Although *res judicata* ('Rechtskraft') is not required but only the enforceability of the judgment, which implies an effect of finality. Provisions to this effect are found in Article 52, prohibiting a review of a foreign judgment as to its substance. The concept *res judicata* was deliberately avoided since judgments in interlocutory proceedings may be recognised, and these do not always have the force of *res judicata*. On the other hand, the binding effect of a domestic judgment is a bar to recognition of another identical foreign judgment (the ground of irreconcilable judgments, Article 45(1)(c) Brussels I bis Regulation). Therefore, attention has been drawn to difficult issues concerning the objective identity of claims. Despite the

[75] Case 42/76, Jozef de Wolf v Harry Cox BV, 30.11.1976, ECLI:EU:C:1976:168.

previous autonomous interpretation of the identity of claims, the differences between the two concepts of 'Streitgegestandsbegriff' still influence the implementation of the Brussels I bis Regulation.[76] The special problem field is irreconcilability due to related claims.[77]

The CJEU has used the term finality and highlighted the importance of the principle of *res judicata* in the Kapferer case.[78]

12.2 Method of Effects' Recognition in Another Member State

Another pressing problem that needs to be addressed is that of clarifying the method of transfer of effects to other Member States. In relation to the answer to this question, three theories have been advanced throughout all legal systems in the world: the extension theory; the theory of equalisation; and the theory of cumulation. From the case law of the CJEU it seems that the effects of a judgment in cross-border situations may involve the application of the law of the Member State of origin, the law of the Member State addressed, and EU law to a greater or lesser extent depending on the type of effect in issue. Following this, it is tempting to question whether the dominating broad doctrine of extension of effects is truly an accurate description of the legal situation within the scope of the Brussels I bis Regulation. Perhaps the time is ripe to clearly decide on the roles that EU law and national law should play in the cross-border circulation of judgments. Moreover, it is unclear how far the principle of adaptation (introduced with Article 54) can go, and further evaluation of different possible situations is necessary.[79] A further problem arises because of the uncertainty of the effects of an enforcement title when legal remedies in the state of origin are still not exhausted.

A problem may arise if, in the Member State of origin, an effect is given to a judgment which is unknown in the Member State of recognition. It becomes necessary to decide which law determines the effects of a foreign judgment. Based on the Jenard Report,[80] the CJEU seems to accept that the law of the Member State where the judgment was rendered decides on the effects of the judgment. But while on the one hand foreign effects are extended to the Member State of recognition, on the other, this State could still seek for the possibility of a partial limitation for unknown effects under its own law. It indicates the use of the cumulative approach.

---

[76] See more on obstacle 'lis pendens' in this volume Rijavec, Pendency Rules.

[77] See more on 'related actions' in this volume Baghrizabehi, Related actions.

[78] Case C-234/04, Rosmarie Kapferer v. Schlank & Schick GmbH, 16.03.2006, ECLI:EU:C:2006:178, para 21; see Section Theories on Finality and Res Judicata of this Chapter; see also in this volume Kennett, Effects of Judgments in Cross-Border Perspective.

[79] See also Ivanc (2018).

[80] Jenard Report. Jenard (1979).

However, Article 54 restricts this approach by ordering the State addressed to adapt measures in order to guarantee their intended purpose. An adaptation without extending the effects of the foreign judgment does not make any sense.

Some German legal authors plead the statement that the extension of effects is not supposed to be unlimited, and that the Brussels Convention of 1968 implies a system of cumulative assessment. But the more widely accepted view is that recognition extends the effects from the state of origin. This is also the practice of the CJEU. It is deemed that the decision settles a dispute in the same manner as in the state of origin and prevents a retrial of the identical claim. A judgment cannot develop more effects in the state of enforcement than it would have in the state of origin. If, for example, in the state of origin a judgment on alimony can be changed it cannot be unchangeable in the state of enforcement. Even effects unknown in the state of enforcement are to be considered provided that they are not in contradiction with domestic public policy ('ordre public'). The same type of judgment may vary in scope and effect in different countries. For example, in France, a judgment against the principal debtor extends also to the guarantor, whereas this is not the case in the Netherlands and Germany. Under Brussels I bis Regulation the effect of enforceability is acknowledged to a foreign enforcement title even where the domestic law of the state of enforcement relating to such a title does not provide for enforceability (provisional enforceable titles).[81]

12.3 Theories on Finality and Res Judicata

The issue of effects is theoretically very demanding, which is reflected in the various points of view in the theoretical treatment of the meaning of finality, in individual types of procedures and in individual concepts or elements of finality. In English terminology there is no direct translation of *res judicata* effect ('Rechtskraft'). Instead, the term 'finality' of judicial and extra-judicial decisions is used. This is a notion related to the need to maintain legal certainty and to the principle of *res judicata*. The oft-stated requirement that a judgment should be 'final and conclusive' is terminology used by English law. The finality of a judgment is contrasted with 'interim' decisions. For a judgment to be used in subsequent proceedings, it must be conclusive on the relevant issue. Thus, Halsbury's Laws of England states that 'Every final judgment is conclusive evidence against all the world of its existence, date and legal consequences'.[82] This terminology is not particularly helpful in discussing *res judicata* in comparative perspective.

Therefore, when discussing the effects of judgments in the EU, the most comprehensible approach is to start with the *res judicata* principle. The term *res judicata*

---

[81] Rijavec et al. (2015), p. 5.

[82] Halsbury's Laws of England is the authoritative source on the laws of England and Wales, LexisNexis, https://www.lexisnexis.co.uk/products/halsburys-laws-of-england.html.

has been used in different ways. It is a portmanteau term which is used to describe a number of different legal principles with different judicial origins'.[83] In modern European civil procedure, however, there is a broad acceptance that a judgment is *res judicata;* 'when ordinary means of recourse are not or are no longer available'.[84] All the legal systems involved in the research recognise two facets of *res judicata*, positive and negative.[85] The positive effect of *res judicata* is that the judgment is binding between the parties. It becomes enforceable (enforceability effect) and may produce other effects (constitutive, declaratory effects). The negative effect of *res judicata* is that it is preclusive of any further litigation with respect to the same '*res*'. The precise preclusive effects of a judgment nevertheless vary from one legal system to another.

Going one step back, two groups of theories concerning *res judicata* may be considered: 'civilistic' and procedural. According to 'civilistic' theories, a final judgment is the new legal basis of a civil law relationship, which means that all judgments have a constitutive effect. Among other things, 'civilistic' theories are accused of failing to explain the situation that arises after a judgment has been issued relating to absolute rights (e.g. property rights). As the judgment is effective only between the parties, the original legal relationship still applies to third parties, even though the judgment finds that it does not exist. According to modern procedural theory, a final judgment does not establish or abolish rights, but only represents an authoritative finding on the content of the disputed legal relationship—the only exceptions are constitutive judgments. Whether the judgment is correct or not, it does not have a direct effect on the existing legal relationship, but in the interest of maintaining the rule of law, it excludes the possibility of reconsidering the same case and binds those concerned.[86]

In the theoretical analysis adopted by the German circle, a further distinction is drawn between formal and substantive *res judicata*. Formal *res judicata* is understood as a position where a decision can no longer be challenged by ordinary legal remedies. By contrast, the term substantive/material *res judicata* means binding the parties and the court in relation to the content of the court decision and the prohibition of a retrial of the same case. The first consequence is the positive side of material *res judicata*, and the second is the negative side of the same phenomenon.

Proponents of a different view consider that the distinction between substantive/material and formal *res judicata* is no longer important for the judicial process.[87] If a judgment can no longer be challenged by ordinary legal means of recourse it does not *per se* mean that the decision is *res judicata. Res judicata* means binding in

[83] Per Lord Sumption in Virgin Atlantic Ltd v Zodiac Seats UK Ltd (2013) UKSC 46.

[84] See ELI-UNIDROIT Model European Rules of Civil Procedure, Rule 148.

[85] The ELI-UNIDROIT Model Rules refer to the positive and negative effects of res judicata in somewhat different terms, see Rule 149.

[86] Wedam Lukić (2009), p. 147.

[87] It is a main approach in Croatia and Austria; Dika (2013), pp. 592–598; Prodinger & Nunner Kraugasser (2020).

relation to the content of the legal protection pronounced by the court, which in the field of mutual material legal relations binds the persons for whom the decision is final. The decision, which can no longer be challenged by ordinary legal remedies (irreversibility), does not yet create any relevant and new effects in the field of finality for the court, participants and third parties. Formal finality thus does not allow the emergence of material *res judicata*, but separates them, both temporally and conceptually. If a legal situation resulting from the loss of the right of one of the parties to challenge a decision by ordinary legal remedies qualifies as final, this brings confusion to the sensitive area of legal terminology and creates an unjustified devaluation of the notion of *res judicata* reserved for other content. These are: the prohibition against relitigating the same matter (*ne bis in idem*), the rule that the decision must be considered genuine (*res iudicata pro veritate habetur*), the rule that a final judgment is an authoritative regulator of legal relations that binds the parties and everyone to whom it refers *(res judicata facit ius inter partes*), the impact of the final decision on the civil law relationship, intervention effect, and other legal consequences (the final decision acts as a legally relevant fact with respect to third parties as well if the occurrence of a certain consequence is related to the final decision).

In Austrian theory, there is a difference between the procedural effects of judgments and the substantive effects of judgments. In Germany 'Feststellungswirkung'/declaratory effect and the enforcement effect belong to the procedural effects, the constitutive effect ('Gestaltungswirkung') and the effect of the findings of facts ('Tatbestandswirkung') belong to the legal effects of substantive law.

Formal legal force (irreversibility or 'Unabänderlichkeit') is not an effect of a judgment, but it is a necessary precondition for the material legal force of the judgment and the constitutive effect ('Gestaltungswirkung') of it. However, formal legal force is not a necessary condition for enforceability. For example, execution can lead to satisfaction (Exekution zur Befriedigung) even where an appeal judgment ('Berufungsurteil') is challenged with an extraordinary appeal ('außerordentliche Revision') (see § 505 (4) Austrian ZPO) and so is not yet final but after exhaustion of ordinary legal remedies has become enforceable. Debtor has a right to ask for a postponment of enforcement.

On the other hand, execution to secure a debt ('Exekution zur Sicherstellung') can generally be initiated by creditor until the enforcement is over even before a judgment has become final and even before the action has been submitted (see §§ 370 ff A EO). A foreign court decision has four procedural effects that can be acknowledged: the effect of material *res judicata*; preclusive effect; constitutive effects (in declaratory judgments); and intervention effects (together with the effect of informing the intervening party of a pending procedure). In addition, a judgment imposing liability can evolve into one having the effect of enforceability that is not subject to recognition under Brussels I bis Regulation but is granted by the court in the state addressed through exequatur. After the abolition of exequatur, the enforceability effect is automatically presumed in the state addressed.[88]

Nevertheless, viewed generally, the binding effect of a judicial decision can be dealt with under the headings of subject matter limit, personal limits, and the time limits of *res judicata*. But the effects vary from Member State to Member State. Even so, the judgment cannot have greater effects than those provided by the law of the Member State addressed.

12.4 Decisions Capable to be Res Judicata

Here, we must refer back to the previous comprehensive categorisation of judgments and decrees in this chapter, where we also explained their ability to become *res judicata* or just enforceable. However, some aspects need to be reconsidered here.

The main category consists of judgments and decisions on the substance of the matter. To obtain *res judicata* status, the final, valid judgment must also be 'on the merits' which means that it is founded on a complete examination of the substantive rights asserted in the case. But on the other hand, judgments rendered on the basis of the parties' right to settle their claim (e.g. default judgment, consent judgment. . .), where a full court decision on the relevant facts and the rights is missing, become *res judicata* too.

The effects of a court decision are not altogether uniform under the legal systems of the Member States. A judgment delivered in one State as a decision on a procedural issue may, in another state, be treated as a decision on a matter of substance. Not just judgments, but also decisions can be rendered on the merits and become *res judicata*.

Some procedural decisions in some countries attain formal *res judicata* effect. In other words, they cannot be challenged by ordinary legal remedies, but they can sometimes be relitigated. Thus, decisions on the admissibility of the entire procedure are capable of becoming *res judicata* and are capable of recognition (e.g. a decision on dismissal of the action for jurisdictional reasons). On the other hand, completely procedural decisions (decisions on interim procedural conduct) do not attain *res judicata* effect and are not capable of recognition. Decisions ordering the execution of an enforcement title by coercive measures are not capable of recognition, and the same is true for decisions on the recognition of a foreign judgment. It is too early to state that enforcement acts are covered by the Brussels I bis Regulation.[89] However, a certain favourable trend can be seen in the case of Realchemie Nederland

---

[88] Prodinger & Nunner-Krautgasser (2020).

[89] Domej (2016), p. 477.

concerning the payment of an order imposing a fine for infringement of intellectual property rights.[90]

12.5 Subject Matter Scope of Res Judicata

The material scope of *res judicata* is determined by reference to the claims for relief in the parties' pleadings, including amendments, as decided by the court's judgment. It embraces a decision on the claims—one or more of them—any counterclaim, and any decision on the defendant's defence of set off. It also covers necessary and incidental legal issues that are explicitly decided in a judgment.[91]

12.6 Binding Effect of Operative Part and Reasoning

The concept of *res judicata* under European Union law does not attach only to the operative part of the judgment in question but also adheres to the ratio decidendi of that judgment, which provides the necessary underpinning for the operative part and is inseparable from it.[92]

The CJEU explicitly explained in the aforementioned case Gothaer allgemeine Versicherung that a judgment by which a court of a Member State has declined jurisdiction on the basis of a jurisdiction clause binds the courts of the other Member States both as regards that court's decision to decline jurisdiction, contained in the operative part of the judgment, and as regards the finding on the validity of that clause, contained in the ratio decidendi which provides the necessary underpinning for that operative part.

12.7 Personal Scope of Res Judicata

Res judicata binds the parties to the process. In some cases, the law orders that the effects of certain judgments also extend to persons who were not involved in the proceedings themselves (e.g. in Austria, a 'wirkungsgebundene

[90] Case C-406/09, Realchemie Nederland BV v Bayer CropScience AG, 18.10.2011, ECLI:EU:C:2011:668, para 43.

[91] See also Content of the operative part of this chapter; ELI-UNIDROIT Model states in Rule 149. Material Scope of res judicata.

[92] Case C-456/11, Gothaer Allgemeine Versicherung AG and Others. The same view is evident from Joined Cases C-442/03 P and C-471/03 P, P & O European Ferries (Vizcaya) and Diputación Foral de Vizcaya v Commission, 01.06.2006, ECLI:EU:C:2006:356, para 44 and Case C-221/10 P Artegodan GmbH v European Commission, 19.04.2012, ECLI:EU:C:2012:216, para 87.

Streitgenossenschaft'—a relationship such that a decision has *in rem* effects). If these (third) persons take part in the proceedings (either as interveners or as co-claimants or co-defendants), because they are included in the effects of the judgment anyway, then it is absolutely necessary to issue a uniform judgment for and against all the parties involved (forming a 'collective litigant'—'einheitliche Streitpartei' according to § 14 Austrian ZPO).

In the following cases, uniform judgments must be given against and for all parties to the dispute. Judgments in favour of actions for nullification ('Nichtigerklärung') of a shareholders' resolution ('Gesellschafterbeschluss') are effective for and by all shareholders (even for those shareholders who have not sued for nullification) (see § 42 (6) Austrian GmbHG, § 198 (1) Austrian AktG).

Other examples of extension of legal effect *ex lege* are universal and individual legal succession ('Gesamt- und Einzelrechtsnachfolge'), various judgments resulting from execution proceedings (see §§ 232 (2), 310 (2) EO)193, and a decision on the correctness and ranking of claims filed and disputed in the insolvency proceedings (see § 112 IO).

Judgments on personal status (for example a decision of divorce) have an effect on everyone (*erga omnes* binding effect). Constitutive judgments ('Rechtsgestaltungsurteile') have an effect on all parties to the legal relationship in dispute that has to be established, annulled or amended by the judgment.[93]

It is a fact that there is always a conflict with Article 6 ECHR when extending the effects of a judgment to persons who have not been heard or have not been heard sufficiently in the proceedings. This problem has not yet been fully discussed in procedural law.

12.8 Time Limits: Issue Preclusion

An area of particular difficulty in comparing national legal systems is the determination of the preclusive effects of a judgment. Broadly speaking, a distinction is drawn between claim and issue preclusion. Preclusive effects are generally accepted with respect to claims, whereas issue preclusion is much less commonly accepted. Nevertheless, precise distinctions between claim and issue preclusion are problematic in a comparative perspective since much depends on the particular structure of the relevant substantive law, and on the way that judgments are drafted. For example, although German law does not recognise issue preclusion with respect to a decision on a preliminary/incidental question, the claimant or defendant who wishes to extend the preclusive effects of a judgment to an incidental decision, is entitled to request a declaratory judgment on relevant preliminary legal relationships such as the existence of a contract etc. (§ 256 (2) German ZPO).

[93] Prodinger & Nunner-Krautgasser (2020), p. 54.

The time limits relevant to *res judicata*, in general, determine the facts at the moment that the court takes into account when issuing a judgment. In Slovenian law, this is the moment of the conclusion of the main hearing, i.e. the last possible time at which the parties can still state the facts and propose evidence that arises during the proceedings. Finality does not relate to and does not cover what happened later (after the main hearing), such as the defendant's payment of a debt, occurring after the end of the proceedings at first instance. The time limits relevant to finality therefore refer only to factual matters, but not to the underlying legal base.[94]

Thus *res judicata* covers the situation of the facts at the conclusion of the main hearing, so the parties are precluded from relitigating all the facts that already existed up to that point. The parties may no longer contest those facts after they have become final except in the context of a reopening of the proceedings and under the conditions laid down for such proceedings. No evidence is admissible that contradicts the correctness of the findings arising from final court decisions. Any objections should be raised by the defendant in the original lawsuit.[95]

12.9 Time of Entry the Effect of Res Judicata

A judgment resulting from an *inter partes* proceeding becomes *res judicata*:

(a) at the moment it is announced/served if it is not subject to any recourse, (e.g. § 310 III Austrian ZPO).
(b) at the moment the period to take recourse against the judgment expired.
(c) at the moment when both parties claimant and defendant waiver of their right to challenge/appeal the judgment.
(d) at the moment one party's withdrawal of a challenge/appeal becomes effective if the period for any further challenge/appeal has already expired.
(e) at the moment the decision following the challenge/appeal becomes *res judicata* if the original judgment is not quashed or the original proceedings are not continued.[96]

[94] Mežnar (2012), p. 47.

[95] Judgment of Slovenian Supreme court VSRS Sodba III Ips 153/2015, 17.11.2016, ECLI:SI:VSRS:2016:III.IPS.153.2015.

[96] Prodinger & Nunner-Krautgasser (2020).

12.10 *Enforceability Effect*

12.10.1 National Requirements

Although there is a significant overlap between the enforceability effect of a judgment and its character as *res judicata* the two are not identical. In principle, a judgment that is not *res judicata* is not enforceable except provisional enforceable judgments, and a judgment that is *res judicata* may not be enforceable until the time allowed for voluntary fulfilment of the claim (delai de grâce) has expired. In all jurisdictions there are, however, exceptions created by rules on provisional enforceability.

An automatic 'grace period' was also provided by Brussels I Regulation and abolished by Brussels I bis Regulation.

12.10.2 Provisional Enforceability

Legal systems vary as to how far they permit provisional enforcement. In some countries, all judgments are in general provisionally enforceable. For example, in Belgium, the lodging of an appeal does not stay the possibility of enforcement. The Belgian legislator has opted for this system because the use of an appeal was often misused to unduly postpone the enforceability of a judgment in order to delay payment.[97]

In Austria, Slovenia, and Croatia the entry of *res judicata* and of the enforceability effect is suspended on the submission of a legal recourse against the first instance judgment. Sometimes provisional enforcement may not be permitted, but only the securing of assets of the debtor pending enforcement. Once a judgment on the merits has been handed down at first instance, but before the judgment becomes final, measures to secure the position of the creditor are commonly available. Thus, the default position may be that a judgment is not provisionally enforceable, but the judgment creditor may apply for provisional enforcement. On the other hand, (as in e.g. France and Belgium) the default position may be that a first instance judgment is provisionally enforceable, and a stay of enforcement may be sought. Security may be required from a creditor seeking to enforce, or from a debtor seeking a stay of enforcement. In Germany, provisional enforceability is generally linked to a security deposit. It should be noted, however, that the Brussels I bis Regulation assumes that the enforcement may not be made dependent on the provision of a security.[98]

For a judgment on the merits of a case, confirmation of enforceability is necessary before enforcement can take place—whether in the form of an endorsement on the judgment or a separate document. In cross-border cases under Brussels I bis

[97] Rys (2020), p. 52.

[98] Prodinger & Nunner-Krautgasser (2020), Kunštek et al. (2020), Rijavec et al. (2020), Wolf et al (2020).

Regulation, Article 33 requires that the judgment is enforceable in the Member States of origin. This is confirmed via the certificate of enforceability (Article 42).

13 Identity of Many Claims

Although the preclusive effects of judgments reduce the scope for relitigation of the same claim, they do not prevent parallel litigation—which may be particularly problematic in the international context. Brussels I bis Regulation, therefore, contains rules to deal with such parallel litigation, primarily based on a principle of temporal priority. In particular, Article 29 regulates the situation where 'proceedings involving the same cause of action and between the same parties are brought in the courts of different Member States'.

The question arises as to how far the requirement of the 'same cause of action' and 'same parties' is correlated to the requirements for claim preclusion.[99]

Same Parties (Personal Identity) In The Tatry, the European Court of Justice (ECJ) ruled, among other things, that the identity of the parties must be understood regardless of their respective position in the two proceedings so that the claimant in the first case can be a defendant in the second case. This is notably relevant in cases where a claim is brought in one Member State and a declaration of non-liability with respect to the same claim (negative declaration) is brought in another Member State.

Same Cause of Action (Objective Identity) In different language versions there are different wording for the objective identity of the claims (Art 29(1) Brussels I bis Regulation): in German 'wegen desselben Anspruchs', in English 'same cause of action', in French 'le même objet et la même cause' and in the Spanish language 'el mismo objeto y la misma causa'. The same wording can be found in the Brussels Convention 1968. Therefore, the matter was dealt with by the European Court of Justice (ECJ) in The Tatry. For the purposes of Article 21 of the Brussels Convention, the 'cause' of the claim includes the facts and the law on which the action is based and the 'object' is the purpose of the action. In that case, 'cause of action' in a case seeking to determine that the defendant was liable for damage and to require him to pay damages was held to be the same as a previous action brought by that defendant to find that he was not liable for that damage.

This decision by the CJEU that proceedings for a negative declaratory action were included with the rule *lis pendens*, overturned the previously held view in some jurisdictions, especially in the Germanic legal community. Until then, the approach of national procedural rules in Germany and Austria was that this was not possible. A negative declaratory claim could not prevent a subsequent claim for performance

[99] In the context of Brussels I bis Regulation see Case C-296/10, Bianca Purrucker v Guillermo Vallés Pérez, 09.11.2010, ECLI:EU:C:2010:665, per View of AG Jääskinen, 4.10.2010, ECLI:EU:C:2010:578.

due to the stand point that a performance action represents the more extensive legal protection in terms of content.

The *lis pendens* principle is universally implemented in EU member states such that the same case cannot be tried in two or more places simultaneously. To understand *lis pendens*, it is first necessary to understand *res judicata*, the principle that a case based on the same merits cannot be tried twice between the same parties, provided a non-appealable decision/judgment has been given. The purpose of *res judicata* is to facilitate a final decision in a dispute and to hinder a party from being forced to retry the same case in absurdum, thus allowing parties to proceed following a dispute knowing that it is legally over.

In the literature, some warnings can be found. It is possible that other issues could arise with respect to the Recast's mechanism for dealing with conflicting proceedings involving third States. First, the requirement in Articles 33 and 34 for the proceedings to have commenced first in a non-EU State creates an incentive to rush to court and could motivate defensive litigation strategies. Secondly, at present the EU does not provide harmonised rules on the recognition and enforcement of non-Member State judgments. Accordingly, the possibility remains for torpedo actions to be instigated by the simple expedient of bringing an action in the court of a Member State that does not recognise a judgment rendered in a third State.[100]

13.1 Related Actions

Article 30 on related actions only requires the actions to be so closely connected that it is expedient to hear and determine them together to avoid the risk of irreconcilable judgments resulting from separate proceedings. It does not contain a requirement for the parties to be the same and a requirement of same cause of action. The CJEU seems to have considered actions related even if they were merely based on different legal bases, e.g. claims in respect of the same loss between the same plaintiff and various defendants, where a claim against one defendant is rooted in contractual liability and a claim against another defendant is rooted in tort.[101] Notion of 'action' used in context with related actions is more comprehensive than the notion of 'claim'. It also considers defences and counter-claims.[102]

Article 30 Brussels I bis Regulation provides that there must be a risk of irreconcilable judgments. How far irreconcilability from this provision corresponds

[100] Cook (2013), p. 87.

[101] Case C-98/06, Freeport plc v Olle Arnoldsson, 11.10.2007, ECLI:EU:C:2007:595; Compare C-145/10, Eva-Maria Painer v Standard VerlagsGmbH and Others, 07.03.2012, ECLI:EU:C:2011:798, para 81; the rationale of that decision is confined to cases where jurisdiction is anchored in rules of jurisdiction *loci delicti comissi*.

[102] Bosters (2017), p. 150; See Research in Motion (UK) Ltd v. Visto Corp [2008] EWCA Civ at 36. 153, 2008 2 All ER (Comm) 650.

with the one in provision of Article 45 (c) Brussels I bis Regulation will be discussed in the next chapter on irreconcilable judgments.

Mainly a distinction from *lis pendens* will be the fact that the parties are different. But the definition of related actions might also cover the cases where the parties are the same, but the cause of action differs slightly.

Moreover, the main difference is in effect that in case of related actions the judge just may stay the proceedings. It is in his discretion to decide when to protect the parties from being involved in the same taking evidence proceeding twice. It is unclear how the provision 'it is expedient to hear and determine cases together' was meant. The Article 30(3) Brussels I bis Regulation also contains a requirement that the national law of the first seised court permits the consolidation. For the rules of Brussels I bis Regulation is deemed that two related actions were submitted in different states. Therefore the consolidation in the meaning of the simultaneous taking evidence process is not foreseen. It is more obvious that the stayed proceedings will remain stayed until the related case is settled. It is unclear how the stayed case should be continued. There are no direct binding effects of the outcome. To avoid the irreconcilability under Article 45(1)(c) the judge should respect the outcome but there is no explicit duty to do so in national law. The benefit might be the use of taking evidence results but it is a problem of using evidence taken in another procedure if the parties had no chance to participate in the process. Here, we can refer to Slovenian rules which contain the solution of model case litigation (Article 279.b Slovenian ZPP) settling some binding effects.

If a large number of lawsuits are filed with the same court, in which the claims are based on the same or similar factual and legal basis, the court may, after receiving the responses to the lawsuits, conduct a model procedure on the basis of one lawsuit, and suspend the remaining procedures.

There is no effect of *res judicata* and the court in other cases is not bound to model decision. However, the sense of the rule is to consider factual and legal findings and positions taken in the model procedure in the other cases where no essential peculiarities exist but under the condition that the party who did not participate in the model procedure does not oppose the transfer of factual ground from another procedure. The party who had the opportunity to participate in the model procedure has no right to opposition.

The sense of related actions can be the inclusion of evidential results from another procedure by more intense cooperation between courts and not in preventing recognition and enforcment of irreconcilable judgments in other Member States.

14 Irreconcilable Judgments

14.1 Mechanisms to Avoid Irreconcilable Judgments

Special *forum connexitatis* in Article 8(1) Brussels I bis Regulation should reduce the risk of irreconcilable judgments.[103] The same aim is introduced in Article 29–34 (*lis pendens* and related actions), and in Article 45(1)(c) and (d) (grounds for refusal of recognition) of the Brussels I bis Regulation.

14.2 Concept of Irreconcilable Judgment

Possible conflicts of judgments are dealt among grounds for refusal of recognition of foreign judgment in Article 45 (1)(c) and (d) and these are :

(c) conflicts with any even later local judgment between the same parties including successors (no same cause of action is mentioned), also outside of Brussels I bis Regulation regime and
(d) conflicts with an earlier judgment given in another Member State or in the third state on the same claim (the same cause of action), between the same parties, provided that the earlier judgment fulfils the conditions necessary for its recognition in the Member State addressed.

In relation to the original Brussels Convention 1968, Jenard reports that the same cause of action in the situation under (c) is not necessarily involved. Thus, for example, a French court in which recognition of a Belgian judgment awarding damages for failure to perform a contract is sought will be able to refuse recognition if a French court has already given judgment in a dispute between the same parties declaring that the contract was invalid. Nevertheless, for an irreconcilable judgment, 'it is not sufficient that there would be a divergence in the outcome of the dispute, but that divergence must also arise from the same situation of fact and law.' The *res judicata* effect is not a requirement for an irreconcilable judgment, 'the words *res judicata* have expressly been omitted.'[104]

Same under Brussels I bis Regulation a foreign judgment can be refused if it is irreconcilable with either (c) a judgment rendered in the enforcement state in a dispute between the same parties or (d) an earlier recognisable judgment rendered in another state in a dispute between the same parties and involving the same cause of action. This ground for review has not been changed, despite criticism in legal

[103] Case 189/87, Athanasios Kalfelis v Bankhaus Schröder, Münchmeyer, Hengst and Co. and others, 27.09.1988, ECLI:EU:C:1988:459, para 12 and case C-539/03, Roche Nederland BV and Others v Frederick Primus and Milton Goldenberg, 13.06.2007, ECLI:EU:C:2006:458, para 20.

[104] Jenard (1979), p. 43.

commentaries and the fact that changes were made in EU regulations that abolished exequatur.

Judgment—meaning of the Brussels I bis Regulation covers all judgments without distinguishing final and interim judgments.

14.3 More on the Scope of Article 45(c) and (d) Brussels I bis Regulatiom

Neither point, (c) or (d) seem to cover the case of related actions. Both provisions namely require the same parties, contrary to Article 30 on related actions which does not contain such a requirement. On the other hand, it neither requires the same cause of action. So, related action might appear if the parties are the same but the claims are not completely identical. Therefore, recognition and enforcement should be refused under Article 45 (1) (c) in case the parties are the same, but the claims are not completely identical, so it would not be possible to refer to pendency rules which require the 'same cause of action', interpreted by the CJEU.

Provisions 45(1)(c) and (d) are broader than Articles 29 to 32 because the decision in conflict may fall outside the scope of the BIR, either because it was rendered in a third State—for Article 45(1) (d)—or because it covers subjects excluded from the material scope of Brussels I bis Regulation—for Article 45(1) (c) and (d).

14.4 The Criticism of Article 45 (1)(c) and (d)

The criticism relates mainly to two issues. The first issue is the priority of a domestic judgment over a foreign judgment even if the foreign judgment was rendered earlier. The second criticism relates to the priority of an earlier judgment regardless of whether it was obtained in violation of the *lis pendens* rule of the Regulation. The discretion of a judge is too comprehensive. He will assess whether from his point of view the legal consequences of the decisions are mutually exclusive.

Therefore provisions 45(c) and (d) should be set in line with the rules on the pendency of the Brussels I bis Regulation to prevent the refusal of recognition of domestic judgment given despite the pendency of the proceedings in the Member State of origin and despite possible violation of exclusive jurisdiction.

One more issue has to be addressed here. Judicial settlements might have the same force as final judgments in the state of origin. They might bring a lawsuit to an end and be enforceable without further formality. However, where the Brussels I bis Regulation and the Lugano Convention are to be applied, 'a judicial settlement, which is essentially contractual in nature in that its content depends first and foremost on the parties' intentions, is not a judgment'. In other words, even for a cross-border lawsuit in which the Brussels I bis Regulation is to be applied and which has been concluded by a judicial settlement having acquired *res judicata* effect, a party to the settlement will not be able to claim irreconcilable judgments as a ground to refuse the recognition (and enforcement) of a judgment from another EU Member State by virtue of Article 45(1)(c) and (d) Brussels I bis Regulation.

It still does not mean that the said judgment will be enforced. There is, at least, a special provision for judicial settlements in Article 59 of the Regulation. However, the chance for two divergent titles in enforcement among the same parties, having the same cause of action, and based on identical facts should be omitted by new rules on court settlements.

15 Court Settlement According to Brussels I bis Regulation

According to CJEU in the case Solo Kleinmotoren GmbH[105] the term court settlement is to be interpreted autonomously. Characteristics of a settlement are its contractual nature, the intention of the parties to end the legal dispute and its effect as an enforcement title (procedural effects of the termination of proceedings and enforceability).

The distinction between procedural settlements and 'consent judgments' presents practical difficulties. In addition, a procedural settlement as an enforcement title must be distinguished from a contractual settlement ('Consent judgments and jugements d'expedient' fall under Article 2(a)).

In general, the court examines whether the result is appropriate and whether certain procedural minimum standards have been complied with. Ultimately, however, what matters it is not the judicial approval of the settlement, but rather its prior conclusion by the parties that creates its binding nature. Thus, the agreement between the parties, not the judicial review, is decisive.[106] But the presence of a judge at the conclusion of the settlement is required.

In both the Slovenian and Croatian legal systems judicial settlements acquire the same *res judicata* effect as actual judgments.[107] Slovenian private international law (PIL) also treats court settlements in the same way as judgments, since a court settlement gains *res judicata* effect. Judicial settlements bring a lawsuit to an end and are enforceable without further formality in Austria, Germany, and the Netherlands.[108]

[105] Case C-414/92, Solo Kleinmotoren GmbH v. Emilio Boch, 02.06.1994, ECLI:EU:C:1994:221.

[106] Hess (2021), p. 480.

[107] See e.g. Supreme Court of Slovenia, judgement in case II Ips 268/2011, 03.04.2011, ECLI:SI:VSRS:2014:II.IPS.268.2011 and Croatian legal writing Dika (2013), pp. 592-598. Prodinger & Nunner-Krautgasser, Wolf et al. (2020) and Sujecki (2020).

[108] Prodinger & Nunner-Krautgasser (2020), Wolf et al. (2020) and Sujecki (2020).

A settlement in the Member State of origin concluded before a court and enforceable may be enforced in another Member State under the Brussels I bis Regulation or can even be confirmed as a European enforcement title (the second paragraph of Article 24 of the EEOR).

At this point, it should be emphasized that, in contrast to the position under the law of Slovenia, foreign judicial settlements often have no *res judicata* effects, but only enforceability effects. According to EU regulations, therefore, a court settlement cannot be considered as a reason for not recognising a foreign court decision within the meaning of point 3 of Article 34 of the Brussels I bis Regulation, even if both enforcement titles are mutually incompatible.

Therefore, where the Brussels I bis Regulation is to be applied, judicial settlement, which is essentially contractual in nature in that its content depends first and foremost on the parties' intentions, is not a judgment.

The primacy of EU law also implies that the term 'judgment' in the Brussels I bis Regulation has an autonomous meaning that is detached from national procedural law. However, such an autonomous definition of the term 'judgment' is bound to create problems in legal orders where judicial settlements produce effects identical to judgments (Slovenia, Croatia).[109]

Court settlements are extraordinarily convenient instruments of amicable dispute resolution. In Slovenia, for example, about one-fifth of civil proceedings conducted annually end with a settlement. Theory attributes to the court settlement a mixed contractual and procedural nature. The contractual side is evident because the settlement has to meet the requirements for a contractual settlement under substantive law as provided in the Slovenian Obligation Code. Slovenian ZPP provides a special lawsuit for the annulment of court settlements and does not give the dissatisfied party the right to appeal in court. On the other hand, the indication of the procedural nature of a settlement is the fact that it terminates the dispute and has immediate effect as a *res transacta*,—which is the same effect as *res judicata* and means the finality of the settlement. Settlements that include imposition of liability also have the effect of enforceability. In relation to a settlement, it would be more natural to speak of an acceptance of liability. However, the settlement as an enforcement title must include an order to which the defendant has agreed.

Slovenian law defines a court settlement as a settlement concluded by the parties in writing before the civil court in the proceedings on the disputed case. It additionally must contain all the elements of an obligation settlement (settlement of substantive law). A court settlement concluded during the proceedings may relate to all or part of the disputed case. It may also include other disputed legal relationships between the parties.[110]

---

[109] Sladič (2018), p. 109.

[110] The court settlement does not automatically terminate all open cases within the commercial dispute between parties. It has the direct effect of concluding the case only in the procedure in which it was concluded. Regarding other open procedures, the parties must agree to withdraw the action; Higher Court of Celje, VSC Sklep III Cpg 54/2021, 14/04/2021, ECLI:SI:VSCE:2021:III.CPG.54.2021.

It is also possible to settle before the start of the litigation, which should prevent the dispute, but this is done before the judge in a special court procedure for a court settlement.

Thus, in Slovenia, as in Austria, there are three main types of court settlements:

- the 'classic' court settlement, which is concluded within an ongoing procedure;
- the praetoric settlement before starting a legal dispute, which can be concluded upon the party's application in the special procedure for court settlement (Article 309 ZPP);
- the settlement as a result of mediation, if the agreement reached in a mediation procedure is afterwards confirmed before a judge in order to be upgraded into *res transacta* and an enforceable court settlement.

All these types of settlements are settlements within the meaning of Article 2 (b) Brussels I bis Regulation (as well as the definition of the CJEU) and thus fall under the regime of Article 59 Brussels I bis Regulation.

According to Article 2(b) Brussels I bis Regulation, a court settlement is a 'settlement which has been approved by a court of a Member State or concluded before a court of a Member State in the course of proceedings.' This definition was broadened in comparison to Article 58 Brussels I Regulation and now leaves no doubt that it covers not only settlements that were reached in court during a proceeding but also settlements that were already reached out of court and rendered enforceable (as provided for in Article 6 of the Directive on certain aspects of mediation in civil and commercial matters).

15.1 Intermediate Conclusion

The lack of a sharp definition may not be a problem in the majority of cases, because the concept of a court settlement is well-known in most Member States (although its concrete form varies between the different Member States).

Scientific literature has proposed several possible standards that might be used to distinguish between a settlement and a decision. One such proposition is a mere formal distinction, according to which it should depend on whether the act in question takes the form of a judgment or a decision, in which case it should not be considered a court settlement. Another dilemma in the literature focuses on the functional role of the court, i.e., whether the court only documents the 'court settlement' and examines it in the light of certain minimum legal requirements or whether it decides on the substance (Article 58 1b Brussels I bis Regulation). Finally, some authors propose a distinction based on the effects of the act in question, where 'judgment-like' effects, such as a *res judicata*-effect, will indicate that it is a judgment.

In our opinion, the most important factor distinguishing a judgment and a court settlement should be whether the legal act created is predominantly contractual (including procedural contracts) or predominantly a sovereign decision. This assessment considers both the formal part of the legal act and the functional role of the court. The effects of the acts in question, however, do not constitute a suitable criterion for delimitation in our opinion, not only because the effects of judgments—as well as of court settlements—may vary strongly in different Member States (and therefore there are no 'exclusive' effects that determine when to consider an act a 'judgment' or a 'court settlement'), but also because court settlements constitute 'judgment surrogates' in some legal systems, potentially generating the same legal effects as judgments (e.g. in Slovenia the effect as *res transacta* is equally binding as *res judicata*. Following from this understanding, if a court of law takes a sovereign decision, then—as a rule of thumb—this legal act is to be considered a 'judgment' for the purposes of the Brussels I bis Regulation, even if it was reached by consensus in the proceedings (for example, if one party had admitted the claim or if the parties had largely predetermined the facts on which the decision is based).[111] Accordingly, Slovenian 'judgments of recognition' or 'judgments based on plaintiff's waiver' are to be classified as 'judgments' in the sense of Article 2(a) Brussels I bis Regulation and not as court settlements.

However, for cross-border enforcement it is important that the law of the Member State of origin enables the specific type of authentic instrument to obtain the status of an enforcement title.

16 Authentic Instrument According to Brussels I bis Regulation

16.1 Concept

A definition of an authentic instrument is given in Article 2(c) of Brussels I bis Regulation. The concept of an authentic instrument with the character of an enforcement title is, pursuant to the CJEU case law, interpreted autonomously at a European level. According to these definitions, an authentic instrument is an instrument that has been established by a public authority or other authority empowered for that purpose by the Member State in which it originates which adopts a certain required form. Its authenticity under national law must relate not only to the signatures but also to the content of the document.[112] The particular designation of a relevant public authority, scope of authority and authentication procedures adopted are a matter of national law.

[111] Anzenberger (2020), p. 12.

[112] See e.g. Directorate General for Internal Policies, Policy Department C: Citizens' Rights and Constitutional Affairs, Comparative Study on Authentic Instruments National Provisions of Private Law, Circulation, Mutual Recognition and Enforcement, Possible Legislative Initiative by the European Union: United Kingdom, France, Germany, Poland, Romania, Sweden (notified under document PE 408.329 (2008).

Obligations arising from authentic instruments are enforceable. In some States this is by operation of law. In other States authentic instruments are enforceable if a specific submission to enforcement is contained in a declaration in the authentic instrument.

16.2 Incompatible Authentic Instruments

If two incompatible authentic instruments occur in enforcement, the question as to which authentic instrument, if any, should be given priority could be assessed using the solution adopted in the Recital 66 of the Regulation on Succession 650/2012. Due to their specific nature, authentic instruments cannot be compared in the same way as irreconcilable judgments. Therefore, the circumstances of the particular case come into play. Where it is not clear from those circumstances which authentic instrument, if any, should be given priority, the question should be determined by the courts having jurisdiction under this Regulation, or, where the question is raised as an incidental question in the course of proceedings, by the court seised of those proceedings. In the event of incompatibility between an authentic instrument and a decision, regard should be had to the grounds of non-recognition of decisions.

16.3 Diversity of Enforceable Authentic Instruments

The notion of a public document clearly includes notarial acts/deeds but not all Member States are familiar with the concept of Latin notaries. It is unknown in the UK, although there are some civil notaries dealing with cross-border issues. In Sweden[113] and Cyprus,[114] notarial deeds are also not acknowledged as authentic instruments that may constitute enforcement titles.[115] However, foreign enforceable notary deeds have to be recognised and enforced according to Brussels I bis Regulation in those countries anyway.

Moreover, even private deeds regarding obligations concerning sums of money contained therein, bills of exchange, and other debt instruments, which are enforcement titles according to some national laws may be enforcement titles under the condition that their authenticity has been certified by a national public authority or by another body vested with the public power to do so in that country. A good example

[113] In Sweden, certain agreements regarding alimony obligations are directly enforceable by the Swedish Enforcement Authority, see Conseil des barreaux européens – Council of Bars and Law Societies of Europe (2011), p. 4, maintenance obligations, however, remain beyond the scope of the research.

[114] Christofi & Loizou (2020), p. 8.

[115] Conseil des barreaux européens – Council of Bars and Law Societies of Europe (2011); Bylander & Linton (2020), p. 38.

is Italy where, bank checks, promissory notes, and also private documents, insofar as a public officer certified the authenticity of their signatures, may be enforcement titles.[116]

This group of authentic instruments also comprises commercial contract policies in Spain ('pólizas de contratos mercantiles') signed by the parties and by a registered trade broker. Although lawyers and solicitors in Portugal have the competence to authenticate documents, private documents may also be authorised and become authentic instruments.

For example, a mediation agreement in Spain ('acuerdo de mediación'), if raised to the status of a public deed, may qualify as an authentic instrument.

Another example of an authentic instrument that is enforceable under the Brussels I bis Regulation is a decision of the Lithuanian Labour Dispute Committee. The Labour Dispute Committee is a mandatory pretrial dispute settlement body that specialises in individual labour disputes. Decisions made by the committee are binding for the parties and enforceable.

In some states, bailiffs are also entitled to issue authentic instruments. One example can be found in France, where the status of authentic instruments has been bestowed upon titles issued by bailiffs in cases of non-payment of cheques. In Sweden, a similar title can be issued by the Enforcement agency (Kronofogdemyndigheit). Under Croatian and North Macedonian law, debenture bonds (zadužnica) serve as authentic instruments. In Spain, bearer or registered financial bonds (títulos al portador) that represent past due obligations and coupons have the status of enforcement titles. This also applies to unexpired certificates (certificados no caducados) issued by the entities responsible for accounting records regarding securities represented by book entries defined in the Securities Market Law.

Such a variety of authentic instruments serving for direct enforcement is undeniably in line with commercial purposes to accelerate business and create safeguards in the face of financial disobedience. On the other hand, they increase the risk for the debtor to be unfairly exposed to recovery. These instruments can be enforced throughout the EU and only subject to the public policy exception (Articles 58-60). The lack of judicial scrutiny could increase the risk of fraud and forgeries, which non-judicial authorities may be ill-equipped to detect. In that regard, some have rightly criticised the abolition of exequatur for authentic instruments, which are even more vulnerable than judicial rulings. Nonetheless, the right of the debtor to contest inaccurately certified claims in the state of enforcement—as opposed to e.g. certified judgments under Article 21(2) EEO—should help to mitigate these risks.[117]

In this context, the Polish Constitutional court found that the right of banks to issue bank enforcement titles constituted a violation of Article 32 sec. 1 of the Polish Constitution—namely the principle of equality in relation to the banks' customers.

[116] Guissani (2018), Kaczorowska et al. (2021).

[117] Hovaguimian (2015), p. 249.

The constitutional court's statement that banks are not public authorities and do not exercise public powers in regard to bank enforcement titles is consistent with the CJEU's ruling in the case Unibank. The CJEU namely explained that: 'an acknowledgment of indebtedness enforceable under the law of the State of origin whose authenticity has not been established by a public authority or other authority empowered for that purpose by that State does not constitute an authentic instrument within the meaning of Article 50 of the Brussels Convention'.[118]

17 Intermediate Conclusion

However, for cross-border enforcement, it is important that the law of the Member State of origin enables the specific type of authentic instrument to obtain the status of an enforcement title. The certificate in Annex II from the state of origin proves that the authentic instrument is enforceable. However, there are still some ambiguities regarding box 5.2.1.1.: 'Short description of the subject matter'.

Another uncertain issue is the provision of Article 58(2) Brussels I bis Regulation: 'authentic instrument produced must satisfy the conditions necessary to establish its authenticity in the Member State of origin.' What requirements are meant here, since the legalisation[119] of documents has been abolished? In Article 61, Brussels I bis Regulation provides that no documentary or similar formalities, not even an apostille, are required for documents issued in a Member State.

On the other hand, the transparency of the requirements that different instruments serving as enforcement titles need to meet must be improved in the interests of the single market and the economy.

The most widespread is the system of notary deeds. The role of the notary is regulated by the State, with strict rules for dealing with documents. The creditor is equipped to start enforcement without litigation, but on the other hand, the debtor can submit a lawsuit to challenge the legal transaction in the notary act. In Slovenia, this lawsuit does not stop enforcement but nevertheless gives the debtor a proportionate legal remedy. It is, therefore, possible to eliminate the concern that allowing persons outside the judicial system to issue enforcement orders in principle increases the risk of unfair debt recovery. The debtor can in fact bring an action regarding the legal transaction in accordance with the jurisdictional rules under Brussels I bis Regulation.

---

[118] See more in this volume Rodziewicz, Authentic Instruments.

[119] For the use of a public document abroad out of the scope of Brussels I bis Regulation, additional administrative formalities are usually required for the authentication of the documents. The traditional method of authentication of public documents for purposes of use abroad is legalisation. Legalisation means a chain of individual document authorizations. The regular legalisation procedure (i.e. full legalisation) provides for the legalisation of the document first by the competent authorities of the issuing State, followed by the embassy or consulate of the country in which it is to be used.

18 National Structural Differences in Enforcement Procedures

Generally taken there are three different systems of civil enforcement in the world. The private system involves an enforcement agent distinct from the courts—whether an independent professional. The other is a court-oriented enforcement system and the third is the one with an administrative enforcement agency. The latter only applies for Sweden and Finland. In Sweden, kronofogde have the same level of qualifications as judges and operate in a 'quasi-judicial' way.

Having non-judicial authorities to carry out the judgment import function without *exequatur* is potentially problematic. It includes questions about the level of training of the competent officer; the fact that expertise is not concentrated in one place,[120] leading to the greater possibility of inconsistent approaches and inefficient procedures; problems relating to the adaptation of the imported judgment; and varying regulation of the instances of recourse in the case of a challenge to the recognition of the judgment; problems of identifying the scope of the adjudicated claim that need to be enforced due to the different types and structures of judgments and due to the problems with the correspondence of the certificate to the judgment itself.

In some Member States, it is anticipated that the enforcement agent will be able to evaluate legally the steps required by the debtor—but this confidence cannot translate across legal systems. Although it has been asserted that the introduction of a very detailed certificate is an indirect way of harmonising national procedures. Kennett notes that procedural autonomy is greater under the Brussels I bis Regulation than before.

The second system, in principle enacted in Slovenia, requires first of all that a Court renders a decree (authorisation of enforcement) as permission for the special type of enforcement that is further performed by a court bailiff or private agent.

Differences in the level of responsibility of enforcement agents have an impact on their scope for initiative and flexibility, which facilitate cross-border collaboration—for example through the creation of networks and through direct communication between enforcement agents. Clarification of the roles and responsibilities of those engaged in the enforcement process will assist in identifying the 'nodes' in the cross-border process.[121]

---

[120] The Swedish Kronofogdemyndighet is a unified agency (although with dispersed offices). Brussels I bis Regulation issues are concentrated in one office (Umea).

[121] See more Kennett (2018), p. 273.

19 Problems of Terminology

Terminological differences between national enforcement systems in relation to functionally similar instruments or procedures also create significant problems in the communication and understanding of instruments. This inevitably hinders cross-border enforcement itself but also frustrates discussions about how to improve cross-border enforcement.[122]

20 Conclusions

Delays in national procedures due to a request for refusal of recognition/enforcement of a foreign enforcement title are an exception to the principle of enforceability of a judgment enforceable in the Member State of origin and the opportunities to lodge applications for refusal, therefore, requires a restrictive interpretation. Before turning to enforcement titles as such, the most general conclusion is that, despite many deficiencies, the changed procedural role of a creditor, which is related to the automatic enforcement of a foreign title under Brussels I bis Regulationis an important step forward in improving the creditor's position for quicker debt collection abroad. For the debtor, however, the Brussels I bis Regulation opens up new defensive strategies but also complicates his options for lodging a challenge to a foreign enforcement title. A necessary goal for the future will be to build uniform standards of due process in all Member States which will enable the abolition of any necessary additional procedures regarding foreign titles. In the longer term, it seems an insufficient solution to introduce an autonomous formal procedure specially designed for reviewing foreign judgments, but it is the only legislative option for now. One cannot other than agree that human rights must prevail, and that in the current situation a review procedure in the Member State addressed is inevitable. Although national enforcement systems are very different from one Member State to another, they still have some common principles which could make it possible to regulate a European procedure for the limited review of foreign judgments. Theoretically, such review could be introduced in the State of origin, but it would not be realistic to expect the court of origin to review its own judgment and national procedure fairly. In the literature, ideas can be found of transnational control of enforcement titles by an appellate review of rights and standards through a common, supranational court at the EU level.[123]

The objective of the Brussels I bis Regulation was to remove obstacles to the circulation of foreign judgments without changing the relevant domestic laws. It is however doubtful if this approach can survive in the long term. In the absence of

[122] See more Drnovšek (2018); Kennett (2018), p. 301.

[123] Hovaguimian (2015), p. 215; Cuniberti and Rueda (2011), p. 316; De Cristofaro (2012), pp. 377–378.

significant harmonisation measures, the rights conferred by community law must be exercised before the national courts following the conditions laid down by national rules. First of all, it is necessary to enact implementing rules as a sort of translation of the regulation's rules. On the other hand, harmonisation is happening all the time due to the influence of European law on national legislators. Civil procedure in the EU is increasingly subject to further Europeanisation. Member states are confronted with a growing body of EU legislation and case law on procedural topics. National legislators are also subject to impacts from other national systems, which are becoming more understandable due to different comparative studies and literature. The impact of good practices from different Member States is important. Nevertheless, such impact is a result of research projects which highlight commonalities and develop arguments that may be useful in all legal systems.

Moreover, this research has demonstrated that one of the greatest problems is that, due to differences in national legal orders, the EU rules are more difficult to implement in some Member States than in others. Conceptual differences in procedures lead to different interpretations, and solutions that seem obvious in one jurisdiction are much less obvious in another. The European legislator might be working from the assumption that it is the courts who deal with disputed issues in all Member States. But it is necessary to consider that in privately orientated enforcement systems, enforcement titles have to be checked by enforcement agents acting outside of the court.

Furthermore, EU Civil Procedure law sometimes challenges the concepts, ideas, and structures of national laws. Depending on the degree of difference, it could be a matter of mere nuance or one of clashes between fundamental concepts, principles, and structures. Problems may ensue where there is a need for radical reforms with potentially momentous consequences.

The structures of the enforcement systems influence the wide range of instruments considered to be acceptable as enforcement titles.

In general, enforcement titles everywhere are divided into groups based on mostly the same factors.

Despite previous case law interpretations by the CJEU of the term 'judgment', difficulties in interpretation remain an urgent problem. This problem is not solved by the rules on adaptation. The European legislator should make a clear distinction between the identification of the obligation or claim subject to enforcement and the specific provisions in a judgment that orders coercive measures. Harmonisation should go further: a judgment should consist of two separated parts, the operative part, and the reasoning, so as to be able to identify the effects of a judgment that are primarily found in the operative part. Good practices will influence the style of reasoning as is discussed above.

The same question arises in relation to the interpretation of provisional measures. When is a provisional order a title to be enforced, and when is it a manifestation of state power to order coercive measures, which may not be imposed on another sovereign state? Freezing orders are an example of a concept that gives rise to confusion. Member States have different approaches to this issue.

The understanding of the terms decree, order, decision, and writ of execution needs further elaboration in Member States. Continental legal theory seems to offer some good solutions as it examines the applicable legal norms (exegetical jurisprudence) and develops recognised legal principles based on the prevailing legal opinions. It thus serves legal certainty and the predictability of court decisions by determining the possibilities and limits of new legal constructions for solving legal problems.

Moreover, the concept of *res judicata* as applied to a judgment under Brussels I bis Regulation should be understood as an effect making the decision binding and conclusive. It is conclusive if the effect is attained in the state of origin because the judgment can no more be challenged by ordinary legal remedies. The binding effect is in most cases the result of the irreversibility of the judgment.[124] On the other hand, enforceability is an effect of a judgment that is binding but not conclusive and is not identical with *res judicata*. The effect of enforceability can attain also the decisions imposing liability which are not final yet, because legal remedies in the state of origin are still not exhausted.

Despite many practical issues, in most systems, we have not found decisions or instruments being problematic in the light of the autonomous definitions. It appears that as long as a decision falls within the scope of civil and commercial matters, all of the decisions mentioned seem to fall within the scope of Article 2(a) of the Brussels I bis Regulation.

National enforcement agents outside the court will also have to assess the ruling and statement of reasons for foreign decisions.

The solution is the improvement of knowledge of foreign enforcement titles within the EU Member States which will result in improved judicial information on the ability and suitability of enforcement titles for recognition and enforcement (the concept, structure, and terminology of enforcement titles, the binding character of the judgment—provisional enforcement of judgments in some jurisdictions—how far does a judgment need to be final before it can be enforced; preclusive effects of judgments).

The degree of precision of the operative parts in foreign judicial decisions, required for the enforcement proceedings, should in principle be assessed in the Member State of origin. If foreign judgments cannot be rendered sufficiently specific, because it would be necessary to violate the prohibition on verifying the content of the judgment, enforcement must be rejected. Nevertheless, the situation is often ambiguous, and the interpretation of the title needs to be further analysed from different perspectives.

Still, the certificates under the Brussels I bis Regulation have their limitations. It is therefore recommended to upgrade the forms for the certificates in Annexes I and II and word them more precisely to be able to reflect the exact status of the judgment or authentic instrument within the Brussels I bis Regulation. Even as things stand the

[124] It corresponds with the concept of formal res judicata; division on formal and material res judicata is accepted in Germany, see Theories on Finality and Res Judicata of this Chapter.

certificate in Annex I or II indicates that the court of origin has to certify that a case is a civil or commercial matter subject to the Brussels I bis Regulation. But a review in the state addressed is not excluded, albeit those concepts have to be interpreted in an autonomous European manner. Another problem with the certificate is the ambiguous rule regarding the extract of the judgment or summary of the authentic instrument in the certificate (Article 42(1)(b) and 60 Brussels I bis Regulation). This concept may have a clear meaning in some Member States but not in others. We would suggest that the box in the Annex for an extract of a judgment should require clarifications of the type and extent of the obligation and the time when it should be performed. They should be followed by a short description of the cause of action (as defined above in the section on *lis pendens* of this Chapter).

The more complex certificate now provided under Brussels I bis Regulationis also binding with regard to the judgment's enforceability in the state of origin, thereby exempting the enforcement authority from further investigation. Nevertheless, court intervention is sometimes necessary even without any complaint of the parties (e.g. with respect to the problem of the unclear scope of the obligation due).

In the future, the certificate could be given mandatory evidential value not allowing any review of the characterisations certified in the state addressed. This implies another legislative adjustment to regulate the remedies for challenge, rectification and withdrawal of the certificate in the country of origin. The certificate of enforceability should further be amended also to provide greater clarification of certain issues e.g., interest rates, or more generally information about how interest should be calculated. It is not unusual for the instruments received to be very unclear as to the actual enforcement steps that need to be taken.

A certificate for an authentic instrument using the form set out in Annex II is issued by the competent authority or court of the Member State of origin at the request of any interested party. The form also contains a box for a summary, this time of the enforceable obligation recorded in the authentic instrument or of the agreement between the parties recorded in the court settlement (Article 60). The previous Brussels I Regulation does not contain any instructions regarding the content of the obligation recorded in an authentic instrument or settlement. In relation to making a summary, there is again a question as how to understand the scope of the summary: nevertheless, for enforcement to take place the exact obligation has to be made clear.

The Brussels regime should introduce mandatory service of the certificate on both parties in the State of origin and require evidence of service (return receipt) as part of the formal requirements to start enforcement of the foreign judgment in the State addressed. This would enable some surprise effect to be maintained in starting enforcement.

About the identity of many claims, concurrent proceedings, court settlements, and authentic instruments the conclusions are incorporated in the intermediate conclusion in the paragraphs above with the same name.

References

Anzenberger P (2020) The cross-border enforcement of court settlements within Brussels Ia regulation: from a European and an Austrian perspective. Lexonomica 12(2):149–162. https://doi.org/10.18690/lexonomica.12.2.149-162.2020
Becker-Eberhard E (2016–2017) Para 260. In: Krüger W, Rauscher T (eds) Munchener Kommentar zur ZPO. C. H. Beck, München
Boscovic O (2018) Provisional measures. In: Rijavec V, Kennet W, Keresteš T et al (eds) Remedies concerning enforcement of foreign judgements: Brussels I Recast. Wolters Kluwer, Alphen aan den Rijn, pp 137–148
Bosters T (2017) Collective redress and private international law in the EU. Asser, The Hague
Brehm W (2012) VIII.A. In: Rijavec V, Jelinek W, Brehm W (eds) Die Erleichterung der Zwangsvollstreckung in Europa, Europäischer Vollstreckungstite. Nomos, Baden Baden
Briggs A (2005) Civil jurisdiction and judgments. Norton Rose LLP, London, Singapore
Bylander E, Linton M (2020) National report for Sweden. Project EU-En4s – JUST-AG-2018/JUST-JCOO-AG-2018.
Christofi D, Loizou D (2020) National report for Cyprus. Project EU-En4s – JUST-AG-2018/JUST-JCOO-AG-2018.
Conseil des barreaux européens – Council of Bars and Law Societies of Europe, Comparative Study on Authentic Acts and Instruments with Comparable Status and Effects According to National Legislation Within The EU, Considering in Particular The Role of Lawyers,. https://www.ccbe.eu/NTCdocument/Report_Authentic_Act1_1302619714.pdf
Cook J (2013) Pragmatism in the European Union: recasting the Brussels I regulation to ensure the effectiveness of exclusive choice-of-court agreements. Aberdeen Student Law Rev 4:76–91
Couchez G, Lagarde X (2014) Procédure civile, 17th edn. Sirey, Paris
Cuniberti G, Rueda I (2011) Abolition of Exequatur: Addressing the Commission's Concerns. Rabels Zeitschrift für ausländisches und internationales Privatrecht
De Cristofaro M (2012) The abolition of Exequatur proceedings: speeding up the free movement of judgments while preserving the rights of the defense. In: Pocar F, Viarengo I, Villata F (eds) Recasting Brussels I: proceedings of the conference held at the University of Milan on November. CEDAM, Padua
de Leval G (2021) Droit judiciaire – Tome 2. Procédure civile. Larcier, Brussels
Dickinson A (2007) The Effect in the European Community of Judgments in Civil and Commercial Matters: Recognition, Res Judicata and Abuse of Process. European Community Framework Programme for Judicial Co-operation in Civil Matters. https://www.biicl.org/files/2976_discussion_paper.pdf
Dika M (2013) Građansko parnično pravo, Sudske odluke i sudska nagodba, IX. Knjiga. Narodne novine, Zagreb
Directorate General for Internal Policies, Policy Department C: Citizens' Rights and Constitutional Affairs, Comparative Study on Authentic Instruments National Provisions of Private Law, Circulation, Mutual Recognition and Enforcement, Possible Legislative Initiative by the European Union: United Kingdom, France, Germany, Poland, Romania, Sweden (notified under document PE 408.329 (2008)
Domej T (2016) Internationale Zwangsvollstreckung und Haftungsverwirklichung. Mohr, Tübingen
Drnovšek K (2018) Financial implications of remedies against foreign enforcement titles and linguistic issues under Brussels I recast. In: Rijavec V, Kennet W, Keresteš T et al (eds) Remedies concerning enforcement of foreign judgements: Brussels I Recast. Wolters Kluwer, Alphen aan den Rijn, pp 227–272
Esplugues Mota C (2016) Article 21. In: Magnus U, Mankowski P (eds) European commentaries on private international law. O. Schmidt, Köln, pp 541–553
European Judicial Atlas in civil matters, European e-Justice Portal. https://e-justice.europa.eu/content_european_judicial_atlas_in_civil_matters-321-en.do

Fasching H (1990) Zivilprozeßrecht, 2nd edn. Manz, Vienna

Ferrand F (2014) Lis Pendence and Res Judicata from national law to a possible European harmonisation? In: Hess B, Kollman S, Adolphsen J (eds) Festschrift für Peter Gottwald zum 70. Geburtstag. C.H. Beck, Munich, pp 144–158

Galič A (2009) Sodba na podlagi odpovedi. In: Ude L, Galič A (eds) Pravdni postopek zakon s komentarjem. GV, Uradni list RS, Ljubljana

Geimer R, Geimer E, Geimer G (2005) Internationales Zivilprozessrecht, 5th edn. Otto Schmidt, Köln

Green Paper on the review of Council Regulation (EC) No 44/2001 on jurisdiction and the recognition and enforcement of judgments in civil and commercial matters, 21.4.2009

Guissani A (2018) National Report for Italy. https://pf.um.si/site/assets/files/3539/national_report_italy.pdf

Halsbury's Laws of England is the authoritative source on the laws of England and Wales, LexisNexis. https://www.lexisnexis.co.uk/products/halsburys-laws-of-england.html

Hess B (2010) Europäisches Zivilprozessrecht: ein Lehrbuch. C. F. Müller, Heidelberg

Hess B (2021) Europäisches Zivilprozessrecht, 2nd edn. De Gruyter, Berlin, Boston

Hess B, Pfeiffer T, Schlosser P (2007) Report on the Application of Regulation Brussels I in the Member States, Study JLS/C4/2005/03. Ruprecht-Karls-Universität, Heidelberg

Hess B et al (2022) Max Planck Institute Luxembourg for Procedural Law Research Paper Series 2022(6):1–35

Hovaguimian P (2015) The enforcement of foreign judgments under Brussels I bis: false alarms and real concerns. J Priv Int Law 11(2):212–251. https://doi.org/10.1080/17441048.2015.1068001/

Ivanc T (2018) Introductory Chapter. In: Rijavec V, Kennet W, Keresteš T et al (eds) Remedies concerning enforcement of foreign judgements: Brussels I Recast. Wolters Kluwer, Alphen aan den Rijn, pp 1–38

Jenard P (1979) Report on the Convention on jurisdiction and the enforcement of judgments in civil and commercial matters signed at Brussels. OJ C 59, 5.3.1979. Also published as Bulletin of the European Communities Supplement 12/79, p 220

Kaczorowska M, Voinich A, Previatello M (2021) National report for Italy. Project EU-En4s - JUST-AG-2018/JUST-JCOO-AG-2018

Kaye P (1999) Law of the European Judgment Convention. Barry Rose Law Publishers, Chichester

Kennett W (2018) Different national enforcement structures and their consequences for cross-border enforcement. In: Rijavec V, Kennet W, Keresteš T et al (eds) Remedies concerning enforcement of foreign judgements: Brussels I Recast. Wolters Kluwer, Alphen aan den Rijn, pp 301–358

Kennett W (2021) Civil Enforcement in comparative perspective. Intersentia, Cambridge, Antwerp, Chicago

Kenton W (2020) Writ of Execution, Investopedia. https://www.investopedia.com/terms/w/writ-of-execution.asp

Kodek G (2015) Article 35–60 EuGVVO 2012. In: Czernich D, Kodek G, Mayr P (eds) Europäisches Gerichtsstands-und Vollstreckungsrecht – Brüssel Ia-Verordnung (EuGVVO 2012) und Übereinkommen von Lugano 20, 4th edn. LexisNexis, Vienna

Kramer X, Ontanu A, de Rooij, M (2018) The application of Brussels I (Recast) in the legal practice of EU Member States, Synthesis Report

Kropholler J (2005) Europäisches Zivilprozessrecht Kommentar, 8th edn. Recht und Wirtschaft GmbH, Frankfurt am Main

Kunštek E, Kunda I, Mihelčič G et al (2020) National report for Croatia. Project EU-En4s - JUST-AG-2018/JUST-JCOO-AG-2018

Mayr P (2004) Das streitige Verfahren (Zivilprozessrecht), https://www.uibk.ac.at/zivilrecht/buch/kap19_0.xml?section-view=true;section=5

Mežnar Š (2012) Objektivne, subjektivne in časovne meje pravnomočnosti v odškodninskem pravu, Pravni letopis, IPP, Ljubljana

Musielak H (2016–2017) Para 300. In: Krüger W, Rauscher T (eds) Munchener Kommentar zur ZPO. C. H. Beck, München
Nagel H, Gottwald P (2007) Internationales Zivilprozeßrecht. O. Schmidt, Köln
Pavčnik T (2015) Koncept in argumentacija sodne odločbe (Concept and argumentation of court decision). Pravosodni bilten, Vrhovno sodišče RS Ljubljana
Prodinger L, Nunner-Krautgasser B (2020) National report for Austria. JUST-AG-2018/JUST-JCOO-AG-2018.
Rechberger W, Simotta D (2009) Zivilprozessrecht. Manz'sche, Wien
Rijavec V (2012) III. B. In: Rijavec V, Jelinek W, Brehm W, Die Erleichterung der Zwangsvollstreckung in Europa, Europäischer Vollstreckungstite. Nomos, Baden Baden, pp 105–120
Rijavec V (2018) Final assessment of effecting and protecting rights in cross-border enforcement of monetary claims under Brussels I Recast. In: Rijavec V, Kennet W, Keresteš T et al (eds) Remedies concerning enforcement of foreign judgements: Brussels I Recast. Wolters Kluwer, Alphen aan den Rijn, pp 359–422
Rijavec V, Sladič J, Gomes J (2015) Introductory chapter. In: Rijavec V, Ivanc T, Keresteš T (eds) Simplification of debt collection in the EU. Kluwer Law International, Alphen aan den Rijn, pp 1–46
Rijavec V, Baghrizabehi B, Drnovšek K et al. (2020) National reports for Slovenia. Project EU-En4s — JUST-AG-2018/JUST-JCOO-AG-2018
Rys M (2020) National report for Belgium. Project EU-En4s — JUST-AG-2018/JUST-JCOO-AG-2018
Schlosser P (1979) Report on the Convention of 9 October 1978 on the Assosiation of the Kingdom of Denmark, Ireland and the United Kingdom of Great Britain and Northern Ireland to the Convenvention on jurisdiction and the enforcement of judgments in civil and commercial matters and to the Protocol on its Interpretation by the Court of Justice. OJ C 59
Schlosser P (2009) EU-Zivilprozessrecht: EuGVVO, AVAG, VTVO, MahnVO, BagatellVO, HZÜ, EuZVO, HBÜ, EuBVO, 3rd edn. Beck, München
Sladič J (2018) Some open issues in determining the scope of enforcement titles in Brussels I Recast. In: Rijavec V, Kennet W, Keresteš T et al (eds) Remedies concerning enforcement of foreign judgements: Brussels I Recast. Wolters Kluwer, Alphen aan den Rijn, pp 95–112
Sujecki B (2020) National report for Netherlands. Project EU-En4s — JUST-AG-2018/JUST-JCOO-AG-2018
Wedam Lukić D (2009) Pravomočnost sodbe: Pojem in pomen pravomočnosti. In: Ude L, Galič A (eds) Pravdni postopek zakon s komentarjem. GV, Uradni list RS, Ljubljana
Wolf C, Volkhausen L (2018) National enforcement titles: a comparative German perspective. In: Rijavec V, Kennet W, Keresteš T et al (eds) Remedies concerning enforcement of foreign judgements: Brussels I Recast. Wolters Kluwer, Alphen aan den Rijn, pp 81–94
Wolf C, Kurth N, Mieszaniec K (2020) National report for Germany. Project EU-En4s — JUST-AG-2018/JUST-JCOO-AG-2018

Enforcement Titles in the EU: Common Core After All?

José Caramelo Gomes and Tomaž Keresteš

Abstract The chapter attempts to identify a common core of shared legal principles, which underline the notions of enforcement titles in both the Common and Civil law systems of Europe. The authors employed a comparative analysis, which demonstrated that the existing lines of difference among the national laws are neither particularly deep nor static. At the functional level, there was no finding off any differences with dramatical consequences. This would present an opportunity for the EU legislator to make bold new steps towards harmonisation efforts.

1 Introduction

In previous years the comparative analysis of law in Europe strongly embraced the concept of 'common core'. For the purpose of this chapter, we understand common core to express the actual findings, if any, about similar rules or institutions, both on a conceptual, abstract approach, or in a functional approach, among different legal systems.[1] Our work in the previous project 'Dimensions of evidence in civil procedure'[2] has already demonstrated that even in the perspective of the pessimistic beholder we should expect a certain degree, regardless how small, of pan-European principles of Civil Procedure.[3] Even though it is difficult to expect that there exist some substantive degree of common principles, terminology and notions within the

[1] Keresteš and Caramelo Gomes (2016), p. 321.

[2] Project DEECP: JUST/2011-2012/JCIV/AG/3434, with financial support from the Civil Justice/Criminal Justice Programme of the European Union.

[3] Keresteš and Caramelo Gomes (2016), p. 345.

J. Caramelo Gomes
University Portucalense Faculty of Law, Porto, Portugal

T. Keresteš (✉)
University of Maribor, Faculty of Law, Maribor, Slovenia
e-mail: tomaz.kerestes@um.si

V. Rijavec et al. (eds.), *Diversity of Enforcement Titles in the EU*, Ius Gentium: Comparative Perspectives on Law and Justice 111,
https://doi.org/10.1007/978-3-031-47108-7_2

Civil Procedure across the whole continent, we can nevertheless expect that States with similar historical, socio-economical and ideological background produce principles of law with sufficient level of closeness that we can call them Common Core after all.[4]

Comparative law has a long history of attempts to classify countries into groups with such similar historical, socio-economical and ideological background and related legal systems. With relevance to the situation in Europe, David and Grasmann distinguished between Romano-Germanic (Continental European), which encompasses also the Nordic legal family, and Anglo-American legal circles.[5] Zweigert and Kötz on the other hand distinguish, again with relevance to the situation in Europe, among the Germanic, Nordic and Romanistic legal families.[6] Glenn finds on the basis of European cultural background the Civilian law[7] and the Common law tradition,[8] while Siems even proposes a term 'Western legal systems', finding important commonalities shared between Common and Civil law systems.[9] This short overview can demonstrate us that even though Samuel calls classification to be one fundamental legal skill of legal science,[10] such taxonomies are far from being mutually accepted. Some of them are even based on myths, such as that a codification can provide an accessible and complete formulation of law etc.[11] This is exactly the reason why the common core approach can offer us some better perspective—instead of concentrating on differences among legal traditions, circles or families, we can concentrate on common traits of various legal systems, regardless to their purported classifications and may try to establish and preserve the collective identity as 'community of culture'.[12] And even if stay true to the "classical" taxonomies we have to admit, that those taxonomies were to a great extent developed on the basis of descriptive and functional analysis of substantive law and institutional differences.

A narrow-targeted analysis focusing specifically on procedural law gives a little bit of a different result. In general, here too we encounter the classical division

[4]Typical such example are Austria, Croatia and Slovenia, which again and again emerges out of the data collected as closely connected systems of Civil Procedure, regardless to the fact that Croatia and Slovenia shared more than 45 years of common socialist law history and Austria did not. Regardless to the socio-economical differences, the common historical legacy (and to certain level also State ideology) survived and created a strong Procedural Common Core.

[5]David and Grasmann (1998), pp. 67 et seq. For the purpose of this contribution, one has to note that considerable differences exist between the version of common law in the United States of America and in law of England and Walles. And this is true also for civil procedure, where some structural differences exist between both systems: Jolowicz (2000), pp. 51 et seq.

[6]Zweigert and Kötz (1992), p. 74.

[7]Patrick Glenn (2014), pp. 132 et seq.

[8]Ibid., pp. 236 et seq.

[9]Siems (2014), p. 68.

[10]Samuel (2003), p. 220.

[11]Markesinis (1997), pp. 36–37.

[12]Frankenberg (2012), p. 128.

between the civil and common law.[13] The common law jurisdictions there is a tendency to centralize the trial, involve parties to the litigation in a set of evidence, and confine the reconsiderations comparing to the civil law countries. However, even though these differences do exist, they seem to have much more theoretically importance than they are in practice. During the process of convergence common and civil law countries borrowed from one another.[14] It is not unusual that scholars try to describe this common cloth through the fundamental principles of civil procedure, even though the results can give very different results.[15] Although there still exist fundamental differences between the civil procedure in common and civil law jurisdictions, the functional analysis shows that very often both systems solve similar functions within their own socio-economical frameworks. Sometimes these differences uncover, and at the same time also establish cultural differences among different countries (and their particular legal systems).[16]

Modern challenges of the common market, but also common area of justice within the EU, is supporting the global trend of transformation of civil procedure.[17] Uzelac describe seven transformation processes that are marking the modern civil procedure: (a) transformation by borrowing from national and transnational sources; (b) transformation by technological modernization; (c) transformation by reorganization of courts and redefinition of court functions, (d) transformation by establishment of multi-dimensional procedure for civil cases, (e) transformation by the pursuit of alternatives to litigation, (f) transformation by the collectivization of decision-making process, and (g) transformation by privatization of judicial tasks.[18] Such transformation produces convergence. It is therefore no surprise that Seidman finds growing similarities between civil and common law civil procedures, including matters concerning the functioning of the trial.[19]

---

[13] Seidman calls this 'divergence within the duopoly', based upon 'study of contrasts'. Seidman (2016), p. 8.

[14] Ghanbari et al. (2016), p. 273.

[15] Such examples are Habscheid (1984), or Keresteš and Caramelo Gomes (2016).

[16] Chase emphasises the words of Franz Klein: 'the squalid, arid, neglected phenomenon of civil procedure is in fact strictly connected with the great intellectual movement of people; and its varied manifestations are among the most important documents of mankind's culture.' Regardless of the convergence some local forms of civil procedure show surprising persistence. This phenomenon can be related to existing cultural differences among different societies and jurisdictions: Chase (1997), pp. 861 et seq.

[17] Uzelac and van Rhee (2018), p. 21.

[18] Ibid., p. 8.

[19] Seidman (2016), pp. 29–30.

2 Res Judicata

Legal systems of Albania,[20] Austria,[21] Belgium,[22] Bulgaria,[23] Croatia,[24] Cyprus,[25] Czech Republic,[26] France,[27] Germany,[28] Italy,[29] Lithuania,[30] Netherlands,[31] North Macedonia,[32] Poland,[33] Portugal,[34] Slovenia,[35] Spain[36] and Sweden[37] are all familiar with the concept of res judicata. Although there exist certain dogmatical differences, the majority of them also make a distinction between the material (substantive) and procedural (formal) res judicata. In countries that are closely related to the legal system of Germany, judgements only attain a formal res judicata effect after the expiry of the period determined for the means of recourse against judgements (Austria, Croatia, Czech Republic, Italy, Lithuania, Netherlands, North Macedonia, Portugal and Slovenia). The same is true also for legal orders of Portugal, Spain and Sweden. The situation is not the same in France and Belgium, where the authority of res judicata is attached to any judgement at the time of its pronouncement.[38] The same is true for the common law jurisdiction of Cyprus.[39] Regarding this criteria a clear line of distinction can be observed between legal system of Germany and those close to Germany (included Italy, Portugal, Spain and Sweden) on one side and legal systems of France and Belgium and the common law jurisdiction of Cyprus on the other side of this line.

Regarding the question to which part of the judgment is res judicata restricted, we can see quite different results. In general, obviously, the operative part is covered by res judicata in every country covered by the research. However, due to the fact that

[20] Kola Tafaj (2020), National Report for Albania, p. 36.

[21] Prodinger and Nunner Krautgasser (2020), National Report for Austria, p. 40.

[22] Rys (2020), National Report for Belgium, p. 42.

[23] Naydenova (2022), pp. 61 et seq.

[24] Kunštek et al. (2020), National Report for Croatia, p. 29.

[25] Christofi and Loizou (2022), pp. 54 et seq.

[26] Valdhans (2020), National Report for Czech Republic, p. 19.

[27] Mensah (2020), National Report for France, p. 30.

[28] Wolf et al. (2020), National Report for Germany, p. 63.

[29] Kaczorowska et al. (2022), p. 49.

[30] Bolzanas et al. (2020), National Report for Lithuania, p. 23.

[31] Sujecki (2020), National Report for Netherlands, p. 27.

[32] Zoroska Kamilovska & Rakočević (2020), National Report for North Macedonia, p. 36.

[33] Gołaczyński et al. (2020), National Report for Poland, p. 40.

[34] Caramelo Gomes et al. (2020), National Report for Portugal, p. 35.

[35] Rijavec et al. (2020), National Report for Slovenia, p. 53.

[36] Bores Lazo and Serrano Ron (2020), National Report for Spain, p. 37.

[37] Bylander and Linton (2020), National Report for Sweden, p. 16.

[38] Even though this is considered a conditional *res judicata*, see Rys (2020), National Report for Belgium, p. 44.

[39] Christofi and Loizou (2022), p. 55.

operative part is usually not enough to individualise the claim, in some countries the grounds of the decision can be covered by "relative" res judicata (e. g. Austria[40] or Germany[41]). However, in some countries some other parts can be covered as well. In Albania[42] bot findings of the facts and application of law is also covered by res judicata. In Belgium[43] the res judicata includes everything that constitutes the necessary basis for the court decision. In France[44] case law does not necessarily exclude reasoning from res judicata. In the Netherlands[45] the reasoning regarding a legal relationship of the parties is also covered by res judicata, but not the pure factual statements that are not used for the reasoning of a legal relationship. In Spain[46] res judicata also covers some points of fact finding.

3 Enforceability

Regarding the enforceability the French law[47] represents a case with a demand for judgments to contain a "command and order to the enforcement officer. Similar situation exists in Italy,[48] where judgments are enforceable only if the "formula esecutiva" that orders their enforcement was inscribed on the instrument by the court registrar or other custodian. This formula does not only acknowledge that the instrument became enforceable, but also commands the enforcement officer and all competent officials to enforce the instrument. In Germany[49] and Poland[50] the enforcement title has to be equipped with a special enforcement clause, which however does not resemble the French order. In other countries no such order exists, and the judgments become enforceable by law whenever the conditions are met.

---

[40] Prodinger and Nunner-Krautgasser (2020), National Report for Austria, p. 42.
[41] Wolf et al. (2020), National Report for Germany, p. 69.
[42] Kola Tafaj (2020), National Report for Albania, p. 38.
[43] Rys (2020), National Report for Belgium, p. 45.
[44] Mensah (2020), National Report for France, p. 31.
[45] Sujecki (2020), National Report for Netherlands, p. 28.
[46] Bores Lazo and Serrano Ron (2020), National Report for Spain, p. 39.
[47] Mensah (2020), National Report for France, p. 37.
[48] Kaczorowska et al. (2022), p. 27.
[49] Wolf et al. (2020), National Report for Germany, p. 94.
[50] Gołaczyński et al. (2020), National Report for Poland, p. 52.

4 Judgment Binding Effects "Erga Omnes"

Normally in the continental legal systems the judgments normally cannot produce in rem (*erga omnes*) binding effects. Exceptions can exist regarding certain types of judgments. However, in Cyprus,[51] a common law jurisdiction, there is a different situation. The judgments in Cyprus can produce in rem binding effects. It seems that a wider exception in this direction exists also in Sweden.[52]

5 Negative Declaratory Action

In general, legal systems of European continent are familiar with the concept of negative declaratory action, even though it does not have the general applicability everywhere (e. g. in Belgium[53] is used mostly in the field of intellectual rights). However, no action or proceeding of merely declaratory nature is allowed in Cyprus.[54]

6 Enforcement Title

Although all legal systems under research are familiar with the concept of enforcement title, they may differ regarding the path to impose enforceability effect on judgment. In this regard we can clearly distinguish the Austrian system[55] where the operative part can be certified as enforceable after the judgment become legally binding and the term for voluntary performance expire. This model is followed by Croatia,[56] Czech Republic[57] and Slovenia.[58] Austrian system of enforcement is a two-tier system, where a separate order of enforcement is obtained in a separate judicial procedure and only on its basis the real enforcement can follow. This is not the case with Germany, where the enforcement is executed based on enforcement clause.

In practically all continental countries there exist a normative list (numerus clausus) of enforcement titles.[59] In general, these are judicial decisions (judgments

[51] Christofi and Loizou (2022), p. 66.
[52] Bylander and Linton (2020), National Report for Sweden, p. 28.
[53] Bylander and Linton (2020), National Report for Sweden, p. 63.
[54] Christofi and Loizou (2022), p. 74.
[55] Prodinger and Nunner-Krautgasser (2020), National Report for Austria, p. 52.
[56] Kunštek et al. (2020), National Report for Croatia, p. 37.
[57] Valdhans (2020), National Report for Czech Republic, p. 26.
[58] Rijavec et al. (2020), National Report for Slovenia, p. 67.
[59] Wolf and Volkhausen (2018). pp. 88 et seq.

and decrees) and court settlements.[60] Where appropriate, authentic instruments are added. Different is situation in Cyprus, which is a common law jurisdiction. There is explicitly provided by law that every court's judgment ordering payment of money is an enforceable title and can be enforced through all or any of the prescribed methods of execution and enforcement directed against the judgment debtor.[61]

7 Concept of Judgment

Certain national differences are observable regarding the notion of judgment. That is the reason why the Brussels Regulations I and I bis tried to overcome national differences with a broad definition of the term 'judgment'. In Brussels Regulation I the judgment was defined in Article 32 as 'any judgment given by a court or tribunal of a Member State,[62] whatever the judgment may be called, including a decree, order, decision or writ of execution, as well as the determination of costs or expenses by an officer of the court.' In Brussels I bis Regulation this provision was restructured in Article 2, which enumerates all enforcement titles (judgments, court settlements and authentic instruments) and defines a judgment as any judgment given by a court or tribunal of a Member State, whatever the judgment may be called, including a decree, order, decision, or writ of execution, as well as a decision on the determination of costs or expenses by an officer of the court. It also includes provisional, including protective, measures ordered by a court or tribunal which by virtue of Brussels Regulation I bis has jurisdiction as to the substance of the matter. However, it does not include a provisional, including protective, measure which is ordered by such a court or tribunal without the defendant being summoned to appear, unless the judgment containing the measure is served on the defendant prior to enforcement.

Firstly we can conclude that under Brussels regime it is not deciding for a judgment that such a name is given to it.[63] The second condition is that the judgment must emanate from a court or a tribunal. This condition is satisfied in case that the decision is given by a body of judicial nature. This covers any body that is part of judicial branch of the State, and which exercises judicial functions.[64] There is also no requirement that the judgment must be res judicata or final and conclusive.[65] The payment orders that exist in some Member States and arise out of special procedures

[60] Which is consistent with principles 23 and 24 of the ALI/UNIDROTI (2006), p. 44.

[61] Christofi and Loizou (2022), p. 7.

[62] With Brexit the United Kingdom revoked the Brussels I and Brussels I bis Regulations and the Lugano Convention also ceased to apply. Briggs (2021), p. 715.

[63] Magnus and Mankowski (2007), p. 536.

[64] Ilmer et al. (2015), p. 96.

[65] Magnus and Mankowski (2016), p. 89.

for summary enforcement are also considered judgments.[66] For obvious reasons of EU unification is the definition in Brussels Regulation I bis quite wide and inclusive. The comparative research shows a very broad palette of different judicial decisions that can be considered judgments that exist in different Member States under different names and in different procedures. Even though the structure of judgments is not the same across Europe, nor are the formal requirements, the notion of a judgment does not seem to be extensively problematic. One could expect that a judge from one jurisdiction should not have to many problems in recognizing and understanding a judgment from other jurisdiction.

8 Interest Rate

One of the noteworthy differences existing among different jurisdictions is a way how the courts state the interests in the operative part of the judgment. This is furthermore complicated by the Forms under the Brussels Regulation I bis, which do not contain a box showing the actual interest rate. In German[67] and Austrian[68] law the interest rate (statutory or contractual) is fixed in the operative part of the judgment. On the basis of this information everyone can calculate the amount of interests. In other states, such as Italy,[69] Netherlands,[70] Croatia[71] and Slovenia,[72] in case of statutory default interests the operative part only refers to the corresponding provisions in the statute, without precisely stating the interest rate. Such information is not sufficient to be able to calculate the amount of interests without consulting the statute or using a specialised calculator.

9 Conclusions: Common Core After All?

Procedural law enables enforcement of personal rights and claims in modern society. By this the procedural law comes in immediate contact with the ranks of citizens. This has an important consequence of directly shaping public perception of legal system's performance and acceptability. This is further reflected in the perception of wider political superstructure. What happens to civil procedural law does therefore have important implications for lives of every citizen, being involved in judicial

[66] Ibid., p. 93.
[67] Wolf et al. (2020), National Report for Germany, p. 50.
[68] Prodinger and Nunner-Krautgasser (2020), National Report for Austria, p. 33.
[69] Kaczorowska et al. (2022), p. 29.
[70] Sujecki (2020), National Report for Netherlands, p. 22.
[71] Kunštek et al. (2020), National Report for Croatia, p. 25.
[72] Rijavec et al. (2020), National Report for Slovenia, p. 39.

proceedings or not. At the time we live in dynamic time when several important processes affect civil procedure. On one hand we are facing progressive harmonisation at the EU level that is ever more penetrating the fortresses of national civil procedure.

Such harmonisation will promote equality among citizens of the EU by white-washing the existing differences between more and less efficient and just system of civil procedure. This process will also overcome the problem of trust. This project clearly demonstrates a shift from 'should we trust' to 'how to better cooperate'. The more do judges and lawyers in general from Member States know and understand the standing of their domestic legal order towards other legal orders from other Member States, the more will they accept the common culture of civil procedure in Europe. Projects like this demonstrate again and again that even though differences exist at descriptive, functional, and cultural level among various types of civil procedure, these differences are not that great, and above all not insurmountable. And this is the power of the new concept of comparative law—the one that builds on what we have in common and not what makes us different.

Procedural law is closely related and incorporated into the wider structure of the State. Profound changes in civil procedure would inevitably cause profound changes in this structure. We can imagine that the this raises quite an opposition. However, at the same time we are facing yet another process of change—the transformation of civil procedure that takes place all over the world and the EU in no exception. As the whole society, the civil procedure has to adopt to new political, economical and societal reality. And this process represents a perfect opportunity for the EU to take control of it and use it as a tool for further harmonisation processes.

The comparative analysis within this project demonstrates that the existing lines of difference are neither that deep nor statical. At functional level we could not find any differences with dramatical consequences. It is true that the common law (with Cyprus as a representative of the system) deviates from the rest of Europe in certain aspects, but not always and not necessarily alone. The lines of division in the world of civil procedure are not statical. Beside the common law system there is possible to identify one legal family based on French procedural law, and other based on German-Austrian tradition. The family based on French law does deviate in certain cases from the German Austrian tradition. However, these differences do not seem to be profound. On the other side the German-Austrian tradition is also not monolithic. Several clear dogmatical differences exist between the civil procedure of Germany and Austria, and each has its followers. However, at functional level all these differences become more or less trivial as it is clear that various legal systems identify the same legal functions and create not that different tools to achieve it. These findings could be related to the fact that the research in this project did not concentrate on such legal procedural ideological issues as the position of parties and court in civil procedure, which would supposedly be decisive for building the taxonomy. These findings are in accordance with findings in the previous project (Dimensions of Evidence in European Civil Procedure).

So, did we find any common core in the aspects of civil procedure that were subject of this project. For sure we can once again confirm that we should be optimist. Firstly, there is a clear solid core of legal systems with close ties to German-Austrian tradition. These are of course countries with strong historical ties (e. g. Austria and Slovenia) or similar socio-economical circumstances. However, it was noted that also the countries from Southern Europe (Portugal, Spain and Italy) often share their characteristics with German-Austrian tradition. One notable exception we found on example of how the statutory interest rate is indicated in the operative part of the judgment. Here Germany and Austria clearly represent an example that is not followed neither by Croatia and Slovenia, which otherwise follow their (especially Austrian) model. Nevertheless, such a deviation is more an exception that proves the rule.

References

ALI/UNIDROIT (2006) Principles of transnational civil procedure. Cambridge University Press – ALI – UNIDROIT, Cambridge – New York – Melbourne

Bolzanas D, Visinskis V, Visinskyte D (2020) National report for Lithuania. Project EU-En4s – JUST-AG-2018/JUST-JCOO-AG-2018

Bores Lazo J, Serrano Ron I (2020) National report for Spain. Project EU-En4s – JUST-AG-2018/JUST-JCOO-AG-2018

Briggs A (2021) Civil Jurisdiction and Judgments, 7th edn. Informa Law from Routledge, Abingdon

Bylander E, Linton M (2020) National report for Sweden. Project EU-En4s – JUST-AG-2018/JUST-JCOO-AG-2018

Caramelo Gomes J, Marques Cebola C, Lucas E et al (2020) National report for Portugal. Project EU-En4s – JUST-AG-2018/JUST-JCOO-AG-2018

Chase GO (1997) Some observations on the cultural dimension in civil procedure reform. Am J Comp Law 45(4):861–870

Christofi D, Loizou D (2022) Diversity of enforcement titles in cross-border debt collection in the EU: National Report Cyprus. University of Maribor University Press, Maribor

David R, Grasmann G (1998) Uvod v velike sodobne pravne sisteme, prva knjiga. Cankarjeva založba, Ljubljana

Frankenberg G (2012) How to do projects with comparative law: notes of an expedition to the common core. In: Monateri GP (ed) Methods of comparative law. Edward Elgar, Cheltenham, pp 120–143

Ghanbari N, Mohseni H, Nassiran D (2016) Comparative study of civil procedure in common law and civil law systems. J Polit Law 9(5):267–282

Gołaczyński J, Rodziewicz P, Kaczorowska M et al (2020) National report for Poland. Project EU-En4s – JUST-AG-2018/JUST-JCOO-AG-2018

Habscheid WJ (1984) The fundamental principles of the law of civil procedure. Comp Int Law J South Afr 17(1):1–31

Ilmer M, Nuyts A, Fitchen J (2015) Scope and definitions. In: Dickinson A, Lein E (eds) The Brussels I regulation recast. Oxford University Press, Oxford, pp 55–111

Jolowicz JA (2000) On civil procedure. Cambridge University Press, Cambridge

Kaczorowska M, Voinich A, Previatello M (2022) Diversity of enforcement titles in cross-border debt collection in the EU: National Report Italy. University of Maribor University Press, Maribor

Keresteš T, Caramelo Gomes J (2016) Common core after all. In: Rijavec V, Keresteš T, Ivanc T (eds) Dimensions of evidence in European civil procedure. Wolters Kluwer, Alphen aan den Rijn, pp 321–350

Kola Tafaj F (2020) National Report Albania. EU-En4s — JUST-AG-2018/JUST-JCOO-AG-2018
Kunštek E, Kunda I, Mihelčić G et al (2020) National report for Croatia. Project EU-En4s — JUST-AG-2018/JUST-JCOO-AG-2018
Magnus U, Mankowski P (2007) European commentaries on private international law, Brussels I Regulation. Sellier, European Law Publishers, München
Magnus U, Mankowski P (2016), European commentaries on private international law, ECPIL: commentary, Vol. I. Brussels Ibis Regulation, Otto Schmidt, Köln
Markesinis SB (1997) Foreign law and comparative methodology: a subject and a thesis. Hart, Oxford
Mensah M (2020) National report for France. Project EU-En4s – JUST-AG-2018/JUST-JCOO-AG-2018
Naydenova D (2022) Diversity of enforcement titles in cross-border debt collection in the EU: National Report Bulgaria. University of Maribor University Press, Maribor
Patrick Glenn H (2014) Legal traditions of the world, 5th edn. Oxford University Press, Oxford
Prodinger L, Nunner-Krautgasser B (2020) National report for Austria. Project EU-En4s — JUST-AG-2018/JUST-JCOO-AG-2018
Rijavec V, Baghrizabehi D, Drnovšek K et al (2020) National report for Slovenia. Project EU-En4s — JUST-AG-2018/JUST-JCOO-AG-2018
Rys M (2020) National report for Belgium. Project EU-En4s – JUST-AG-2018/JUST-JCOO-AG-2018
Samuel G (2003) Epistemology and method in law. Ashgate, Burlington
Seidman IG (2016) Comparative civil procedure. In: Picker BC, Seidman IG (eds) The dynamism of civil procedure – global trends and developments. Springer International Publishing, Cham, pp 3–17
Siems M (2014) Comparative law. Cambridge University Press, Cambridge
Sujecki B (2020) National report for Netherlands. Project EU-En4s — JUST-AG-2018/JUST-JCOO-AG-2018
Uzelac A, van Rhee CH (2018) The metamorphoses of civil justice and civil procedure: the challenges of new paradigms—unity and diversity. In: Uzelac A, van Rhee CH (eds) Transformation of civil justice: unity and diversity. Springer International Publishing, Cham, pp 3–21
Valdhans J (2020) National report for Czech Republic. Project EU-En4s — JUST-AG-2018/JUST-JCOO-AG-2018
Wolf C, Volkhausen L (2018) National enforcement titles: a comparative German perspective. In: Rijavec V, Keresteš T, Ivanc T, Kennett W (eds) Remedies concerning enforcement of foreign judgements: Brussels I Recast. Wolters Kluwer, Alphen aan den Rijn, pp 81–94
Wolf C, Kurth N, Mieszaniec K (2020) National report for Germany. Project EU-En4s – JUST-AG-2018/JUST-JCOO-AG-2018
Zoroska Kamilovska T, Rakočević M (2020) National report for North Macedonia. Project EU-En4s — JUST-AG-2018/JUST-JCOO-AG-2018
Zweigert K, Kötz H (1992) Introduction to comparative law. Claredon Press, Oxford

Part II
Judgment

Types of Judgments According to Different Criteria

Eric Bylander and Marie Linton

Abstract The purpose of this chapter is to form a 'European classification' of judgments by highlighting and evaluating certain types of judgments in civil and commercial matters issued in some EU Member States, according to different criteria. The aspiration is to reveal differences and similarities concerning the different criteria and to relate them to Brussels I bis Regulation. The criteria identified as significant are: (1) The title and contents of a decision. (2) The basis of a decision. (3) Decision makers and procedural stages. (4) Effects of judgments. The definition of a judgment is EU autonomous and has its own meaning common to all Member States, irrespective of definitions in national laws. The concept has a wide meaning. However, the exemption concerning court settlements is identified as problematic. The concept court is also EU autonomous. Besides 'regular' courts, the concept may also include other adjudicatory authorities. Within the framework of a national legal system, a judgment may have different effects, i.e. *res judicata* effect. Recognition under Brussels I bis Regulation means that the judgment produces effects in the whole EU. In practice the so-called doctrine of extension means that a national court may have to investigate the doctrine of *res judicata* according to the law of the Member State of origin. What is most striking about the results are the many similarities, not the discrepancies. There is a high degree of consistency between the identified factors in different countries. Further, there is reason to believe that much of what appears as peculiarities actually has its counterparts. The report ends with five conclusions, in brief: (1) The contents and effects of a decision or judgment, not how it is labelled, are significant for the circulation of judgments under Brussels I bis Regulation. (2) It could be argued that it would have been more accurate if Brussels I bis Regulation referred to the all-inclusive

Parts of this report contain conclusions from a book in Swedish by Marie Linton (2023) Erkännande och verkställighet av utländska domar i förmögenhetsrätt (Recognition and Enforcement of Foreign Judgments in Private and Commercial Matters), Norstedt Juridik, Stockholm.

E. Bylander · M. Linton (✉)
Uppsala University, Faculty of Law, Uppsala, Sweden
e-mail: Eric.Bylander@jur.uu.se; Marie.Linton@jur.uu.se

V. Rijavec et al. (eds.), *Diversity of Enforcement Titles in the EU*, Ius Gentium: Comparative Perspectives on Law and Justice 111,
https://doi.org/10.1007/978-3-031-47108-7_3

expression 'decision' instead of 'judgment'. (3) The EU legislator should consider including court settlements in the concept of judgment in Brussels I bis Regulation. (4) The doctrine of extension is too complicated in practice. (5) True mutual trust needs to be furthered in the EU and its Member States.

1 Introduction

Before we journey into the topic, it is essential to frame the question relevant to this part of the book. Its purpose is to form a 'European classification' of judgments by highlighting and, concisely, evaluating certain types of judgments issued in some EU Member States, according to different criteria. The aspiration is to reveal differences and similarities with regard to judgments in civil and commercial matters, and to relate them to the Regulation (EU) No 1215/2012 of the European Parliament and of the Council of 12 December 2012 on jurisdiction and the recognition and enforcement of judgments in civil and commercial matters.[1]

The criteria we have identified as significant to this report are:

- Title and contents. The title of a decision may vary significantly, although terminology should not matter within the EU in terms of free circulation of judgments under Brussels I bis Regulation. The contents should be in focus.
- The basis of decisions. This refers to factors such as whether or not the decision was taken following an adversarial procedure. It could also refer to matters such as whether the decision was made on the basis of a party's failure to act, a consent or an admission, or following an examination of the merits, which may have been more or less thorough.
- Decision makers and procedural stages. National decision makers are generally courts, organised in a certain hierarchy with diverse competences, to provide access to justice. A decision maker does not need to be a court in the formal conventional meaning. In certain EU Member States, authorities other than courts have the power to issue binding decisions in civil and commercial matters, irrespective of the procedural stage.
- Effects of judgments. Nationally, issues relating to the effects of judgments trigger doctrines of *res judicata*. The use of the concept *res judicata* has deliberately been avoided in a European context, and in the Brussels I bis Regulation. The reason is that it is a nationally varied concept with diverging contents. Instead, recognition is the notion of importance in Brussels I bis Regulation.

In this chapter, we are only concerned with judgments delivered in a judicial procedure in civil litigation, and, in principle, not in criminal matters. It should be

[1]Regulation (EU) No 1215/2012 of the European Parliament and of the Council of 12 December 2012 on jurisdiction and the recognition and enforcement of judgments in civil and commercial matters, OJ L 351, 20.12.2012 (hereinafter 'Brussels I bis Regulation'). The principle of continuity between the Brussels instruments is laid down in indent (34) of Brussels I bis Regulation.

mentioned that a common feature to some Member States is that it is possible to pursue a civil action in a criminal procedure; typically, it is an action for damages suffered by an injured party. Judgments of this kind can also fall within the scope of Brussels I bis Regulation.[2] In this chapter we are not concerned with authentic instruments.[3] These instruments are enforceable, but do not produce a *res judicata* effect.

In carrying out our task, we have based the research on a systematic screening of information provided in the National Reports previously conducted in the EU-project EU-En4s, i.e., reports provided by Albania, Austria, Belgium, Bulgaria, Croatia, Cyprus, the Czech Republic, France, Germany, Italy, Lithuania, the Netherlands, North Macedonia, Poland, Portugal, Slovenia, Spain, and Sweden.[4] In addition, some other materials and explanatory reports have been used.

We approach the task with the selected criteria mentioned above; the criteria have also determined the outline of this report. In addition, comparative elements are employed. The techniques used are both descriptive and explanatory in nature.[5] Embarking on a comparative journey can be compared to a legal quagmire, where the over-arching objective is to guarantee effective and rapid cross-border circulation of judgments under the consideration of the European principles of mutual recognition and mutual trust.

The review has been carried out by comparing the different answers to the question. Similar responses have been combined, whilst more divergent responses have been dealt with separately. Many details may have been lost through this approach; however, it has increased the overall view. The result can be compared to a map at a scale that allows a picture of the whole of Europe to fit on a book page like this. Such a map is difficult or even useless for navigation in a single European country, but it is certainly useful for studying overall relationships between different countries and regions.

Every ground for categorisation of different types of decisions is linked to other classification grounds. The question has to be raised, what is sufficiently distinct to be addressed separately. For example, decisions concerning the costs of proceedings are similar even though they are given by authorities at different levels.

An important distinction that should be noted is, on the one hand, decisions on the main petitions and, on the other hand, decisions on accessory claims. Both types of decisions are different from decisions concerning the management of the procedure. As will be seen, in many jurisdictions, the concept 'judgment' and its equivalents are often reserved for the first type of court decision. However, when it comes to

---

[2] See Art. 7(3) Brussels I bis Regulation.

[3] Authentic instruments are regulated in Ch. IV of Brussels I bis Regulation.

[4] The answers to the following questions have mainly been in focus: Question 1.4 on domestic decisions, Question 1.5 on the definitions I B IA, and Question 1.6 on preliminary rulings in CJEU of National Reports under the Project EU-En4s – JUST-AG-2018/JUST-JCOO-AG-2018.

[5] Private international law and international procedural law has always enjoyed close cooperation with comparative law, because dealing with cross-border disputes requires knowing about the legal systems at hand, see Husa (2021), p. 746.

clarifying the category of 'decision' or similar concepts, a closer examination of the precise content is needed.

What is most striking about the results are the many similarities, not the discrepancies that are quite few. The division between judgments and different kind of decisions, is found in almost all the jurisdictions. A common core of what is considered significant for a judgment is similar to the definition 'judgment' for the purpose of the Regulation in Article 2 a) of the Brussels I bis Regulation, see Sect. 2.4.1 below.

There are several factors affecting the numerous discrepancies, including the national assumptions. For example, a national reporter from one country would mention arbitral awards when asked (as in Question 1.4) to present the types of domestic decisions, which may be rendered/issued 'under your Member State's civil procedure', while others would not even consider arbitration to be part of a 'Member State's civil procedure'.

One reason may be that presumptions play a big part. There is reason to believe that much of what appears as peculiarities has its counterparts. If a particular factor is handled nationally, in such a way that the question did not prompt the respondent to think about it, it has not influenced the answer. The high degree of consistency between the factors in different countries is consistent with the fact that relatively few questions for a preliminary ruling (Article 263 of Treaty of the Functioning of the European Union (hereinafter 'TFEU') have been addressed to the Court of Justice of the European Union (hereinafter 'CJEU') regarding the notion of 'Judgment'.

2 Titles

2.1 Variations in Terminologies

It is important to bear in mind that certain decisions should not be classified by their names only. In relation to certain Member States, it is difficult to find suitable English translations for the entire categories of domestic decisions, and the English translation may not correspond well to certain national concepts.

Judgments are particular decisions, which apply only to particular persons and, in general, they bind no others; they vary depending on the circumstances in which they are found. The contentious issues, both facts and laws, are those which have been presented by the parties to the courts for resolution. The judgment is the result of the full examination of all these. As a main principle, in order to be valid, a judgment must have been issued by a court (or a competent judge) having jurisdiction at a time and place, specified by law and in the form that the law requires. The judgment must confine itself to the motion and cause of action raised before the court. By and large, the judgment cannot go beyond it.

2.2 Judgments in National Laws[6]

In almost all the Member States surveyed, the courts can issue judgments on the merits. In Italy, the equivalent concept seems to be 'Sentenza', in Spain 'Sentencias' and in Portugal 'Sentença'. In Portugal the term judgment is used for a decision of the collegial courts. In Germany, a judgment ('Urteil') can only be issued by a court if there has been a prior oral hearing. In Sweden, an oral hearing is not a pre-requisite for a court to issue a judgment ('Dom'). In some Member States, a judgment can only be issued by a court of first instance. This seems to be the case in Belgium, Hungary, Cyprus, France and Lithuania. Only in Bulgaria, the concept judgment is reserved for civil claims in a criminal procedure. In Bulgaria, the court normally issue court decision ('Решение'), which appears to be equivalent to the concept of judgment.

In higher courts a decision/judgment is called a ruling ('Arrest/Arrêt') in Belgium, and an 'Arrêt' in France. In the Czech Republic, a ruling ('Usnesení') is a decision by a court that is not a judgment, and it is commonly used in procedural matters, but may also be a decision on the merits of the case, if specified by law.

Judgments from the Member States may be final, non-final, interim, and in terms of content they may be condemnatory, declaratory or constitutive. Special kinds of judgments are default judgments, summary judgments, waiver judgments and interim judgments, e.g., in Austria, Cyprus, Germany and Sweden.

2.3 Decisions, Orders, Etc. in National Laws[7]

In many Member States, courts can issue formal decisions or orders. The precise meaning to these concepts varies. But often they are decisions on procedural matters, as in Austria, Belgium, Cyprus, Lithuania, North Macedonia, Portugal and Sweden, or is the concept for a decision in summary proceedings, e.g., in Belgium.

In Germany, orders ('Beschluss') can be issued by a court without an oral hearing, or under exempted oral hearing or in accordance with an explicit statutory provision, such as the approval of legal aid or the suspension of enforcement proceedings.

In Lithuania, the expression order ('Teismo įsakymas') is used to include first instance summary procedure on monetary issues, whereas in the Netherlands orders ('beschikking') are issued in proceedings of a non-contradictory kind ('verzoekschriftprocedures'). However, in Dutch practice, the differentiation between orders and judgments are not always clear. As a main rule the distinction is based on the contentious (judgment) versus the non-contentious (order) of a case. Nonetheless, an order may also be issued in contradictory proceedings. In North

---

[6] Question 1.4 of the National Reports, Project EU-En4s – JUST-AG-2018/JUST-JCOO-AG-2018.

[7] Question 1.4 of the National Reports, Project EU-En4s – JUST-AG-2018/JUST-JCOO-AG-2018.

Macedonia, the concept decision ('пресуда') is reserved for decisions in civil claims in criminal proceedings.

In Croatia, decrees ('rjesenje') can be issued. It appears to be equivalent to formal decisions and orders in the sense that decrees are ordered with regard to court proceedings as well as other issues, both inside and outside a main hearing. Certain types of Croatian decrees may be enforcement titles. In Italy, a decree ('decreto') is a type of final order, used in special proceedings, particularly those conducted ex parte. In Poland, decrees ('postanowienie') are decisions that determine the substance of the case, commonly concerning a formal matter, outside a trial or within a trial if the law does not provide for issuing a judgment or a payment order.

In Slovenia, decrees regularly refer to decisions on administrative measures, or decisions on procedural costs. In Spain, decrees are judicial ('auto') or non-judicial ('decretos'). Judicial decrees are issued to solve appeals against decisions or orders regarding particular issues, e.g., the admission or dismissal of evidence, a mediation agreement or provisional and protective measures. Non-judicial decrees can, for example, be a decision on the costs of the procedure.

In France, some decisions are regarded as enforceable although they are not issued by a court. That is the case with titles issued by bailiffs for the payment of unpaid checks, and 'constraints' issued by certain administrative authorities.

In the Czech Republic, a ruling ('Usnesení')—similar to an order—is commonly a decision in procedural matters, but it may also be a decision on the merits of the case, if specified by law. In France, the concept 'ordonnance' is used to describe a provisional decision or an administrative decision. In Germany, the concept ruling is a decision of a judge that usually contains procedural measures.

2.4 *Judgments in Brussels I bis Regulation*

2.4.1 An EU Autonomous Concept

Article 2 a) of Brussels I bis Regulation contain a definition of the concept judgment for the purpose of the Regulation. A judgment means:

> any judgment given by a court or tribunal of a Member State, whatever the judgment may be called, including a decree, order, decision or writ of execution, as well as a decision on the determination of costs or expenses by an officer of the court.
>
> For the purposes of Chapter III, 'judgment' includes provisional, including protective, measures ordered by a court or tribunal which by virtue of this Regulation has jurisdiction as to the substance of the matter. It does not include a provisional, including protective, measure which is ordered by such a court or tribunal without the defendant being summoned to appear, unless the judgment containing the measure is served on the defendant prior to enforcement.

The concept contains three parts: a 'judgment' given by a 'court or tribunal' in a 'Member State'. The definition of judgment under Article 2 a) of Brussels I bis Regulation is rather wide-ranging, but not very precise. According to the

Explanatory Schlosser Report the concept of judgment is 'designed to cover only court judgments which either determine or regulate the legal relationship of the parties'[8] The CJEU stated in a preliminary ruling that in order to be a judgment, a decision must have been, or could have been, the object of adversarial proceedings.[9]

The concept of judgment in Brussels I bis Regulation comprises many different national forms of decisions, i.e. judgments for specific performances (positive and negative), declaratory judgments, part (separate) judgments, intermediate judgments, default judgments,[10] orders and decisions that falls within the scope of civil and commercial matters.[11] Moreover, payment orders[12] and orders on assistance, as well as certain interim measures, including security measures, are covered by the concept in Brussels I bis Regulation.[13] Decisions on interim measures must have been issued in contradictory proceedings in order to benefit from the rules of free circulation in Brussels I bis Regulation. Decisions on interim measures delivered *ex parte* can only be enforced under Brussels I bis Regulation if the decision has been served on the defendant prior to enforcement.[14] A general understanding in the doctrine has been that exequatur decisions are not included in the concept (*exequatur sur exequatur ne vaut*), but territorially limited to the Member State where they are issue.[15] However, in the case H Limited[16] the CJEU held that an order for payment made by a court of a Member State on the basis of final judgments delivered in a third State constitutes a judgment that can benefit from the free circulation under the Brussels I bis Regulation.

The definition of a judgment is EU autonomous and has its own meaning common to all Member States, irrespective of definitions in national laws. In the case Gothaer Allgemeine Versicherung,[17] the CJEU held that an extensive and autonomous interpretation of the concept judgment is explained by the mutual trust that national courts in the Member States show each other, irrespective of how that judgment is categorised under the law of the Member State of origin. In this preliminary ruling, the CJEU seems to be against the opinion that there are national decisions falling outside the system of Brussels I bis Regulation: Brussels I bis

[8] Schlosser (1979), p. 126.

[9] See Case C-125/79, Bernard Denilauer v. SNC Couchet Frères, 21.5.1980, ECLI:EU:C:1980:130.

[10] Cf. also the General Advocate's opinion in C-394/07, Marco Gambazzi v. Daimler Chrysler Canada Inc. and CIBC Mellon Trust Company, 2.4.2009, ECLI:EU:C:2008:748.

[11] See also Briggs (2015), pp. 682, 683; Torremans (2017), pp. 611–613.

[12] For example, according to a decision from the German Oberlandesgericht (OLG) Celle, an Italian payment order (decreto ingiuntivo) was deemed to be a judgment covered by the concept of judgment under Brussels I bis Regulation: OLG Celle, Beschluss vom 3.1.2007 – 8 W 86/06.

[13] See Art. 3 Brussels I bis Regulation.

[14] See case 125/79, Bernard Denilauer v. SNC Couchet Frères, 21.5.1980, ECLI:EU:C:1980:130.

[15] Pålsson (2008), p. 268.

[16] Case C-568/20, J v. H Limited, 7.4.2022, ECLI:EU:C:2022:264.

[17] Case C-456/11, Gothaer Allgemeine Versicherung AG v. Samskip GmbH, 15.11.2012, ECLI:EU:C:2012:719.

Regulation should include as many decisions as possible.[18] The concept has a wide meaning.[19]

2.4.2 Excluded Judgments

Several judgments in civil and commercial matters fall outside the scope of Brussels I bis Regulation, because they are explicitly excluded according to Article 1.2 (e.g., arbitral awards). Other decisions may also be excluded for various reasons relating to the substantive, temporal or territorial scope of Brussels I bis Regulation. Other excluded decisions are decisions issued in the course of proceedings, such as decisions determining the date of hearing, decisions regarding evidence, witnesses, etc. These exempted decisions are not enforceable against a party as it only concerns the proceedings. However, certain decisions issued during proceedings that regulates the relationship between the parties can be covered by the concept.[20]

A more problematic exemption, developed by the CJEU in the preliminary ruling Solo Kleinmotoren[21], concerns court settlements. According to the CJEU, foreign court settlements are not judgments, because it is the parties and not the court that determines the contents of the settlement, see Sect. 2.5.2 below.

2.4.3 Final and Non-Final Judgments

A court decision on the merits, which is final is, of course, a judgment covered by the Brussels I bis Regulation. The question is if a decision not on the merits or which is not final is covered by the concept of judgment in Brussels I bis Regulation. According to Hartley, a final decision can mean different things. A distinction needs to be made between a decision, which is final in the court that issued it, and a decision, which is final within the legal system as a whole. A decision may be effective until the court of origin decides otherwise, such a decision is not final in the court that delivered it. Decisions that cannot be altered by the court of origin, but which can be appealed, are indeed final in the court of origin, but not in the legal system as a whole. If no ordinary remedies are available, the judgments/decisions are final within that legal system.[22]

Case law of the CJEU illustrates that the concept of judgment may also include a decision that is not on the merits or which is not final. Provisional measures, including protective measures, issued prior to a decision on the merits or prior to

[18] Sjövall and Rudvall (2018), p. 41.

[19] Hartley (2017), p. 291.

[20] See, e.g., Case C-39/02, Mærsk Olie & Gas A/S v Firma M. de Haan en W. de Boer, 14.10.2004, ECLI:EU:C:2004:615.

[21] C-414/92, Solo Kleinmotoren GmbH v. Emilio Boch, 2.6.1994, ECLI:EU:C:1994:221.

[22] Hartley (2017), p. 292.

enforcement,[23] a court's official decision on litigation costs,[24] a court's decision on its competence,[25] decisions limiting liability in maritime law,[26] imposition of a conditional fine (a foreign imposition of a conditional fine is only enforceable if the fine has finally been determined by the court of origin),[27] and an order for sequestration issued short of the court of origin have decided on the merits,[28] are all examples of decisions that may well be within the scope of the concept of judgment in Brussels I bis Regulation.

2.5 Some Concise Reflections

2.5.1 Decisions Delivered *Ex Parte*

The most obvious example of decisions that do not benefit from the rules of recognition and enforcement in Brussels I bis Regulation are decisions delivered *ex parte*, e.g., security measures, where a defendant is not heard prior to the measure. According to the preliminary ruling by the CJEU in Denilauer,[29] decisions on security measures issued in non-adversarial proceedings, and which are enforceable without prior service, are not within the scope of the concept of judgment in the Brussels I bis Regulation. The explanation is basically that the administration of justice (adjudication) shall be adversarial and safeguard the right to a fair trial.

Hence, decisions on provisional measures do not produce *res judicata* effect, and are issued provisionally, awaiting a judgment on the merits or its enforcement. Decisions of this kind can, for example, be issued in Austria, Hungary, Croatia, Germany, the Netherlands, Poland, Slovenia and Sweden. The same *ex parte* character is found in Albanian enforcement orders, as well as Belgian and Bulgarian orders for immediate execution.

For a creditor it is therefore important to make strategic choices before an application for security measures is made. If it is crucial to 'surprise' the debtor,

[23] See, i.e., Case 125/79, Bernard Denilauer v. SNC Couchet Frères, 21.5.1980, ECLI:EU:C:1980:130.

[24] The concept has its origin in German law where decisions on litigation costs are determined by a 'Rechtspleger', see Jenard (1979), p. 42, hereinafter 'the Jenard Report'.

[25] See, i.a., Case C-456/11, Gothaer Allgemeine Versicherung AG v. Samskip GmbH, 15.11.2012, ECLI:EU:C:2012:719.

[26] See, i.a., Case C-39/02, Maersk Olie & Gas A/S v. Firma M de Haan en W de Boer, 14.10.2004, ECLI:EU:C:2004:615.

[27] See Art. 55 of Brussels I bis Regulation; and Case C-406/09, Realchemie Nederland BV v. Bayer CropScience AG, 18.10.2011, ECLI:EU:C:2011:668.

[28] Case C-27/17, AB 'flyLAL-Lithunian Airlines' v. 'Starptautiskā lidosta 'Rīga' VAS and 'Air Baltic Corporation' AS, 15.7.2018, ECLI:EU:C:2018:533.

[29] See Case C-125/79, Bernard Denilauer v. SNC Couchet Frères, 21.5.1980, ECLI:EU:C:1980:130.

he or she should apply for an *ex parte* measure. As the measure cannot circulate under Brussels I bis Regulation, the application should be filed in the Member State where a forthcoming decision needs to be enforced, usually in the Member State where the debtor has assets.

2.5.2 Court Settlements

A more challenging issue concerns foreign court settlements. In some Member States, court settlements are seen as judgments. For example, under Croatian national private international law, a foreign court settlement can be considered to be a judgment if a judge homologated the agreement, in which case, it has the same value as a judicial judgment.

In Solo Kleinmotoren,[30] however, the CJEU found that a court settlement is not a judgment, 'even if it was reached in a court of a Contracting State and brings legal proceedings to an end, because settlements in court are essentially contractual in that their terms depends first and foremost on the parties' intention. In the case Gambazzi,[31] the Advocate General held that a settlement recorded by the court is not equal to a judgment, as the settlement primarily has a contractual character determined by the parties' will and not the by the court. The court's involvement is limited to officially recognizing the settlement. Even though a court settlement cannot circulate under Brussels I bis Regulation, it might possibly circulate under national law in the requested Member State.

In some cases, it may be difficult to determine if a legal instrument emanating from a court is a settlement or a judgment. To determine this, one has to consider the legal effects that the instrument has according to the law of the Member State of origin. In our view, if the legal effects are the same as a judgment in general it must be considered to be a judgment within the meaning of Brussels I bis Regulation. Moreover, many Member States' national laws contain rules where a judgment can be issued after a party's admission. In this case the contents of the judgment is also, as in the case with court settlements, formed by the will of the parties. The court's assessment of the circumstances is limited to the same degree as a court settlement, taking place in an adversarial procedure.

Not to recognise court settlements means that they have no effect (they are not recognised) under Brussels I bis Regulation, although they may acquire legal force under national law in the Member State of origin. This could appear as contrary to

---

[30] Case C-414/92, Solo Kleinmotoren GmbH. v. Emilio Boch, 2.6.1994, ECLI:EU:C:1994:221.

[31] Case C-394/07, Marco Gambazzi v. Daimler Chrysler Canada Inc. and CIBC Mellon Trust Company, 2.4.2009, ECLI:EU:C:2009:219.

the purpose of Brussels I bis Regulation with mutual trust,[32] and the wide interpretation given to the concept of judgment by the CJEU.[33]

These arguments may speak in favour of 'adding' court settlements to the various types of decisions already covered by the concept of judgment in Brussels I bis Regulation.

3 Decision Makers and Procedural Stages[34]

Under Brussels I bis Regulation, a decision only constitutes a judgment for the purpose of recognition or enforcement in another Member State if it was issued by a court or tribunal of a Member State. In the case Solo Kleinmotoren[35] the CJEU declared that a judgment refers solely to judicial decisions given by a court or tribunal deciding on its own authority on the issues between the parties. Furthermore, according to Owens,[36] it must be a decision from a court or other adjudicatory body in a Member State.

The concept court is an EU autonomous concept, common to all Member States.[37] The concept consequently specifies that a judgment is issued by a governmental and independent body/authority in a proceeding of a legal nature that secures the adversarial principle.[38] Besides 'regular' courts, the concept may also include other adjudicatory authorities, if they are competent in civil and commercial matters. This means that decisions from common courts in the Union, such as the Benelux court or the Common European Patent Court,[39] can be decision makers whose decisions are eligible for circulation under Brussels I bis Regulation.[40]

In another context, the CJEU has held that a court in the sense of Article 267 TFEU implies that the body is established according to law, is of a lasting character, that its' competence is mandatory in nature, that the proceedings are

[32] See e.g., Case 145/86, Horst Ludwig Martin Hoffmann v. Adelheid Krieg, 4.2.1988, ECLI:EU:C:1988:61.

[33] See also the Jenard Report, Jenard (1979), p. 43.

[34] Question 1.3 of the National Reports. Project EU-En4s – JUST-AG-2018/JUST-JCOO-AG-2018.

[35] Case C-414/92, Solo Kleinmotoren GmbH v. Emilio Boch, 2.6.1994, ECLI:EU:C:1994:221.

[36] Case C-129/92, Owens Bank Ltd v. Fulvio Bracco and Bracco Industria Chimica SpA, 20.1.1994, ECLI:EU:C:1994:13.

[37] Art. 2 a) Brussels I bis Regulation.

[38] Cf. Magnus and Mankowski (2023), Article 2, p. 83–84.

[39] See The Unified Patent Court (2022), About the Court. https://www.unified-patent-court.org/.

[40] Indent (11) Brussels I bis Regulation: 'For the purposes of this Regulation, courts or tribunals of the Member States should include courts or tribunals common to several Member States, such as the Benelux Court of Justice when it exercises jurisdiction on matters falling within the scope of this Regulation. Therefore, judgments given by such courts should be recognised and enforced in accordance with this Regulation'.

adversarial, and that the body/authority applies legal rules/law and has an independent position.[41]

In reference to the Member States compared, there are many types of courts with shifting jurisdiction, acting in different capacity and in different instances: general courts (district courts, regional courts or courts of appeal and supreme courts, courts of cassation and constitutional courts), as well as administrative courts (administrative courts, administrative courts of appeal and supreme administrative court). The Member States surveyed also have a number of specialised courts, e.g., labour courts, tax courts, military courts, police courts etc., which may issue decisions in civil and commercial matters.

How a certain Member State 'labels' a court is irrelevant for the free circulation of judgments under Brussels I bis Regulation. The important issue is that the court's decision is in a civil and commercial matter that falls under the substantive and temporal scope of Brussels I bis Regulation.

4 Effects of Judgments[42]

4.1 In National Laws of Some Member States

Within the framework of a national legal system, a judgment may have different effects. It can create, determine, adjust or distinguish a legal obligation or a relationship. Furthermore, a judgment may exclude or limit the parties' options to take further or other measures, because of a judgment's negative effects. For reasons of certainty, the effect of a judgment usually means that the same action shall not be tried twice (*ne bis in idem*). The parties must be able to act confidently in accordance with the judgment, that it will not be altered in a new proceeding. Furthermore, it would not be economically viable to conduct several proceedings on the same matter. Finally, the judgment may have effect as evidence in subsequent proceedings.

What are the national effects of *res judicata*, and which part of a judgment has legal force; the operative part and/or the reasoning of a judgment? The Member States compared are Belgium, Bulgaria, France, Poland, Portugal and Sweden.

In many Member States, a final judgment enjoys some form of *res judicata* effect. The effects associated with *res judicata* may, however, differ. According to Swedish, Belgian and Portuguese law, *res judicata* means that a prior judgment can be

[41] See for example cases C-49/13, MF 7 a.s. v. MAFRA a.s., 14.11.2013, ECLI:EU:C:2013:767; C-54/96, Dorsch Consult Ingenieurgesellschaft mbH v. Bundesbaugesellschaft Berlin mbH, 17.9.1997, ECLI:EU:C:1997:413; and C-53/03, Synetairismos Farmakopoion Aitolias & Akarnanias (Syfait) et al. v. GlaxoSmithKline plc and GlaxoSmithKline AEVE, 31.5.2005, ECLI:EU:C:2005:333.

[42] Questions 5.1.1, 5.1.4 and 5.5.2.1 of the National Reports, Project EU-En4s – JUST-AG-2018/JUST-JCOO-AG-2018.

used as a basis for a subsequent action, producing a positive effect. *Res judicata* also implies a negative effect in these States: a court cannot try the case again, as it has already been determined by another court. Therefore, the initial judgment constitutes a procedural hindrance and a second claim on the same issue shall be dismissed. Polish law shows some similarities concerning the negative effects: *res judicata* precludes the same case from being adjudicated again. If a subsequent claim is filed, it shall be dismissed. Under Portuguese law, *res judicata* has two effects concerning a judgment on the merits. *Res judicata* means that it has force within as well as outside the proceedings (substantive *res judicata*). *Res judicata* can also mean that a decision on procedural matters cannot be modified after it has been delivered; this is the formal 'Portuguese side' of *res judicata*. Also, according to Bulgarian law, *res judicata* concerns the 'irrevocability' of a judgment and serves the interests of the parties so that they know how to act in the future, and the effect of *res judicata* bars new proceedings and possibilities to appeal.

A common feature to Swedish, French, Polish and Portuguese national laws is that only the operative parts of a judgment obtain *res judicata*, and it does not extend to the reasoning of a judgment. Hence, a judgment cannot be appealed because a judgment debtor finds that the reasoning 'is wrong'. A court is, therefore, in principle not formally bound by the reasoning in a previous judgment delivered by another court. However, French case law is not unanimous on excluding the reasoning from the *res judicata* effect. Under Polish law there are some exceptions, i.e. *res judicata* can only be extended to the reasoning if it is necessary to clarify the scope of the operative part. From Article 236 para. 2 of the Polish CPC, it follows that the reasoning and the decision of the court are two different things.

Bulgarian law is contradictory. In case law dating back to the 1950's the Bulgarian Supreme Court held that not only the operative parts of judgments require *res judicata*, but also the main reasoning of a judgment. The question on how to deduce the main reasoning was, however, not clarified by the Bulgarian Supreme Court. Nowadays, the reasoning of a judgment does not acquire *res judicata*.

Belgian law provides an interesting exception concerning the effects of a judgment. According to Belgian law, the effect of *res judicata* is not merely restricted to the operative part of a judgment, it also extends to the reasoning of a judgment.[43]

In many of the compared national legal orders, the effect of a judgment is described in terms of *res judicata*, entailing a positive and a negative side. The judgment can be relied upon in other proceedings, and it constitutes a bar to new proceedings on the same matter. In most Member States, the *res judicata* effect appears to be limited to the operative parts of a judgment.

[43]Cf. Cass. 14 May 1982, Arr.Cass. 1981-82, 1140.

4.2 In Brussels I bis Regulation According to the CJEU

In a European, cross-border perspective, legal force is connected to the concept of recognition. Recognition under Brussels I bis Regulation means that a judgment produces positive and negative effects, i.e. the judgment has finally decided the disputed issues, and it bars new proceedings in the same cause of action.[44] This means that the judgment produces effects in the whole Union.

In Hoffmann,[45] the CJEU reiterated the so-called doctrine of extension from the Jenard Report, i.e., 'recognition must have the result of conferring on judgments the authority and effectiveness accorded to them in the State in which they were given'.[46] In practice, this means that a national court may have to investigate the doctrine of *res judicata* according to the law of the Member State of origin. The findings have consequences and determine the effects that the judgment will have in the recognising Member State. It could concern which parties are obliged by the judgment, whether the judgment has effect against third parties, if a judgment against a debtor also binds his or her creditor, and so on.[47] This position deviates from the position in some Member States' national laws, for example Sweden, where a recognised judgment is believed to produce the same effects as a domestic judgment in force.

In the case Gothaer Allgemeine Versicherung,[48] the CJEU made an 'exception' to the doctrine of extension. This case concerns an issue of jurisdiction under the 2001 Brussels I bis Regulation.[49] A Belgian court had rejected a claim, because the disputed contract contained—according to the Belgian court—a valid choice-of-court agreement appointing an Icelandic court (which meant the application of the 2007 Lugano Convention's parallel rules). The question at hand was, if a court of another Member State (Germany), where an application later was filed, was bound by the Belgian decision to reject the claim and, if so, the consequences of that.

The CJEU found that the decision should be recognised, and that it obliged courts within the whole Union. What's more, the CJEU held that the court of a Member State before which 'recognition is sought of a judgment by which a court of another Member State has declined jurisdiction on the basis of a jurisdiction clause is bound by the finding – made in the grounds of a judgment, which has since become final, declaring the action inadmissible – regarding the validity of that clause'.

This autonomous determination requires national courts in the Member States to take into account, recognise and follow the operative part of the judgment, and also

---

[44] See, *e.g.*, Dickinson and Lein (2015), pp. 375–383.

[45] Case 145/86, Horst Ludwig Martin Hoffmann v. Adelheid Krieg, 4.2.1988, ECLI:EU:C:1988:61.

[46] See the Jenard Report, Jenard (1979), p. 43.

[47] Cf. Magnus and Mankowski (2023), pp. 795–798.

[48] Case C-456/11, Gothaer Allgemeine Versicherung AG v. Samskip GmbH, 15.11.2012, ECLI:EU:C:2012:719.

[49] OJ L 12/1, 16.1.2001. See also indent (34) of Brussels I bis Regulation with regard to the principle of continuity between the Brussels instruments.

the reasoning that prompted the decision. In Gothaer Allgemeine Versicherung, this meant that the Belgian court's assessment of the validity of the jurisdiction clause was binding and should be recognised by German courts.

The outcome of this preliminary ruling seems to be that when determining jurisdictional issues under Brussels I bis Regulation, a minimum level concerning legal force must be observed so that national rules of *res judicata* does not deprive a judgment its effect in other Member States. The 'value' of this preliminary ruling has been much discussed in literature, and it probably does not extend beyond its scope.[50] Therefore, the doctrine of extension still prevails as a main rule.

5 Five Conclusions

1. How a decision or judgment is labelled is irrelevant, it is its contents and effects that are significant for the European circulation of judgments under Brussels I bis Regulation. Consequently, Member States can keep their 'national procedural identities' when it comes to titles and decisions makers.
2. It could be argued that it would have been more accurate if Brussels I bis Regulation referred to the all-inclusive expression 'decision' instead of 'judgment', in order to identify the wide variety of national decisions actually covered by the Brussels I bis Regulation.
3. The EU legislator should consider including court settlements in the concept of judgment in Brussels I bis Regulation.
4. The doctrine of extension is too complicated in practice.
5. True mutual trust needs to be furthered in the EU and its Member States.

References

Briggs A (2015) Civil Jurisdiction and Judgments, 6th edn. Informa Law, Routledge

Dickinson A, Lein E (2015) The Brussels I Regulation Recast. Oxford University Press, Oxford

Hartley T (2017) Civil Jurisdiction and Judgments in Europe: The Brussels I Regulation, the Lugano Convention, and the Hague Choice of Court Convention. Oxford University Press, Oxford

Husa J (2021) Merging International Law and Comparative Law: Balancing Between Normative and Non-Normative. Rabels Zeitschrift 85(4):745–774

Jenard P (1979) Report on the Convention on jurisdiction and the enforcement of judgments in civil and commercial matters signed at Brussels. OJ C 59, 5.3.1979. Also published as Bulletin of the European Communities Supplement 12/79

Magnus U, Mankowski P (Eds) (2023) Brussels Ibis Regulation: Commentary, 2nd edn. Verlag Dr. Otto Schmidt, Köln

[50] See, e.g., Hartley (2017), p. 395; Dickinson and Lein (2015), pp. 384, 385.

Pålsson L (2008) Bryssel I-förordningen jämte Bryssel- och Luganokonventionerna: Domstols behörighet samt erkännande och verkställighet av domar i privaträttsliga ämnen inom EU/EFTA-området. Norstedts Juridik, Stockholm
Schlosser P (1979) Report on the Convention on the association of the Kingdom of Denmark, Ireland and the United Kingdom of Great Britain and Northern Ireland to the Convention on jurisdiction and the enforcement of judgments in civil and commercial matters and to the protocol on its interpretation by the Court of Justice, OJ C 59/71
Sjövall F, Rudvall S (2018) De europeiska civilprocessförordningarna: En kommentar. Norstedt Juridik, Stockholm
The Unified Patent Court (2022) About the Court. https://www.unified-patent-court.org/
Torremans P (Ed) (2017) Private International Law, 15th edn. Oxford University Press, Oxford

Is a Judgment Always a Judgment? A Dutch-Belgian Comparative Perspective

Marielène Wertenbroek and Marta Pertegás Sender

Abstract This chapter describes the enforcement titles of the Netherlands and Belgium. It focuses on the characterising features of outgoing titles originating from the Netherlands and Belgium and provides helpful indicators to those entrusted with the proper identification and characterisation of such enforcement titles in a cross-border perspective.

1 Introduction

The diversity of enforcement titles in the European Union (EU) is both the triggering factor and the major challenge of the cross-border circulation of such titles. In line with the findings of previously completed work under the coordination of the University of Maribor,[1] the consortium made further progress in mapping out the existing diversity of enforcement titles under the aegis of the EN4s Project.[2] In particular, this project achieved a new milestone in facilitating the identification of such enforcement titles in a cross-border context. Thanks to a multidisciplinary collaboration between legal and IT experts, new software was developed and made available to the practitioners who should ensure the interoperability of legal titles across borders.

[1] Rijavec et al. (2014, 2018, 2020).

[2] EU-En4s project 'Diversity of Enforcement Titles in cross-border Debt Collection in EU', Faculty of Law, under the coordination of the University of Maribor (Prof. dr. V. Rijavec). Project website is Vesna Rijavec, Diversity of Enforcement Titles in cross-border Debt Collection in EU, Faculty of Law University of Maribor (3 December 2021, 22,35 PM EDT), http://pf.um.si/en/acj/projects/pr09-eu-en4s.

M. Wertenbroek (✉) · M. P. Sender
Maastricht University, Faculty of Law, Maastricht, The Netherlands
e-mail: m.wertenbroek@student.maastrichtuniversity.nl; m.pertegassender@maastrichtuniversity.nl

V. Rijavec et al. (eds.), *Diversity of Enforcement Titles in the EU*, Ius Gentium: Comparative Perspectives on Law and Justice 111,
https://doi.org/10.1007/978-3-031-47108-7_4

Contributing to this mapping exercise of differences in either the structure, the content or the effects of judgments in a selected number of Member States, this chapter zooms in the enforcement titles of two neighbouring Member States the authors are relatively familiar with, i.e., the Netherlands and Belgium. This contribution focuses on the characterising features of outgoing titles originating from the Netherlands and Belgium and offers the flipside of a previous contribution by our Maastricht colleague F. Fernhout, who dealt with the treatment of incoming foreign titles that seek enforcement in the Netherlands.[3] Both perspectives may provide helpful indicators to those entrusted with the proper identification and characterisation of such enforcement titles in a cross-border perspective.

2 Enforcement Titles Originating in the Netherlands or Belgium

Both jurisdictions under review know enforcement titles other than judgments, which is the focus of the following sections.

In the Netherlands, the Dutch Code of Civil Procedure (hereinafter 'CCP', *Wetboek van Burgerlijke Rechtsvordering* in Dutch) is the primary source to describe what qualifies as an enforcement title under Dutch law.

Article 430 CCP distinguishes among three categories of enforceable titles originating in the Netherlands: court judgments, authentic instruments and other titles designated by law as enforceable.

Enforceable court judgments from the Netherlands are easily identifiable because they contain the coined expression 'In the name of the King' (*In naam van de Koning* in Dutch) at the top right corner of the judgment.

The enforceable version of a judgment with the abovementioned affix is delivered to the creditor who, incidentally, could be either party in the original proceedings. The creditor, in the context of the enforcement, is the party who seeks the enforcement ('*executant*'). If needed, the creditor is provided with several copies containing the same affixed royal reference and no fees are charged for the issuing of these copies (Article 231 CCP). No distinction is made between the judgments of civil, administrative or criminal courts, nor between the type of judgments (as further described below).

The second category of enforcement titles under Dutch law is that of authentic instruments. According to Article 156(2) CCP, these are documents in pre-established forms drawn up by officials with the power to issue such instruments on the basis of their actions or observations. Notarial deeds are authentic

[3] Fernhout (2020), pp. 153–178. This contribution is primarily based on the national chapters on respectively Belgium and the Netherlands for the EU-En4s Project. The main authors of these two national chapters contributed by Maastricht University are Mateusz Rys (Belgium) and Bartosz Sujecki (the Netherlands).

instruments, but also the writs issued by a process server, the acts of the registrar of the Registry of Births, Deaths and Marriages, or the court minutes drawn up by judges and court clerks. These titles become enforceable when they carry the words 'In the name of the King', a reference that can only be added by authorised officials. For instance, notaries are authorised to affix this expression on the basis of Article 50 of the Notary Act.

There is a third 'catch-all' group of enforceable titles originating from the Netherlands. For instance, for debt recovery purposes, a court settlement that is transcribed to the court minutes and signed by the parties can be enforceable. For this purpose, the minutes are issued in accordance with the legal requirements (Article 87(3) CCP) so that the 'In the name of the King' formula can be added, which makes this title directly enforceable. We could also refer to the arbitral awards for which a Dutch judge has granted enforceability (this task is entrusted to the summary proceedings judge (*voorzieningenrechter*)) who will issue an *exequatur* in accordance with Article 1062 CCP).

In Belgium, enforcement titles are those legal instruments that are drawn up in accordance with a specific form (*formulier van tenuitvoerlegging / formule exécutoire*).[4] The precise formulation stems from a 1971 Royal Decree[5] that was last revised in 1993.[6]

Under Belgian law, Article 1386 of the Judicial Code ('Gerechtelijk Wetboek') refers to the in-principle enforceability of judgments and acts (*vonnissen en akten*) drawn up in accordance with the form referred to in the previous paragraph. Enforcement titles with Belgium as the state of origin may include court decisions, consent orders,[7] arbitral awards, notarial acts and administrative documents which are enforceable by operation of the law. An example of such an administrative document is a tax assessment register issued by the tax authorities.[8]

[4] De Valkeneer (2002), p. 58.

[5] Royal Decree establishing the form of enforcement of judgments, verdicts, orders, court orders or deeds contributing to immediate enforcement ('Koninklijk besluit tot vaststelling van het formulier van tenuitvoerlegging van de arresten, vonnissen, beschikkingen, rechterlijke bevelen of akten die dadelijke tenuitvoerlegging medebrengen').

[6] Royal Decree of 9 August 1993 amending the Royal Decree of 27 May 1971 establishing the form of enforcement of judgments, verdicts, orders, court orders or deeds contributing to immediate enforcement ('Koninklijk besluit van 9 augustus 1993 tot wijziging van het koninklijk besluit van 27 mei 1971 tot vaststelling van het formulier van tenuitvoerlegging van de arresten, vonnissen, beschikkingen, rechterlijke bevelen of akten die dadelijke tenuitvoerlegging medebrengen', Belgian Official Journal (B.S.) 21 July 2013, p. 45654, available at http://www.ejustice.just.fgov.be/cgi/summary.pl.

[7] Article 1046 Judicial Code.

[8] Cass. 17 June 1929, Pas. 1929, I, 246.

3 Judgments

Among the diverse enforcement titles listed above, this section focuses on judgments as the most frequent and important type of enforceable title originating from either the Netherlands or Belgium. A typology of judicial decisions is presented.

In Dutch civil procedure, judicial decisions can be classified according to the issuing institution. A judgment (*vonnis/jugement* or, in appeal proceedings: an *arrest/arrêt*), is a judicial decision that is rendered in the context of contradictory proceedings (the so-called *dagvaardingsprocedures*). The second type of judicial decision is an order (*beschikking*), which is initiated by a unilateral petition (*verzoekschriftprocedure*). For such orders, further attention must be paid to the way proceedings were conducted: if those are exclusively *ex parte* proceedings, and the resulting order is a provisional (including protective) measure, the limitation resulting from Article 2 (a) 2nd para Brussels I bis Regulation applies.

There is, indeed, a distinction to be made between a final judgment (*eindvonnis/ jugement définitif*) which represents the end of the proceedings and interim judgments. The latter are rendered while the proceedings are pending and will therefore be referred to as an interlocutory judgment (*tussenvonnis*). In cross-border cases, Dutch courts may, for instance, resolve case management issues, or procedural questions such as their international jurisdiction or the applicable law, in such interlocutory judgments.[9] An interlocutory judgment where a partial final decision is given is called a partial judgment (*deelvonnis*).

It is also possible to categorise judgments based on their effects. A general distinction is made between awarding and rejecting decisions. Awarding decisions include the following subcategories: a constitutive (*constitutief*) judgment confers a new legal status, such as, for instance, in a divorce case. A declaratory (*declaratoir*) judgment provides a definitive statement on the legal relationship between parties. A condemnatory (*condemnatoir*) judgment mandates the judgment debtor to perform a certain action. Conversely, rejecting decisions include declaratory judgments, as well as declarations of inadmissibility (*niet-ontvankelijkheidsverklaring*).[10]

Finally, in a cross-border setting, it is important to sketch the conditions for a judgment to become enforceable in the Netherlands. This is because, according to Article 39 Brussels I bis Regulation, a judgment given in the Netherlands needs to be enforceable in this country to claim mirror effects abroad on the basis of the Regulation.

For enforceability in the Netherlands, the main rule is that the judgment may only be enforced by the party in whose favour the judgment was rendered, provided no further legal remedies are possible. If, for example, a party is ordered to pay a sum of money, the party is required to pay this amount *after* the term for appeal has expired. The judgment is thus enforceable after the expiration of this time.

[9]For instance, see Case C/10/526115/HA ZA 17-440, Rechtbank Rotterdam, 20.1.2018, ECLI:NL: RBROT:2018:7852.

[10]Groeneveld-Tijssens (2015), p. 19.

However, it is possible for the court to grant provisional enforceability (*uitvoerbaar bij voorraad*) to a judgment. If provisional enforceability is granted, the judgment becomes immediately executable. It is up to the claimant to request the provisional enforceability and, if granted, the defendant must immediately comply with the judgment.[11] Next, there is voluntary enforcement by the debtor or, in the absence thereof, a party can start the enforcement procedure by instructing the court bailiff to serve the judgment on the counterparty. In case of a money debt (to be enforced in the Netherlands), the debtor is given two days to make the payment. The debtor can make the payment voluntarily, and if they fail to do so, the court bailiff has the authority to freeze the debtor's assets.[12]

In terms of typology of judgments, Belgian civil procedure does not show significant differences compared to Dutch civil procedure.

With regard to the issuing instance, a judgment (*vonnis*) is a decision rendered by a court in the first instance, while an 'arrest' is the decision rendered by a higher court, for example, the Court of Cassation or a Court of Appeal. Judicial decisions are referred to as orders (*beschikking*) when they are rendered in summary proceedings (*in kort geding/en référé, zoals in kort geding/comme en référé*), or when they refer to case management issues.[13]

With regard to the effects of a judgment, a distinction is made between a final decision (*eindvonnis*), a decision before adjudicating (*vonnis alvorens recht te doen*), a provisional decision (*provisioneel vonnis*)[14] and procedural decisions (*maatregelen van inwendige aard*).[15] In contrast to procedural judgments in Germany[16] or the Netherlands (see above), it seems unlikely that such procedural decisions (such as the setting of the hearing dates or the granting of additional time for parties' submissions) produce cross-border effects.

It is also possible to distinguish between final judgments (*eindvonnis*) and interlocutory[17] judgments (*tussenvonnis*). A judgment may be final on certain contentious issues and interlocutory on other issues, for example when it grants damages on the merits and appoints an expert to issue an opinion on the amount of such damages. Such judgments are referred to as 'mixed' judgments.

---

[11] Article 233 Wetboek van Burgerlijke Rechtsvordering (CCP).

[12] Margetson and Margetson (2021).

[13] Laenens et al. (2019), pp. 151–152.

[14] Laenens et al. (2019), p. 151.

[15] Article 19 and 1046 Judicial Code.

[16] Case C-456/11, Gothaer Allgemeine Versicherung AG and Others v Samskip GmbH, 15.11.2012, ECLI:EU:C:2012:719.

[17] Taelman and Van Severen (2018), p. 99.

4 Characterising Features and Structure of Judgments

When Belgian or Dutch judgments need to cross borders for the purposes of enforcement, it is important that they are readily identified as enforcement titles. In principle, this identification will be facilitated by the mandatory certificate concerning a judgment in civil and commercial matters required on the grounds of Article 53 Brussels I Regulation (or similar certificates for other cross-border cases).

In addition, this section sketches the standard structure and characterising features of a judgment in the Netherlands and Belgium, respectively.

In the Netherlands, Article 121 of the Dutch Constitution sets out two constitutional requirements. First, the judgment must be motivated by the court, or, in other words, it must set out the grounds on which it rests. Second, the judgment must be issued in public. These requirements are further clarified in the CCP. In particular, Article 28 CCP sets out the requirement that a decision must be given in public and Article 30 CCP refers to the requirement of motivation.

These general requirements are complemented with the requirements set out in Article 230 CCP for a judgment (*vonnis* or *arrest*) and in Article 287 in combination with Article 230 CCP for an order (*beschikking*).

Based on these several requirements, the Dutch Judiciary has developed a blueprint for (civil) judgments in the Netherlands, which contains the following characterising features:

*4.1 Judgment (*Vonnis *or, in Appeal Proceedings,* Arrest*)*

Article 230 para 1 CCP states that the judgment must state the names and place of residence of the parties, as well as the names of their counsels or legal representatives. Secondly, the type of judgment is specified (*vonnis* or *arrest*). Thirdly, there is a paragraph about the claim, as formulated in the writ of summons, together with the main arguments of the parties.

Where applicable, the claim and the statements of the Public Prosecutor will be referred to next (although this is rather infrequent in civil and commercial cases).

Most importantly, the judgment shall contain the statement of reasons or motivation. The motivation precedes the substantive decision and the allocation of costs. Finally, the name of the judge and, if the judgment is rendered by a chamber, the name of the president of the chamber, as well as the date of the judgment, are referred to.

In practice, these requirements have led to the following sequence:

- The text *'In the name of the King'* (*'In naam van de Koning'*) only in cases of a final decision;
- Type of decision;

- Name of the court issuing the decision;
- Case number;
- Name of the parties, place of residence, role in the procedure and name of the representatives;
- The course of the procedure (documents that were exchanged by the parties, hearings etc.);
- Facts of the case as determined by the court;
- The claim as laid down in the writ of summons and, where applicable, the counterclaim;
- The statement of reasons (regarding the claim and, where applicable, the counterclaim);
- The decision (it may contain instructions to the parties);
- Name and signature of the judge and the registrar;
- Date of the judgment.

*4.2 Order (***Beschikking***)*

The blueprint of an order (*beschikking*), on the basis of Article 287 and Article 230 CCP, is as follows:

- Type of decision;
- Name of the court issuing the decision;
- Case number;
- Name of the parties, place of residence, role in the procedure and name of the representatives;
- The course of the procedure (documents that were exchanged by the parties, hearings etc.);
- Facts of the case as determined by the court;
- The petition;
- The statement of reasons;
- The decision;
- Name and signature of the judge and the registrar and the date of the judgment.

In Belgium, we notice a similar judicial practice to follow a standard structure for judgments. A Belgian judgment typically has five main sections:

i. The preamble or the introductory part in which the identity of the parties and their respective counsel is stated. The preamble also clarifies the capacity of each party. Additionally, the docket number and the name of the court or tribunal is stated in the preamble.
ii. An overview of the facts is provided.
iii. The claims of the parties are stated.

iv. The reasoning of the judge is set out.
v. The Operative Part of the judgment is presented.[18]

This structure stems from Article 780 of the Judicial Code, which refers to judgments but is actually understood to refer to other judicial decisions as well.[19]

The first paragraph of Article 780 specifies that the judgement needs to contain the statement of reasons as well as an Operative Part. In addition, the same Article 780 refers to additional information that must be included: the judge or court that delivered the judgment, the names of the judges that decided the case (if applicable, the name of the public prosecutor), and the name of the registrar at the time of delivery of the judgement, the requirements with regard to the parties, the object of the civil claim, the statements of claim of the parties, the date of the judgment.

Additionally, the judgment must also be signed by the judges who ruled on the issue.[20] Specific to Belgium is a reference pertaining to the use of the language in the procedure. Belgium has three official languages (Dutch, French and German), and the proceedings may in principle be initiated in any of them. The language in which the proceedings have been initiated determines the language in which the judgment shall be written. Each judgment must explicitly state that the provisions of the law of 15 June 1935 regarding the use of language in judicial proceedings have been complied with.

A graphic overview of the common characterising features of a judgment in the Netherlands or Belgium is shown in Fig. 1.

5 Binding Effects of a Judgment

It is debated whether European civil procedure includes an autonomous concept of *res judicata* for the application of the relevant Regulations on cross-border circulation of judgments. While this question is further debated, it is important to give consideration to the effects of a judgment as attributed by the Member State of origin.

We therefore examine how the *res judicata* effects are conferred in respectively Dutch and Belgian civil procedure. It is already anticipated that no essential differences are noticeable among these two legal systems.

In the Dutch civil procedure, Article 236 para 1 CCP states that the decisions regarding a dispute as set out in the judgement (*vonnis*) are binding in another procedure between the same parties. This applies to decisions against which no legal remedy, such as an appeal or another remedy, is available.

[18] Van Ransbeeck (2014), pp. 49–50. It is possible for the Operative Part, understood as the judge/judges'decision on a contentious issue, to be segmented throughout the judgment: Cass. 10 November 1987, *Pasicrisie*, 1988, 301; Cass. 29 March 2001, Larcier Cas. n°618.

[19] Laenens et al. (2019), p. 513.

[20] Laenens et al. (2019), p. 515.

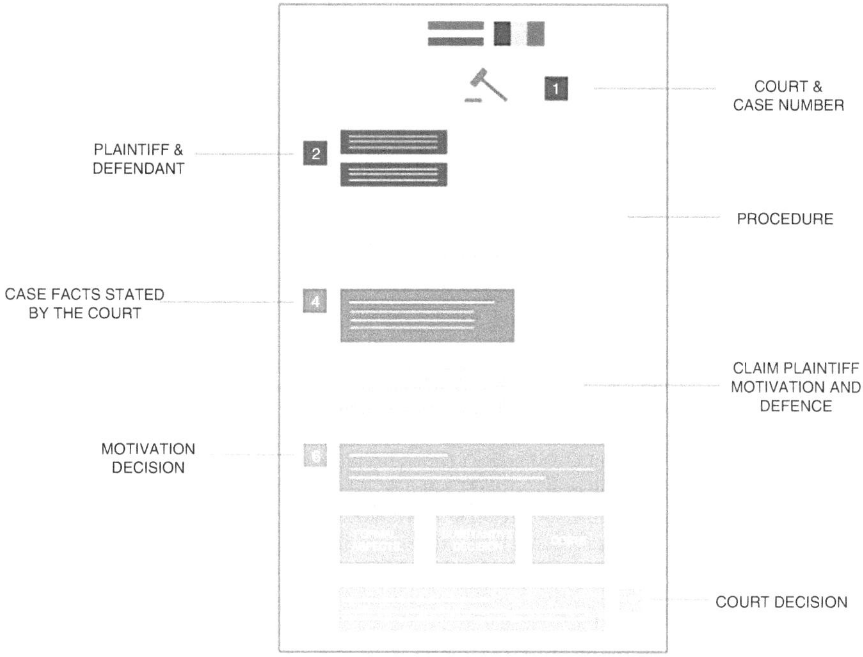

Fig. 1 Visualisation of characteristics. Source: Based on the presentation by Dr. Bartosz Sujecki and Prof. Marta Pertegas given on 10 September 2020 during the Portorož Conference of the EN4s project (https://www.youtube.com/watch?v=9PTrF7ZF6h0)

The binding effect is conferred not only to the operational part of the judgment but also to the statement of reasons included in the judgment. These same elements of interlocutory judgments have a binding effect as well.

In Belgium, all final decisions within a judgment (*eindbeslissing*) can become res judicata. This means that both a judgment and an order can be granted res judicata effects, provided there is a final determination on a contentious matter. A contentious matter is defined as a point at which the parties had a dispute and at which they had an exchange of opinions.[21]

It is the final nature of the judicial decision that, according to Article 24 of the Judicial Code, confers res judicata effects. Conversely, certain decisions do not become res judicata. A preliminary decision (*vonnis alvorens recht te doen*) is an example of a judgment that does not become res judicata as it does not hold a final decision. However, judgments relating to the admissibility of a claim are final decisions and therefore res judicata.[22] Judgments in summary proceedings (*kort*

[21] Cass. 14 June 2018, P&B 2018, afl. 5-6, 200.

[22] Cass. 7 November 1994, Arr.Cass. 1994, 931.

geding) can have res judicata effects when the judge makes a final decision on the disputed matter.[23] Additionally, *kort geding* judgments hold res judicata as well.[24]

The *res judicata* effect is conferred not only to the decision of the court but also to all elements that, following the filing of the case, were argued (even implicitly) by the parties, and that constitute the necessary basis for the court decision.[25] As such, the statement of reasoning can possess *res judicata* effects.

References

De Valkeneer R (2002) Précis Du Notariat. Bruylant, Brusselles

Fernhout F (2020) Enforcing foreign titles regarding monetary claims in the Netherlands. In: Rijavec V, Drnovšek K, van Rhee C (eds) Cross-border enforcement in Europe: national and international perspectives. Intersentia, Cambridge, pp 153–178

Groeneveld-Tijssens N (2015) De verklaring voor recht. Wolters Kluwer

Laenens J, Scheers D, Thiriar P et al (2019) Handboek gerechtelijk recht, 5th edn Intersentia

Margetson N, Margetson N (2021) Litigation and enforcement in the Netherlands: overview. Thomson Reuters Practical Law. https://uk.practicallaw.thomsonreuters.com/w-015-9107?transitionType=Default&contextData=(sc.Default)&firstPage=true

Rijavec V, Kereteš T, Ivanc T (2014) Simplification of debt collection in the EU. Wolters Kluwer

Rijavec V, Kennet W, Kereteš T et al (2018) Remedies concerning enforcement of foreign judgements: Brussels I Recast. Wolters Kluwer, Alphen aan den Rijn

Rijavec V, Drnovšek K, van Rhee C (2020) Cross-border enforcement in Europe: national and international perspectives. Intersentia, Cambridge

Taelman P, Van Severen C (2018) Civil procedure in Belgium. Wolters Kluwer

Van Lersberghe P (2010) Het gezag van gewijsde in burgerlijke zaken. In: Engels C, Lecocq P (eds) Rechtskroniek voor de Vrede- en Politierechters. Bruges, Die Keure, pp 329–350

Van Ransbeeck R (2014) Standaardisatie van vonnissen en arresten: opportuniteiten en valkuilen bij de digitalisering van justitie. Orde van de Dag: Criminaliteit en Samenleving 2(66):49–57

[23]Van Lersberghe (2010), p. 343.

[24]Cass. 6 February 1930, Pas. 1930, I, 87.

[25]Laenens et al. (2019), p. 152; Cass. 14 May 1982, Arr.Cass. 1981-82, 1140.

Comparative View on the Divergence of Structure and Substance of Judgements

Katja Drnovšek

Abstract Even though enforcement procedure under Brussels I bis Regulation regime is undoubtedly a considerable step forward in pursuing simplified cross-border procedures, the participants in such proceedings regularly encounter foreign enforcement titles drafted in an unfamiliar language and form. While difficulties arising from the use of language can be overcome by translation, the unfamiliar structure of enforcement titles remains another significant source of possible confusion. It is true that in most cases, the information contained in the certificate should suffice for the competent authority in the Member State of enforcement to carry out enforcement without resorting to the enforcement title itself, and that Article 52 of Brussels I bis Regulation further eliminates the need to re-examine the enforcement title by prohibiting the court of enforcement to review its substance. However, if the debtor decides to oppose enforcement, they—and the court of enforcement—will unavoidably have to face the foreign enforcement title itself. Deviations in the structure of national judgements and other enforcement titles may lead to situations where the information needed is hidden in a different part of the document, making it easy to miss or misinterpret, or even omitted, making certain procedural acts difficult or impossible. Such misplacement might also result in different legal consequences than those intended by the court drafting the judgement (e.g., regarding *res judicata*). Therefore, the issue of divergent structure and substance of judgements drafted in different jurisdictions should not be overlooked in the context of cross-border judicial cooperation. The chapter focuses on the examination and comparison of national judgements in terms of their basic structure at a macro level (division into elementary parts), as well as on certain selected issues that might arise at a micro level as a result of different national requirements for drafting judgements (e.g. the inclusion of time-limits for voluntary fulfilment, the threat of enforcement, the value of the dispute, the assessment of procedural requirements, etc.). Following the analysis of relevant data compiled in the form of national reports and manuals within the scope of the project Diversity of Enforcement Titles in cross-border Debt

K. Drnovšek (✉)
University of Maribor, Faculty of Law, Maribor, Slovenia
e-mail: katja.drnovsek@um.si

V. Rijavec et al. (eds.), *Diversity of Enforcement Titles in the EU*, Ius Gentium: Comparative Perspectives on Law and Justice 111,
https://doi.org/10.1007/978-3-031-47108-7_5

Collection in EU (EU-EN4s), the comparative research first concentrates on synthesising the collected data in an attempt to determine similarities and shared characteristics of national judgements. Afterwards, it highlights deviations and national particularities, especially concerning the more detailed elements of a judgement where these differences become more apparent and greater in number. Finally, it assesses their implications both at national and cross-border levels.

1 Introduction

Despite all attempts undertaken to simplify cross-border enforcement procedures at international and EU levels, participants in such proceedings will still regularly encounter foreign legal acts and documents drafted in an unfamiliar language and an unfamiliar form. For example, two documents are needed for enforcement proceedings conducted in accordance with Brussels I bis Regulation,[1] which is already incredibly simplified compared to previously available enforcement options: a copy of the judgement and the certificate issued pursuant to Article 53, certifying that the judgement is enforceable and containing an extract of the judgement (as well as, where appropriate, relevant information on the recoverable costs of the proceedings and the calculation of interest) (Article 42(1) of Brussels I bis Regulation). It is true that the information contained in the certificate should in most cases suffice for the competent authority in the Member State of enforcement to carry out enforcement without resorting to the judgement itself, and that Article 52 of Brussels I bis Regulation adamantly states that under no circumstances may a judgement given in a Member State be reviewed as to its substance in the Member State addressed, thus further eliminating the need to examine it. However, if the debtor decides to seek a remedy or to oppose enforcement, they—and the court of enforcement—will unavoidably have to face the foreign enforcement title itself. In other proceedings not falling within the scope of the regulation (e.g. those conducted pursuant to the Hague Convention or national rules regulating enforcement of foreign judgements), where no such standardised certificates are provided, a detailed examination of foreign judgements is basically inevitable. Difficulties arising from the use of language can be overcome (more or less easily) with the help of translation;[2] however, the unfamiliar structure of enforcement titles still has the potential to confuse the court of enforcement, the debtor and/or their representatives and other participants in proceedings. Not only is it possible for the information they would need to pursue their procedural rights to be hidden in a different part of the document, which might make it easy to miss or misinterpret, or to be even omitted altogether, which would make certain procedural acts difficult or impossible, but

[1]Regulation (EU) No 1215/2012 of the European Parliament and of the Council of 12 December 2012 on jurisdiction and the recognition and enforcement of judgments in civil and commercial matters, OJ L 351, 20.12.2012, 1–32.

[2]For more on that, see, for example, Drnovšek (2018), pp. 227–271.

such misplacement could also lead to different legal consequences than those intended by the court drafting the judgement (e.g., regarding *res judicata*). Therefore, the issue of divergent structure and substance of judgements drafted in different jurisdictions should not be overlooked in the context of cross-border judicial cooperation.

The present chapter focuses on the examination and comparison of national judgements in terms of their basic structure at a macro level (division into elementary parts), as well as on certain selected issues that might arise at a micro level as a result of different national requirements for drafting judgements (e.g. the inclusion of time-limits for voluntary fulfilment, the threat of enforcement, the value of the dispute, the assessment of procedural requirements, etc.). Following the analysis of relevant data compiled in the form of national reports and manuals within the scope of the project Diversity of Enforcement Titles in cross-border Debt Collection in EU (EU-EN4s),[3] the comparative research first concentrates on synthesising the collected data in an attempt to determine similarities and shared characteristics of national judgements. Afterwards, it highlights deviations and national particularities, especially concerning the more detailed elements of a judgement where these differences become more apparent and greater in number. Finally, it assesses their implications both at national and cross-border levels.

Some disclaimers are necessary concerning the subsequent comparative analysis. Due to the unavoidable constraints regarding the scope and length of the chapter, the discussion is limited to the comparison of monetary judgements issued by national courts of the first instance. The term 'judgement' in the context of this chapter is used to denote any such act issued by a court or tribunal in the respective country, regardless of what it might be called in the national legal system.[4] Other enforcement titles, judgements issued by appellate courts and judgements ordering some other type of performance are mentioned only sporadically, where this is beneficial for the discussion at hand or necessary for a proper understanding of the issue. This choice was made because, unlike in the case of other enforcement titles (e.g. authentic instruments) where the regulation differs significantly between jurisdictions, a judgement is universally established as the standard act containing a final decision granted by the court on the case before it and, as a consequence, the most typical enforcement title. As judgements in all jurisdictions serve a universal purpose and pursue the same goal, it is expected that their basic structure and substance would also be similar or at least similar enough to be comparable. Furthermore, in terms of available resources, the analysis relies heavily (sometimes exclusively) on national reports and manuals compiled in the scope of the project EU-EN4s, some of which might have provided more detailed information regarding certain aspects of the

[3]Diversity of Enforcement Titles in cross-border Debt Collection in EU, https://www.pf.um.si/en/acj/projects/pr09-eu-en4s/.

[4]In line with Article 2(a) Brussels I bis Regulation and its interpretation by CJEU. See also Case C-551/15, Pula Parking d.o.o. v. Sven Klaus Tederahn, 9.3.2017, ECLI:EU:C:2017:193 and case C-484/15, Ibrica Zulfikarpašić v. Slaven Gajer, 9.3.2017, ECLI:EU:C:2017:19.

structure of judgements and their implications than others. Therefore, it should be emphasised that it is not the purpose of the chapter to provide a comprehensive overview and comparison of every single element of national judgements for all eighteen participating jurisdictions, which would not even be possible within its limited scope. Instead, it attempts to identify and assess some prominent similarities and differences that would most likely affect the courts and the parties in cross-border proceedings and provide a starting point for future and more detailed research in this area.

2 Structure of Judgements

2.1 Regulation of the Structure of Court Documents

In most legal systems, the formal structure of judgements and other judicial decisions is considered critical enough in the pursuit of legal certainty to justify special attention at a legislative level. Correspondingly, procedural legislation in most jurisdictions examined in the course of the project contains specific provisions regulating the elements, structure and content of these court documents (the exceptions being Poland and the Republic of Cyprus, see below). While the extent of provided details and a precise division into particular units comprising a judgement somewhat vary, the following provisions determine at least the basic structure of judgements drafted in respective countries (Table 1):

Worth noting are two exceptions to the legislative approach, Poland and the Republic of Cyprus, where the structure of judgements issued by national courts is not exhaustively regulated under provisions adopted by legislative authority. In Poland, the established structure of court decisions is mainly a result of developments in judicial practice since Polish independence in 1918. Nonetheless, Polish judgements were recently standardised with the implementation of the Regulation of the Minister of Justice of 18 June 2019—Regulations governing the operation of courts of law, and Direction of the Minister of Justice of 19 June 2019 on the organisation and scope of operation of court offices and other divisions of court administration, as well as with the use of IT systems supporting court operations.[5] In the Republic of Cyprus, in line with its common-law tradition, the structure of judgements is not regulated by law either and thus fails to follow a formal structure. However, certain elements composing any civil court judgement can also be derived from court practice.[6]

Even in some jurisdictions where the structure of judgements is imposed by law, the courts themselves have played an important role in their standardisation in certain cases. In Slovenia, for example, a more detailed standardised structure than

[5] Gołaczyński et al. (2020), p. 17.

[6] Christofi & Loizou (2022), p. 11.

Table 1 Legal provisions regulating the structure of judgements

Albania	Article 310 of Albanian Civil Procedure Code (*Kodi i Procedurës Civile*)
Austria	§§ 417, 417a, 418 of Austrian Code of Civil Procedure (*Zivilprozessordnung*, ZPO)
Belgium	Article 780 of Belgian Judicial Code (*Gerechtelijk Wetboek, Code Judiciaire*)
Bulgaria	Article 236 (1) of Bulgarian Civil Procedure Code (*Граждански процесуален кодекс*)
Croatia	Article 338 of Croatian Civil Procedure Act (*Zakon o parničnom postupku*), Article 62 of Court Ordinance (*Sudski poslovnik*)
Republic of Cyprus	*No legal provisions, developed through court practice*
Czech Republic	§ 157 of Czech Civil Procedure Code (*Občanský soudní řád*)
France	Article 454 of French Code of Civil Procedure (*Code de procédure civile*)
Germany	§313 of German Code of Civil Procedure (*Zivilprozessordnung*, ZPO)
Italy	Articles 132, 134 and 135 of Italian Code of Civil Procedure (*Codice di procedura civile*)
Lithuania	Article 270 of Lithuanian Code of Civil Procedure (*Civilinio proceso kodeksas*)
Netherlands	Article 230 of Dutch Code of Civil Procedure (*Wetboek van Burgerlijke Rechtsvordering*, Rv)
North Macedonia	Article 327 of North Macedonian Civil Procedure Act (*Закон за парничната постапка*)
Poland	*Developed through court practice, standardised by the Minister of Justice acts of 2019*
Portugal	Article 607 of Portuguese Civil Procedure Code (*Código de Processo Civil*)
Slovenia	Article 324 of Slovenian Civil Procedure Act (*Zakon o pravdnem postopku*)
Spain	Articles 208 and 209 of Spanish Code of Civil Procedure (*Ley de Enjuiciamiento Civil*, LEC)
Sweden	Chapter 17 Section 7 of Swedish Code of Judicial Procedure (*Rättegångsbalk*, RB)

the one provided by law has developed in court practice, and considerable efforts have been made in recent years to regulate these rules in a more official manner. The Court Rules ('Sodni red') thus delegated the task and authority to the Slovenian Supreme Court to adopt a (mandatory) style to be used in judicial writings by all Slovenian courts. In turn, the Supreme Court issued the Instructions for the unification of style to be used in court decisions and other judicial writings of 29 March 2010. Furthermore, several courts issued internal rules on the use of standards for uniform drafting of decisions (e.g. the rules issued by the Supreme Court of the RS of 26 January 2009, the rules issued by the Higher Court in Maribor of 1 December 2011, etc.) and prepared a standard template to be used by courts. These rules and templates regulate in great detail the content for each part of a judgement, together with examples of proper phrasings, style of citations, as well as graphic requirements (font, spacing, size, margins, etc.).[7] Similarly detailed is the standardised formatting of Croatian judgements, as defined in Article 62 of the Court Ordinance ('Sudski poslovnik').[8] The Netherlands is another country where the structure of judgements is broadly stipulated by law, but the courts have further developed the structure of their decisions by applying these requirements in practice with the aim to standardise their form and improve the quality. These developments were then adopted in the form of guidelines published by the Dutch Council for the Judiciary ('Raad voor de Rechtspraak').[9] Belgian Judicial Code also stipulates certain formalities that need to be considered but fails to determine a detailed structure; nonetheless, most Belgian judgements follow a similar structure developed by judicial tradition.[10]

2.2 *Level of Standardisation*

Since a resounding majority of examined jurisdictions (with the above-discussed exceptions of the Republic of Cyprus and Poland) stipulates at least basic elements comprising a judgement, frequently in great details, it is not surprising that most participating national reporters consider judgements in their respective countries adequately standardised in terms of their formal structure.[11] This holds true even for countries with such complicated governance structures as Spain, where the content and structure of judgements remain uniform across the country despite its division into seventeen autonomous regions and the use of four official languages.[12]

In addition to legislative solutions, which are thus generally viewed in a positive light, some other measures and contributing factors to the uniformity of court documents were emphasised as being especially helpful; namely, special recommendations or guidelines issued by the ministries, supreme courts or other relevant institutions addressing formal requirements for the drafting of written judgements,[13] as well as solutions offered by the use of IT support. Both North Macedonian and

[7] Rijavec et al. (2020), p. 17.

[8] Kunštek et al. (2020), p. 11.

[9] Sujecki (2020), p. 13.

[10] Rys (2020), p. 15. See also Raf Van Ransbeeck (2014), pp. 49, 50.

[11] See, for example, Kolaj Tafaj F (2020), p. 17, Prodinger and Nunner-Krautgasser (2020), p. 17; Valdhans (2020), p. 9; Wolf et al. (2020), p. 26; Kaczorowska et al. (2022), p. 17; Sujecki (2020), p. 14; Caramelo Gomes et al. (2020), p. 16; Rijavec et al. (2020), p. 18 etc. Despite the lack of legal rules regulating the structure of judgements, national reporter for the Republic of Cyprus also finds the structure of judgements adequately standardised, as a judgement will always encompass certain elements, even though the length and detail provided by the judgement with respect to each element will vary depending on the circumstances and the legal issues arising. Christofi & Loizou (2022), p. 11.

[12] Bores Lazo & Serrano Ron (2020), p. 23.

[13] Bolzanas et al. (2020), p. 12; Rijavec et al. (2020), p. 17.

Polish reporters recounted their experience with the implementation of uniform IT systems where the templates of judgements are created that can be used by judges when preparing a written issue of the judgement.[14] In Poland, the employment of such IT system especially seemed to compensate for the lack of legal provisions in accomplishing a high level of standardisation (along with regulatory support by the Ministry of Justice and well-established judicial practice).[15] To a similar effect, Slovenian courts at all levels use uniform templates, which ensure not only a standardised structure, wording and content but also consistent font, spacing, graphic design, etc.[16] National reporters for these countries noted that most of the remaining differences between the structures of individual judgements are a logical consequence of diverging particularities of each case.

The only national report that explicitly regarded the standardisation of national judgements as inadequate was the Belgian report. Even though the structure of Belgian judgements is derived from tradition and certain formalities are provided by law, there is no proper standardisation, which is why each court uses a different form, font or other formatting elements.[17] Furthermore, some reporters pointed out that the lack of more detailed rules regulating the structure and content of the reasoning part of a judgement may result in differences between judgements or even certain missing elements that would constitute a severe violation of the rules of civil procedure. Most notably, the Croatian reporter suggested that it would be beneficial to introduce a legal solution for 'the substructure of the reasoning' so that judgements would become more uniform.[18]

3 Main Elements of a Judgement

The more the analysis of judgements focuses on their structural details and case-related particulars, the more differences can be identified; however, while individual units comprising a judgement naturally differ from country to country, their basic structure remains prominently similar. With some exceptions explained below, most judgements issued by national courts are broadly divided into the following sections: (a) the header or introduction, (b) the operative part, (c) the reasoning. In some countries, the reasoning is further divided into clearly separated parts addressing the facts of the case or the parties' statements and those justifying and explaining the

[14] Zoroska Kamilovska & Rakočević (2020), pp. 13–14; Gołaczyński et al. (2020), p. 17.

[15] Gołaczyński et al. (2020), p. 17.

[16] Rijavec et al. (2020), pp. 17–18.

[17] Rys (2020), p. 16.

[18] Kunštek et al. (2020), p. 12. See also Naydenova (2022), p. 17.

findings of the court (e.g. France,[19] Germany,[20] Italy,[21] Portugal,[22] Spain).[23] One should note that the order of these basic sections in national judgements might vary, with jurisdictions evenly split between those where the introductory part (which, by definition, is always at the beginning) is followed by the operative part, with the reasoning part coming last (e.g. Austria, Croatia, Germany, Slovenia, Sweden), and those where the reasoning precedes the operative part of the judgement (e.g. Albania, Belgium, France, Italy, Portugal, Spain).[24] Some judgements include legal instructions regarding available remedies (generally including the type of legal remedy available, the period of time within which the remedy shall be submitted, the authority to which it shall be submitted, the required number of copies that shall be submitted, and the consequences of submitting a late or incomplete remedy).[25] While not necessary explicitly listed amongst the parts of the judgement, a signature

[19]The judgement contains the statement of the dispute (facts, claims and arguments of the parties; factual and legal matters subject to the judge's analysis), which delimitates the subject matter of the trial, as well as motivation or the reasoning (by which the judge engages in the analysis of facts, legal qualification, the assessment of the means of proof, the application of the relevant rules of law and the solution derived based on these elements). Mensah (2020), p. 13.

[20]The part of the judgement called "Tatbestan" addresses the facts of the case (the essential content, the claims asserted and the means of challenge or defence, as well as the reference to procedural history), while the "Entscheidungsgründe" is the part of the judgement on which a ruling is based (a brief summary of the considerations of the facts and circumstances of the case and the legal aspects on which the decision is based). Wolf et al. (2020), pp. 23–24.

[21]Italian legislation explicitly lists the conclusions of the public prosecutor and those of the parties and a concise explanation of the factual and legal reasons for the decision as separate elements of a judgement. Kaczorowska et al. (2022), p. 16.

[22]Portuguese judgements are divided into four parts: report (summary of the process: the parties, the claim, the reasons for the claim, information about service, the grounds for defence, information about a prior hearing and a final hearing, a statement that the case is still in order and meets procedural requirements, identification of issues to be considered by the court), reasoning of facts (indicates proven and unproven facts, provides reasons for judge's conviction and decision on facts), reasoning of law (states legal grounds and applies the law to the proven facts), and the operative part. Caramelo Gomes et al. (2020), p. 15.

[23]Spanish judgements separate between the part with factual background (claims of the parties, facts supporting the claims, evidence proposed and taken, proven facts) and the part with the findings of law (factual and legal facts established by the parties, reasons and legal grounds for court's ruling on disputed questions, rules applicable to the case). Bores Lazo & Serrano Ron (2020), pp. 21–22.

[24]For more, see respective national reports under point 2.1. Note that in Belgium, while the operative part is generally located at the end of the judgement, it may also be placed within the statement of reasons. Rys (2020), p. 28.

[25]For example, Naydenova (2022), p. 15; Valdhans (2020), p. 8; Wolf et al. (2020), pp. 24–25; Rijavec et al. (2020), p. 16; Bores Lazo & Serrano Ron (2020), pp. 21–22; Bylander & Linton (2020), p. 5. Compare with Kunštek et al. (2020), p. 12. In Croatia, legal instruction is not mentioned in Article 338 of Civil Procedure Act, which defines the structure of a judgement. However, it nevertheless forms a part of the decision pursuant to Article 66 of Court Ordinance, which requires that in all decisions against which the remedy is allowed, the instruction on the legal remedy is placed under the signature of the president of the council or the judge.

by a judge (or the members of judicial panel or council) issuing the judgement is also required.[26]

There are certain deviations from these generalisations in national legal systems to which special attention should be paid. For example, in Belgium, where court proceedings can in principle be initiated in any of the three official languages (thus also determining the language in which the judgement shall be written), there is a legal requirement for each judgement to contain a reference pertaining to the use of language in particular proceedings. Each judgement must explicitly state that the provisions of the law of 15 June 1935 regarding the use of language in judicial proceedings have been complied with to guarantee that the rules regarding the use of language in judicial proceedings have been adhered to.[27] This reference is thus considered an obligatory part of Belgian judgements.

Most deviations, however, are related to the reasoning part of the judgement and the possibility to omit or reduce it. In an attempt to simplify the drafting of judgements and facilitate more efficient and rational court operations (saving both money and time), several jurisdictions provide for exceptional circumstances under which the reasoning may be drafted in an abridged form or even omitted altogether. Such is the case of default judgements, judgements based on the acknowledgement of the claim and judgements based on the relinquishment of the claim in, for example, Austria, Croatia, North Macedonia and Slovenia, which may be issued in shortened forms. Generally, this means that the reasoning contains only reasons that justify the rendering of such judgement.[28] Austrian legislation also allows the court to issue a judgement containing a statement of grounds limited to the essential arguments of the parties and the reasoning of the court in so far as such information is necessary to assess the *res judicata* of the judgement, if a judgement has been delivered orally in the presence of both parties and if neither party has lodged an appeal against the judgement in due time.[29] In Poland, a judgement will only contain a statement of reasons upon a party's request.[30] While Bulgarian legislation requires the court to provide reasoning for its decision (indicating requests and objections of the parties, the assessment of evidence, factual findings and legal conclusions), national reporter for Bulgaria emphasised that the reasoning, in fact, is not considered part of the judgement, even though it is materialised together with it in the same document. The legal acts in their capacity of declarations of will are different from

[26] See for example, Kolaj Tafaj F (2020), p. 16; Prodinger and Nunner-Krautgasser (2020), p. 15; Rys (2020), p. 15; Wolf et al. (2020), p. 25; Kaczorowska et al. (2022), p. 16; Bores Lazo & Serrano Ron (2020), pp. 21–22, etc.

[27] Rys (2020), p. 15.

[28] Rijavec et al. (2020), p. 16; Kunštek et al. (2020), p. 11; Zoroska Kamilovska & Rakočević (2020), p. 12.

[29] § 417a ZPO; Prodinger and Nunner-Krautgasser (2020), p. 17.

[30] Gołaczyński et al. (2020), p. 17.

the considerations upon which the legal act is based. Even if the judgement is not motivated, it is, therefore, not null and void but revocable.[31]

Judgements issued in the Republic of Cyprus stand out as the least typical compared to other examined court documents. As the structure of judgements was established by court practice and is not explicitly determined by legal provisions, it might vary depending on the circumstances of the case and legal issues arising therein. However, a civil court judgement is generally comprised of the following elements: the title (listing the case number, the court hearing the case, the names of the judge, parties and their representatives), introduction/history of the case, claims of both parties (may be included in the introductory part of the judgement), testimony, the assessment of testimony (and its probative value), legal aspect (setting out relevant law, case-law and elaboration on the legal issues), interest, conclusion/outcome (including legal costs). At the same time, the template of the judgement may vary depending on the formatting tools and personal writing style of the individual judge (e.g. some judgements incorporate headings while others do not; some judgements contain numbered paragraphs, footnotes or even a table of contents; there is no consistent font style and size).[32] Despite these particularities and inconsistencies, it should be emphasised that Cyprus judgements provide basically the same information as judgements issued by courts of other countries, even if their formal structure is less rigid.

Legal requirements discussed above refer to the structure of judgements; however, most national regulations have adopted a similar approach when regulating the structure of other court documents or decisions, either by including separate provisions describing the structure of different types of documents or by referring to provisions regulating the structure of judgements, which are to be applied in a manner that takes into account special characteristics of the respective document. For example, in Italy, judicial decisions encompass sentences (judgements), orders and decrees. In comparison to sentences, orders are succinctly reasoned, while decrees contain reasoning only if expressly prescribed by law.[33] Similarly, a decree in North Macedonia contains only the introductory and operative part, while the statement of reasons is necessary only if the decree dismissed a party's motion, decided on the contradicting motions of the parties, or in other cases determined by law. In this regard, Article 327 of the North Macedonian Civil Procedure Act, which refers to judgements, is also applicable to other types of decisions unless otherwise determined by law.[34] In Belgium and the Netherlands, articles regulating the

[31] Naydenova (2022), p. 17.

[32] Christofi & Loizou (2022), pp. 10-11. See also Alpha Bank Cyprus Ltd *v*. Prestos Confectionery Ltd and others, Case no. 330/06, 30/1/2015.

[33] Kaczorowska et al. (2022), p. 16.

[34] Zoroska Kamilovska & Rakočević (2020), p. 12.

structure of judgements (Article 780 of Judicial Code in Belgium and Article 287 Rv in the Netherlands) are also applicable to other types of decisions.[35]

4 Introductory Part and Other General Information

The introductory part of a judgement is invariably intended to provide basic information about the case (e.g. case reference number, sometimes the type of proceedings or the type of decision), the court deciding the case, the names of judges and other participating court personnel (e.g. secretaries, clerks or registrars), personal information about the parties and their representatives and the date of decision (if not included at the end of the judgement). The date on which the judgement was issued and the date of the main hearing might be stated separately (e.g. in Croatia, North Macedonia, Poland, Slovenia).[36]

The introduction might also indicate the subject matter of the dispute (e.g. in Austria, Croatia, North Macedonia, Slovenia),[37] while in Albania, it also contains *petitum*, the parties' claims and the opinion of the prosecutor (if applicable).[38] Furthermore, a majority of examined judgements contains a solemn proclamation that they are issued in the name of the republic (e.g. Austria,[39] Croatia,[40] the Czech Republic,[41] Poland),[42] in the name of the people (e.g. Bulgaria,[43] France,[44] Germany,[45] Italy,[46] Slovenia),[47] in the name of the citizens (North Macedonia),[48] or in the name of the king (the Netherlands),[49] thus reflecting a system of government in a particular country.

[35] Rys (2020), p. 14; Sujecki (2020), p. 13. See also Laenens et al. (2019), p. 513.

[36] Kunštek et al. (2020), p. 10; Zoroska Kamilovska & Rakočević (2020), p. 12; Gołaczyński et al. (2020), p. 16; Rijavec et al. (2020), p. 16.

[37] Prodinger and Nunner-Krautgasser (2020), p. 15; Kunštek et al. (2020), p. 10; Zoroska Kamilovska & Rakočević (2020), p. 12; Rijavec et al. (2020), p. 16.

[38] Kolaj Tafaj F (2020), p. 15.

[39] Im Namen der Republik. Prodinger and Nunner-Krautgasser (2020), p. 18.

[40] U ime Republike Hrvatske. Kunštek et al. (2020), p. 11.

[41] Valdhans (2020), p. 8.

[42] Gołaczyński et al. (2020), p. 15.

[43] Naydenova (2022), p. 16.

[44] Au nom du peuple français. Mensah (2020), p. 13.

[45] Im Namen des Volkes. Wolf et al. (2020), p. 23.

[46] Kaczorowska et al. (2022), p. 11.

[47] V imenu ljudstva. Rijavec et al. (2020), p. 16.

[48] Zoroska Kamilovska & Rakočević (2020), p. 12.

[49] In denaam van de Koning. Sujecki (2020), p. 12.

4.1 Personal Information of the Parties

In order to determine clearly and precisely the parties to the case that shall be bound by a particular judgement, national courts are required to provide personal data allowing for such identification. Most often, the parties are identified at least by their first name and family name, their place of residence and a personal identification number (e.g. personal identification number or the number of the identification document in Albania,[50] national registry or company number in Belgium,[51] unique civil number (UCN) in Bulgaria,[52] OIB (previously JMBG) in Croatia,[53] national ID number or date of birth (or company ID) in the Czech Republic,[54] fiscal code in Italy,[55] unique (personal) identification number in Lithuania,[56] Unique Personal Identification Number (EMBG) for natural persons and Unique Registration Number of the Subject of Registration (EMBS) for legal entities in North Macedonia,[57] tax number (NIF) in Portugal,[58] EMŠO (natural persons), registration number (legal entities), tax ID number or a date of birth in Slovenia).[59] In Albania, judgements additionally specify the parties' paternity and/or motherhood, place of birth and nationality,[60] in Portugal, they include the parties' civil (marital) status,[61] while in Austria, they also state the parties' occupation and status as a party in proceedings, the parties' date and place of birth (in personal status cases), the affected parties' date of birth (for entry into the land register), or the commercial register number (legal entity).[62] On the other hand, it is only mandatory to specify the name and surnames of the parties (and, when applicable, the status of a legal representative) in Spain,[63] while in the Netherlands, the parties must only be identified by their last name, their initials and the place of residence (or their legal form, the name and place of establishment in the case of legal entities).[64]

There are no provisions in Sweden on personal information that has to be specified in the judgment to identify the parties to the dispute; however, in court practice, the names, personal identity numbers/company registration numbers, and

[50] Kolaj Tafaj F (2020), p. 19.
[51] Rys (2020), p. 19.
[52] Naydenova (2022), p. 21.
[53] Kunštek et al. (2020), p. 15.
[54] Valdhans (2020), p. 11.
[55] Kaczorowska et al. (2022), p. 20.
[56] Bolzanas et al. (2020), p. 13.
[57] Zoroska Kamilovska & Rakočević (2020), p. 17.
[58] Caramelo Gomes et al. (2020), p. 19.
[59] Rijavec et al. (2020), pp. 22–23.
[60] Kolaj Tafaj F (2020), p. 19.
[61] Caramelo Gomes et al. (2020), p. 19.
[62] Prodinger and Nunner-Krautgasser (2020), p. 21. See also Gitschthaler (2019) para 75, Rz 1 ff.
[63] Bores Lazo & Serrano Ron (2020), p. 25.
[64] Sujecki (2020), p. 16.

addresses are usually included.[65] Polish legislation also contains no provisions that would detail how the parties to proceedings should be identified in the judgment; instead, the law stipulates that the parties must be identified in the submission that initiates the proceedings (e.g. the claimant must be identified in the action). In the case of natural persons, the personal identification number (PESEL) or tax identification number (NIP) is required, while legal entities should provide their National Court Register number (KRS). The judgement usually describes both parties only using their names and surnames, while the parties' PESEL, NIP or KRS numbers are specified only in the writ of execution, allowing enforcement officers, who also have access to PESEL, CEIDG and KRS databases, to verify again the identity of a given party and institute enforcement action against that person.[66]

Legislation in most countries allows the protection of the parties' personal data under certain circumstances (e.g. omission of the place of residence in Austrian judgements, anonymisation with initials in published judgements in Sweden).[67] Stating personal information in the introductory part of the judgement generally eliminates the need to repeat such information in other parts of the judgement, with rare exceptions (e.g. North Macedonia, where the personal information is usually repeated in other parts of the judgement).[68] While the main reason to provide personal information of the parties is to establish the personal scope of *res judicata*, the parties' representatives and attorneys should also be designated with enough information to ensure control over proper representation and service of documents.[69]

4.2 Indicating the Amount in Dispute and the Underlying Legal Relationship

National practices somewhat vary regarding the requirement of whether (as well as how and where) the amount in dispute and the underlying legal relationship should be indicated within the judgement. Generally, the claimant is responsible for determining the amount in dispute (the value of the claim) when filing the action, which is then repeated either in the introductory part or in the reasoning part of the written judgement.[70] Naturally, the value of the claim as asserted by the claimant may differ

---

[65] Bylander & Linton (2020), p. 7.

[66] Gołaczyński et al. (2020), p. 21.

[67] See, for example, Prodinger and Nunner-Krautgasser (2020), p. 21; Bylander & Linton (2020), p. 7.

[68] Kolaj Tafaj F (2020), p. 19; Wolf et al. (2020), p. 31; Caramelo Gomes et al. (2020), p. 19 cf.; Zoroska Kamilovska & Rakočević (2020), p. 17.

[69] See, for example, Wolf et al. (2020), p. 31; Feskorn (2020b) para 313.

[70] Kolaj Tafaj F (2020), p. 19; Prodinger and Nunner-Krautgasser (2020), p. 21; Rys (2020), p. 19; Naydenova (2022), p. 21; Kunštek et al. (2020), p. 16; Wolf et al. (2020), pp. 32–33; Bolzanas et al. (2020), p. 13; Sujecki (2020), p. 16; Zoroska Kamilovska & Rakočević (2020), p. 17; Rijavec et al. (2020), p. 23.

from the value of the claim as determined by the court when deciding on the just compensation in a particular case. The latter value would be included in the operative part of any judgement arising from the pecuniary claim as one of its most important elements.[71]

When establishing the amount in dispute in the case of pecuniary claims, most jurisdictions are consistent in considering only the value of the principal claim as stated in the action; interests, additional claims, litigation costs, penalty charges, etc., are not relevant for this purpose (unless they are part of the principal claim).[72] However, in the case of non-pecuniary claims, national rules on assessing the amount in dispute vary significantly, as each legal system provides its own method for calculating the value of the claim and elements that should be considered in this calculation. For illustration, in Austria, if the subject of the dispute has no monetary value, the claimant must assess its value in terms of property; otherwise, the amount in dispute will be assumed at EUR 5000. The value of disputes without assets does not have to be established (e.g. for a status action).[73] In North Macedonia, if the claim arises from a property dispute, the amount in dispute is assessed based on the property's market value. In all other cases, it is determined as the amount of the fee base.[74] In Albania, the value of the claim in immovable property disputes is also calculated based on the market value of the property or of the rights claimed on his property, while the amount in dispute related to the existence, validity or dissolution of a legal obligation relationship is determined on the basis of that part of the *ratio* which is under dispute. If the lease contract is terminated, the value is determined based on the amount of requested rent, whereas if the continuation of the lease contract is being contested, the value is determined by adding up lease payments for the contested period. In the case of a division of property, the value of the requested part represents the amount in dispute.[75] When establishing the amount in dispute, all claims filed in the same proceedings against the same party (joinder of claims) should be considered and summed up.[76]

Asserting a proper value of the dispute when initiating court proceedings is important for several reasons; for example, it might determine the subject-matter jurisdiction, the composition of the court, the type of proceedings (e.g. regular proceedings vs small claims procedure), the amount of court fees, or the attorney tariff.[77] If the claimant has manifestly set the amount in dispute too low (e.g. with the

[71] For example, Kolaj Tafaj F (2020), p. 20; Gołaczyński et al. (2020), pp. 21–22; Bores Lazo & Serrano Ron (2020), p. 25.

[72] For example, Prodinger and Nunner-Krautgasser (2020), p. 21; Rechberger and Simotta (2017), p. 62, Kunštek et al. (2020), p. 16; Zoroska Kamilovska & Rakočević (2020), p. 17. See also Rijavec et al. (2020), pp. 23–24; Bores Lazo & Serrano Ron (2020), p. 25.

[73] Prodinger and Nunner-Krautgasser (2020), p. 21; Rechberger and Simotta (2017), p. 133.

[74] Zoroska Kamilovska & Rakočević (2020), p. 17.

[75] Kolaj Tafaj F (2020), p. 20.

[76] For example, Kolaj Tafaj F (2020), p. 19; Kaczorowska et al. (2022), p. 20; Wolf et al. (2020), p. 33.

[77] See also Rijavec et al. (2020), p. 23; Kunštek et al. (2020), p. 16.

intention to pay lower court fees) or too high (e.g. with the intention to intimidate the defendant financially), national regulations usually grant the defendant and/or the court the option to adjust the amount. For instance, in Austria, the defendant may object to the improperly stated amount in dispute until the end of the preparatory hearing (*vorbereitende Tagsatzung*). If the parties can not agree on the proper amount, the assessment is done by the court with a decision that is not subject to appeal.[78] Similarly, in Slovenia and in North Macedonia, the court may establish a proper amount *ex officio* or upon the defendant's request.[79] In Albania, a special appeal may be submitted in case of the wrong assessment of the amount in dispute.[80]

The amount in dispute can also be affected if the claimant amends it by increasing the value of the claim, by submitting an additional claim, or by partially withdrawing the claim. Such changes can be accompanied by other—more significant—legal consequences concerning the change of jurisdiction or the payment of court fees. In Slovenia, for example, the reduced value of the claim does not affect the subject-matter jurisdiction, even if the case is adjudicated before the district court, and the new amount would place the case under the county court's jurisdiction (*perpetuation fori*). However, if the case fell under the jurisdiction of the county court when initiated and the claim was later increased, the case has to be relegated to the district court if it falls under its jurisdiction after the amendment.[81] In Germany, the claim may be amended if the defendant has agreed to it or if the court believes such modification to be expedient (§ 263 ZPO). If the amount in dispute increases, the court fees are calculated according to the highest value. If the amount was reduced, however, and the higher costs have already been paid, a decision on these costs had to be issued under the rules of § 269 III ZPO (abandonment of action) at the expense of the claimant or in accordance with § 91a ZPO.[82] On the contrary, in Albania, the claimant is required to pay higher court fees after increasing the amount of the claim but is not entitled to the reimbursement of court fees if the claim is reduced instead.[83] If the amount in dispute was amended in the course of proceedings, such change is also reflected in the written copy of the judgement. Croatian, Czech and Dutch national reporters all emphasised that if the claimant amends the value of the claim, the last effective value is stated as the amount in dispute, while the court may address the amendment in more detail in the reasoning part of the judgement.[84] In Slovenia, every amendment of the amount in dispute is marked on the case file (by crossing out the previous amount and replacing it with the new one) in addition to amending the

[78] Prodinger and Nunner-Krautgasser (2020), p. 21. See also Rechberger and Simotta (2017), p. 133.

[79] Rijavec et al. (2020), p. 23; Zoroska Kamilovska & Rakočević (2020), p. 17.

[80] Kolaj Tafaj F (2020), p. 20.

[81] Rijavec et al. (2020), pp. 23–24.

[82] Wolf et al. (2020), p. 33. See also Herget (2020), para 3, margin 16; Roth (2016), para 263, margin 34.

[83] Kolaj Tafaj F (2020), p. 20.

[84] Kunštek et al. (2020), p. 16; Valdhans (2020), p. 11; Sujecki (2020), p. 16.

amount stated in the introductory part of the judgement. Procedural acts and decisions that lead to the amendment are addressed in the reasoning and, where relevant, included in the operative part.[85] In Albania, the amendment is specified within the reasoning part of the judgement,[86] while in Belgium, it is included in the special part of reasoning dedicated to the parties' claims.[87] In Sweden and in North Macedonia, the amendment is reflected in the formulation of the operative part, e.g. with an indication 'as finally determined' or 'the modified claim is satisfied or dismissed', respectively.[88]

Concerning the legal relationship upon which the claim or the decision are based, national reports for several countries (e.g. Austria, the Netherlands, North Macedonia, Poland, Portugal, Slovenia, Sweden) stated that the courts are generally not required to include any such information in the operative part of the judgement; instead, the reasoning is the part of the judgement that provides a legal assessment of the dispute and explains how legal provisions were applied to the established facts of the case to justify the final decision.[89] Croatia, however, is an example of a country where the underlying legal relationship may also be discernible from the operative part of the judgement (but may also always be determined based on the reasoning). For instance, in maintenance disputes, the term 'on the basis of maintenance' ('na ime uzdržavanja') appears in the operative part.[90] Even where the examination of legal relationship is considered a standard part of the judgement (reasoning or otherwise), the claimant is not responsible for providing their own legal assessment of the dispute, as the court is presumed—and required—to know the law (*iura novit curia*). If the claimant nevertheless expresses their views on which legal provision should be applied in a particular case, the court is not bound by their proposal but is required to examine all possible legal grounds that could be relevant for the decision on the merits of the claim.[91]

Rather than stating the underlying legal relationship, judgements in certain legal systems indicate the subject matter of the dispute, which is generally included in the introductory part of the judgement. For example, in North Macedonia, the introductory part contains a brief description of the subject matter, thus mentioning, for instance, general damages, maintenance, divorce, remuneration for work, etc. This information helps the enforcement agent determine the nature of the claim and whether limitations to the scope of the attachable part of the assets are applicable

[85] Rijavec et al. (2020), p. 24.

[86] Kolaj Tafaj F (2020), p. 20.

[87] Rys (2020), p. 19.

[88] Bylander & Linton (2020), p. 7.

[89] See, for example, Prodinger and Nunner-Krautgasser (2020), p. 22; Sujecki (2020), p. 16; Zoroska Kamilovska & Rakočević (2020), p. 18; Gołaczyński et al. (2020), p. 22; Caramelo Gomes et al. (2020), p. 20; Rijavec et al. (2020), pp. 24–25; Bylander & Linton (2020), p. 7.

[90] Kunštek et al. (2020), p. 17.

[91] For example, Rijavec et al. (2020), p. 24; Galič (2006), p. 134.

in such a case.[92] Likewise, in Poland, every judgement, decree or payment order contains information on the subject matter of the case (e.g. child maintenance, remuneration for work, compensation, general damages), based on which the enforcement officer can ascertain whether there is any basis for limiting the enforcement action.[93] The subject matter is also explicitly displayed in Austrian,[94] Croatian[95] and Slovenian judgement.[96]

4.3 Time Limits for Voluntary Fulfilment

As far as the requirement to specify time limits for a voluntary fulfilment of obligations imposed with the judgement is concerned, examined jurisdictions can be broadly organised into three groups. Croatia, North Macedonia and Slovenia form a group of legal systems where civil judgements ordering the performance of a certain obligation contain the specification of the time period within which the obligation has to be voluntarily fulfilled. The aim of including this information, which constitutes a mandatory element of the operative part of the judgement, is to prevent the claimant from seeking involuntary enforcement against the defendant until the time limit expires. In some cases, the judgement becomes enforceable upon becoming final (i.e. it may no longer be challenged by an appeal); however, in cases where the court has to include the time period for voluntary fulfilment of the claim, it only becomes enforceable if it has become final and if this time period has already expired. As a rule, the court will set this time period for positive obligations or omissions, but not in the case of a decision that the defendant is required to endure certain claimant's conduct—in such cases, the judgement is immediately enforceable. If the judgement does not contain the time period for a voluntary fulfilment of the obligation, it will be set by the court of enforcement in the enforcement order. The time period for the performance of the obligation starts to run on the first subsequent day following the service of the judgement upon the defendant.[97]

[92] For example, Article 117, para1 of Enforcement Act imposes limitations to the scope of the attachable part of the income; enforcement for claims based on legal maintenance, compensation for damage caused due to illness, reduction or loss of working capacity and compensation for lost maintenance due to the death of the maintenance payer, may be implemented up to the amount of one half of the salary or pension, while for claims based on other grounds, it may be implemented up to the amount of one third of the salary or pension. Zoroska Kamilovska & Rakočević (2020), p. 18.

[93] Gołaczyński et al. (2020), p. 22.

[94] Prodinger and Nunner-Krautgasser (2020), p. 15.

[95] Kunštek et al. (2020), p. 10.

[96] Rijavec et al. (2020), p. 16.

[97] Kunštek et al. (2020), p. 14; Zoroska Kamilovska & Rakočević (2020), p. 16; Rijavec et al. (2020), pp. 21–22; Ude (2009), p. 55. See also Rijavec (2003), p. 109; Triva and Dika (2004), pp. 585–586. In Slovenia and in North Macedonia, the time limit for the performance of the obligation is fifteen days unless otherwise provided by special regulations; however, the court may set a longer time period in the case of non-monetary obligations (when it would be unrealistic to expect that the defendant could fulfil his or her obligation within 15 days, e.g. in the case of unfulfilled obligations under construction contract). In disputes involving bills of exchange and cheques, this time period is eight days.

On the contrary, judgements in several countries do not contain any such specifications. This does not mean that such a time limit does not exist at all, but that it is generally set either by law or by the enforcement officer after the enforcement proceedings are initiated, instead of by the court rendering the enforcement title. For example, in Sweden, the judgement creditor has to apply to the Enforcement Authority (*Kronofogdemyndigheten*) for enforcement. Under Swedish Enforcement Code (*UB*), notification of the case shall be sent to the debtor by post or given in an appropriate manner before attachment may take place, giving the debtor sufficient time to protect their rights. Accordingly, the Enforcement Authority notifies the judgement debtor, usually by mail, that enforcement measures will take place if the debt is not paid voluntarily within a specific time (usually 14 days).[98] A similar solution is provided in the Albanian legal system. At the commencement of enforcement proceedings, the enforcement officer issues to the debtor a notice for voluntary enforcement of the obligation contained within the enforcement order, designating for this purpose a timeframe of five days when the judgement involves a salary or an order for maintenance and ten days for all other judgements. Mandatory enforcement cannot start before these time limits for voluntary enforcement have expired unless there is a danger that enforcement will no longer be possible.[99] In Italy, enforcement must be preceded by serving on the debtor the enforcement title and a notice to comply. The notice to comply is a formal warning by the creditor to the debtor that if they do not fulfil their obligation within a given period (not less than ten days), enforcement proceedings will be initiated. A notice to comply expires if enforcement proceedings are not commenced within ninety days after its service; however, if the debtor takes steps to contest its validity, the ninety-day period is suspended until the objection is resolved.[100] In Lithuania, the bailiff likewise notifies the debtor to fulfil their obligation with the deadline of ten days voluntarily.[101] In Spain, the time period within which the judgement may not be enforced is specified under Civil Procedural Law; the judgement only becomes enforceable twenty days after becoming final.[102] In Austria, ZPO requires both the time limit for an appeal and a 14-day period for the performance of debt to expire before the judgement becomes enforceable.[103] Belgium and Bulgaria are other examples of legal systems where no time limits for voluntary enforcement are stated in the judgement.[104]

---

[98] Bylander & Linton (2020), p. 6.

[99] Kolaj Tafaj F (2020), pp. 18–19.

[100] Kaczorowska et al. (2022), p. 19.

[101] Bolzanas et al. (2020), p. 16.

[102] Bores Lazo & Serrano Ron (2020), pp. 24–25. In Spain, a judgement can be (judicially) enforced only by initiating a new procedure with a petition for execution, except for actions for evictions, which can be executed without additional proceedings.

[103] Prodinger and Nunner-Krautgasser (2020), p. 20; Neumayr and Nunner-Krautgasser (2018), p. 68.

[104] Rys (2020), p. 18; Naydenova (2022), p. 20.

The third category loosely combines those legal systems where the time period within which the obligation is to be voluntarily fulfilled may be specified within the operative part of the judgement, but as it is not considered its mandatory element according to relevant legislation, it may also be omitted. Such is the case of the Czech Republic, where the time period may or may not be specified in a judgement; if it is not, the provisions of the Czech Civil Procedure Code apply, requiring the obligation to be fulfilled within three days or, in the case of eviction, within fifteen days after the judgement became final and conclusive. The court may specify a longer period or decide that the debt can be paid in instalments and under specified payment conditions. In any case, the period of voluntary performance starts after the judgement is served upon the defendant.[105] Under German ZPO, the claimant may demand that the court determines a time limit for the defendant to fulfil their obligation and include it in the judgement. The length of this period—which starts with the *res judicata* of the judgement—may be set by the claimant or left to the court's discretion.[106] In Portugal, the claimant may similarly request that the court sets such time limit, but the judge may only decide in accordance with the request. Otherwise, the court decision can be enforced immediately, as long as it meets all the conditions of enforceability.[107] In the Netherlands, the courts regularly state in their decisions that the obligation has to be fulfilled within a certain amount of time after the service of the judgement upon the defendant. If the time period is not specified, the obligation has to be fulfilled as soon as the judgement is being enforced based on the rule of enforcement. In practice, the parties' counsels first try to negotiate whether the judgement debtor is willing to fulfil their obligation voluntarily before actually initiating enforcement.[108] In the Republic of Cyprus, it is understood in practice that the obligation in the operative part is to be fulfilled by the defendant immediately unless the operative part specifies otherwise; if it does, enforcement may not commence until the period expires.[109] Although it is not usually done in practice, it is also possible to specify the time limit for voluntary performance in Poland and Lithuania.[110]

Other than constraints imposed by setting the time period for voluntary performance of debtor's obligations, none of the examined legal systems contains any specifications of the time period within which the final judgement may not be enforced; after the time for voluntary fulfilment of the claim expires, the enforcement may invariably commence. Moreover, no jurisdiction could be identified where

[105] Valdhans (2020), p. 10.

[106] Wolf et al. (2020), p. 30. See also Feskorn (2020a), para 255, margin 4.

[107] Caramelo Gomes et al. (2020), pp. 18–19.

[108] Sujecki (2020), p. 15.

[109] Christofi & Loizou (2022), p. 14.

[110] Gołaczyński et al. (2020), p. 20; Bolzanas et al. (2020), p. 13.

national judgement specifies the time period after which it may no longer be enforced (statute of limitation for the enforcement of a particular claim). This does not necessarily mean that enforcement proceedings may be initiated indefinitely, but that time limits should be sought in relevant legislation instead of the judgement itself, as demonstrated by the following examples. Slovenian Obligations Code and North Macedonian Law on Obligations both provide that all claims determined by a final court ruling or by a ruling by another relevant authority or through settlement before the court or another relevant authority shall become statute-barred after ten years (including those for which the statute of limitations stipulates a shorter period).[111] The same time limits apply to Belgian judgements,[112] while the limitation periods under the Swedish Act of Statute of Limitation could be three or ten years.[113] According to French legislation, the limitation period for enforcement titles is also set at ten years, but it may be interrupted and thus re-started due to certain court decisions against the debtor. In the case of enforcement titles issued by a court, there are no limits to how many times it can be postponed due to such interruptions, while in the case of enforcement titles issued by a notary of bailiff, the total limitation period may not exceed twenty years.[114] In Spain, the limitation period for the enforcement of sentences, judgements, court settlements, arbitration awards or mediation agreements is five years after they become final.[115] Under the Portuguese Civil Code, obligations imposed by judgements expire after twenty years unless the judgement refers to payments not yet due; in such cases, the limitation period is five years.[116] In the Republic of Cyprus, the enforcement period regulated by the Civil Procedure Rules was extended from ten to twelve years in 2020.[117] Albanian law does not explicitly provide a statute of limitations for the enforcement of judgements; however, the Albanian Civil Code implies that the limitation period depends on the nature of disputes regarding which they have been granted.[118] There are also some specific rules referring to the enforcement of a particular type of obligations; e.g. Austrian enforcement titles regarding inventories (e.g. eviction order) must be enforced within six months since the eviction period expired,[119] and Croatian decrees concerning the disturbance of possession must be enforced within thirty days since the period in which a certain action was to be performed under such decree expired.[120] None of these limitations is explicitly mentioned in national judgements.

---

[111] Zoroska Kamilovska & Rakočević (2020), p. 16; Rijavec et al. (2020), p. 22.

[112] Rys (2020), p. 18; Laenens (2019), p. 156.

[113] Bylander & Linton (2020), p. 6.

[114] Mensah (2020), p. 16.

[115] Bores Lazo & Serrano Ron (2020), p. 25.

[116] Caramelo Gomes et al. (2020), p. 19.

[117] Christofi & Loizou (2022), p. 15.

[118] Kolaj Tafaj F (2020), p. 19.

[119] Prodinger and Nunner-Krautgasser (2020), p. 20; Neumayr and Nunner-Krautgasser (2018), p. 68.

[120] Kunštek et al. (2020), p. 15.

5 Operative Part of the Judgement

The operative part is the most important part of any judgement, as it determines the content and scope of legal protection granted to the claimant against the defendant and thus provides a solution to the dispute. It is especially important when determining subjective and objective limits to the legal effect of the judgement, as the content of the operative part falls under *res judicata* and becomes final. A standard operative part contains a decision by which the court satisfies or dismisses the claims (and counterclaims) of the parties relating to the main subject of dispute, as well as ancillary claims (especially the costs of proceedings) and, if applicable, the court's decision on the existence or non-existence of the claim asserted for the purpose of setoff.[121] It may also state a time period for voluntary fulfilment of the obligation (see Sect. 4.3 above), the right to appeal (e.g. Albania, Lithuania),[122] the decision on (provisional) enforceability (e.g. Albania, Germany, the Netherlands),[123] and similar. In most jurisdictions, at least the basic content of the operative part is determined by law. However, this is not the case in Belgium, where the Judicial Code stipulates that each judgement must contain the operative part but fails to provide any legal specification or definition of its content and form. The operative part simply needs to answer all claims invoked by the parties.[124] The same is true for the Republic of Cyprus, where the operative part briefly presents the court's decision with reference to the relief sought in the claim (and, where relevant, the counterclaim).[125]

A question might be posed of possible issues arising from different phrasing used in operative parts across Europe, particularly in the case of condemnatory judgements. While in some legal systems, the operative part explicitly states that the defendant is *ordered* or *condemned* (Croatia,[126] Belgium,[127] France,[128] Germany,[129]

---

[121] See Kunštek et al. (2020), pp. 19–20; Mensah (2020), p. 20; Wolf et al. (2020), p. 40; Zoroska Kamilovska & Rakočević (2020), p. 21; Rijavec et al. (2020), pp. 28–29, and others.

[122] Kolaj Tafaj F (2020), p. 24; Bolzanas et al. (2020), p. 16.

[123] Kolaj Tafaj F (2020), p. 24; Wolf et al. (2020), p. 40; Sujecki (2020), p. 18.

[124] Rys (2020), p. 23. See also Laenens (2019), p. 514.

[125] Christofi & Loizou (2022), p. 27.

[126] 'The defendant is ordered to pay…' ('nalaže se tuženiku plaćanje iznosa od…"). Kunštek et al. (2020), p. 25.

[127] The wording 'condamne à payer' is often used in judgements drafted in French and the wording 'veroordeelt […] om te betalen' is used in judgements drafted in Dutch. Rys (2020), p. 29.

[128] The court is asked to 'condemn [the debtor] to pay the sum of [amount]'. Mensah (2020), p. 24.

[129] 'The defendant is ordered to …' (‚Der Beklagte wird verurteilt …'). Wolf et al. (2020), p. 49; Feskorn (2020b), para 313, margin 9.

Italy,[130] the Netherlands,[131] Poland,[132] Spain)[133] to fulfil their obligation as determined in the judgement, there are several jurisdictions where the operative parts are phrased to read that the defendant is *liable* to pay a certain amount (or perform a particular obligation), giving the impression of a declaratory relief (Albania,[134] Austria,[135] Bulgaria,[136] the Republic of Cyprus,[137] Lithuania,[138] North Macedonia,[139] Slovenia,[140] Sweden).[141] However, all national reporters coming from countries where the defendant is held liable instead of ordered to pay have emphasised that despite such phrasing, the 'liability' of the debtor is clearly understood to mean a duty to perform in their respective legal order. It is universally understood that such judgement is condemnatory, and there are no problems or misunderstandings in practice. While it is possible that such wording could lead to confusion in the context of cross-border enforcement, especially with participants who might not be familiar with the particularities of such phrasing, no case law could be identified where that would actually be the case.

5.1 Threat of Enforcement

Legal systems in participating countries do not require the operative part of a judgement to include a threat of enforcement in order to meet formal conditions for its validity, with the exception of Germany, where the operative part contains a decision on the enforceability or provisional enforceability of a judgement pursuant

[130] 'The court declares the defendant to be liable and orders him to pay the claimant the sum of . . .' ('Il Tribunale dichiara tenuta e condanna la parte convenuta al pagamento, nei confronti di parte attrice, della somma di Euro . . .'). Kaczorowska et al. (2022), p. 30.

[131] 'The court orders Party X to pay Party Y an amount of . . .'. Sujecki (2020), p. 22.

[132] 'The court orders the defendant to . . .' or 'the court awards the claimant . . . from the defendant'. Gołaczyński et al. (2020), pp. 29–30.

[133] 'The debtor is condemned to. . .' ('debo/debemos condenar a . . .'). Bores Lazo & Serrano Ron (2020), p. 30.

[134] 'the obligation of the Defendant to pay in favour of the Claimant'. Kolaj Tafaj F (2020), p. 29.

[135] 'the debtor is liable to pay/perform' ('. . . ist schuldig . . . zu leisten'). Prodinger and Nunner-Krautgasser (2020), pp. 32–33.

[136] 'the debtor is obliged to pay'. Naydenova (2022), p. 33.

[137] 'the debtor is liable to pay. . .'. Christofi & Loizou (2022), 12.

[138] In Lithuania, both expressions are possible. Bolzanas et al. (2020), p. 18.

[139] 'The defendant is obliged to. . .' ('Се задолжува тужениот да. . .'). Zoroska Kamilovska & Rakočević (2020), p. 27.

[140] 'The defendant is liable to pay to the claimant. . .' ('Tožena stranka je dolžna tožeči stranki plačati. . .'). Rijavec et al. (2020), p. 36.

[141] Different formulations are used in Sweden, e.g. that the debtor shall pay a certain amount to the claimant. Bylander & Linton (2020), p. 12.

to § 708 ZPO and § 709 ZPO.[142] In other countries, similar formulations might have developed in judicial practice, but the inclusion or the omission of such threats has no effect on the enforceability of the judgement. For instance, Austrian judgements usually contain the following phrase: 'The defendant is obliged to pay the claimant XX EUR and 4% interest since XX within 14 days, otherwise it will be enforced'.[143] Similarly, in Croatia, North Macedonia and Slovenia, courts developed a practice of including a threat of enforcement within the operative part of condemnatory judgements, even though this is not explicitly required under national legislation. For example, the operative part of a judgement ordering performance of a certain obligation would be phrased in the following manner: 'The defendant is obliged to pay the claimant the outstanding debt in the amount of XX, together with interests from XX until the date of payment, within 15 days, under a threat of enforcement/to avoid enforcement' ('pod prijetnjom ovrhe' in Croatia, 'под закана/страв од присилно извршување' in North Macedonia, 'pod izvršbo/pod grožnjo izvršbe' in Slovenia).' However, despite this phrase becoming a standard part of a judgement, its omission by the court bears no legal consequence and does not constitute an appealable defect, as judgements already become enforceable by law.[144] In Italy, the operative part may contain an expression' sentence provisionally enforceable by law' (*sentenza provvisoriamente esecutiva per legge*),[145] while Belgian national report suggested that it would be possible for a Belgian judgement to include a threat of enforcement since there are no specific rules regarding the structure and content of the operative part.[146] In Albania, the Czech Republic, the Republic of Cyprus, France, Lithuania, the Netherlands, Poland, Portugal or Sweden, the operative part does not refer to enforcement, nor does it provide any threat thereof.[147] Even more, the Bulgarian Civil Procedural Code, which regulates the content of court decisions, does not allow for the operative part to contain a threat of enforcement. The reason is that the right of enforcement is not considered a right of the creditor against the debtor, but a public-law procedural power; this procedural right is addressed to the enforcement body in the CPC enforcement proceedings, namely to the bailiff.[148]

[142] Wolf et al. (2020), p. 40.

[143] Prodinger and Nunner-Krautgasser (2020), p. 32.

[144] Kunštek et al. (2020), p. 20; Zoroska Kamilovska & Rakočević (2020), p. 21; Rijavec et al. (2020), p. 29. See also Galič (2006), p. 128.

[145] Kaczorowska et al. (2022), p. 25.

[146] Rys (2020), pp. 23–24.

[147] Kolaj Tafaj F (2020), p. 25; Valdhans (2020), p. 13; Christofi & Loizou (2022), p. 21; Mensah (2020), p. 21; Bolzanas et al. (2020), p. 16; Sujecki (2020), p. 18; Gołaczyński et al. (2020), p. 25; Caramelo Gomes et al. (2020), p. 23; Bylander & Linton (2020), p. 9. Note that National report for Sweden mentions an exception in the case of eviction from the property, where the defendant is threatened to be evicted by force if they do not voluntarily leave the property according to the judgement.

[148] Naydenova (2022), p. 26.

5.2 Formal Rigidity of the Operative Part

One of the main principles underlying all examined national civil procedures is the principle of party disposition (disposition maxim), which means that the claimant determines the content and scope of judicial protection by specifying the claim contained in the action. Consequently, national courts are bound by the claim and may not exceed its limit, even if the claimant would be entitled to a more beneficial outcome under provisions of substantive law. This prohibition encompasses decisions *extra petitum* (excess in a qualitative sense) or *ultra petitum* (excess in a quantitative sense); however, a court may always grant the claimant less than requested (e.g. if only a part of the claim is justified). On the flip side, the courts are also required to address every part of the claim and may not refuse to render a decision concerning the claim within their jurisdiction.[149] In terms of the formal structure of a judgement, this means that the courts do not have much discretion when formulating the operative part of the judgement and are only rarely allowed to deviate from the claim as set out by the claimant (or counterclaim, setoff, etc., as framed by the defendant, if applicable). There are some exceptions to this rule; for example, Belgian national report notes that a judge may rule *ultra petitum* in matters that would violate public policy,[150] Bulgarian report states that the court may deviate from the claim when drafting the operative part of its decision in some special proceedings in family law cases (especially in divorce proceedings affecting underage children),[151] Polish report mentions deviations in cases concerning maintenance and cases concerning employment,[152] and Portuguese report likewise acknowledges a possibility to deviate from the original claim in labour disputes.[153] It is also acceptable for the court to deviate from the exact wording of the claim in order to draft a clearer, more explicit and more accurate operative part, as long as it remains within limits set by the parties (e.g. by clarifying an unspecified claim to include specifications that can be perfectly deducted from the underlying factual argument, even if they are not explicitly contained within the claim).[154] Other discrepancies between the claim and the operative part, which are not allowed under the law,

[149] See, for example, Rijavec et al. (2020), pp. 42–43; Galič (2005), p. 30; Zobec (2009), p. 460; Wolf et al. (2020), pp. 55–56; Feskorn (2020a), para 30, margin 2. See also Kolaj Tafaj F (2020), p. 33; Prodinger and Nunner-Krautgasser (2020), pp. 35–36; Rys (2020), p. 38; Kunštek et al. (2020), p. 27; Valdhans (2020), p. 16; Christofi & Loizou (2022), p. 31; Kaczorowska et al. (2022), p. 33; Mensah (2020), p. 27; Sujecki (2020), p. 24; Caramelo Gomes et al. (2020), p. 31; Bores Lazo & Serrano Ron (2020), p. 33; Bylander & Linton (2020), p. 14.

[150] Rys (2020), p. 38.

[151] Naydenova (2022), p. 38.

[152] Gołaczyński et al. (2020), pp. 34–35.

[153] Caramelo Gomes et al. (2020), p. 31.

[154] See, for example, Zoroska Kamilovska & Rakočević (2020), p. 32, Prodinger and Nunner-Krautgasser (2020), p. 36; Fucik (2018), Rz 7.

constitute a violation of national procedural rules, usually with severe legal consequences (setting aside the judgement, retrial, etc.).[155]

While the courts are bound by the formulation of the claim as provided by the claimant when drafting the operative part of a judgement, the enforcement authorities are bound in turn by the formulation of the operative part as framed by a court issuing the enforcement title. Slovenian legal theory calls this requirement a principle of strict formal legality, which prevents the court of enforcement from (re)-examining the legality and correctness of the enforcement title or changing its contents in any way; instead, it must enforce the claim as framed in the operative part of the judgement. Any decision-making regarding the merits of the claim is reserved for the litigation phase, while the role of the court of enforcement is limited to executing decisions precisely as specified in the judgement. For that reason, the operative part of the judgement must not leave any doubts regarding the claim or require any further legal reasoning to determine its content. If the debtor's obligation is insufficiently determined, the enforcement will not be possible, as the court of enforcement is not authorised to remedy any deficiencies in this regard.[156] Most other national reports similarly stated that the debtor's obligation has to be specified and finalised by the court in a civil judgement instead of being left to later procedures or authorities, at least as far as the principal claim and the costs of proceedings are concerned. Enforcement authorities have to adhere to the formulation of the operative part when enforcing the judgement or another enforcement title (e.g. Albania, Austria, Belgium, Croatia, the Czech Republic, France, Germany, Lithuania, the Netherlands, North Macedonia, Poland, Portugal, Spain, Sweden).[157]

Some deviations from these restrictions concern the types or elements of the obligation that cannot be precisely determined or specified at the time the court issues its decision. Most notably, such is the case of interest, the total payable amount of which depends on how much time has passed until the debtor repays the debt or fulfils the obligation imposed in the judgement. The national report for North Macedonia explains in detail that while the due amount of main debt and the costs of proceedings are precisely specified in the operative part of the judgement, in a final and conclusive way, the specification of interest is somewhat different. Thus, the court defines interest in the operative part of the judgement with a formula stating the interest rate and the time period for which interest is to be paid (from XX until XX), whereas the final amount is determined on the day when the debtor fulfils the obligation of monetary payment, either voluntary or by force. Accordingly, in the

[155] See, for example, Rijavec et al. (2020), p. 43; Zobec (2009), pp. 461–462; Prodinger and Nunner-Krautgasser (2020), p. 36; Kodek and Mayr (2018), Rz 899; Rechberger and Simotta (2017), p. 517.

[156] Rijavec et al. (2020), pp. 29–30. For more, see Galič (2006), pp. 123–124.

[157] Kolaj Tafaj F (2020), p. 25; Prodinger and Nunner-Krautgasser (2020), p. 35; Rys (2020), p. 24; Kunštek et al. (2020), pp. 20–21; Valdhans (2020), p. 13; Mensah (2020), p. 21; Wolf et al. (2020), p. 41; Bolzanas et al. (2020), p. 16; Sujecki (2020), p. 19; Zoroska Kamilovska & Rakočević (2020), pp. 22–23; Gołaczyński et al. (2020), pp. 25–26; Caramelo Gomes et al. (2020), p. 24; Bores Lazo & Serrano Ron (2020), p. 27; Bylander & Linton (2020), p. 9.

case of enforcement proceedings, the final amount of interest is determined by the enforcement agent on the day of realisation of the obligation set by the judgement (enforcement title). The same applies to contractual penalties when they are not determined in the contract as a total amount but as a percentage.[158] Croatian national report emphasised that it is not just the final payable amount of interest that shall be determined later, but that the interest rate could also be amended. According to Croatian Enforcement Act, if the interest rate is changed after rendering the decision, the court may render a decree upon request by a party ordering payment of statutory interests at a different rate for the period when it applies. Therefore, the enforcement may be carried out for the interest calculated under a different rate than the rate specified in the operative part of the decision that is being enforced, which is an exception to the principle of strict formal legality.[159] In Poland, the court determines the interest rates of contractual interest, the date from which it is due, and the principal amount; however, in the case of statutory interest, the interest rate is not specified in the judgement and is instead calculated by the enforcement agency. The enforcement officer is also responsible for converting any amounts of money specified in a foreign currency into Polish złoty in the course of enforcement proceedings.[160]

6 Reasoning

The reasoning (i.e. the statement of reasons) is the part of the judgement that justifies decisions stated in the operative part and allows both the parties and the appellate court to review and understand the court's reasons for its conclusions regarding the case. Requiring the judge to explain in detail the rationale behind all elements of their findings and opinions, it remains one of the most important deterrents against arbitrariness. For that reason, it is not surprising that all examined national jurisdictions consider the reasoning a necessary part of any standard judgement (with some deviations in the form of special types of judgements, e.g. in the case of acknowledgement or withdrawal of the claim, in summary proceedings, etc.; see Sect. 3 above). However, unlike the structure of the operative part, which is overall strictly regulated—not surprisingly, considering its *res judicata* effects—the structure of reasoning is rarely set out in much detail by procedural legislation, as it is mainly determined by the circumstances of a particular case. In some jurisdictions, the law only refers to the reasoning as being an essential part of a judgement but refrains from defining its content; for instance, French CPC simply states that 'the judgement must be reasoned',[161] while the Swedish Code of Judicial Procedure (RB) is only

[158] Zoroska Kamilovska & Rakočević (2020), pp. 22–23.

[159] Kunštek et al. (2020), pp. 20–21. See also Mihelčić (2015), pp. 160–165.

[160] Gołaczyński et al. (2020), pp. 25–26.

[161] Mensah (2020), p. 28.

slightly more informative with a provision asserting that a judgement shall be in writing and shall specify the reasoning in support of the judgement, including a statement of what has been proven in the case.[162] Neither Dutch nor Belgian legislation provides a specific structure of the reasoning that needs to be adhered to. Instead, the courts are required to address all issues and questions raised by the parties. They basically need to follow the structure of the claim as formulated by the claimant in the writ of summons.[163] It is worth emphasising that in the Netherlands, the reasoning part contains only the grounds for the decision and that the facts of the case, as well as the claims of the parties, are included in a separate part of the judgement.[164]

Most national laws nonetheless provide at least some principal requirements regarding the basic structure, content and elements that should be met within the reasoning. Standard reasoning[165] would generally have to include the claims raised by the parties, the facts asserted by the parties to support these claims and the court's assessment of these facts, the assessment of evidence (including justifications if any proposed evidence was rejected or not considered credible), and the law applied in the rendering of the judgement.[166] Procedural rules in some countries are slightly more detailed; for example, Austrian, where the reasoning is prescribed to contain the following parts under ZPO: the arguments and requests of the party, determinations regarding the existence of procedural requirements, and, if applicable, the handling of procedural complaints, the evidence provided and an explanation for rejected requests for evidence, the findings of facts (the undisputed facts are followed by the facts accepted by the court as facts in the present case, the assessment of evidence (why the court accepted the facts it had established as proven), the legal assessment (the subordination of the established facts under the legal parameters and the examination of the question whether the requested legal consequence can be concluded from the established facts), the reasoning for the decision on costs.[167] Under Spanish LEC, the reasoning comprises a factual

[162] Bylander & Linton (2020), pp. 14–15.

[163] Note that in Belgium, Judicial Code provides a pattern that needs to be adhered to by the counsel when drafting their respective statements of the case. If they fail to do so, the court does not need to answer to the points of law presented in a different manner. Rys (2020), p. 39.

[164] Sujecki (2020), pp. 24–25.

[165] In the case of default judgements, judgements on the basis of acknowledgement or relinquishment of a claim, judgements based on absence, judgements in small claims procedure, etc., the reasoning does not necessarily have to include all listed elements but can instead be drafted in a brief form or even altogether omitted. Usually, it would provide only reasons justifying the rendering of that specific (brief) judgement. See, for example, Kunštek et al. (2020), p. 27; Rijavec et al. (2020), pp. 43–44; Zoroska Kamilovska & Rakočević (2020), p. 32.

[166] See, for example, Rijavec et al. (2020), p. 43; Zoroska Kamilovska & Rakočević (2020), p. 32; Naydenova (2022), pp. 38–39; Gołaczyński et al. (2020), p. 36; Kunštek et al. (2020), p. 27; Kolaj Tafaj F (2020), p. 34; Caramelo Gomes et al. (2020), p. 32; Bolzanas et al. (2020), p. 21; Christofi & Loizou (2022), pp. 35–36.

[167] Prodinger and Nunner-Krautgasser (2020), pp. 36–37. See also Rechberger and Simotta (2017), p. 518; Kodek and Mayr (2018), Rz 901.

background, which records the claims of the parties or interested parties (with clarity and conciseness and in separate and numbered paragraphs), the facts on which they are based (that have been alleged in a timely manner and are related to the issues to be resolved), the proposed and taken evidence, and proven facts, if applicable; as well as the findings of law, which express factual and legal grounds established by the parties and those that posed controversial questions, and provide reasons and legal grounds for the ruling, with the concrete expression of rules applicable to the case (again in separate and numbered paragraphs).[168] On the other hand, procedurals laws in several countries only require the reasoning to include factual findings and legal assessment, without prescribing any subdivisions of these two parts.[169]

Regardless of how elaborately or vaguely the requirements for the structure and content of reasoning are phrased in national legislation, more is generally expected of the courts. As noted in the National report for Slovenia, the court that would only satisfy these rudimentary requirements would prevent the party from getting sufficiently acquainted with the reasons for the court's decision and from properly exercising their right to appeal.[170] For that reason, the judicial practice has played an important role in most jurisdictions in standardising the more precise structure of the reasoning by determining in more detail which elements should be included and properly addressed in particular circumstances.[171] All in all, it is evident that despite different approaches adopted by national legislators and some minor particularities arising from both differences in national rules and specifics of the case, the foundational structure of reasoning in all examined national judgements is very similar in practice.

6.1 The Length of Reasoning

While the reasoning is by and large the most detailed and elaborate part of the majority of judgements, its precise length will depend on the particularities of each case. Factors emphasised by national reporters as having the most impact on the length of reasoning include, *inter alia*, the type of the judgement (e.g. a meritory judgement would usually have lengthier reasoning than a judgement on procedural issues), the complexity of the case, factual issues raised by the parties, legal considerations, evidence proposed and evidence taken, the number of claims, the type and level of the court (e.g. judgements issued by a court of appeal are on average shorter than judgements issued by a court of the first instance), the personal

[168] Bores Lazo & Serrano Ron (2020), p. 34.

[169] See, for example, Valdhans (2020), p. 17; Wolf et al. (2020), p. 56; Kaczorowska et al. (2022), p. 33.

[170] Rijavec et al. (2020), p. 43.

[171] See also Bylander & Linton (2020), p. 15; Rijavec et al. (2020), p. 44; Wolf et al. (2020), p. 56; Grunsky and Jacoby (2018), p. 212.

writing style of the judge, etc.[172] Besides listing the basic elements and issues that have to be addressed within the reasoning (see above), national rules generally do not attempt to provide any specific limits to the length of the reasoning, which might vary significantly as a consequence.

National reporters hold very different views on whether the resulting length is appropriate, which, interestingly, do not always reflect the customary length of judgements in their respective legal systems. Several participating experts expressed concerns about their national judgements not being detailed enough, regardless of whether the reasoning in their country is objectively detailed or brief,[173] while others criticised needless additions to the volume of judgements in the form of unnecessary elements and repetitions. For instance, Albanian judgements in practice vary in length from five to ten pages, and Albanian national reporter considers such length adequate.[174] Lithuanian reporter stated that the reasoning in Lithuanian judgements is very detailed, five to thirty pages in length, but even this is not always enough, as parties commonly appeal judgements on the grounds of insufficient legal arguments. On the other hand, in very exceptional cases, courts sometimes refer to too many court precedents and tend to simply repeat such paragraphs (which may take dozens of pages in areas like intellectual property) without including much actual reasoning. The reporter suggested that it would make more sense to limit such listings to the most relevant cases where *ration decidendi* coincide and refer to the others only in footnotes.[175] In Slovenia, the reasoning for very complicated cases could be spread across tens of pages (even though such judgements are rare in litigation), and even reasoning in the least complex cases would have to be at least a few pages long to address all necessary elements. To a certain extent, the Slovenian national report regards such detailed reasoning necessary; it allows the appellate court to re-assess the arguments and to establish whether the conclusions reached by the court of the first instance are correct or not, it gives the parties a better understanding of the outcome of the case (which promotes their right of a fair trial) and contributes to the development of case law and law in general. On the other hand, the reasoning that includes too much unnecessary information, repetition, uncritical copying of

[172] See, for example, Kolaj Tafaj F (2020), p. 34; Prodinger and Nunner-Krautgasser (2020), p. 38; Rys (2020), p. 39; Naydenova (2022), p. 39; Valdhans (2020), p. 18; Mensah (2020), p. 28; Sujecki (2020), p. 25; Zoroska Kamilovska & Rakočević (2020), p. 33; Rijavec et al. (2020), p. 45; Bores Lazo & Serrano Ron (2020), p. 34; Bylander & Linton (2020), p. 15.

[173] For instance, Belgian, French, Portuguese national reports stated that judgements in their legal system are very detailed, while Austrian, Dutch, North Macedonian and Swedish reports noted that it depends on the case whether the reasoning is very detailed or rather short, and Bulgarian report considered reasoning in national judgements brief. See Rys (2020), pp. 39-40; Mensah (2020), p. 28; Caramelo Gomes et al. (2020), p. 32; Prodinger and Nunner-Krautgasser (2020), p. 38; Sujecki (2020), p. 25; Zoroska Kamilovska & Rakočević (2020), pp. 33-34; Bylander & Linton (2020), p. 15; Naydenova (2022), p. 39.

[174] Kolaj Tafaj F (2020), p. 34.

[175] Bolzanas et al. (2020), p. 21.

statements and cliché phrases is considered wasteful of time and human resources.[176] Other national reporters are of similarly mixed opinions. Belgian reporter noted that although the reasoning can be very technical and detailed, Belgium has had numerous initiatives to increase the legibility and the length of the reasoning provided by the courts, which is why this was a step in the right direction, providing for a balance between the need for proper motivation and the judicial backlog.[177] Portuguese reporter remarked that with the possibility of 'copy and paste', the judgements have become more extensive recently, but that the possibility of judgement annulment for the lack of reasoning justifies the judge dedicating more space to this part.[178] Similarly, the reporter for North Macedonia pointed out that even though the article of the North Macedonian Civil Procedure Act defining the elements of the statement of reasons has remained the same for decades, the court practice has recently undergone significant changes, and there is now a trend towards increasing the length of the statement of reasons.[179] Spanish and Swedish reporters declared that the reasoning in their respective legal systems is not too detailed (or should sometimes be even more detailed), while Austrian reporter likewise praised high standards for the explanation of the reasoning set by Austrian law.[180] The national reporter for the Republic of Cyprus pointed out that the issue frequently faced by the Supreme Court is not whether the reasoning is too detailed, but whether it sufficiently conveys the deliberations of the court for reaching its verdict, and whether any gaps or omissions in the reasoning undermine the logical consistency of the judgement. On such occasions, the verdict is a nullity, and, therefore, the judgement is set aside.[181] It is clear that in attempting to find the balance between time-saving concise judgements and detailed justification of as many arguments as possible, the courts in these countries tend to err on the side of caution and provide longer judgements when that could convince the court of appeal or the parties of their accuracy.

On the contrary, some other jurisdictions have tackled the issue of lengthy reasoning and ineffective arguments, which can be a drain on human resources without providing any added value for the parties, by calling for concise and brief judgements. For example, German ZPO explicitly prescribes brief reasoning ('brief summary of the considerations of the facts and circumstances of the case', § 313 III ZPO), which is understood as a presentation that omits everything not necessary to sufficiently justify the decision taken. However, such brevity must not be at the expense of comprehensibility, and the court is still required to answer questions that

[176] Rijavec et al. (2020), pp. 46–47.

[177] Rys (2020), p. 40.

[178] Caramelo Gomes et al. (2020), p. 32.

[179] Zoroska Kamilovska & Rakočević (2020), pp. 33–34.

[180] Bores Lazo & Serrano Ron (2020), p. 34; Bylander & Linton (2020), p. 15; Prodinger and Nunner-Krautgasser (2020), p. 38.

[181] Christofi & Loizou (2022), p. 35. See also Hambou and others v Michael and another (1981) 1 CLR 618, 619.

are of central importance to the proceedings and regarding which the parties submitted their position. The judgement thus requires explanations that are limited to the essentials and precisely worded, yet not incomplete.[182] The Italian Code of Civil Procedure was amended in 2009 to also promote shorter judgements. Following the amendment, judges can resolve legal points of a dispute simply by referring to existing precedents, which allows them to deal with 'serial' cases quickly. Moreover, they are expressly prohibited from quoting academic writing in their legal reasoning; instead, they generically refer to the 'best doctrine' without mentioning specific authors or books.[183] Another example of a country where the law explicitly requires reasoning to be drawn up concisely is Poland. This includes the requirement for the court to limit its deliberations by refraining from quoting extensive fragments of case law and doctrine and only specifying the opinions that formed the basis for its judgement. However, as this is only a postulate and not a mandatory instruction, it seems not to be functioning well in practice. Polish national reported criticises statements of reason as being too detailed, mainly in parts where the court is required to reconstruct in detail the factual circumstances of the case and clearly state which evidence it accepted and why, as well as which evidence it found to lack credibility and why. It is also a practice of Polish courts to include a description of the parties' positions, which may sometimes take up several pages, even though such description is not required under the law.[184]

Regardless of whether the reasoning is comparatively brief or lengthy, it is evident that it is not the length of reasoning as such that is considered problematic by the authors of national reports but the amount of information that does not contribute to the clarification of court decisions and thus has no other impact than to cause backlogs and wastes available resources.

6.2 Addressing Procedural Issues

The length of reasoning is, naturally, affected by the amount of information provided and explained, including procedural aspects of the case. In this regard, considerable differences can be identified between national approaches to which procedural issues should be addressed or re-addressed in the final judgement, both in terms of procedural prerequisites that have to be met for the case to commence and proceed and in terms of procedural decisions issued in the course of proceedings.

Aside from Lithuania and Albania, where procedural prerequisites do not have to be addressed within the final judgement at all,[185] most other jurisdictions either

[182] Wolf et al. (2020), p. 58. See also Prüttung (2020), para 331, margin 20.

[183] Kaczorowska et al. (2022), p. 34.

[184] Gołaczyński et al. (2020), p. 37.

[185] See Bolzanas et al. (2020), p. 22 and Kolaj Tafaj F (2020), p. 35. Note that although there is no requirement to include procedural prerequisites in Albanian judgements, there are some judges that nonetheless address—very shortly—some procedural prerequisites, such as jurisdiction, competence, etc.

explicitly require their courts to make a note of these prerequisites as a standard part of the reasoning, or they impose such requirement in the case of specific issues being raised by the parties. In Austria, for example, the reasoning includes all arguments and applications (including procedural prerequisites), regardless of whether they were made when the action was filed or afterwards, as long as they were brought forward until the end of the hearing.[186] The same is true of Italian judgements, where procedural prerequisites and applications are referred to in the reasoning if they prove relevant for resolving the dispute; thus, all the issues that the court has considered must be addressed in the reasoning.[187] In Germany, procedural prerequisites are addressed within the part of reasoning dealing with the 'admissibility of the action'. Some are reviewed *ex officio*,[188] and others are examined upon the party's motion.[189] Which procedural prerequisites are necessary depends on the action filed, as some actions require special procedural prerequisites, and the courts may leave the statement regarding the admissibility out of the judgement in cases where no procedural prerequisite is problematic or disputed. Applications made after filing the claim are considered at the beginning of the reasoning within the part' other preliminary inquiries'.[190] In Portugal, procedural conditions are generally assessed at the intermediate stage of proceedings (by an order called 'Despacho Saneador'),[191] but in any case, the judgement must contain a statement that all the procedural conditions are maintained or have been remedied.[192] French judgements address procedural prerequisites before the reasoning (which is intended for the judge to provide reasons in support of their decisions and not for procedural prerequisites), but they are included nonetheless.[193]

---

[186] Prodinger and Nunner-Krautgasser (2020), pp. 38–39.

[187] Kaczorowska et al. (2022), p. 35.

[188] German jurisdiction or the international jurisdiction of German courts ('deutsche Gerichtsbarkeit'), legal responsibility ('Rechtswegzuständigkeit'), factual, local and functional competence ('sachliche, örtliche und funktionelle Zuständigkeit'), the capacity to be a party to court proceedings and the capacity to sue and to be sued ('Partei- und Prozessfähigkeit'), in the event of incapacity to sue, the legitimisation of a legal representative ('wirksame gesetzliche Vertretung'), the required authorisation to pursue legal proceedings ('Prozessführungsbefugnis'), the proper filing of an action ('ordnungsgemäße Klageerhebung'), the lack of other lis pendens ('mangelnde anderweitige Rechtshängigkeit'),the lack of other res judicata ('mangelnde anderweitige Rechtskraft'), the need and interest for legal protection ('Rechtsschutzbedürfnis'), where applicable, conciliatory proceedings ('Güteverhandlung'). Wolf et al. (2020), pp. 60–61. See also Grunsky and Jacoby (2018), pp. 125–126.

[189] The plea of arbitration and the plea of lack of security regarding the reimbursement of costs.

[190] Wolf et al. (2020), p. 61.

[191] This is not necessary in certain abbreviated procedures, in particular for debt recovery, where there is no such intermediate stage and the judge assesses and decides procedural issues in the final judgement.

[192] Caramelo Gomes et al. (2020), p. 33.

[193] Mensah (2020), p. 29.

Most other jurisdictions require the courts to include their assessments of procedural requirements in the judgement only when these prerequisites are disputed and only to the extent of such objections. This is often the case in those national procedures where procedural prerequisites are examined separately under national legislation in earlier stages of the proceedings. For example, in Slovenia, the courts would mainly address procedural prerequisites with special decrees, before issuing the final judgement or even before the main hearing. After an action is submitted, the court carries out preparations for the main hearing (preliminary examination of the action, service of the action on the defendant, setting a date for the main hearing) and may already render a decision concerning certain procedural issues (e.g. regarding the parties' capacity to sue, party representation, the lack of jurisdiction, the lack of standing to sue, *lis pendens*, on amending the action, stay of proceedings due to withdrawal of action, joinder of claims, etc.). If the court renders these decisions by issuing a special decree, procedural prerequisites are already justified within the reasoning of the respective decree and are not repeated within the final judgement. However, certain decrees concerning the procedural requirements may be issued together with the final judgement, resulting in a combined judgement and decree (e.g. a decree (partially) rejecting the action due to the lack of jurisdiction, due to an incomplete action, due to the lack of legal interest for a declaratory judgement, due to the expiry of time limits for the filing of the action, etc.). Any such decision has to be addressed in the reasoning of the combined judgement and decree.[194] Similar is true in North Macedonia, Poland, Croatia and the Republic of Cyprus, where the court may decide on certain procedural requirements or procedural objections separately or together with the main subject of dispute. The court must address these issues in the reasoning of the final judgement only if such objections had not already resulted in issuing a particular decree at an earlier stage of proceedings.[195] In Spain, procedural prerequisites are usually examined in earlier separate decisions as well, unless the defendant raises certain objections in the counterclaim or the answer to the claim; in such case, the court may issue an absolutory sentence without making any decision on the merits of the case and address procedural matters in the reasoning, but only in such situation.[196] In Dutch civil proceedings, procedural prerequisites might be addressed with a separate interlocutory judgement if they form a preliminary question (mainly in the case of disputed jurisdiction). Otherwise, they are dealt with in the reasoning of the judgement.[197] The Czech Republic, Bulgaria, Sweden and Belgium are other examples of jurisdictions where procedural prerequisites are addressed in the reasoning of the judgement only in certain situations.[198]

[194] Rijavec et al. (2020), p. 48.

[195] Kunštek et al. (2020), p. 28; Zoroska Kamilovska & Rakočević (2020), pp. 34–35; Gołaczyński et al. (2020), p. 39; Christofi & Loizou (2022), p. 36.

[196] Bores Lazo & Serrano Ron (2020), p. 35.

[197] Sujecki (2020), p. 26.

[198] For more, see Valdhans (2020), p. 18; Naydenova (2022), p. 41; Bylander & Linton (2020), p. 15; Rys (2020), pp. 40–41.

As far as independent procedural rulings delivered in the course of proceedings are concerned, the countries could be logically divided into two groups; those where the courts have to re-address all such rulings within the reasoning and those where only certain kinds of rulings are incorporated into the final judgement. Some representatives of the former group are Belgium, Croatia, France, Lithuania and the Netherlands.[199] National report for the Netherlands explains in more detail that if the court has rendered an independent procedural ruling, this decision will also be mentioned in the summary of the final judgement, and, if necessary, the court will refer to this ruling in the final judgement as well.[200] Belgian judgements also refer to independent procedural rulings preceding the judgement, which is often done in the preamble of the judgement after a phrase 'the court observes' ('de rechtbank neemt in acht').[201] In other legal systems, there are some limitations to the requirement of which procedural rulings have to be included in the judgement (and its reasoning) and which may be omitted. In several jurisdictions, procedural decisions that can be appealed against independently do not necessarily have to be included in the judgement, unlike decisions that can not be appealed against independently, against which a special appeal is allowed, but have not yet been rendered in writing prior to the final judgement, or certain types of procedural decisions that affect the final decision.[202] Such procedural decisions must generally be included in the operative part and justified in the reasoning, which gives the parties a fair possibility to challenge them before the appellate court, as the latter can examine the reasons for such decisions. In the case of procedural decisions against which the parties were allowed to file an independent appeal, this safeguard is unnecessary, and the repetition of the court's previous rulings would be redundant. Such is the practice in Albania, Austria, North Macedonia, Poland and Slovenia,[203] while Czech, Portuguese, Spanish and Swedish national reporters similarly noted that procedural rulings generally do not need to be re-addressed in the judgement unless they have

[199] Rys (2020), p. 41; Kunštek et al. (2020), p. 29; Mensah (2020), p. 29; Bolzanas et al. (2020), p. 22; Sujecki (2020), p. 26.

[200] Sujecki (2020), p. 26.

[201] Rys (2020), p. 41.

[202] For example, decisions that affect the structure of judgements, such as judgement on the joinder of the proceedings, judgement on the admission of counterclaim, etc. (see Kolaj Tafaj F (2020), p. 35), decrees on whether a given matter is subject to legal recourse, jurisdiction, court competence (see Gołaczyński et al. (2020), p. 39), decrees (partially) rejecting the action, e.g. due to the lack of jurisdiction, an incomplete action, the lack of legal interest for a declaratory judgement, the expiry of time limits for the filing of action (see Rijavec et al. (2020), pp. 48–49), decisions on the amount of dispute, evidence or the refusal to testify (see Wolf et al. (2020), pp. 61–62), and similar.

[203] Kolaj Tafaj F (2020), p. 35; Prodinger and Nunner-Krautgasser (2020), p. 39; Zoroska Kamilovska & Rakočević (2020), p. 35; Gołaczyński et al. (2020), p. 39; Rijavec et al. (2020), pp. 48–49.

not been rendered before for the lack of elements (Portugal)[204] or unless they directly affect the final decision (Spain and Sweden).[205]

6.3 *The Distinction Between the Parties' Statements and the Court's Assessments*

Since the parties' statements are (more or less extensively) summarised or transcribed in judgements in all examined legal systems, it is worth exploring whether any problems might occur in practice regarding a distinction between the parties' positions and the court's arguments and findings. While the former provide factual grounds and frame the scope of proceedings without necessarily being true or correct, the latter justify and support the court's decision as phrased within the operative part, with other accompanying legal implications (see above). Having different purposes and effects, it is important for both the appellate court and the parties to be able to easily differentiate between what was the party's one-sided opinion and what was accepted by the court as being established as true. This distinction is the most clear-cut where the parties' statements are incorporated as a separate part of a judgement, sometimes even announced with special headings or titles. Headings are used, for instance, in Albanian,[206] Italian,[207] Lithuanian[208] and Polish judgements,[209] while in Germany, the parties' statements are mostly provided in the '*Tatbestand*', with a distinction being made between the statements of the claimant and those of the defendant. In the reasoning, the courts distinguish between the parties' statements through the use of language and proper formulations.[210] In Austrian judgements, the court's assessments are usually given a separate heading, but even when that is not the case, the reasoning clearly indicates the facts on which the court based its decision and the arguments put forward by the party. In addition, the courts express the parties' statements in the conditional tense so that the grammar already shows what comes from the party and what comes from the court.[211] The use of language is also the main tool used by other national courts that are not in the habit of using headings or separate sections to designate the parties' statements

[204] Caramelo Gomes et al. (2020), p. 33.

[205] Bores Lazo & Serrano Ron (2020), p. 35; Bylander & Linton (2020), p. 15.

[206] Kolaj Tafaj F (2020), p. 35.

[207] The description of the parties' statements may be preceded by a heading 'The course of proceedings' (Svolgimento del processo), while the court's assessment may be preceded by a heading 'Reasons for the decision' (Motivi della decisione). Kaczorowska et al. (2022), p. 35.

[208] Bolzanas et al. (2020), p. 21.

[209] Gołaczyński et al. (2020), pp. 37–38.

[210] Wolf et al. (2020), p. 60.

[211] Prodinger and Nunner-Krautgasser (2020), p. 38.

(e.g. Belgium, France, Portugal).[212] In Slovenia and North Macedonia, the parties' statements are summarised at the very beginning of the reasoning, ahead of the court's assessment, but even when they are further addressed in other parts of reasoning and intertwined with the court's arguments, the judges also use specific phrases and formulations to ensure that a distinction between these elements is evident.[213] Where the use of linguistic means is the main technique applied to determine to whom a certain view should be ascribed, it is crucial that judges develop good judgement-drafting skills, as a judgement with vague reasoning that lacks proper justification of decisive facts cannot be reviewed.[214] In any case, regardless of whether the parties' statements and the court's findings are separated with headings or linguistic formulations, all national reporters firmly claimed that such distinction is always clear and unproblematic in practice.[215]

7 Conclusions

The first and most important conclusion that should be drawn based on the conducted analysis is that at a macro level, the formal structure of national judgements is remarkably similar in all participating countries. Regardless of whether the structural elements were determined by legislative provisions or have instead been developing through judicial practice, most judgements issued by national courts broadly comply with the following generalised structure: (a) the header or introduction, (b) the operative part, (c) the reasoning. It should be noted that the order of these basic sections in national judgements might vary, with jurisdictions split between those where the introductory part (which, by definition, is always at the beginning) is followed by the operative part, with the reasoning part coming last (e.g. Austria, Croatia, Germany, Slovenia, Sweden), and those where the reasoning precedes the operative part of the judgement (e.g. Albania, Belgium, France, Italy, Portugal, Spain). However, as these parts are clearly discernable, a different arrangement of basic parts should not pose many difficulties for participants in enforcement proceedings. This is true even for judgements issued in the Republic of Cyprus, which stand out as the least typical as their structure was established by court practice in the common-law tradition, but nonetheless provides basically the same information as judgements issued by courts in other countries.

[212] See, for example, Rys (2020), p. 40; Caramelo Gomes et al. (2020), p. 33; Mensah (2020), p. 29.

[213] Rijavec et al. (2020), p. 47; Zoroska Kamilovska & Rakočević (2020), p. 34.

[214] See, for example, Rijavec et al. (2020), pp. 47–48 and Christofi & Loizou (2022), p. 36.

[215] See also Kunštek et al. (2020), p. 28; Valdhans (2020), p. 18; Mensah (2020), p. 29; Sujecki (2020), p. 26; Bores Lazo & Serrano Ron (2020), p. 35; Bylander & Linton (2020), p. 15.

Furthermore, the fundamental substance of each of these elements is also very much alike. For example, the introductory part of a judgement is universally intended to provide basic information about the case, the court deciding the case, the names of judges and other participating court personnel, personal information about the parties and their representatives, the date of the decision and possibly the date of the main hearing, even if the precise information included somewhat vary. The operative part determines the content and scope of legal protection granted to the claimant against the defendant, thus providing a solution to the dispute. It generally contains a decision by which the court satisfies or dismisses the claims of the parties relating to the main subject of dispute, as well as ancillary claims (especially the costs of proceedings) and, if applicable, the court's decision on the existence or non-existence of the claim asserted for the purpose of setoff, a time period for voluntary fulfilment of the obligation, the right to appeal, the decision on (provisional) enforceability, and similar. The reasoning (i.e. the statement of reasons) justifies decisions stated in the operative part and allows both the parties and the appellate court to review and understand the court's reasons for its conclusions regarding the case. Standard reasoning generally includes the claims raised by the parties, the facts asserted by the parties to support these claims and the court's assessment of these facts, the assessment of evidence (including justifications if any proposed evidence was rejected or not considered credible), and the law applied in the rendering of the judgement. While these descriptions are broad generalisations and certain exceptions and deviations can undoubtedly be identified—as provided in the chapter above—it is evident that functional necessities related to the purpose and effects of judgements have resulted in a similar outcome across different jurisdictions.

Naturally, such parallels between foreign judgements could not be established if the judgements were not already highly standardised within the national context. In addition to the legal regulation of their structure, some examples of good practices are especially worth emphasising as being a contributing factor to the uniformity of court documents; namely, special recommendations or guidelines issued by ministries, supreme courts or other relevant institutions that address formal requirements for drafting written judgements, as well as solutions offered by the use of uniform IT systems, in which the templates of judgements are created that can be used by judges when preparing a written issue of the judgement (e.g. approaches adopted in North Macedonia, Poland or Slovenia). Given that such solutions seem to have considerably reduced deviations between judgements within individual jurisdictions, it is worth considering whether further steps could be taken at a cross-border level to bring the structure of enforcement titles even closer together. This idea is not new. There have been several attempts in the past to identify the common core of procedural legislation of the EU Member States and to propose harmonisation or unification of national regulations, arguably the most prominent and successful being EU civil procedures (e.g. European Order for Payment Procedure and the European Small Claims Procedure). Amongst the recent notable efforts undertaken by institutions other than the EU, the joint ELI/UNIDROIT project is especially worth mentioning, as it resulted in a comprehensive proposal for the European Rules of Civil Procedure, which aim to reconcile the differences among various national rules of civil procedure and can be considered as 'a model for reform in domestic legislation'.[216] So far, these rules have not had a significant influence on national jurisdictions but are nonetheless a welcome initiative with potential future impacts. In terms of the structure of judgements, Rule 131 states that a structure of a judgement must contain (a) the court's designation and composition; the place and date of the judgement; (b) the names of the parties and, if applicable, of their lawyers; the relief claimed; the order of the court; (c) the legal and factual grounds for the judgement; (d) the signature of the judge or judges, if necessary; (e) the signature of the court clerk, if necessary; and (f) where relevant, information on formal requirements of any available means to challenge the decision. When compared to national judgements examined in this chapter, it is clear that they already contain all the required elements, just not necessarily in the same order or structured into the same units. Therefore, the slight adaptation of the structure of judgements that would be required if these—admittedly broad—rules (or any similar attempts) were indeed implemented in the future should not pose any significant problems.

In the context of cross-border enforcement within the EU, it thus seems unlikely that differences in the basic structure and substance of judgements would cause many difficulties on their own (and not, for example, as a result of *res judicata* issues or ambiguities regarding interests). Hypothetically, certain particularities and deviations in the structure could cause the enforcement to be manifestly contrary to public policy in the state of enforcement. For example, the French Court of Cassation already established in its past judgements that the recognition of an unjustified foreign decision (i.e. not containing the statement of reasons) is contrary to the French conception of the international public order of procedure when other documents are not produced that could be considered equivalent in the case of missing motivation.[217] However, as already explained, no such significant deviations could be detected in the scope of this research at a macro level.

On the other hand, some aspects of the structure or substance of judgements at a micro-level should be examined more carefully. It is evident that the range of differences between judgements begins to increase once the focus is turned towards the more detailed aspects and more specific elements. Some of these distinctions, even if palpable, are not expected to cause any problems in cross-border enforcement, as they reflect mainly aesthetic or practical conventions without significant legal effects. Such are the differences regarding the requirement to indicate the amount in dispute, the underlying legal relationship, the type of personal data provided to identify the parties (as long as they are identifiable enough to establish the personal scope of *res judicata*), the requirement to include the threat of

[216] ELI/UNIDROIT, The European Rules of Civil Procedure, The Rules, accompanied by Comments, were finalised and approved in 2020, https://www.unidroit.org/wp-content/uploads/2021/06/English-integral.pdf.

[217] Cass. 1ère civ., 28.11.2006, n ° 04-19.031; Cass. 1ère civ., 22.10.2008, n ° 06-15.577. See also Mensah (2020), 28.

enforcement within the operative part or the need to (re)address procedural prerequisites within the reasoning, etc. For example, the amount in dispute is doubtlessly a piece of important information that might determine the subject-matter jurisdiction, the composition of the court, the type of proceedings (e.g. regular proceedings vs small claims procedure), the amount of court fees, or the attorney tariff, etc. However, as far as cross-border enforcement is concerned, it is irrelevant whether this information is provided within the introductory part, the operative part, or the reasoning of the judgement and how exactly it is framed. What is important in the enforcement phase is the amount granted by the court within the operative part of its final and enforceable decision. Likewise, the inclusion of the threat of enforcement has no actual legal effect, even though it is a standard part of how the operative part of the judgement is traditionally phrased in several jurisdictions, as the enforceability is already provided by law and not established (or affected) by such wording or the lack thereof. Notwithstanding, some other variations could cause more significant issues. Such is the case of different wording used in the operative parts of condemnatory judgements. While in some legal systems, the operative part explicitly states that the defendant is *ordered* or *condemned* (e.g. Croatia, Belgium, France, Germany, Italy, the Netherlands, Poland, Spain) to fulfil their obligation as determined in the judgement, there are several jurisdictions where the operative parts are phrased to read that the defendant is *liable* to pay a certain amount (or perform a certain obligation), giving the impression of a declaratory relief (e.g. in Albania, Austria, Bulgaria, the Republic of Cyprus, Lithuania, North Macedonia, Slovenia, Sweden). Within these jurisdictions, no problems occur in practice, as it is clearly understood that the 'liability' of the debtor means a duty to perform. However, a possibility can not be excluded that such wording could cause confusion in the context of cross-border enforcement, especially with participants who might not be familiar with the particularities of such phrasing, or even in the case of inaccurate translations arising from these differences. Furthermore, the court of enforcement could face difficulties in the case of obligation that cannot be precisely determined or specified at the time the original judgement is issued. Especially problematic in this regard is the method of calculating the interest, the total payable amount of which depends on how much time passes until the debt is repaid. In most cases, the court defines interest in the operative part of the judgement with a formula stating the interest rate (contractual or statutory) and the time-period for which interest is to be paid (from [date] until [date]), whereas the final amount is determined on the day when the debtor fulfils the obligation of monetary payment, either voluntary or by force. The same would apply to contractual penalties when they are not determined in the contract as a total amount but as a percentage. As a rule, Article 52 of Brussels I bis Regulation prevents the court of enforcement from reviewing the substance of foreign judgements (under any circumstance) in line with the principle of legal certainty, pursuant to which the creditor may claim only the debt as determined with the enforcement title. The concretisation of a foreign enforcement title is thus possible only where necessary calculation can be done on the objective basis of foreign laws, judgements or statistical documents. If a concretisation of a foreign judgement would constitute the prohibited verification of the content of a judgement, the enforcement must be rejected.[218] In practice, discrepancies and deviations mentioned in this paragraph are somewhat mitigated with the standardised certificate issued pursuant to Article 53 of Brussels I bis Regulation using the form set out in Annex I, which should ensure that the court of enforcement is provided with all information necessary to conduct enforcement proceedings successfully; however, issues resulting from these differences can not be altogether excluded. All in all, though, it can be concluded that the structure and substance of the examined monetary judgements are comparable and similar enough that major problems in this regard are not expected in most cases of cross-border enforcement, with some less consequential ambiguous areas where there is still some room for improvement.

References

Bolzanas D, Visinskis V, Visinskyte D (2020) National report for Lithuania. Project EU-En4s – JUST-AG-2018/JUST-JCOO-AG-2018
Bores Lazo J, Serrano Ron I (2020) National report for Spain. Project EU-En4s – JUST-AG-2018/ JUST-JCOO-AG-2018
Bylander E, Linton M (2020) National report for Sweden. Project EU-En4s – JUST-AG-2018/ JUST-JCOO-AG-2018
Caramelo Gomes J, Marques Cebola C, Lucas E et al (2020) National report for Portugal. Project EU-En4s – JUST-AG-2018/JUST-JCOO-AG-2018
Christofi D, Loizou D (2022) National report for the Republic of Cyprus. Project EU-En4s – JUST-AG-2018/JUST-JCOO-AG-2018
Drnovšek K (2018) Financial implications of remedies against foreign enforcement titles and linguistic issues under Brussels I Recast. In: Rijavec V, Kennett W, Keresteš T et al (eds) Remedies concerning enforcement of foreign judgments: Brussels I Recast. Wolters Kluwer, Alphen aan den Rijn, pp 227–272
Feskorn C (2020a) Para 308. In: Zöller R (ed) Zöller Zivilprozessordnung Kommentar. Otto Schmidt
Feskorn C (2020b) Para 313. In: Zöller R (ed) Zöller Zivilprozessordnung Kommentar. Otto Schmidt
Fucik R (2018) Rz 7. In: Fasching H, Konecny A (eds) Kommentar zu den Zivilprozessgesetzen Bd III/2. Manz
Galič A (2005) 2. Člen. In: Ude L, Galič A (eds) Pravdni postopek, zakon s komentarjem, 1. knjiga. Uradni list, GV Založba, Ljubljana
Galič A (2006) 180. člen. In: Ude L, Galič A (eds) Pravdni postopek, zakon s komentarjem, 2. knjiga. Uradni list. GV Založba, Ljubljana
Gitschthaler E (2019) para 75 ZPO Rz 1 ff. In: Rechberger W, Klicka T (eds) Kommentar zur Zivilprozessordnung. Verlag Österreich
Gołaczyński J, Rodziewicz P, Kaczorowska M et al. (2020) National report for Poland. Project EU-En4s – JUST-AG-2018/JUST-JCOO-AG-2018
Grunsky W, Jacoby F (2018) Zivilprozessrecht. Verlag Franz Vahlen
Herget K (2020) Para 3. In: Zöller R (ed) Zöller Zivilprozessordnung Kommentar. Otto Schmidt
Kaczorowska M, Voinich A, Previatello M (2022) National report for Italy. Project EU-En4s – JUST-AG-2018/JUST-JCOO-AG-2018

[218] Rijavec (2018), pp. 359–421, 370. See also Sladič (2018), pp. 95–112.

Kodek G, Mayr P (2018) Zivilprozessrecht. Facultas
Kolaj Tafaj F, National Report for Albania (2020) Project EU-En4s – JUST-AG-2018/JUST-JCOO-AG-2018
Kunštek E, Kunda I, Mihelčić G et al (2020) National report for Croatia. Project EU-En4s – JUST-AG-2018/JUST-JCOO-AG-2018
Laenens J, Scheers D, Thiriar P et al (2019) Handboek gerechtelijk recht. Intersentia
Mensah M (2020) National report for France. Project EU-En4s – JUST-AG-2018/JUST-JCOO-AG-2018
Mihelčić G (2015) Komentar Ovršnog zakona. Organizator
Naydenova D (2022) National report for Bulgaria. Project EU-En4s – JUST-AG-2018/JUST-JCOO-AG-2018
Neumayr M, Nunner-Krautgasser B (2018) Exekutionsrecht. Manz
Prodinger L, Nunner-Krautgasser B (2020) National report for Austria. Project EU-En4s – JUST-AG-2018/JUST-JCOO-AG-2018
Prüttung H (2020) Para 331. In: Krüger W, Rauscher T (eds) Münchener Kommentar zur Zivilprozessordnung, 1st edn. C. H. Beck
Rechberger W, Simotta D-A (2017) Zivilprozessrecht: Erkenntnisverfahren. Manz
Rijavec V (2003) Civilno izvršilno parvo. GV založba, Ljubljana
Rijavec V (2018) Final assessment of effecting and protecting rights in cross-border enforcement of monetary claims under Brussels I Recast. In: Rijavec V, Kennett W, Keresteš T et al (eds) Remedies concerning enforcement of foreign judgments: Brussels I Recast. Wolters Kluwer, Alphen aan den Rijn, pp 359–422
Rijavec V, Baghrizabehi D, Drnovšek K et al. (2020) National report for Slovenia. Project EU-En4s – JUST-AG-2018/JUST-JCOO-AG-2018
Roth H (2016) Para 263. In: Bork R, Roth H (eds) Stein/Jonas Kommentar zur Zivilprozessordnung, 3rd edn. Mohr
Rys M (2020) National report for Belgium. Project EU-En4s – JUST-AG-2018/JUST-JCOO-AG-2018
Sladič J (2018) Some open issues in determining the scope of enforcement titles in Brussels I Recast. In: Rijavec V, Kennett W, Keresteš T et al (eds) Remedies concerning enforcement of foreign judgments: Brussels I Recast. Wolters Kluwer, Alphen aan den Rijn, pp 95–112
Sujecki B (2020) National report for the Netherlands. Project EU-En4s – JUST-AG-2018/JUST-JCOO-AG-2018
Triva S, Dika M (2004) Građansko parnično procesno pravo, 7th edn. Narodne novine
Ude L (2009) 313. člen. In: Ude L, Galič A (eds) Pravdni postopek, zakon s komentarjem, 3. knjiga. Uradni list, GV Založba, Ljubljana
Valdhans J (2020) National report for the Czech Republic. Project EU-En4s – JUST-AG-2018/JUST-JCOO-AG-2018
Van Ransbeeck R (2014) Standaardisatie van vonnissen en arresten: opportuniteiten en valkuilen bij de digitalisering van justitie. Orde van de Dag: Criminaliteit en Samenleving 66:49–57
Wolf C, Kurth N, Mieszaniec K (2020) National report for Germany. Project EU-En4s – JUST-AG-2018/JUST-JCOO-AG-2018
Zobec J (2009) 357. člen. In: Ude L, Galič A (eds) Pravdni postopek, zakon s komentarjem, 3. knjiga. Uradni list, GV Založba, Ljubljana
Zoroska Kamilovska T, Rakočević M (2020) National report for North Macedonia. Project EU-En4s – JUST-AG-2018/JUST-JCOO-AG-2018

Comparative Issues Concerning the Determination of Interest

Maria Dymitruk and Maria Kaczorowska

Abstract Establishing a legal framework for the determination and calculation of interest lies within the competences of the Member States of the European Union. Of relevance in the context of European cooperation in civil and commercial matters is the need to ensure a clear and unambiguous enforcement procedure in each Member State, which requires transparent rules on how adjudicated or settled interest is to be calculated. In practice, difficulties in determining the amount of interest and identifying the legal basis for its calculation hamper the free circulation of enforcement titles in the European Union. The present chapter discusses comparatively legal solutions adopted in this respect in particular jurisdictions, with a focus on the types of interest, interest calculation methodology, currency and limitations in interest calculation. Based on the comparative analysis, conclusions have been drawn on the possible improvements to be implemented in the field of the determination of interest for the purpose of cross-border enforcement.

1 Introduction

European Union legislation neither defines the notion of interest nor contains specific regulation on how interest payments on debts shall be made. As a result, the issue is subject to the national regulations of each Member State.[1] The notion of interest remains undefined in most, if not all Member States' legal systems, which rightly recognise the notion as one that is understood consistently—both in legal practice and theory. Interest shall be characterised as an additional pecuniary performance to be rendered by a debtor who uses a creditor's funds. The use of money

[1] Even in eurozone countries (the Member States that apply the Euro as their common currency), interest regulation is neither unified nor harmonised. See Rijavec et al. (2018), para 5.02.

M. Dymitruk (✉) · M. Kaczorowska
University of Wroclaw, Faculty of Law, Administration and Economics, Wroclaw, Poland
e-mail: maria.dymitruk@uwr.edu.pl; maria.kaczorowska@uwr.edu.pl

V. Rijavec et al. (eds.), *Diversity of Enforcement Titles in the EU*, Ius Gentium: Comparative Perspectives on Law and Justice 111,
https://doi.org/10.1007/978-3-031-47108-7_6

or other things specified to their kind by the debtor, the interest rate, and the passage of time are the structural elements of the notion.[2] Interest constitutes remuneration for the use of another party's money (or less frequently, other assets) or compensation for a delay in the performance of an obligation, calculated as a percentage of the value of the main performance, according to the duration of the use or delay.[3]

In the context of European cooperation in civil and commercial matters (mostly within the scope of enforcement of judgments, court settlements, and authentic instruments under Brussels I bis Regulation), the most sizeable challenge is the need to ensure a clear and unambiguous enforcement procedure in each Member State. This requires transparent rules on how adjudicated or settled interest is to be calculated, as practical concerns have been expressed by practitioners who frequently work with foreign enforcement titles.[4] Difficulties in determining the amount of interest and identifying the legal basis for its calculation hamper the free circulation of enforcement titles in the European Union. In response, some postulate that an official solution that enables the calculation of interest claimed in a foreign state should be devised.[5] This goal has motivated the EU-En4s project, which aims to create an innovative IT tool (Interest Calculator) that outputs exact numerical values on interest for enforcement titles that originate in each participating Member State. The tool will utilise correct and current data on interest rates and applicable statutes, thereby removing the obstacles mentioned above.

2 Comparative Analysis

Brussels I bis Regulation only once mentions the notion of interest explicitly. Article 42 paragraph 1 letter b of Brussels I bis Regulation requires a person who wishes to enforce a judgment in another Member State to provide a competent enforcement authority with the certificate mentioned in Article 53 of the regulation and provided for in Annex 1 to the regulation. The certificate should contain, *inter alia*, a calculation of interest. In accordance with point 4.6.1.5. of Annex I, for the purposes of enforcement in a Member State of a judgment given in another Member State, it is necessary for such a certificate to specify:

---

[2]See Lemkowski (2007), pp. 38–46. The author cites both Polish and German literature on the definition of 'interest', as well as the relevant case law.

[3]Lemkowski (2007), p. 38 et seq.

[4]See e.g.: the minutes of the national workshop on identification of open issues regarding theory and practice on types and effects of judgments and other decisions equally treated as judgments within the scope of application of Brussels I bis Regulation held on 24 September 2019 at the University of Wroclaw as a part of the EU-En4s project's activities.

[5]Ibid., pp. 2–3.

a. an amount or rate (as a percentage) of interest;
b. an interest period indicated in the following manner: 'interest due from ... (date [dd/mm/yyyy] or event) to ... (date [dd/mm/yyyy] or event)';[6]
c. information on whether statutory interest shall be calculated and if so, the relevant statute that lays down the specific rules in this regard;
d. information on the possible capitalisation of interest (together with further detailed information).

The above applies analogously to interest on the cost of judicial proceedings (see point 4.7.4. of the Annex I), as well as to that established in an authentic instrument or court settlement in civil and commercial matters (see point 5.2.1.5. of Annex II). This implies that the European Union legislators treat the interest stipulated in judgments the same way as that established in documents, such as authentic instruments and court settlements, that have not necessarily been produced by the court.

Interestingly, neither of the certificates in Annexes I and II to Brussels I bis Regulation contains any specific requirement to provide information on the method of calculation of statutory interest. Although it is obligatory to indicate '*the relevant statute laying down the specific rules in this regard*', it is not always sufficient in practice for the debtor (in the case of voluntary performance of an obligation) or the enforcement agent in another Member State (in the case of compulsory execution) to undisputedly and correctly calculate the interest due. Although the reasons for this vary, legal provisions do not always lay down rules concerning interest that are specific enough to determine its exact amount. Many such rules derive from nonlegal documents, or even from practice. Correct calculation of interest, or even knowledge of the correct interest rate, frequently proves impossible without prior understanding of the technical aspects of interest calculation (including its methodology) and the consultation of relevant economic data. When international cooperation in civil and commercial matters and interest calculation performed by foreign debtors or enforcement agents are considered, the difficulty this entails for debtors and enforcement agents becomes one that may inhibit the free flow of enforcement titles in the European Union and undermine the effectiveness of Brussels I bis Regulation.

2.1 Types of Interest

2.1.1 Statutory and Contractual Interest

Member States' legal systems distinguish at least two basic types of interest: statutory and contractual.[7] In accordance with freedom of contract, parties entering

[6] If more than one interest period is specified, information for all periods shall be included.

[7] See e.g.: Article 1907 of the French Civil Code ('Interest is statutory or conventional. Statutory interest is fixed by statute. Conventional interest may exceed statutory interest whenever a statute does not so prohibit. The rate of conventional interest must be fixed in writing'), https://www.

into an agreement may determine the legal relation at their own discretion (including determining interest in the event of lending money or delaying repayment of a debt); this, however, does not always entail unfettered discretion. Possible limitations may occur in such cases, as provisions of maximum interest rate often apply.[8] Conversely, statutory interest is applied in situations in which parties to proceedings have not agreed a specific interest rate.

Statutory interest can be determined either in accordance with the rate that is precisely and numerically indicated in the legal provision (e.g., § 1000 of the General Civil Code of Austria)[9] or with reference to the rates published by national central banks (interesting examples can be found within the laws of European Union candidate countries, such as North Macedonia and Albania). A hybrid method that combines both approaches can be observed in Member States' legislation: statutory interest may be determined in the legal provision; it is not numerically mentioned but indicated with reference to a base rate (commonly, the one set by a national central bank[10] or the European Central Bank).[11]

Differentiation between statutory and contractual interest is particularly relevant in cases of compulsory enforcement in an addressed Member State. With regard to contractual interest, judgments usually determine the exact interest rate that was previously established at the parties' discretion (the wording of the operative part may be as follows: 'the court awards the claimant contractual interest from the defendant, charged at a rate of 3.5% per annum on the amount of PLN 50,000 from 05/05/2018 until 31/03/2020',[12] or 'the defendant is liable to pay to the claimant the amount of 10 000 EUR, together with contractual interest under a fixed annual

legifrance.gouv.fr/download/pdf/legiOrKali?id=LEGITEXT000006070721.pdf&size=1,3%20 Mo&pathToFile=/LEGI/TEXT/00/00/06/07/07/21/LEGITEXT000006070721/LEGITEXT000006070721.pdf&title=Code%20civil; or Article 359 para 1 of the Polish Civil Code (Ustawa z dnia 23 kwietnia 1964 r. – Kodeks cywilny, unified text: Journal of Laws of 2020 item 1740) ('The interest on a pecuniary sum shall be due only where it results from a juridical act or from a statute (...)'), https://isap.sejm.gov.pl/isap.nsf/download.xsp/WDU19640430296/U/D19640296Lj.pdf.

[8] See e.g.: Section 33 of the Cypriot Court of Justice Law of 1960, Article 26 of the Croatian Obligations Act or Article 359 para 2 of the Polish Civil Code ('A maximum yearly interest rate resulting from a juridical act may not exceed four-times the amount of the Lombard rate of the National Bank of Poland (maximum interest)').

[9] Allgemeines Bürgerliches Gesetzbuch of 1811 (JGS No. 946/1811, as last amended BGBl. I No. 175/2021), hereinafter 'ABGB'.

[10] As is the case, for example, in Poland (See Article 359 para 2 of the Polish Civil Code: 'If the amount of interest is not specified elsewise the statutory interest in the amount equal to the reference rate of the National Bank of Poland and 3.5 percentage points shall be due').

[11] As is the case in Germany (See Section 247 para 1 of the German Civil Code; Bürgerliches Gesetzbuch (BGBl. I S. 42, 2909; 2003 I S. 738, as last amended BGBl. I S. 5252, 2021), hereinafter 'BGB': 'The basic rate of interest is 3.62%. It changes on 1 January and 1 July each year by the percentage points by which the reference rate has risen or fallen since the last change in the basic rate of interest. The reference rate is the rate of interest for the most recent main refinancing operation of the European Central Bank before the first calendar day of the relevant six-month period').

[12] A Polish example, see Gołaczyński et al. (2020), p. 31.

interest rate of 8.5% from 15/04/2020 until the date of payment, within 15 days to avoid enforcement').[13] The resultant calculation method is rather simple, as it is based purely on arithmetic.

Statutory interest, by contrast, often demands enforcement agents from Member States other than the state of origin to perform more detailed analysis of the interest debt due. The absence of a sufficiently determined operative part of a judgment regarding interest for the purposes of enforcement in an addressed state (namely, the absence of numerical indication of a statutory interest rate) creates difficulty for enforcement agents in ensuring the correct calculation of interest. It is highly likely that the agent assigned to a particular case is unfamiliar with the calculation method applied in the Member State of origin of the enforcement title. As a result, they are forced to take 'crash courses' in foreign regulation on interest—often with modest success.

Many EU Member States are insufficiently strict in determining the interest debt in judgments. The absence of precision is visible most frequently in cases of statutory interest. Most of the Member States confine themselves to set out in judgments that 'statutory interest' or 'interest as provided by the law' applies. The wording of the operative part of such judgments may be, in that case, as follows:

- 'the judgment is issued in favour of the claimant and against the defendant for the sum of 2 377 EUR **plus interest as provided by the law**';[14]
- 'the court orders that the claimants are to pay **the statutory interest due** for these costs after the expiry of fourteen days from the date of this judgment';[15]
- 'the defendant is liable to pay the amount of 5 056.76 EUR with **statutory** default **interest** from 15 August, 2008 until the day of payment, all within fifteen days, to avoid enforcement';[16]
- 'the court orders the defendant (. . .) to pay the claimant (. . .) PLN 32 900, including **statutory interest** from 10 November, 2015 to 31 December, 2015'.[17]

Statutory interest is determined similarly in Italy,[18] Belgium,[19] Portugal,[20] and Spain.[21]

---

[13] A Slovenian example, see Rijavec et al. (2020), p. 38.

[14] A Cypriot example, see EU-EN4S Blog (2019). Cyprus. http://blog.pf.um.si/enforcement-titles/cyprus/.

[15] A Dutch example, see EU-EN4S Blog (2019). Netherlands. http://blog.pf.um.si/enforcement-titles/netherlands/.

[16] A Slovenian example, see EU-EN4S Blog (2019). Slovenia. http://blog.pf.um.si/enforcement-titles/slovenia/.

[17] A Polish example, see EU-EN4S Blog (2019) Poland. http://blog.pf.um.si/enforcement-titles/poland/.

[18] Kaczorowska et al. (2022), pp. 29-30.

[19] Rys M (2020), pp. 30–31.

[20] Caramelo Gomes et al. (2020), p. 29.

[21] Bores Lazo and Serrano Ron (2020), p. 31.

On the other hand, some Member States do not refer in the operative part of their judgments to the notion of statutory interest but indicate a numerical rate of interest (a specific percentage) – even in cases in which contractual interest does not apply. In such cases, court rulings might be as follows:

- 'the defendant is liable to pay the claimant 100,000 Euros within 14 days, **plus 4% interest** since 28.7.2010, otherwise the claim will be executed'[22] (this is an Austrian example, in which 4% is the 'legal rate' defined explicitly in Section 1000 of the ABGB; the operative part of the judgment is not limited, however, to the indication of 'interest at the legal rate', but always states the exact percentage);
- 'the defendant is obliged to pay the plaintiff the amount of CZK XY together with **interest in the amount of 3%** per month from the amount of CZK XY from [DATE] until payment';[23]
- 'the defendant shall pay **5% interest** from the day the claim was submitted until the debt is fully recovered'.[24]

The reason most of the Member States decline to specify exact rates of statutory interest is that such rates often rely on economic parameters that alter over time; consequently, the statutory interest rate may change between the date a judgment is issued and the date it is enforced. If the operative part of a judgment specifies the numerical percentage of the statutory interest rate, how it changes over time is indiscernible to the judgment's reader.

The provisions of Brussels I bis Regulation offer a partial solution to the problem of indication in the operative part of judgments solely of the notion of 'statutory interest' (without more precise specification). The provisions establish the requirement that parties provide information on the exact amount of applicable interest or, alternatively, its precise rate (see points 4.6.1.5.1.2.1 and 4.6.1.5.1.2.2 of Annex I, and points 5.2.1.5.1.2.1 and 5.2.1.5.1.2.2 of Annex II in the case of court settlements and authentic instruments). As a result, the certificate needed to execute an enforcement title in an addressed Member State may be more precise than the enforcement title itself. Even when a judgment, court settlement, or authentic instrument uses the notion of 'statutory interest' without numerical indication of the interest rate, such a certificate should contain the detailed information. For example, if a Polish enforcement title states that a defendant is obliged to pay PLN 32 900 to a plaintiff, including statutory interest from 10 November 2015 to 31 December 2015, the certificate should indicate that the interest rate is 8% per annum. If a certificate contains no clear indication of the rate or amount of interest, an enforcement agent must investigate the legal regulations of the certificate's Member State of origin. This might also prove insufficient, as interest calculation methods are often not shaped solely by legal provisions.

[22] Prodinger and Nunner-Krautgasser (2020), p. 33.

[23] Valdhans J (2020), p. 16.

[24] Bolzanas et al. (2020), p. 19.

2.1.2 Default Interest

As indicated above, interest constitutes remuneration for the use of others' assets (interest on capital) or compensation for a delay in the performance of a monetary obligation, such as interest for a late payment or default interest. All Member States provide for default interest, which is partially a result of the implementation of Directive 2000/35/EC of the European Parliament and of the Council of 29 June 2000 on combating late payment in commercial transactions,[25] and its successor, Directive 2011/7/EU of the European Parliament and of the Council of 16 February 2011 on combating late payment in commercial transactions (recast). [26] The national transposition of the directives[27] has strengthened the position of creditors, but its applicability is limited to commercial transactions.[28] For this reason, most Member States differentiate the default interest in commercial transactions (see the Polish example of the Act of 8 March 2013 on preventing excessive delay in commercial transactions,[29] Section 456 of the Austrian Commercial Code[30] or Article 6:119a of the Dutch Civil Code),[31] and standard non-business cases of default interest (see Article 481 of the Polish Civil Code,[32] Section 1333 of Austrian ABGB or Article 6: 119 of the Dutch Civil Code).[33, 34] Differentiation between the interest imposed on natural persons and that on legal persons can also be found in the legal systems of

[25] Official Journal of the European Communities, L 200, Volume 43, 8.8.2000, pp. 35–38.

[26] Official Journal of the European Union, L 48, Volume 54, 23.2.2011, pp. 1–10.

[27] See in respect of Directive 2000/35/EC of the European Parliament and of the Council of 29 June 2000 on combating late payment in commercial transactions, OJ L 200, 8.8.2000; in respect of Directive 2011/7/EU of the European Parliament and of the Council of 16 February 2011 on combating late payment in commercial transactions Text with EEA relevance, OJ L 48, 23.2.2011.

[28] The scope of application of both directives is limited (see Articles 1 and Articles 2 of the Directives).

[29] Ustawa z dnia 8 marca 2013 r. o przeciwdziałaniu nadmiernym opóźnieniom w transakcjach handlowych, Dz. U. z 2021 r. poz. 424, 2317, https://isap.sejm.gov.pl/isap.nsf/download.xsp/WDU20130000403/U/D20130403Lj.pdf.

[30] Bundesgesetz über besondere zivilrechtliche Vorschriften für Unternehmen (Unternehmensgesetzbuch – UGB), StF: dRGBl. S 219/1897 (GBlÖ Nr. 86/1939).

[31] Burgerlijk Wetboek of 1992 (NLD-1992-L-91671). Article 6:119 par 1. 'The compensation for damages, chargeable because of a delay in payment of a sum of money, consists, in the case of a commercial agreement, of the statutory interest on the unpaid part of that sum from the day following the date that has to be considered as the expiry date for payment under the agreement up until and including the day on which the debtor has paid the amount chargeable to him. (. . .)'.

[32] Article 481 para 1 of the Polish Civil Code: 'If a debtor is late with a monetary performance, the creditor may demand interest for the period of delay even if he has not suffered any damage and even if the delay was due to circumstances for which the debtor is not liable'.

[33] Article 6:119 para1. 'The compensation for damages, chargeable because of a delay in payment of a sum of money, consists of the statutory interest on the unpaid part of that sum over the time that the debtor is in default of complying with his obligation'.

[34] This is also the case in Belgium, Bulgaria, Germany, Spain, Lithuania, Luxemburg and Portugal.

Member States (see the Lithuanian example).[35] Interestingly, some Member States—including Slovenia,[36] Estonia,[37] and France[38]—make no distinction between the interest imposed on consumers and that on commercial entities, and opt to apply a single universal interest rate.

Default interest can be based on statutory and contractual rates; this means that all of Sect. 2.1.1 on how Member States determine interest in their enforcement titles remain valid. In the case of delayed performance of a monetary obligation, when the parties have not agreed on a specific default interest rate, most Member States apply the 'statutory interest rate' and specify no further details. A calculator of the statutory default interest in commercial transactions is publicly available on the Your Europe website.[39] Useful information on statutory interest in Member States can be also found on the e-Justice Portal.[40]

2.2 Interest Calculation Methodology

In addition to the difficulties that arise from the variety of means of specifying interest in enforcement titles, the methodology of interest calculation also remains an issue in European Union Member States. Generally, Member States have adopted the linear method of interest calculation—an approach based on annual interest rates. Some of the countries that have adopted such methods, however, have opted not to explicitly indicate that fact in the wording of operative parts. As a result, in most of the Member States examined in the EU-En4s project—including Austria, Belgium, Cyprus, France, Germany, Italy, Lithuania, the Netherlands, Poland, Portugal, Slovenia, and Spain—enforcement titles determine the annual statutory interest rate implicitly; Czech judgments, however, tend to specify explicitly that the annual rate is applied. In the case of contractual interest, a time unit (e.g., per month, per day) should always be clearly indicated and employed to calculate interest; the parties are entitled to determine the legal obligation between them freely, and may wish to apply an interest rate other than the annual one in their case.

In adopting the linear method of interest calculation, leap years, which last 366 days, present a challenge. Two solutions are possible: such calculations can be based on all-equal years (every year is assumed to contain a standard number of

[35] Bolzanas et al. (2020), p. 19.

[36] Merc (2021), p. 86.

[37] European e-Justice: Interest Rates: Estonia. https://e-justice.europa.eu/404/EN/interest_rates?ESTONIA&member=1.

[38] Rijavec et al. (2018), para 6.03.

[39] Your Europe: Interest Calculator. https://europa.eu/youreurope/business/finance-funding/making-receiving-payments/late-payment/index_en.htm.

[40] European e-Justice: Interest Rates, https://e-justice.europa.eu/404/EN/interest_rates?BELGIUM&member=1. It is possible to change the Member State by clicking the flag in the frame on the left.

days), or they can be based on the actual number of days in a given year, (leap years contain 366 days and common years contain 365). In Croatia,[41] Czechia,[42] Germany,[43] Lithuania,[44] and the Netherlands,[45] the calculation method is always based on the actual numbers of the days in a year. This means that interest calculation in these countries differs between common and leap years. Conversely, Cyprus,[46] Portugal,[47] and Poland[48] have adopted fixed rules stating that the 'standard year' always contains 365 days—regardless of whether it is a regular or a leap year. One interesting example can be found in Bulgaria,[49] where a 'standard year' is defined as 360 days. Information on the calculation method adopted is offered neither in enforcement titles nor in the certificates contained in Annexes I and II of Brussels I bis Regulation.

2.3 *Currency*

When considering the rules that underlie the determination of interest in enforcement titles, the currency in which interest is to be paid must also be addressed. This is imperative for cross-border legal relations and possible doubts related thereto. For this reason, currency conversion in the context of contractual freedom enshrined in national laws will be discussed from a comparative perspective. Specific rules on the currency of pecuniary liabilities provided for in substantive law are reflected in procedural provisions on the rendering of judgments, as well as the conduct of enforcement proceedings.

Party autonomy is widely accepted with respect to the selection of the currency of payment in European legal systems; thus, payment may be effected in both domestic and foreign currencies. Unless explicitly provided otherwise by the parties, debtors are usually allowed to render payment in domestic currency—even if the debt is expressed in a foreign currency. As a rule, when a debtor makes use of their right to pay in domestic currency, provisions on the relevant exchange rate apply.[50] According to Article 358 paragraph 1 of the Polish Civil Code, if the object of an obligation being performed on the territory of the Republic of Poland is a pecuniary sum expressed in a foreign currency, a debtor may render performance in Polish

[41] Interest rate calculator questionnaire for Croatia, p. 8.
[42] Interest rate calculator questionnaire for Czech Republic, p. 8.
[43] Interest rate calculator questionnaire for Germany, p. 8.
[44] Interest rate calculator questionnaire for Lithuania, p. 8.
[45] Interest rate calculator questionnaire for the Netherlands, p. 8.
[46] Interest rate calculator questionnaire for Cyprus, p. 8.
[47] Interest rate calculator questionnaire for Portugal, p. 8.
[48] Interest rate calculator questionnaire for Poland, p. 8.
[49] Interest rate calculator questionnaire for Bulgaria, p. 8.
[50] Martens (2018), p. 1048.

currency [złoty], unless a statute, a court decision that acts as the source of the obligation, or a juridical act reserves the performance of an obligation exclusively in foreign currency. The value of the foreign currency shall be calculated according to the average exchange rate announced by the National Bank of Poland on the day the claim becomes due, unless a statute, court decision, or juridical act provides otherwise (Article 358 paragraph 2 of the Polish Civil Code). If a debtor delays rendering a performance, the creditor may demand performance in Polish currency according to the average exchange rate announced by the National Bank of Poland on the day the payment is made (Article 358 paragraph 3 Polish Civil Code). Similar legal solutions have been adopted, *inter alia*, in Austria (Section 907b of the ABGB), Italy (Articles 1278 and 1279 of the Italian Civil Code),[51] Germany (Section 244 paragraph 1 of the BGB), and the Netherlands (Article 6:121 of the Dutch Civil Code).

The above rules also cover the payment of interest. Given that interest is qualified as ancillary (accessory) performance, if a principal performance is expressed in a foreign currency, the interest thereon should also generally be expressed in the same currency;[52] different rules may result, however, from a special legal provision or an agreement between the parties. With regard to Polish law, default interest is payable both on pecuniary performance expressed in Polish złoty and on that expressed in foreign currencies. In the latter case, default interest shall also be due in the foreign currency, unless otherwise stipulated by the parties or provided for by law. If the amount of such interest is unspecified in a contract, the provisions on statutory default interest shall apply.[53]

In cases of pecuniary performances expressed in foreign currencies to be rendered in domestic currency, currency conversion, in accordance with the relevant regulations regarding enforcement proceedings, is necessary. Under Polish law, in principle, if a specific amount of money in a foreign currency is awarded by the court, the enforcement agent is responsible for converting that amount into Polish złoty in the course of enforcement proceedings.[54] Pursuant to Article 798 paragraph 1 of the Polish Code of Civil Procedure,[55] if an enforcement title covers a pecuniary performance in a foreign currency, the enforcement agent shall convert the awarded amount into Polish currency at the average exchange rate announced by the National Bank of Poland on the date a plan to distribute proceeds obtained in enforcement is prepared, or, if such a plan has not been prepared, on the date the amount is paid to the creditor. The provision of paragraph 1 shall not apply if an enforcement title

[51] Codice civile (Regio Decreto 16 marzo 1942, n. 262, Gazzetta Ufficiale n. 79 of 4 April 1942, as amended).

[52] See Machnikowski (2021), Article 358, para 2.

[53] See Borysiak (2021), Article 481, para 11; Szanciło (2020) Article 481, para 3; Lemkowski (2007), p. 67 et seq.; Karasek (2001), p. 103. See also resolution of the Polish Supreme Court of 12 June 1981, V PZP 3/81.

[54] See Gołaczyński et al., National Report for Poland, pp. 25–26; Gil (2021) Article 798.

[55] Ustawa z dnia 17 listopada 1964 r. – Kodeks postępowania cywilnego, unified text: Journal of Laws of 2021 item 1805.

indicates that a pecuniary performance may only be rendered in a foreign currency.[56] In such cases, the enforcement agent shall purchase the currency from the bank. On initiating enforcement, the enforcement agent shall set the debtor a one-week time limit to specify a bank; if the debtor fails to specify a bank, the enforcement agent shall request the creditor to do so within one week; if neither the debtor nor the creditor specifies a bank, the duty to do so shall rest with the enforcement agent. The bank specified by the creditor or the enforcement agent may not be the creditor (Article 798 paragraph 2 of the Polish Code of Civil Procedure). It must be emphasised that an enforcement agent's duty to convert foreign currency into Polish złoty also derives from the enforcement clause. As follows from Article 783 paragraph 1 sentence 2 of the Polish Code of Civil Procedure, unless otherwise provided for by specific regulations, the court shall issue an enforcement clause for an enforcement title involving payment in a foreign currency, and shall oblige the enforcement agent to convert the amount awarded into Polish currency at the average exchange rate of the foreign currency issued by the National Bank of Poland on the date a plan for the distribution of proceeds is prepared, or, failing that, on the date the relevant amount is paid to the creditor.[57]

The question of currency conversion with regard to interest awarded in foreign judgments arises against the backdrop of cross-border enforcement of judgments under Brussels I bis Regulation. As already indicated above in this chapter, the entitlement to interest depends on and is generally specified in judgments issued in the Member State of origin. Relevant information on the calculation of interest shall be provided in a certificate stating that the judgment is enforceable, issued according to Article 53 of Brussels I bis Regulation by the court of origin at the request of any interested party.[58] These issues will be illustrated by the examples presented below.

Within the Italian legal framework, creditors are entitled to interest at the rate set in a foreign judgment, and it is unnecessary to convert the value of such judgment into domestic currency. If the sum due is set in a currency that is not legal tender in the state, the debtor can pay in a legal currency at the exchange rate of the due date and in the place established for the payment, as laid down in Article 1278 of the Italian Civil Code.[59] Similarly, in the Netherlands, the value of a foreign judgment need not be converted into domestic currency.[60] Under Belgian law, a conversion of foreign currency into domestic currency is not required in (enforcement) judgments

[56] In this context, it is noteworthy that by virtue of art. 319 of the Polish Code of Civil Procedure, if a statute, a court decision that serves as the source of an obligation, or a juridical act provide for a performance to be rendered only in a foreign currency, the court shall, when upholding the action, stipulate that the performance shall only be rendered in a foreign currency. See e.g. Rudkowska-Ząbczyk (2021), Article 319.

[57] See Gołaczyński et al. (2020), National Report for Poland, p. 71; Modrzejewski and Potasz (2021).

[58] See Goździaszek (2015), Article 53, para 6; Kramer (2016) Article 58, pp. 968–969.

[59] See Batini and Traverso (2021); Ascarelli (1959), Articles 1277–1284, p. 368.

[60] González Nicolás et al. (2021).

themselves. According to Article 562 of the Belgian Code of Civil Procedure,[61] foreign currency shall be converted into Euros at the highest exchange rate on the date of payment.[62] If enforcement of a foreign judgment that requires the payment of a sum in foreign currency is conducted in France, that sum shall be converted into Euros by the enforcement agent.[63]

The Slovenian legal system demonstrates an unusual consideration of the currency of interest in its rules on currency conversion: interest arising from a Slovenian enforceable title shall be executed at the interest rate specified in Slovenian legislation; that arising from a foreign enforceable title shall be determined on the basis of a foreign substantive provision. For domestic enforcement titles, the Slovenian courts use publicly-available software to calculate statutory default interest. The software assumes that interest can be calculated only from principals or debt in domestic currency, and not from those denominated in foreign ones. As a consequence, when calculating statutory default interest from foreign currency, that currency must first be converted, according to the exchange rate defined by the Bank of Slovenia, into Euros on the day of payment; the interest is then calculated using domestic currency. During an enforcement procedure, statutory default interest cannot be recovered at the rate established under Slovenian law if the creditor applies for enforcement based on a foreign enforceable title. According to Article 1 paragraph 1 of the Statutory Default Interest Rate Act,[64] the default interest rate is the annual rate at which pecuniary obligations are remunerated between the date of the debtor's default and the date of payment. The above provision applies only to Slovenian enforcement titles containing foreign currency, such as notarial deeds.[65]

2.4 *Limitations in Interest Calculation*

The differences between national regulations on interest are also visible in the context of limitations in calculating interest. These restrictions may take the form of interest rate limitations (maximum interest rate) or limitations in interest capitalisation (embodying a general prohibition of compound interest or a rule that interest on late payment ceases to run when the amount of accrued and unpaid interest equals the principal amount owed). Both kinds of limitations of the amount of interest aim to protect the debtor against excessive interest payment.

The first mentioned, the institution of maximum interest restricts the amount of interest that can be levied from the debtor by reducing (in most cases contractual) interest rate because the national legislator considers it to be excessive. For example,

[61] Code judiciaire/Gerechtelijk Wetboek, 10.10.1967.

[62] Devos and Nijns (2021).

[63] Poisson et al. (2021).

[64] Zakon o predpisani obrestni meri zamudnih obresti (Official Gazette of the Republic of Slovenia, No. 56/03, as amended).

[65] See Merc (2021), pp. 74–75.

according to art. 359 § 2^1 of the Polish Civil Code, the maximum interest rate resulting from a juridical act (most often contractual interest rate) may not exceed annually double the amount of statutory interest (maximum interest). If the rate of interest resulting from a juridical act exceeds the rate of maximum interest, the maximum interest shall be due. Contractual provisions may not exclude nor limit provisions on maximum interest even where the foreign law has been chosen as applicable. In such a case the statutory provisions shall apply (art. 359 paragraphs 2^2–2^3 of the Polish Civil Code). Similar rules preventing usury have been adopted, i. a., in France. They relate, however, exclusively to consumer transactions.[66] In other countries, such as Germany and Slovenia, usury is prohibited by way of judicial interpretation of a general clause.[67]

Moreover, as already indicated, there are rules in many jurisdictions establishing a prohibition on the awarding of compound interest (interest on interest, anatocism), and allowing the payment of only simple interest. Some legislations permit compound interest in certain circumstances. This is generally the case in Poland. Pursuant to art. 482 paragraph 1 of the Polish Civil Code, one may demand interest for a late payment on the outstanding interest only from the moment of instituting an action for it, unless following the accrual of the arrears the parties have agreed to add the outstanding interest to the amount due. An amendment of 2018 resulted in the repeal of art. 482 paragraph 2 of the Polish Civil Code which provided for another exception to the prohibition of anatocism, regarding long-term loans granted by financial institutions.[68] The German Civil Code prohibits a contractual clause allowing interest to be added 'in advance' to the principal sum outstanding. However, some exceptions have been stipulated as well.[69] Under Italian law, in turn, compound interest is available when there has been prior usage or a prior agreement as long as interest has been due for at least six months (art. 1283 of the Italian Civil Code).[70]

An instrument of protection of the debtor that should also be mentioned is the *ne ultra alterum tantum* rule, deriving from Roman law. According to this rule, interest ceases to run when the amount of interest accrued but not paid reaches the amount of

[66] As follows from Article L313-3 of the French Consumer Code (*Code de la consummation*), any contractual loan granted at an annual percentage rate which, at the time of its granting, is more than one third higher than the average percentage rate applied by the credit institutions during the previous quarter for loans of the same type presenting a similar risk factor, constitutes a usurious loan.

[67] See Lemkowski (2007), pp. 343 et seq.; Mojak (2018), p. 6; Reifner et al. (2010), pp. 42, 80.

[68] See e.g. Dybowski and Pyrzyńska (2019), p. 330.

[69] According to Section 248 of the German Civil Code, an agreement reached in advance that interest due should in turn bear interest is void. Savings banks, credit institutions and owners of banking businesses may agree in advance that interest not collected on deposits should be held to be fresh interest-bearing deposits. Credit institutions entitled to issue interest-bearing bonds for the amount of the loans granted by them may, for such loans, have commitments made to them in advance to pay interest on interest in arrears. Moreover, as follows from Section 289 of the German Civil Code, default interest is not to be paid on interest. The right of the obligee to compensation for damage caused by the default remains unaffected.

[70] See Lemkowski (2007), pp. 372 et seq.; Gotanda (2004); Reifner et al. (2010), pp. 97 et seq.

the principal. The prohibition on accruing interest *ultra alterum tantum* is basically not foreseen in contemporary European countries' legislation and applies only to contractual relations.[71] A noteworthy example in this respect is Slovenian law. In 2002, the *ne ultra alterum tantum* rule was introduced in art. 376 of the Slovenian Civil Code,[72] relating to the calculation of both contractual and default interest. It caused a lot of confusion with regard to the latter and was being misused by the businesses. After a series of decisions of the Constitutional Court the above provision needed to be corrected by the legislator in 2007, and since then the rule covers only contractual interest.[73]

Unfortunately, the presented provisions on the interest limitations do not seem to be always reflected in the content of national enforcement titles. At the same time, these issues should be clearly presented at least in the certificate provided for in Annex 1 to Brussels I bis Regulation.

As far as maximum interest rate is concerned, it should be numerically indicated already in the enforcement title. Therefore, the enforcement agent in the Member State addressed does not need to know if in a particular case the maximum interest rate was applied. He is only interested in the exact interest rate, and as long as it does not exceed the national maximum interest rate, the interest calculation runs smoothly. So, if the parties have agreed on 20% annual interest, and it exceeds the current maximum interest rate, the court should apply the maximum interest rate instead of the agreed one. As a result, the enforcement title indicates only the correct (maximum) interest rate, and the enforcement agent in the Member State addressed calculates the debt using this correct (maximum) interest rate. The only obstacle occurs when the maximum interest rate changes after the issuance of the enforcement title. If this change is not mentioned at least in the certificate, the enforcement agent is often unable to correctly calculate the interest.

As to the limitations in interest capitalisation (the application of the *ne ultra alterum tantum* rule or the prohibition of anatocism), they are less likely to be visible in the content of the enforcement title. However, they should be clearly indicated in the certificate provided for in Annex 1 to the Regulation in the section devoted to the information on the possible capitalisation of interest (together with further detailed information). The lack of empirical research in this context makes it hard to determine if actually the detailed information on limitations in interest capitalisation is always provided in the certificate and if not, how the situation can be improved.

[71] See Lemkowski (2007), pp. 385–386.

[72] Obligacijski zakonik (Uradni list RS, št. 97/07 – uradno prečiščeno besedilo, 64/16 – odl. US in 20/18 – OROZ631).

[73] See Možina and Vlahek (2019), Introdutction to the Law of Contracts, § 2.II.37; Možina (2010), pp. 1–7. See also Case C-256/15 Drago Nemec v Republika Slovenija, ECLI:EU:C:2016:954.

3 Conclusions

As demonstrated by this comparative overview of the national regulations that govern the determination of interest for the purpose of enforcement proceedings, an approach that is common in some respects for the majority of European countries can be identified. With regard to other specific issues, however, the legal solutions that exist in particular jurisdictions covered by this analysis present considerable dissimilarities.

The methods of specifying and expressing the interest rates in a judgment that orders payment vary depending on whether the interest is contractual or statutory. With regard to contractual interest, generally, the operative parts of judgments specify the rate agreed by the parties. In some jurisdictions, statutory default interest rates are indicated explicitly as percentages in the operative parts of judgments; other national laws provide that rates be specified by reference to the relevant legal provisions by which interest is to be calculated, or by reference to the rates announced by national banks. Alternatively, general wording that merely includes the term 'statutory (legal) interest' may be employed. In such cases, it is the responsibility of the enforcement agent to calculate the amount of interest. Statutory interest rates are generally subject to fluctuations over time, depending on economic factors and domestic monetary policy.

Within another widely used typology, interest is divided between interest on capital and default interest. Moreover, most legal systems distinguish between their default interest rates in civil and commercial matters (in relation to natural persons and legal entities, respectively). Regulations that pertain to default interest in commercial transactions have been introduced in European Union Member States by implementation of the European Union Directives on combating late payment in commercial transactions.

The linear method has been adopted widely for interest calculation in the European Union Member States. Based on the annual interest rate, this method causes the interest rate to be distributed equally among all days in a year, and multiplied by the number of days to which a calculation applies. Depending on the jurisdiction, the annual statutory interest rate may be determined either implicitly or explicitly. Differences in national legislation can also be observed in terms of interest calculation in the case of leap years. One calculation method requires the use of standard (equal) years—usually comprising 365 days. Other countries calculate interest on the basis of the actual number of days in a year; in other words, they make a distinction between leap years and common years.

In line with commonly accepted rules, the payment of a sum expressed in a foreign currency may be rendered in a country's domestic currency. This applies both to the principal sum and interest thereon. Numerous examples exist of national regulations that provide for the requirement of currency conversion for the purpose of conducting enforcement proceedings, with the exception of cases in which it is explicitly stated in the enforcement title that a specific amount shall be paid exclusively in a foreign currency.

What is more, regulations governing limitations of the amount of interest vary to a great extent among European countries, as shown by the examples regarding maximum interest, compound interest and the *ne ultra alterum tantum* rule.

Due to the complexity of the legal solutions on the determination and calculation of interest adopted in European jurisdictions, as well as significant differences among them, knowledge of the relevant national rules is of high relevance from the perspective of cross-border enforcement. Specific regulations and practicalities regarding methods of interest calculation are frequently unclear from enforcement titles that originate in particular European countries. The same applies to certificates provided for under Brussels I bis Regulation.

In this context, the contribution of the research undertaken as part of the EU-En4s project to improving the understanding of the legal and practical aspects of the payment of interest adjudicated in judgments issued in European Union Member States is crucial. The Interest Calculator software being developed by the project partners—the aim of which is to provide a simple user interface for interest calculation based on principal, date, and state information—is particularly worthy of attention.

References

Ascarelli T (1959) Obbligazioni pecuniarie. Art. 1277–1284. In: Scialoja A, Branca G (eds) Commentario del Codice civile. Libro IV – Delle obbligazioni. Zanichelli, Bologna, Società Editrice del Foro Italiano, Roma

Batini A, Traverso S (2021) Enforcement of Judgments and Arbitral Awards in Italy: Overview, https://uk.practicallaw.thomsonreuters.com/1-619-4633?transitionType=Default&contextData=(sc.Default)&firstPage=true

Bolzanas D, Visinskis V, Visinskyte D (2020) National Report for Lithuania. Project EU-En4s — JUST-AG-2018/JUST-JCOO-AG-2018

Bores Lazo J, Serrano Ron I (2020) National Report for Spain. Project EU-En4s — JUST-AG-2018/JUST-JCOO-AG-2018

Borysiak W (2021) Commentary on art. 481 Civil Code. In: Osajda K (ed) Kodeks cywilny, Komentarz. Beck Online Komentarze

Caramelo Gomes J, Marques Cebola C, Lucas E (2020) National Report for Portugal. Project EU-En4s — JUST-AG-2018/JUST-JCOO-AG-2018

Devos L, Nijns J (2021) Enforcement of Judgments and Arbitral Awards in Belgium: Overview, https://uk.practicallaw.thomsonreuters.com/2-619-4133?navId=2A59C77262C9653D1DB47A62B4168A8C&comp=pluk&transitionType=Default&contextData=%28sc.Default%29

Dybowski T, Pyrzyńska A (2019) Świadczenie. In: Osajda K (ed), System prawa prywatnego, vol. 5: Prawo zobowiązań – część ogólna. Wydawnictwo C.H. Beck, Warszawa

European e-Justice: Interest Rates, https://e-justice.europa.eu/404/EN/interest_rates?BELGIUM&member=1

European e-Justice: Interest Rates: Estonia, https://e-justice.europa.eu/404/EN/interest_rates?ESTONIA&member=1

Gil I (2021) Commentary on art. 798 Code of Civil Procedure. In: Marszałkowska-Krześ E (ed) Kodeks postępowania cywilnego, Komentarz. Beck Online Komentarze

Gołaczyński J, Rodziewicz P, Kaczorowska M, Dymitruk M (2020), National Report for Poland, Project EU-En4s — JUST-AG-2018/JUST-JCOO-AG-2018

González Nicolás R, Verkerk R, Hoek G, et al (2021) Enforcement of Judgments and Arbitral Awards in The Netherlands: Overview, https://uk.practicallaw.thomsonreuters.com/w-024-3617?navId=88D2DDEB9028E69A7AAE6D3A5F60CCF2&comp=pluk&transitionType=Default&contextData=%28sc.Default%29
Gotanda J Y (2004) Compound Interest in International Disputes. Oxford University Comparative Law Forum, https://ouclf.law.ox.ac.uk/compound-interest-in-international-disputes/
Goździaszek Ł (2015) Commentary on art. 53 Brussels I Recast Regulation. In: Gołaczyński J (ed) Jurysdykcja, uznawanie orzeczeń sądowych oraz ich wykonywanie w sprawach cywilnych i handlowych. Rozporządzenie Parlamentu Europejskiego i Rady (UE) Nr 1215/2012, Komentarz. Wydawnictwo C.H. Beck, Warszawa
Interest rate calculator questionnaire for Bulgaria, Project EU-En4s – JUST-AG-2018/JUST-JCOO-AG-2018
Interest rate calculator questionnaire for Croatia, Project EU-En4s – JUST-AG-2018/JUST-JCOO-AG-2018
Interest rate calculator questionnaire for Cyprus, Project EU-En4s – JUST-AG-2018/JUST-JCOO-AG-2018
Interest rate calculator questionnaire for Czech Republic, Project EU-En4s – JUST-AG-2018/JUST-JCOO-AG-2018
Interest rate calculator questionnaire for Germany, Project EU-En4s – JUST-AG-2018/JUST-JCOO-AG-2018
Interest rate calculator questionnaire for Lithuania, Project EU-En4s – JUST-AG-2018/JUST-JCOO-AG-2018
Interest rate calculator questionnaire for Poland, Project EU-En4s – JUST-AG-2018/JUST-JCOO-AG-2018
Interest rate calculator questionnaire for Portugal, Project EU-En4s – JUST-AG-2018/JUST-JCOO-AG-2018
Interest rate calculator questionnaire for the Netherlands, Project EU-En4s – JUST-AG-2018/JUST-JCOO-AG-2018
Kaczorowska M, Voinich A, Previatello M (2022) National Report for Italy. Project EU-En4s — JUST-AG-2018/JUST-JCOO-AG-2018
Karasek I (2001) Świadczenia wyrażone w walutach obcych w egzekucji, układzie i upadłości. Transformacje Prawa Prywatnego 1:97–106
Kramer X (2016) Commentary on art. 58. In: Magnus U, Mankowski P (eds) Brussels Ibis Regulation: Commentary. Verlag Dr. Otto Schmidt, Köln
Lemkowski M (2007) Odsetki cywilnoprawne. Wolters Kluwer Polska, Warszawa
Machnikowski P (2021) Commentary on art. 358 Civil Code. In: Gniewek E (ed) Kodeks cywilny, Komentarz. Wydawnictwo C.H. Beck, Warszawa
Martens S (2018) Performance. In: Jansen N, Zimmermann R (eds) Commentaries on European contract law. Oxford University Press, Oxford
Merc I (2021) Recovery of the interest in enforcement procedure in the Republic of Slovenia. Lexonomica 13(1):69–90
Modrzejewski J, Potasz A (2021) Enforcement of Judgments and Arbitral Awards in Poland: Overview, https://uk.practicallaw.thomsonreuters.com/0-619-3441?transitionType=Default&contextData=(sc.Default)&firstPage=true
Mojak J (2018) Ekspertyza prawna w sprawie odsetek od umownych zobowiązań pieniężnych w wybranych systemach prawnych. Kancelaria Senatu, Warszawa
Možina D (2010) Ne ultra alterum tantum in evropsko pravo. Podjetje in Delo 3–4:497–509
Možina D, Vlahek A (2019) Contract law in Slovenia. Kluwer Law International, Alphen aan den Rijn
Poisson E, Stoyanov M, Mautray Q et al (2021) Enforcement of Judgments and Arbitral Awards in France: Overview, https://uk.practicallaw.thomsonreuters.com/w-023-4113?navId=CD1CB6A78EA68149F9D61915576E4417&comp=pluk&transitionType=Default&contextData=%28sc.Default%29

Prodinger L, Nunner-Krautgasser B (2020) National Report for Austria. Project EU-En4s — JUST-AG-2018/JUST-JCOO-AG-2018

Reifner U, Clerc-Renaud S, Knobloch M (2010) Study on Interest Rate Restrictions in the EU: Final Report, Project No. ETD/2009/IM/H3/87, https://www.cnb.cz/export/sites/cnb/en/supervision-financial-market/.galleries/legislation/cnb_opinions/download/urokove_sazby_studie.pdf

Rijavec V, Kennet W, Keresteš T et al (eds) (2018) Remedies Concerning Enforcement of Foreign Judgements: Brussels I Recast. Wolters Kluwer International

Rijavec V, Baghrizabehi D, Drnovšek K et al (2020) National Report for Slovenia. Project EU-En4s — JUST-AG-2018/JUST-JCOO-AG-2018

Rudkowska-Ząbczyk E (2021) Commentary on art. 319 Code of Civil Procedure. In: Marszałkowska-Krześ E (ed) Kodeks postępowania cywilnego, Komentarz. Beck Online Komentarze

Rys M (2020) National Report for Belgium. Project EU-En4s — JUST-AG-2018/JUST-JCOO-AG-2018

Szanciło T (2020) Commentary on art. 481 of the Civil Code. In: Załucki M (ed) Kodeks cywilny, Komentarz. Wydawnictwo C.H. Beck, Warszawa

Your Europe: Interest Calculator, https://europa.eu/youreurope/business/finance-funding/making-receiving-payments/late-payment/index_en.htm

Part III
Effects of Judgments

Effects of Judgments in Cross-Border Perspective

Wendy Kennett

Abstract This chapter is concerned with the enforceability effects of judgments within the scope of the Brussels I bis Regulation. It examines how far enforcement action is authorised, or may be delayed or stayed, following the issue of a judgment at first instance: a judgment that may later be revised or quashed. Although the starting point is that a judgment should be final before it can be enforced, in practice Member States provide for the provisional enforceability of judgments under certain circumstances even before they become final. This chapter first provides a comparative overview of the provisional enforceability of judgments under the national laws of selected Member States. In particular, it looks at the role of the certificate of enforceability required by national laws before enforcement can take place, and it explores how far the certificate is relevant to the material enforceability of the judgment. The paper then explores some of the problems that arise in cross-border cases with respect to the certificate of enforceability provided for by Art. 53 of Brussels I bis. There is a growing case law concerning the role and effects of the certificate. National expectations as to the enforceability effects of judgments and the functions of a certificate of enforceability may help to explain the interpretative difficulties that have arisen.

1 Introduction

This chapter is concerned with the enforceability effects of judgments within the scope of Brussels I bis Regulation.[1] It first provides a comparative overview the national laws of selected Member States, and then explores the problems that may

[1]Regulation (EU) No. 1215/2012 of the European Parliament and of the Council of 12 December 2012 on jurisdiction and the recognition and enforcement of judgments in civil and commercial matters, OJ L 351, 20.12.2012.

W. Kennett (✉)
Cardiff University, Cardiff, UK
e-mail: kennettw@cardiff.ac.uk

V. Rijavec et al. (eds.), *Diversity of Enforcement Titles in the EU*, Ius Gentium: Comparative Perspectives on Law and Justice 111,
https://doi.org/10.1007/978-3-031-47108-7_7

arise in cross-border cases. In practice, an important aspect of cross-border enforcement is the question whether the judgment in question is entitled to recognition, or whether one of the defences to recognition may be asserted. This question has been analysed in many publications. The focus of the present paper is the extent to which enforcement action itself is authorised, or may be delayed or stayed, following the issue of a judgment at first instance. It requires consideration of a series of issues:

1. Is a first instance judgment provisionally enforceable before it becomes final? And if so, are there ways of challenging a decision that the judgment is enforceable?
2. What procedures exist under Member State laws for verifying the enforceability of domestic judgments and dealing with changes in circumstances that affect whether and how a judgment can be enforced and the identity of the parties to the enforcement proceedings?
3. What are the implications of any differences in national laws for cross-border enforcement under Brussels I bis Regulation?

2 Provisional Enforceability

Legal systems differ in the way that they structure their approach to the effects of judgments[2] and the different effects that they recognise at different points in proceedings. As far as the 'enforceability effect' of judgments is concerned, an appropriate starting point is to say that a judgment is enforceable when it becomes final, and any period allowed for voluntary compliance (typically payment) has passed. Enforceability effects may then be brought forward, by allowing (provisional) enforcement immediately, before the judgment becomes final, or they may be deferred, by granting a further grace period for compliance. In some countries, first instance judgments are immediately enforceable as of right, leading to full satisfaction of the judgment creditor. It is assumed that appeals will not often be successful and that a first instance decision is reasonably secure. [3] In other countries, provisional enforcement is available, but the judgment creditor must make a separate application for it and may have to provide security. In both these cases the further question arises as to when enforcement may be suspended in the case of an appeal on the merits. In a third group of countries, enforcement—in the sense of full satisfaction of the creditor—is not available in most cases. Steps may nevertheless be taken to secure the assets of the judgment debtor pending full execution.

---

[2]Much of what is said in this article is also applicable to other enforcement titles, but reference is here restricted to judgments for ease of discussion. The commonest case is a money judgment, and so the parties are referred to as creditor and debtor.

[3]For this reason, it will not normally be necessary for the judgment creditor to provide security, although the court may order otherwise in appropriate cases.

Although these categories are distinct in principle, in practice there is a spectrum of approaches that blur the distinctions. Thus, jurisdictions that deny the immediate enforceability of judgments as a general principle have exceptions to that principle that may be more or less extensive. Moreover, the difference between judgments being immediately enforceable as of right and judgments being enforceable in appropriate cases on an individual application is also limited if provisional enforcement is permitted on a regular basis and is customarily sought by claimants during the proceedings on the merits. Distinctions may nevertheless exist in terms of cost, complexity of procedure and a possible requirement to provide security. The following paragraphs have categorised jurisdictions based on what appears to be the 'general' position in each jurisdiction, while recognising that these categorisations may deserve adjustment in the light of practice.

2.1 *First Instance Judgment Immediately Enforceable as of Right*

France provides an example of the first approach to enforceability. According to Article 501 CPC, a judgment is enforceable once it becomes final ('passe en force de chose jugée') subject to two exceptions: on the one hand enforcement may be deferred if a 'délai de grâce' has been granted; and on the other hand, enforcement may be brought forward if the judgment[4] is provisionally enforceable. But in fact, following recent reforms to the law, first instance decisions are immediately (provisionally) enforceable as of right, unless otherwise provided by law or in the decision itself (Article 514 CPC).[5] Thus, in an individual case, a judge may conclude that provisional enforcement is 'incompatible with the nature of the case' (Article 514-1 CPC). Under Article 514 CPC is not necessary for the judgment creditor to provide any security to protect the position of the judgment debtor: a review of the desirability of provisional enforceability only arises if an appeal is lodged or an application is made to set aside the judgment ('opposition'). If an appeal is lodged, the first president of the appeal court can hear an application to stop provisional enforcement if there is a serious argument for annulling or revising the decision and enforcement risks causing 'manifestly excessive' consequences. (Article 514-3 CPC). In this situation, rejection of the application to stop provisional enforcement may be made subject to the provision of security (Article 414-5 CPC).

A similar approach, providing for the provisional enforceability of first instance judgments, can be found in Belgium. Article 1397 CJ states that (except where an exception is provided for by the law or a judicial decision) 'jugements définitifs' are provisionally enforceable—irrespective of any appeal and without the need to

---

[4] Décret n° 2019-1333 du 11 décembre 2019 réformant la procédure civile (2019), Article 3.

[5] Article 514 CPC: 'Les décisions de première instance sont de droit exécutoires à titre provisoire à moins que la loi ou la décision rendue n'en dispose autrement.'

provide security unless the court so orders.[6] Subject to any exceptions provided for by the law or a judicial decision, however, an appeal or application to set aside a judgment will suspend enforcement in the case of a default judgment.

In some jurisdictions where the general principle is that first instance judgments are not provisionally enforceable as of right, certain types of judgment are nevertheless identified as being provisionally enforceable—for example, awards of maintenance,[7] judgments in cases in which the defendant admits the claim,[8] default judgments,[9] decisions awarding payment to employees under labour law regulations.[10]

2.2 *Decision on Provisional Enforceability in the Individual Case*

As noted above, the second category of cases blends into the first, in so far as provisional enforcement is regularly ordered by courts. Differences will nevertheless exist as to the circumstances justifying provisional enforcement and any requirement of security. This can be illustrated by a few examples.

In the Netherlands, Article 233 Rv provides that a first instance judgment may be declared provisionally enforceable (unless the law or the nature of the case dictates otherwise). A provisional declaration of enforceability may concern the entire judgment or part of it, and the court may make the declaration subject to the provision of security. In fact, although the court may order *ex officio* that the creditor must provide security, this only occurs if one of the parties requests it. Article 350 Rv then deals with the position in the case of an ordinary appeal. The default position is that if provisional enforcement has not been ordered, enforcement is suspended by the appeal. The judgment creditor may nevertheless seek provisional enforcement (Article 234 Rv), and where provisional enforcement has already been ordered, the judgment debtor may apply for enforcement to be suspended (Article 351 Rv).

---

[6]See National Report for Belgium, para 152 as to this policy decision to prevent the abusive use of appeals procedures.

[75] E.g., Poland, Article 333(1) KPC (maintenance payments that became due prior to bringing the action and due for a period of no longer than 3 months); Czech Republic § 162(1) OSR; Lithuania, Article 282(2)(1) CPK.

[8]E.g., Poland, Article 333(1) KPC.

[9]E.g., Poland, Article 333(1) KPC; Sweden, chapter 3, section 5(2) UB. In fact, chapter 3 sections 5–9 UB provide for a range of other situations in which provisional enforcement is possible, and in principle this extends to other money judgments with certain provisos.

[10]E.g., Poland, Article 4772(1) KPC (cases concerning matters regulated by labour law when the judgment awards a sum of money to an employee which does not exceed a full 1 month's salary of that employee); Czech Republic, § 162(1) OSR (remuneration for the 3 months prior to the delivery of the judgment); Lithuania, Article 282(2)(2) CPK (award of work pay—the parts of judgements not exceeding an average monthly wage).

Moreover, Article 235 Rv permits a cross-appeal for security in cases where provisional enforcement of a judgment has been permitted without security and then an appeal has been lodged against that judgment.

Provisional enforcement is also considered in the individual case in Germany. Arguments on provisional enforcement and provision of security should be made during the main proceedings and will then be addressed by the judge dealing with the merits. Provisional enforcement is typically ordered against provision of security. The decision on provisional enforcement may be the subject of an appeal: §§ 708 et seq. ZPO.

Provisional enforcement is not the general rule in Poland, the Czech Republic or Lithuania but is granted *ex officio* by the court in some cases where it is authorized by statute[11] and may be ordered in individual cases where a delay would prevent or significantly hamper the enforcement of the judgment or put the claimant at the risk of incurring damage.[12] Swedish law provides more generally that provisional enforcement may be ordered 'if there is a reason for doing so'.[13]

Spain permits provisional enforcement after an appeal is lodged *except* in the case of judgments that are specifically excluded (notably judgments relating to family matters, those that declare the expiration or annulment of intellectual property rights, and those that require a declaration of will).[14] The judgment debtor can challenge provisional enforcement, but in the case of monetary judgments they cannot lodge a general opposition to enforcement. They can only oppose specific methods of enforcement and offer alternatives.

In Portugal, a distinction is drawn in the Code of Civil Procedure between appeals that have a merely devolutive effect and those that have a suspensive effect. The default position is for appeals to have a devolutive effect, with the result that provisional enforcement is possible.[15] Appeals have suspensive effect where a legal provision so provides. This includes cases concerned with the status of persons, and those concerned with the ownership or possession of a dwelling house.[16] Moreover, in addition to the cases specifically provided for by law, an appellant may request that the appeal have a suspensive effect if enforcement will cause them considerable damage.[17]

---

[11] See above at n. 6–9.

[12] Poland, Article 333 § 3 KPC; Czech Republic § 162(2) OSR (the party would be in danger of suffering damage that is significant or difficult to compensate). A more extensive list of situations is provided for Lithuania, Article 283(1) CPK.

[13] Chapter 17, section 14 RB, which also provides for the immediate enforceability of decisions made during the proceedings that cannot be appealed against separately, and lists other immediately enforceable decisions concerning procedural matters, detention of persons and protective measures.

[14] Article 524 ff LEC.

[15] Article 647 CPC and see also Article 704 CPC.

[16] Article 647(3) CPC.

[17] Article 647(4) CPC.

In some jurisdictions, provisional enforcement may be conditional on the judgment creditor providing appropriate security,[18] but alternatively in the situations where provisional enforcement is permitted the judgment debtor who lodges an appeal may be required to provide security in order to obtain a stay of enforcement.[19] The judgment creditor who seeks enforcement takes the risk that the judgment may be overturned on appeal. In addition to the restitution of payment made, compensation may be payable to the judgment debtor if provisional enforcement causes them any additional loss or damage.[20]

2.3 Provisional Enforcement Limited to Security Measures

In other jurisdictions, provisional enforcement—in the sense of full satisfaction of the judgment creditor ('Exekution zur Befriedigung')—is not ordinarily permitted. Nevertheless, certain decisions may be immediately enforceable, and it may be possible to apply for protective measures pending the time when the judgment becomes final.[21]

In Austria, the general position is that an appeal against a judgment on the merits ('Berufung', ordentliche Revision) has suspensive effect, and so no Exekution zur Befriedigung is available.[22] Certain forms of appeal do not, however, have suspensive effects ('auβerordentliche Revision'). [23] And protective seizure to secure a debt

[18]Sweden, chapter 17 section 14 RB. See also Poland, Article 334 § 1 KPC but note that Article 335 § 1 KPC provides that a judgment may not be rendered provisionally enforceable, even where security is deposited, if the enforcement of the judgment could result in the defendant incurring irrecoverable damage.

[19]E.g., Spain, Articles 528–530 LEC (National Report for Spain, para 6.1.2.1.). In Portugal, the provision of security may be required from a judgment debtor under Article 647(4) CPC as a condition for suspending enforcement. However, in the case of provisional enforcement, seized property may be sold but without the resulting payment being transferred to the judgment creditor. If the creditor wants to receive it, they have to provide a guarantee: Article 704(3) CPC.

[20]See National Reports at 6.1.2. and e.g., Belgium, Article 1398 CJ; Poland, Article 338 KPC; Netherlands, Hoge Raad 19.5.2000, Nederlandse Jurisprudentie 2000, 603; Hoge Raad 1.4.2016, Nederlandse Jurisprudentie 2016, 189; Sweden, chapter 3, section 22 UB. Portugal, Article 858 CPC requires proof of intention and is not of great utility in practice.

[21]Cf the intermediate position in Portugal under Article 647(4) CPC as stated in text accompanying n. 16.

[22]The National Report for Austria explains the formal and material requirements for enforceability, para 6.2. The formal requirements are checked by the court that gave judgment on the merits before it issues a confirmation of enforceability (Vollstreckbarkeitsbestätigung). The material requirements are checked by the enforcement court before it issues an enforcement order (Exekutionsbewilligung). See below at II (b).

[23]§ 505(4) ZPO.

('Exekution zur Sicherstellung') is generally available.[24] As well as preventing a dissipation of assets, protective seizure preserves rank among creditors.

A similar approach has been adopted in Slovenia.[25] According to Article 19 ZIZ, a court decision is enforceable if it has become final and if the deadline for voluntary fulfilment of the debtor's obligation has expired.[26] Enforcement is also allowed by the court on the basis of a court decision that has not yet become final, if the law stipulates that the appeal does not suspend its enforcement. Otherwise, only protective seizure is possible pending the time when the decision becomes final.[27]

3 Obtaining Formal Certification of Enforceability

Before a judgment can be enforced, even if it is immediately enforceable in principle, formal confirmation of enforceability must normally be obtained.[28] This typically take the form of a seal or endorsement on the face of the judgment itself, although it may be contained in a separate document.

The formal confirmation is provided by the court that issued the decision. It is regulated in national laws with varying degrees of formality and may involve administrative or judicial personnel. By way of example, a comparison may be drawn between the procedures in Germany, Austria and France.

3.1 Germany

Germany adopts a particularly formal approach to the issue of a certificate of enforceability. Enforcement takes place on the basis of an enforceable execution copy of the judgment ('vollstreckbare Ausfertigung').[29] Both the formal and substantive requirements for enforcement are checked in one distinct, formal civil procedure ('Klauselerteilungsverfahren') with its own competent authority and specific remedies (§§ 724 ff ZPO). In the most straightforward cases the clerk of the court office for the court that issued the enforcement title ('Prozessgericht') can issue the certificate if a judgment is immediately enforceable ('einfache Klausel').[30] But in cases where there are further issues to be considered—as in cases of

[24] §§ 370–377 EO.

[25] National Report at 6.1.1. For the historical close connections between Austrian and Slovenian civil enforcement law see Kennett (2021), pp. 489–520.

[26] Time starts to run on the day following the day on which the decision was served on the debtor.

[27] Rijavec (2003), pp. 210 et seq.

[28] There are exceptions to this principle, notably in the case of protective measures.

[29] § 724 ZPO.

[30] § 724(2) ZPO.

succession in title or assignment of rights, or where enforcement is subject to proof that a condition has been satisfied by the creditor (§§ 26–29 ZPO)—it is the Rechtspfleger[31] at the 'Prozessgericht' who is competent to issue the 'Vollstreckungsklausel' ('qualifizierte Klausel') and the debtor is entitled to be heard.[32] In more complex cases, where there is no official document to prove the creditor's right to bring enforcement proceedings and further proof-taking is necessary, § 731 ZPO provides for an action for the issue of a 'Vollstrekungsklausel'.

The approach adopted by German law is the consequence of its bifurcated system of enforcement. Depending on the enforcement measure sought, application may be made to the competent enforcement court ('Vollstreckungsgericht'[33]) or to the 'Gerichtsvollzieher'—a figure based historically on the French 'huissier de justice' but whose regulation and functions have developed in ways that are quite distinct from those of their French counterpart.[34] The 'Gerichtsvollzieher' has a lower level of education and more limited competences, but nevertheless plays an important role in procedures requiring personal contact with the debtor, such as service of enforcement documents, settlement negotiations and seizure of tangible movable property. To reflect expectations of the 'Gerichstvollzieher', the procedure for obtaining a Vollstreckungsklausel is intended to provide clarity on the parties to the enforcement procedure and the obligation owed by the debtor.

The fact that a formal procedure exists for the issue of a certificate of enforceability is reflected in the remedies available to both creditor and debtor.[35] Moreover, the importance of this procedure to ensure that the 'Gerichtsvollzieher' is in no doubt about how to act also helps to explain why German law has further procedures in the first instance court (rather than in the course of enforcement proceedings) to deal with changes in circumstances that arise after a 'Vollstreckungsklausel' has been obtained.[36]

The ZPO provides several different possibilities for challenging the issue of a 'Vollstreckungsklausel'.[37] But it is significant that any issues as to the material enforceability of the judgment, and the impact of any new facts arising after the close of the hearing in the original proceedings that was the last opportunity for objections

---

[31] A senior judicial administrator. For further details see Kennett (2021), pp. 489–520.

[32] §§ 26–30 ZPO. See also § 20 Nr. 12 RPflG. If enforcement is dependent on the provision of security by the creditor, this is not something that needs to be checked by the Rechtspfleger. Instead, the procedure in § 24 II ZPO applies. The provision of security will by checked by the enforcement agent later in accordance with § 751 II ZPO. There are other cases in which checking that a condition is satisfied are sufficiently straightforward that the procedure in § 26 does not need to apply—such as where performance of an obligation becomes due on a particular date.

[33] A section of the lowest level first instance court (Amtsgericht).

[34] See further Kennett (2021), pp. 521–564.

[35] Klage auf Erteilung einer Vollstreckungsklausel (§ 731 ZPO); Erinnerung (§ 573 ZPO); sofortige Beschwerde (§ 567 II ZPO; § 567 I Nr. 2 ZPO, § 11 I RPflG).

[36] §§ 323, 767 ZPO.

[37] For further discussion of means of recourse see Brox and Walker (2017), pp. 81 et seq. See also Wolf et al. (2018), p. 18.

to be asserted, must be raised in the 'Prozessgericht' by means of a 'Vollstreckungsgegenklage' under § 767 ZPO. This is therefore the way to proceed if the debtor argues that the claim has been paid, set off or remitted, that some payment arrangement has been made or that the identity of creditor or debtor has changed—for example as a result of an assignment.[38] Third party claims with respect to seized assets—for example an assertion of ownership of the asset—are also brought by way of an action on the merits, rather than a dispute in enforcement proceedings (§ 771 ZPO).

3.2 *Austria*

By contrast, in Austria, the requirements for enforceability are checked at two different procedural stages. Initial certification of enforceability ('Vollstreckbarkeitsbestätigung') by the court that issued the judgment is confined to checking the formal requirements for enforceability under § 7 EO.[39] These are:

- The enforcement title must have been properly served on the debtor[40]
- Time limits for appeals with suspensive effect must have expired[41]
- The time allowed for performance (which is usually 14 days from the judgment) must have expired[42]
- Where performance is due at a point in time later than the issue of the judgment, the due date must have passed[43]
- The enforcement title must not have expired due to the passage of time.

[38] § 767(2) limits the operation of this article to situations where the grounds of action arose after the close of the hearing in the original case. Note also that where the debtor has been ordered to make recurrent payments, § 323 permits them to make an application in the Prozessgericht for the order to be modified on the basis of a material change in factual or legal circumstances that has arisen after the hearing in the original proceedings.

[39] For discussion of these requirements, and in particular the requirement that performance must have become due (Fälligkeit), see especially Angst and Oberhammer (2015), para 7.

[40] § 416 ZPO.

[41] §§ 464 (1), 466, 505 (2)–(4) ZPO.

[42] § 409(1) ZPO in conjunction with § 7(2) EO.

[43] § 7(2) EO. The question whether performance is due (Fälligkeit) is sometimes a matter of material enforceability—for example when the performance of the debtor depends on the fulfilment of a condition by the creditor and the satisfaction of that condition must be verified before enforcement can take place. But when the date for performance is given in (or can be calculated from) the original judgment, modern jurisprudence considers the question of Fälligkeit to be evidenced by the Vollstreckbarkeitsbestätigung. Indeed, this approach is required by legislation in certain cases (§ 43 Abs 3 AußStrG). See further Angst and Oberhammer (2015), EO § 7; Burgstaller and Deixler-Hübner (2019), § 7 EO Rn 151.

According to § 16(1) no. 2 RpflG, a Rechtspfleger is usually responsible for issuing the certificate of enforceability ('Vollstreckbarkeitsbestätigung').[44] A 'Vollstreckbarkeitsbestätigung' issued unlawfully or incorrectly shall, either ex officio or at the request of one of the parties, be revoked by decision ('Aufhebungsbeschluss').[45] This decision must be served on all parties and, in contrast to the certificate of enforceability itself, is open to appeal.[46]

For enforcement to take place, an application must then be made to the competent enforcement court which likely to be the court for the domicile of the debtor.[47] That court, again acting through a 'Rechtspfleger', relies on the 'Vollstreckbarkeitsbestätigung' as proof that the formal requirements for enforcement are satisfied. But in accordance with § 7(1) EO[48] it must check that the material requirements for enforcement are met before issuing an enforcement order ('Exekutionsbewilligung') as the first stage in the enforcement process. In other words, the identity of the person entitled to enforcement, and the person against whom enforcement is to take place, must be certain as well as the object, nature, scope and time of the performance owed.

The procedure for checking that the material requirements for enforcement are satisfied is *ex parte* and based on the documents presented by the creditor. Austrian law allows only limited opportunities to dispute the issue of the 'Exekutionsbewilligung', but further procedures exist that enable the debtor or a third party to challenge enforcement. Objections to the 'Exekutionsbewilligung' can be made via an 'Impugnationsklage' (§ 36 EO), which enables the debtor to assert that enforcement should not have been authorized—for example, because performance has not yet become due, or because there is a legal objection to using the selected method of enforcement, or because the identity of the debtor or creditor has changed. Going beyond this, if new facts have arisen after the issue of the enforcement title[49] that impact the continued existence of the creditor's claim (*nova producta*), those facts may be raised in an 'Oppositionsklage' (§ 35 EO) in the court where the 'Exekutionsbewilligung' was issued.[50] Such new facts may include payment of the judgment debt, or an agreement between debtor and creditor on a payment arrangement.[51] If a third-party claims rights in a seized asset, the

[44] See further Neumayr and Nunner-Krautgasser (2018), p. 75.

[45] § 7(3) EO.

[46] § 517(1) Z 6 ZPO.

[47] See §§ 4–6 EO for alternatives.

[48] In conjunction with § 36 (1) Z 1 EO.

[49] Or in the case of a judgment, after the point in time at which those facts could be raised in the original proceedings.

[50] In the case of facts that arose before the issue of the enforcement title but were not discoverable or provable in time to be taken into account (nova reperta), a Wiederaufnahmsklage (§ 530 ZPO) exists as a remedy that permits the reopening of the original proceedings. See § 35(2) for the jurisdictional rules in the case of employment or maintenance cases.

[51] Angst and Oberhammer (2015), § 35 EO Rn 3, pp. 12–14.

implications of this for enforcement may also be resolved in proceedings in the enforcement court (§ 37 EO).[52]

3.3 France

The procedures in Austria and Germany for issuing a certificate of enforceability or order for enforcement may be compared with the French system, where similar concerns for about the immediate enforceability of the enforcement title, service on the judgment debtor, identification of the parties to the enforcement proceedings and the grant of time to pay also apply, but responsibility for undertaking or checking these factors is allocated differently. An enforcement title must be endorsed as immediately enforceable—through the application of the 'formule exécutoire'—before enforcement can take place. A 'greffier' (court registrar) is responsible for checking whether a judgment is enforceable. But service of the judgment is a matter for the 'huissier de justice' on the instructions of the creditor.[53] And once a creditor, in possession of an enforcement title endorsed with the 'formule exécutoire', employs a 'huissier de justice' to enforce that title, the *huissier* must first give the debtor time to pay by issuing a 'commandement de payer'. Issues arising in the process of enforcement will typically be referred the 'juge d'exécution' (JEX).

> The JEX has sole competence to determine issues relating to enforcement titles and disputes that arise in the course of forced execution, even if they relate to substantive issues unless they fall outside the competence of courts of the 'ordre judiciaire' (Article L213-6 Code de l'organisation judiciaire)

The competence of JEX extends to 'the reality of the executory character of the title, or its correct notification, the possibility that it no longer produces effects, or its nullity or to judge its regularity if the enforcement title is one other than a judgment'.[54] They can rule on disputes relating to the debt owed—including the amount and whether it is due as well as questions of the interest payable. They can also determine questions relating to the identity of the debtor or creditor.[55]

Nevertheless, a 'huissier de justice' may also sometimes play a significant role in clarifying substantive issues. Thus, in the case of the death of a debtor, delay on the part of an heir in accepting the inheritance can be combatted through the

---

[52] Any assertion of rights going beyond the implications for enforcement requires a separate action on the merits. For the nature of the recourse provided by § 37 EO (Exszindierungsklage) see Ibid § 37 EO Rn 51.

[53] Article 675 of the Code de procédure civile states that judgments are notified by way of signification unless the law provides otherwise. Signification is formal service by a huissier de justice (from 1 July 2022, Commissaire de justice).

[54] Fricero (2021), p. 68. The JEX cannot modify a judgment or stay its enforcement, but they can grant a 'delai de grâce'.

[55] Ibid.

employment of a 'huissier' to serve on the heir a requirement to opt whether to accept the inheritance or not (with the presumption that no response indicates acceptance of the inheritance and therefore the debts of the deceased).

4 Application to Brussels I bis Regulation

It is apparent from the foregoing that challenges to the enforceability of an enforcement title may arise in various different ways and at different points in proceedings. It may be that service of the judgment in question has not taken place. It may be that a judgment is not enforceable because the time allowed for lodging an appeal has not yet expired. It may be that the competent authority has not made a payment request to the debtor prior to commencing enforcement proceedings; or it may be necessary to prove that a particular condition has been satisfied before the judgment is enforceable. It may be that a question arises as to right of the alleged creditor to act, or as to the person against whom enforcement should take place—and depending on the relevant national procedure and the time at which the issue arises, this may affect the enforcement title and the certificate of enforceability. The procedure for challenging enforceability will therefore vary depending on the ground of challenge and the legal system in question.

The certificate of enforceability issued for the purpose of enforcement under Brussels I bis Regulation (henceforth 'Article 53 certificate') is a relatively detailed document that provides information about the court in the state of origin, the identities of debtor and creditor, and details of the judgment including questions of service, enforceability, subject matter, principal amount payable and payment arrangements, currency, joint or several liability, costs and interest. Debates about the procedure for issue of the Article 53 certificate and possible challenges have to be seen against the background of the varying national approaches to the enforceability of a judgment and the certification of enforceability.

4.1 A Tendency to Assimilate the Article 53 Certificate to National Certificates of Enforceability

National courts have tended to see the certificate of enforceability issued under Regulation 44/2001 and the Article 53 certificate through the lens of their own procedures for certification of enforceability. Thus, the Austrian OGH has stated that the certificate issued under Article 54 of Regulation 44/2001 is 'nothing other than an extended form of the 'Vollstreckbarkeitsbestätigung' that is already familiar under national law'.[56] It draws from that the conclusion that the national law

[56] OGH 3Ob152/15x (2015) at 3.1 et seq.

provisions relevant to challenging a 'Vollstreckbarkeitsbestätigung' are also applicable to a certificate of enforceability issued under Article 54 of Regulation 44/2001. A similar parallelism between national law and EU law can be found in Germany. Wolf and Volkshausen describe the certificate as 'a functional equivalent' of a 'vollstreckbare Ausfertigung' of a judgment.[57] § 1110 ZPO provides that the courts or notaries competent to issue an enforceable copy of an enforcement title are also competent to issue the certificate of enforceability under Articles 53 and 60 of Brussels I bis Regulation. § 1111(1) ZPO provides for the possibility of a hearing of the debtor in the situations identified in §§ 726–729 ZPO in the context of the issue of a 'Vollstreckungsklausel'. And § 1111(2) ZPO states that the provisions concerning challenges to a decision to issue a 'Vollstreckungsklausel' apply by analogy to the decision to issue an Article 53 certificate.[58]

The issue of Article 53 certificate in Germany or Austria may thus be in the hands of the clerk of the court or the 'Rechtspfleger'. In France, issue of the certificate is regulated by the French Code de Procedure Article 509. According to Article 509-1, applications for certification of French enforcement titles, for their recognition and enforcement abroad under Brussels I bis Regulation should be made to the 'directeur de greffe' for the court that gave judgment or approved a settlement of the dispute. Under Article 509-7 a refusal to issue the certificate may be referred to the President of the 'tribunal judiciaire' who gives a final decision on the application.[59, 60]

4.2 Preliminary References Concerning the Interpretation of Article 53

4.2.1 Admissibility of the Reference

Several decisions of the CJEU have recently addressed the nature of the procedure for issuing the Article 53 certificate. The nature of the procedure is significant because it determines whether an application for a preliminary ruling is admissible in the case. Under Article 267 TFEU a national court can only refer a question to the CJEU if there is a case pending before it and if it is called upon to give judgment in

[57] Wolf et al. (2018), pp. 14 et seq.

[58] For further comment see Schlosser and Hess (2021), Article 53; Wolf et al. (2018), pp. 16 et seq.

[59] The applicant and the authority that has refused to issue the certificate are given a hearing.

[60] Richard (2020), pp. 1, 149 and 154 notes that the judgment of the CJEU in Case C-300/14, Imtech Marine Belgium NV v. Radio Hellenic SA, 17.12.2015, ECLI:EU:C:2015:825 led to the reform of French law on EEOs so that the certification was given by a judge, not a greffier. But Article 509-1 still places the issue of an Article 53 certificate in hands of the greffier. In fact, in several jurisdictions, senior administrators have taken on certain functions formerly performed by judges. This is also true of greffiers, although to a lesser extent than their counterparts in Germany and Austria (Rechtspfleger) and Spain (Letrados de la Administración de Justicia). See further Kennett (2021).

proceedings intended to lead to a decision of a judicial nature.[61] The characterisation of the procedure for issuing a certificate had previously arisen in the context of European Enforcement Orders (EEOs). According to Article 5 of Regulation 805/2004:

> A judgment which has been certified as a European Enforcement Order in the Member State of origin shall be recognised and enforced in the other Member States without the need for a declaration of enforceability and without any possibility of opposing its recognition.

To be certified as an EEO, a judgment must meet certain criteria that are set out in the Regulation. The CJEU therefore concluded, in Case C-300/14, Imtech Marine Belgium NV v. Radio Hellenic SA,[62] that certification 'requires a judicial examination of the conditions laid down by Regulation No 805/2004'. It observed that

> [t]he legal qualifications of a judge are essential to the correct assessment – in a context of uncertainty as to the observance of the minimum requirements intended to safeguard the debtor's rights of defence and the right to a fair trial – of the remedies under national law. . . . Moreover, only a court or tribunal within the meaning of Article 267 TFEU is capable of ensuring, by means of a reference for a preliminary ruling to the Court of Justice, that the minimum requirements laid down by Regulation No 805/2004 are interpreted and applied uniformly throughout the European Union.

On the other hand, it considered that the formal act of issuing a certificate after certification of a judgment as an EEO was a matter that could be left to a registrar.

It will be apparent from the discussion at (II) above that Member States vary significantly in the procedure they adopt for the issue of an Article 53 certificate and the organ competent to issue the certificate. In straightforward cases, it may be that a registry official can issue the certificate. In more complex situations, decision-making competence may be required. The reasoning in the case law of the CJEU in cases concerned with certification of a judgment as an EEO can thus be extended—at least in some cases—to the Article 53 certificate.

Although this issue first arose in Case C-579/17, Gradbeništvo Korana,[63] more recent clear expression of the approach adopted by the CJEU can be found in Case C-347/18, Salvoni v. Fiermonte.[64] The CJEU stated that

> [T]he role of the certificate provided for in Article 53 of Regulation No 1215/2012 in the system established by that regulation warrants, where some of the information which must be provided in the certificate is not in the judgment whose enforcement is sought, or requires an interpretation of that judgment or is of a contentious nature, the exercise of judicial

[61] See Case C-511/14, Pebros Servizi Srl v. Aston Martin Lagonda Ltd, 16.06.2016, ECLI:EU:C:2016:448.

[62] Case C-300/14, Imtech Marine Belgium NV v. Radio Hellenic SA, 17.12.2015, ECLI:EU:C:2015:825.

[63] Case C-579/17, BUAK Bauarbeiter-Urlaubs- u. Abfertigungskasse v. Gradbeništvo Korana d.o.o., 28.02.2017, ECLI:EU:C:2019:162.

[64] Case C-347/18, Alessandro Salvoni v. Anna Maria Fiermonte, 4.9.2019, ECLI:EU:C:2019:661. The question raised in this case was whether the court asked to issue a certificate of enforceability could consider of its own motion whether the judgment at issue had been given in compliance with the rules of Brussels I bis Regulation relating to jurisdiction in consumer disputes.

functions by the court of origin. In such cases, that court forms part of the continuity of the previous judicial proceedings, ensuring the full effectiveness thereof, in so far as, in the absence of certification, a judgment may not freely be enforced within the European judicial area. Such a conclusion responds to the need to ensure rapid enforcement of court judgments while ensuring the legal certainty which is the basis of mutual trust in the administration of justice within the European Union.

But the court also stated that Article 53

does not provide, in any way, that it is for that court to examine the aspects of the dispute which fall outside the scope of that provision, such as questions of substance and jurisdiction which have already been dealt with in the judgment enforcement of which is sought. Moreover, it follows from the case-law of the Court that the delivery of that certificate is almost automatic . . .[65]

The implication of this approach is that the procedure for the issue of a certificate of enforceability is judicial in character if involves a decision on an issue that was not decided in the original proceedings—but is not judicial if all relevant issues were decided in the original proceedings.

4.2.2 The Function of the Article 53 Certificate

The function identified for the Article 53 certificate necessarily impacts on the interpretation of rules concerning its issue and effects. This function has, in fact, been addressed by the CJEU in Case C-579/17, Gradbeništvo Korana,[66] but only in an oblique way. At paragraph 37 of its judgment, the Court stated that the certificate 'forms the basis for implementation of the principle of direct enforcement of judgments delivered in the Member States'.[67] It refers in this context to para 44 of the Opinion of AG Bot in the case,[68] and the Advocate General elaborates on this idea in paragraph 45 by saying that the certificate 'was designed as a substitute for that judgment, without a translation of the certificate, or even of the judgment to be enforced, being required in all cases'. This confers a particularly important role on the certificate when combined with the fact that

[t]he system established by Regulation No 1215/2012 is based on the abolition of exequatur, which implies that no control is exercised by the competent court of the requested Member

[65] At para 38 of Case C-619/10, Trade Agency Ltd v. Seramico Investments Ltd, 6.9.2012, ECLI: EU:C:2012:531.

[66] Case C-579/17, BUAK Bauarbeiter-Urlaubs- u. Abfertigungskasse v. Gradbeništvo Korana d.o. o., 28.02.2017, ECLI:EU:C:2019:162.

[67] Cf. for the function of the certificate of enforceability under Regulation 44/2001, Case C 619/10, Trade Agency Ltd v. Seramico Investments Ltd, 6.9.2012, ECLI:EU:C:2012:531, para 41: 'the function ascribed to the certificate is specifically to facilitate, in the first stage of the procedure, the adoption of the declaration of enforceability of the judgment given in the Member State of origin, making its delivery almost automatic.'

[68] Opinion of AG Yvesa Bota in Case C-579/17, BUAK Bauarbeiter-Urlaubs- u. Abfertigungskasse v. Gradbeništvo Korana d.o.o., 28.02.2017, ECLI:EU:C:2019:162.

> State, since only the person against whom enforcement is brought can oppose the recognition or enforcement of the judgment affecting him.[69]

Several decisions of the CJEU have addressed questions concerning the enforceability of a judgment in the State of origin. These indicate that the Court interprets the requirement of enforceability as meaning formal enforceability. Thus, in Case C-267/97, Coursier,[70] a case decided under the 1968 Brussels Convention, the CJEU stated that the term 'enforceable' in Article 31 of the Convention 'refers solely to the enforceability, in formal terms, of foreign decisions and not to the circumstances in which such decisions may be executed in the State of origin'.

Issues of material enforceability or alterations in factual circumstances affecting the creditor's claim are thus matters for the enforcement State. This is emphasised in Case C-139/10, Prism Investments BV v. Jaap Anne van der Meer[71] in which the judgment debtor sought to resist cross border enforcement on the basis that it had already complied with the judgment at issue. According to the CJEU:

> [C]ompliance with a judicial decision does not in any way deprive that decision of its enforceable nature, or lead to its being given, at the time of its enforcement in another Member State, legal effects that it would not have in the Member State of origin. Recognition of the effects of such a judgment in the Member State in which enforcement is sought, which is precisely the subject of the enforcement procedure, concerns the specific characteristics of the judgment in question, without reference to the elements of fact and law in respect of compliance with the obligations arising from it. Such a ground may, by contrast, be brought before the court or tribunal responsible for enforcement in the Member State in which enforcement is sought.[72]

In the light of the fact that Brussels I bis Regulation removes the *exequatur* procedure, it cannot be assumed that judgments concerning the certificate of enforceability issued under Regulation 44/2001 can automatically be transposed to this new regime. In particular, the distinctive approach of German law to the emergence of new facts and circumstances following the close of the hearing in the original proceedings that was the last opportunity for objections to be asserted (§ 767 ZPO), and the place of the German *Gerichtsvollzieher* within the enforcement system, do not provide a smooth fit with the vision of enforcement proceedings espoused by the CJEU. In Case 220/84, AS-Autoteile Service GmbH v. Pierre

---

[69] Case C-579/17, BUAK Bauarbeiter-Urlaubs- u. Abfertigungskasse v. Gradbeništvo Korana d.o. o., 28.02.2017, ECLI:EU:C:2019:162, para 36. In fact, there are examples in several Member States of courts conducting a review of the application for enforcement to ensure, at least, that it falls within Brussels I bis Regulation. See Kennett (2018), pp. 273–299.

[70] Case C-267/97, Eric Coursier v. Fortis Bank and Martine Coursier, née Bellami, 29.04.1999, ECLI:EU:C:1999:213.

[71] Case C-139/10, Prism Investments BV v. Jaap Anne van der Meer, 13.10.2011, ECLI:EU: C:2011:653.

[72] At paras 39–40. See also para 37 'no provision of Regulation No 44/2001 permits the refusal or revocation of a declaration of enforceability of a judgment that has already been complied with because such a situation does not deprive that judgment of its enforceable nature, which is a characteristic specific to that judicial act.'

Malhé,[73] the CJEU has already characterised § 767 ZPO as a part of 'proceedings concerned with the enforcement of judgments' for the purposes of Article 16(5) of the Brussels Regulation 1968 (now Article 24(5) of Brussels I bis Regulation). But it is perhaps of interest that the Advocate General in that case, AG Lenz, was a German lawyer who did not think that the issue was sufficiently discussed in the proceedings to permit the Court to define exactly to what extent actions under § 767 ZPO fell within the exclusive jurisdiction of the enforcement State.

Should any modification in the approach of the CJEU to the certificate of enforceability be thought desirable, it must nevertheless be borne in mind that the new procedure is intended to further facilitate the free movement of judgments and so any change in interpretation or practice needs to reflect that objective.

4.2.3 Emerging Questions: In the State of Origin

In fact, a proposal for enhancing the information provided with the certificate has recently been made in a request for a preliminary ruling (C-135/18, Logistik XXL GmbH v. CMR Transport & Logistik)—although the request was later withdrawn.[74] The case concerned an application for an Article 53 certificate in respect of a judgment of the LG Berlin. The judgment had been declared provisionally enforceable, subject to the provision of security, but the judgment creditor had not provided the designated security. Under German law, this does not prevent the issue of a copy of the judgment with a 'Vollstreckungsklausel'. It simply means that enforcement is restricted to protective measures securing the debtor's assets until the required security is provided by the judgment creditor or the judgment becomes final.[75] § 726 ZPO regulates the issue of a 'vollstreckbare Ausfertigung' in cases where enforcement is conditional on the creditor proving certain facts.[76] But proof of provision of security is specifically excluded from the operation of this article. This not normally a matter for the court: compliance with a requirement of security is checked by the 'Gerichtsvollzieher' during the enforcement process. This nuanced approach to the question whether enforceability is subject to a condition does not fit easily into the regime established by Brussels I bis Regulation.[77]

[73] Case 220/84, AS-Autoteile Service GmbH v. Pierre Malhé, 4.07.1985, ECLI:EU:C:1985:302. The case was concerned with enforcement under the Brussels Convention 1968 and involved the interpretation of Article 16(5) (current Article 24(5)).

[74] The judgment debtor was successful in an appeal against the judgment sought to be enforced.

[75] §§ 720a, 724–726 ZPO.

[76] Requiring such proof to take the form of 'public records or documents, or records or documents that have been publicly certified.'

[77] Differences in national approaches to the provisional enforcement of judgments did not arise in quite the same way under Regulation 44/2001, since the court in the enforcement State could determine whether security should be provided (Article 46). The Regulation also limited enforcement to protective measures until such time as any disputes about recognition had been decided. A

Point 4.4. of the Article 53 certificate seeks confirmation that the judgment at issue is enforceable without any further conditions being met: it does not make any reference to the provision of security. There was therefore debate in Germany as to whether a judgment that had been declared provisionally enforceable subject to the provision of security could be issued with an Article 53 certificate—even though enforcement measures could be taken in the State of origin. In its decision to request a preliminary ruling, the BGH observed that:

'[t]he form in Annex I of the EuGVVO does not sufficiently take into account the differences between final and non-final judgments in terms of enforcement law. Therefore, there are doubts as to how, under national law, the special requirements provided for enforcement of judgments that have not yet become final are to be classified. This applies in particular if these regulations—as in German law—offer different enforcement options for judgments that are not yet final.'[78]

The BGH then referred to the earlier CJEU decision in Coursier.[79] If the Article 53 certificate was concerned with the question whether a judgment was enforceable 'in formal terms', the BGH considered that there were good arguments in favour of a conclusion that the judgment at issue was not enforceable in the absence of the provision of security. If, on the other hand, the focus was on the actual effects that the judgment had in the State of origin, confirmation should be given in point 4.4. of the certificate that the judgment was enforceable.

This produced a policy dilemma. On the one hand, the freedom of movement of decisions would be jeopardized if a judgment creditor was prevented from implementing security measures in the enforcement State even though security enforcement was easily possible in the country of origin. But on the other hand, the Article 53 certificate did not provide any opportunity to clarify the scope of enforceability and to explain that it was limited to protective measures. There was therefore a risk that the judgment might have greater effects in the State addressed than in the State of origin. The reference submitted by the BGH for a preliminary ruling suggested various possible ways of dealing with this problem, in particular suggesting that the way forward might be to include with the certificate information concerning the rules of the State of origin as the scope of enforceability of the judgment and the requirement of security.

---

somewhat different dynamic was therefore at work in enforcement proceedings under the earlier legislation.

[78]Federal Court of Justice of German, DE-3568, ECLI:DE:BGH:2018:250118BIXZB89.16.0, para 15.

[79]Case C-267/97, Eric Coursier v. Fortis Bank and Martine Coursier, née Bellami, 29.04.1999, ECLI:EU:C:1999:213.

4.2.4 Emerging Questions: In the Enforcement State

A recent reference picks up the question of the most appropriate forum for dealing with issues around provisional enforcement and the possible requirement of security. Case C-393/21, Lufthansa Technik AERO Alzey GmbH c Arik Air Ltd (Lithuania) concerned a European Enforcement Order (EEO) certificate under Regulation 805/2004, rather than an Article 53 certificate under Brussels I bis Regulation but it raised questions that were also relevant to an Article 53 certificate. A decision of the AG Hünfeld had been certified as an EEO, and enforcement was sought in Lithuania. The request for a preliminary ruling did not explain the enforcement steps taken in Lithuania, but the implication was that assets had been seized. The judgment debtor then applied to the LG Frankfurt am Main for withdrawal of the EEO certificate and termination of enforcement. It claimed that the certificate had been issued unlawfully because the relevant procedural documents had not been duly served on it, causing it to miss the time limit for lodging objections. It also requested a stay of enforcement pending a decision on its application. The response of the 'Landgericht' was that enforcement would only be stayed pending its decision if the judgment debtor provided security of € 2 million. This scenario placed the judgment debtor in a difficult situation: if assets had been seized in the State addressed, and security was also sought in the State of origin before the enforceability of the judgment was suspended, there was an excessive restriction of the debtor's assets.

The judgment debtor requested the bailiff in Lithuania to stay the enforcement proceedings. The bailiff refused, on the basis that the Lithuanian Code of Civil Procedure gave him a limited discretion to stay proceedings, and that discretion did not extend to the situation that had arisen (i.e. a claim for withdrawal of an EEO certificate before a court of the State of origin). The judgment debtor challenged this refusal in the Lithuanian courts, eventually leading to the request for a preliminary ruling by the Lithuanian Supreme Court.

The court posed several questions concerning the interpretation of Article 23(c) of Regulation 805/2004[80] and, in addition, it asked about the effect that should be given to any judgment in the State of origin concerning the suspension or cancellation of enforceability. Should such a judgment be recognised without any special procedure being required (by analogy with Article 36(1) Brussels I bis Regulation) or was a 'legal regime similar to that specified in Article 44(2)' of Brussels I bis Regulation applicable.[81] In the end the CJEU reformulated the question to focus only on

[80]This provision allows a competent court or authority in the Member State of enforcement to stay the enforcement proceedings 'under exceptional circumstances' when the debtor has applied for the withdrawal of an EEO certificate (under Article 10 of Regulation 805/2004). Clarification was needed because the reference to 'exceptional circumstances' indicated that something more than merely an application for withdrawal of the certificate was required but gave no guidance as to what kinds of factors could be taken into consideration.

[81]Article 44(2) states: 'The competent authority in the Member State addressed shall, on the application of the person against whom enforcement is sought, suspend the enforcement proceedings where the enforceability of the judgment is suspended in the Member State of origin'. It

Regulation 805/2004. Nevertheless the question posed highlights the fact that litigation around certificates of enforceability is taking on a life of its own, creating judgments which themselves may be entitled to recognition and enforcement under Brussels I bis Regulation, and, more generally, it draws attention to the need to ensure co-ordination between the security measures and further enforcement steps that can be taken in the State of origin and in the enforcement State, and to the implications of any order for the suspension or stay of proceedings.[82]

5 Conclusions

With the passage of time since Brussels I bis Regulation came into force, questions concerning the enforceability effect of judgments and the way this is evidenced by the Article 53 certificate have begun to emerge.

Member States take distinctively different approaches to the enforceability effect of judgments that remain subject to appeal. Such judgments may automatically be immediately enforceable—leading to full satisfaction of the judgment creditor—without the need for the provision of security. Alternatively, they may be declared enforceable in the individual case—with or without provision of security—or it may be that only protective measures to secure the judgment debtor's assets are available. These different approaches are not adequately considered in the design of the Article 53 certificate. From a policy perspective, the free movement of judgments is best furthered by rules that ensure a judgment produces the same effects in the State addressed as in the State of origin. The Article 53 certificate does not, however, provide any mechanism for clarifying the scope of the enforceability of a judgment if it is conditional on the provision of security.

As to the procedures for issuing the certificate and for dealing with disputes arising out of the issue of the certificate, these are also matters on which the laws of the Member States differ substantially. There is a natural tendency for national laws to treat the Article 53 certificate as comparable to the domestic certification of enforceability of a judgment, and to regulate it in an analogous way. But, as observed at (II) above, domestic regulation is shaped by the relationship between courts and enforcement institutions. Thus, in Austria the enforcement institution is a court and can resolve issues concerning material enforceability that arise during enforcement. In Germany, the main enforcement institution is the *Gerichtsvollzieher*, a civil servant external to the courts with limited qualifications and competences. As a result, German law ensures that the trial court determines questions concerning the

is not obvious that the enforceability of the judgment is suspended in Germany in the absence of evidence that the required security has been provided.

[82] AG Pikamäe gave his opinion on 22 October 2022 and took the view that Art. 11 of Reg. 805/2004 did in fact supply the answer to the question posed. He concluded that the enforcement proceedings should be suspended if the enforceability of the judgment was suspended in the Member State of origin.

material enforceability of a judgment. And in France, the main enforcement institution is the *huissier de justice* who can seek guidance from the JEX in cases in which it becomes necessary to decide legal questions relevant to enforcement. Thus, although the onus may often be on the debtor to raise objections to enforcement, the *huissier de justice* also has obligations in this respect.

In Brussels I bis Regulation cases the allocation of decision-making responsibility to the trial court or the court with responsibility in enforcement matters plays out in a cross-border context, with plenty of scope for confusion as to respective competences of the courts in the State of origin and the enforcement State. This is likely to prove problematic for debtors with limited resources and litigation experience. The differences between Member State laws suggest that further research may need to be done to clarify how Member States handle questions of the formal and material enforceability of judgments (and other enforcement titles) and the impact of changes in factual and legal circumstances—both to appreciate where confusion may arise and to consider whether modifications to the Article 53 certificate may be advisable to address specific problems.

In Lufthansa Technik AERO Alzey GmbH v. Arik Air Ltd (Lithuania) the Lithuanian Supreme Court observed that

> the need to analyse the legal rules of another Member State on appealing against judgments, taking into account differences between the legal systems and linguistic differences, may be very resource-consuming, and this may not always be compatible with the objective of prompt enforcement of a judgment of another Member State. Therefore, it is important to ascertain how these values should be reconciled and the extent of the assessment that the competent authorities of the Member State of enforcement should carry out.[83]

While this observation was made in the context of the application of Article 23(c) of Regulation 805/2004, it seems to be of general relevance. As disputes concerning the issue of Article 53 certificate emerge, greater attention needs to be paid to the appropriate forum for resolving questions concerning the enforceability effect of a judgment to promote the equal treatment of creditors and debtors in different Member States with respect to their access to both enforcement measures and measures to protect against enforcement.

References

Angst P, Oberhammer P (2015) Kommentar zur Exekutionsordnung. MANZ Verlag, Wien

Brox H, Walker W (2017) Zwangsvollstreckungsrecht, 11th edn. Vahlen, München

Burgstaller A, Deixler-Hübner A (2019) Exekutionsordnung: Kommentar, 28th edn. LexisNexis ARD ORAC

Fricero N (2021) Procedures civiles d'exécution. Gualino

[83] Summary of the request for a preliminary ruling in Case C-393/21, Lufthansa Technik AERO Alzey, 28.06.2021, para 16.

Kennett W (2018) Different national enforcement structures and their consequences for cross-border enforcement. In: Rijavec V, Kennett W, Keresteš T et al (eds) Remedies concerning enforcement of foreign judgments: Brussels I recast. Wolters Kluwer, Alphen aan den Rijn, pp 301–358

Kennett W (2021) Civil enforcement in a comparative perspective: a public management challenge. Intersentia

Neumayr M, Nunner-Krautgasser B (2018) Exekutionsrecht, 4th edn. MANZ Verlag, Wien

Richard V (2020) L'office du juge certifiant une décision rendue en droit de la consummation. Revue critique de droit international privé 1:149–157. https://doi.org/10.3917/rcdip.201.0149/

Rijavec V (2003) Civilno izvršilno pravo. GV Založba, Ljubljana

Schlosser P, Hess B (2021) EU-Zivilprozessrecht: EuZPR, 5th edn. C.H. Beck

Wolf C, Volkshausen L, Zeibig N (2018) Cross border enforcement of monetary claims - interplay of Brussels IA regulation and national rules: national report: Germany

Searching for *Res Judicata* at the Edges of National Procedural Autonomy

Denis Baghrizabehi

Abstract This chapter explores the autonomous understanding of *res judicata* in the (civil procedure) law of the EU. It does so by referencing mainly two distinct prongs of EU law. First, the Brussels regime on cross-border recognition and enforcement, where an autonomous interpretation has recently been explicitly established in CJEU case law, albeit in a narrow (restrictive) sense. This is contrasted by the interpretation of the scope of *res judicata* in the second prong of EU law, namely, the case law of the CJEU on the limits of national procedural autonomy. The chapter attempts to reconcile the two interpretations. The results show that the gradual evolution of both prongs has produced disparities, which, for the time being, do not provide for a common understanding of *res judicata* in EU law.

1 Introduction

Apart from rare exceptions, the European Union (EU) lacks legislative competence to regulate Member States' rules of (civil) procedure. The (private) enforcement of EU law thus hinges on a decentralised system,[1] where a national judge acts as the judge of the EU (*juge du droit commun*).[2] In the absence of EU regulation, national courts are free to apply the procedural rules laid down in their respective Member State, as long as those rules do not conflict with the principle of effectiveness of EU

[1] Dougan (2004), pp. 1–3.
[2] Fennelly (2013), p. 62.

D. Baghrizabehi (✉)
University of Maribor, Faculty of Law, Maribor, Slovenia
e-mail: denis.baghrizabehi@um.si

V. Rijavec et al. (eds.), *Diversity of Enforcement Titles in the EU*, Ius Gentium: Comparative Perspectives on Law and Justice 111,
https://doi.org/10.1007/978-3-031-47108-7_8

law (*effet utile*). This maxim has become known as the principle[3] of 'national procedural autonomy'.[4]

National rules on *res judicata* may significantly hinder the principle of effectiveness if a final judgment contains an infringement of EU law. In a growing body of case law, the CJEU has gradually outlined the limits of national procedural autonomy in relation to the various *res judicata* doctrines of the Member States. By virtue of 'negative harmonisation',[5] the CJEU has arguably developed an autonomous understanding of *res judicata*.

One notable exception to the lack of legislative competence of the EU concerns the area of judicial cooperation in civil matters having cross-border implications, as laid down in Article 81 TFEU. The latter provides for the adoption of measures aimed at, *inter alia*, the mutual recognition and enforcement of judgments between Members States. The crowning achievement within this area has been the enactment of the Brussels Ia Regulation, which enables an exequatur-free system of recognition and enforcement of judgments. Although it might appear necessary that a regime, which provides for the free movement of judgments, would require a robust approach to the concept of *res judicata* and its emanating features, i.e. binding and preclusive effects, this is not the case.

Admittedly, the CJEU has expounded on the principle of *res judicata* as far back as De Wolf v Cox,[6] stating that it would be incompatible with the purpose of the rules on the recognition of judgments if Member States would admit actions raised by the same parties concerning a subject-matter already decided-upon by a judgment delivered in another Member State.[7] However, this rationale has not given birth to a euro-autonomous *res judicata* concept that national courts would apply *sua sponte*. Instead, *res judicata* has long remained a procedural issue vested in national law.[8] Its effects can cross Member States' jurisdictions in line with the theory of extension of effects (German: 'Grundsatz der Wirkungserstreckung'),[9] whilst the system of

[3]It should be emphasized that certain authors do not consider national procedural autonomy to be a legal principle, since it bears no limit to the possibility of the EU to regulate aspects of national procedures. See Widdershoven (2019), p. 12.

[4]The term was initially coined by theory, while it saw its first use by the CJEU in C-201/01 Delena Wells. See Case C-201/01, The Queen on the application of Delena Wells v Secretary of State for Transport, Local Government and the Regions, 7.1.2004, ECLI:EU:C:2004:12.

[5]This term is used to describe the case law of the CJEU whereby the latter induces convergence across national legal systems by striking down national legislation that is at variance with EU law, by abolishing the differences with regard to interpretation of EU law, by establishing minimum standards and by removing barriers to EU integration. See Jaremba (2013), pp. 48–49.

[6]Case C 42-76, Jozef de Wolf v Harry Cox BV, 30.11.1976, ECLI:EU:C:1976:168.

[7]It should be mentioned that the Court of Justice made no explicit reference to 'res judicata', but rather based its reasoning on the rationale stemming from the rules on lis pendens, referring to the risk of incompatible judgments. See Case C 42-76, Jozef de Wolf v Harry Cox BV, 30.11.1976, ECLI:EU:C:1976:168, paras 10–13.

[8]Ferrand (2014), pp. 143–133.

[9]Voulgarakis (2020), pp. 451–453.

recognition and enforcement defers to rules on *lis pendens* and irreconcilability of judgments for their respective purposes.

This long-lasting paradigm was disrupted when the CJEU issued the judgment in Gothaer. There it introduced a euro-autonomous understanding of *res judicata* for judgments that contain decisions regarding international jurisdiction over a dispute. The Gothaer judgment gives rise to legitimate speculation that this euro-autonomous concept of *res judicata* might contain further dimensions, which could become apparent in future rulings and integration efforts.

This chapter will attempt to clarify whether the two bodies of case law are in the process of converging or diverging. The prospects for reconciling the concepts were examined in pioneering work by Kornezov,[10] who concluded that *res judicata* in the case law on national autonomy seemed to converge with the *lis pendens* rules in the cross-border context. By applying the same methodological approach, we will demonstrate that developments in case law indicate that the concepts are in fact drifting apart. The chapter will first describe the principle of effectiveness as the progenitor of harmonisation (Sect. 2). This will be followed by a concise overview of the main differences in the scope of *res judicata* doctrines in the Member States and the case law on negative harmonisation of the CJEU (Sect. 3). Next, we will examine the *res judicata* concept in the cross-border context, together with the related *lis pendens* rule (Sect. 4). Differences in the dimensions of both concepts show that they have diverged; nonetheless, they allow for cross-fertilisation of ideas (Sect. 5).

2 The Limits of National Procedural Autonomy

In the absence of EU law provisions, the enforcement of EU law at the national level is governed by the institutional[11] and procedural rules of the Member States, subject to two limitations: the principle of equivalence and the principle of effectiveness (*effet utile*). Equivalence requires that the Member States shall not discriminate between claims based on national law and claims arising out of EU law.[12] Effectiveness requires that national 'procedural'[13] rules do not render the enforcement of

[10] Kornezov (2014), pp. 809, 842.

[11] Member States enjoy institutional autonomy, according to which Member States retain sovereignty regarding their own institutional (e.g. judicial) set-up, and this leads to institutional heterogenety within the EU. It is a consequence of a lack of federal institutions in the EU. In the same way, procedural autonomy gives rise to procedural heteronomy in the EU and is a consequence of the lack of the legislative competence of the EU to regulate procedural law. See Van Cleynenbreugel (2011), pp. 511, 543.

[12] See Baghrizabehi (2016), pp. 15, 16.

[13] It must be emphasized, that the notion of national procedural autonomy encompasses both procedural rules stricto sensu and rules on legal remedies. In EU law, remedies are to be understood as classes of action, intended to make good infringements of the (subjective) rights concerned, in accordance with 'procedures' governing the exercise of such classes of action and intended to make

EU law excessively difficult. More recently, the CJEU has also established limits based on the principle of effective judicial protection. Since national rules on *res judicata* are applied uniformly for claims based on EU law as well as those based on national law, this venue is not devoted further attention. Much more perplexing are the limitations imposed through the principle of effectiveness because there is a lack of clear-cut criteria on resolving conflicts between the effectiveness of EU law on the one hand and the scope of national procedural autonomy on the other.

2.1 Absence of EU Law Provisions

At the outset, it should be emphasised that the prerequisite for exercising national procedural autonomy is the absence of EU procedural rules (Member States retain 'procedural competence'[14] where no EU regulation is imposed). In addition, it would be irrelevant if the EU were conferred the (shared) competence to regulate a specific area of procedural law, but it had not (yet) acted on it. In both cases, the enforcement of EU law takes place through national procedural law, since EU law displaces national rules only to the extent the EU has exercised its powers.[15] If, however, EU legislation is enacted, in the form of a Regulation, then the latter will supersede the application of national law due to the principle of primacy; a conflicting national rule should be disapplied.[16] In general, the 'absence of EU law provisions' accurately describes the *status quo*, precisely due to the lack of competence of the EU to regulate the procedural laws of the Member States. However, upon closer inspection, some tangible forms of competence do manifest themselves.

The starting point for any investigation into EU competence is the Treaties. In line with Article 5(1) TFEU, which elucidates the principle of conferral, the EU may act only within the limits of the competence conferred upon it by the Member States in the Treaties to attain the objectives set out therein. (Legislative) competence is thus rooted in a system of attributed competence.[17] The Treaties do not provide any

the remedy concerned operational. See Van Gerven (2000), pp. 501, 502. This approach, developed in the case law of the CJEU, mirrors the common law understanding of procedures and remedies and is not widely accepted in civil law systems, where remedies are considered 'by-products' of the subjective rights. See Franziska and Franz (2019), p. 5. Some authors make a distinction when speaking about the remedial aspects of the principle of procedural autonomy, prompting the creation of 'remedial autonomy'. See Franziska and Franz (2019), p. 5; Giliker (2014), p. 10.

[14]Van Gerven (2000), p. 502; Galetta (2010), p. 9.

[15]Halberstam (2021), pp. 128, 143.

[16]Theory has developed at least two models to explain the interplay of the principles of primacy and direct effect with national law. According to the primacy model, the principle of primacy is independent of other principles and serves mainly the exclusionary effect (setting aside of national law). According to the trigger model, on the other hand, primacy is the trigger for the direct effect of an EU provision taking place (where the provision is directly effective). In most cases, however, the outcome according to both models is the same. See Dougan (2007), pp. 931, 936.

[17]See Craig and de Búrca (2015), p. 73.

direct, general legal ground, be it exclusive or shared, for legislating 'genuine' national procedural law (i.e. law intended to regulate purely domestic matters). On the other hand, opinions differ as to whether the Treaties nevertheless provide for an implicit competence of the EU in this area.[18] Evidence for implicit competence stems from the phenomenon described as 'incidental proceduralisation' or 'proceduralisation through the back door'. This form of harmonisation of procedural laws describes the insertion of procedural rules in secondary EU law measures adopted on the basis of provisions enabling the EU to develop a substantive policy.[19] The antitrust 'Damages Directive'[20] is a prime example of such proceduralisation through Europeanisation, since it contains a plethora of rules harmonising the domestic rules of civil procedure. Furthermore, a quasi-implicit competence stemming from the principle of effectiveness of EU law is argued to exist.[21] In any case, it is clear that there is a spill-over effect of EU substantive policies into procedural law,[22] mainly due to the (speaking in reductionist terms) ancillary or instrumental character of procedural law.

The spill-over effect is a consequence of the need for an enforcement mechanism of EU law. More precisely, the need for EU regulation in the area of civil procedural law stems from three identifiable sources of EU policy. Firstly, in certain instances EU law creates rights for individuals, which have direct effect. The enforcement of these rights takes place in national courts due to a lack of a federal judiciary in the EU. Areas such as competition law, consumer contract law and product liability law are prime examples of such instances. However, national procedural law might not provide for effective procedural and remedial rules to enforce these rights. Secondly, the EU declares itself to constitute an area of justice with respect for fundamental rights and the different legal systems and traditions of the Member States, wherein the EU shall facilitate access to justice (Article 67 TFEU). According to Article 47 of the EU Charter of Fundamental Rights, everyone whose rights and freedoms, guaranteed by the law of the EU are violated, has the right to an effective remedy and is entitled to a fair and public hearing within a reasonable time. The EU thus necessitates the effective judicial protection of individuals for claims based on EU

[18] Galleta is of the opinion, that such competence does not exist, while Hess seems to acknowledge it. See Galetta (2010), pp. 9–11; Hess (2012), pp. 164–166. This can further be elaborated if one subscribes to the idea of the normative trinity of EU law (substance, procedure and remedy). Given the trinity of legal normativity, the direct conferral of substantive competences of the Union includes the implied conferral of the necessary attendant procedural and remedial competences as well. See Halberstam (2021), pp. 128, 143.

[19] Eliantonio (2015), pp. 177, 204.

[20] Directive (EU) 2014/104/EU of the European Parliament and of the Council of 26 November 2014 on certain rules governing actions for damages under national law for infringements of the competition law provisions of the Member States and of the European Union Text with EEA relevance, OJ L 349, 5.12.2014.

[21] Galetta (2010), pp. 9–11.

[22] The 'spill-over' effect of substantive primacy into procedural law, has led some authors to develop the notion of 'EU procedural primacy'. See Delicostopoulos (2004), pp. 599, 613.

law.[23] Thirdly, the creation of the internal market and its four freedoms entails that entities can efficiently engage in cross-border trade. It is important that cross-border civil or commercial litigation does not disrupt the proper functioning of the internal market. Thus, a fifth freedom tacitly forms part of the internal market—'free movement of judgments'.[24]

The first and second of the above-described areas of law are susceptible to procedural harmonisation based on the implicit competence of the EU to regulate national procedural law. This takes place through sectoral regulation or negative harmonisation by the CJEU. In contrast, matters having cross-border implications are the sole area where the EU enjoys competence to introduce acts through Article 81 TFEU. Judicial cooperation in cross-border matters is a shared competence of the EU, requiring the EU legislator to observe the principle of subsidiarity and proportionality before acting. Once the EU has adopted acts, it effectively pre-empts the competence of Member State to regulate the area further.[25]

Importantly, the competence to regulate matters having cross-border implications cannot intrude into the Member State's 'genuine' civil procedure law but remains restricted to the cross-border context. Granted, Article 81 TFEU no longer requires (as did Article 65 TEC) justification in view of the 'proper functioning' of the internal market to adopt acts. The renewed approach must be viewed in the context of moving EU integration beyond the market focus towards encompassing EU citizenship. Despite this paradigm shift, the requirement of a cross-border element has been maintained, which means that EU involvement in civil justice is possible only if there are cross-border elements in a case.[26] Arguments have been raised that a broad interpretation of Article 81(2)f TFEU may form the basis of an approximation of the civil procedural laws of the Member States, irrespective of the cross-border character of litigation. It could be claimed that differences between the procedural laws of the Member States always have cross-border implications, e.g. in the sense that businesses may be affected by these differences when deciding where to produce and market their products. Nevertheless, this interpretation of Article 81 TEU is currently politically unacceptable for the Member States.[27] Still, it would be wrong not to mention that instruments adopted on the basis of Article 81 TFEU generate indirect harmonisation of the national laws of the Member States, either by providing a 'model' basis for national law or through the introduction of acts, serving as an interface between national and EU law.[28]

---

[23] Storskrubb (2008), pp. 1–4.

[24] Hazelhorst (2017), pp. 3–6.

[25] Mangiameli (2013), Article 2 TEU, pp. 198, 222–224.

[26] Mańko (2015); Tulibacka (2009), p. 1562.

[27] Van Rhee (2012), pp. 39–43.

[28] Krans and Nylund (2020), pp. 236–239.

2.2 *The Foremost Criteria of Effectiveness: The Procedural 'Rule of Reason'*

The scope of national procedural autonomy is limited by the principle of the effectiveness of EU law. The scope of one, necessarily determines the scope of the other. Accordingly, some authors argue that there is no real 'autonomy', since national procedural law is under the perpetual mandate to accommodate the effective enforcement of EU law[29] or that procedural autonomy is merely a 'presumption',[30] which is valid as long as the national rule does not collide with EU law. National procedural law can collide with EU law directly or indirectly. The former is of little concern, as it pertains to situations where the EU introduces procedural rules of its own. Indirect collision, although regular in this area of case law, is both hard to identify and resolve,[31] since national procedural rules can deprive an EU substantive rule of effect in a variety of constellations, e.g. short limitation periods to bring an action, rigorous rules on standing and rules on taking evidence, limiting rules on invoking points of EU law *ex officio*, strict rules on *res judicata* and reopening of cases etc.[32]

Historically speaking, the scope of the two principles of procedural autonomy and effectiveness has oscillated. Three generations of CJEU case law on the subject are discernible. In the early period, the CJEU was keen on respecting the autonomy of Member States, intervening only inasmuch the enforcement of EU law would prove practically impossible. This lenient approach was contrasted in the second generation, where procedural autonomy was stressed to its limits, evidenced by the CJEU arguably introducing *de novo* remedies in national law. As with any extremes, a balance was struck in the third and latest generation, by recognising the shortcomings of the conservative approach and abstaining from the intrusive effects of the second generation. The chronology of this development has already been well documented.[33]

[29] Bobek (2012), p. 12. Furthermore, the prefaratory wording employed by the CJEU ('in the absence of EU rules') implies that the CJEU does not consider the area of procedural law ultra vires, in respect of the competence of the EU, but rather that there is a politically contingent absence of rules. This becomes evident when compared with the prefatory wording of the CJEU in other areas of law ('as Community law currently stands'). See Halberstam (2021), pp. 128, 143; Eliantonio (2015), p. 180.

[30] Sowery (2017), pp. 1168, 1169. Furthermore, the prefatory wording employed by the CJEU ('in the absence of EU rules') implies that the CJEU does not consider the area of procedural law ultra vires, in respect of the competence of the EU, but rather that there is a politically contingent absence of rules. This becomes evident when compared with the prefatory wording of the CJEU in other areas of law ('as Community law currently stands'). See Halberstam (2021), pp. 128, 143.

[31] For a general overview of problems incurred in indirect conflict. See Ortlep and Verhoeven (2012), pp. 2–4.

[32] See e.g. Kakouris (1997), pp. 1398, 1404.

[33] See e.g. Smith (2010), pp. 412–421.

What is more important, is the extrapolation of the criteria the CJEU used to delimit autonomy from effectiveness. To elaborate: effectiveness of EU law can be viewed as a standard with differential criteria. Reflecting the above-mentioned generational approach, three distinct sets of criteria are identifiable.[34]

First, the traditional Rewe/San Giorgio test. This test is in essence a recapitulation of the CJEU's decision in both cases, where it stated that national law cannot render enforcement of EU law excessively difficult[35] or impossible in practice[36] (although the former is an *a fortiori* expression of the latter). This statement is nowadays accepted as the standard definition of scope of procedural autonomy.[37]

Second, the *full effectiveness* criterion. This criterion can be described the most rigorous and is emblematic of the second-generation case law for setting aside provisions of national law. The CJEU has made frequent references to the need to guarantee the *full effectiveness* of EU law in a number of landmark cases; including the Simmenthal, Francovich, Köbler, Courage and Factortame cases. The Factortame case is especially important to note, as some scholars have commented that in that case the CJEU went so far as to create new remedies, thereby overstepping the 'no new remedies'[38] prerogative it had developed beforehand.

Third, the procedural 'rule of reason' test, which marks the third and latest generation of case law. This term was first introduced by Prechal[39] in comments on the Van Schijndel case, where the CJEU had to decide whether a national court should take EU law into consideration *ex officio*. The test requires that 'each case which raises the question whether a national procedural provision renders application of EU law impossible or excessively difficult must be analysed by reference to the role of that provision in the procedure, its progress and its special features, viewed as a whole, before the various national instances'.[40] The national court must conduct a balancing test between the competing interests and ascertain whether the rule pursues a legitimate aim and is proportionate to reach that aim. This expresses the idea that the protection of EU law rights does not take precedence over all other

[34]Schütze (2012), pp. 389–390.

[35]Case C-33-76, Rewe-Zentralfinanz eG and Rewe-Zentral AG v Landwirtschaftskammer für das Saarland, 16.12.1976, ECLI:EU:C:1976:188.

[36]Case 199/82, Amministrazione delle Finanze dello Stato v SpA San Giorgio, 9.11.1983, ECLI: EU:C:1983:318.

[37]Case C-234/17, XC and Others v Generalprokuratur, 24.10.2018, ECLI:EU:C:2018:853.

[38]The CJEU has established in earlier case law that the Treaties were not intended to create new remedies. See Case 158/80, Rewe v Hauptzollamt Kiel, 7.7.1981, ECLI:EU:C:1981:163.

[39]Prechal (1998), pp. 681, 706. The test is also referred to as the 'objective justification model'. See Dougan (2004), p. 30.

[40]Joined cases C-430/93 and C-431/93, Jeroen van Schijndel and Johannes Nicolaas Cornelis van Veen v Stichting Pensioenfonds voor Fysiotherapeuten [1995] E.C.R. I-04705, Case C-312/93, Peterbroeck, Van Campenhout & Cie SCS v Belgian State, 14.12.1995, ECLI:EU:C:1995:437, Case C-276/01, Joachim Steffensen, 10.4.2003, ECLI:EU:C:2003:228, Case C-125/01, Peter Pflücke v Bundesanstalt für Arbeit, 18.9.2003, ECLI:EU:C:2003:477.

interests that procedural rules are set to achieve.[41] For example, the right of access to court may be limited by the setting of time limits for bringing a claim.[42] The right of one party to be heard may be limited in order to ensure that the other party can exercise its right of protection of business secrets.[43] The rule of reason test is not a self-standing test but is used to help elucidate the 'excessively difficult' criterion stemming from the traditional Rewe/San Giorgio test.[44] The interests of the EU are weighed against the basic principles of the domestic judicial system, such as protection of the rights of defence, the principle of legal certainty and the proper conduct of the procedure.[45] Although not explicitly, this weighing sometimes takes the form of comparing the restrictive procedural rule under scrutiny to similar rules in other Member States, which are then used as yardsticks to measure its 'restrictiveness' (e.g. comparing limitation periods).[46]

Not surprisingly—as will be seen below—the 'rule of reason' has been used in case law related to the scope of national *res judicata*, where the latter was weighed against the principle of effectiveness as a corollary of the principle of legal certainty.

The 'rule of reason' balancing between the competing principles of effectiveness on the one hand and procedural autonomy on the other bears a striking resemblance to 'practical concordance' (ger. 'Praktische Konkordanz')[47] as established in German constitutional theory.[48] The aim of practical concordance in situations concerning conflicting rights is to avoid, to the fullest extent possible, sacrificing one right against the other, and instead seeking a compromise between the rights in conflict which will respect their respective claims, by 'optimising' each of the rights against the other.[49]

Part of EU procedural theory considers the pure Rewe/San Giorgio test to gravitate towards a reductionist view of procedural law, where the latter is servile to substantive law. To be precise, in Rewe/San Giorgio there is a fundamental disregard of the 'independent virtues and values' inherent in procedural law itself. On the other hand, the rule of reason better accommodates the goals of procedural justice and is thus better suited for resolving conflicts between *res judicata* and effectiveness.[50] Despite this, the procedural rule of reason has been criticised

---

[41] Engström (2011).

[42] Case C-63/08, Virginie Pontin v T-Comalux SA, 29.10.2009, ECLI:EU:C:2009:666.

[43] Case C-450/06, Varec SA v Belgian State, 14.2.2008, ECLI:EU:C:2008:91, para 51, Case C-438/04, Mobistar SA v Institut belge des services postaux et des télécommunications (IBPT), 13.7.2006, ECLI:EU:C:2006:463, Reneman (2014), p. 44.

[44] Wennerås (2007), p. 88.

[45] Case C-312/93, Peterbroeck, Van Campenhout & Cie SCS v Belgian State, 14.12.1995, ECLI:EU:C:1995:437, para 10.

[46] Komnios (2007), p. 137.

[47] The principle of practical concordance has been most prominently theorised by the German constitutional jurist Konrad Hesse. See Hesse (1995).

[48] Voß (2019), p. 111; Halberstam (2021), pp. 128, 143.

[49] De Schutter and Tulkens (2008), pp. 169–216.

[50] Schebesta (2014), p. 859.

because it leads to a lack of predictability and legal certainty due to its necessarily casuistic nature. Furthermore, the rule of reason is not being applied by the CJEU in each instance of assessing the scope of the principle of procedural autonomy. Referencing the case law on the rule of reason is thus fairly complicated. In addition, the Rewe/San Giorgio criteria have been argued to intrinsically encompass the balancing formula found within the rule of reason anyway.[51] Indeed, even in the seminal Rewe case, the CJEU has weighed the principle of effectiveness against that of legal certainty.[52]

In more recent times, the CJEU has increasingly begun assessing the scope of national procedural autonomy not through the traditional Rewe/San Giorgio principle of 'effectiveness', but through the principle of 'effective judicial protection', which is enshrined in Article 47 of the Charter of Fundamental Rights of the EU and in Article 19(1) TEU.[53] The principle of effective judicial protection requires that individuals should be able to enforce all rights conferred on them by EU law before a court of law. In cases with an EU law dimension, the national courts should offer a complete system of legal remedies, necessary to respect the rule of law.[54] The 'rule of law', seems to be the defining feature that distinguishes the principle of effective judicial protection from the principle of effectiveness.[55] While the former is intended to protect individuals from infringements of their (substantive or procedural) rights (especially by depriving them of effective remedies) committed on the part of the Member State, the latter aims at providing EU law with its due effect in the jurisdictions of the Member States and is more concerned with the 'objective' relationship between EU law and national law. That is also why the principle of effectiveness (in contrast to effective judicial protection) can be either beneficial or detrimental to the legal situation of the individual.[56] The case law defining the relationship between the two principles is, however, still in its infancy and subject to debate.[57]

[51] Reneman (2014), p. 102.

[52] Case C-33-76, Rewe-Zentralfinanz eG and Rewe-Zentral AG v Landwirtschaftskammer für das Saarland, 16.12.1976, ECLI:EU:C:1976:188, para 5.

[53] Widdershoven (2019), p. 6.

[54] Lenaerts et al. (2014), p. 2.

[55] Widdershoven (2019), pp. 15, 18.

[56] For instance, in vertical disputes, the individual will be able to rely on both principles. For example, a national procedural rule may be depriving the individual of standing, which also means that the EU right he or she is enforcing remains unenforced. It also possible that the Member State is trying to enforce EU law obligations against an individual, but national procedural law makes it difficult. Naturally, the Member State would rely the principle of effectiveness for the national court to set aside the conflicting procedural law. It would be hard to imagine, however, how the Member State could rely on effective judicial protection in this case.

[57] Prechal (1998), pp. 681, 706.

2.3 The Pitfalls of Autonomy and Negative Harmonisation

The decentralised system of enforcing EU law, coupled with the principle of national procedural autonomy appears to run contrary to contemporary regulatory theories that suggest that effective enforcement should be an integral part of a successful regulatory system. The procedural diversity among the Member States often leads to an 'enforcement deficit'.[58] Additionally, it leads to a disparity among EU citizens when attempting to enforce their EU rights in national courts:[59]

- parties are subject to different procedural rules, meaning they must approach different litigation rules and devise different litigation strategies;
- parties have to deal with different obstacles, meaning that the potential for enforcement is different under the same set of EU (substantive) rules;
- judges issue different judgments because of different procedural rules.[60]

As already mentioned, the enforcement deficit is curtailed either through sectoral regulation or through the negative harmonisation of the CJEU. The decisions of the CJEU in preliminary ruling procedures (Article 267 TFEU) inform us of the scope of the principle of procedural autonomy vis-à-vis they communicate minimum standards and clarify which national rules need to be subjected to the principle of consistent interpretation or ultimately set aside (disapplied) if the limits of consistent interpretation are exhausted (to the point where such interpretation is *contra legem*).[61] Potential shortcomings of this approach may lie with 'judicial activism'[62] on part of the CJEU. Admittedly, judicial law-making of the CJEU seems to be a potent tool of legal integration. Firstly, because the Treaties can be considered as incomplete contracts, which should be specified not only by legislative, but also judicial means; and secondly, because the market freedoms equip the CJEU with a near unrestricted potential to advance integration as almost all fields of public policy share a plausible connection to the internal market. Through its rulings, the CJEU can steer the policy outcomes of future legislative processes by promoting policy ideas and strengthening the position of some political groups over others. The CJEU often acts as a unitary, rational competence-maximiser, while the legislator is a heterogeneous actor without stable and distinct preferences.[63] Judicial activism can

[58] Tulibacka (2009), pp. 1527, 1565.

[59] Grashof (2016), p. 231.

[60] In actuality these disparities do occur, although the CJEU stated already back in van Gend en Loos that the goal is to secure a uniform interpretation of the Treaty by national courts. See Case C-26-62, NV Algemene Transport- en Expeditie Onderneming van Gend & Loos v Netherlands Inland Revenue Administration, 5.2.1963, ECLI:EU:C:1963:1.

[61] Case C-268/06, Impact v Minister for Agriculture and Food and Others, 15.4.2008, ECLI:EU:C:2008:223, para 100.

[62] What is meant with the term is a claim that a court oversteps its boundaries, either in relation to national law or in relation to functions of the political sphere. See Dawson et al. (2013), p. 9.

[63] Wasserfallen (2010), pp. 1131, 1135. For an in-depth analysis of the legal and political science aspects of the CJEU position in law-making. See Alter (1998), pp. 109, 138.

therefore be considered a welcome phenomenon. However, that might not always be the case. The CJEU may introduce policy ideas prematurely or promote those ideas on uncertain doctrinal grounds. Indeed, as will be discussed below, this might be a legitimate concern for the CJEU's concept of *res judicata*.

3 National Procedural Autonomy and the Scope of Res Judicata

Res judicata ('a matter decided')[64] refers to the various ways in which one judgment exercises a binding effect on another.[65] The full Roman law maxim *res judicata pro veritate habetur* ('an adjudicated matter is regarded as the truth'),[66] conveys that the matter decided by the judgment must be held as true and thus binding. A particular matter once settled by a judgment must be regarded as final and the matter cannot be re-litigated between the persons bound by the judgment (*ne bis in idem*).[67] Therefore, in addition to binding effects, a final judgment also has preclusive effects.

If we are to describe the scope of an EU *res judicata* principle, as constructed by the CJEU in its case law on procedural autonomy, we require comparative cues from national laws on this subject. The national doctrines on *res judicata* contextualise the binding and preclusive effects by reference to different 'models'. We can use these models to approximate their likeness to the EU principle. Subsequently, solutions from the most approximate model can then be used to resolve the unknowns and lacunae in the EU principle.

In several Member State,[68] the distinction is made between 'positive *res judicata*' for the binding effects of the judgment and 'negative *res judicata*' for the preclusive effects. It is essential to determine what is affected in both cases, i.e. *what* is it that courts and parties in subsequent proceedings are obliged to observe and *what* is it that cannot be re-litigated.[69] In essence, the '*what*' describes the 'matter adjudicated'. We can identify the '*what*' by describing its subjective and objective dimensions. The subjective (personal) dimension informs us which persons are affected by the *res judicata*. However, the present contribution will focus on the objective dimension that tells us which legal and factual findings of the court bind or are precluded from being re-litigated between those persons. In addition, it could be posited that there is a third, i.e. temporal dimension, which tells us 'when' *res*

[64] Law (2018), p. 430.

[65] Sinai (2011), pp. 353–400.

[66] The maxim is traced back to Ulpianus' commentary on Lex Julia et Papia, later compiled in Justinian's Digest (D 1, 5, 25).

[67] Schaffstein (2016), p. 10.

[68] Germany, Sweden, Switzerland, Romania, Sweden, Slovenia Croatia. See Van de Velden and Stefanelli (2006), p. 14.

[69] Christian (2020), pp. 5–6.

judicata takes effect and which findings within a specific timeframe it covers. However, the temporal dimension can also be considered part of the objective dimension because it ultimately helps us distinguish which legal and factual findings are relevant. Furthermore, it is vital to determine which parts of the judgment become *res judicata*, since the court may communicate its findings in different parts of the judgment. Together, this analysis will provide us with an answer to the 'scope' of national *res judicata* principles.

Methodologically, we will avoid the pursuit of unified concepts to describe the objective dimension of *res judicata*, due to the sheer variety of approaches applied under national doctrines. For example, common law jurisdictions draw a line between 'claim preclusive effects' and 'issue preclusive effects'. The former affects the re-litigation of claims, which are considered to have already been adjudicated, while the latter relates to preclusion with regard to points of fact or law, which a legal system regards as having already been determined in earlier proceedings.[70] This distinction, although useful on its own merits, will not be employed for the purposes of the present research since it distils the object of study beyond what is necessary. Similarly, national doctrines may operate with concepts such as 'identity of claims', 'object' or 'subject-matter' of the dispute, which may not necessarily translate well across jurisdictions. Reducing national doctrines to unified concepts is also not necessary, since we are not conducting a direct comparative study between them. Another caveat worth taking into account is that some of the elements forming the objective dimension of *res judicata* might not necessarily have both binding and preclusive effects or might have them only in certain combinations. In any case, all of the doctrinal approaches are sufficiently comparable to communicate the objective dimensions of *res judicata* in general terms, especially if we apply the descriptive method to pronounce their meaning. The study is also necessarily limited. National doctrines are subject to evolving internal discrepancies and a variety of particularities, which cannot be taken into account due to constraints in resources and in the interest of brevity, clarity and relevancy. Only the main and prevailing doctrinal approaches are considered. After presenting the national framework, we will move to the analysis of *res judicata* in the CJEU case law regarding procedural autonomy.

3.1 Prevailing Models

3.1.1 German Model

The objective dimensions of 'substantive *res judicata*' ('materielle Rechtskraft')[71] in Germany are delimited according to the procedural 'two-part' ('zweigliedrige')

[70] See Loizou and Christofi (2021), pp. 141, 144.

[71] As opposed to 'formal res judicata' ('formelle Rechtskraft'), which means that a judgment is final and cannot be contested with remedies (procedural recourses). Similar considerations of substantive

theory,[72] which is concurrently used to determine the subject-matter of the dispute (*Streitgegenstand*). The two parts comprise, firstly, the relief sought ('Antrag'), and secondly, the circumstances from which the claimant derives his right ('Lebenssachverhalt'). More precisely, these circumstances, as their name suggests, contain a set of facts, which can be rounded-up into a single 'life' or 'historical' event. Subsequent actions that cumulatively contain the same request for relief based on the same event will be barred on the basis of the preclusive effects of the first judgment. It should be emphasised that the relief sought is incorporated into the operative part ('Tenor') of the judgment and that the latter is the only part of the judgment that becomes *res judicata*. This means that factual findings, legal classifications and determinations on preliminary legal questions (contained in the reasoning of the judgment) are not precluded from being re-litigated, nor do they (in principle) produce binding effects. Granted, decisions on preliminary legal questions can become *res judicata*, but only if invoked by a separate request for (interim) declaratory relief ('Zwischenfestellungsklage'). The identification of the objective dimensions of substantive *res judicata* should therefore not be confused with the scope of binding and preclusive effects—factual and legal findings are taken into account for the purposes of identifying the objective dimension, however, they do not, on their own, have preclusive effects. A minority of the doctrine subscribes to the 'one-part' ('eingliedrige') theory, where only the relief sought is relevant for determining the subject-matter of the dispute, or the 'three-part' ('dreigliedrige') theories, which incorporate (in one way or another) elements of legal classification.

Similar models to the German one are found in Austria,[73] Slovenia[74] and Croatia.[75] The Swedish model is similar in that it limits *res judicata* to the operative part, with limited recourse to the claims and defences.[76]

3.1.2 French Model

In France, three elements are crucial for determining the scope of *res judicata*, hence the 'triple-identity' test of 'parties, cause et objet'. Excluding the personal dimension, the objective dimension is determined by the 'cause et objet', namely, the same legal grounds and the same relief.[77] If one of these elements is missing, a subsequent

res judicata are found in Italian law (cosa giudicata sostanziale) and Spanish law ('cosa juzgada material').

[72] Theory supplements the statutory wording of Article 322(1) of the Zivilprozessordnung: 'Judgments are able to attain legal validity only insofar as the complaint or the claims asserted by counterclaims have been ruled on'.

[73] Prodinger & Nunner-Krautgasser (2020), pp. 41–44.

[74] Rijavec et al. (2020), pp. 56–59.

[75] Kunštek et al. (2020), pp. 31–32.

[76] Bylander & Linton (2020), pp. 17–18; BIICL (n.d.-c), pp. 17–21.

[77] BIICL (n.d.-a), p. 22.

action is not barred.[78] These considerations are of course only basic. For example, the traditional doctrinal position was that it was possible to raise a new claim for the same relief with new grounds; however, the Cour de cassation has more recently diverged from this position, effectively instituting the principle of 'concentration of grounds'.[79] Similarly, the Cour de cassation has introduced uncertainty with regard to the parts of the judgment that become *res judicata*. To elaborate, under French law (480 CPC) only the operative part ('dispositif') is a *res judicata*. This is further emphasised in Article 455 CPC, which provides that the judgment states the decision in the form of a final order. A reading of the 'dispositif' should thus suffice for determining the scope of *res judicata*. Conversely, the reasons ('motifs') are not usually regarded as *res judicata* and should not be consulted in the identification of the objective dimension. However, waters are muddied when it comes to 'motifs decisifs', which are reasons that are indispensable for understanding the operative part. Case law extends the *res judicata* effect to them, but several decisions of the Cour de cassation adopt an opposite solution.[80]

Similar 'triple identity tests' are found in Belgium and Luxembourg.[81] Bulgaria seems also to subscribe to the triple identity test;[82] however, uncertainty remains over the parts of the judgment endowed with *res judicata effects*. In its earlier case-law, the Bulgarian Supreme Court has held that, in addition to the operative part of judgments, main 'motives',[83] i.e. motives justifying the operative part determining the decision, also obtain res judicata force. Nevertheless, the Bulgarian Supreme Court gave no answer as to which motives can be classified as 'main'. In its more recent practice, the Bulgarian Supreme court takes the view that only the direct findings on the disputed right are of such force.[84]

Spain seems to follow a 'triple identity test' as well, with certain modalities and many issues open to interpretation.[85] The subjective dimension of *res judicata* is naturally determined by looking at the parties to the dispute. To determine the objective dimension of *res judicata*, one must refer to the claims raised by the parties, the specific relief sought (*petitum*), and the foundation of that relief (a combination of legally relevant elements that substantiate the claim, i.e. the *causa petendi*). Legal and factual issues which could have been raised, but were not, are also covered. The latter approach also determines the parts of judgments having *res judicata* effects—it is not only the operative part that is covered, but also other points of the legal and factual findings. However, care must be taken when

[78] Kornezov (2014), p. 815.

[79] BIICL (n.d.-a), p. 24.

[80] Ferrand (2014), p. 149.

[81] Kornezov (2014), p. 816.

[82] Kornezov (2014), p. 816.

[83] Motives state the factual and legal findings by which the court accepts or denies certain facts. See National report for Bulgaria, p. 45.

[84] National report for Bulgaria, pp. 45–46.

[85] Kornezov (2014), p. 816.

determining exactly which points these are, since not all are covered by the *res judicata* principle. Doctrine considers that only the legally relevant facts, those that identify and individualise the *causa petendi* of the specific claim are covered by *res judicata* effects (*ratio decidenci*).[86]

3.1.3 Italian Model

Italian law provides for a broad interpretation of the scope of *res judicata*, made possible by the general wording of Article 2909 Codice civile. As in Germany, the law distinguishes formal and substantive *res judicata*.[87] The objective dimension of *res judicata* seems to consist of the subject matter of the case as set out in the relief sought (*petitum*) and the *causa petendi* (the factual and legal basis on which the relief is sought).[88] Prejudicial issues (*questione pregiudizale*) that have not been subject to a specific claim do not have *res judicata* effect, if not raised by the parties as a special claim, similar to the German model.[89] However, in some cases, case law admits that reasons which decide on certain issues closely (necessarily) connected with the final order ('*antecedenti logici necessary della decision*') do have (implicit)[90] *res judicata* effect, if the parties were given opportunity to discuss these issues. This applies only where the prejudicial issue regards the right at stake.[91] Moving forward to the parts of the judgment having *res judicata* effect—the operative part of the judgment has binding and preclusive effects, together with the above-mentioned closely connected reasons.[92]

3.1.4 Netherlands Model

The objective dimension of *res judicata* in Netherlands law seems to be framed rather broadly. It requires the 'identity of claims', wherein that identity concerns the identity of the factual cause of action of the relief claimed. It does not refer to the 'legal' cause of action, nor to the type of relief claimed. The court's finding on the claim entails the court's answer to the question whether the claim for relief follows from the applicable legal cause of action in view of the factual cause of action.[93] This should not be confused, however, with the notion that purely factual findings of the court can exert *res judicata* effects on their own; the court must necessarily decide on

[86]Bores Lazo & Serrano Ron (2020), p. 38.
[87]Kaczorowska et al. (2022), p. 36.
[88]Kornezov (2014), p. 816.
[89]Ferrand (2014), p. 151.
[90]Kaczorowska et al. (2022), p. 37.
[91]Ferrand (2014), p. 151.
[92]Kornezov (2014), p. 816.
[93]BIICL (n.d.-b), pp. 42–43.

a 'legal' relationship between the parties, which is, however, determined by the factual cause of action.[94]

3.1.5 Intermediary conclusion

Even though we have focused on a select number of jurisdictions, it is obvious that there are several competing models regarding the scope of *res judicata* within the EU. The findings allow us to paint a picture with broad brush strokes, generalising an otherwise complex subject. A distinction can be made between models employing a narrow scope of *res judicata*, where the objective dimension is restricted to the operative part (German and French model) and those employing a broader scope, where the reasoning of the judgment is also encompassed (Italian model). There also seem to be competing visions with regard to determining the objective dimension. On the one hand, the German model relies on the subject-matter of the dispute, defined as the relief sought and interpreted through factual grounds, while the French model relies on the triple identity test. The Italian model seems to more broadly approximate the French one. The model employed in the Netherlands is rooted in a broad understanding based on a factual assessment of the identity of claims.

3.2 National Res Judicatae in Procedural Autonomy Case Law

The case-law of the CJEU on the limits of national *res judicata* doctrines is paramount for the study of national procedural autonomy since the interests safeguarded by *res judicata* doctrines present the last bastion of legal certainty. More specifically, *res judicata* is an expression of public interest (*interest reipublicae ut sit finis litium*) and of private benefit to individual litigants (*nemo debet bis vexari pro una et eadem cause*).[95] It is in the public interest for there to be an end to litigation to ensure legal certainty. Private interest is expressed in the need to protect individuals from being tried more than once on the same matter. *Res judicata* is one of the essential characteristics of judicial institutions in the modern State and a *sine qua non* condition of the trust placed by parties in the authority of the courts.[96] Thus, when the CJEU applies the 'rule of reason' test, it balances the interests of the infringed EU provision against the interests protected by the national rules on *res judicata*. By doing so, the EU is indirectly carving out an autonomous understanding of *res judicata*.

[94] Sujecki (2020), p. 27.
[95] Von Moschzisker (1929), pp. 299, 334.
[96] Araceli (2021), pp. 361, 362.

At the outset, it should be mentioned that the EU legal order recognises the importance of *res judicata* as an important and basic principle or the 'expression'[97] of the principle of legal certainty found in the laws of the Member States. Unsurprisingly, the 'rule of reason' balancing test is regularly kicked-off by the expression of the CJEU's respect for *res judicata* with the following phrasing 'attention should be drawn to the importance', both in the legal order of the EU and in national legal systems, of the principle of *res judicata*.[98]

3.2.1 Köbler

The first case to draw the line of EU conforming objective dimensions of national *res judicata* was Köbler.[99] The case concerned the objective dimension of an Austrian judgment rendered by the administrative court ('Verwaltungsgerichtshof'). Mr Köbler applied for a length-of-service salary increment for university professors. He claimed that, although he had not completed 15 years' service as a professor at Austrian universities, he had completed the length of service required in universities of other Member States. He claimed that fixing the condition by reference to service performed solely in Austrian universities amounted to indirect discrimination unjustified under EU law.[100] The 'Verwaltungsgerichtshof' rejected his claim. Due to a lack of means of recourse, Mr Köbler brought an action for damages against Austria for reparation of the loss, which he allegedly suffered as a result of the infringement of EU law. The Austrian, the French and the UK governments maintained that a Member State cannot be held liable for a breach of EU law attributable to a court. They relied, *inter alia*, on *res judicata* and the principle of legal certainty. Austria in particular argued that a re-examination of the legal appraisal by a court adjudicating at last instance would be incompatible with the

[97] Case C-126/97, Eco Swiss China Time Ltd v Benetton International NV, 1.6.1999, ECLI:EU:C:1999:269, para 46.

[98] Case C-234/04, Rosmarie Kapferer v Schlank & Schick GmbH, 16.3.2006, ECLI:EU:C:2006:178, para 20, Case C-2/08, Amministrazione dell'Economia e delle Finanze and Agenzia delle entrate v Fallimento Olimpiclub Srl, 3.1.2009, ECLI:EU:C:2009:506, para 22, Case C-505/14, Klausner Holz Niedersachsen GmbH v Land Nordrhein-Westfalen, 11.11.2015, ECLI:EU:C:2015:742, para 38, Case C-234/17, XC and Others v Generalprokuratur, 24.10.2018, ECLI:EU:C:2018:853, para 52, Case C-676/17, Oana Mădălina Călin v Direcţia Regională a Finanţelor Publice Ploieşti – Administraţia Judeţeană a Finanţelor Publice Dâmboviţa and Others, 11.1.2019, ECLI:EU:C:2019:700, para 26, Case C-69/14, Dragoş Constantin Târşia v Statul român and Serviciul Public Comunitar Regim Permise de Conducere si Inmatriculare a Autovehiculelor, 6.10.2015, ECLI:EU:C:2015:662, para 28.

[99] Case C-224/01, Gerhard Köbler v Republik Österreich, 30.1.2003, ECLI:EU:C:2003:513.

[100] Case C-224/01, Gerhard Köbler v Republik Österreich, 30.1.2003, ECLI:EU:C:2003:513, paras 5–6.

function of such a court since the purpose of its decisions is to bring a dispute to a definitive conclusion.[101]

Importantly, in the opinion of AG Léger, the 'prevailing traditional definition' of *res judicata* is the triple identity test. He argued on this basis that a claim raised for damages (reparations) caused by a breach of EU law does not share a threefold identity with the anterior judgment on Mr Köbler's request for the salary increment.[102] The CJEU seemingly adopted AG Léger's rationale. Proceedings seeking to render a Member State liable do not have the 'same purpose' and do not necessarily involve the 'same parties' as the proceedings resulting in the decision, which has acquired the status of *res judicata*. Granting damages would not necessarily be invalidating the status of *res judicata* of the judicial decision responsible for the damage.[103]

It would seem the CJEU based its decision on the triple identity test in order to resolve the quandary on the admissibility of a damages claim for EU law infringements. The Court made reference to the same parties and the same purpose ('objet'); impliedly leaving out the legal ground ('cause').[104] The approach of the court follows the AG's opinion, which seems to be rooted in the French model. One point of interest should be raised on that note; namely, the evaluation of the triple identity test as the 'prevailing traditional definition'. Neither the AG, nor the CJEU provided any background as to the determination of this factor nor any other indications as to the sources of their consideration.

3.2.2 Lucchini

The facts of the case concerned Lucchini, who applied for state aid with the Italian authorities. This aid measure was notified to the Commission, which had to assess its compatibility with EU law. The Commission eventually issued its decision, declaring the aid intended for Lucchini incompatible with the internal market. Prior to this decision, however, Lucchini had instituted civil litigation against the competent Italian authorities to establish its right to the payment of the aid. The 'Tribunale civile e penale di Roma' held that Lucchini was entitled to the aid in question and ordered the competent authorities to pay the amounts claimed. None of the parties raised points of EU (state aid) law, nor the Commission decision which had been issued in the meantime. The judgment was confirmed on appeal and became *res judicata* and the aid was disbursed to Lucchini. After an exchange of correspondence

---

[101] Case C-224/01, Gerhard Köbler v Republik Österreich, 30.1.2003, ECLI:EU:C:2003:513, paras 5–6.

[102] Opinion of AG Leger in Case C-110/05, Commission of the European Communities v Italian Republic, 9.7.2008, ECLI:EU:C:2008:386, para 101.

[103] Case C-224/01, Gerhard Köbler v Republik Österreich, 30.1.2003, ECLI:EU:C:2003:513, para 39.

[104] Case C-160/14, João Filipe Ferreira da Silva e Brito and Others v Estado português, 9.1.2015, ECLI:EU:C:2015:565, para 55.

between the Commission and the Italian authorities, the latter decided to revoke the national grounds for the aid scheme and ordered Lucchini to repays the aid. The matter was referred to the Consiglio di Stato' which had no doubt as to the *res judicata* effect of the judgment issued by the 'Tribunale civile e penale di Roma' and that that effect precludes, in principle, considerations of EU law, which could have (or should have) been raised (or observed) in the litigation process. Nevertheless, such an understanding of *res judicata* could conflict with the Commission decision.[105]

The CJEU started off its assessment with reference to Article 2909 of the Italian Civil Code, which precludes not only the reopening, in a second set of proceedings, of pleas in law which have already been expressly and definitively determined but also precludes the examination of matters which could have been raised in earlier proceedings but were not. One of the consequences of such an interpretation of that provision may be that effects are attributed to a decision of a national court which exceed the limits of the jurisdiction of the court in question as laid down in EU law. In the case at hand, the national court had violated the exclusive jurisdiction of the Commission on assessing the compatibility of aid. The application of Article 2909 to its fullest extent would frustrate the application of EU law in so far as it would make it impossible to recover unlawful State aid granted. The CJEU went on to stress that the national court is under duty to apply the principle of consistent interpretation of national law, if necessary refusing of its own motion to apply any conflicting national provision. Thus, the CJEU went on to state that EU law precludes the application of national provisions, such as Article 2909 of the Italian Civil Code, which seeks to lay down the principle of *res judicata* in so far as the application of that provision prevents the recovery of illegal State aid.[106]

The judgment by the CJEU indicates, first, that the broad Italian model of *res judicata* is problematic in the light of EU law, as it endangers the effective application of EU law. The CJEU noted that national courts are under an obligation to guarantee the 'full effect'[107] of EU law, either through consistent interpretation or setting aside the *res judicata* rules. Secondly, the rationale employed by the CJEU seems to indicate that the Italian judgment should be considered a 'null judgment' ('wirkungsloses Urteil'). To elaborate, the Italian court blatantly exceeded its jurisdiction; such a manifest deficiency should render it without any effect.[108] The rather unconditional language used by the CJEU is also understandable due to the implications a lenient approach to the issue would have—national courts could effectively

[105] Case C-119/05, Ministero dell'Industria, del Commercio e dell'Artigianato v Lucchini SpA, 18.7.2007, ECLI:EU:C:2007:434, paras 17–39.

[106] Case C-119/05, Ministero dell'Industria, del Commercio e dell'Artigianato v Lucchini SpA, 18.7.2007, ECLI:EU:C:2007:434, paras 59–62.

[107] Case C-119/05, Ministero dell'Industria, del Commercio e dell'Artigianato v Lucchini SpA, 18.7.2007, ECLI:EU:C:2007:434, para 61.

[108] Kornezov (2014), p. 816. The rationale of the judgment has more recently been reaffirmed in Case C-586/18P. See Case C-586/18P, Buonotourist Srl v European Commission, 4.3.2020, ECLI: EU:C:2020:152, paras 88–96.

overrule the primacy of EU law and exclusive jurisdictions of the EU authorities through *res judicata*. An individual cannot, in such circumstances, rely on the interests protected by *res judicata*, namely legal certainty or legitimate expectations. In fact, State aid law has proven to be an area, where regard for the interests of the beneficiary is of least concern.[109] Thus, the CJEU had not conducted a precise balancing test.

3.2.3 Fallimento Olimpiclub

While the CJEU abstained from a detailed balancing test in Lucchini, this would change in Olimpiclub. There, a contract involving Olimpiclub was found to circumvent the relevant legislation in order to obtain a VAT advantage. The Italian tax authorities accordingly adjusted their tax notices, which Olimpiclub successfully challenged before the Provincial Tax Court. On appeal, the Regional Tax Court confirmed the decision. Another challenge was filed, where the issue of *res judicata* became apparent, since Olimpiclub essentially relied on the two previous judgments, which had acquired *res judicata* status and which did not find the contract unlawful. Although those judgments related to different tax periods, the findings in those judgments and the approach adopted were—again—binding in accordance with Article 2909 of the Italian Civil Code.

AG Mazák noted that 'Lucchini' is not singular in the sense that EU law can preclude national *res judicata* solely in cases of exclusive competence of the EU (on the other hand, the area of VAT is only partially harmonised). In the opinion of AG Mazák, the Italian scope of *res judicata* was rather 'unorthodox'.[110] He went on to qualify the 'same matter' as being 'commonly understood' as the same 'subject-matter, legal basis and parties',[111] again seeming to imply a triple identity test, with some modification in the language employed. He then submitted that the *res judicata* effects of the prior Italian judgments should not extend to the dispute that gave rise to the preliminary reference and that the principle of legal certainty was subsequently also limited in scope.

The CJEU first expressed the view that national *res judicata* rules are subject to the general limits of procedural autonomy, i.e. the principle of effectiveness. It then made a distinction between Olimpiclub and Lucchini, where the issue was of division of competence between the Commission and the national court. In Olimpiclub, however, the issue was, in essence, whether the broad Italian model of *res judicata* is compatible with *effet utile*. The CJEU conducted the 'rule of reason' test—more specifically, it inquired whether the interpretation of Article 2909

[109] Merola (2020), pp. 267–271.

[110] Opinion of AG Mazak in Case C-280/08, Deutsche Telekom AG v European Commission, 22.4.2010, ECLI:EU:C:2010:212, para 67.

[111] Opinion of AG Mazak in Case C-280/08, Deutsche Telekom AG v European Commission, 22.4.2010, ECLI:EU:C:2010:212, para 68.

of the Italian Civil Code may be justified with a view of protecting legal certainty. The CJEU found that the provision not only prevents the challenge of a *res judicata* decision in breach of EU law, but also prevents any finding on a fundamental issue common to other cases, contained in a judicial decision which has acquired the force of *res judicata*, from being called into question in the context of judicial scrutiny of another decision taken by the relevant tax authority in respect of the same taxpayer or taxable person, but relating to a different tax year. This would basically preclude any rectification of an abusive practice, which would persist for every subsequent tax year.[112] Thus, Article 2909 of the Italian Civil Code should be left unapplied by the national court.

We can gather from Olimpiclub that the CJEU confirms Köbler inasmuch as it does not share the same concept of the objective dimension of the Italian *res judicata*.[113] It also seems to confirm that the parts of the judgment covered by *res judicata* should not cover the closely connected issues found in the reasoning of the judgment.[114] This basically confirms the ruling in Lucchini; however—as made clear by the CJEU—not for the same reasons. The main reason for striking down the broad scope in Lucchini pertained to the principle of primacy, while the main reason in Olimpiclub pertains to the principle of effectiveness.[115]

3.2.4 Klausner Holz

In this case, the CJEU had once more to deal with an infringement of EU State aid law, as a consequence of a *res judicata* judgment; however, this time in relation to the German model of *res judicata* and a more nuanced background than Lucchini. In essence, Klausner Holz concluded an agreement for the purchase of wood from a German federal State in successive amounts. Due to financial difficulties affecting Klausner Holz, the federal State rescinded the contract, prompting Klausner Holz to submit an action for positive declaratory effect, which succeeded. The declaratory judgment held that the contracts remained in force. It was confirmed on appeal,

[112] Case C-2/08, Amministrazione dell'Economia e delle Finanze and Agenzia delle entrate v Fallimento Olimpiclub Srl, 3.1.2009, ECLI:EU:C:2009:506, paras 24–29.

[113] It can also be held that the temporal dimension of Italian res judicata is too broad. See Araceli (2021), p. 377.

[114] Kornezov (2014), p. 823.

[115] More recently, the CJEU had to deal with a similar case concerning the broad application of Article 2909 of the Italian Civil Code, which effectively creates a tax precedent for coming years. The CJEU reiterated that EU law must be interpreted as meaning that a national court, in a dispute relating to VAT, may not apply the principle of the authority of res judicata where that dispute does not relate to a tax period identical to the one which was at issue in the dispute which gave rise to the judicial decision having the authority of res judicata, does not have the 'same subject matter' as that dispute, and where the application of that principle would prevent that court from taking into account EU legislation on VAT. See Case C-424/19, Cabinet de avocat UR v Administrația Sector 3 a Finanțelor Publice prin Direcția Generală Regională a Finanțelor Publice București and Others, 16.7.2020, ECLI:EU:C:2020:581, para 34.

becoming *res judicata*. Klausner Holz then instituted new proceedings, claiming performance of the contract, payment of damages and submission of information. This time, the federal State, as defendant, raised the argument that the performance of the contract would present a breach of State aid law, as the sale amounted to unlawful State aid. These arguments were previously not raised in the first-instance or appellate proceedings. If the argument was accepted, the underlying contract would be considered null and void, since this was the accepted consequence for civil contracts in breach of EU State aid law, and Klausner Holz's claim would be rejected. However, the national court was precluded from reaching such a conclusion, due to the previous declaratory judgment obtained by Klausner Holz declaring the contract in force. The question was, therefore, whether the principle of effectiveness trumps *res judicata*.

The CJEU began by carefully extrapolating the effects of § 322(1) of the German ZPO. It found that the declaratory judgment did not concern 'either principally or incidentally' the State aid characteristics of the contract, so that the latter was not examined by the appellate court. Secondly, it pointed out, that the dispute that gave rise to the preliminary reference sought condemnatory relief (claim for damages and performance) while the previous judgment sought declaratory relief. The CJEU then recognised that *res judicata* under German law has 'subjective, objective and temporal limitations' which encompass questions that could have been raised but were not.[116] The CJEU went on to remind the referring German court of the principle of consistent interpretation, under which the national court should check if § 322 (1) ZPO, together with other provisions of national law, nevertheless allows for another interpretation. The CJEU specifically referred back to the observations it had made regarding the difference between the declaratory and condemnatory nature of the subject-matter of the dispute and the lack of any principal or incidental application of State aid law in the declaratory judgment. Furthermore, the CJEU pointed out that under § 322(1) ZPO, judgments are able to become *res judicata* only in so far as a ruling has been given on the complaint made in the 'action or on a counterclaim'.[117] In the end, the CJEU applied the 'rule of reason' test, restating what was already established in Olimpliclub that *res judicata* should, in such circumstances, give way to the principle of effectiveness, if no solution is found though consistent interpretation.[118]

It is immediately clear that the CJEU conducted a full examination of the national doctrine of *res judicata*.[119] The objection raised by the defendant regarded the

[116] Case C-505/14, Klausner Holz Niedersachsen GmbH v Land Nordrhein-Westfalen, 11.11.2015, ECLI:EU:C:2015:742, paras 28–30.

[117] Case C-505/14, Klausner Holz Niedersachsen GmbH v Land Nordrhein-Westfalen, 11.11.2015, ECLI:EU:C:2015:742, paras 35–36.

[118] Case C-505/14, Klausner Holz Niedersachsen GmbH v Land Nordrhein-Westfalen, 11.11.2015, ECLI:EU:C:2015:742, paras 41–46.

[119] The CJEU did not fully embrace the approach used in Lucchini. This can be explained, if we take into account the fact that the Klausner Holz judgment did not challenge the authority of a Commission decision and secondly, that 'nullity' of unlawful State aid contracts is not prescribed

validity of the underlying contract, which had already been determined with binding effect, regardless of the fact that neither of the parties argued any point of EU State aid law as grounds for nullity, nor did the national court raise this issue of its own motion. Apparently, the CJEU does not necessarily accept the preclusion of issues, which could have or should have been invoked in prior proceedings but were not. In addition, it suggests that declaratory and condemnatory relief should not be considered identical in determining the objective dimension of *res judicata*. Interestingly, the CJEU made no effort to curtail the scope of the German model by relying on the 'prevailing traditional definition' of the triple identity test but instead suggested that the national court should adopt a restrictive interpretation of § 322(1) ZPO, limiting the understanding of a 'claim' in German procedural law. Indeed, upon referral to the national court, the latter concluded that in order to effectively enforce EU law, it is permissible to interpret § 322 ZPO in such a way that national *res judicata* does not cover a violation of EU (State aid) law.[120]

3.2.5 Finanmadrid

In Finanmadrid the rules of Spanish *res judicata* were scrutinised. Under the Spanish rules of civil procedure, an order for payment can become *res judicata*. In enforcement proceedings, this prevents the (re)examination *ex officio* by the enforcement court of unfair consumer contract terms, as mandated by EU consumer protection law (Directive 93/13).

The CJEU reflected its previous case law by first stating that the rules implementing the principle of *res judicata* are a matter for the national legal order; however, in line with the principle of national procedural autonomy, those rules must still comply with the principles of equivalence and effectiveness. In the words of the CJEU, *res judicata* makes it impossible to check for unfair terms at the stage of enforcement of an order, simply because the consumers have not lodged an objection to the order within the time limit prescribed. The CJEU held that the rules implementing res judicata in the context of the order for payment procedure appear to run counter to the principle of effectiveness, in so far as they make it impossible or excessively difficult to ensure the protection conferred on consumers by Directive 93/13.[121]

The CJEU provided no detailed explanation in striking down the objective dimension of national *res judicata*, apart from stating its general incompatibility with the principle of effectiveness. The case is peculiar, since the issue as to whether

---

by EU law but derived from national law. EU law allows for other effective remedies, that is why the CJEU prompted the national court to explore other venues of national law to remedy the situation.

[120] LG Münster, Urteil vom 21.06.2018—011 O 334/12, §151.

[121] Council Directive 93/13/EEC of 5 April 1993 on unfair terms in consumer contracts, OJ L 95, 21.4.1993.

decisions issued in *ex parte* proceedings should be endowed with the force of *res judicata* was raised in argument. At least impliedly, we can gather that infringements of EU consumer contract law that should have been checked by the national court *ex officio* but were not, should not be covered by the scope of *res judicata*.

3.2.6 Intermediate Conclusion

Up until Klausner Holz, the CJEU appeared to have been operating with an autonomous concept of *res judicata* when sizing up the national counterparts. This concept seemed to follow the 'triple identity test', which is prevalent in France, Spain and other jurisdictions. At the same time it was fairly narrow; limited to the operative part of the judgment. However, in Klausner Holz, the court did not refer to this concept but suggested that the German court should restrict its own interpretation of *res judicata*. Even though the particularities of these cases differ significantly, a general trend can be observed at the macro level; the CJEU is becoming more comfortable developing solutions which, without going as far as requiring exceptions to the finality of judicial decisions, require a detailed engagement with domestic procedural law.[122]

4 Res Judicata in the Brussels Regime

For the majority of its existence, the Brussels Regime deferred to national law, when it came to the effects of *res judicata*, coupled with the theory of extension of effects as developed in Hoffman v Krieg.[123] The inherent problem with the aforementioned theory is the inconsistency it produces in a contained legal system. For instance, in Germany, a decision on preliminary questions of law will generally not become *res judicata* if not raised in a separate claim, whereas other jurisdictions may extend to them *res judicata* by default. In some jurisdictions, decisions on procedural issues do not become *res judicata*, while in others, they do, or they are not considered as procedural judgments in the first place etc.[124]

[122] Araceli (2021), p. 380.

[123] Extension of effects means that a recognized foreign judgment has the same effects in the forum that it has in the foreign country, subject to practical feasibility and the forum's public policy. See Harder (2013), p. 443.

[124] Voulgarakis (2020), p. 453.

4.1 The Scope According to Gothaer

The procedural landscape changed when the CJEU defined an autonomous 'EU' concept of *res judicata* in Gothaer.[125] The latter case concerned German claimants who filed an action against a German defendant in a Belgian court. That court declared itself to have no authority to hear and decide the case. In essence, it held that the claimants were bound by a jurisdiction clause, which provided that Icelandic courts had exclusive jurisdiction. The Belgian judgment became *res judicata*. The claimants then instituted proceedings before German courts, where the defendant submitted that the actions were inadmissible inasmuch as the Belgian judgment produced legal effects not only as regards the Belgian courts' lack of jurisdiction but also as regards the finding that jurisdiction lay with the Icelandic courts. Under the theory of extension of effects, any such effect should be reviewed under Belgian law. The CJEU explained that the recognition of judgments handed down by courts of Member States, declining jurisdiction under the Brussels regime, is governed by a *sui generis* system.[126] This reasoning was based on the principle of mutual trust, the need for enforcing common rules of jurisdiction and the prohibition of reviewing the jurisdiction of the Belgian courts. Moreover, according to the CJEU, the concept of *res judicata* under EU law attaches not only to the operative part of the judgment in question, but also to the *ratio decidendi* of that judgment, which provides the necessary underpinning for the operative part and is inseparable from it.[127] This latter explanation was provided by the court as a response to the arguments of the claimants which alleged that the *res judicata* effect should be restricted to the operative part.

Logically, the question arises, which situations—apart from *prorogatio fori*—are *mutatis mutandis* covered by this autonomous concept. The answer must be ascertained through the underlying reasons provided by the CJEU; namely, the strengthening of mutual trust, the need to enforce common rules of jurisdiction and the prohibition of any review of the grounds for jurisdiction. It is logical, then, that when jurisdiction is determined by any of the 'common rules' provided in the Brussels I bis Regulation, the decision of the court of origin should also be subject to this autonomous conception of *res judicata*. For instance, if a party institutes proceedings in the court of Member State A on the jurisdictional grounds established by Article 7(1)(b) Brussels I bis Regulation and the court declines jurisdiction because it considers that the place of performance is in Member State B, then the courts of Member State B should be bound by that determination, while courts in other

[125] The judgment's rationale was recently analogously extended in the domain of the Succession regulation. See Case C-422/20, RK v CR, 9.1.2021, ECLI:EU:C:2021:718, para 44.

[126] Case C-456/11, Gothaer Allgemeine Versicherung AG and Others v Samskip GmbH, 15.11.2012, ECLI:EU:C:2012:719, para 42.

[127] Case C-456/11, Gothaer Allgemeine Versicherung AG and Others v Samskip GmbH, 15.11.2012, ECLI:EU:C:2012:719, para 38.

Member States should reject jurisdiction.[128] This outcome is not, however, entirely certain when jurisdiction is to be determined by both the common rules of jurisdiction and deference to national law, e.g. when a determination is made as to whether an individual is domiciled in a Member State (Article 62 Brussels I bis Regulation).

Furthermore, it is highly doubtful whether the autonomous concept of *res judicata* applies when it is not the formal validity of the jurisdictional clause that is at stake, but its substantive validity (e.g. whether 'one-sided' jurisdictional clauses can be considered valid).[129] On the other hand, an obvious exception to the autonomous conception of *res judicata* is found in rules which provide exceptions from the prohibition of any review of the jurisdiction of the court of origin (e.g. consumer, insurance and employment contracts).

It must be emphasized that a distinction should be drawn between the finding of facts for the purposes of jurisdiction (e.g. determining the place of performance or of a tort (Article 7 Brussels I bis Regulation)) and for the decision on the merits. Consider, for example, the situation where a court dismisses an action for lack of jurisdiction after assessing that the *forum loci delicti* or the place of performance is located in another Member State. As already mentioned, this would bind those courts to accept jurisdiction. It should, however, in no case preclude those courts from ultimately determining that no tortious act was committed or that the contract that needed to be performed was invalid, thus rejecting the claim on its merits.[130]

Following Gothaer, it is now possible in practice for a national court that does not have jurisdiction to establish a binding referral of a dispute by means of a 'procedural judgment' (*Prozessurteil*). The CJEU has departed from its long-lasting Hoffman v Krieg paradigm. It has now established a two-tier *res judicata* system. On the one hand, a national judge is under an obligation to observe the EU concept of *res judicata* when it comes to the assessment of jurisdiction; on the other hand, that judge must follow the national concept of *res judicata* for the assessment of other binding and preclusive effects. This also generates a further paradox. Namely, in Member States that accord a narrow scope to the matters that are scope of *res judicata*, e.g. those with the German model, a judgment which is issued in respect of jurisdiction will have effects in another Member State which it does not have in its own.[131]

It is also important to observe how the CJEU derived the autonomous definition. Namely, it referred to the *res judicata* concept which it applies for determining the effects of its own judgments.[132] Under the latter conception, the principle of *res judicata* extends to matters of fact and law actually or necessarily settled by the

[128] Voulgarakis (2020), pp. 456–457.

[129] Voulgarakis (2020), pp. 450–461.

[130] Klöpfer (2015), p. 215; Zogg (2013), pp. 39, 71.

[131] Torralba Mendiola and Rodríguez Pineau (2014), p. 425.

[132] Case C-456/11, Gothaer Allgemeine Versicherung AG and Others v Samskip GmbH, 15.11.2012, ECLI:EU:C:2012:719, para 38.

judicial decision in question.[133] It has been submitted that this solution still leaves some issues unclear; namely, whether the autonomous *res judicata* effects extend only to the *ratio decidendi* in a strict sense, i.e. the reasons which are 'absolutely' necessary to reach the conclusions in the operative part of the judgment, or whether *res judicata* extends to other reasons given which may not be as decisive but nevertheless lead to the same outcome, and contribute to it.[134] These concerns are amplified by the rather underdeveloped doctrine of *res judicata* in the CJEU's own rulings. In any case, it has been argued[135] that this approach mimics the French model of *res judicata*; however, we have already established that 'motifs decisifs' are not uniformly accepted as *res judicata* in French doctrine. In any case, it is certain that the rather broad concept utilized by the CJEU is at odds with the German model, which does not extend *res judicata* beyond the operative part.

4.2 *Lis pendens and the Triple Identity Test*

For the time being, the *res judicata* concept from the Gothaer judgment has not spilled over to substantive considerations, which remain in the domain of the theory of extension of effects. Nevertheless, in the past, arguments were raised that the Wolf v. Cox judgment at least partially provides for preclusion of claims which were already adjudicated upon. Following that judgment, a successful party cannot be compelled to relitigate *res judicata* claims in another Member State. On the other hand, the triple identity test is firmly established for the purposes of determining the 'same cause of action', in line with Brussels I bis Regulation rules on *lis pendens*. The triple identity test could also be used to provide an objective dimension of EU *res judicata*. This would prevent unsuccessful parties from relitigating disputes in other Member States.[136]

Be that as it may, we will consider the *lis pendens* determination for the purposes of the final assessment of convergence/divergence of concepts. The rather broad scope of the triple identity test is discussed in detail in other parts of this report. It should suffice to say that the 'same cause of action' under *lis pendens* rules encompasses not only the causes of the action *stricto sensu*, but also their object—'-même cause et même objet'. The cause of action, on the one hand, is formed by the factual and legal grounds that support the claim. As to the object, on the other hand,

---

[133] Lenaerts et al. (2014), p. 782; Case C-277/95 P, Erika Lenz and Volker Lenz v Commission of the European Communities, 28.11.1996, ECLI:EU:C:1996:456, Case C-310/97 P, Commission of the European Communities v AssiDomän Kraft Products AB, Iggesunds Bruk AB, Korsnäs AB, MoDo Paper AB, Södra Cell AB, Stora Kopparbergs Bergslags AB and Svenska Cellulosa AB, 14.1.1999, ECLI:EU:C:1999:407, para 54, Case T-333/01, Karl L. Meyer v Commission of the European Communities, 13.2.2003, ECLI:EU:T:2003:32, paras 22–27.

[134] Torralba Mendiola and Rodríguez Pineau (2014), p. 426.

[135] Klöpfer (2015), p. 213.

[136] Dickinson (2010), p. 17.

it is to be understood in a broad sense, not as the relief sought or the remedy requested, but as the main objective or purpose (the same end in view) of the claim (also known as the 'Kernpunktstheorie').[137] For example, in Gubisch, an action to enforce a contract and another for its rescission, were considered to share the cause of action. In The Tatry, an action for negative declaratory relief, i.e. that there is no liability, and an action for damages, shared the cause of action (same factual and legal grounds) and object (determination of liability).[138]

5 Conclusion

In the introduction we mentioned that the pioneering study conducted by Kornezov found a convergence between the autonomous *res judicata* concept in procedural autonomy case law and the *lis pendens* rules in the Brussels I bis Regulation. More specifically, after analysing the Köbler, Lucchini and Olimpiclub judgments, Kornezov concluded that the CJEU operates with a narrow triple identity test for determining the scope of national *res judicata*, wherein *res judicata* is limited to the operative part, mimicking the French model. He remarks that this bears a striking resemblance to the *lis pendens* rules under Brussels I bis Regulation. However, at that time, neither the Klausner Holz, nor Gothaer judgments were issued. These two judgments markedly changed the approach taken by the CJEU.

Firstly, the Klausner Holz judgment departed from the CJEU's previous case law. In Klausner Holz, the CJEU indicated that the action for performance and damages does not share the same subject matter as the prior declaratory judgment and suggests to the national court that the German rules on *res judicata* are too broadly framed to accommodate the effective enforcement of EU law. However, the CJEU does not resolve the issue by relying on an autonomous understanding of *res judicata*, as it did in Köbler and Lucchini. This might be understood if we take into account what a resolution under the triple identity test would actually entail. The action for a declaratory relief was directed at obtaining a declaration of validity of the contract. In the subsequent proceedings, the claimant attempted, on the basis of the valid contract, to obtain, on the one hand, damages for non-fulfilment of the valid contracts and, on the other hand, the future performance of delivery claims. These proceedings therefore dealt with the substantive consequences of the determination of the validity of the contractual relationship. Applying the broad concept of the 'Kernpunktstheorie' developed in *lis pendens* case law, one will have to come to the conclusion that both proceedings were ultimately about the validity or realisation of the concluded contract and the purpose was directed towards the fulfilment of the same.[139] Thus, if the CJEU referred to its case law on the triple identity test, as

[137] Gascón Inchausti and Barragán Schumann (2021), pp. 15, 29.

[138] Pippa (2015), Article 29, p. 326.

[139] Voß (2019), p. 137.

developed in the *lis pendens* case law and infused in national autonomy case law, it would not be able to guarantee the effective application of EU law. Contrary to Köbler and Lucchini, the Klausner Holz case would share the same subject matter with the declaratory judgment, which has become *res judicata*. Additionally, the Klausner Holz judgment seems to be at odds with the Gothaer judgment as well. The latter is rooted in the *res judicata* effect ascribed to the CJEU's own judgments according to which *res judicata* extends to the *ratio decidendi* of judgments. The issue of validity of the underlying contract is a preliminary question of law, absolutely necessary to determine the outcome of the case. However, it has already been resolved in independent proceedings. If *res judicata* were to extend to it in incidental circumstances, then it must *a fortiori* extend to it when raised as the relief sought in independent proceedings. In sum, the Klausner Holz case demonstrates that there is an internal inconsistency in the autonomous understanding of *res judicata* in case law pertaining to national procedural autonomy. This inconsistency may be necessary to guarantee the effectiveness of EU law, however, it is an inconsistency nonetheless, posing a detriment to legal certainty in EU law.

Secondly, the Gothaer judgment disrupts the narrow approach on *res judicata* employed by the CJEU in national autonomy case law. In the latter case law, the CJEU essentially struck down the broad scope of *res judicata* as defined in Article 2909 of the Italian Civil Code and interpreted by case law. This can be contrasted with Gothaer, where the CJEU introduced a relatively broad concept of *res judicata* which encompasses not only the operative part but also the *ratio decidendi* of the judgment. This seems to be in direct contradiction to its case law on procedural autonomy. This straightforward conclusion can be somewhat alleviated by adopting the perspective that the problem with the Italian model did not strictly lie in its objective dimension, but perhaps rather its temporal dimension.

In more general terms, the case law of the CJEU points to a fragmented concept of *res judicata* in EU law. While initial developments showed a gradual convergence towards the French model of *res judicata*, recent case law seems to demonstrate a more casuistic approach. The reasoning of the CJEU in prior judgements might also be scrutinized for the light application of the triple identity test. The inclination towards this approach is understandable, considering its use in international law, however, it can also be said to somewhat neglect the differences between the legal traditions and systems of the Member States (granted, the EU membership is fluctuating over time and the prevalence of one legal tradition is chained to the number of Member States subscribed to it). Similarly, more recent and watershed judgements, such as that in Gothaer, provide lacklustre arguments for the adoption of EU *res judicata* in the field of cross-border recognition and enforcement, making reference to the CJEU's own understanding of the concept. *Res judicata* is considered a general principle of EU law. The CJEU derives general principles of EU law from the general principles common to the laws of the Member States.[140]

[140]Communication from the Commission—Commission Notice on the recovery of unlawful and incompatible State aid, OJ C 247, paras. 23, 44.

Accordingly, care should be taken to derive the EU concept of *res judicata* from the laws of the Member States. Otherwise, the risk of judicial activism and intrusion into national procedural autonomy will increase.

References

Alter K (1998) Who are the 'Masters of the Treaty'?: European governments and the European Court of Justice. Int Organ 52(1):121–147

Araceli T (2021) National res judicata in the European Union: revisiting the tension between the temptation of effectiveness and the acknowledgement of domestic procedural law. Common Mark Law Rev 58(2):361–390

Baghrizabehi D (2016) The current state of national procedural autonomy: a principle in motion. InterEULawEast 3(1):13–30

BIICL (n.d.-a) National report for France. https://www.biicl.org/files/3481_france_final_c.pdf

BIICL (n.d.-b) National report for Netherlands. https://www.biicl.org/files/3483_netherlands_final_c.pdf

BIICL (n.d.-c) National report for Sweden. https://www.biicl.org/files/3486_sweden_final_c.pdf

Bobek M (2012) Why there is no principle of national procedural autonomy. Intersentia, Cambridge

Bores Lazo J, Serrano Ron I (2020) National report for Spain. Project EU-En4s — JUST-AG-2018/JUST-JCOO-AG-2018

Bylander E, Linton M (2020) National report for Sweden. Project EU-En4s — JUST-AG-2018/JUST-JCOO-AG-2018

Christian K (2020) Europäischer Rechtskraftbegriff. Mohr Siebeck, Tübingen

Craig P, de Búrca G (2015) Text, cases and materials, 6th edn. Oxford University Press, Oxford

Dawson M, De Witte B, Muir E (2013) Judicial activism at the European Court of Justice. Edward Elgar Publishing, Cheltenham

De Schutter O, Tulkens F (2008) The European Court of Human Rights as a pragmatic institution. In: Brems E (ed) Conflicting between fundamental rights. Intersentia, Cambridge

Delicostopoulos J (2004) Towards European procedural primacy in national legal systems. Eur Law J 9(5):599–613

Dickinson A (2010) The effect in the European Community of judgments in civil and commercial matters: recognition, Res Judicata and abuse of process: report of England and Wales

Dougan M (2004) National remedies before the Court of Justice. Bloomsbury Publishing

Dougan M (2007) When worlds collide! Competing visions of the relationship between direct effect and supremacy. Common Mark Law Rev 44(4):931–963

Eliantonio M (2015) Concluding thoughts: legitimacy, rationale and extent of the incidental proceduralisation of EU law. Rev Eur Adm Law 8(1):175–204

Engström J (2011) The principle of effective judicial protection after the Lisbon Treaty

Fennelly N (2013) The National Judge as Judge of the European Union. The Court of Justice of the European Union, The Court of Justice and the Construction of Europe: analyses and perspectives on sixty years of case-law - La Cour de Justice et la Construction de l'Europe: Analyses et Perspectives de Soixante Ans de Jurisprudence. Asser, Springer, The Hague, pp 61–79

Ferrand F (2014) Lis pendens and Res Judicata. From national law to a possible European harmonization? In: Hess B, Kollman S, Adolphsen J (eds) Festschrift für Peter Gottwald zum 70. Geburtstag. C.H. Beck, Münich, pp 144–158

Franziska K, Franz H (2019) Law of remedies. Intersentia, Cambridge

Galetta D (2010) Procedural autonomy of EU Member States: paradise lost? Springer

Gascón Inchausti F, Barragán Schumann G (2021) The rules on lis pendens and on res judicata in the ELI/UNIDROIT model European rules of civil procedure. Ius Dictum 5:15–29

Giliker P (2014) The Europeanisation of English Tort Law. Hart Publishing, Oxford

Grashof F (2016) National procedural autonomy revisited. Europa Law Publishing
Halberstam D (2021) Understanding national remedies and the principle of National Procedural Autonomy: a constitutional approach. Camb Yearb Eur Leg Stud 23:128–158. https://doi.org/10.1017/cel.2021.12
Harder S (2013) The effects of recognized foreign judgments in civil and commercial matters. Int Comp Law Q 62(2):441–461
Hazelhorst M (2017) Free movement of civil judgments in the European Union and the right to a fair trial. Springer
Hess B (2012) Procedural harmonisation in a European context. In: Kramer XE, Van Rhee CH (eds) Civil litigation in a globalising world. Asser, Spinger, The Hague, pp 159–174
Hesse K (1995) Grundzüge des Verfassungsrechts der Bundesrepublik Deutschland. C. H. Beck, München, p 1972
Jaremba U (2013) National judges as EU law judges: the Polish civil law system. Martinus Nijhoff Publishers
Justinian's Digest
Kaczorowska M, Voinich A, Previatello M (2022) National report for Italy. Project EU-En4s — JUST-AG-2018/JUST-JCOO-AG-2018
Kakouris C (1997) Do the Member States possess judicial procedural "autonomy". Common Mark Law Rev 34(6):1389–1412
Klöpfer M (2015) Unionsautonome Rechtskraft klageabweisender Prozessurteile – Paradigmenwechsel im Europäischen Zivilverfahrensrecht. Zeitschrift für das Privatrecht der Europäischen Union 12(5):210–218
Komnios A (2007) EC private antitrust enforcement: decentralised application of EC competition law by national courts. Hart Publishing, Oxford
Kornezov A (2014) Res Judicata of national judgments incompatible with EU law: time for a major rethink. Common Mark Law Rev 51(3):809–842
Krans B, Nylund A (2020) Procedural autonomy across Europe. Intersentia
Kunštek E, Kunda I, Mihelčić G et al (2020) National report for Croatia. Project EU-En4s — JUST-AG-2018/JUST-JCOO-AG-2018
Law J (2018) A dictionary of law, 9th edn. Oxford University Press, Oxford
Lenaerts K, Maselis I, Gutman K (2014) EU procedural law. Oxford University Press, Oxford
Loizou D, Christofi D (2021) The concept of Res Judicata in the common law system with emphasis on Cypriot and UK perspectives. Lexonomica 13(2):135–150
Mangiameli S (2013) The Treaty on European Union (TEU): a commentary
Mańko R (2015) Europeanisation of civil procedure: towards common minimum standards? Publications Office. https://data.europa.eu/doi/10.2861/670
Merola M (2020) Remedies for violation of State aid rules under EU law: reasons for reform and its scope. In: Gerard D, Komninos A (eds) Remedies in EU competition law: substance, process and policy. Kluwer International Law, pp 255–309
Ortlep R, Verhoeven M (2012) The principle of primacy versus the principle of national procedural autonomy. Netherlands Adm Law
Pippa R (2015) Article 29. In: Dickinson A, Lein E (eds) The Brussel I Regulation recast. Oxford University Press, Oxford
Prechal S (1998) Community law in national courts: the lessons from Van Schijndel. Common Mark Law Rev 35(3):681–706
Prodinger L, Nunner-Krautgasser B (2020) National report for Austria. Project EU-En4s — JUST-AG-2018/JUST-JCOO-AG-2018
Reneman M (2014) EU asylum procedures and the right to an effective remedy. Bloomsbury Publishing
Rijavec V, Baghrizabehi D, Drnovšek K et al (2020) National report for Slovenia. Project EU-En4s — JUST-AG-2018/JUST-JCOO-AG-2018
Schaffstein S (2016) The doctrine of res judicata before international commercial arbitral tribunals. Oxford University Press, Oxford

Schebesta H (2014) Procedural theory in EU law. In: Purnhagen K, Rott P (eds) Varieties of European economic law and regulation: Liber Amicorum for Hans Micklitz. Springer, New York, pp 851–862
Schütze R (2012) European constitutional law. Oxford University Press, New York
Sinai Y (2011) Reconsidering Res Judicata: a comparative perspective. Duke J Comp Int Law 21: 353–400
Smith C (2010) Remedies for breaches of EC law in national courts: legal variation and selection. In: Craig P, de Búrca G (eds) The evolution of EU law. Oxford University Press, Oxford
Sowery K (2017) Reconciling primacy and environmental protection: Association France Nature Environnement. Common Mark Law Rev 54(4):1157–1177
Storskrubb E (2008) Civil procedure and EU law: a policy area uncovered. Oxford University Press, Oxford
Sujecki B (2020) National report for Netherlands. Project EU-En4s — JUST-AG-2018/JUST-JCOO-AG-2018
Torralba Mendiola E, Rodríguez Pineau E (2014) Two'S company, Three'S a crowd: jurisdiction, recognition and Res Judicata in the European Union. J Priv Int Law 10(3):403–430
Tulibacka M (2009) Europeanization of civil procedures: in search of a coherence approach. Common Mark Law Rev 46(5):1527–1565
Van Cleynenbreugel P (2011) Transforming shields into swords: the VEBIC judgment, adequate judicial protection standards and the emergence of procedural heteronomy in EU law. Maastricht J Eur Comp Law 18(1):511–547
Van Gerven W (2000) Of rights, remedies and procedures. Common Mark Law Rev 37(3):501–536
Van Rhee C (2012) Harmonisation of civil procedure: an historical and comparative perspective. In: Van Rhee C, Kramer X (eds) Civil litigation in globalising world. Springer, pp 39–63
Von Moschzisker R (1929) Res judicata. Yale Law J 38(3):299–334
Voß C (2019) Die Durchbrechung der Rechtskraft nationaler Zivilgerichtsurteile zu Gunsten des unionsrechtlichen "effet utile"? Nomos, Baden-Baden
Voulgarakis K (2020) Reflections on the scope of "EU res judicata" in the context of Regulation 1215/2012. J Priv Int Law 16(3):451–464
Wasserfallen F (2010) The judiciary as legislator? How the European Court of Justice shapes policy-making in the European Union. J Eur Public Policy 17(8):1128–1146
Wennerås P (2007) The enforcement of EC environmental law. Oxford University Press, Oxford
Widdershoven R (2019) National procedural autonomy and general EU law limits. Rev Eur Adm Law 12(2):5–34
Zogg S (2013) Accumulation of contractual and tortious causes of action under the judgments regulation. J Priv Int Law 9(1):39–76
Van de Velden J, Stefanelli J (2006) Comparative report: The Effect in the European Community of Judgments in Civil and Commercial Matters: Recognition, Res Judicata and Abuse of Process. British Institute of International and Comparative Law
Naydenova D (2020) National report for Bulgaria. Project EU-En4s - JUST-AG-2018/JUST-JCOO-AG-2018

The Effects of Judgments and Court Settlements in Cross-border Collective Redress and the Brussels I bis Regulation: Houston, We Have a Problem!

Jerca Kramberger Škerl

Abstract EU Member States offer a colourful plethora of collective redress mechanisms available in different cases of mass harm. The article focuses on the recognition and enforcement of titles stemming from such proceedings in a cross-border setting, where the Brussels I bis Regulation is called into action. Namely, said Regulation is applicable, but not (yet) adapted to cross-border collective redress. Several issues need urgent attention. First, the collective redress unveils the already problematic qualification of court settlements in the Brussels I bis Regulation, or, more specifically, their treatment in the chapter on recognition and enforcement. The latter arguably does not allow the courts to look at the specific coming into existence and effects of the court settlement at hand, but automatically demands the application of the rules from the special chapter devoted to court settlements and authentic instruments. Its most notable deficiency is the lack of talk of recognition (it only provides the possibility of enforcement), but also the further restriction of the possible grounds for refusal of enforcement. When a court settlement has, under national law, the same effects as judgments, such treatment in the Brussels I bis Regulation is not justified. There is also the open question of the qualification of out-of-court settlements approved by the court: are they deemed to be dealt with as court settlements, as judgments, as neither? The second challenging issue is the binding effect of judgments and court settlements regarding individual members of the class, most notably in the so-called opt-out collective redress proceedings. If the binding effect is established, the opt-out mechanisms can still be problematic from the point of view of the regularity of service of the introductory document. Courts will have to interpret, on a case-by-case basis, the wording of Article 45 1) (b) of the Brussels I bis Regulation. If the strict conditions of that article are not met, there is still a possibility to apply the public policy defence from Article 45 1) (a), which, under the CJEU case-law, also covers the violations of fundamental procedural guarantees. The third important issue is the irreconcilability of final decisions in collective redress proceedings, where they consider the same defendant and the same (type

J. Kramberger Škerl (✉)
University of Ljubljana, Faculty of Law, Ljubljana, Slovenia
e-mail: jerca.kramberger@pf.uni-lj.si

V. Rijavec et al. (eds.), *Diversity of Enforcement Titles in the EU*, Ius Gentium: Comparative Perspectives on Law and Justice 111,
https://doi.org/10.1007/978-3-031-47108-7_9

of) harm, but different claimants. The rules of the Brussels I bis Regulation do not deal with these issues. As to the court settlements, the rules of the Regulation do not allow for a refusal of enforcement on grounds of irreconcilability, however, the situation could, in the view of the author, be tackled via the public policy exception. If the current wording of the Brussels I bis Regulation can, to a certain extent, be 'bent' in a way to accommodate cross-border collective redress, the author recommends tackling these issues in a new recast of the Brussels I Regulation and provides ideas for such improvements.

1 Introduction

In the common European market, it is not unusual that mass harm events affect people in different EU Member States, who would then profit from the possibility of joining their efforts in demanding compensation from the perpetrator. What is more, many times, single victims would not only face more difficulties in pursuing their own claim, but would, predicting the said difficulties, decide against pursuing such claim.[1] This, in turn, could result in more unsanctioned breaches of law, in thwarted competition, damaged environment etc. In order to prevent such consequences and facilitate collective actions, Member States have enacted different mechanisms.[2] The term 'collective redress' does not refer to one specific type of collective action, but rather describes a group of mechanisms enabling victims of the same event, of the same product default etc., to step together and initiate common court proceedings, and, in such a way, optimize their costs and efforts, as well as chances of success. The cross-border element of collective redress adds to the complexity of such multiparty proceedings and demands special legislative attention.

2 (Cross-border) Collective Redress and the EU

In its 2013 Recommendation,[3] the European Commission advised that Member States adopt the so-called 'representative action' model, where the collective action is brought by a designated or certified non-profit entity in the name of the victims. For injunctive collective redress (i.e. for temporary and preservation measures), the Commission encouraged Member States above all to provide rapid proceedings. For compensatory collective redress (i.e. for damage claims), the Commission's

[1] Rielaender speaks about the 'rational apathy' of consumers when their individual harm is trivial: Rielaender (2021), p. 4.

[2] See e.g. Amaro et al. (2018).

[3] Commission Recommendation of 11 June 2013 on common principles for injunctive and compensatory collective redress mechanisms in the Member States concerning violations of rights granted under Union Law, OJ L 201, 26.7.2013.

probably most important recommendation was that the so-called 'opt-in' principle is adopted, i.e. that only victims who expressly join the scheme are considered claimants, contrary to those who decline or remain passive.

In 2018, 'the Amaro Study' found that Member States did not all entirely follow the Commission's recommendations in enacting their national collective redress mechanisms.[4] On the basis of such developments, action was taken towards the new Consumer Collective Redress Directive (CCRD),[5] adopted in 2020. The CCRD was undoubtedly a great achievement, however, one of its most prominent weak spots is precisely the lack of rules regarding cross-border collective redress.[6] Despite the calls to include these issues,[7] no suitable compromise could yet be found, apart from the mutual recognition of legal standing of 'the qualified entities', i.e., entities entitled to represent consumers in collective redress. Entities wishing to bring a 'cross-border representative action' must fulfil very strict conditions, *inter alia* as to their non-profit status, their experience and their funding.[8] Among the provisions of the CCRD, facilitating cross-border collective redress, Rielaender mentions also the promotion of cooperation and the exchange of information between qualified entities and, notably, the mandatory opt-in mechanism for consumers from EU Member States other than the forum state.[9]

The CCRD also brought a European definition of cross-border collective action. Article 3(7) of the CCRD provides: 'cross-border representative action' means a representative action brought by a qualified entity in a Member State other than that in which the qualified entity was designated.' Furthermore, Article 9(3) of the CCRD defines what Hess[10] calls 'quasi domestic cases': 'Notwithstanding paragraph 2, Member States shall ensure that individual consumers who are not habitually resident in the Member State of the court or administrative authority before which a representative action has been brought have to explicitly express their wish to be

[4] Amaro (2018), pp. 47–48.

[5] Directive (EU) 2020/1828 of the European Parliament and of the Council of 25 November 2020 on representative actions for the protection of the collective interests of consumers and repealing Directive 2009/22/EC (Text with EEA relevance), OJ L 409, 4.12.2020.

[6] The Directive (EU) 2020/1828 thus states: "This Directive should not affect the application of rules of private international law regarding jurisdiction, the recognition and enforcement of judgments or applicable law, nor should it establish such rules. Existing instruments of Union law should apply to the procedural mechanism for representative actions required by this Directive. In particular, Regulation (EC) No. 864/2007(6), Regulation (EC) No. 593/2008(7) and Regulation (EU) No. 1215/2012(8) of the European Parliament and of the Council should apply to the procedural mechanism for representative actions required by this Directive" (Recital 21) and "This Directive is without prejudice to Union rules on private international law, in particular rules regarding jurisdiction and the recognition and enforcement of judgments in civil and commercial matters and rules on the law applicable to contractual and non-contractual obligations" (Article 2(3), point 3).

[7] Rielaender (2021), pp. 1–32.

[8] Articles 4(3), 5 and 6 of the CCRD.

[9] Rielaender (2021), p. 3.

[10] Hess (2021a).

represented in that representative action in order for those consumers to be bound by the outcome of that representative action.' Within the scope of the recognition and enforcement of judgments from other EU Member States, the latter rule can prove of great importance, since it only permits the 'opt-in' system regarding consumers who reside outside of the country of origin of the judgment. Namely, we will see that the 'opt-out' system is one of the most important possible obstacles for the recognition and enforcement of judgments in cross-border collective redress, therefore, the reduction of its use can prevent negative outcomes of such proceedings.

2.1 The Applicability of the Brussels I bis Regulation in Cross-border Collective Redress

Against the described background, the issues arising in cross-border collective redress must be tackled via the existing EU Private International Law mechanisms. It is, however, common knowledge that the EU Private International Law, specifically the Brussels I bis Regulation,[11] does not appropriately (or in any way, for that matter) address such issues,[12] despite warnings and urges from the doctrine to address collective redress in the Recast version of the Regulation.[13]

It is interesting to note that the European Commission suggested, in its proposal of 2010 for the recast of the Brussels I Regulation, that judgments issued in collective redress proceedings (as well as those regarding defamation and privacy rights) be excluded from the abolition of exequatur and continue to be submitted to the exequatur system of the original version of the Brussels I Regulation.[14] It seems that this exclusion was meant to only be temporary, namely, in Article 37(4) of the Proposal the Commission reserved itself the right to 'propose at any time' the extension of the common rules on the abolition of exequatur also to judgments in collective redress cases, 'in view of the state of convergence of national laws and of the development of Union law'. Furthermore, the Commission promised that, 'three years after the entry into force of this Regulation, or earlier in case the Commission proposes further harmonisation', it would 'submit to the European Parliament, the Council and the European Economic and Social Committee a report reviewing the continuing need to maintain the procedure for recognition and enforcement for judgments given in matters referred to in paragraph 3(b)'. Given that the adopted

[11]Regulation (EU) No. 1215/2012 of the European Parliament and of the Council of 12 December 2012 on jurisdiction and the recognition and enforcement of judgments in civil and commercial matters, OJ L 351, 20.12.2012.

[12]See e.g. Rielaender (2021), pp. 1–32; Danov (2010), pp. 359, 393.

[13]See e.g. Danov (2010), pp. 359, 393.

[14]Proposal for a Regulation of the European Parliament and of the Council on jurisdiction and the recognition and enforcement of judgments in civil and commercial matters, 14.12.2010, Article 37 (3) b).

Brussels I bis Regulation eventually did not contain any special treatment of the collective redress, the latter promises also never became binding. In the hindsight, a precious occasion might have been missed for the Commission to specifically focus on collective redress proceedings from the viewpoint of the recognition and enforcement of judgments.

In result, the Brussels I bis Regulation contains no special jurisdictional norms and no rules on recognition and enforcement specific to the cross-border collective redress. Since such proceedings are not excluded from the scope of application of the Regulation,[15] its general rules are fully applicable.[16] However, since they are not adjusted to the specificities of collective redress, problems arise both regarding jurisdiction and regarding enforcement of judgments and court settlements, which in turn undermines consumer protection, product liability and data protection litigation, EU antitrust law,[17] climate change litigation, human rights and good administration of justice in general.[18]

In recent times, European legislative action in the field of cross-border collective redress is becoming ever more pressing. The practical importance of the collective redress in the EU is beginning to show, *inter alia*, in the recent Court of Justice of the EU (CJEU) case law.[19] The report on the application of the Brussels I bis Regulation, which was due, on the basis of Article 79 of the Regulation, to be presented by the Commission by 11 January 2022 is still expected at the time of writing of this paper; relevant information and propositions as to the collective redress will hopefully be included. The named Article expressly states that the report should 'include an evaluation of the possible need for a further extension of the rules on jurisdiction to defendants not domiciled in a Member State'. This could be of interest also for collective redress proceedings against such defendants, for example regarding the human rights litigation in the field of business.[20] Hess notes that, among other issues, a possible next recast of the Brussels I bis Regulation should address the definitions

---

[15] In the Case C-73/19, Movic, 16.7.2020, ECLI:EU:C:2020:568 the CJEU found that a consumer collective action fell into the scope of civil and commercial matters under the Brussels I bis Regulation.

[16] Rielaender (2021), p. 6, draws attention to the 'international character' of the claim, which is a prerequisite for the application of the Brussels I bis Regulation, namely that the definition from the CCRD of 'cross-border representative action' must not be adopted as a criterion for the claim to be considered cross-border in light of the Brussels I bis Regulation.

[17] Regarding jurisdiction for the place of damage under Article 7(2) of the Brussels I bis Regulation, see Case C-30/20, RH v. AB Volvo, 15.7.2021, ECLI:EU:C:2021:604.

[18] For a quick though thorough overview of the current issues in collective redress, see Hess (2021a).

[19] Case C-191/15, Verein für Konsumenteninformation v. Amazon EU, 28.7.2016, ECLI:EU:C:2016:612; Case C-498/16, Schrems v. Facebook Ireland, 25.1.2018, ECLI:EU:C:2018:37; Case C-343/19, Verein für Konsumenteninformation v. Volkswagen, 9.7.2020, ECLI:EU:C:2020:534; Case C-709/19, Vereniging van Effectenbezitters v. BP, 12.5.2021, ECLI:EU:C:2021:377. Cf. Hess (2021b), p. 7.

[20] Hess (2021b), p. 7.

of 'courts' and 'settlements',[21] which are of importance also in cross-border collective redress. The new recast, so Hess, should also clarify the relationship between the Brussels I bis Regulation and the sectorial EU instruments touching upon collective redress, such as the General Data Protection Regulation (GDPR)[22] and the CCRD.[23]

This article focuses on enforcement titles stemming from collective redress proceedings, therefore jurisdictional issues will only be addressed as far as they influence or sometimes cause difficulties in the enforcement stage. Already at this point, it might be important to note that, like in any other civil proceedings, the claimants in collective redress can be successful or unsuccessful. Enforcement will be sought against the unsuccessful party from the judgment: sometimes against the defendant as the perpetrator of the mass harm event, and sometimes against the claimants who will become debtors of procedural costs.[24] Furthermore, judgments resulting from collective redress proceedings, can be of condemnatory nature (i.e., they order the unsuccessful party to give, do, omit or allow something), or else of a declaratory nature (for example, the trader brings an action against a qualified entity seeking the declaration that they are not liable for damages).[25] Since many collective redress scenarios are resolved via a collective settlement, it is particularly interesting to examine how the Brussels I bis Regulation deals with such documents.

3 The Collective Settlements Under the Brussels I bis Regulation

3.1 Collective Court Settlements

The Brussels I bis Regulation differentiates two regimes of recognition and enforcement, one for judgments and the other for court settlements and authentic instruments. In this two-tier system, the court settlements are dealt with in an unsatisfactory way. Namely, the Regulation does not take into consideration the substantial differences among the effects and the coming into existence of the court settlements in different EU Member States. Specifically, it fails to accept that, in certain national legal orders, court settlements are approved by the court in proceedings which guarantee procedural fairness and basic substantive regularity, and

[21] Hess (2021b), p. 4.

[22] Regulation (EU) No. 2016/679 of the European Parliament and of the Council of 27 April 2016 on the protection of natural persons with regard to the processing of personal data and on the free movement of such data, and repealing Directive 95/46/EC, OJ L 119, 4.5.2016.

[23] Hess (2021b), p. 4.

[24] For example, the CCRD requests the Member States to implement the 'loser pays' principle regarding procedural costs in cross-border proceedings (Article 12). The same rule is applied in several national procedural laws of the Member States (for example in Slovenia).

[25] Cf. Rielaender (2021), p. 16.

therefore obtain enforceability and even the res judicata effect (such is, for example, the case in Slovenia).[26] The effects of such settlements are aligned with those of judgments and they are enforced in the same manner as judgments. In other legal systems, court settlements are indeed a category which differs considerably from a judgment in their coming into existence and in their effects. Those effects are more similar to authentic instruments than to judgments. In squeezing all types of court settlements into one single category, together with authentic instruments, is therefore problematic.

The approach of the 2019 Hague Judgments Convention is different and could be considered in a future recast of Brussels I Regulation. Namely, in Article 11 the Convention deals with court settlements in a pragmatic way, subsuming them to the category of judgments if a court has approved them and if they are, in the country of origin, enforceable 'in the same manner as a judgment'.[27] This shows that it is possible to circumvent a difficult or impossible definition which would encompass and treat 'fairly' all court settlements in the EU Member States. On the contrary, the recognition and enforcement regime should follow the effects of the court settlement in the country of origin, in that such settlement is either submitted to the judgments' regime, or else, to the authentic instruments' regime. Being that a new recast is not even planned yet and court settlements are a very common way of resolving cross-border collective redress disputes, the question is how to deal with their recognition and enforcement under the current rules of the Brussels I bis Regulation.

One possibility would be to follow the grammatical interpretation (i.e., 'when the words are clear, there is nothing to interpret'). If the document at hand corresponds to the definition from Article 2(b) of the Brussels I bis Regulation ('court settlement' means a settlement which has been approved by a court of a Member State or concluded before a court of a Member State in the course of proceedings), then its recognition and enforcement is carried out under the rules of Chapter IV of the Regulation. This option leads to the problems described above.

But is there a second option? The recent CJEU case-law on the notion of 'judgment', introducing quite a broad interpretation of that notion (judgments in Zulfikarpašić,[28] Pula parking,[29] Obala i lučice[30]) might be of help. Namely, it could be argued that court settlements, which correspond to the Regulation's (Article 2(a)) and CJEU's broad definition of 'judgment' could actually 'move' from the category of 'court settlements' to the category of 'judgments'. The Regulation namely

[26] Article 308 of the Slovenian Civil Procedure Act (Official Gazette of the Republic of Slovenia No. 26/99 of 15 April 1999, with further amendments) provides that if the court discovers, during civil proceedings, that a court settlement was already concluded concerning the same subject matter, the claim has to be declared inadmissible.

[27] Similar approach can also be found in Article 94(2) of the Slovenian Private International Law and Procedure Act (Official Gazette of the Republic of Slovenia No. 56/99 of 13 July 1999, with further amendments).

[28] Case C-484/15, Ibrica Zulfikarpašić v. Slaven Gajer, 9.3.2017, ECLI:EU:C:2017:199.

[29] Case C-551/15, Pula Parking d.o.o. v. Sven Klaus Tederahn, 9.3.2017, ECLI:EU:C:2017:193.

[30] Case C-307/19, Obala i lučice d.o.o. v. NLB Leasing d.o.o., 25.3.2021, ECLI:EU:C:2021:236.

expressly allows for the 'judgment' to not necessarily be called 'judgment'. Such interpretation is, however, improbable, precisely because of the rules applying explicitly to court settlements (i.e., there is no apparent *lacuna*). It would definitely be welcome if the next recast of the Regulation tackled this issue clearly.

3.2 Collective Out-of-Court Settlements

Another common way of resolving cross-border issues are the out-of-court settlements. While they do not fall into the scope of application of the Brussels I bis Regulation, the question arises what to do if such settlements are later approved by the court. Are those to be considered as 'court settlements' or even as 'judgments', since confirmed by the court? Hess deems that the court's approval should not be interpreted as transforming an out-of-court settlement into a judgment.[31] Therefore, such approval can only transform an out-of-court settlement into a court settlement.[32]

On the contrary, Arons deems that the approval of the court of the out-of-court settlements results in treating such settlements as 'judgments' under the Brussels I bis Regulation.[33] Therefore, parties to collective settlements approved by a court in an opt-out system could object the enforcement on the ground of Article 45(1) b) of the Brussels I bis Regulation, which sanctions the lack of service of the introductory document in the proceeding, naturally only if the parties were in fact not appropriately served.[34] An example of a possibly problematic procedure could be, so Arons, the Dutch system of judgments declaring a settlement binding to all interested parties which did not opt-out, whereas all parties do not, under certain conditions, need to be served personally.[35] Danov describes a similar system in England, where court decisions 'recording the consent of the parties' are called 'judgments by consent' and are considered as 'judgments' for the purposes of the application of the Brussels I bis Regulation.[36]

In this author's opinion, the situation described above regarding the opt-out system is indeed possibly problematic from the point of view of the fundamental procedural rights and recognition (of a declaratory judgment) and enforcement should be able to be refused in case of establishment of severe deficiencies. The

---

[31] Hess (2021b), p. 12.

[32] Cf. Kramer (2014), p. 266; Rielaender (2021), p. 28.

[33] Arons (2020), p. 37.

[34] Ibid.

[35] Ibid. The author speaks about declaratory judgments issued under the Dutch Collective Settlement of Mass Damage Act (WCAM). Contra: Kramer, who deems that in general, the WCAM proceedings comply with the demands of the Brussels I and the Service Regulations. Kramer (2014), p. 270.

[36] Danov (2010), p. 385.

qualification of the court approval as a 'judgment' or else as a 'court settlement' should, however, not result in a different treatment of this particular procedural issue. Namely, the lack of service of the introductory document in the proceedings is probably the most prominent breach of procedural public policy, which, since the Krombach judgment[37] in 2000, is included in the public policy defence from Article 45(1) of the Brussels I bis Regulation. And public policy is protected both regarding 'judgments' and regarding 'court settlements'.

What can indeed prove problematic if we apply the rules regarding court settlements is that Article 59 of the Brussels I bis Regulation only speaks of enforcement and not of recognition. If the court approval is, as in the case of the 'notorious' Dutch WCAM proceedings,[38] intended to confer on the settlement the preclusive effect, then what is sought by the interesting parties is recognition and not enforcement.[39] To characterize (only) such court approved settlement as 'judgments' under the Regulation, so as to also provide for recognition, seems a bit far-fetched and we will probably have to wait for another recast to solve this problem.[40]

4 The Binding Effect of Judgments and Court Settlements in Cross-border Collective Redress

Hess notably wrote that the most prominent issue that arises in the field of recognition and enforcement of judgments (and court settlements) in collective redress is the binding effect of such decisions (especially in the case of an 'opt-out' mechanism).[41]

4.1 The Res Judicata Effect of Decisions in Collective Redress

In order to 'profit' from the circulation of judgments regime in the Brussels I bis Regulation, the decision in the collective redress proceedings has to be a 'judgment'

[37] Case C-7/98, Dieter Krombach v. André Bamberski, 28.3.2000, ECLI:EU:C:2000:164.

[38] Dutch Collective Settlement Act (Wet Collectieve Afwikkeling Massaschade) entered into force on 27 July 2005.

[39] Kramer (2014), p. 267.

[40] Cf. Rielaender (2021), p. 28, who deems that 'at present, there is thus a considerable risk that individual consumers on whose behalf a settlement is entered into and approved by a court might still be able to assert further claims in accordance with the applicable lex causae'. Cf. Danov (2010), p. 386, who specifically addresses the situation where the enforcement of a foreign class judgment is sought in England, while this judgment is irreconcilable with a foreign collective settlement; he deems that the English court could not refuse enforcement on the basis of irreconcilability nor on the basis of public policy.

[41] Cf. Hess (2021b), p. 7.

or a 'court settlement' in the sense of the Brussels I bis Regulation.[42] The material and personal scope of the binding effect (*res judicata*) of the judgment is, however, defined by the national law of the Member State of origin of the judgment.[43] Numerous papers and monographs have dealt with different collective redress mechanisms in the EU Member States and the different effects of the decisions in such proceedings.[44] Arons notes that the Jenard and the Schlosser[45] Reports give such a wide interpretation of 'judgments' that they also include declaratory judgments in Dutch collective action proceedings.[46]

It is important to emphasise that the binding effect of a judgment or a court settlement regarding the parties in the enforcement proceedings instituted in another EU Member State is just a prerequisite for the triggering of the Brussels I bis Regulation mechanism. This does not preclude the defendant from filing a request for refusal of enforcement, citing, for example, the contrariety to the procedural public policy of the Member State of enforcement because of the use of the opt-out system in the collective redress proceedings.

The least 'problematic' from the binding effect point of view are judgments in collective proceedings based on the opt-in mechanism. Only persons who explicitly expressed their wish to participate and be bound by the judgment will be able to demand cross-border recognition and enforcement, and the latter will only be possible against such parties.

In the so called 'representative action' proceedings, national law has to be consulted, in order to define the personal scope of the binding effect of the judgments. For example, in Dutch law, the declaratory judgment resulting from the national collective action procedure, is only binding between the claimant entity and the defendant and there is no legal binding of the individual members of the group whose interests were represented by the entity.[47]

---

[42] Cf. Arons (2020), p. 36.

[43] Jenard (1979). The basic rule in the recognition of judgments is that, by recognising a judgment, is effects are 'broadened' to other countries, and are not to be altered in any way (with the exception of the need of adaptation of certain measures).

[44] See e.g. Arons (2020), pp. 1–39.

[45] Schlosser wrote: 'The provisions of the 1968 Convention governing recognition and enforcement are in general designed to cover only court judgments which either determine or regulate the legal relationships of the parties.' Schlosser (1979).

[46] Arons (2020), p. 36.

[47] Id. Arons explains that courts confronted by individual claims 'try to avoid deviating from the collective ruling'.

4.2 The Evidentiary Effect of the Foreign Judgments and Court-Settlements

Another issue has to be tackled regarding the binding force of a judgment or a court settlement from another EU Member State: the use of such judgment or court settlement merely as evidence in court proceedings in a country other than the country of origin. In such cases, the party producing the foreign judgment or court settlement does not aspire for a binding effect of such a document in the sense of *res judicata*. The aim of producing such document in the proceedings is to prove the veracity of an asserted fact. For example, if the claimant asserts that the defendant admitted to receiving a certain sum of money in the foreign proceedings, and the defendant denies ever doing that, the claimant can produce the foreign judgment, which includes a notice of the defendant's admission. Such evidence will usually have a very strong evidentiary power, since it is a public document. However, it will not acquire the *res judicata* effect.

Article 15 of the CCRD, entitled 'Effects of final decisions', states: 'Member States shall ensure that the final decision of a court or administrative authority of any Member State concerning the existence of an infringement harming collective interests of consumers can be used by all parties as evidence in the context of any other action before their national courts or administrative authorities to seek redress measures against the same trader for the same practice, in accordance with national law on evaluation of evidence'. It is important to note that this Article only regulates the evidentiary use of final decisions from other EU Member States, and not the recognition and enforcement of such decisions in the sense of Private International Law. Moreover, the named Article is problematic even within its scope of application. As noted by Hess, it is possibly contrary to Article 47 of the Charta of Fundamental Rights, since it seems to provide 'a binding effect concerning findings obtained in a third party procedure'.[48]

5 Grounds for Refusal of Recognition and Enforcement in Cross-border Collective Redress

Article 45 of the Brussels I bis Regulation provides four grounds for refusal of recognition and enforcement of judgments issued in an EU Member State, in other EU Member States. These are: the contrariety to the public policy of the addressed Member State; the lack of service of the introductory document in the proceedings, when a default judgment was issued; the irreconcilability of judgments; and the

[48] Hess (2021a).

non-compliance with certain jurisdictional rules, namely with protective and exclusive jurisdictions.

Court settlements are, as already mentioned, subject to the same enforcement regime as authentic instruments, i.e., Chapter IV of the Brussels I bis Regulation applies. Article 58 states that the 'enforcement of the authentic instrument may be refused only if such enforcement is manifestly contrary to public policy (*ordre public*) in the Member State addressed'. No other grounds for refusal of enforcement are available, contrary to judgments, where multiple grounds for refusal can be invoked. Pursuant to Article 59, 'a court settlement which is enforceable in the Member State of origin shall be enforced in the other Member States under the same conditions as authentic instruments.' Article 58 further provides that the following rules of the Regulation apply to authentic instruments and court settlements: the provisions of Section 2 (procedural rules concerning enforcement), Subsection 2 of Section 3 (Refusal of enforcement), and Section 4 (Common provisions) of Chapter III shall apply as appropriate. Given that the sole ground for refusal of enforcement of authentic instruments and court settlements is cited in Article 58, other grounds for refusal of Article 45 do not apply.

The two most prominent possible reasons for refusal of recognition and enforcement will be addressed: the incorrect service of the introductory document in the proceedings in the case of an opt-out system, and the irreconcilability of judgments and/or court settlements in cases where they concern the same defendant and the same event, but different claimants. Naturally, other reasons for refusal are not excluded, such as, for example, the (substantial) public policy defence in cases of punitive damages, and the violation of jurisdictional rules protecting weaker parties.

5.1 Opt-Out Systems and the Lack of Correct Service of the Introductory Document in the Proceedings (Article 45(1) a) and b) of the Brussels I bis Regulation)

A possible weak point of certain collective redress proceedings is the questionable guaranteeing of the right to be heard of all members of the class. More specifically, issues can arise when the proceedings are conducted under the opt-out system where, additionally, a personal service in due time is not always requested.[49] As emphasised by Danov, in cases where service can be made by public notice and without an obligatory personal identification of the addressees, the EU Service Regulation is not applicable (Article 1(2)). The national law thus applies and the result of such application has to be examined by the addressed court in another Member State. When there is question of due service of the introductory document, the court will first examine the applicability of Article 45 1) (b) of the Brussels I bis Regulation. The wording of this ground for refusal is, however, fairly specific and does not cover

[49] Cf. Danov (2010), p. 388.

all instances of incorrect service and its consequences.[50] In case the indent (b) is not applicable, the violations of fundamental procedural rights can also be dealt with under Article 45 1) (a). As confirmed by the CJEU in *Krombach*,[51] the breaches of Article 6 of the European Convention of Human Rights (ECHR) can trigger the public policy exception from the Brussels I bis Regulation.

All EU Member States are also parties to the ECHR and the Brussels I bis Regulation only applies to recognition and enforcement of judgments, court settlements and authentic instruments from other EU Member States, so the judgment in question will be necessarily issued by a State bound by the ECHR. It must, however, be emphasised that the criteria for applying the public policy exception regarding a foreign judgment are arguably a little more lenient (a necessity of a 'manifest', 'flagrant' breach) than the criteria applicable in inner-State relations and proceedings.

The multi-party setting brings additional complexity also to the examination of the respect of procedural guarantees. First, the rules regarding specific collective redress proceedings can allow for multiple ways of service, which will be used for different claimants; some of them problematic from the point of view of procedural fairness, and some of them not. And second, the same manner of service can prove in conformity with Article 6 ECHR regarding one claimant, and contrary to this Article in another case, depending on the circumstances of each case.

Furthermore, as emphasised by Danov, the possible breach of Article 6 operates differently when the claimants are successful than when they are unsuccessful. Namely, when a successful claimant, although served by public notice and without personal identification (and who maybe even did not hear about the proceedings before they were already over), requests enforcement against the defendant, the defendant will not be able to oppose such enforcement on grounds of a defectuous service. On the contrary, when a successful defendant will demand recognition of a foreign class judgment as an obstacle to instituting new collective proceedings by plaintiffs who did not opt-in in the foreign proceedings, the latter will be able to invoke the public policy defence.[52] Another such situation would occur if a successful defendant demanded enforcement of a foreign class judgment in order to get procedural costs from the unsuccessful claimants. There are therefore serious issues of *res judicata* and *lis pendens*, to name just two.[53]

Since public policy under the Brussels I bis Regulation is a category of national law, we can also expect a possibly different treatment of the same judgment in different EU Member States. Article 6 ECHR surely is the basis (the procedural 'Magna Charta'), however, Member States can (and are encouraged to) define higher standards. Such standards can then oppose the recognition and enforcement of a judgment from a Member State, which adopted a 'lower' protection of procedural

[50] Cf. Pogorelčnik Vogrinc (2021), p. 319.

[51] Case C-7/98, Dieter Krombach v. André Bamberski, 28.3.2000, ECLI:EU:C:2000:164.

[52] Danov (2010), p. 389.

[53] Cf. Ibid., p. 391.

rights.[54] The CJEU does not get involved, unless the interpretation of public policy defence exceeds the common European frame.[55]

It would be easy to conclude that the opt-in system should always be preferred in cross-border settings. However, there is a substantial downside of this system, namely the possibility that the claimants who did not opt in, institute parallel proceedings in another country regarding the same defendant and the same infringement (for such situations, see irreconcilability, *infra*).[56]

5.2 Irreconcilability of Judgments and Court Settlements (Article 45(1) c) and d) of the Brussels I bis Regulation)

Irreconcilability of judgments from Article 45(1) c) and d) is a real threat in cases of mass damage events, given that Brussels I bis Regulation does not effectively prevent parallel proceedings in collective redress. Namely, when individual claimants suffered harm in different Member States (such is mostly the case in consumer disputes), the only common place for them to institute proceedings together will be in the Member State of the defendant's domicile, under Article 4 of the Regulation. Being that consumers enjoy protective jurisdiction under Article 18 in the place of their domicile, it is not realistic to expect that they will opt to sue in another Member State, just to be able to join other claimants, unless of course this option would be made attractive (or obligatory) for them by the law. Article 7 does not allow for a consolidation of claims for example in the place where one of the plaintiffs suffered damage (para. 2) or else in the place of characteristic performance in one of the litigious contracts (para. 1). Article 8 only provides for joinder of claims when there are multiple defendants and in three other very specific situations, neither of which is particularly relevant for collective redress. The lack of a jurisdictional provision aiming at an easier access to justice in cross-border collective redress can thus result in a dispersion of claims against the same defendant, regarding the same or identical harm.[57]

Since, in the Regulation, irreconcilability is defined in a relatively strict manner, judgments regarding different claimants cannot be subject to a refusal of enforcement on such grounds. However, problems arise in situations, where an individual claimant pursued their claim against the defendant in one proceedings, and then also joined the collective proceedings or is deemed to have joined them (in an opt-out mechanism). Rielaender argues that it is possible to construe the term 'the same parties' in Article 29(1) regarding *lis pendens* in a broad manner, 'meaning that a

[54] Cf. Ibid.

[55] Most notably in Case C-38/98, Régie nationale des usines Renault SA v. Maxicar SpA and Orazio Formento, 11.5.2000, ECLI:EU:C:2000:225. See also Kramberger Škerl (2011), pp. 461, 490.

[56] Cf. Danov (2010), p. 392.

[57] Cf. Rielaender (2021), p. 5.

beneficiary represented in a collective action pending in one Member State is precluded from suing the same defendant with respect to the rights asserted in the prior proceedings in the courts of another Member State', namely on the basis of the Drouot judgment of the CJEU,[58] where the Court treated the insurer and the insured party as 'the same parties', as well as on the basis of Article 9(4) of the CCRD. [59] Equally, if the same individual is represented in two separate collective proceedings against the same claimant and regarding the same claims (for example one instituted in the place of the defendant's domicile, and the other in the place where the damage occurred), we are in presence of *lis pendens*.

However, if the mechanism of *lis pendens* from Article 29 does not eliminate one of the parallel proceedings and the judgments are issued, the rules of Article 45 (1) c) and d) kick in and one or the other of the judgments will not be able to be enforced in cross-border environment, under the same logic as regarding the *lis pendens*, described above. [60] In the end, it must be prevented that the tortfeasor is obliged to compensate the same victim twice.[61]

Another possible situation is that two collective proceedings target the same defendant because of the same illegal practice or harm, however, by two different groups of plaintiffs. Is there irreconcilability in the sense of Article 45 c) or d)? Rielaender deems that, in such cases, we are in presence of 'related actions' pursuant Article 30 of the Brussels I bis Regulation,[62] another mechanism aiming at preventing precisely irreconcilable judgments. If this mechanism fails, may the courts refuse recognition and enforcement on the basis of Article 45? This author deems that this is not possible on the basis of the current wording of the said Articles. Danov suggests that a new rule should be added in Brussels I Regulation regarding the irreconcilability of judgments in collective redress; namely, that the recognition of a foreign class judgment may be refused if it concerns the same defendant and the same infringement, but a different plaintiffs' class.[63] In that author's view, such rule would not only prevent incompatible judgments to co-exist in the same EU Member State, but would also encourage consolidation of related actions at an earlier stage of the proceedings.[64]

Rielaender draws attention to judgments for negative declaratory relief, brought by a trader against the qualified entity, representing a group of consumers, where question arises which consumers are, in the event of success of the plaintiff, bound

---

[58] Case C-351/96, Drouot assurances SA v. Consolidated metallurgical industries (CMI industrial sites), Protea assurance and Groupement d'intérêt économique (GIE) Réunion européenne, 19.5.1998, ECLI:EU:C:1998:242.

[59] Rielaender (2021), p. 15.

[60] Cf. Ibid., p. 16.

[61] In this sense also Article 9(4) CCRD: 'Member States shall also lay down rules to ensure that consumers do not receive compensation more than once for the same cause of action against the same trader'.

[62] Rielaender (2021), p. 18.

[63] Danov (2010), p. 393.

[64] Ibid.

by such judgment.[65] The same author argues that it is only those who expressly accepted to be bound, i.e. who opted in, by analogy with Article 9(4) of CCRD, which prescribes obligatory opt-in for consumers from other Member States.[66]

As already mentioned, the Brussels I bis Regulation does not provide for irreconcilability to possibly stand in the way of (recognition and) enforcement of court settlements. The question arises whether in cases where the foreign judgment conflicts with a domestic or foreign court settlement regarding the same parties and the same cause of action, the recognition and enforcement can be refused via the public policy defence. This author deems that this is possible. Having two binding but conflicting resolutions of the same conflict in force in the same state territory, is certainly contrary to fundamental values of all national legal orders, specifically the predictability and legal safety. In this sense, Danov describes, that English courts would refuse the enforcement of a foreign court settlement, conflicting with a class judgment rendered in England, on the basis of the public policy defence.[67]

The same author, however, warns that in case of conflicting judgments (for example a foreign class judgment conflicting with an English class judgment) the public policy defence might not be applicable, in view of the Hoffmann judgment,[68] in which the CJEU stated that incompatibilities of judgments are to be dealt with within the special ground for refusal devoted to these issues; however, it could also be argued (and this author agrees) that the special provisions do not apply, when the parties are not the same and thus, the way for the public policy defence is (re)-opened.[69] Danov further argues that public policy could not be applicable when the incompatibility existed between two foreign judgments.[70] The author does not explicitly give reasons for this opinion, however, it might be based on the understanding, by English courts, of the public policy exception. Public policy is a predominantly national category,[71] therefore interpretations in different Member States might differ. Nevertheless, this author sees no 'European' obstacle[72] for a Member State to find contrary to its public policy the recognition and enforcement of a foreign class judgment incompatible with another foreign class judgment, involving the same defendant and the same infringement, but a different class of claimants. It would, however, without any doubt, be much better if the European legislators tackled such situations explicitly in the next recast of the Brussels I bis Regulation.

---

[65] Rielaender (2021), p. 17.

[66] Ibid.

[67] Danov (2010), p. 385.

[68] Case 145/86, Horst Ludwig Martin Hoffmann v. Adelheid Krieg, 4.2.1988, ECLI:EU:C:1988:61.

[69] Danov (2010), p. 387.

[70] Ibid., pp. 387–388.

[71] Case C-38/98, Régie nationale des usines Renault SA v. Maxicar SpA and Orazio Formento, 11.05.2000, ECLI:EU:C:2000:225.

[72] Ibid.

6 Conclusion

EU Member States offer a colourful plethora of collective redress mechanisms available in different cases of mass harm. These are civil litigation mechanisms, which, however, depart from the basic model of two-party structure to which most civil procedural rules are adapted. This, in turn, results in the need to modify the existing rules or else develop and add new rules, taking into account the specificities of these multi-party civil proceedings. Many procedural rules have to be looked at from such different perspective, for example the litigation funding, the service of court documents, the binding effect of judgments and court settlements, etc.

The landscape gets even more complex, when a cross-border element is involved. In the common European market, this is not a rare scenario. A seller sold damaged goods to consumers from different Member States, a factory polluted a river causing harm in different Member States where this river flows, to name just two possible hypotheses. The typical Private International Law questions thus arise and instruments of EU Private International Law are called into action. Regarding the recognition and enforcement of judgments and court settlement, this will be the Brussels I bis Regulation of 2012.

Unfortunately, one quickly notices that, in spite of the EU long-time enhancement of collective redress mechanisms, (almost) no work has been done on the EU level regarding the cross-border effects of such mechanisms. The Brussels I bis Regulation is applicable, but not adapted to cross-border collective redress. Thus, the courts, including the CJEU, are left with the hard work of trying to interpret the rules of the Regulation in such a way that the wording and the intentions of the regulative text are not thwarted, but the collective redress case is nevertheless resolved in a sensible and just manner.

In recognition and enforcement of judgments and court settlements, several issues need urgent attention. First, the collective redress unveils the already problematic qualification of court settlements in the Brussels I bis Regulation, or, more specifically, their treatment in the chapter on recognition and enforcement. The latter arguably does not allow the courts to look at the specific coming into existence and effects of the court settlement at hand, but automatically demands the application of the rules from the special chapter devoted to court settlements and authentic instruments. Its most notable deficiency is the lack of talk of recognition (it only provides the possibility of enforcement), but also the further restriction of the possible grounds for refusal of enforcement. When court settlements have, under national law, the same effects as judgments, such treatment in the Brussels I bis Regulation is not justified. There is also the open question of the qualification of out-of-court settlements approved by the court: are the deemed to be dealt with as court settlements, as judgments, as neither?

The second possibly problematic issue is the binding effect of judgments and court settlements regarding individual members of the class, most notably in the so-called opt-out collective redress proceedings. If the judgment or settlement do not bind a specific party, then recognition or enforcement cannot be requested against such a party. Furthermore, if the binding effect is established, the opt-out mechanisms can pose a challenge to the regularity of service of the introductory document. Such service will have to be dealt with on a case by case basis. Courts will have to interpret the wording of Article 45 1) (b): 'if the defendant was not served with the document which instituted the proceedings or with an equivalent document in sufficient time and in such a way as to enable him to arrange for his defence', where service was made via a public notice, for example, as is common in opt-out mechanisms. Also, the incorrect service cannot be invoked, if 'the defendant failed to commence proceedings to challenge the judgment when it was possible for him to do so'. If the strict conditions of Article 45 1) (b) are not met, there is still a possibility to apply the public policy defence from Article 45 1) (a), which, under the CJEU case-law, also covers the violations of fundamental procedural guarantees.

The third important and unresolved issue is the irreconcilability of final decisions in collective redress proceedings, where they consider the same defendant and the same (type of) harm, but different claimants. The rules of the Brussels I bis Regulation do not deal with these issues. As to the court settlements, the irreconcilability rules of the Regulation do not allow for a refusal of (recognition and) enforcement, however, the situation could, in the view of this author, be tackled via the public policy exception.

If the current wording of the Brussels I bis Regulation can, to a certain extent, be 'bent' in a way to accommodate cross-border collective redress, this author's opinion is aligned to those pressing for an effort to provide explicit rules of EU Private International Law regarding collective proceedings. Since the fragmentation of EU Private International Law is already a problem in itself, we would strongly recommend tackling these issues in a new recast of the Brussels I Regulation, rather than in a separate and specialized EU regulation.

References

Amaro R, Azar-Baud M, Corneloup S et al (2018) Collective redress in the Member States of the European Union. Policy Department for Citizens' Rights and Constitutional Affairs Directorate General for Internal Policies of the Union. https://www.europarl.europa.eu/RegData/etudes/STUD/2018/608829/IPOL_STU(2018)608829_EN.pdf

Arons T (2020) Cross-border dimension of collective proceedings in the Brussels Ibis Regime: jurisdiction, lis pendens and related actions. In: Mankowski P (ed) Research handbook on the Brussels Ibis Regulation. EE Elgar Online, pp 1–39

Danov M (2010) The Brussels I Regulation: cross-border collective redress proceedings and judgments. Priv Int Law 6(2):359–393

Hess B (2021a) Collective redress in the European Union and private international law - current developments. https://cjbl.lu/wp-content/uploads/2021/06/Presentation_Hess-1.pdf

Hess B (2021b) Reforming the Brussels Ibis Regulation: perspectives and prospects. MPILux Research Paper, Series 4

Jenard P (1979) Report on the Convention on jurisdiction and the enforcement of judgments in civil and commercial matters, OJ C 59

Kramberger Škerl J (2011) European public policy (with an emphasis on exequatur proceedings). J Priv Int Law 7(3):461–490

Kramer X (2014) Securities collective action and private international law issues in Dutch WCAM settlements: global aspirations and regional boundaries. Glob Bus Dev Law J 27(2):235–279

Pogorelčnik Vogrinc N (2021) Public policy as grounds for refusal of recognition and enforcement under Regulation 2016/1103 and Regulation 2016/1104. Actualidad Jurídica Iberoamericana 15:308–323

Rielaender F (2021) Aligning the Brussels regime with the representative actions directive. Int Comp Law Q 71:107–138. https://doi.org/10.1017/S0020589321000403

Schlosser P (1979) Report on the Convention on the Association of the Kingdom of Denmark, Ireland and the United Kingdom of Great Britain and Northern Ireland to the Convention on jurisdiction and the enforcement of judgments in civil and commercial matters and to the Protocol on its interpretation by the Court of Justice, OJ C 59

Enforceability and Enforcement Appeals: Continental Law

Bettina Nunner-Krautgasser

Abstract This article is dedicated to the presentation of the different regulations of enforcement titles in the legal systems of the EU Member States with regard to their (provisional) enforceability and contestability. For this purpose, a comparative law analysis is carried out.

The legal systems of selected states from the Roman, German, Mixed Romano-Germanic and Nordic Legal Family are subject of the legal comparison. The extent to which the legal systems differ with regard to their provisions concerning the enforceability of enforcement titles is examined. Furthermore, the differences in the respective national enforcement periods and the structure of provisional enforceability within these member states are shown. In addition, the legal remedies against enforcement titles available in the respective legal systems are presented.

For this purpose, the legal systems of France and Spain as members of the Roman legal family, and Germany and Austria as representatives of the German Legal Family were used. Furthermore, the Dutch as part of the Romano-Germanic Legal Family and the Swedish as Nordic legal order were dealt with. The results of this comparison show that the European legal systems included differ considerably with regard to their provisions on the enforceability of enforcement titles. Divergent regulations can be found both in states with legal orders from different legal families and within legal families. Because of this divergent design of the enforceability provisions, the existing differences in the legal remedies provided against enforcement are consistent.

B. Nunner-Krautgasser (✉)
Institute of Civil Procedure and Insolvency Law, University of Graz, Faculty of Law, Graz, Austria
e-mail: bettina.nunner@uni-graz.at

V. Rijavec et al. (eds.), *Diversity of Enforcement Titles in the EU*, Ius Gentium: Comparative Perspectives on Law and Justice 111,
https://doi.org/10.1007/978-3-031-47108-7_10

1 Introduction

The following article provides an overview of how enforceability and appeals against enforcement titles are defined and structured in various national legal systems within the EU. For this purpose, the enforcement laws of six EU Member States were analysed from a comparative law perspective, thereby identifying similarities and differences among the relevant legal systems. For a better comparability, the legal systems are classified into legal families (Roman, German, Mixed Romano-Germanic and Nordic Legal Family), each being represented by one or two Member States.[1]

The focus of this study is on two main areas: On the one hand, the enforceability of enforcement titles is examined, with a particular focus on relevant time limits for enforcement and on the concept of provisional enforceability. On the other hand, this article explores how enforcement titles can be challenged (appeals against enforcement titles).[2]

2 Enforceability

2.1 Enforceable Title

2.1.1 Roman Legal Family

In the following, the enforcement title in the Roman legal family—the 'legal system of the Code Napoleon'[3]—will be examined, using France and Spain as examples.[4]

In France, the enforcement title is regulated in Article L 111-3 of the Code of Civil Enforcement Procedures ('Code des procédures civiles d'exécution', hereinafter referred to as 'CPC').[5] Accordingly, court decisions as well as certain notarial deeds are regarded as suitable enforcement instruments. Likewise, acts of certain legal entities under public law, such as administrative authorities, tax offices or social security institutions, are recognised enforcement instruments, provided the law grants them the effect of a judgment.

[1]The legal situation in Common Law countries is not discussed.

[2]The legal statements in this paper are largely based on the national country reports within the framework of the EU-En4s project. Additional information was obtained from the European Justice Portal see European e-Justice (n.d.-a).

[3]Kischel (2015), para 4, p. 169; Hertel (2009), p. 157.

[4]Kischel (2015), para 7, p. 16; Hertel (2009), p. 162.

[5]République Française, Légifrance, https://www.legifrance.gouv.fr/codes/section_lc/LEGITEXT000025024948/LEGISCTA000025934278/#LEGISCTA000025934278.

In Spanish law, the enforcement title is defined in § 517 of the Spanish Code of Civil Procedure ('Ley de Enjuiciamiento Civil', hereinafter referred to as 'LEC').[6] It merely states that 'the enforcement action must be based on a title that is linked to execution'.[7] This rather vague definition of an enforcement title was clarified by the Spanish Legal Dictionary of the Royal Language Academy. Accordingly, an enforcement title is a 'document to which the Law expressly grants force enough to obtain from the Courts the compliance of the obligation integrated in its content'.[8] Even though the definition contained in § 517 LEC only gains significance through this interpretation, § 517 LEC does still have relevance, since it includes a list of all enforcement instruments. Enforcement titles therefore include, for example, (usually final) court decisions as well as 'authentic instruments'.[9] Among these, particular attention must be paid to § 517 Nr. 9 LEC which serves as a kind of 'catch-all clause'. Thus, 'other procedural decisions and documents which are enforceable under this or another law'[10] also constitute enforcement titles.

In French and Spanish enforcement law, some striking features can be found in the list of enforcement titles, such as in Article L 111-3 5° CPC. In France, the bailiff, who has a monopoly for undertaking compulsory enforcement,[11] can in fact issue an enforcement in the following two cases: (1) if a cheque has not been paid or, in the case of the invalidity of the cheque, if there is a confirmation of non-payment from the bank;[12] (2) in the case of an agreement between the debtor and the creditor for claims with low amount in dispute, subject to the conditions set out in Article L 125-1 CPC. In Spanish enforcement law, notarised arbitral awards, duplicates of public deeds under certain conditions, specific bearer or registered securities, certain securities and notarised commercial contracts signed by the contracting parties and a certified commercial broker are also considered to be enforcement titles according to § 517 LEC.[13]

In France, a title containing an obligation to (1) pay, (2) do or refrain from doing something or (3) give or return can be enforced.[14] The Spanish enforcement title can be used to enforce a claim for payment or to demand an act or omission from the debtor.[15]

Under French Law, the right of enforcement concerns only the debtor's assets. Enforcement against persons does not exist.[16] Thus, bending penalties for the

---

[6] European e-Justice (n.d.-f).

[7] National Report for Spain (2020), p. 12.

[8] Spanish Royal Academy (2021); National Report for Spain (2020), p. 12.

[9] National Report for Spain (2020), p. 12.

[10] European e-Justice (n.d.-f).

[11] European e-Justice (n.d.-c).

[12] National Report for France (2020), p. 9.

[13] National Report for Spain (2020), p. 12.

[14] National Report for France (2020), p. 9.

[15] National Report for Spain (2020), pp. 30 et seq.

[16] European e-Justice (n.d.-c); National Report for France (2020), p. 9.

fulfilment of an unjustifiable act or for acquiescence and omission are inadmissible because they are not directed at the property but directly against the person itself.[17] However, if the debtor refuses to comply with certain obligations, for example maintenance obligations, in French law, he is guilty of a criminal offence. This can lead to criminal prosecution and, as a consequence, to imprisonment.[18] Since it is prohibited to physically force a person to perform an obligation to do or to refrain from doing something, the debtor is encouraged to perform those obligations by the handing down of a pecuniary penalty by the court. Obligations to pay, to give or to return are also interpreted as obligations to do something, therefore they may also be combined with a pecuniary penalty in addition to other compulsory enforcement measures.[19]

If an executory title has been issued in France or Spain, it is usually enforceable without the need for an additional legal act.[20] The immediate enforceability is justified from the Spanish point of view by the fact that through the conviction ('the debtor is condemned to do something') the obligation of the debtor and thus the enforceability of the title is legally recognised.[21] In French and Spanish law (final) decisions of ordinary courts are immediately enforceable. However, this 'immediate enforceability' does not mean that the creditor is released from his obligation to file an application for enforcement;[22] rather, executory measures can only be initiated upon application.[23] Although in the Spanish legal system the final title—without the need for further procedural steps—is per se immediately enforceable, a separate procedure must be initiated in order to take enforcement actions.[24]

Arbitral awards are excluded from the system of immediate enforceability in France. These must first be recognised as enforceable by the President of the Judicial Tribunal ('Tribunal Judiciaire') in a specific *exequatur* procedure.[25] In contrast, arbitration decisions are immediately enforceable in Spanish enforcement law according to § 517 LEC—without any intervening proceedings. Court settlements, on the other hand, must first be declared enforceable by the judge in both countries, France and Spain.[26]

[17] European e-Justice (n.d.-c).

[18] European e-Justice (n.d.-c).

[19] European e-Justice (n.d.-c).

[20] European e-Justice (n.d.-c); National Report for Spain (2020), pp. 30 et seq.

[21] National Report for Spain (2020), pp. 30 et seq.

[22] European e-Justice (n.d.-c); National Report for Spain (2020), p. 25.

[23] European e-Justice (n.d.-c); National Report for Spain (2020), pp. 30 et seq.

[24] National Report for Spain (2020), p. 47.

[25] National Report for France (2020), p. 11.

[26] National Report for France (2020), p. 47; National Report for Spain (2020), p. 59.

2.1.2 German Legal Family

The legal situation of enforceable titles in the German legal family is illustrated on the basis of German and Austrian Law.[27]

In Germany, the enforcement title is defined as an official document declaring a substantive legal claim enforceable.[28] The enforcement title empowers the creditor to carry out the enforcement; the enforcement title determines the content and scope of the enforcement. Thus, the enforcement title is the basis of the German enforcement proceedings.[29]

According to § 704 of the German Code of Civil Procedure ('Zivilprozessordnung', hereinafter referred to as 'ZPO_DE'), such enforcement titles are above all final judgments that have become final or have been declared enforceable. Other enforcement titles are governed by § 794 ZPO_DE. It includes, *inter alia*, court settlements (section 1), decisions declaring certain arbitral awards enforceable (section 4a) and certain deeds of a German court or German notary public.[30]

Pursuant to § 724 ZPO_DE, the enforcement title in Germany must in principle contain an enforcement clause before enforcement actions can be initiated.[31] This means that the enforcement title is not immediately enforceable; rather, its enforceability must first be confirmed with an enforceable copy of the judgment.[32] This is attached at the end of the judgment, signed and stamped by an official for the court (§ 725 ZPO_DE). In contrast to Austrian law, in German law there exists no further proceeding for the granting of enforcement.[33]

In Austria, the enforcement title is an official document by which a certain claim can be realized by execution. The enforcement title thus gives the creditor the right to demand execution. If all the conditions for execution are met, the state is obliged to execute the claim. Without an enforcement title, the creditor has no right to enforcement, even if he is entitled to a material claim. The enforcement title must always have a clear content, i.e. it must be directed to a specific performance, acquiescence or omission. The execution title is the basis for the application for execution and the execution permit. These must not exceed the title in their content and scope. It determines the parties to the proceedings and, indirectly, the type of execution: If, for example, a monetary claim is to be brought in, only an execution for a monetary claim can be considered.[34] § 1 of the Austrian Execution Act ('Exekutionsordnung', hereinafter referred to as 'EO') regulates the execution titles. They can be roughly

[27] Kischel (2015), para 7; Hertel (2009), p. 164.

[28] Rosenberg et al. (2010), p. 142.

[29] National Report for Germany (2020), p. 7.

[30] National Report for Germany (2020), pp. 7 et seq.

[31] Rosenberg et al. (2010), p. 146.

[32] National Report for Germany (2020), pp. 94 et seq.

[33] European e-Justice (n.d.-d).

[34] Neumayr and Nunner-Krautgasser (2018), pp. 65 et seq.

divided into court titles (titles issued by an ordinary civil or criminal court), administrative titles and documents not issued by an administrative authority (e.g. enforceable notarial acts).[35]

In Austrian law, most titles need an additional confirmation of enforceability according to § 7 (3)–(6) EO. This confirmation is an official certification by title court or title authority that the title is enforceable. In the course of issuing the confirmation of enforceability, only the formal requirements for enforcement are checked (esp. the proper service of the title, the expiry of time limits for appeals with suspensive effect and the expiry of the performance period).[36] The substantive conditions for enforcement, however, are only reviewed later by the court of execution during the so-called authorisation procedure in which the court issues an enforcement authorisation. This is an essential difference to the German procedural structure with its dominant enforcement clause.[37]

2.1.3 Romano-Germanic Legal Family

Since the Netherlands can no longer be clearly assigned to the Roman legal family, they are attributed to the Romano-Germanic legal family.[38]

In Dutch law, domestic enforcement titles are governed by Article 430 of the Dutch Code on Civil Procedure ('Wet van Burgerlijke Rechtsvorderingen', hereinafter referred to as 'Rv'). Accordingly, court judgments and orders issued by a Dutch court as well as public judgments issued in the Netherlands can be enforcement titles. Furthermore, as in Spanish enforcement law, there is a kind of 'catch-all clause' according to which any title that is *ex lege* declared enforceable is an enforcement title.[39]

In the case of court decisions, it is irrelevant for the enforcement effect whether the judgments are issued by a civil or an administrative court. However, a prerequisite for the enforceability of court decisions is that they are issued in a special form of enforcement ('grosse') and in the name of the King ('In de naam van de Koning'). Public deeds only obtain enforceability if they are issued and signed by a holder of a public office (such as a notary or civil servant), specifically describe the debtor's obligation and serve as evidence. The 'catch-all clause', declaring titles enforceable by law, includes, for example, minutes of court hearings and court settlements. Furthermore, also arbitral awards issued in the enforcement form ('grosse') are enforceable in the Netherlands.[40]

---

[35] Neumayr and Nunner-Krautgasser (2018), p. 71; National Report for Austria (2020), p. 7.

[36] National Report for Austria (2020), pp. 52 et seq.

[37] National Report for Austria (2020), p. 53.

[38] Hertel (2009), pp. 166 et seq.

[39] National Report for Netherlands (2020), p. 6.

[40] National Report for Netherlands (2020), p. 6.

The previously mentioned special form of enforcement ('grosse'), which confers enforceability on Dutch court decisions, is similar in its function to the German enforcement clause. Without this form, the title cannot have any enforcement effect; the bailiff may not carry out any executory measures. In contrast to the German system, however, the enforcement clause is not issued as a stamp or special clause in the judgment; rather, the 'grosse' is a certified copy of the judgment confirming enforceability. The enforcing creditor receives it free of charge; the enforceable certified copy of the judgment is served on the debtor by the bailiff before taking executory measures.[41]

2.1.4 Nordic Legal Family

Chapter 1 Section 1 first paragraph of the Swedish Enforcement Code ('Utsökningsbalken', hereinafter referred to as 'UB') states that an enforcement title is the basis of any enforcement of a payment or other obligation. The enforcement titles are listed in Chapter 3 Section 1 UB; among these, the enforcement title according to Section 7 first paragraph should be highlighted as a special feature in European comparative law: According to Section 7 first paragraph, a decision issued by the Swedish enforcement authority itself ('Kronofogdemyndigheten') can also constitute an executory title. However, it must be an order for payment or a decision related to a request for legal assistance.[42] The Swedish enforcement authority is not only responsible for the actual execution of titles; it also decides which executory measures are to be taken.[43] This competence is reserved to judges in most other jurisdictions, such as Austria, Spain or France;[44] in Sweden, on the other hand, the task is assigned to officials of the enforcement authority.[45]

As in Roman Law,[46] the legally binding title is immediately enforceable in Sweden: Once an enforceable title has been issued, there is no need for any further decision by a court or other authority in order for enforcement to be initiated.[47] Therefore apart from filing an application, no further legal action is required in order to initiate enforcement actions.[48] The application for enforcement may be submitted to the enforcement authority in writing or orally, the latter requiring the personal

[41] European e-Justice (n.d.-e).

[42] National Report for Sweden (2020), p. 2.

[43] European e-Justice (n.d.-g).

[44] Neumayr and Nunner-Krautgasser (2018), p. 81; European e-Justice (n.d.-f); European e-Justice (n.d.-c).

[45] European e-Justice (n.d.-g).

[46] European e-Justice (n.d.-c); National Report for Spain (2020), pp. 30 et seq.

[47] European e-Justice (n.d.-g).

[48] National Report for Sweden (2020), p. 22.

appearance of the creditor seeking enforcement.[49] In contrast to Roman law,[50] court settlements that have been confirmed by the court are immediately enforceable in Sweden; no additional judicial act is necessary.[51]

2.2 *Time Limits*

In most of the legal systems analysed in this paper, enforceability is suspended until a title becomes final. Accordingly, a title is not enforceable as long as an appeal is still admissible (regarding the exception of provisional enforceability). In addition to time limits that determine the start of enforceability, there are also provisions that stipulate time limits after the expiry of which enforcement is no longer permissible.

2.2.1 Roman Legal Family

In Spanish law, enforcement titles are only enforceable after they have become final.[52] The debtor is additionally granted an absolute time limit of 20 days from the date of *res judicata* (Article 548 LEC).[53] The purpose of this waiting period is to induce the obligated person to voluntarily fulfil the respective obligation.[54] However, payment need not be demanded before the initiation of enforcement actions. The request for payment is sufficiently expressed by the final decision and the application for enforcement; the 20-day deadline from the date of the final decision gives the debtor a generous period of time to fulfil the obligation.[55] This waiting period in addition to the period until the decision becomes final works strongly in favour of the debtor. Regarding the end of enforceability, Spanish enforcement law provides for a period of 5 years from the date of *res judicata* after which an enforcement request will lapse (Article 518 LEC).[56]

In France, enforcement titles are in principle immediately enforceable; accordingly, no time limit suspends the enforceability of the title. Article L 111-4 CPC provides that in French law titles can be enforced within 10 years. This period begins when an enforcement measure is initiated on the basis of that title, in detail depending on the type of enforcement title.[57] This limitation period may be

---

[49] European e-Justice (n.d.-g).

[50] National Report for France (2020), p. 47; National Report for Spain (2020), p. 59.

[51] National Report for France (2020), p. 30; National Report for Sweden (2020), p. 37.

[52] National Report for France (2020), p. 30; National Report for Spain (2020), p. 37.

[53] National Report for Spain (2020), pp. 24 et seq.

[54] European e-Justice (n.d.-f).

[55] National Report for Spain (2020), pp. 24 et seq.

[56] National Report for Spain (2020), pp. 24 et seq.

[57] European e-Justice (n.d.-c).

interrupted by the pendency of certain court proceedings; however, this interruption effect may not cause the limitation period to exceed 20 years.[58]

2.2.2 German Legal Family

According to § 255 (1) ZPO_DE, a time limit can be determined in the judgment within which the debtor has to fulfil his performance. Either the creditor seeking enforcement or the court may determine the time limit at its discretion. No enforcement actions may be taken until the expiry of this period. This time limit only starts to run from the date of *res judicata*;[59] it is therefore to be distinguished from the suspension of enforceability until the expiry of an appeal period.

The time limit from which a decision can no longer be enforced in Germany is based on the 30-year limitation period pursuant to § 197 of the German Civil Code ('Bürgerliches Gesetzbuch', hereinafter reffered to as 'BGB'). According to this, enforcement measures to enforce legally established claims as well as claims from enforceable settlements or deeds can be initiated within 30 years.[60]

In Austria, the formal requirements for enforcement are already checked by the title court when the confirmation of enforceability is issued: In particular, the enforcement title must have been properly served on the debtor pursuant to § 416 (1) of the Austrian Code of Civil Procedure ('Zivilprozessordnung', hereinafter referred to as 'ZPO_AT'), time limits for appeals with suspension effect must have expired (see § 464 (1) ZPO_AT) and the performance period (which is usually 14 days) must have expired (see § 409 (1) ZPO_AT).

Deadlines, which are to be set within the applications for enforcement, are in principle not provided in Austria. The most notable exception is the eviction order pursuant to § 575 ZPO_AT. However, the debtor can counter the enforcement with an objection of a statute of limitations which has already entered into force. The statutory period of limitation for claims for which there is a legally binding title of enforcement ('claims awarded by enforceable judgement') is generally 30 years from the date of the enforcement title coming into force. If the enforcement title is based on the rights of legal entities governed by public or private law, this limitation period is extended to 40 years. Regarding services which are only to be paid in the future, there exists an exception, provided that the general limitation provisions stipulate a shorter period of limitation. The statute of limitations is interrupted by any legally binding enforcement authorization and begins anew with the last enforcement step or the termination of enforcement. In some cases, temporary barriers are

[58] National Report for France (2020), p. 16.

[59] National Report for Germany (2020), p. 30.

[60] European e-Justice (n.d.-d).

provided for a further enforcement application or the continuation of the enforcement procedure.[61]

2.2.3 Romano-Germanic Legal Family

In Dutch Law, the judgment does not contain a time limit within which the judgment may not be enforced or after which the judgment is no longer enforceable. However, if an obligation to perform is imposed, the judgment contains a time limit within which the obligation must be fulfilled by the debtor. The lawyers of the parties usually consult with each other to determine whether the debtor is willing and able to fulfil the obligation voluntarily. The parties have a discretionary power here.[62]

2.2.4 Nordic Legal Family

In Sweden, neither the law itself nor the judgment contains a time limit during which a judgment is not yet or no longer enforceable. However, Chapter 4 Section 11 UB indicates the following: After the creditor has filed an application for enforcement, the debtor will be informed of the initiation of enforcement measures by post. The notification should be made in a timely manner so that the debtor still has sufficient time to protect his rights. On average, the debtor then has 14 days to pay his debt.[63] However, the fact that Swedish law does not contain any provisions on the time limits of the writ of execution or the underlying judgment seems to be a notable characteristic of Swedish enforcement law.

2.3 Provisional Enforceability and Res Judicata

Provisional enforceability means that enforcement actions can take place before a title becomes final. Because this instrument counteracts the suspensive character of legal remedies, however, it is generally only applied under certain conditions. If an appeal is brought against the decision on which enforcement is based, this may also have an impact on provisional enforceability. This chapter is dedicated to issues related to provisional enforceability (but not to legal consequences regarding provisional enforceability if the writ of execution itself is challenged).

---

[61] European e-Justice (n.d.-b).

[62] National Report for Netherlands (2020), p. 15.

[63] National Report for Sweden (2020), p. 6.

2.3.1 Roman Legal Family

Both French and Spanish enforcement law are familiar with the instrument of *provisional enforceability*. In France, according to Article 514 CPC, first instance decisions are only not provisionally enforceable if the law or the decision issued provides otherwise.[64]

In Spain, on the other hand, provisional enforceability, which is regulated in Articles 524 ff LEC, only applies under certain conditions that limit its applicability. Provisional enforceability is intended to prevent the creditor from incurring losses in the period between the issuance of the judgment and its *res judicata*.[65] However, provisional enforceability only applies if resources are claimed in abuse of rights and if the respective decision is amenable to provisional enforceability. For example, judgments relating to rights of a highly personal nature (filiation, annulment of marriage, legal capacity, etc.) or decisions directed at the making of a declaration of intent cannot be enforced.[66]

The different basic attitude to provisional enforceability in the Roman Legal Family necessarily leads to different legal consequences if an appeal is lodged against the title. As in the French legal system provisional enforceability is the rule, a request to lift provisional enforceability must be addressed to the president of the court if an appeal is lodged. In contrast, in Spanish law, decisions—except the cases described above—are generally not enforceable until they have become final. Therefore, provisional enforceability must be applied for additionally if an appeal is brought against the title. The application can be filed in the period from the lodging of an appeal until the final decision; the debtor has a 5-day right of appeal against the approval of the application.[67]

2.3.2 German Legal Family

According to § 704 ZPO_DE, the principle that only final decisions are enforceable also exists in Germany;[68] however, practice shows that the opposite has prevailed.[69] The prerequisite for provisional enforceability is that the court has confirmed provisional enforceability with a clause. The titles mentioned in § 708 ZPO_DE are provisionally enforceable without the provision of security, whereas the titles of § 709 ZPO_DE are provisionally enforceable only against the provision of security.[70]

[64] National Report for France (2020), p. 22.

[65] European e-Justice (n.d.-f).

[66] National Report for Spain (2020), p. 45.

[67] National Report for Spain (2020), p. 45.

[68] Rosenberg et al. (2010), p. 175.

[69] Rosenberg et al. (2010), p. 269.

[70] National Report for Spain (2020), p. 84.

If the debtor opposes the decision on which enforcement is based, this does not affect the provisional enforceability of the decision. This is justified by the fact that the debtor could otherwise delay enforcement by filing an appeal even in hopeless cases.[71] Nevertheless, if an appeal is lodged, the debtor may file an application for the suspension of provisional enforceability pursuant to § 719 ZPO_DE.[72]

In Austria, there is also the principle that a judgment has to be final to be enforceable. However, there are exceptions: For example, even before an appeal judgment becomes final, enforcement can lead to satisfaction if the judgment is challenged with an extraordinary appeal (see § 505 (4) ZPO_AT). An enforcement to merely secure a debt can generally be initiated before a judgement has become final (see §§ 370 ff EO).[73]

Court orders, on the other hand, are generally enforceable before they become final (see § 524 (1) ZPO_AT). However, the court may grant the remedy against the order a suspensive effect if this does not result in a disproportionate disadvantage to the other party and the purpose of the remedy is not otherwise frustrated (see § 524 (2) ZPO_AT).[74]

Disputes at the Labour and Social Court are a special feature in Austria: In such disputes, the filing of an appeal only suspends the formal legal force, but not the enforceability of the judgment (see § 61 Labour and Social Court Code—'Arbeits- und Sozialgerichtsgesetz', henceforth 'ASGG'). So only here, provisional enforceability is the rule. This exception results from the fact that remuneration claims from employment relationships usually affect the livelihood of the person concerned.[75]

2.3.3 Romano-Germanic Legal Family

As in French law, provisional enforceability is the rule in the Netherlands. However, if an ordinary appeal is lodged, the enforceability of the title is suspended until it becomes final. The creditor can file an application for provisional enforceability, which is granted in most cases. This means that the decision can be provisionally enforced despite the lodging of an appeal. Upon application, the court may also declare the decision provisionally enforceable in advance—even in cases in which appeals are still admissible (Article 233 para 1 Rv). However, the creditor seeking enforcement must provide security first.[76]

[71] Brox and Walker (1996) p. 41; National Report for Germany (2020), pp. 84 et seq.

[72] National Report for Germany (2020), pp. 84 et seq.

[73] National Report for Austria (2020), p. 49.

[74] National Report for Austria (2020), p. 50.

[75] National Report for Austria (2020), p. 50.

[76] National Report for Netherlands (2020), p. 32.

2.3.4 Nordic Legal Family

In Sweden, titles can only be enforced when the underlying decision has become final (Chapter 3 Section 3 of the UB). However, this principle does not apply without exception. On the one hand, according to the Code of Judicial Procedure ('rättegångsbalken', hereinafter referred to as 'RB'), decisions rendered during proceedings and not separately appealable are provisionally enforceable (Chapter 17 Section 14 RB). The same chapter lists other procedural decisions that are provisionally enforceable. On the other hand, the UB also states that non-final judgments can be enforced, provided they fulfil the requirements of sections 5–9 (Chapter 3 Section 4 UB).[77] For example, judgments in bill of exchange or cheque disputes and default judgments are usually provisionally enforceable (Chapter 3 Section 5 UB). Other judgments imposing an obligation to pay are also enforceable before *res judicata* if the debtor has not provided a security deposit, whether at the enforcement authority or as a pledge at the bank (Chapter 3 Section 6 UB). Similarly, judgments determining that a payment obligation is time-barred are in principle provisionally enforceable (Chapter 3 Section 7 UB). The same applies to judgments obliging the debtor to surrender, insofar as this is not an obligation arising from a criminal offence and security has been provided (Chapter 3 Section 7 UB). In addition, any judgment can be enforced before it becomes final if required by law or ordered by the judge.[78]

Provisional enforcement is not automatically suspended if an appeal is lodged—unless the UB or the court prescribes otherwise. The debtor then usually has two options: He can file an application for the suspension of enforcement actions or alternatively deposit a security. In certain cases, however, the court itself may also suspend enforcement if an appeal is lodged against an enforcement title that has been issued without a hearing. Finally, it should be noted that in Swedish law only the enforcement actions are suspended; the enforcement title itself remains unaffected.[79]

3 Enforcement Appeals

This final section illustrates how the debtor can challenge the writ of execution or the executory measures (but not the decision underlying the enforcement).

[77] National Report for Sweden (2020), p. 22.

[78] National Report for Sweden (2020), p. 23.

[79] National Report for Sweden (2020), pp. 23 et seq.

3.1 Roman Legal Family

Since the French Execution Code provides for the immediate enforceability of execution titles, the bailiff can usually start the attachment immediately after the application for enforcement has been granted. However, the debtor can file an objection against the attachment; only then does a judge decide on the legality of the attachment. The situation is different in the case of attachments for which the creditor does not yet have an enforcement title, in the case of attachments of earned income and immovable assets. In these cases, the enforcement must be approved by a judge before the bailiff attaches the property.[80] The decisions of the judge can be appealed to the Court of Appeal ('Cour d'Appel') or the Court of Cassation ('Cour de Cassation'), depending on the amount in dispute.[81]

In Spain, the debtor can bring an objection against the enforcement under §§ 556 ff LEC. In doing so, the debtor can invoke substantive grounds, for example that he has already paid the debt, or procedural deficiencies. Adversary proceedings follow, which end with the annulment or confirmation of the writ of execution. An appeal against this decision is allowed to the regional court ('Audiencia Provincial').[82]

3.2 German Legal Family

Since there is no proceeding in Germany for the confirmation of the enforceability of a title, apart from the enforceability clause there is no writ of execution that can be challenged. The debtor only has a legal remedy against the manner of the enforcement actions taken. However, the lodging of the appeal has no suspensive effect; as a result, the enforcement measures are not stopped for the time being.[83]

In Austria, the right of appeal is granted against the enforcement authorization. The appeal is to be addressed to the appeal court (higher regional court), but is lodged with the court of first instance (district court). The appeal must be lodged within 14 days. Representation by a lawyer is generally required. The appeal process is a purely written procedure.[84]

There are other remedies as well: Esp. the fact that the debtor has already paid the claim can be invoked with an opposition motion or an action to oppose enforcement (and not with an appeal against the authorisation of enforcement). The complaint must be lodged with the court that has issued the enforcement authorization. An application for deferment of enforcement can be combined with the complaint.

[80] European e-Justice (n.d.-c).

[81] European e-Justice (n.d.-c); National Report for France (2020), p. 11.

[82] European e-Justice (n.d.-f).

[83] European e-Justice (n.d.-d).

[84] European e-Justice (n.d.-b).

Should enforcement have been granted under the simplified authorisation procedure, the debtor can show—through an appeal—that an enforcement title covering the enforcement is missing, including confirmation of enforceability, or that the enforcement title does not correspond to the information contained in the application for enforcement. The appeal has to be lodged with the court that that has issued the enforcement authorisation in the first instance. When the appeal is lodged, the court examines whether an enforcement title covering the claim to be recovered is available. The time limit for remedies is 14 days.[85]

3.3 *Romano-Germanic Legal Family*

In the Netherlands, the debtor can take action against the enforcement itself; the rules for this are found in Art 438 Rv on enforcement disputes ('executiegeschillen'). The subject matter of the proceedings is not the decision on which the enforcement is based, but merely the meaning and scope of the writ of execution and executory acts. The district court has jurisdiction over enforcement disputes, regardless of the instance that has issued the decision.[86]

3.4 *Nordic Legal Family*

If the decision of the Swedish enforcement authority ('Kronofogdemyndigheten') on the initiation of enforcement measures is challenged, the appeal must also be lodged with this enforcement authority. This is because the enforcement authority also has the power to decide on the appeal and thus on the suspension of the executory measures taken. Consequently, the Swedish enforcement authority is not only entrusted with the decision on the initiation of enforcement measures; it also acts as an appellate authority.[87] This is a specific feature in comparison to other countries, as in other legal systems this function is reserved for judicial bodies.

With regard to time limits, it is particularly striking in Sweden that a writ of execution of earned income can be appealed for an unlimited period of time. The appeal period for granting or refusing enforcement of other assets is 3 weeks after the writ of execution has been served; third parties, in contrast, are not subject to any time limit.[88] If, on the other hand, it is not the writ of enforcement, but the underlying

[85] European e-Justice (n.d.-b).

[86] European e-Justice (n.d.-e).

[87] European e-Justice (n.d.-g).

[88] European e-Justice (n.d.-f).

executory title that is successfully challenged and consequently set aside, the enforcement shall be stopped immediately.[89]

4 Conclusion

The present study has shown that there are considerable differences between the legal systems of the EU Member States with regard to the enforceability of titles; this is true even within legal families. The heterogeneous picture is not least due to the fact that the respective enforcement systems already differ greatly from one another. These considerable differences necessarily lead to major differences in the system of remedies against enforcement as well.

References

Bores Lazo J, Serrano Ron I (2020) National report for Spain. Project EU-En4s — JUST-AG-2018/JUST-JCOO-AG-2018

Brox, Walker (1996) Zwangsvollstreckungsrecht. Carl Heymanns Verlag KG

Bylander E, Linton M (2020) National report for Sweden. Project EU-En4s — JUST-AG-2018/JUST-JCOO-AG-2018

European e-Justice (n.d.-a) https://e-justice.europa.eu/home?init=true&action=home&plang=en

European e-Justice (n.d.-b) How to enforce a court decision – Austria. https://e-justice.europa.eu/52/EN/how_to_enforce_a_court_decision?GERMANY&init=true&member=1

European e-Justice (n.d.-c) How to enforce a court decision – France. https://e-justice.europa.eu/52/DE/how_to_enforce_a_court_decision?FRANCE&member=1

European e-Justice (n.d.-d) How to enforce a court decision – Germany. https://e-justice.europa.eu/52/EN/how_to_enforce_a_court_decision?GERMANY&init=true&member=1

European e-Justice (n.d.-e) How to enforce a court decision – Netherlands. https://e-justice.europa.eu/52/EN/how_to_enforce_a_court_decision?NETHERLANDS&init=true&member=1

European e-Justice (n.d.-f) How to enforce a court decision – Spain. https://e-justice.europa.eu/52/EN/how_to_enforce_a_court_decision?SPAIN&init=true&member=1

European e-Justice (n.d.-g) How to enforce a court decision – Sweden. https://e-justice.europa.eu/52/EN/how_to_enforce_a_court_decision?SWEDEN&init=true&member=1

Hertel C (2009) Rechtskreise im Überblick. Notarius International 1-2:157–170

Kischel U (2015) Rechtsvergleichung. C.H. Beck

Mensah M (2020) National report for France. Project EU-En4s — JUST-AG-2018/JUST-JCOO-AG-2018

Neumayr M, Nunner-Krautgasser B (2018) Exekutionsrecht. Manz

Prodinger L, Nunner-Krautgasser B (2020) National report for Austria. Project EU-En4s — JUST-AG-2018/JUST-JCOO-AG-2018

Rosenberg L, Gaul H, Schilken E et al (2010) Zwangsvollstreckungsrecht. Verlag C.H. Beck, München

[89] European e-Justice (n.d.-f).

Spanish Royal Academy (2021) Spanish legal dictionary – definition of enforcement title. https://dpej.rae.es/lema/t%C3%ADtulo-ejecutivo
Sujecki B (2020) National report for Netherlands. Project EU-En4s — JUST-AG-2018/JUST-JCOO-AG-2018
Wolf C, Kurth N, Mieszaniec K (2020) National report for Germany. Project EU-En4s — JUST-AG-2018/JUST-JCOO-AG-2018

Pendency Rules

Vesna Rijavec

Abstract The aim of this chapter is a profound analysis of conflicting parallel proceedings in cross-border cases starting with a difficult definition of the 'identity ratione materiae' of two claims. Even the language versions of the provision of Article 29 Brussels I bis Regulation reflect different national approaches using wording the of 'same cause of action', 'same claim' and even two elements, namely 'same object and same cause of action'. The CJEU, although only partially in a few cases, simply stated and interpreted all of the above in the same way. Furthermore, the CJEU explained the requirement of 'the same end in view' and defined the negative declaratory action. An object of the subsequent action for a negative declaration might well have been introduced as a defence to the previous action. On the EU level, a *lis pendens* exists even in cases where the claims are not completely the same, but they are mutually exclusive. Mutually exclusive claims exist when the grant of the first claim automatically means that the second claim is excluded, and similarly, when the rejection of the first claim automatically implies that the second claim is justified. Therefore, the relationship between a positive action and a negative declaratory action is a typical example of mutually exclusive claims. Nevertheless, the cross-border cases still demonstrate unsolved complexity of the first pending negative declaratory actions. The author analyses the requirements from Brussels I bis Regulation which are not entirely regulated at the unified level and refer to national law (legal interest for declaratory action, the necessary precision of the negative declaratory claim, beginning of pendency, requests to the claimant in order to achieve the effect of *lis pendens*, later amendments of a lawsuit, which procedural act constitutes acceptance of jurisdiction, the conduct of the second court becoming cognisant of a prior proceeding, the conduct of the second court after the first court accepts its jurisdiction. Special issues are also if the later positive action for performance being stopped by negative declaratory action may then be submitted as a counterclaim. The author also discusses the position of the defendant in litigation initiated by negative declaratory action regarding his claim,

V. Rijavec (✉)
Faculty of Law, University of Maribor, Maribor, Slovenia
e-mail: vesna.rijavec@um.si

V. Rijavec et al. (eds.), *Diversity of Enforcement Titles in the EU*, Ius Gentium: Comparative Perspectives on Law and Justice 111,
https://doi.org/10.1007/978-3-031-47108-7_11

considering the statute of limitations. Finally, the author finds the Brussels I bis Regulation regime still unsatisfactory in the prevention of the risk of forum Shopping and forum running.

1 Introduction

Concurrent proceedings between the same parties before the courts of different Member States having the same subject-matter, can lead to inconsistent judgments and subject the parties to incompatible obligations. They raise problems and delays in the initial stage of the litigation and create potential legal obstacles to the recognition of judgments. Problems arise in the context of the grounds for non-recognition. That is, Article 45(1) lit (c) and (d) prioritise any domestic or recognisable judgment of another Member State in the Member State of enforcement. This provision is in contradiction with the rules on pendency of the Brussels I bis Regulation. It enables refusal of recognition even when the domestic judgment was given despite the pendency of proceedings in the Member State of origin. Parallel instruments such as Article 22 of the European Payment Order Regulation and the European Small Claims Order Regulation address this situation in a different way that preserves the priority of pendency. Therefore, Article 45(1)(c) of the Brussels I bis Regulation should be adapted accordingly.[1]

Parallel proceedings are also problematic because they diminish 'public faith in the judicial system'. A litigant may file parallel proceedings solely as a means of unduly bypassing or harassing the opposing party.[2]

2 The Identity Ratione Materiae and Ratione Personae of Two Claims

The EU has tried to resolve this problem using a traditional civil law solution. If another court is already seized of a matter, the second court seized must decline jurisdiction (now Article 29 Brussels I bis Regulation). There must be two concurrent proceedings that share the same cause of action; those proceedings must involve the same parties.

Identity is important not only for *lis pendens*, but also for modification of a claim and subsequently for determining the objective scope of *res judicata*.

[1]Hess (2021), p. 13.
[2]Bisello et al. (2015), p. 4.

2.1 *Identity of Object and Cause of Action*[3]

One of first problems of interpretation in practice still concerns the requirement that the two claims present the same object and the same cause of action. The precise notion is problematic due to the wide variety of conceptions that can be found in the legal literature of the Member States on this issue.

The different language versions of the Brussels I bis Regulation thus present varying terminology: 'wegen desselben Anspruchs', 'samma sak', 'le même objet et la même cause', 'el mismo objeto y la misma causa'. . . This English phrase 'cause of action' is particularly problematic since it is used in different ways in the relevant legislation and case law.[4] In the following discussion it is used in the way it has been used by the CJEU—to translate the French notion of *cause*.

The CJEU addressed the problem of interpretation of the European rules on *lis pendens* in 1987 in Gubisch Maschinenfabrik v Palumbo. [5]

The Court began by observing that even though the requirement was formulated in different terms in the various linguistic versions of the Brussels Convention, as it is now in those of Brussels I bis Regulation, it was possible to identify a uniform meaning of the different terms adopted, encompassing the unitary German notion of 'denselben Anspruchs', and the more common two-element approach, referring to the 'object' of the action[6] and its 'cause of action'. In particular the CJEU relied on the fact that most versions of the European rules at that time used a two-element approach.

2.2 *The Notions of 'Cause of Action'*

For the purposes of *lis pendens* rule, the 'cause of action' comprises the facts and the rule of law relied on as the basis of the action and the 'object of the action' means the end the action has in view.[7] An action seeking to have the defendant held liable for causing loss and ordered to pay damages has the same cause of action and the same object as earlier proceedings brought by that defendant seeking a declaration that he is not liable for that loss.

---

[3] In German 'objektive Identität des Anspruchs'.

[4] Thus, in English law usage it refers to the facts that are necessary to support a claim to a particular remedy, and so combines objet and cause. The English version of Brussels I Regulation therefore simply refers to 'proceedings involving the same cause of action'.

[5] C-144/86, Gubisch Maschinenfabrik KG v Giulio Palumbo, 8.12.1987, ECLI:EU:C:1987:528.

[6] The English language version of Gubisch Maschinenfabrik refers to the 'subject-matter' of the action rather than the 'object', but the 'object of the action' is now the standard terminology.

[7] C-111/01, Gantner Electronic GmbH v Basch Exploitatie Maatschappij BV, 8.5.2003, ECLI:EU:C:2002:724, para 25.

From an English law perspective, technically the cause of action refers to the facts underlying the claim (although in practice it often gets mingled with the legal basis of the claim—particularly in contract cases where the existence of a contract inevitably draws in legal constructs). In spite of Brexit, therefore, writing in English can lead to confusion because it is not clear whether the term ‘cause of action’ has its ‘English’ meaning or its ‘European’ meaning.

As an example, from the common law, we can consider the Cypriot legal order. There a ‘cause of action’ has a similar meaning as in England and is therefore (in domestic cases) a unitary concept rather than part of a two-element concept. There, in domestic cases, the term ‘cause of action’ is defined in Article 2 of Law 14/60 as follows: ‘A cause of action includes the total of facts that found the right to bring a claim, but in contractual claims, this does not necessarily mean the whole cause of action’. The cause of action in each case is determined based on the case file. Thus, the cause of action is decided based on the facts of the case that constitute the claim and are included in the report of the claim. In addition, a claim may have more than one cause of action. In the case Radiofoniko Idrima Kiprou and others v Androu Nikolaidi, it was stressed that Order 13 of the Cyprus Civil Procedure Rules allow several causes of action in the same action and ‘where two or more causes of action are united in the same legal action, the substance of action is the sum of the causes of the action’.[8]

In the Netherlands, on the other hand, the concept of a ‘cause of action’ as laid down in the internal national provisions (Article 12 Rv) is also highly similar to the concept ‘cause of action’ as laid down in the Brussels I bis Regulation.

The joinder of claims in a civil action in contemporary civil law systems also means multiple causes of action.

2.3 The Notion of ‘the Same Claim’, ‘Wegen derselben Anspruchs’

The EU case law on the same ‘cause of action’ also covers the ‘same claim’ terminology.

If we return to the language versions, we need to consider the rules and theories in the German legal circle including Slovenia and Croatia.

The Slovenian civil procedure act (hereinafter ‘ZPP’) resembles Article 29 Brussels I bis Regulation in the German version. While the action is pending, no litigation can be initiated between the same parties on the same claim; the court shall reject any action brought to initiate such litigation (Article 189/3 ZPP).

---

[8] Christofi & Loizou (2020).

Two theories on the subject matter identity of claims exist in Slovenia. So-called 'pure procedural theory'[9] and 'procedural equivalence theory'.[10] Under the pure procedural theory, the court only compares claimants' requests for relief to determine identity of claims. If the request in the pending action is the same as the request in the second-filed action, then *lis pendens* is established. An exception to this rule lies in requests for money or generic goods. There, the court, in addition to the request for relief, has to look at the facts of the case in order to determine whether the two claims refer to the same amount of money or generic goods (*genus*).

Under the prevailing procedural equivalence theory, the court must look at both the request for relief and the 'grounds of the claim', these are the facts and the legal basis. According to the majority of academics, the grounds encompass all facts constituting the same 'historic event'.[11] The procedural equivalence theory also corresponds with the autonomous concept used in the Brussels I bis Regulation.

Similar in Sweden there exist two views in the legal literature regarding how to determine what is meant by 'samma sak'. According to one view, the decisive criterion is whether the two actions concern the 'same course of events' or the 'same set of facts'. According to the other view, the decisive question is whether the two actions concern the same 'remedy'. The Swedish Supreme Court has, with certain modifications, embraced the latter view.[12]

In Austria, the theory of a two-part dispute is used to determine an identical subject matter in dispute. According to this theory, identity of the claims exists if it is clear from the facts that have been brought forward and the request derived from them that both requests for relief are aiming at the same goal of legal protection. In addition, the claims must be derived from the same facts that give rise to the rights. Both elements must be cumulative: The mere equality of the facts that give rise to the rights does not in itself establish an identity of the claims, nor does the mere equality of the claims.[13]

2.4 Two Elements: 'Object' and 'Cause' of Action

In determining the precise meaning of the 'two-elements' versions, the ECJ has also stressed the need to pursue an autonomous and uniform interpretation, capable of transcending the peculiarities of domestic legal conceptions. In establishing such an interpretation, the ECJ referred to the essential aim of the rules on *lis pendens*, that is to prevent conflicting judgments, which would create an obstacle to the free circulation of judgments among the Member States. Consequently, the autonomous

[9] Ude (2017), p. 215.

[10] Ude et al. (2010), p. 223.

[11] Ude et al. (2009), p. 161.

[12] Bylander & Linton (2020).

[13] Prodinger & Nunner-Krautgasser (2020).

interpretation of both notions of 'object' and 'cause' of the two actions had to be conceived broadly, so as to ensure to the largest extent possible the attainment of that aim. Therefore, the 'object' of the action is in principle identified with the substantial aim pursued by the plaintiff with his claim, rather than with the specific form of relief requested, which might vary according to the legal system concerned. The 'cause' embraces facts and rule of law relied on as the basis of the action.

As one of the main consequences of this interpretation is that, as stated by the ECJ in the Gubisch case, an action for a negative declaration and an action for the performance of the contract should be considered as having the same cause of action. From the Gubitsch case it must be quoted: 'According to its wording Article 21 applies where two actions are between the same parties and involve the same cause of action and the same subject-matter; it does not lay down any further conditions. Even though the German version of Article 21 does not expressly distinguish between the terms 'subject-matter' and 'cause of action', it must be construed in the same manner as the other language versions, all of which make that distinction the German version of Article 21 does not expressly distinguish between the terms 'subject-matter' and 'cause of action', it must be construed in the same manner as the other language versions, ali of which make that distinction'.

The relationship between *lis pendens* and the 'ne bis in idem' effect as a negative reflection of formal finality can provide an answer. If, after the conclusion of the first procedure, a particular further procedure is unlikely to be permissible, because of the 'ne bis in idem' effect of the first decision, then there is also no reason to permit this particular procedure while the first procedure is pending. If the court would dismiss the debtor's action for negative declaratory relief as unfounded, the claimant would not be automatically entitled to an enforcement title and the continuance of his action for performance should therefore be permitted. The court will only be bound by the decision on the dismissal of the negative declaratory effect with regard to preliminary questions of law. On the other hand, it could be argued that once the action for performance is instituted, the debtor loses legal interest for maintaining the declaratory proceedings.

2.5 The Requirement 'the Same End in View' as Expressed by the CJEU

This has been stated in several CJEU decisions and has to do with determining the subject matter identity of the parallel disputes.[14] A possible way to understand it is to consider that it means the effects which the judgments would have should they be rendered in the parallel proceedings. The same end would exist if the judgments in the parallel proceedings might become contradictory to each other.

---

[14] CJEU in Gubisch case (as per English translation) talked about the 'subject-matter' of the action to translate 'objet'. In The Tatry, it talks about the 'object' of the action.

2.6 Essential Common Points of Two Actions (Kernpunkttheorie)

The ECJ held in the Gubisch case[15] that because the enforceability of the same contract was at the heart of the two actions ('Kernpunkttheorie'),[16] which were in fact aimed either at affirming or at denying enforceability of the contract, the actions were to be assumed as having the same object and the same cause of action for the purposes of the Convention, even though pursuant to the domestic legal conceptions of the relevant Member States the identity of the object of the two actions could apparently not be affirmed. The Court further observed that the solution reached was justified because the object of the subsequent action for a negative declaration might well have been introduced as a defence to the previous action for the enforcement of the contract since it did not extend the limits of the object of the dispute as set by the latter action.

2.7 Identity of the Parties

For the *lis pendens* mechanism to be applicable, there is a requirement for the parties in each of the actions to be the same. The term 'same parties' has an independent or autonomous meaning, as established in The Tatry case. Where there are more than two parties (joinder of parties), issues can arise as to whether the same parties are involved in both cases.

If the case involves indispensable co-litigants, those co-litigants must be considered as relevant parties for purposes of identity, even if they are not nominated as proper parties in the action, i.e. they are 'third persons'[17] (e.g., if A institutes proceedings against B, but due to the nature of their legal relationship, the judgment will have the same effect for the legal position of C as well, then A cannot institute separate proceedings against C as well; conversely, C cannot institute proceedings against A, but he may intervene as an indispensable co-litigant).

The court must also observe rules on successors of parties (a universal successor, i.e. heirs, restructured companies, will generally assume the position of a party, while singular successors, e.g., cessionary, will generally not). Also, judgments on

[15]The Gubisch case presented, on the one hand, an action for the performance of a sales contract, whereby the seller sought payment of the price from the buyer. On the other hand, it presented an action for a negative declaration, whereby the buyer sought a declaration holding either that the contract was null and void or that the seller had committed a fundamental breach of the contract, discharging the buyer from his obligations. Bisello et al. (2015), p. 7.

[16]Martiny (2009): 'Miteinander unvereinbar sind etwa eine Klage auf Kaufpreiszahlung und eine solche auf Auflösung des ihr zugrunde liegenden Vertrags. Sie haben die gleiche 'Grundlage', beziehen sich auf dieselben Kernpunkte des Streits'.

[17]See Ude et al. (2006), p. 222.

erga omnes rights (*in rem* rights on property law) do not of their own accord produce *erga omnes* effects regarding the personal boundaries of the pending case (A may first institute proceedings against B, claiming he is the owner of property and then initiate proceedings against C with the same request for relief, i.e. that he is the owner).[18]

Whether the parties are the same cannot depend on the procedural position of each of them in the two actions, so whether they act as the claimant or the defendant in case set of proceedings is irrelevant.

Two parties will be the same where their interests are identical and indissociable in relation to the subject matter of the two disputes concerned. In terms of legal entities, whether they are identical may depend on whether 'there is such a degree of identity between the interests of the entities that a judgment given against one of them would have the force of *res judicata* as against the other'.[19]

According to the CJEU case law, no identity can be found between the parties of the two sets of proceedings unless it is proved that they are acting in the pursuit of the same indivisible legal interests so that the judgment is to be pronounced in respect of the former would be *res judicata* with respect to the latter. However, a 'cautious' understanding of the same end in view could be advocated. The importance of individual access to court has to be observed.[20]

The case Drouot determined by the CJEU, concerned the issue of personal identity. The claimant in case 1 was the owner of a cargo on a sunken vessel (that was later salvaged) and an insurer that had insured the cargo. The defendant in case 1 was the ship owner and its charterer. In case 2 the claimant was an insurer that had issued an insurance on hulls concerning the sunken and salvaged vessel. The claim was brought against the claimants in case 1. Hence, the parties were not the same in case 1 and case 2: the owner of the vessel and its charterer were not parties to case 2, and the insurer on hulls was not a party to case 1. However, it was claimed that identity between the parties existed, apparently because they had the same interests.

The CJEU did not exclude the possibility that an insurer and a policy holder could be regarded as one and the same party in certain cases, when it comes to the provisions on *lis pendens* in the Brussels instruments. However, in this case the CJEU held that it did not appear that the interests of the insurer of the hull of the vessel could be considered to be identical to and indissociable from those of its insured, the owner and the charterer of that vessel. Nevertheless, it was for the national court to ascertain whether that was in fact the case.

---

[18] Ude et al. (2006), p. 222.

[19] C-351/96, Drouot Assurances SA v Consolidated metallurgical industries and Others, 19.05.1998, ECLI:EU:C:1998:242, para 19.

[20] Bylander & Linton (2020).

2.8 Collective Redress

From the perspective of the Brussels I bis Regulation, collective redress raises issues of jurisdiction and of pendency and relatedness (with regard to the claimants represented and the moment of pendency) and of recognition (regarding the binding effects of judgments and court-approved settlements on parallel claims). Some basic clarifications in this area are still required and; upgrade of Brussels I bis Regulation is recommended. Regarding pendency, there should be a rule that only cross-border collective claims based on (explicit) opt-in are permissible. Furthermore, Article 30 of the Brussels I bis Regulation should be made mandatory in order to avoid overlapping collective claims. Finally, the moment of pendency (Article 32 Brussels I bis Regulation) should be clarified in the sense that the relevant moment in time should be identified in the application to be admitted as a (lead) claimant in a collective case. As a general rule, the first step in filing a collective lawsuit should be decisive.[21]

3 Negative Declaratory Action

While discussing the identity of the object of two claims a more detailed insight into the nature of a negative declaratory action is necessary. Generally, a declaratory judgment creates a 'prejudice' for potential further disputes between the parties since the courts are bound by the determination of the (non)existence of a right or legal relationship. Declaratory relief cannot be requested to determine facts or just to determine certain individual prerequisites of a legal right (e.g., a party cannot request that a court finds that it did not act contrary to law: contravening the law is merely a prerequisite for establishing liability).[22] A party can, however, request declaratory relief in the form of a finding that it has no liability.

These points are controversial and should be weighed against the backdrop of the debtor's request. If the debtor requests the finding that there exists no underlying legal relationship between him and the creditor, then this claim should not be considered a cause for *lis pendens*, nor produce binding effects. Such a finding is not identical nor contradictory to the request for performance raised by the creditor (it is considered *aliud*). A condemnatory judgement decides on performance; the grounds are merely explained in the reasoning, which is not encompassed by finality. If, on the other hand, the debtor seeks declaratory relief wherein he negates the particular right (or validity) of the creditor's claim, then this decision would—if raised as a preliminary question of law—bind the court entertaining the action for performance.

---

[21] Hess (2021), p. 8.

[22] Ude et al. (2009), p. 181.

In The Tatry, the CJEU also states that it sees an identity between an action for damages and a previously filed action finding that the defendant is not liable for the damage.[23]

This decision that the *lis pendens* rule covers proceedings with a negative declaratory action has changed the perception in many places, especially in German legal circles. Before, the approach of national procedural law in Germany and Austria used to be that a negative declaratory claim could not prevent a subsequent positive condemnatory action because the condemnatory action is, in essence, a more comprehensive legal protection.[24]

On the EU level, a *lis pendens* exists even in cases where the claims are not completely the same, but they are mutually exclusive. Mutually exclusive claims exist when the grant of the first claim automatically means that the second claim is excluded, and similarly, when the rejection of the first claim automatically implies that the second claim is justified. Therefore, the relationship between a positive action and a negative declaratory action is a typical example of mutually exclusive claims. However, two positive declaratory actions are not necessarily mutually exclusive claims.[25]

In this context, a recent Slovenian case should be mentioned.[26] After heavy rainfall in 2012 in Austrian Carinthia, the hydroelectric power plant is supposed to have neglected the proper management of excessive waters that causes floods on the Drava River banks in Slovenia. The injured parties submitted actions based on the optional international jurisdiction rules of Brussels I bis Regulation in the place where the tort/*delict* occurred or may occur against the power plant, which overtook them with negative declaratory action. In the aforementioned case between the

---

[23] In Case C-406/92, The owners of the cargo lately laden on board the ship "Tatry" v the owners of the ship "Maciej Rataj", 6.12.1994, ECLI:EU:C:1994:400, an action for a negative declaration was instituted in the Netherlands by the owners of a ship, wherein they tried to exclude their liability for damage to the ship's cargo before the owners of the cargo sued them in England to recover damages. The Tatry's facts are reversed from those in Gubisch: in The Tatry the action for a negative declaration preceded that for performance so that it could not be said that the object of the latter action could have been introduced as a defence in the first proceedings. In fact, in accordance with the domestic legal conceptions of various Member States, the object of the latter action appeared broader than that of the former. Nonetheless, the Court still held that the same question lay at the heart of the two actions (the shipowners' liability for damage to the cargo) and believed that the subsequent claim for damages might well be considered dependent on a ruling finding the shipowners liable, as that was the main object of the action subsequently introduced by the owners of the cargo; Bisello et al. (2015), p. 7.

[24] Ude et al. (2006), p. 221.

[25] E.g.: Judgment of the Supreme Court of Slovenia II Ips 652/92 of 20.5.1993, judgment and decision II Ips 171/95 of 8.10.1997: 'If the plaintiff requests that the existence of a legal relationship (joint property) be established, the defendant cannot claim that this relationship does not exist', e.g., A's claim against B to establish 'that A is the owner of thing X' and B's claim against A to establish 'that B is the owner of thing X'. Admitting the first claim automatically means that the second claim is unfounded, but the opposite is not true: if the court rejects the claim to establish A's property right, it does not automatically mean that he is the owner of B. Both actions are therefore admissible.

[26] VSMB, I Cpg 263/2016, 15.07.2016, ECLI:SI:VSMB:2016:I.CPG.263.2016.

insurance company and the power plant, the Slovenian court, upon the defendant's objection, suspended the proceedings because proceedings were pending before the Austrian court between the same litigants, in which the defendant claimed that it was not liable for the flood events in November 2012 (negative declaratory action).

Nevertheless, the Austrian court first denied its jurisdiction in favour of the Slovenian court, dismissed the action, and issued a decision to that effect. If this decision became final, the obstacle to *lis pendens* would disappear *ex tunc*, and there would no longer be any obstruction to proceedings in the Slovenian court. However, in the second and third Austrian instances, the opposite decision was reached and Austrian jurisdiction was accepted. The Slovenian court continued to stay its procedure and issued a decision that denied Slovenian jurisdiction but did not dismiss the action.

3.1 Legal Interest for Declaratory Action

According to Slovenian law, a claimant must have a legal interest before he can initiate a declaratory action. A claimant lacks such interest if he is already entitled to claim performance of an obligation that became due. However, that does not mean that the debtor does not have an interest in a negative declaratory action. By means of the negative action, the non-existence of a specific legal relationship is asserted to prevent liability for the debt. The negative declaratory action's particular nature also implies that negative facts cannot be proved. The negative declaratory action involves the reversal of party roles (the debtor here is the claimant and not the defendant as in all other actions), but this does not affect the allocation of the burden of proof.

The German system presents the same requirement that the claimant has an interest in a declaratory judgment (§ 256 ZPO). In contrast to a declaratory judgment, a judgment ordering performance is enforceable. So, the existence of an interest in a declaratory judgment is typically denied because it is not as effective as an action for performance. But the German system differentiates between the matter in dispute in a declaratory action and the matter in dispute in an action for performance. In the Brussels I bis Regulation there is no difference between the matter in dispute in these two actions. Nevertheless, it might be a good solution to the problem of 'torpedo' actions if a special interest was required before a declaratory action could be brought—and especially prior to an action for negative declaratory relief.[27]

[27] Galle et al. (2016).

3.2 *Sufficient Determination of the Negative Declaratory Claim*

The burden of proof for facts proving the valid establishment of a legal relationship lies on the creditor (defendant). On the other hand, the debtor (claimant in this litigation) bears the burden of proving the facts on which he bases his objections regarding the termination or non-existence of the legal relationship or obligation.

However, an action in which the claimant generally (without specifying the specific legal relationship, the existence of which must otherwise be claimed by the claimant) seeks a declaration that he owes nothing to the defendant is inadmissible. The term legal relationship presupposes the existence of a concrete factual situation between identified parties and not an abstract hypothetical case.

A claim that which is based on possible future compensation payments is also not suitable for a decision since the legal relationship that the court is supposed to decide on is not sufficiently specified.

According to the CJEU approach, based on the 'Kernpunkttheorie',[28] a negative declaratory action is, in principle, an obstacle to a later condemnatory action. Still, it is also necessary to verify the identity of object of the two claims in the light of the content of the action brought.

Therefore, the identity problem for negative declaratory actions might be the content of the claim. According to Slovenian jurisprudence, the action must contain a description of the legal relationship, stating its specific elements to such an extent that it cannot be confused with any other legal relationship. Therefore, it is inadmissible for an action by which the claimant in general (without stating the specific legal relationship, the existence of which is otherwise claimed by the defendant) seeks a declaration that he does not owe the defendant anything. In the Drava case, the defendant alleged concrete damages in the settlement offer. However, the claimant in the claim only requires a finding that he does not owe anything from a particular very broad life event.

4 Beginning of Pendency

Brussels I bis Regulation provides a definition that overcomes national differences[29] regarding the start of the procedure. A court is seised at the time when the document instituting the proceedings or an equivalent document is lodged with the court,

[28]Martiny (2009): 'Miteinander unvereinbar sind etwa eine Klage auf Kaufpreiszahlung und eine solche auf Auflösung des ihr zugrunde liegenden Vertrags. Sie haben die gleiche 'Grundlage', beziehen sich auf dieselben Kernpunkte des Streits'.

[29]E.g., in Croatia the litigation is pending as of the day the claim is served on the defendant. If the request has been raised by the party in the course of the proceedings, it is pending once the counterparty has been informed of the request. Article 194 (1, 2) CPA. The same applies in Slovenia.

provided that the claimant has not subsequently failed to take the steps he was required to take to have service effected on the defendant; or if the document has to be served before being lodged with the court, at the time when it is received by the authority responsible for service, provided that the claimant has not subsequently failed to take the steps he was required to take to have the document lodged with the court (Article 33 Brussels I bis Regulation).

5 What Must the Claimant Do to Achieve the Effect of 'Lis Pendens'?

To create a *lis pendens*, the claimant must subsequently take the steps he was required to take to have service effected on the defendant (Article 32 (1) Brussels I bis Regulation). All the measures incumbent on him, particularly the necessary advances on costs (in Germany according to Article 12 GKG), must be paid immediately. However, Article 32 presupposes that the document submitted names the claimant and the defendant and provides an address for service. If the lawsuit is later expanded or otherwise changed, there is a dispute as to whether the point when the amended lawsuit was filed or when the original lawsuit was filed is relevant. The purpose of Article 32, to avoid competing proceedings, should be based on the point in time at which the original action was filed.[30]

According to Austrian procedural law, obtaining a translation is the claimant's duty and not that of the court. However, the Austrian court's final decision[31] found that the claimant fulfilled his duty to facilitate valid service of the claim under Article 32 (1) even if he had not provided the translation on his own initiative but after the court expressly required it from him.

Regulations 1393/2007 and 2020/1784 on the service of documents do not resolve this issue. However, they stipulate that 'the applicant shall bear any costs of translation prior to the transmission of the document, without prejudice to any possible subsequent decisions by the court or competent authority on liability for such costs' (Article 5(2) of Regulation 1393/2007 and Article 9(2) of Regulation 2020/1784). The requesting party is the court. In litigation, the court transfers the necessary procedural acts as well as the translations of the documents to the party whose document is to be translated. This also follows from the provision on free legal assistance, including translation costs, if the party cannot pay them. According to Austrian law, the court only handles translations for deaf people (§ 73a ZPO, sign language interpreters).

[30] Gottwald (2017), Article 32.

[31] Beschluss Republik Österreich Oberster Gerichtshof, N 1 Ob 63/20a, https://rdb.manz.at/document/ris.just.JJT_20200428_OGH0002_0010OB00063_20A0000_000/formats/ris.just.JJT_20200428_OGH0002_0010OB00063_20A0000_000.pdf.

The first act in the proceedings must enable the defendant to inform himself about the decisive grounds of the lawsuit.[32] This means that the procedural relationship is established if the minimum standard for the lawsuit is met. The claim must contain a specific request, the facts on which the claim is based as to the main and ancillary matters, evidence to prove the facts, and the other information that each request must contain (see e.g., § 226 ZPO, Article 180 ZPP—Slovenian Code of Civil Procedure).

In the case of an incomplete or incomprehensible lawsuit, the court must deal with the application in the same way as with any similar application (Article 108 ZPP, § 85 ZPO). The claimant must be required to remedy the defects if the claim is insufficiently definite. If the deficiencies are not remedied or cannot be rectified within the time limit, the court will reject the application. The first court must nevertheless devote much attention to the consistency of a claim.

Suppose a claimant deliberately submits an incorrect lawsuit to delay the proceedings. In that case, no order for improvement is to be issued, but the claim is to be rejected immediately.[33]

6 Amendments of a Lawsuit

It should be noted that the claimant can not remedy a defective action by amending the action. If a claim changes during the proceedings, its priority with respect to a condemnatory action is lost.

At the given time, the court may begin proceedings only concerning the claims asserted at that time, and not concerning anticipated claims and issues. The plaintiff should not be permitted to tamper with the claim as a means of preserving the jurisdiction of the first court for subsequent claims, and the procedural consequences of subsequent claims should be considered. In the case-law of the national courts, such a focus on the dispute is consistent with the position of the UK Supreme Court.[34]

There is another point of view, but the CJEU has not yet ruled on it.[35]

---

[32] Schlosser (2009), p. 151; Geimer (2004), p. 361.

[33] Ballon et al. (2013), paras 84, 85.

[34] Mankowski and Magnus (2016), para 757: The court can be seised at a given moment only in relation to claims advanced at that moment, not in relation to anticipated issues. Again, the principle suggests that a claimant should not be allowed to treat the issue of the claim as a means of reserving the first court's jurisdiction over claims advanced later, and should be held to the procedural consequences of subsequently changing its case. This fragmental view of a dispute would also appear to be consistent with the position of UK Supreme court.

[35] Mankowski and Magnus (2016), para 757.

7 Which Procedural Act Constitutes a Determination of Jurisdiction

Brussels I bis Regulation does not require a specific act for accepting jurisdiction. This issue has various interpretations in the literature. Acceptance of jurisdiction is already in place if the defendant has started to address the matter of a case and has not objected to lack of jurisdiction (Article 26(1) of the Brussels I bis Regulation). The view that jurisdiction is considered accepted if a there is a judicial decision to that effect it is convincing. Such a decision is formally final because it can no longer be challenged by legal means.[36]

8 Conduct of the Second Court Becoming Cognisant of a Prior Proceeding

The decision to stay the proceedings on the grounds of *lis pendens* shall be made of the court's own motion, thus even if none of the parties requests it.

Any later courts seised are obliged to stay their proceedings and wait, without any time limit, until the court first seised has established whether it has jurisdiction or not. If the court first seised concludes that it has jurisdiction, all the other courts must decline jurisdiction even if they believe that the court's conclusion was erroneous.[37]

The CJEU ruled in the Gasser case: 'The Brussels Convention must be interpreted as meaning that, where the jurisdiction of the court first seised is contested, the court second seised may, if it does not decline jurisdiction, only stay proceedings and may not itself examine the jurisdiction of the court first seised'. The Court stated that its ruling was without prejudice to the case where the court second seised has exclusive jurisdiction under the Convention and in particular under Article 16 thereof. Brussels I bis Regulation later enacted a new rule introducing false exclusive jurisdiction for agreed jurisdiction (prorogatio fora). If in case there is an agreement on jurisdiction, only the agreed court has jurisdiction, which prevents from negative declaratory actions.

However, the two courts might not have the same opinion on the identity of claims and priority of action. It is still an open question as to what happens if both courts demand priority or if the latter court finds no identity and continues its proceedings. The decision to stay the procedure depends on one of the parties raising an objection or the court's knowledge that there is another identical action. The second court stays its proceedings and issues a decision which is subject to an appeal in which the issue of the identity of the claims might be raised. Therefore, in the second State, the decision may prove to be different from the decision in the first

[36] Schlosser (2009), p. 149.

[37] Bisello et al. (2015), p. 10.

State. However, both states are obliged to give an autonomous European interpretation of the requirements of Brussels I bis Regulation.

Further, it is still worth asking how the second court is to find out when a foreign court has reached a decision on its jurisdiction and whether it must dismiss the action. The Brussels I bis Regulation does not stipulate the obligation of a foreign court to send a notice of acceptance of jurisdiction, nor of its refusal. The Brussels I bis Regulation only stipulates that all courts except the one that first initiated the proceedings shall suspend their proceedings *ex officio* until the jurisdiction of the court that first initiated the proceedings is established. At the same time, it establishes a duty for courts to inform one another, but just on request, of the date when they were seised (in accordance with Article 32). This makes it possible to determine which court has priority (paragraphs 1 and 2 of Article 29 of the Brussels I bis Regulation). Here, too, practice will provide a way of communication, as the Brussels I bis Regulation does not prescribe anything more detailed regarding cooperation between courts.[38]

The potential that there may be a '*lis pendens*' is under Slovenian law considered *ex officio*, but in fact, the defendant always raises the issue from his own interest. The Brussels I bis Regulation does not specify anything about this.[39]

Staying a procedure is regulated according to national rules and the ZPP provides for a special formal possibility of suspension of proceedings if another law, e.g., the Brussels I bis Regulation, so provides (Item 6 of paragraph 1 of Article 205 of the ZPP).

9 Conduct of the Second Court Seised When the First Court Accepts Its Jurisdiction

According to the ZPP, the suspended procedure is continued on a party's proposal as soon as the reason for the suspension ceases (paragraph 3 of Article 208 of the ZPP).

Rejection (dismissal on procedural grounds) of the subsequent action is the method of terminating a case under Slovenian law when the Slovenian court has no jurisdiction. A positive decision on jurisdiction by a foreign State relating to the procedural issue of jurisdiction must be recognised under the Brussels I bis Regulation and is binding.

However, Brussels I bis Regulation only says that the second court shall decline jurisdiction in favour of the court first seised, if the latter has established its jurisdiction. According to a literal interpretation of Brussels I bis Regulation, this might be understood as meaning that the court just issues a declaratory decision. On the other hand, national legal systems may require the dismissal/rejecting of the

[38]The solution follows the Green Book, Cf: Rogerson (2015), p. 330.

[39]Rogerson (2015), p. 330.

claim ('Zurückweisung der Klage') in order to create a procedural barrier of *lis pendens*.[40]

Since Article 29(3) Brussels I bis Regulation only leads to jurisdiction being 'declined', it is unclear what happens to the pending action that was not dismissed/ rejected. Is the litigation still pending and de facto suspended until the end of the procedure for a negative declaratory action? When so, can the procedure revive if the negative declaratory claim is refused or dismissed? In the opposite situation, if the negative declaratory action is justified, should the still exiting condemnatory action be withdrawn by the claimant or dismissed by the court? The Slovenian rules do not support such a solution but simply impose the rejection of the action if the court has no international jurisdiction.

A condemnatory action presents more comprehensive protection than a declaratory one. The '*res judicata*' effect of a negative declaratory decision does not embrace the claim for performance if the negative declaratory action is rejected. Therefore, it might be possible to advocate a solution to keep the pending proceedings in the second court suspended until a decision is made upon the first lawsuit.[41]

10 Counterclaim

According to CJEU case law[42] a counterclaim is an active defence of a defendant who seeks the pronouncement of a separate judgment or decree. It does not apply to the situation where a defendant raises, as a pure defence, a claim that he allegedly has against the plaintiff. The defences which may be raised and the conditions under which they may be raised are governed by national law.[43]

Thus, a counterclaim, in substance, is a separate claim seeking a judgment against the claimant, which may be made for an amount exceeding that claimed by the claimant, and can be proceeded with even if the claimant's claim is dismissed. As the Advocate General observes in point 39 of her Opinion in Case-185/15 (Kostanjevec v F&S Leasing GmbH), the counterclaim must therefore be separable from the claimant's action and seek a separate judgment. On the facts of that case, a claim for reimbursement of the payment made in the enforcement of an original decision—which was later set aside by the Supreme Court—constituted a separate claim by the lessee seeking for a separate judgment to be given against the lessor to repay what

[40] Slovenian and Austrian civil procedure rules.

[41] Schlosser (2009), p. 146.

[42] C-341/93, Danværn Production A/S v Schuhfabriken Otterbeck GmbH & Co, 13.7.1995, ECLI: EU:C:1995:239.

[43] Ibid.

was wrongly paid to him. Such a claim is not therefore a mere defence to the action for payment brought by the other party.[44]

Lis pendens rules must also be considered for counterclaims,[45] as well as for claims the debtor invokes for set-off (compensation in judicial proceedings).[46] The debtor cannot raise separate actions for these claims. Furthermore, partial *lis pendens* is also possible, where only part of a claim is the subject of ongoing litigation.

11 Statute of Limitations

The general question is how the defendant protects himself from the expiration of the statute of limitations period in case the condemnatory action is dismissed for lack of jurisdiction.

The limitation period is qualified as a substantive law matter under Slovenian law governed by the applicable law, not, like in some other states, as a procedural question governed by *lex fori*.

According to the substantive law e.g., Obligations code (hereinafter 'OZ') (Article 367), a new lawsuit filed within 3 months after the dismissal of the lawsuit for jurisdictional reasons causes the statute of limitations period to remain interrupted by the first lawsuit.

It may be resubmitted only if the obstacle due to which the action was dismissed/rejected (e.g., end of the first proceeding without granting the claim) later fell away.

In Slovenian substantive law, the limitation period is not interrupted only by filing a lawsuit but by any other activity of the creditor against the debtor before a court or other competent authority to establish, secure, or recover the claim (Article 365 OZ). In a negative declaratory action, the active party is the debtor. The creditor only defends himself. However, his actions before the court, even if only in response to the lawsuit, in my opinion, imply his claim is being addressed in the sense of Article 365 OZ and interrupt the statute of limitations period. In the case of a negative declaratory action, the court may issue a judgment and grant the declaration. The decision implies that there is no obligation. On the other hand, if the court rejects the claim, it means that the obligation under the merits definitely exists.

Therefore, submitting another identical condemnatory action this time in the State where the negative declaratory action is pending just to interrupt the statute of limitations period seems unnecessary and even questionable. A new condemnatory claim in the state where the negative declaratory action is pending can still be burdened by the obstacle of *lis pendens* and the same condemnatory counterclaim to the negative declaratory action. On the other hand, in purely national cases Brussels I bis Regulation does not apply. In Austria for example a condemnatory

[44] C-185/15, Marjan Kostanjevec v F&S Leasing GmbH, 12.10.2016, ECLI:EU:C:2016:763.

[45] VSRS sodba in sklep II Ips 7/2012, 19.12.2016, ECLI:SI:VSRS:2016:II.IPS.7.2012.

[46] VSRS sklep II Ips 906/2008, 05.04.2012, ECLI:SI:VSRS:2012:II.IPS.906.2008.

action offers more extensive legal protection than a negative declaratory action. It would therefore be considered that two claims are not identical, and a new condemnatory action would be admissible.

12 The Risk of Forum Shopping and Forum Running

However, current rules in the Brussels I bis Regulation regarding *lis pendens* still encourage tactics designed to delay the lawsuit from proceeding in the forum prescribed by the Regulation. The improvement introduced by the rule in the Brussels I bis Regulation that the jurisdiction expressly agreed by parties has an exclusive nature only solved a small part of the problem.

The Brussels I bis Regulation has a weak point regarding the abuse of the right to choose where to commence proceedings (abusive reliance on the *lis pendens* and Article 29 of the Brussels I bis Regulation). There is a hint in the literature that there a quite a few opportunities available to create further avenues for filing negative declaratory actions.[47]

Nevertheless, the Brussels I bis Regulation in general prohibits the abuse of procedural rights. Abuses are activities that are intended to achieve unjustified advantages. The unjustified advantage might also include the fact that the claimant creates for himself the status of a domestic litigant. Some of the party's motives are, per se, morally questionable (e.g., the motive of achieving success that could not be expected in another country, achieving the highest possible compensation, silencing critical public voices, and preventing public interest debate). It is however, difficult to assess in what context they are abusive enough for court intervention.

The CJEU has ruled that a claimant's attempt to avoid a foreign court in a race to hijack a forum (forum running) because he does not trust the other forum is justified. But, in that case, the court seised was an English court. Because of its different common law system, with its specific rules of procedural management and usual procedural deadlines, it was difficult for a continental litigant to accept the jurisdiction of the English courts.

The aforementioned Drava case concerning concurrence between the Austrian and Slovenian courts also initiated a dispute on the illegitimate assumption of jurisdiction for a negative declaratory action. In this case there are no essential differences between the systems as in the English case. Therefore, the excuse is not the fear of being judged at a Slovenian court but gaining the unjust advantage of litigating on home territory, which could be considered an illegitimate goal. The maneuver of a negative declaratory action namely in principle unreasonably delays the resolution of the case even if the courts are not particularly slow. The claimant's intention is that the long delay, together with the potential costs and inconveniences

[47] Nuyts (2007), p. 70.

of taking part in court proceedings abroad, will make the other party give up his claim or accept a settlement favorable to the former.

Moreover, it is a problematic tactic to take advantage of the other party's willingness to negotiate by taking the opportunity to commence proceedings first, whether or not the action is properly prepared for litigation, and whether or not the disputed relationship can be described with precision. By seising jurisdiction in this way, the claimant violates the universal fundamental principles of diligence and honesty, as the defendant approached the negotiations fairly to avoid costly litigation.[48]

Abuse of rights can generally be defined as exercising a right for a purpose other than the right was created for, and it is generally prohibited. The CJEU encountered the problem of abuse of rights concerning the torpedo lawsuit in the Gasser case.[49] The court avoided deciding on the violation of the right to a trial within a reasonable time under Article 6 of the ECHR, which was put at risk by the torpedo, lawsuit since this question was not the matter of interpretation of any provision of Brussels I bis Regulation. However, it emphasized that proceedings in another Member State, exclusively under the provisions of *lis pendens* within the Brussel's regime, do not release Member States' courts from the protection of fundamental rights, e.g., due to the length of the procedure. Even when applying EU rules, national courts retain the duty to examine the possibility of abuse by the parties.[50] Article 47 of the European Charter of Human Rights now embeds this right as part of EU law.

[48]It would be interesting to survey Europe wide case law/articles on this subject which was not possible for this chapter.

[49]Case C-116/02, Erich Gasser GmbH v MISAT Srl., 9.12.2003, ECLI: EU: C: 2003: 657, shows that the ECJ had the opportunity to decide on the misuse of a torpedo lawsuit in breach of Article 6 of the ECHR.

[50]Nuyts (2007), p. 70: If the court did not address as such the issue of the abuse of the process, a silence which cannot be criticised since this question was not raised by referring court and since there was under specific circumstances true, the court did rule that delaying and running for forum tactics are not as such the question of the interpretation of any provision of Brussels I Regulation as deduced from its wording and purpose but that should not be as such a subject for disapproval. Indeed, this seems to be plainly correct and in accordance with settled case law: the way the EU rules are interpreted is not to be altered only because there is a possibility that, under such interpretation some parties might engage in abusive actions or behaviour. But at the same time the national courts keep the residual power, or even duty, to verify in view of that all that has taken place in law and fact, that the rules EU are not relied upon abusively by the parties. Pursuant to the EU general principle of abuse of right, which under the most recent case law seems to have received a general scope of application, the national courts are entitled to even required, when a manifest abuse occurs, to deny the abusing party the benefit of the provision of EU law he seeks to rely upon.

13 Conclusions

The mechanisms of *lis pendens* still too negatively influence access to justice. Even if the procedures of the court first seised are not particularly slow, parallel proceedings cause unavoidable delays. The first stage—waiting for the acceptance of jurisdiction—may require decisions in more than one instance in both countries. Each time, the *lis pendens* rule obliges the court second seised to stay proceedings until the court first seised makes up its mind about its jurisdiction.

For the sake of legal certainty, the rules of jurisdiction must be clear, as their interpretation must ensure a certain and reliable criterion of jurisdiction. A multiplicity of courts having jurisdiction as regards the same legal relationship might be avoided, including: the avoidance of alternative courts having jurisdiction with respect to the same legal relationship; the avoidance of different courts having jurisdiction as regards various aspects of the same legal relationship; the avoidance of fragmentation of proceedings. To reach this position it is necessary to have: (1) an interpretation of concepts constituting the connecting link to jurisdictions that is not too broad or multifarious and an interpretation of concepts constituting the substantive scope of jurisdictions that is not too restrictive; (2) a power in national courts to decide quickly without hesitation whether they are competent to hear a case.[51]

During the last years, different solutions have been elaborated to face the Torpedo proceedings' threat and prevent the abuses of the *lis pendens* rule.[52] The proposals discussed include the granting of an anti-suit injunction by the court and introducing the forum non-conveniens doctrine, but these were found to be unacceptable. Another proposal was to expressly exclude the option of negative declaratory action as a reason of *lis pendens*. This solution was quickly rejected as it would encourage parallel proceedings leading to possible irreconcilable judgments and eroding the principle of mutual trust in the EU Member States judicial System.[53]

The most promising solution to the problem posed by the abusive use of negative declarative actions may be the careful control of the admissibility of those actions, performed directly by the judge seised. This solution consists of a preliminary and fast examination of the jurisdictional issue by the judge concerned in a summary proceeding. This proposal could be connected with the idea of assigning national judges a time limit for reaching a final decision on jurisdiction in transnational litigation. it has been objected procedural deadlines, which remain distinct from the issue jurisdiction, are left to the national rules of procedure.

Anyhow, direct communication and cooperation between the two courts involved in parallel proceedings should be strengthened so that the court second seised is constantly informed about the development and the time needed for the conclusion

---

[51] Bisello et al. (2015), p. 11.

[52] Granting anti-suit injunctions by the court, forum non conveniens doctrine, eliminating the option of negative declaratory action and improving the existing system of dealing with parallel proceedings.

[53] Bisello et al. (2015), p. 12.

of the first proceedings. Cooperation and communication between the courts would help mutual understanding and mutual trust.

References

Ballon O et al (2013) Paras 84–85. In: Fasching H, Konecny A (eds) Kommentar zu den Zivilprozessegesetzen. MANZ Verlag, Wien

Bisello G, Cognetti C, Lo Gerfo F (2015) Deactivating the Italian Torpedo. https://www.ejtn.eu/Documents/Themis%20Luxembourg/Written_paper_Italy3.pdf

Bylander E, Linton M (2020) National report for Sweden. Project EU-En4s — JUST-AG-2018/JUST-JCOO-AG-2018

Christofi D, Loizou D (2020) National report for Cyprus. Project EU-En4s — JUST-AG-2018/JUST-JCOO-AG-2018

Galle M, Hosseinian Sereshki A, Romero S (2016) The race to the court in the light of the Brussels I recast – an improvement in preventing the torpedo tactics? https://www.ejtn.eu/PageFiles/14777/Written%20paper_Germany.pdf

Geimer (2004) Lis pendens in der Europäischen Union. In: Coester M, Sonnenberger H (eds) Festschrift für Hans Jürgen Sonnenberger zum 70. Geburtstag

Gottwald P et al (2017) Münchener Kommentar zur ZPO, 5th edn. Ia-VO, Brüssel

Hess B (2021) Reforming the Brussels Ibis Regulation: perspectives and prospects. Max Planck Institute Luxembourg for Procedural Law Research Paper, Series 4

Mankowski M, Magnus U (2016) European commentaries on private international law ECPIL. Otto Schmidt, München

Martiny D (2009) Rechtshängigkeit. HWB-EuP

Nuyts A (2007) The enforcement of jurisdiction agreements further to gasser and the community principle of abuse of right. In: De Vareilles-Sommières P (ed) Forum shopping in the European judicial area. Bloomsbury Publishing, Oxford

Prodinger L, Nunner-Krautgasser B (2020) National report for Austria. Project EU-En4s — JUST-AG-2018/JUST-JCOO-AG-2018

Rogerson P (2015) Lis pendens and related actions. In: Dickinson A, Lein E (eds) The Brussels I Regulation recast. Oxford University Press, Oxford, pp 321–355

Schlosser P (2009) EU-Zivilprozessrecht, 3rd edn. C. H. Beck

Ude L (2017) Civilno procesno pravo. Uradni list RS, Ljubljana

Ude L, Betetto N, Galič A et al (2006) Pravdni postopek: zakon s komentarjem, 2.knjiga. Uradni list RS, GV Založba, Ljubljana

Ude L, Betetto N, Galič A et al (2009) Pravdni postopek: zakon s komentarjem, 3. Knijga. Uradni list RS, GV Založba, Ljubljana

Ude L, Betetto N, Galič A et al (2010) Pravdni postopek: zakon s komentarjem, 4. knjiga Uradni list RS, GV Založba, Ljubljana

Related Actions

Denis Baghrizabehi and Tjaša Ivanc

Abstract The chapter deals with the rules on related actions found in Article 30 of Brussels I bis Regulation. At the outset, the authors attempt to describe the nuances of the autonomous understanding of the concept, both regarding the relatedness of actions and the powers of the national courts to stay proceedings. The authors demonstrate that gaps in the conceptual understanding of the rules contribute to an underutilization of said rules. The chapter continues to describe a lack of functional approximates of the rules on related actions in national laws, which are more concerned with guaranteeing efficiency and avoiding irreconcilability in the narrow sense (i.e. *lis pendens*). The authors finally use a case example from Slovenia to demonstrate the difficulties faced by national courts in applying the rules on related actions and the errors, which may occur in the process.

1 Introduction

Article 30 of Brussels I bis Regulation contains provisions on related actions, which may apply when the conditions set out for *lis pendens* are not met, however, a risk of 'irreconcilable' judgments nonetheless exists. To avoid said risk, the first paragraph of Article 30 provides any court other than the court first seized the possibility to stay its proceedings. In addition, the second paragraph of Article 30 provides that any other court may, on the application of the parties, decline jurisdiction if the court first seized has jurisdiction over the actions in question and its law permits for consolidation thereof.

In practice, national courts do not seem inclined to exercise the discretion of staying proceedings and rarely identify actions as related in the first place. The problem of defining 'relatedness' and the lack of incentives to stay proceedings are probably the main causes for the underutilisation of the rules on related actions.

D. Baghrizabehi (✉) · T. Ivanc
University of Maribor, Faculty of Law, Maribor, Slovenia
e-mail: denis.baghrizabehi@um.si; tjasa.ivanc@um.si

V. Rijavec et al. (eds.), *Diversity of Enforcement Titles in the EU*, Ius Gentium: Comparative Perspectives on Law and Justice 111,
https://doi.org/10.1007/978-3-031-47108-7_12

This contribution attempts to bring clarity to the concept of related actions and provide some guidance on the use of the national courts' discretionary powers to stay proceedings. First, we will analyse the concept and mechanism of related actions within the framework of EU law. We will then proceed with a succinct overlook of national case law on the topic, including a more in-depth analysis of a string of case law arising from a singular damaging event (the floods of river Drava). It is worth noting that leading scholarly works in this area draw heavily from English case law, while we will look to the laws of continental Member States.[1] Finally, we provide concluding remarks on the state of play regarding the concept and the mechanism of related actions.

2 Defining Related Actions as an Autonomous Concept

2.1 *The 'Irreconcilability' of Actions*

There is no doubt that the concept of related actions is a (euro)autonomous concept.[2] The rule contained in paragraph 3 of Article 30 is the starting point for its (literal) interpretation. Actions are deemed related where they are so closely connected that it is expedient to hear and determine them together to avoid the risk of irreconcilable judgments resulting from separate proceedings.

The Brussels I bis Regulation employs the term of 'irreconcilable' judgments as one of the deciding factors in assessing relatedness. However, the meaning of irreconcilable judgements in Article 30 should be considered more flexible[3] from the meaning of irreconcilable judgements as cause for refusal of recognition under Article 45(1)(c) and less strict than the rules on *lis pendens* under Article 29 of Brussels I bis Regulation.[4,5] That much is clear from the judgement in The Tatry, where the CJEU elaborated that the objective of the rules on related actions is to improve coordination of the exercise of judicial functions within the EU and to avoid *conflicting and contradictory* decisions, even where the separate enforcement of each of them is not precluded.[6] Moreover, the risk of conflicting decisions may arise

[1]Following Brexit, it is reasonable to assume that the influence of English case law in the matter will gradually subside.

[2]Leible (2006), p. 505; Rogerson (2015), p. 332.

[3]Rogerson (2015), p. 332; Briggs (2021), p. 384.

[4]Law (2022), p. 485.

[5]The function of the rules on *lis pendens* is prophylactic in relation to the rules on refusal, inasmuch the risk of irreconcilable judgments is concerned. See Case C-351/89, Overseas Union Insurance, 27.6.1991, ECLI:EU:C:1991:279, para 16.

[6]Case C-406/92, Tatry v Maciej Rataj, 6.12.1994, ECLI:EU:C:1994:400, para 55.

without necessarily involving the risk of giving rise to mutually exclusive legal consequences.[7,8]

The CJEU reached the above conclusion on the basis of the purposive method of interpretation, as evidenced by recourse to the Opinion of AG Tesauro.[9] The CJEU apparently also applied the comparative and linguistic methods, since it highlighted that the German and Italian versions of the (then) Brussels Convention do not make use of the same terms for the 'irreconcilability'.[10] Purely from the standpoint of the principle of legal certainty, the use of the same term for different concepts in certain linguistic versions is suboptimal and can be considered a source of confusion. In this regard, some academics seem to advocate the notion of *inconsistent* rather than *irreconcilable* judgements resulting from the misapplication of the rules on related actions.[11] Notwithstanding the differences, it is clear that the manifestations of irreconcilability found under the rules of *lis pendens* and related actions serve the overarching interest of the harmonious administration of justice as set out in Recital 21 of Brussels I bis Regulation.[12]

As indicated above, the rules on related actions apply where the requirements of the 'triple identity' test as set out in Gubisch[13] are not satisfied. Therefore, actions may be related where the parties are the same, but the cause of action differs, or where the cause of action is the same, but the parties differ.[14] One should also take account of the fact that the notion of 'action' is more comprehensive than the notion of 'claim'. In their assessment of irreconcilability, courts should thus take into consideration claims, defences and counter-claims.[15] The broader framing entails a subsidiary (residual) nature of the provision in relation to that of *lis pendens*. In other words, if the national court fails to find that the situation adheres to *lis pendens*, it should consider whether the actions are related.[16]

It is as of yet unclear whether irreconcilability is concerned with 'primary' or 'essential' rulings, i.e. those, which the courts seized are required to decide on, or

---

[7] Ibid., para 58.

[8] It has been argued that the provision off Article 30 has a supplemental function to regulations on the conflict-of-law rules. The goal of avoiding irreconcilable judgements runs parallel to the uniform application of law, regardless of the International forum; both sets of rules are thus in service of guaranteeing an international consistency of decisions (German: *internationale Entscheidungseinklang*). See Eichel (2021), para 6.2.

[9] Opinion of AG Tesauro in Case C-406/92, Tatry v Maciej Rataj, 13.7.1994, ECLI:EU:C:1994:289, paras 27–28.

[10] Case C-406/92, Tatry v Maciej Rataj, 6.12.1994, ECLI:EU:C:1994:400, para 56.

[11] See e.g. Bosters (2017), p. 150.

[12] See also Fentiman (2007), pp. 480–481.

[13] Case C-144/86, Gubisch Maschinenfabrik KG v. Palumbo, ECLI:EU:C:1987:528.

[14] Bosters (2017), p. 150.

[15] Bosters (2017), p. 150; See Research in Motion (UK) Ltd v. Visto Corp [2008] EWCA Civ at 36. 153, 2008 2 All ER (Comm) 650.

[16] See Wagner (2022), p. 141; Eichel (2021), para 7; Van Calster (2016), p. 182; D'Alessandro (2010), p. 7.

also ancillary observations made *obiter dicta* and which may not be strictly necessary for the decision of the court.[17] In a string of cases, which, admittedly, do not primarily relate to the field of related actions, but rather to the risk of irreconcilable judgements in multiparty litigation under the rules of jurisdiction,[18] the CJEU seems to have indicated that the outcome of the judgments is not the determining factor of 'conflicting' judgments in itself; the divergence must also exist in the situation of law and fact.[19] Later, the CJEU seems to have considered actions related even if they were merely based on different legal bases, e.g. claims in respect of the same loss between the same plaintiff and various defendants, where a claim against one defendant is rooted in contractual liability and a claim against another defendant is rooted in tort.[20,21] The extend of the applicability of these considerations for the interpretation of the rules on related actions proper, remains uncertain.[22]

---

[17] Fentiman (2016), p. 742; Briggs (2021), p. 349. One should note that this was a leading issue in an often cited English decision, where it was noted, first, that the Brussels I bis Regulation and the CJEU case law do not contain grounds for a limiting interpretation; second, that confining irreconcilability to primary issues comes dangerously close to equating related actions and *lis pendens*; and third, that limiting the notion in such a way would in essence erode the autonomous character of the EU concept and infuse it with domestic (English) notions. See Sarrio S.A. v. Kuwait investment authority. [1997] 1 Lloyd's Rep. 113.

[18] Article 8(1) of Brussels I bis Regulation provides that a person domiciled in a Member State may also be sued where he is one of a number of defendants, in the courts for the place where any one of them is domiciled, provided the claims are so closely connected that it is expedient to hear and determine them together to avoid the risk of irreconcilable judgments resulting from separate proceedings.

[19] Case C-539/03, Roche Nederland and Others, 13.6.2006, ECLI:EU:C:2006:458, para 26.

[20] Case C-98/06, Freeport, 11.10.2007, ECLI:EU:C:2007:595; compare Case C-145/10, Painer, 1.12.2011, ECLI:EU:C:2011:798, para 81. To note, Hess lists the situation where actions are based on different legal bases as an example of no relatedness (Hess 2021, p. 422). This observation is true when considering Réunion européenne (C-51/97, Réunion européenne, 27.10.1998, ECLI:EU:C:1998:509). However, as elaborated in Freeport, the rationale of that decision is confined to cases where jurisdiction is anchored in rules of jurisdiction *loci delicti commissi*.

[21] Stone (2010), pp. 201–202.

[22] In her Opinion in Painer, AG Trstenjak first points out that the text of the two provisions is identical and reiterates that the interpretation of (what is now) Article 8(1) is derived from references of the CJEU to (what is now) Article 30 of Brussels I bis Regulation. However, she stresses that a full transplantation of the rationale from Article 30 is not possible, due to divergent outcomes predicted by both sets of rules. Namely, Article 8 is a jurisdictional rule largely dependent on the actions of the plaintiff, while Article 30 does not provide a basis of jurisdiction of its own accord and leaves the discretion of staying proceedings to the court, permitting consolidation only if an application is made by a party. It should be assumed that a national court will take the decisions for which it is empowered under Article 30, in particular having regard to the need for the harmonious administration of justice. In contrast, the decision whether jurisdiction for related actions is applied rests solely with the claimant who will not be guided by the needs for the harmonious administration of justice, but according to the jurisdiction, which is more favourable to him. Because of that, sufficient account must be taken of the defendant's interests in order to check the risk of possible abuse. Consequently, higher requirements are to be applied to the notion of connection in Article 8(1) of the regulation than to the notion of connection under Article 30. See Opinion of AG Trstenjak in Case C-145/10, Painer 12.4.2011, ECLI:EU:C:2011:239.

2.2 *The Risk of Irreconcilability*

While the notion of irreconcilability is the focal point of Article 30(3) of Brussels I bis Regulation, the rule contains other factors, which jointly define the relatedness of actions.

Firstly, actions are related not only if the irreconcilability (whatever its intensity) is inevitable; they may be related when there is already a 'risk' of producing irreconcilable judgments. However, it is not clear, what degree of risk is sufficient to trigger this provision. Taking account of the CJEU's inclination toward a broad interpretation of Article 30, one could suggest that 'any' degree of risk suffices.[23] If one adopts a broad interpretation of both irreconcilability and its risk, then the threshold for relatedness is met with ease. Obviously, this might not be the optimal solution, since any risk of conflicting *obiter dicta* findings would render the actions related. On the other hand, a broad understanding of 'risk' relieves the national judge of engaging in more a complex prognosis of what a 'material' or 'substantial' level of risk might entail.[24]

2.3 *Expediency*

A further factor, which needs to be taken into account, is that the above risk would be avoided if the actions would be heard and determined together (the expediency requirement). As pointed out by Briggs, this wording is problematic, since Article 30(2) covers this exact situation (consolidation of actions); thus, the requirement on its own is either bereft of meaning or implies to have an autonomous one. In any case, the expediency requirement is directed at the interests of coherence of adjudication, which is not to be confused with cost-efficiency of proceedings.[25]

3 The Powers of the Court(s) Subsequently Seized (the Mechanism of Related Actions)

When faced with a related action, the court(s) subsequently seized may provide one of the following reliefs:

[23] Fentiman (2016), p. 742.

[24] In a leading English case, the national court indicated that a bare assessment of a possibility is not sufficient. See Research in Motion (UK) Ltd v. Visto Corp [2008] EWCA Civ. 153, 2008 2 All ER (Comm) 650.

[25] Briggs (2021), p. 348.

- they may stay their proceedings,
- they may proceed without ordering the stay,
- they may, inasmuch the related action at the court first seized is pending at first instance, on the application of one of the parties, decline jurisdiction, if the court first seized has jurisdiction over the actions and its law permits the consolidation thereof.

The first two options are merely opposite outcomes of the court's discretion to stay proceedings, stemming from Article 30(1) of the Brussels I bis Regulation. The third option is envisaged in Article 30(2) and is dependent on the active involvement of a party and the provisions of the national law of the Member State of the court first seized. This provision does not create a jurisdictional basis for the court first seized to entertain the second action, as elaborated by the CJEU in Elefanten Schuh.[26] Additionally, it seems clear that the option of declining jurisdiction is not to be exercised if the court subsequently seized holds exclusive jurisdiction to hear the case.[27]

It is unclear which objectives and circumstances national courts should take into account when exercising their discretion. In this regard, the Opinion of AG Lenz in Owens Bank v Bracco is often referenced; according to the latter, the court should consider:[28]

- the extent of the relatedness and the risk of mutually irreconcilable decisions,
- the stage reached in each set of proceedings, and
- the proximity of the courts to the subject-matter of the case.[29]

As specified by AG Lenz, this list is non-exhaustive. It has been suggested in theory and practice that the following objectives and circumstances may also be considered:[30]

- the interests of the parties (party autonomy),[31]
- procedural economy (efficiency),
- the existence of a choice-of-court agreement in favour of the court subsequently seized,[32]

[26]Case C-150/80, Elefanten Schuh GmbH v Jacqmain, 24.6.1981, ECLI:EU:C:1981:148.

[27]Stone (2010), p. 203.

[28]Opinion of AG Lenz in Case C-129/92, Owens Bank v Bracco, 20.1.1994, ECLI:EU:C:1993:363.

[29]This consideration should not be as widely interpreted as the English doctrine of *forum non conveniens*. See: Rogerson (2015), pp. 332–333.

[30]See Leible (2006), p. 508; Eichel (2021), para 7.

[31]The court should, however, not grant stay if this would enable tactical forum shopping or would contravene the right to a public hearing within a reasonable time. See: Fentiman (2016), p. 746; D'Alessandro (2010), p. 9.

[32]This has been the case in English case law. See: JP Morgan Ltd. V. Primacom AG [2005] 2 Lloyd's Rep. 665. The latter consideration can be considered a corollary of party autonomy.

– the applicability of the court's own national law on the merits of the case, whereas the court first seized applies it merely as a foreign law.[33,34]

Turning back to the Opinion AG Lenz—the latter seems to have also suggested that, in case of doubt, the objectives of Brussels I bis Regulation, namely—the prevention of parallel proceedings and avoidance of conflicting decisions—favoured the decision to stay the proceedings.[35] It is unclear whether this entails a (rebuttable) presumption in favour of a stay.[36] Nothing in the literal interpretation of the rule would suggest such an approach. In any case, it should be possible for the court second seized to stay the proceedings only in part where the actions are related partially,[37] and to order the continuation of the proceedings if the reason for the stay (the factors of relatedness) has ceased (e.g. due to party dispositions in the first set of proceedings).[38]

From a practical perspective, the courts will often exercise discretion with regard to the significance that the resolution of the dispute pending before the court first seized bears on the action pending with the court subsequently seized. For example, if related actions are taking place between different parties (e.g. only one party is the same in both actions), but share the same cause of action, the judgment rendered by the court first seized—although recognised in the Member state where the court second seized is located—will generally not bind the parties in the second set of proceedings. To elaborate, the judgment was not given against the parties in the second set of proceedings (personal boundaries of the judgment are restricted to the parties of the dispute), nor was one of the parties given the right to be heard in the first set of proceedings. On the other hand, it may prove prudent to stay proceedings where the parties are the same, yet the cause of action somewhat differs.[39] Granted, if the resolution of the first set of proceedings does indeed affect the second

[33] This consideration (inasmuch we consider it separately from the courts proximity to the subject-matter of the case) might be considered controversial, since the principle of mutual recognition would dictate that the courts of Member States apply foreign law universally.

[34] Another consideration previously pointed out in theory was the potential of the non-recognisability of the judgment by the court first seized. See: D'Alessandro (2010), p. 9; Leible (2006), p. 507. After the abolishment of exequatur with the Brussels I bis Regulation, these considerations would seem to have lost some appeal due to the principled automatic recognition of foreign judgments.

[35] See Opinion of AG Lenz in Case C-129/92, Owens Bank v Bracco, 20.1.1994, ECLI:EU:C:1993:363, para 75. His argument seems to be inspired by an English case (Virgin Aviation Services Limited v CAD Aviation Services, [1991]), in which the court held that there was a strong presumption in favour of allowing an application. This argument is also somewhat supported by the Jenard report, where it is expressed that the first duty of the court is to stay proceedings. See: Jenard P, Report on the Convention on jurisdiction and the enforcement of judgments in civil and commercial matters, OJ C 59/1, 5.3.1979, p. 41.

[36] Fentiman (2016), p. 745; Rogerson (2015), p. 333.

[37] Gottwald (2022), para 2.

[38] Leible (2006), p. 508.

[39] Briggs (2021), p. 352.

set of proceedings and the court second seized does not stay its proceedings, this may trigger a rush to judgment to have it recognised.[40] A prominent example, which speaks in favour of a stay, is when the court first seized is deciding on a matter, which involves a 'preliminary claim'. in the sense that the resolution of the second action, between the same parties, depends on the decision of the court first seized.[41] Similarly, where both parties had the opportunity to be heard on matters of fact, which are common to both sets of proceedings, the court second seized might give weight to the determinations made by the court first seized. The latter consideration provokes, or rather—points—to the duality of national procedural laws applied to the decision on the exercise of discretion. On the one hand, the significance of the decisions made by the court first seized will, in line with the theory of extension of effects, be determined by the concept of *res judicata* under the law of the Member state of the court first seized. On the other hand, the court second seized could make recourse to its own procedural law, inasmuch that law contains mechanisms that would allow that court to take into consideration the findings of the court first seized.[42]

4 Case Law of National Courts and Doctrinal Approaches

Since related actions are an autonomous concept of EU law, national courts should refrain from employing nominally or functionally similar rules found in national law. On the one hand, the arguably sparse and vague language used to describe the relatedness of actions seems to unintentionally prompt national courts to seek guidance in their national laws. On the other hand, it also seems to intentionally grant the national courts a wide discretion in assessing relatedness. The scarce case law of the CJEU on the autonomous understanding of the concept does not markedly aid the efforts of national courts in applying the correct (autonomous) interpretation of the rule. In the following paragraphs, we will briefly address the application and understanding of the concept by national courts.

[40] Stone (2010), p. 202.

[41] D'Alessandro (2010), pp. 6–7. The latter author also argues that CJEU has created such an obligation of stay in the are of patent law through its ruling in Case C-4/03, GAT, 13.6.2006, ECLI: EU:C:2006:457.

[42] See D'Alessandro (2010), p. 5.

4.1 *National Mechanisms Approximating the Functions of Related Actions*

As with many (euro)autonomous concepts, the introduction of related actions into the predecessor Brussels Convention[43] was inspired by a national provision. In fact, the concept is based on Article 30 of the Belgian Judicial Code.[44] The Brussels I bis Regulation seems to be more or less a verbatim adoption of said article. In line with Belgian jurisprudence, the assessment of a sufficiently close connection between actions is a matter for the court to decide,[45] regardless of the cause of action ('oorzak') or the identity of the parties.[46] The assessment of relatedness should be made at the initiation of the proceedings so that a possible change in the actions cannot lead to the actions no longer being regarded as related.[47]

Other national legal orders taken into consideration do not seem to operate with an equivalent notion. National legal orders contain rules on consolidation of proceedings, which are not employed for the same objectives. In Austria, § 187 öZPO[48] allows for several proceedings (with partial party identity) pending before the same court, to be heard together in order to accelerate and simplify the proceedings. According to § 192 öZPO, the finding of the connection as well as its reversal is at the discretion of the court, whose order is incontestable.[49] It must be stressed that an action under § 187 öZPO provides only for the joint hearing of the cases, which retain their legal independence. Essentially the same rules apply in Slovenia through the operation of Article 300 sZPP[50] and in Croatia through Article 313 hZPP.[51,52]

---

[43] 1968 Brussels Convention on jurisdiction and the enforcement of judgments in civil and commercial matters, OJ L 299, 31.12.1972.

[44] Jenard P, Report on the Convention on jurisdiction and the enforcement of judgments in civil and commercial matters, OJ C 59/1, 5.3.1979, p. 42.

[45] Rys (2020), p. 64.

[46] Cass., 15 mei 1981, Arr. Cass., 1980-81, 1073; Pas., 1981, I, 1073; Cass., 28 September 1984, Arr. Cass., 1984-85, 165; Pas., 1985, I, 141).

[47] Rys (2020), p. 64.

[48] Gesetz vom 1. August 1895 über das gerichtliche Verfahren in bürgerlichen Rechtsstreitigkeiten (Zivilprozessordnung), RGBl. Nr. 113/1895.

[49] Prodinger & Nunner-Kraugasser (2020), p. 62.

[50] Zakon o pravdnem postopku (Uradni list RS, št. 73/07 – uradno prečiščeno besedilo, 45/08 – ZArbit, 45/08, 111/08 – odl. US, 57/09 – odl. US, 12/10 – odl. US, 50/10 – odl. US, 107/10 – odl. US, 75/12 – odl. US, 40/13 – odl. US, 92/13 – odl. US, 10/14 – odl. US, 48/15 – odl. US, 6/17 – odl. US, 10/17, 16/19 – ZNP-1, 70/19 – odl. US, 1/22 – odl. US in 3/22 – ZDeb).

[51] Kunštek et al. (2020), p. 43.

[52] Zakon o parničnom postupku, SL SFRJ 4/77, 36/77, 6/80, 36/80, 43/82, 69/82, 58/84, 74/87, 57/89, 20/90, 27/90, 35/91, i NN 53/91, 91/92, 58/93, 112/99, 88/01, 117/03, 88/05, 02/07, 84/08, 96/08, 123/08, 57/11, 148/11, 25/13, 89/14, 70/19, 80/22.

German law provides for consolidation through the operation of § 147 dZPO[53] and requires that proceedings be legally connected (often the case with counter-claims). The legal connection can be identified through the same factual circumstances (e.g. reciprocal damage claims arising out of the same traffic accident);[54] different factual circumstances but interdependent claims (e.g. a claim following from the validity of the contract and the counterclaim arising out of the purported invalidity of the same contract);[55] a sufficient connection can also be established, if the proceedings concern different legal relationships that have arisen out of related circumstances which economically and considering their purpose from the point of view of a reasonable third person belong together, such as different contracts within an ongoing business-relationship.[56,57] Italian law provides that actions are related for the purposes of consolidation, if they involve the same parties and the same object (*petitum*), or are based on the same grounds (*causa petendi*).[58] Certain legal orders allow for consolidation, which appear to mimic the concept of related actions to an extent. For instance, in Swedish law, closely related actions may be joined in one proceeding if they are 'based essentially on the same grounds" and if partial party identity is provided. The actions have to be pending at the same court, however, an action may be transferred from one court to another pursuant a Supreme court order, if the action is related to an action pending in another court.

By and large, the primary objectives of the consolidation of proceedings are aimed at guaranteeing procedural efficiency. The harmonious administration of justice may be considered a by-product of the consolidation. This is, *inter alia*, evidenced through the restriction of consolidation to cases pending at the same court, which seems to be the general rule in all observed jurisdictions.

In addition to consolidation of proceedings, one should consider another mechanism as functionally approximate to related actions; namely, a stay of proceedings for the purposes of awaiting a judgement rendered in another set of proceedings, where that judgment decides on a preliminary issue for the pending procedure. This is the case, for example, in Germany (§ 148 dZPO), Slovenia (Article 206 sZPP) and Italy ('cause pregiudiziali di merito').

[53]Zivilprozessordnung in der Fassung der Bekanntmachung vom 5. Dezember 2005 (BGBl. I S. 3202; 2006 I S. 431; 2007 I S. 1781), die zuletzt durch Artikel 2 des Gesetzes vom 7. November 2022 (BGBl. I S. 1982) geändert worden ist.

[54]BGH, Urteil v 13 March 2007 - VI ZR 129/06, NJW 2007, p. 1753.

[55]BGH, Urteil v 21 February 1975 – V ZR 148/43.

[56]BGH, Versäumnisurteil v 7 November 2001 – VIII ZR 263/00.

[57]Wolf et al. (2020), pp. 111–112.

[58]Kaczorowska et al. (2021), p. 51.

4.2 The Understanding of Relatedness by National Courts

Although Article 30 Brussels I bis Regulation is underutilized in practice (in fact, some Member States report no cases of application),[59] the rare instances where it is applied, reveal a diverse, if not—inconsistent—understanding. The following is a summarisation of national case law, focusing specifically on the understanding of the 'relatedness' of actions. Of note, we shall be omitting mere repetitions of the CJEU's interpretations, made by the national courts.

The concept of related actions as interpreted by Austrian courts, may pertain to so-called 'procedural set-off' objections raised during proceedings between the same parties abroad.[60] Additionally, Austrian courts consider the possibility of related actions where different claims arise from the same contract and are litigated in different Member States.[61] In German case law, courts have held that the necessary connection between actions was not met in a case where both actions shared the same factual grounds, because the actions were nevertheless based on the violation of different intellectual property rights.[62] In another German decision, the court did not stay the proceedings concerning the violation of a European trademark due to a negative declaratory action concerning the same trademark that was previously initiated in Belgium. The court held that the possibility that two courts of different Member States come to different conclusions towards the extent of protection of a European trademark is not covered by Article 30 of the Brussels I bis Regulation, thus, did not give rise to the danger of contradictory decisions.[63]

Recent Italian case law reveals that an action filed in Poland, for the payment of the purchase price on the basis of a certain contract was deemed related to another action, filed in Italy, seeking liability on a warranty on the basis of the same contract. The actions were regarded as related because they were based on the same core issue. Indeed, in both cases courts had to assess whether the parties had correctly performed the obligations laid down in the contract.[64] Furthermore, an action for payment of the purchase price on the basis of a certain contract filed against a British undertaking was deemed related to another action brought against the same defendant, seeking compensation for non-contractual liability stemming from unfair competition.[65] On the opposite spectrum, the Italian Supreme Court elaborated

[59] Those Member States seem to be Croatia, Portugal and Poland.

[60] Prodinger & Nunner-Krautgasser (2020), p. 63, citing: OGH 25.5.1999, 1 Ob 115/99i EvBl 1999/187 = ZfRV 1999/70; RIS-Justiz RS0112099.

[61] Prodinger & Nunner-Krautgasser (2020), p. 63, citing: OGH 25.5.1999, 1 Ob 115/99i EvBl 1999/187 = ZfRV 1999, 70; 22.2.2001, 6 Ob 295/00a ZfRV 2001/58 = JBl 2001, 796; RIS-Justiz RS0112099.

[62] Wolf et al. (2020), p. 114, citing LG Düsseldorf, Beschluss v 17 March 2009 – 4b O 218/08, juris at margin n. 51.

[63] Wolf et al. (2020), p. 114, citing LG Düsseldorf, Urteil v 5 June 2008 – 4a O 27/07.

[64] Kaczorowska et al. (2021), p. 53, citing Tribunale di Padova, 15 October 2014.

[65] Kaczorowska et al. (2021), citing case Cass. civ. Sez. Unite, 28/10/1993, n. 10704.

that the risk of irreconcilable judgments is excluded where actions are based on different factual circumstances, *in concreto* where the first action is filed against an investment fund on the basis of non-contractual liability while the second action is filed by an investment fund against another for contractual liability.[66]

Sparse Swedish case law reveals that the courts did consider actions, which were based on similar agreements and the same underlying legal relationship, but negotiated separately, as related.[67] On the other hand, in a case where two actions were based on the same commitment to pay, they were deemed related, when taking into account the principle of procedural economy.[68]

In Cyprus, courts have entertained several related actions, however, no specific definition on their relatedness vis-à-vis irreconcilability has been provided, apart from referring to mutually exclusive legal consequences.[69]

The Belgian reporter cited an example of a case where actions were not deemed related under the Brussels I bis Regulation. It references an action before a Belgian court for a preliminary payment of invoices and an action before a French court for the termination of an exclusive distribution agreement. Beyond the scope of Brussels I bis Regulation, related actions under Belgian law encompass, for instance, an action relating to a divorce and an action relating to the determination of parenthood.[70]

In Slovenia, a court considered actions related, where an Austrian claimant filed an action for damages (arising from a vehicular accident) against the tortfeasor (driver) in Slovenia and a separate action against the torteasors insurance company in Austria.[71]

4.3 *The Exercise of Discretion*

The available case law of the Member States on the issue of the exercise off discretion to stay proceedings is sparse. Only German, Italian and Slovenian reports provided detailed insight into the court's arguments.

In Germany, one court observed that Article 30 Brussels I bis Regulation contains no rules as to the exercise of the discretion. It subsequently deferred to national law to determine the requirement, specifically to § 148 dZPO. As explained above, this rule governs the stay of proceedings if a decision in a preliminary matter is anticipated.[72] Another court denied the stay of a proceedings initiated in Germany

[66] Kaczorowska et al. (2021), citing Cass. Sez. Unite ord. 8 April 2011 n. 8034.

[67] Bylander & Linton (2020), citing Supreme Court decision NJA 2001 s. 386.

[68] Bylander & Linton (2020), citing Supreme Court case NJA 2007 s. 1000.

[69] Christofi et al. (2020), p. 56.

[70] Rys (2020), p. 65.

[71] VSM Sklep I Cp 473/2017, ECLI:SI:VSMB:2017:I.CP.473.2017.

[72] Wolf et al. (2020), p. 115, citing LG Erfurt, Teilurteil v 30 December 2005 – 2 HKO 69/04.

seeking the handover of movable property due to a proceeding initiated in France concerned with a claim for the protection against dismissal and a payment claim. The court found that the handover claim did not depend on the validity of the contract of employment and, therefore, the results from the French proceeding would hardly have been relevant for the German proceeding. Furthermore, the claimant's interest in a swift decision concerning the international jurisdiction outweighed potential reasons speaking in favour of a stay of the proceeding.[73] Yet another German court considered as relevant circumstances the inability to estimate the time required by the court first seized to render its decision and the proximity of the courts to the damaging location (*loci delicti*). That court also rules that a potential of overcompensation by the claimant was not the concern of Article 30, as this would not be a contradictory decision.[74]

The Italian Supreme court held that Article 30 assumes no obligation of the courts to stay proceedings. Since the national court is vested with full discretion, its decision on stay, could and not to decline jurisdiction could not be appealed under Italian law.[75] Another Italian court elaborated that the decision to stay proceedings is not dependent upon any request made by the parties, but is approximate to Art. 295 of the Italian Code of Civil Procedure, which envisaged the so-called 'sospensione necessaria', which is—as with German law—concerned with a stay of proceedings if a decision in a preliminary matter is anticipated.[76]

5 Case Example: The Court Saga of the River Drava

An interesting string of cases arose in Slovenia and Austria, in relation to damages arising from a flood in 2012. It may serve as an illustration of the difficulties facing national courts in the application of the rules on related actions in light of their vagueness.

The flooding in the cases at hand took place alongside the riverbanks of the river Drava (Drau) that flows into Slovenia southwards from Austria, with many towns, villages and agrarian communities erected by its riverside. The floods were caused by centennial rainfall and plaintiffs alleged that the Austrian operator of the hydroelectric power plants on the river mismanaged the situation by negligently regulating the water levels—relaxing turbines only after the water levels rose severely, thereby causing damage downstream, in Slovenia. A rush to court occurred, where the Austrian operator filed an action before Austrian courts for negative declaratory

[73] Wolf et al. (2020), pp. 115–116, citing LAG Niedersachsen, Urteil v 29 June 2016 – 13 Sa 1152/15, juris.

[74] Wolf et al. (2020), pp. 116–117.

[75] Wolf et al. (2020), p. 54, citing Cass. civ. Sez. Unite, 26/11/1990, n. 11363.

[76] Wolf et al. (2020), p. 54, citing Tribunale di Firenze in case 07/05/1987 Agostini c. GEB Schuhgrosseinkaufsbund.

relief against the Republic of Slovenia, alleging no liability for damages. Later, the Republic of Slovenia, as well as a myriad of private claimants initiated (individual) actions for (pecuniary) damages against the Austrian operator in Slovenian courts. The Slovenian courts found *lis pendens* in actions where the Republic of Slovenia acted as claimant.[77] At least three courts stayed proceedings in regards to the actions raised by the private litigants, deeming them related actions, due to the possibility of producing contradictory judgments on the liability issue.[78] On appeal, all three decisions to stay were reversed.

The appellate court found that none of the parties proposed the stay of proceedings. Parties are *dominus litis* and according to the assessment of the appellate court, at least one of the first instance courts breached this maxim, when it decided (in contrast with the will of the parties) to stay proceedings. The appellate court found partial party identity in the defendant (the Austrian operator). It went on to explain that the identity of parties is not comparable to The Tatry case, where the parties involved were either claimants or defendants in all of the relevant proceedings, involving a singular causal event and the same adverse consequences. All of the involved parties in the The Tatry had the possibility to steer the outcome of the proceedings by providing the court with procedural materials in each of the pending proceedings. The Brussels I bis Regulation speaks of joint hearing and determination. This was not the case in the Slovenian and Austrian proceedings. Following the rationale of the contested decision of the court of first instance, the proceedings would only be stayed until the final judgement rendered by the Austrian court. However, there was no need for a joint hearing or determination. The procedure under consideration should continue to be a stand-alone, separate procedure. The final Austrian judgement would have no effect - nor could it produce any effect - on the Slovenian proceedings. As the appellate courts phrased it, factual and legal questions of the proceedings pending in Slovenia and Austria do not reach the required 'intensity" regarding their mutual identity. The procedural materials in both cases may be similar, but they are not identical. In fact, in the Austrian proceedings, the parties to the dispute are not the same as in the Slovene proceedings. In Austria, the operator was attempting to exclude its liability against the Republic of Slovenia on grounds of an international convention (stipulated between the former Yugoslavia and Austria), which it cannot use to substantiate its non-liability in Slovenian proceedings. The appellate court concluded by referring to the principle of *res judicata ius facit inter partes*. A court's decision takes effect only between the parties to the concrete proceedings and cannot bind persons who did not participate in the proceedings and could not influence the proceedings.[79]

---

[77] See VSM sklep I Cpg 273/2016, ECLI:SI:VSMB:2016:I.CPG.273.2016; VSM sklep I Cpg 263/2016, ECLI:SI:VSMB:2016:I.CPG.263.2016.

[78] See VSM Sklep I Cpg 10/2018, ECLI:SI:VSMB:2018:I.CPG.10.2018.

[79] See VSM Sklep I Cpg 208/2017, ECLI:SI:VSMB:2017:I.CPG.208.2017, VSM Sklep I Cpg 197/2017, ECLI:SI:VSMB:2017:I.CPG.197.2017, VSM Sklep I Cpg 10/2018, ECLI:SI: VSMB:2018:I.CPG.10.2018.

The reasoning of the appellate court demonstrates the problems faced by courts in applying the rules on related actions. First, the appellate court does not attempt to explain in detail, how the actions are related. It mentions that the parties are not the same and that the intensity of the mutual identity of the actions is not sufficient to render them related. It is true that the circumstance of only partial party identity may speak against the relatedness of actions, however, the appellate court intertwines this circumstance with the assessment of the decision to stay of proceedings. Furthermore, the rejection of the 'intensity" of mutual identity may be well founded; however, this finding contributes little value on its own. By employing such language, the court alludes to the identity of the claim (the cause of action) as is usual in *lis pendens* arguments. As one Slovenian commentator pointed out, unrefined comparisons to *lis pendens* appear to be a staple in Member States, which do not operate with the notion of 'related actions" simply because of the similar objectives of the two instruments.[80] In other words, national courts attempt to explain away the vague framing of the rules on related actions with reference to *lis pendens*, because they are skilful in applying the latter instrument and not the former. Secondly, the appellate court does not engage in separate analysis of the elements, which comprise the rules on related actions, i.e. the irreconcilability, the risk of irreconcilability, the expediency. Thus, any such decision becomes harder to contest. The degree of risk of irreconcilability and the assessment of the stay seems to be especially intertwined. Thirdly, the decision of the appellate court appears to be greatly motivated by considerations of national law. The court ultimately reached its conclusion on the stay (perhaps also on the relatedness) through recourse to national *res judicata* doctrine and its personal boundaries. In light of the vagueness of the EU rules on related actions, such recourse can be expected. While this approach guarantees the observance of national procedural autonomy it also means that there will be a diversity of outcomes and that the rules on related actions will not be uniformly applied in the Member States. Fourthly and lastly, in the absence of particular guidance on the discretion to stay proceedings, the appellate court put great emphasis to the maxim of parties being *dominus litis*. While party autonomy may be taken into consideration, such elevation of party autonomy can hardly be reconciled with the goals of proper administration of justice. Certainly, a contravening decision of the first instance court should not be considered a breach of the courts powers to stay proceedings.

6 Conclusion

The rules on related actions remain in practice underutilized. This can most probably be attributed to the unfamiliarity of the concept in the majority of Member States, which rely on *lis pendens* rules to avoid irreconcilable judgments in the narrow sense. On the one hand, the sparse case law of the CJEU provides for a broad

[80] Sladič (2018), pp. 226–230.

interpretation of related actions, empowering national courts to apply the rule and exercise the discretion to stay; on the other hand, the very vagueness (or broad understanding) of the rules, dissuades national court from their application. We believe that the lacklustre doctrinal framework, which often overlaps the individual elements of the rules on related actions, will need to be expanded in further detail in order to make the instrument more appeasing to national courts or—alternatively—the EU legislator will have detail the rule through legislative intervention.

References

Bosters T (2017) Collective redress and private international law in the EU. Asser, The Hague

Briggs A (2021) Civil jurisdiction and judgments. Routledge, New York

Bylander E, Linton M (2020) National report for Sweden. Project EU-En4s - JUST-AG-2018/JUST-JCOO-AG-2018

Christofi D, Loizou D, Agapiou N (2020) National report for Cyprus. Project EU-En4s - JUST-AG-2018/JUST-JCOO-AG-2018

D'Alessandro E (2010) Related actions in Europe under Article 28 of the Brussels I Regulation: a critical approach, available on: https://papers.ssrn.com/sol3/papers.cfm?abstract_id=1623853

Eichel (2021) Brüssel Ia-VO Art. 30 [Im Zusammenhang stehende Verfahren]. In: Vorwerk V, Wolf C (eds) BeckOK ZPO, 46th edn

Fentiman R (2007) Article 30. In: Magnus U, Mankowski P (eds) European commentaries on private international law: Brussels I Regulation. Sellier European Law Publishers, München

Fentiman R (2016) Art. 30. In: Magnus U (ed) European commentaries on private international law: ECPIL: commentary. Vol. 1, Brussels Ibis Regulation. O. Schmidt, Köln

Gottwald P (2022) Brüssel Ia-VO Art. 30 [Im Zusammenhang stehende Verfahren]. In: Krüger W, Rauscher T (eds) Münchener Kommentar zur ZPO, 6th edn. C.H. Beck, Berlin

Hess B (2021) Europäisches Zivilprozessrecht, 2nd edn. De Gruyter, Berlin

Kaczorowska M, Voinich A, Previatello M (2021) National report for Italy

Kaczorowska M, Voinich A, Previatello M (2021) National report for Italy. Project EU-En4s - JUST-AG-2018/JUST-JCOO-AG-2018

Kunštek E, Kunda I, Mihelčić G et al (2020) National report for Croatia. Project EU-En4s – JUST-AG-2018/JUST-JCOO-AG-2018

Law S (2022) Art. 30. In: Requejo Isidro M (ed) Brussels I Bis: A Commentary on Regulation (EU) No 1215/2012. E. Elgar Publishing, Cheltenham

Leible S (2006) Art. 28 Brüssel I-VO. In: Rauscher (ed) Europäisches Zivilprozeßrecht Kommentar, 2nd edn. Sellier European Law Publishers, München

Prodinger L, Nunner-Krautgasser B (2020) National report for Austria. Project EU-En4s – JUST-AG-2018/JUST-JCOO-AG-2918

Rogerson P (2015) Lis pendens and related actions. In: Dickinson A, Lein E (eds) The Brussels I Regulation Recast. Oxford University Press, Oxford, pp 321–355

Rys M (2020) National report for Belgium. Project EU-En4s – JUST-AG-2018/JUST-JCOO-AG-2018

Sladič J (2018) Uredba 1215/2012 o mednarodni pristojnosti in priznanju ter izvrševanju sodnih odločb v civilnih in gospodarskih zadevah – Bruseljska uredba I bis. In: Repas M, Rijavec V (eds) Mednarodno zasebno pravo Evropske unije. Uradni list, Ljubljana

Stone P (2010) EU private international law, 2nd edn. E. Elgar Publishing, Cheltenham

Van Calster (2016) European private international law, 2nd edn. Hart Publishing, Oxford

Wagner R (2022) Grundzüge der EuGVVO – unter besonderer Berücksichtigung der EuGH-Rechtsprechung – Teil 3, Juristische Ausbildung, no. 2, pp 140–147

Wolf C, Kurth N, Mieszaniec K (2020) National report for Germany. Project EU-En4s – JUST-AG-2018/JUST-JCOO-AG-2918

Provisional Measures with a Cross-Border Element: Their Issuance, Co-existence, Recognition, and Enforcement

Neža Pogorelčnik Vogrinc

Abstract The chapter begins by outlining the rules regarding the two-track jurisdiction for issuing provisional measures and the different requirements for their cross-border recognition and enforcement in another Member State. It then touches upon some of the relevant issues related to provisional measures, drawing on (and at the same time questioning to a considerable extent) the recent case law of the Court of Justice of the EU (specifically Case C-581/20, Skarb Państwa Rzeczypospolitej Polskiej reprezentowany przez Generalnego Dyrektora Dróg Krajowych i Autostrad v TOTO SpA - Costruzioni Generali and Vianini Lavori SpA of date 6 October 2021). Furthermore, it analyses the relationship between several provisional measures or the procedures for issuing them (*lis pendens*). It examines the validity and direct and indirect effects of the parties' choice-of-court agreement for jurisdiction to issue a provisional measure. In the last section, the chapter deals with the problem of provisional measures that are substantively the same as the claim.

1 Introduction

Regulation (EU) No 1215/2012 of the European Parliament and of the Council of 12 December 2012 on jurisdiction and the recognition and enforcement of judgments in civil and commercial matters[1] (as well as its predecessors: the Brussels Convention on jurisdiction and the enforcement of judgments in civil and commercial matters[2] and Council Regulation (EC) No 44/2001 of 22 December 2000 on

[1] Regulation (EU) No 1215/2012 of the European Parliament and of the Council of 12 December 2012 on jurisdiction and the recognition and enforcement of judgments in civil and commercial matters, OJ L 351, 20.12.2012 (hereinafter 'Brussels I bis Regulation').

[2] Brussels Convention on jurisdiction and the enforcement of judgments in civil and commercial matters, OJ 1972 L 299, 31.12.1972 (hereinafter 'Brussels Convention').

N. P. Vogrinc (✉)
University of Ljubljana, Faculty of Law, Ljubljana, Slovenia
e-mail: neza.pogorelcnik@pf.uni-lj.si

V. Rijavec et al. (eds.), *Diversity of Enforcement Titles in the EU*, Ius Gentium: Comparative Perspectives on Law and Justice 111,
https://doi.org/10.1007/978-3-031-47108-7_13

jurisdiction and the recognition and enforcement of judgments in civil and commercial matters[3]) uses the term 'provisional, including protective measures'[4] in its English version. It does not provide for a definition of 'provisional, including protective measures' and does not contain a list of national protective measures that would fall under this term. As a result, it is determined on a case by case basis whether the character of a specific national measure corresponds to the CJEU interpretations of 'provisional, including protective measures'.[5] As the CJEU has stated, what all provisional measures have in common, is that they 'are intended to preserve a factual or legal situation so as to safeguard rights the recognition of which is sought elsewhere from the court having jurisdiction as to the substance of the matter'.[6] The CJEU further reiterated this, in particular with regard to provisional measures issued by a court having jurisdiction according to national rules. These are 'intended to avoid causing loss to the parties as a result of the long delays inherent in any international proceedings'.[7] Their purpose is to 'meet specific practical needs relating to provisional and interim judicial protection'.[8] They enable the creditor to obtain security in the Member State where the property subject to the security is located.[9] This means that it is practical for the provisional measure to be issued in the Member State where it will be enforced. This avoids the inconvenience of transferring the provisional measure (issued by the court having jurisdiction as to the substance) to another Member State under the rules on recognition and enforcement as laid down in Brussels I bis Regulation. The procedure in the latter is indeed simplified (even more so than in its predecessors), but certain procedural steps still have to be taken. Moreover, as will be explained below, the surprise effect is lost. However, there are also benefits to issuing a provisional measure in the Member State with jurisdiction as to the substance. The court in such a state might already be

[3]Council Regulation (EC) No 44/2001 of 22 December 2000 on jurisdiction and the recognition and enforcement of judgments in civil and commercial matters, OJ 2001 L 12, 16.1.2001 (hereinafter 'Regulation 44/2001').

[4]For the difficulties encountered in the different national versions of the translation of this term, see Pogorelčnik Vogrinc (2020), pp. 131 et seq. In order to avoid confusion and for the sake of brevity, only the term 'provisional measures' will thus be used in this chapter.

[5]See, for example, Case C-186/19, Supreme Sites Services and Others, 3.9.2020, ECLI: EU: C:2020:638, para 49.

[6]Case C-261/90, Reichert and Kockler v Dresdner Bank, 26.3.1992, ECLI:EU:C:1992:149, para 34; Case C-391/95, Van Uden Maritime BV, trading as Van Uden Africa Line, and Kommanditgesellschaft in Firma Deco-Line and Another, 17.11.1998, ECLI:EU:C:1998:543, para 37; and recently also Case C-186/19, Supreme Sites Services, para 50.

[7]Case C-104/03, St. Paul Dairy Industries NV v Unibel Exser BVBA, 28.4.2005, ECLI: EU: C:2005:255, para 12.

[8]The Opinion of AG Rantos in Case C-581/20, Skarb Państwa Rzeczypospolitej Polskiej reprezentowany przez Generalnego Dyrektora Dróg Krajowych i Autostrad v TOTO SpA – Costruzioni Generali, Vianini Lavori SpA, 9.9.2021, ECLI:EU:C:2021:726, para 36.

[9]The Opinion of AG Rantos in Case C-581/20, Skarb Państwa Rzeczypospolitej Polskiej reprezentowany przez Generalnego Dyrektora Dróg Krajowych i Autostrad v TOTO SpA – Costruzioni Generali, Vianini Lavori SpA, 9.9.2021, ECLI:EU:C:2021:726, para 37.

familiar with the case and can therefore decide on the measure more quickly and easily.

The chapter begins by outlining the rules regarding the two-track jurisdiction for issuing provisional measures and the different requirements for their cross-border recognition and enforcement in another Member State. It then touches upon some of the relevant issues related to provisional measures, drawing on (and at the same time questioning to a considerable extent) the recent case law of the Court of Justice of the EU. Furthermore, it analyses the relationship between several provisional measures or the procedures for issuing them (*lis pendens*). It examines the validity and direct and indirect effects of the parties' choice-of-court agreement for jurisdiction to issue a provisional measure. In the last section, the chapter deals with the problem of provisional measures that are substantively the same as the claim.

2 Jurisdiction, Recognition, and Enforcement of Provisional Measures

In order to analyse certain specific (and—in the light of recent CJEU case law—also topical) issues concerning provisional measures, it is necessary first to discuss the basic scheme of the life of provisional measures.

Unlike main claims (see Chapter II of Brussels I bis Regulation), Brussels I bis Regulation, does not establish unified rules regarding the jurisdiction to issue provisional measures. The only article that addresses this issue is Article 35, providing the jurisdiction of the courts of a Member State to issue a provisional measure if possible under the law of that Member State. Article 35 explicitly allows for such jurisdiction according to national laws despite the situation that the courts of another Member State have jurisdiction as to the substance of the matter.[10] Therefore, this article indirectly establishes a two-track system of jurisdiction, which could previously also be found in Regulation 44/2001 and the Brussels Convention.[11]

[10] Thus, although they are closely linked to enforcement, provisional measures do not fall within the scope of enforcement matters for which exclusive jurisdiction is provided in Art. 24(V) of Brussels I bis Regulation. It states that 'in proceedings concerned with the enforcement of judgments, the courts of the Member State in which the judgment has been or is to be enforced'.

[11] The CJEU has confirmed the two-track system of jurisdiction in several of its decisions. See Case C-391/95, Van Uden Maritime BV, trading as Van Uden Africa Line, and Kommanditgesellschaft in Firma Deco-Line and Another, 17.11.1998, ECLI:EU:C:1998:543, para 19, and Case C-99/96, Hans-Hermann Mietz v Intership Yachting Sneek BV, 27.4.1999, ECLI:EU:C:1999:202, paras 38 and 40.

2.1 *Provisional Measures Issued by a Court Having Jurisdiction as to the Substance of the Matter*

Even if only in passing, Article 35 of Brussels I bis Regulation makes it clear that courts having jurisdiction as to the substance of the matter can issue a provisional measure.[12] From the European legislature's point of view, the exception is apparently the jurisdiction of other courts (which do not have jurisdiction as to the substance), which therefore needs to be explicitly provided for in the regulation. The competence of the court having jurisdiction as to the substance also to issue a provisional measure derives from the connection between the main procedure and the provisional measure, the purpose of which is usually to protect the latter.[13] AG Rantos similarly noted that the jurisdiction to adopt provisional or protective measures 'flows naturally from its familiarity with the case'.[14] A court that has jurisdiction for something more (the main dispute) also has jurisdiction for something less (a provisional measure).[15] Such jurisdiction exists even if, in this specific case, the court having jurisdiction as to the substance does not have jurisdiction for a provisional measure according to its national law.[16] The jurisdiction as to the substance is enough for the court to ground also its jurisdiction to issue a provisional measure. This is true even if the court procedure regarding the main dispute is not or will not actually be pending in this Member State. It is important to point out that each court (irrespective of the basis of its jurisdiction) issues a provisional measure according to its national material rules, thus verifying that the conditions required by the *lex fori* are met.

The recognition and enforcement of provisional measures issued by a court having jurisdiction as to the substance in another Member State are explicitly mentioned in Article 2(a) of Brussels I bis Regulation. It states that for the purposes of using the provisions on recognition and enforcement in Brussels I bis Regulation, provisional measures ordered by a court or tribunal which by virtue of this Regulation has jurisdiction as to the substance of the matter are treated as judgments. This signifies that the provisional measures are recognised and enforced in accordance with the simplified procedure determined in Brussels I bis Regulation. However, an additional requirement is determined. Article 2(a) explicitly requires that for such provisional measures to be subject to the provisions on recognition and enforcement, the defendant has to be summoned to appear unless the judgment containing the

[12] Recital 33 of Brussels I bis Regulation, on the other hand, expressly provides for this.

[13] The provisional measures protect the effectiveness of the main procedure by either securing the effectiveness of the future enforcement of the creditor's claim or providing temporary regulation of the legal relation in dispute.

[14] The Opinion of AG Rantos in Case C-581/20, Skarb Państwa Rzeczypospolitej Polskiej reprezentowany przez Generalnego Dyrektora Dróg Krajowych i Autostrad v TOTO SpA – Costruzioni Generali, Vianini Lavori SpA, 9.9.2021, ECLI:EU:C:2021:726, footnote 16.

[15] Pertegás Sender and Garber (2016), p. 789.

[16] Pogorelčnik Vogrinc (2020), p. 135.

measure is served on the defendant prior to enforcement. The situation regarding these measures is regulated under Brussels I bis Regulation the same way as it was under its predecessors. Although Regulation 44/2001 and the Brussels Convention did not make the debtor's participation in a procedure or their awareness of the measure an explicit requirement (as does Brussels I bis Regulation), this requirement was established in the CJEU case law.[17] A provisional measure issued by the court having jurisdiction as to the substance of which the debtor has not been informed cannot, therefore, be transferred to the other Member States.

However, another conclusion can be drawn by a grammatical interpretation of Recital 33 of Brussels I bis Regulation. Recital 33 reads: 'However, provisional, including protective, measures which were ordered by such a court without the defendant being summoned to appear should not be recognised and enforced under this Regulation unless the judgment containing the measure is served on the defendant prior to enforcement. This should not preclude the recognition and enforcement of such measures under national law'. On this basis, it could be concluded that provisional measures ordered *ex parte* by a court having jurisdiction as to the substance can be recognised and enforced in another Member State using the private international law of such a state and not the relevant provisions of Brussels I bis Regulation. Even allowing for such an interpretation, such a cross-border flow of measures issued *ex parte* and their surprise effect is possible in theory, but not so much in practice. The possibility of recognising and enforcing foreign provisional measures is rarely (if ever) to be found in the private international law of individual Member States. In reality, despite the theoretical possibility of crossing Member States' borders, these measures will therefore only have effects in the issuing state.

Besides taking away the surprise effect, there are no other requirements that must be met for a provisional measure to 'cross the border' using the rules of Brussels I bis Regulation. However, it is necessary to emphasise again that the application of the provisions of Chapter III of Brussels I bis Regulation on recognition and enforcement for provisional measures is enabled only regarding measures issued by the court having jurisdiction as to the substance. Only these measures benefit from the rules on recognition and enforcement laid down in Brussels I bis Regulation.

2.2 *Provisional Measures Issued by a Court Having Jurisdiction According to National Law*

Besides the court having jurisdiction as to the substance, a provisional measure can also be issued by any court having jurisdiction for such on the basis of its national law. This is possible even if exclusive jurisdiction is conferred for the decision on the

---

[17] Case C-125/79, Bernhard Denilauler v SNC Couchet Frères, 21.5.1980, EU: ECLI:C:1980:130, para 18.

main matter.[18] Such a provision, namely, provides for jurisdiction only over the main matter (and the court having exclusive jurisdiction may also grant a provisional measure), which does not, however, exclude jurisdiction under Article 35. Thus, in addition to the court having (exclusive) jurisdiction as to the substance, the courts having jurisdiction according to national law may also grant provisional measures.

The creditor can therefore search for the most suitable provisional measure and propose its issuance in the EU Member State that regulates it. As this would enable *forum shopping*, the CJEU severely limited the possibilities of the cross-border recognition and enforcement of provisional measures issued by a court having jurisdiction according to national law during the time of Regulation 44/2001 and the Brussels Convention. In order to use their provisions on recognition and enforcement, a real connecting link between the subject matter of the measure and the territorial jurisdiction of the Member State of the court issuing the measure must have existed.[19] The CJEU did not further define the content of this condition, and its interpretation was left to the court to assess the circumstances of each specific case. However, in most cases, meeting this condition meant that the provisional measure was enforced in the Member State of origin.

Additionally, if the provisional measure was of the same content and effects as the main claim, the CJEU required two additional conditions.[20] Firstly, the provisional measure could be issued only regarding property located in the territory of the court of issuance.[21] Secondly, to avoid irreversibility, the creditor had to provide the defendant with a guarantee that the sum awarded would be repaid. Such a possibility of the repayment of the sum awarded guaranteed reversibility if the plaintiff was later unsuccessful regarding the substance of their claim.[22] In addition to all of the above, as already mentioned, a request for the debtor's participation was also necessary. All of these conditions had to be met in order for a foreign measure issued by the court having jurisdiction according to national law to be subject to the provisions of the relevant European regulations. The conditions had to be met at the time of the issuance of the individual measure, but their fulfilment was only verified at the stage

[18]Case C-616/10, Solvay SA v Honeywell Fluorine Products Europe BV and Others, 12.7.2012, ECLI:EU: C:2012:445, para 40.

[19]Case C-391/95, Van Uden Maritime BV, trading as Van Uden Africa Line, and Kommanditgesellschaft in Firma Deco-Line and Another, 17.11.1998, ECLI:EU:C:1998:543, para 40.

[20]Rijavec (2018a), p. 402 emphasizes that provisional measure issued prior to the decision as to the substance might deprive the debtor of the right to a defense. Therefore, only in exceptional cases can a provisional measure be equivalent to the main claim. For a detailed analysis of requirements needed in such cases, see Pogorelčnik Vogrinc (2020), p. 142.

[21]Nuyts (2016), p. 366, para 12.30 emphasises the aim of such a requirement as: 'imposing the condition that assets be located within the territory of the granting court is meant to ensure that the defendant will have access to some resources in this territory which guarantee that he will get his money back if he is ultimately successful.

[22]Case C-391/95, Van Uden, Van Uden Maritime BV, trading as Van Uden Africa Line, and Kommanditgesellschaft in Firma Deco-Line and Another, 17.11.1998, ECLI:EU:C:1998:543, para 47.

of recognition or enforcement. The cross-border flow of provisional measures issued by the court having jurisdiction according to national law was therefore impeded and, in practice, more or less impossible. In comparison, a court having jurisdiction as to the substance could, without any additional limits (except for the debtor's participation), also issue a provisional measure.[23]

When adopting the recast of Regulation 44/2001, the European legislature decided in favour of a different approach. While the cross-border flow of provisional measures issued by the court having jurisdiction as to the substance is still possible using the provisions of its Chapter III, the same is entirely impossible for provisional measures issued by the court having jurisdiction according to national law. This can be concluded from Article 2(a), which makes no mention of such a possibility. Provisional measures issued by the court having jurisdiction according to national law, therefore, cannot be recognised and enforced in another Member State. Such measures necessarily have to be enforced in the Member State of their issuance. If this is possible, a connection between the provisional measures and the state of their issuance obviously exists. Brussels I bis Regulation, therefore, excludes the possibility of the cross-border transfer of such provisional measures, which was in fact already implicitly established by the CJEU by establishing the requirement of the existence of a real connecting link.

If enforcement in the Member State of its issuance is not possible and the creditor actually wanted to (mis)use the benefits of exorbitant jurisdiction, such a measure cannot be recognised and enforced abroad using the simplified procedure provided for in Brussels I bis Regulation.[24] The question arises whether such a provisional measure can be recognised and enforced abroad by applying the private international rules of the Member State of enforcement. By a grammatical interpretation of Recital 33, this is not the case. The latter provides for such an option only for provisional measures issued *ex parte* in a Member State having jurisdiction as to the substance. Moreover, Recital 33 expressly states that a provisional measure ordered by a court of a Member State that does not have jurisdiction as to the substance should, in accordance with Brussels I bis Regulation, be limited to the territory of that Member State. However, it could be interpreted as meaning that recognition is possible under rules outside Brussels I bis Regulation. However, as already mentioned, in practice, such an option is almost non-existent. It is (almost?) impossible to find a state whose private international rules allow and provide for the recognition and enforcement of foreign provisional measures. Thus, it can be generally concluded that the recognition and enforcement of such provisional measures outside the state of their issuance are practically not viable.[25]

---

[23]The CJEU emphasised in Case C-99/96, Hans-Hermann Mietz v Intership Yachting Sneek BV, 27.4.1999, ECLI:EU:C:1999:202, para 41, that 'the court having jurisdiction as to the substance of a case also has jurisdiction to order provisional or protective measures, without that jurisdiction being subject to any further conditions'. For more details, see subchapter 2.

[24]Brussels I bis Regulation pursues the objective of preventing forum shopping. Rijavec (2018a), p. 29.

[25]For a thorough analysis of this issue, see Pogorelčnik Vogrinc (2020), pp. 144–147.

3 The Existence of Several Provisional Measures

The court having jurisdiction as to the substance can issue a provisional measure prior to the court procedure that concerns the main substantive claims, during such a procedure,[26] or even after it. This is also possible in cases where the main procedure is pending in another[27] Member State, which is justifiable, given the fact that in the Van Uden case, the CJEU speaks of 'jurisdiction as to the substance' and not of 'proceedings as to the substance (which) are pending'.[28] Each court having jurisdiction as to the substance of the matter according to Articles 4–26 Brussels I bis Regulation can therefore issue a provisional measure. If jurisdiction on the merits of the case is granted to the courts of several Member States (see, for example, Article 7 of Brussels I bis Regulation), each of them can issue a provisional measure as the one having jurisdiction as to the substance.[29] If the main claim has been brought before a court in one of the alternative Member States, a provisional measure may therefore also be granted in another Member State whose courts also have jurisdiction but where the claimant has not initiated the main procedure. The opposite interpretation, i.e., that a court otherwise having jurisdiction as to the substance of the matter cannot issue a provisional measure if the main court procedure is already pending in another Member State might lead to a race to the court.[30]

Therefore, the creditor can choose between the courts of several Member States having jurisdiction as to the substance and decide which of them to apply to (not only for the main claim but also) for a provisional measure. The options are even wider if we take into account the possibility of (applying for and) the issuance of provisional measures before the courts having jurisdiction according to the national law. Consequently, this raises the possibility that a creditor will seek a provisional measure in multiple Member States at once.

It is important to note that the situation becomes problematic only when the same provisional measure is proposed between the same parties[31] in several Member States. This issue does not emerge if the content (effects) of the security provided by the various provisional measures differs. The same is true if the creditor alleges in a subsequent application facts that occurred after the decision on the first application.[32]

---

[26] Pertegás Sender and Garber (2016), pp. 791–792, para 29.

[27] Rijavec (2018b), p. 240; Pertegás Sender and Garber (2016), p. 793.

[28] Heinze (2011), pp. 607–608. A similar opinion can also be found in Pertegás Sender and Garber (2016), pp. 791–792, para 29.

[29] Pertegás Sender and Garber (2016), p. 792, para 31; Cuniberti and Rueda (2016), p. 854, para 18.

[30] Nuyts (2016), p. 102.

[31] Undoubtedly, both provisional measures have to be issued between the same parties; however, it is not obligatory that both of the parties participate in both of the provisional measures in the same way or in the same role. A similar opinion can also be found in Fitchen (2016), p. 471, para 13.359.

[32] The Opinion of AG Rantos in Case C-581/20, Skarb Państwa Rzeczypospolitej Polskiej reprezentowany przez Generalnego Dyrektora Dróg Krajowych i Autostrad v TOTO SpA –

However, special caution should be exercised when assessing the content of provisional measures. Typically repetition of applications for the same provisional measure can occur in the case of repeated refusals, where the creditor will, again and again, apply to courts in new Member States with the same proposal.[33] However, there is also a risk of the incompatibility of provisional measures in a more disguised case. This occurs when a creditor proposes and is granted a provisional measure, while the debtor in another Member State proposes a measure with the exact opposite content. For example, the creditor may seek a provisional order forbidding the debtor from performing specific conduct, while the debtor may propose an order enabling them to perform the same act. On the outside, these are not the same measures, but the legal consequences of the two must be compared. In Case C-145/86, Hoffmann, the CJEU explicitly emphasised that 'in order to ascertain whether two judgments are irreconcilable within the meaning of Article 27(3), it should be examined whether they entail legal consequences that are mutually exclusive'.[34] As the CJEU has stated in Case C-80/00, Italian Leather, 'a foreign decision on interim measures ordering an obligor not to carry out certain acts is irreconcilable with a decision on interim measures refusing to grant such an order in a dispute between the same parties in the State where recognition is sought'.[35] Therefore, all that matters are the legal consequences and not the applicable national standards for admissibility, substantive requirements, and the issuance procedure, which determine whether a decision can be rendered and which can differ from one Member State to another.[36]

Mutual exclusivity is thus the criterion to be applied in order to determine whether the same matter is being adjudicated on again and (as will be seen in the next subchapters) to interpret the term 'the same cause of action', which can be found in the provisions regarding *lis pendens* (Article 29(1) of Brussels I bis Regulation) and the grounds for the refusal of recognition and enforcement (Article 45/I(d) of Brussels I bis Regulation).

Costruzioni Generali, Vianini Lavori SpA, 9.9.2021, ECLI:EU:C:2021:726, footnote 56, emphasises: 'By their very nature, measures of that type are adopted or refused on the basis of the facts presented to the court at a specific moment. If those facts change, an initial refusal does not preclude the subsequent grant of an application.'

[33] In Case C-80/00, Italian Leather SpA v WECO Polstermöbel GmbH & Co., 6.6.2002, ECLI:EU:C:2002:342, after the Landgericht Koblenz had refused to issue a provisional measure, the Tribunale di Bari granted Italian Leather's request to restrict WECO from using the LongLife brand name for the marketing of its leather products and therefore decided on an identical case by the same plaintiff against the same defendant.

[34] Case C-145/86, Horst Ludwig Martin Hoffmann v Adelheid Krieg, 4.2.1988, ECLI:EU:C:1988:61, para 22. The cases were decided regarding the Brussels Convention; however, its Article 27 is similar to the relevant Article 45 of Brussels I bis Regulation and the argumentation of the CJEU in the decision is therefore still suitable.

[35] Case C-80/00, Italian Leather SpA v WECO Polstermöbel GmbH & Co., 6.6.2002, ECLI:EU:C:2002:342, para 47.

[36] Ibid, para 44.

3.1 *Lis Pendens*

Brussels I bis Regulation is clear and explicit in stating that there can be no simultaneous proceedings regarding the same cause of action (and between the same parties). For such cases, Article 29 determines that 'any court other than the court first seized shall of its own motion stay its proceedings until such time as the jurisdiction of the court first seized is established'.

In applying Article 29, there is no doubt that the *lis pendens* rule does not apply to the relationship between the main proceedings and the proceedings for the provisional measure. Therefore, the rule does not establish *lis pendens* between two parallel proceedings, one of which is a procedure for the provisional measure, even if the measure is for interim relief (payment).[37] The purpose of a provisional measure (even if it is an interim relief) is to support and secure the main proceedings. As a result, the fact that interim relief is proposed or issued in another Member State has no effect on the main proceedings. The court seized, therefore, must not stay the main proceedings.

The question of whether the *lis pendens* rule applies to several procedures for provisional measures arises. They are not explicitly covered by the rule of Article 29. However, they are usually issued in a timely manner, and the possibility of two parallel provisional proceedings pending at the same time is practically non-existent. Nonetheless, the question of the application of the *lis pendens* rule may arise in theory.

Furthermore, there is a question of whether the answer is affected by the type of jurisdiction of two (or more) courts before which the proceedings regarding provisional measures are pending. Jurisdiction as to the substance and jurisdiction according to national rules are not equivalent. They differ as regards the possibility of the provisional measure being transferred to other Member States and, consequently, as regards the possibility of a surprise effect on the debtor occurring. While in the main proceedings, the jurisdictions are equivalent in this respect (i.e., the possibility of the recognition and enforcement of the judgment in other Member States will be the same irrespective of the Member State in which it is issued), these effects are different in the case of provisional measures. However, despite these differences, the main guiding principle should be that there must not be provisional measures with conflicting effects. This might come true when several provisional procedures regarding the same content subject to security are pending.

One of the goals of Brussels I bis Regulation is to prevent or eliminate the possibility of contradictory court decisions. The CJEU has repeatedly stated that: 'multiplication of the bases of jurisdiction in relation to one and the same legal relationship ... is contrary to the aims of the Convention'.[38] To this end, the provision on *lis pendens* has also been amended and improved in the recast of the

[37] Fentiman (2016), p. 724, para 28.

[38] Case C-104/03, St. Paul Dairy Industries NV v Unibel Exser BVBA, 28.04.2005, ECLI:EU:C:2005:255, para 20.

Regulation. If the European legislature is thus striving for as coherent a situation as possible with regard to judgments, there is no reason why the same should not also apply to provisional measures. Such an interpretation argues in favour of legal protection and legal certainty, which are undoubtedly the objectives of Brussels I bis Regulation.[39] A plurality of proceedings should be avoided to prevent conflicting decisions and to prevent a party from trying to be granted a measure in different countries until it succeeds in one. Therefore, such a plurality of proceedings must be prevented, even in the case of procedures for the issuance of provisional measures.

The relevant sections of Brussels I bis Regulation regulating *lis pendens* can thus be applied to provisional measures.[40] The same opinion is shared by AG Rantos: 'The principle of priority which, in the section headed "Lis pendens – related actions" of Regulation No 1215/2012, governs multiple proceedings between the same parties and involving the same cause of action, in accordance with Article 29 of the regulation, may, in my view, be applied to the interim stage of those proceedings'.[41] This means, as determined in Article 29 of Brussels I bis Regulation that any court other than the one first seized with the procedure for the issuance of the provisional measure shall of its own motion stay its proceedings regarding the same provisional measure between the same parties until such time as the jurisdiction of the court first seized is established.

[39] On legal certainty as an objective of the Brussels Convention, see Case C-38/81, Effer SpA v Hans-Joachim Kantner, 4.3.1982, ECLI:EU:C:1982:79, para 6; Case C-440/97, GIE Groupe Concorde and Others v. The Master of the Vessel Suhadiwarno Panjan and Others, 28.9.1999, ECLI:EU:C:1999:456, para 23; Case C-256/00 Besix SA and Wasserreinigungsbau Alfred Kretzschmar GmbH & Co. KG (WABAG), Planungs- und Forschungsgesellschaft Dipl. Ing. W. Kretzschmar GmbH & Co. KG (Plafog), 19.2.2002, ECLI:EU:C:2002:99, para 24.

[40] Different views can be found on this. See Hess (2010), p. 370; Hess (2021), p. 420; Rijavec (2018a), p. 403.

[41] The Opinion of AG Rantos in Case C-581/20, Skarb Państwa Rzeczypospolitej Polskiej reprezentowany przez Generalnego Dyrektora Dróg Krajowych i Autostrad v TOTO SpA – Costruzioni Generali, Vianini Lavori SpA, 9.9.2021, ECLI:EU:C:2021:726, para 42. In the author's opinion, AG Rantos expressed himself inaccurately in the mentioned Opinion, para 40: 'the co-existence of applications for provisional measures before a court with jurisdiction as to the substance and another ... which is seised pursuant to Article 35 ... provides the party concerned with an option to avoid the delays that are usually associated with importing into one Member State a measure ordered in another.' While it is true that proposing a provisional measure in a certain state relieves the creditor of the disadvantages associated with the cross-border recognition and enforcement of a provisional measure, this is not enabled by the co-existence of applications for provisional measures, but by the co-existence of the possibilities to propose a measure at courts with different jurisdictions. The co-existence of applications for provisional measures is, in the author's opinion, not allowed.

3.2 Irreconcilable Provisional Measures

Even if the principle on *lis pendens* should generally prevent this, intentional or unintentional non-compliance with this rule can lead to the existence of conflicting provisional measures. What if proposals for the recognition and enforcement of both of them are then filed in the same Member State, or recognition and enforcement are proposed in the Member State in which a provisional measure with mutual exclusive legal effects had previously been issued.

As regards judgments issued in main procedures, the situation in Brussels I bis Regulation is again clear. The irreconcilability of a judgment with another judgment between the same parties makes it impossible to recognise and enforce in a particular Member State. Article 45(I) determines that upon the application of any interested party, the recognition of a judgment shall be refused 'if the judgment is irreconcilable with a judgment given between the same parties in the Member State addressed' (para. c) or 'if the judgment is irreconcilable with an earlier judgment given in another Member State or a third State involving the same cause of action and between the same parties, provided that the earlier judgment fulfils the conditions necessary for its recognition in the Member State addressed' (para. d). With regard to Article 46 of Brussels I bis Regulation, the same applies with regard to enforcement.

The question arises whether the court can or should apply Articles 45 and 46 and therefore refuse to recognise and enforce also the relevant provisional measure. If this is disallowed, the creditor may file the same request in another Member State to try to gain a favourable conclusion after the proposal for a provisional measure has been rejected.[42] If successful, they can later propose that the latter measure be recognised and enforced in other Member States.

Concerns regarding whether the provisional measures obtain *res judicata* effect or become final (seemingly) obstruct the path to an answer. In this regard, legal theory has questioned whether a court decision must obtain the *res judicata* effect in order to prevent another judgment from being recognised and enforced.[43] The relevant provisions of Brussels I bis Regulation only mention that the judgment must have been *issued*, which could be seen as indicating that the decision does not have to be final. Nonetheless, there is no denying that provisional measures obtain a certain degree of finality.[44] Furthermore, under Article 2(a), the term 'judgment' may under certain circumstances also include provisional, including protective, measures. This is enabled for the purposes of Chapter III on recognition and

[42] Of course, this would have to take into account the rules on jurisdiction to issue protective measures and the rules on which protective measures may be subject to recognition and enforcement in another Member State.

[43] Francq and Mankowski (2016), p. 920, para 64, and p. 925, para 69.

[44] See the Opinion of AG Rantos in Case C-581/20, Skarb Państwa Rzeczypospolitej Polskiej reprezentowany przez Generalnego Dyrektora Dróg Krajowych i Autostrad v TOTO SpA – Costruzioni Generali, Vianini Lavori SpA, 9.9.2021, ECLI:EU:C:2021:726, para 78.

enforcement, which also includes Articles 45 and 46, which deal with grounds for the refusal of recognition and enforcement.

Therefore, it can be argued that the rule on the refusal of recognition and enforcement can also be applied to provisional measures. It would not make sense to prevent the same measure from being decided by various courts in different Member States while at the same time disregarding the existence of already issued measures in the phase of their recognition and enforcement. The provisions of Brussels I bis Regulation on grounds for the refusal of recognition and enforcement are therefore also applied for provisional measures. As the CJEU has confirmed in Case C-80/00, Italian Leather:

> It is unimportant whether the judgments at issue have been delivered in proceedings for interim measures or in proceedings on the substance. As Article 27(3) of the Brussels Convention, following the example of Article 25, refers to 'judgment' without further precision, it has general application. Consequently, decisions on interim measures are subject to the rules laid down by the Convention concerning irreconcilability in the same way as the other 'judgments' covered by Article 25.[45]

This is true even if the national requirements for the issuance of a provisional measure in both of the relevant Member States are different, e.g., if the court that issued the first provisional measure had stricter requirements for its issuance, which the creditor was unable to demonstrate, but was able to demonstrate more lenient conditions that are required for the issuance of the provisional measure in the Member State where they proposed it subsequently.[46] It can therefore be concluded that the court of the Member State in which recognition and/or enforcement is sought must clearly refuse to recognise and/or enforce a foreign provisional measure if it finds that its substance is incompatible with a provisional measure issued by a court of the first Member State in a dispute between the same parties.[47] The same is true for the situation regarding the irreconcilability of the provisional measure with an earlier provisional measure given in another Member State or in a third State involving the same cause of action and between the same parties, provided that the earlier measure fulfils the conditions necessary for its recognition in the Member State addressed.

However, it should be remembered that only provisional measures imposed by the court with jurisdiction as to the substance can be recognised and enforced in another Member State under the requirements of Brussels I bis Regulation.

[45] Case C-80/00, Italian Leather, Italian Leather SpA v WECO Polstermöbel GmbH & Co., 6.6.2002, ECLI:EU:C:2002:342, para 41.

[46] Case C-80/00, Italian Leather, Italian Leather SpA v WECO Polstermöbel GmbH & Co., 6.6.2002, ECLI:EU:C:2002:342, para 42.

[47] Ibid, para 52.

3.3 To Summarise

A combination of the two situations described above is also possible. This is a situation entailing the filing of a new proposal for a provisional measure where a measure with the same content has already been issued. This is exactly the situation of the recent CJEU Case C-581/20[48] (hereinafter 'TOTO'). The Polish court, which also had jurisdiction as to the substance and before which the main proceedings were pending at the time, refused to grant a provisional measure with certain content.[49] The creditor subsequently applied to the Bulgarian court for the same provisional measure. The case had a connection with the Bulgarian court as its subject matter made use of guarantees issued by a Bulgarian insurance company. The jurisdiction of the Bulgarian court, according to its national rules, was not raised as a matter of dispute. The matter which came to light as a matter of dispute was whether the Bulgarian court must declare that it did not have jurisdiction to adopt the provisional measure sought when an identical application was made before the court seized as to the substance of the main proceedings and that court refused to grant it.[50] Or the contrary: whether the court having jurisdiction according to Article 35 of Brussels I bis Regulation can issue such a provisional measure if the court having jurisdiction as to the substance has previously declined to do so. This raises two concerns.

Firstly, the question has been formulated in such a way that it questions whether the court has jurisdiction under Article 35 if the main court has rejected a proposal for a provisional measure. In the author's opinion, it makes no difference whether the court denied the proposal for a provisional measure or granted it. What matters is that it has already been decided on, regardless of the content of the decision. It is true that if a creditor has already been granted a provisional measure in one Member State, they will not file another proposal for the same provisional measure in another Member State. A debtor, on the other hand, can propose an opposite measure in another Member State, the consequence of which, if implemented, would neutralise the effects of the first measure. As mentioned above, the mutual exclusivity of legal consequences should be examined. A situation like this can be seen in the TOTO case. Initially, the creditor requested that the debtor abstains from certain actions for a certain period of time. On the contrary, the debtor proposed to be allowed to perform the same actions in the meantime. Again, this is a case of deciding twice on the same measure. Thus, the question to be decided would have to be whether the

[48] Case C-581/20, Skarb Państwa Rzeczypospolitej Polskiej reprezentowany przez Generalnego Dyrektora Dróg Krajowych i Autostrad v TOTO SpA - Costruzioni Generali and Vianini Lavori SpA, 6.10.2021, ECLI:EU:C:2021:808.

[49] The detailed content of the security proposed by the creditor is irrelevant for the purposes of this chapter.

[50] This is exactly how AG Rantos understood and partly reworded the question. See the Opinion of AG Rantos in Case C-581/20, Skarb Państwa Rzeczypospolitej Polskiej reprezentowany przez Generalnego Dyrektora Dróg Krajowych i Autostrad v TOTO SpA - Costruzioni Generali and Vianini Lavori SpA, 6.10.2021, ECLI:EU:C:2021:808, para 75.

measure can be decided again (in another Member State) if it has already been decided.

Secondly, the CJEU understood this as a question of the hierarchy among courts. It pointed out that—although it is therefore apparent from the scheme of Brussels I bis Regulation that the effects of provisional measures given by the courts of the Member State having jurisdiction as to the substance and those of provisional measures given by the courts having jurisdiction according to national law are different—the fact remains that Brussels I bis Regulation does not establish a hierarchy between those courts.[51] The CJEU further observes that it does not follow from the wording of Article 35 of that regulation that it confers jurisdiction for provisional measures in principle on the courts of the Member State having jurisdiction as to the substance. The latter would namely mean that the courts of other Member States would not have jurisdiction to issue such measures if proposals for such measures have already been brought before the courts of the first-mentioned Member State or if those courts have already decided on such a proposal.[52] The CJEU concluded that Article 35 of Brussels I bis Regulation must be interpreted as meaning that a court of a Member State which is seized of a proposal for a provisional measure under that provision does not have to declare that it lacks jurisdiction if a court of another Member State having jurisdiction as to the substance has already decided on the same provisional measures between the same parties.[53]

In the author's opinion, the CJEU's understanding of the problem is incorrect. It is not a question of establishing (or not) a hierarchy between both types of courts (i.e., those having jurisdiction as to the substance and those having jurisdiction according to national law). It is not that the CJEU needed to clarify that the court having jurisdiction as to the substance does not have priority over the courts having jurisdiction according to their national law. In the author's view, the case and the question raised should be understood as to whether the rules of *lis pendens* (and indirectly also the effects of already issued measures) also apply to provisional measures. The issue, therefore, concerns the relationship between the measures themselves, not the relationship between the courts issuing them.

The situation (and the question) would be the same if the original decision on the provisional measure had been issued by a court having jurisdiction according to national law, but now a second proposal was made before a court of another Member State (also having jurisdiction according to its national law). The same would apply if the original provisional measure had been granted by the court having jurisdiction as to the substance, and then an application for the same provisional measure was filed with another court that, under Brussels I bis Regulation, would also have jurisdiction as to the substance. Finally, the same would apply if the initial

[51] Case C-581/20, Skarb Państwa Rzeczypospolitej Polskiej reprezentowany przez Generalnego Dyrektora Dróg Krajowych i Autostrad v TOTO SpA - Costruzioni Generali and Vianini Lavori SpA, 6.10.2021, ECLI:EU:C:2021:808, para 59.

[52] Ibid, para 60.

[53] Ibid, para 61.

provisional measure was issued by a court having jurisdiction according to its national law and a proposal for the same provisional measure was subsequently filed before the court having jurisdiction as to the substance (i.e., the reverse of the situation in the TOTO case).[54]

It is true, as the CJEU states, that there is no hierarchy between the two types of courts having jurisdiction to issue provisional measures. This should not be interpreted so as to infer that a creditor can propose a provisional measure before a court having jurisdiction according to national law even if the same measure has already been decided by a court having jurisdiction as to the substance, as the CJEU has indicated. The absence of a hierarchy, in the author's opinion, should be interpreted as implying that there is no rule dictating before which court the creditor must propose the measure first. The opening of the main proceedings in the Member State having jurisdiction does not necessarily mean that a party must also propose a protective measure there. However, if it does, then the *lis pendens* rule applies.

The absence of a hierarchy should be interpreted as suggesting that the creditor is free to propose a provisional measure before any of several competent courts. The existence of a hierarchy (i.e., the rule that the creditor must always bring the action before the court with certain jurisdiction—for example, the court having jurisdiction as to the substance) combined with the *lis pendens* rule would nearly invariably entail that the action would be decided by that (primarily designated) court.

The fact that several courts have jurisdiction to issue a provisional measure causes some risks. It enables several parallel court proceedings regarding the same matter, on the one hand, or a risk of irreconcilable decisions, on the other, or, as has been mentioned, a combination of both. The question remains whether a measure that has already been decided on in one (competent) Member State can subsequently be proposed and decided on in another (competent) Member State. In conclusion, as already explained, in the author's view, the provisions of Regulation 1215/2012 on *lis pendens* in the narrower sense and, by implication, the provisions on the refusal of recognition and enforcement in the case of multiple measures can also be applied to provisional measures.

The same conclusions can also be found in older national case law. A similar case can be found before the French *Cour de cassation* in Case 4. 5. 2011–10–13712.[55] The Greek court first declined to grant a provisional measure, claiming that the required circumstances had not been met. A year later, the creditor in France proposed a provisional measure with the same content, requiring the establishment of more lenient conditions for the approval of the proposed national provisional measure. The case made it to the Supreme Court, which determined that there was an obligation to respect the Greek decision.

[54]This was, for example, the situation in Case C-80/00, Italian Leather, Italian Leather SpA v WECO Polstermöbel GmbH & Co., 6.6.2002, ECLI:EU:C:2002:342.

[55]For an analysis of the case, see Schlosser (2012), pp. 88–91.

4 The Choice-of-Court Agreement

Previous sections analysed the situation in which provisional measures can be granted by the court in a Member State (or several of them) having jurisdiction as to the substance under Brussels I bis Regulation (Articles 4–26) and by the courts having jurisdiction according to national law (in accordance with Article 35). It was concluded that there is no hierarchy between them and that the creditor is free to choose from which of the several courts to seek a provisional measure. The situation might slightly differ when the parties have concluded a choice-of-court agreement. In the latter, they normally agree on the specific jurisdiction of the court having jurisdiction to decide on disputes deriving from a specific legal relationship. It usually does not specify whether the agreement on jurisdiction also applies to procedures for the issuance of provisional measures. If such an agreement exists, the question arises which court has jurisdiction to issue provisional measures.

If the parties agree on jurisdiction over the main matter, this is transferred to the agreed court. Such jurisdiction is considered to be exclusive (Article 25(1) of Brussels I bis Regulation), and therefore, only this court can decide on the substance of the case. The issue is raised whether such an agreement is also deemed to transfer jurisdiction for provisional measures to the agreed court. No doubts regarding this exist when the jurisdiction agreement explicitly mentions the jurisdiction regarding provisional measures. In order to eliminate doubts, it is recommended that the parties explicitly state in the jurisdiction agreement their intention as to its validity regarding provisional measures. However, where the agreement is silent on this matter, the question arises whether it can be interpreted as meaning that, by agreeing on jurisdiction over the main matter, the parties also intended to agree on jurisdiction over provisional measures. Two related issues arise. Firstly, is it possible to interpret the agreement as meaning that they wished to bring before the agreed court any disputes that might arise out of the particular legal relationship? Secondly, did they at the same time prevent the courts in all the other Member States from issuing a provisional measure?

As regards the first question, there is a question of whether or not the agreement is presumed to include jurisdiction over provisional measures, given the fact that it is silent on that. While it is possible to find opposite opinions,[56] the author opines that it is not appropriate to conclude that by agreeing on the jurisdiction for the main action the parties also intended to confer on this court jurisdiction to grant provisional measures. It is reasonable to claim that the parties did not enter into the choice-of-

[56] Magnus (2016), p. 660, para 152, states that the jurisdiction agreement has a prorogation impact in terms of jurisdiction on provisional measures. The same can also be found in the Opinion of AG Rantos in Case C-581/20, Skarb Państwa Rzeczypospolitej Polskiej reprezentowany przez Generalnego Dyrektora Dróg Krajowych i Autostrad v TOTO SpA - Costruzioni Generali and Vianini Lavori SpA, 6.10.2021, ECLI:EU:C:2021:808, paras 59–60, who says that: 'In the absence of clear intent, it could be presumed that a choice of forum clause drafted in general terms extends the jurisdiction chosen to the adoption of provisional, including protective, measures. Logically, the presumption would be rebuttable'.

court agreement with provisional measures in mind, and thus did not intentionally consent to a waiver of jurisdiction over such.[57] Regardless of the different starting points of the opposing opinions, the result is the same. The transfer of jurisdiction over the main case indirectly entails the transfer of jurisdiction over provisional measures. The transfer of jurisdiction over the main procedure means that the court that has agreed jurisdiction (as the court having jurisdiction as to the substance) now also has jurisdiction over provisional measures. It is not that the parties are deemed to have agreed by the stipulation that they will also transfer jurisdiction over provisional measures. But, since they have transferred jurisdiction over the main matter, the jurisdiction over provisional measures (of the court having jurisdiction over the main matter) has also been de facto transferred. Therefore, if a creditor wants to propose a provisional measure at the court having jurisdiction as to the substance, it is not appropriate to look to Brussels I bis Regulation to determine which court has jurisdiction in the main proceedings, but they must necessarily comply with the agreement and propose the provisional measure before the agreed court. This can be argued by the fact that the court having jurisdiction as to the substance also has jurisdiction over provisional measures because it already knows the matter and will decide on the provisional measure quickly and easily. If a choice-of-court agreement is concluded, there is, therefore, no point checking Brussels I bis Regulation to determine the jurisdiction as to the substance for issuing a provisional measure.

Regardless of the prorogation effect of a jurisdiction agreement (also) on the jurisdiction for provisional measures, the author opines that such an agreement does not also have a derogation effect on jurisdictions according to national law (deriving from Article 35). It would be a stretch to interpret an agreement on jurisdiction regarding the main claim as also excluding 'national' jurisdictions for provisional measures. If the agreement also included an explicit agreement on jurisdiction for provisional measures, the situation would be different. The parties' explicit will to assign jurisdiction to issue provisional measures to only one court (or the courts of only one Member State) would have to be respected.[58] If only the jurisdiction regarding the main matter is agreed on, however, jurisdiction under national law

[57]The Opinion of AG Rantos in Case C-581/20, Skarb Państwa Rzeczypospolitej Polskiej reprezentowany przez Generalnego Dyrektora Dróg Krajowych i Autostrad v TOTO SpA - Costruzioni Generali and Vianini Lavori SpA, 6.10.2021, ECLI:EU:C:2021:808, paras 65–67, emphasises that parties conclude a jurisdiction agreement to be applied to disputes deriving from a particular legal relationship. Consequently, such an agreement does not apply to specific cases that parties could not have anticipated when concluding the agreement. Nevertheless, in the specific TOTO Case, the parties could have (in Rantos' opinion) "reasonably foreseen" the specific dispute and consequently that one of them might apply for a related provisional measure. This is, in his opinion, the reason that the agreed-on jurisdiction as to the substance also entails jurisdiction for a provisional measure (as jurisdiction as to the substance).

[58]The same can be found in Garcimartin (2016), p. 304, footnote 203, who states that: 'There is no convincing reasons to deprive the parties of the power to limit that jurisdiction to the chosen court, and there may actually be cases where they have a legitimate interest in doing so'.

(as defined in Article 35) must be accepted for granting provisional measures.[59] As has been confirmed above, even if the court has exclusive jurisdiction as to the substance (regardless of the origin of its exclusivity), a provisional measure can be issued by any court having jurisdiction, therefore on the basis of its national law.[60]

Interestingly, the situation described (the choice-of-court agreement not mentioning jurisdiction regarding provisional measures) was also at issue in the CJEU Case C-581/20, TOTO. In the latter, a jurisdiction agreement was concluded, giving jurisdiction as to the substance to Polish courts. Regarding the derogation effects of a jurisdiction agreement regarding provisional measures, AG Rantos opines that the decision should be made by the court with jurisdiction under national law before which the provisional measure application was filed.[61] Para. 64 of the Opinion of AG Rantos can be understood as allowing national courts to evaluate whether a jurisdiction agreement relating to the main dispute has any effect on derogating jurisdiction under Article 35. However, in the author's opinion, this point should be interpreted differently. It implies that the national court has the authority to interpret the jurisdiction agreement and, as a result, to determine whether the parties intended to include jurisdiction for provisional measures in the agreement. The national courts before which it is invoked, therefore, have the authority to interpret and decide on the scope of a jurisdiction agreement.[62] If it is decided that the jurisdiction clause does not explicitly also include jurisdiction regarding provisional measures, the prorogated jurisdiction indirectly still applies to them (as explained above via jurisdiction as to substance). Nevertheless, in accordance with Article 35, provisional measures can also be proposed at the court having jurisdiction according to national law.

---

[59] The same can be found in Magnus (2016), p. 660, para 152: 'In order not to contradict the aims of Art. 35 – to facilitate prompt relief – the jurisdiction agreement should not be given effect to derogate from the jurisdiction courts would have under their national law'.

[60] Case C-616/10, Solvay SA v Honeywell Fluorine Products Europe BV and Others, 12.07.2012, ECLI:EU:C:2012:445, para 40. This is indirectly confirmed also in the Opinion of AG Rantos in Case C-581/20, Skarb Państwa Rzeczypospolitej Polskiej reprezentowany przez Generalnego Dyrektora Dróg Krajowych i Autostrad v TOTO SpA - Costruzioni Generali and Vianini Lavori SpA, 6.10.2021, ECLI:EU:C:2021:808, paras 57 and 58: 'the question could be asked whether a choice of forum excludes, systematically, the right laid down in Article 35 ... The judgment in Italian Leather clarified, in any event, that the jurisdiction referred to in Article 35 can co-exist with that of a different court chosen by the parties to give a definitive ruling on the dispute'.

[61] The Opinion of AG Rantos in Case C-581/20, Skarb Państwa Rzeczypospolitej Polskiej reprezentowany przez Generalnego Dyrektora Dróg Krajowych i Autostrad v TOTO SpA - Costruzioni Generali and Vianini Lavori SpA, 6.10.2021, ECLI:EU:C:2021:808, paras 63–64.

[62] Case C-222/15, Hőszig Kft. v Alstom Power Thermal Services, 7.7.2016, ECLI:EU:C:2016:525, para 28.

5 Provisional Measures with the Same Content as the Main Claim

Different Member States have different types of provisional measures, which can be issued under various conditions and have different effects. These also include provisional measures that are substantively the same as the claim.[63] This means that a provisional measure provides the creditor with the satisfaction of the claim that they would otherwise obtain in a final judgment. A typical example is an interim relief, where the plaintiff sues the defendant for a certain amount but at the same time asks the court to order the defendant to provisionally pay the amount for the time when the court proceedings are still pending. This type of measure is also possible in respect of non-monetary claims. For example, the plaintiff sues for the delivery of a certain object but at the same time seeks by way of a provisional measure its delivery while the court proceedings are still pending. The same is the situation wherein a claimant sues for the establishment of a certain legal situation but at the same time seeks the same thing by way of a provisional measure. What they all have in common is that their goal is to temporarily regulate the legal relationship at hand rather than to secure the possibility of future enforcement.

There are several risks when the content and effects of the provisional measure are the same as those of the main claim. Firstly, such provisional measures might pre-empt the decision on the substance of the case. A provisional measure establishes a certain legal situation that can be maintained for a considerable period of time. When the court decides on the main claim, it is thus inclined to adopt the same decision as it did on the provisional measure. However, such a measure has typically been adopted in a short procedure with a lower standard of proof than is normally required in litigation. As a result, such a decision having an influence on the substance is undesirable. The CJEU has pointed out the risk that if 'the plaintiff were entitled to secure interim payment of a contractual consideration before the courts of the place where he is himself domiciled, where those courts have no jurisdiction over the substance of the case ... and thereafter to have the order in question recognised and enforced in the defendant's State, the rules of jurisdiction laid down by the Convention could be circumvented'.[64]

Secondly, there is a risk that, once the desired legal situation has been temporarily implemented, it will be impossible to return to the pre-provisional-measure state if

[63] Merrett (2016), p. 95, para 21, clarifies that the term 'provisional and protective' measures can include different types of measures—among others also interim payments.

[64] Case C-391/95, Van Uden Maritime BV, trading as Van Uden Africa Line v Kommanditgesellschaft in Firma Deco-Line and Another, 17.11.1998, ECLI:EU:C:1998:543, para 46. Similar can be found in Case C-99/96, Hans-Hermann Mietz v Intership Yachting Sneek BV, 27.04.1999, ECLI:EU:C:1999:202, para 47, and Case C-104/03, St. Paul Dairy Industries NV v Unibel Exser BVBA, 28.04.2005, ECLI:EU:C:2005:255, para 18. The same position can also be found in the recent Opinion of AG Rantos in Case C-581/20, Skarb Państwa Rzeczypospolitej Polskiej reprezentowany przez Generalnego Dyrektora Dróg Krajowych i Autostrad v TOTO SpA - Costruzioni Generali and Vianini Lavori SpA, 6.10.2021, ECLI:EU:C:2021:808, para 32.

the claim is subsequently dismissed. Thirdly, there is a risk of *forum shopping* in combination with exorbitant bases of jurisdiction in cross-border cases. In order to obtain this type of provisional measure, the claimant is interested in finding a Member State where such a measure can be granted under relatively simple conditions. In this manner, the claimant obtains the early establishment of a specific legal relationship and then transfers it to other Member States. The rules on the recognition and enforcement of foreign measures prove to be important in this respect.

Despite some considerations indicating that a court having jurisdiction under national law should not grant a provisional measure with the same content as the main claim, it has been held that this is possible. As already mentioned above, when Regulation 44/2001 was in force, the CJEU established several requirements that had to be met in order for foreign provisional measures to be recognised and enforced in other Member States.

In addition to the possibility of the debtor contesting the provisional measure (during or after its issuance, but in any event before its recognition and enforcement in another Member State),[65] which was necessary for all provisional measures regardless of the Member State of issuance, the CJEU also laid down additional requirements for the cross-border recognition and enforcement of provisional measures issued by a court having jurisdiction according to its national rules. The existence of a 'real connecting link between the subject matter of the measure sought and the territorial jurisdiction of the court'[66] issuing the measure was required for such measures to be recognised and enforced in another Member State under the simplified rules of Regulation 44/2001.

Furthermore, the CJEU imposed additional conditions for the application of the provisions of Regulation 44/2001 on recognition and enforcement to the cross-border transfer of provisional measures that were substantively the same as the claim in the action and which were issued by a court having jurisdiction according to national law.[67] Firstly, it is necessary that the object of the provisional measure is

[65] Case C-125/79, Bernard Denilauler v SNC Couchet Frères, 21.05.1980, ECLI:EU:C:1980:130, para 18. The decision interpreted the Brussels Convention, but the relevant provisions were comparable with those in Regulation 44/2001. See also Geimer and Schütze (2010), p. 581, paras 97 and 98; Ekart and Rijavec (2010), p. 104; Rijavec (2018b), p. 239, points out that the service of the measure on the debtor must, in any event, be carried out in the Member State of origin, since the form of the certificate has a section in which the court of origin certifies that there is proof of service of the measure on the defendant where the measure was ordered without the defendant being summoned to appear.

[66] Case C-391/95, Van Uden Maritime BV, trading as Van Uden Africa Line v Kommanditgesellschaft in Firma Deco-Line and Another, 17.11.1998, ECLI:EU:C:1998:543, para 40. For more, see Pogorelčnik Vogrinc (2020), p. 142.

[67] Case C-391/95, Van Uden Maritime BV, trading as Van Uden Africa Line v Kommanditgesellschaft in Firma Deco-Line and Another, 17.11.1998, ECLI:EU:C:1998:543, para 47. The CJEU interpreted this to mean that measures with such content do not qualify as 'provisional, including protective, measures' if they do not meet the conditions outlined above (and consequently, the rules on recognition and enforcement do not apply to them).

in the territory of the court of its issuance.[68] Such a requirement nearly always resulted in a provisional measure being enforced in the Member State of its issuance, obviating the necessity of cross-border recognition and enforcement. The second requirement removed the risk of the impossibility of restoration to the earlier situation if the main claim was subsequently rejected. The CJEU required the creditor to provide the debtor in proceedings[69] for the granting of a provisional measure a guarantee[70] of the repayment of the amount awarded. The fulfilment of all of these conditions was checked in the Member State of recognition and enforcement. A provisional measure that did not meet all of the conditions could not be subject to the rules of Regulation 44/2001 on recognition and enforcement.

The sum of these rules posed a significant impediment to the issuance of provisional measures. In most cases, it has resulted in measures being issued by courts with jurisdiction according to national rules and subsequently being enforced in that Member State. In such cases, the court did not, in principle, require the lodging of a guarantee (as provided for by the terms of the CJEU) at the enforcement stage of the domestic measure if it was not otherwise required under national rules. As already mentioned, Brussels I bis Regulation only codified the *ex parte* condition regarding provisional measures, but not also the others. The court of origin (having jurisdiction according to the national rules) requires and verifies the existence of the national requirements for the issuance of a provisional measure. Under Brussels I bis Regulation, measures issued by a court having jurisdiction under national rules can no longer be recognised and enforced in another Member State. These provisional measures are only enforceable and enforced in the Member State of origin. This might imply that the requirements mentioned above might no longer be relevant. However, different opinions can be found in legal theory.

Some opine that the described requirements are still applicable for provisional measures issued by the court having jurisdiction according to the national law, i.e., that such a court can issue an interim order only if repayment of the amount to the defendant is guaranteed and the measure is issued regarding the assets located in the territory of the court of origin.[71] This is grounded upon the fact that the requirement of a guarantee is necessary to strike a balance between the two parties,[72] while such a guarantee is apparently not needed when the court issuing a provisional measure has jurisdiction as to the substance[73] (unless required by the national law applicable in the specific case).

---

[68] It can be argued that this is a more precise interpretation of the requirement for a real connecting link. A similar opinion can also be found in Cuniberti and Rueda (2016), p. 853, para 15.

[69] Geimer and Schütze (2010), p. 565, para 15.

[70] However, the CJEU did not determine any additional details with regard to this guarantee. As a result, it was left to each individual court to decide what kind and how much of a guarantee to impose.

[71] Pertegás Sender and Garber (2016), p. 803, para 63, p. 791, para 27, and p. 787, para 11.

[72] Ibid, p. 803, para 64.

[73] Ibid, 791, para 27.

Such a standpoint on the application of both requirements is justified in legal theory by the CJEU case law mentioned above. Previously, the CJEU case law on provisional measures issued in relation to Article 24 of the Brussels Convention or Article 31 of Regulation 44/2001 was generally applied to its successor, i.e., Regulation 44/2001 or Brussels I bis Regulation. Given the (almost) identical wording of the relevant provisions of all of these legal instruments, it has been useful to transpose the CJEU's interpretations and conditions in this regard.[74] Thus, on the one hand, it is understandable that the application of the conditions laid down for the granting of provisional measures by courts having jurisdiction under Article 35 was also transposed; on the other hand, there are certain concerns in this respect.

The requirements regarding the guarantee and asset location must be verified at the stage of the recognition or execution of the provisional measure. According to Article 2(a) of Brussels I bis Regulation, measures issued by a court having jurisdiction according to national rules are no longer subject to recognition and enforcement in another Member State (at least not under the rules of Brussels I bis Regulation on recognition and enforcement). It appears illogical to require that both conditions be met when the provisional measure is issued, even if it will be enforced in the Member State where it was issued. Whereas previously, these conditions were imposed in order to mitigate the risks that arose in relation to precautionary measures issued by courts having jurisdiction under national rules, these risks no longer exist now that Brussels I bis Regulation applies. As a consequence, in the author's opinion, such a restriction on the issuance of provisional measures that will only have effect in the issuing State is neither necessary nor sensible.

As a result, the legal theory provides interpretations that emphasise the application of conditions while somehow relaxing the need to do so. It is, therefore, possible to find the view that a 'systematic request for a claimant deposit may become an excessive burden'[75] and that it consequently 'seems appropriate that the court balances the interests of the respective parties',[76] as well as the interpretation that it is not obligatory to provide a guarantee if the main case is based on a non-contractual relationship.[77]

While thus far there has only been discussion on whether the requirements as to a guarantee and asset location still apply in the context of Brussels I bis Regulation, the same question applies with regard to the requirement of a real connecting link. Interestingly, it is possible to find opposite conclusions regarding this. Cuniberti and Rueda, for example, conclude that the requirement of a certificate containing a description of the measure and certifying that the court has jurisdiction as to the

[74] Case C-581/20, Skarb Państwa Rzeczypospolitej Polskiej reprezentowany przez Generalnego Dyrektora Dróg Krajowych i Autostrad v TOTO SpA - Costruzioni Generali and Vianini Lavori SpA, 6.10.2021, ECLI:EU:C:2021:808, and Case C-186/19, Supreme Site Services GmbH and Others v Supreme Headquarters Allied Powers Europe, 03.09.2020, ECLI:EU:C:2020:638 are the only two that the CJEU has thus far ruled on regarding Article 35 of Brussels I bis Regulation.

[75] Pertegás Sender and Garber (2016), p. 800, para 51.

[76] Ibid., p. 800, para 51.

[77] For more, see Ibid., p. 804, para 65.

substance of the matter (Article 42(2)(b)(i) of Brussels I bis Regulation) replaces the requirement of a real connecting link.[78] However, contrary to the author's view, the CJEU suggests in its recent TOTO decision that the requirement of a real connecting link should still be tested.[79] The same view is shared by Nuyts, who requires the existence of a real connecting link as one of the two basic conditions for being granted a provisional measure under Article 35 of Brussels I bis Regulation.[80] Such an interpretation would lead to the conclusion that a real connecting link is a requirement that complements the national rules of all EU Member States in the part in which they regulate the conditions for all of the provisional measures known to them under their national law. In the event of a cross-border dispute, national courts, when issuing protective measures to be subsequently enforced in the same country, would have to verify, in addition to the national conditions, an additional one imposed by the CJEU.

Provisional measures issued by courts having jurisdiction according to the national law can no longer be recognised or enforced under the rules set out in Brussels I bis Regulation. Such measures will be enforced in the Member State of origin, where they will secure future enforcement (which, with regard to the location of the assets, will in the future also take place in that state). It is also true that, in light of the provisions of Brussels I bis Regulation, *forum shopping* is no longer possible. As a result, the majority of the risks related to the issuance of provisional measures that are substantively the same as the claim have been eliminated. The only remaining risk is the difficulty in ensuring *restitutio in integrum*, which is often addressed (and resolved with the requirement of a guarantee) by the *lex fori*.[81] It is true that such a provisional measure does have a cross-border element since it will be issued in a different Member State than the one in which the main proceedings are to be conducted. Nonetheless, it is possible to conclude that the CJEU's additional conditions for the cross-border recognition and enforcement of provisional measures are no longer applicable. The CJEU established them for the sole purpose of limiting the cross-border transfer of provisional measures, which is now no longer possible. As a consequence, these requirements are no longer relevant.

---

[78] Cuniberti and Rueda (2016), p. 854, paras 16–17.

[79] Case C-581/20, Skarb Państwa Rzeczypospolitej Polskiej reprezentowany przez Generalnego Dyrektora Dróg Krajowych i Autostrad v TOTO SpA - Costruzioni Generali and Vianini Lavori SpA, 6.10.2021, ECLI:EU:C:2021:808, para 52.

[80] Nuyts (2016), p. 363, para 12.18.

[81] For example, the Slovenian Enforcement and Security Act (Official Gazette of the Republic of Slovenia, No. 51/98 of 17 July 1998 with subsequent changes) in its Art. 275(2) provides for the possibility of the court requesting, in order to grant an interim injunction (začasna odredba), that the creditor deposit a security deposit even if they have proven that there is a likelihood that the claim and the risk exist. At the same time, the Constitutional Court of the Republic of Slovenia, in Decision Up-275/97, 16 July 1998, confirmed the existence of regulatory interim injunctions that correspond in substance to the claim in the action and made this conditional on the requirement that it would be possible to restore the previous situation at a later date. Since then, the requirement has been required in the case law in the event of the issuance of an interim injunction of such content, despite the fact that the Slovene legislature has not included the requirement in the relevant Act.

6 Conclusion

Provisional measures are a special tool in the hands of the creditor. They provide creditors with legal protection at a time when they are not yet protected by a final court decision. This is particularly important in the event of cross-border disputes, where legal protection is even more difficult to obtain. In these disputes, the cross-border recognition and enforcement of security measures are also important, and the different national regimes have necessitated regulation at the European level. When the recast of Regulation 44/2001 was drafted, its proposal foresaw the possibility of the cross-border recognition and enforcement of provisional measures issued by the court having jurisdiction as to the substance, without prior notification of the debtor being necessary. However, despite the original plans, the requirement of their being an adversarial procedure was added to Brussels I bis Regulation, which does not make the creditor's situation any easier. The substantial change also with regard to provisional measures issued by a court with jurisdiction according to the national rules raises some doubts as to the application of the conditions developed in the case-law of the CJEU. However, the final solution would be a European provisional measure issued under uniform conditions and a predefined procedure. The European Account Preservation Order is a positive start, but there is hope for a more comprehensive approach that also covers other content subject to security.

References

Cuniberti G, Rueda I (2016) Articles 39–44. In: Magnus U, Mankowski P (eds) ECPIL: European Commentaries on Private International Law: Commentary, Brussels Ibis Regulation. Otto Schmidt, pp 836–863

Ekart A, Rijavec V (2010) Čezmejna izvršba v EU. GV Založba, Ljubljana

Fentiman R (2016) Articles 29–34. In: Magnus U, Mankowski P (eds) ECPIL: European Commentaries on Private International Law: Commentary, Brussels Ibis Regulation. Otto Schmidt, pp 725–778

Fitchen (2016) The refusal of recognition. In: Dickinson A, Lein E (eds) The Brussels I Regulation Recast. Oxford University Press, Oxford, pp 432–480

Francq S, Mankowski P (2016) Article 45. In: Magnus U, Mankowski P (eds) ECPIL: European Commentaries on Private International Law: Commentary, Brussels Ibis Regulation. Otto Schmidt, pp 863–953

Garcimartin (2016) Prorogation of Jurisdiction - Choice of Court Agreements and Submission (Arts. 25–26). In: Dickinson A, Lein E (eds) The Brussels I Regulation Recast. Oxford University Press, Oxford, pp 277–311

Geimer R, Schütze R (2010) Europäisches Zivilverfahrensrecht: Kommentar. Verlag C. H. Beck

Heinze C (2011) Choice of court agreements, coordination of proceedings and provisional measures in the reform of the Brussels I Regulation. Rabels Zeitschrift für ausländisches und internationales Privatrecht 75:581–618. https://doi.org/10.1628/003372511796351368

Hess B (2010) Europäisches Zivilprozessrecht. C. F. Miller

Hess B (2021) Europäisches Zivilprozessrecht, 2nd edn. De Gruyter

Magnus U (2016) Article 25. In: Magnus U, Mankowski P (eds) ECPIL: European Commentaries on Private International Law: Commentary, Brussels Ibis Regulation. Otto Schmidt, pp 584–669

Merrett L (2016) Article 2. In: Magnus U, Mankowski P (eds) ECPIL: European Commentaries on Private International Law: Commentary, Brussels Ibis Regulation. Otto Schmidt, pp 86–103
Nuyts A (2016) Provisional, including protective measures (Art. 35). In: Dickinson A, Lein E (eds) The Brussels I Regulation Recast. Oxford University Press, Oxford, pp 357–372
Pertegás Sender M, Garber T (2016) Article 35. In: Magnus U, Mankowski P (eds) ECPIL: European Commentaries on Private International Law: Commentary, Brussels Ibis Regulation. Otto Schmidt, pp 778–813
Pogorelčnik Vogrinc N (2020) Provisional security of creditors in cross-border civil and commercial matters. Lexonomica 12(2):129–148
Rijavec V (2018a) Final Assessment of Brussels I Recast. In: Rijavec V, Kennett W, Keresteš T et al (eds) Remedies Concerning Enforcement of Foreign Judgmenents, Brussels I Recast. Wolters Kluwer, pp 359–421
Rijavec V (2018b) VI. Začasni ukrepi. In: Repas M, Rijavec V (eds) Mednarodno zasebno pravo Evropske unije. Uradni list Republike Slovenije, Ljubljana, pp 236–244
Schlosser P (2012) Aus Frankreich Neues zum transantionalen einstweiligen Rechtsshutz in der EU. Iprax 1:88–91

Part IV
Court Settlements and Authentic Instruments

The European Dimension of Court Settlements: Open Issues and Regulatory Needs

Philipp Anzenberger

Abstract The legal framework on the international aspects of court settlements is currently rather scarce and inhomogeneous, which can cause a variety of problems: The European Regulations, to start with, contain no satisfactory definition of a court settlement, so that it is not clear for all legal acts in question whether the rules on judicial settlement apply to them. Furthermore, the lack of a uniform regulatory framework raises questions on the applicable regime for recognition and enforcement when rights and legal relationships from different areas of law are laid down in a single court settlement. Other open questions concern international jurisdiction for the conclusion of court settlements as well as the possible effects of *lis pendens* on the admissibility of a court settlement. And finally, the different European Regulations contain a rather divergent set of rules on recognition and enforcement of court settlements, which can be questioned from the perspective of legal policy. All these topics shall be addressed in this article.

1 Introduction

Court settlements are one of the core instruments for amicable dispute resolution before court in many European countries.[1] A European legislator that aims to promote consensual conflict resolution must therefore *enable the free circulation of court settlements* within the European area of justice. The legal situation in the individual Member States is very heterogeneous in this regard: there is a multitude of different mechanisms for amicable dispute resolution before court in the respective procedural systems, not only regarding the formal rules for their conclusion (such as

[1]For Austria cf. Anzenberger (2020a), p. 1; for Germany cf. Wolfsteiner (2020), para 794 ZPO, margin 1.

P. Anzenberger (✉)
University of Innsbruck, Faculty of Law, Innsbruck, Austria
e-mail: philipp.anzenberger@uibk.ac.at

V. Rijavec et al. (eds.), *Diversity of Enforcement Titles in the EU*, Ius Gentium: Comparative Perspectives on Law and Justice 111,
https://doi.org/10.1007/978-3-031-47108-7_14

‘consent judgments’ or amicable settlements during or even before the proceedings), but also in their dogmatic construction (often, but not necessarily, court settlements are understood as dual-functional procedural acts,[2] meaning, that they consist of a procedural and a substantive part). However, the regulatory framework on a European level is rather loose regarding court settlements, which can be problematic in certain scenarios (although in many cases the parties will comply with the settlements they concluded, so that the current deficiencies often do not come to light). This article will outline some of the issues that may occur during the conclusion and circulation of court settlements in a cross-border context and will analyze whether and to what extent the current regulatory framework offers satisfactory solutions. More precisely, we will address questions of the *legislative technique* of the European Regulations (Sect. 2), issues arising during the *conclusion of court settlements* in a cross-border context (Sect. 3; such as the question of international jurisdiction), as well as problems with the *cross-border circulation of court settlements* (Sect. 4; especially regarding their cross-border enforceability, but also the possible transfer of other effects of a court settlement).

2 Issues Regarding the Legislative Technique

2.1 No Uniform Regulatory Framework

Typically, the national legislators allow the conclusion of court settlements in many *different areas of private law*.[3] Since the procedural provisions for those different areas of law are laid down in separate regulations, the European legislator has therefore also assigned rules on recognition and enforcement of court settlements to those respective regulations: Rules on enforcement (and partly also on recognition) can be found in Art. 59 Brussels Ia-Regulation,[4] Art. 65 Brussels

[2]For example, in Bulgaria (National report for Bulgaria, p. 66), in Germany (National report for Germany, p. 118), or in Slovenia (National report for Slovenia, p. 86); also cf. Anzenberger (2020a), pp. 24–71; Klicka (2015), para 206 ZPO, margin 8; Rechberger and Simotta (2017), margin 689.

[3]Cf. National report for Bulgaria, pp. 67–68; National report for Croatia, p. 45; National report for Cyprus, p. 58; National report for Czech, p. 33; National report for Germany, p. 122; National report for Italy, p. 50; National report for Poland, p. 63; National report for Slovenia, p. 87; National report for Sweden, p. 36.

[4]Regulation (EU) No. 1215/2012 of the European Parliament and of the Council of 12 December 2012 on jurisdiction and the recognition and enforcement of judgments in civil and commercial matters, OJ L 351, 20.12.2012.

IIb-Regulation,[5] Art. 24 of the Enforcement Order Regulation,[6] Art. 48 of the Regulation on Maintenance Obligations,[7] Art. 61 of the Regulation on Matters of Succession,[8] Art. 60 of the Regulation on Matrimonial Property Regimes[9] and Art. 60 of the Regulation on Property Consequences of Registered Partnerships.[10] This leads to *considerable fragmentation of the legal framework* for court settlements on a European level: While some regulations, for example, explicitly provide for the recognition of court settlements (e.g., Art. 65 Brussels IIb-Regulation; Art. 48 para. 1 of the Regulation on Maintenance Obligations), others merely contain rules on the enforcement of court settlements. Also, the modalities of enforcement vary significantly between the regulations: This concerns, in particular, the necessity of a declaration of enforceability, but also the grounds for a refusal of enforcement in another Member State (cf. in more detail Sect. 4.1).

This fragmentation can cause practical problems: As a matter of fact, it is possible for court settlements to regulate several rights and legal relationships that, if regulated separately, would *fall within the scope of different European regulations.*[11] Under Austrian law, for example, a single court settlement could contain claims arising from a bike accident and maintenance claims between two divorced spouses.[12] In such a case, it is necessary to identify which rules apply to the enforcement (and possibly to the recognition[13]) of this specific settlement. As long as the respective rights and legal relationships can be identified and separated (e.g., because they are listed individually in the court settlement), each claim can be assigned to the corresponding European Regulation and subjected to the respective

[5] Council Regulation (EC) No. 2201/2003 of 27 November 2003 concerning jurisdiction and the recognition and enforcement of judgments in matrimonial matters and the matters of parental responsibility, repealing Regulation (EC) No. 1347/2000, OJ L 338, 23.12.2003.

[6] Regulation (EC) No. 805/2004 of the European Parliament and of the Council of 21 April 2004 creating a European Enforcement Order for uncontested claims, OJ L 143, 30.4.2004.

[7] Council Regulation (EC) No. 4/2009 of 18 December 2008 on jurisdiction, applicable law, recognition and enforcement of decisions and cooperation in matters relating to maintenance obligations, OJ L 7, 10.1.2009.

[8] Regulation (EU) No. 650/2012 of the European Parliament and of the Council of 4 July 2012 on jurisdiction, applicable law, recognition and enforcement of decisions and acceptance and enforcement of authentic instruments in matters of succession and on the creation of a European Certificate of Succession, OJ L 201, 27.7.2012.

[9] Council Regulation (EU) 2016/1103 of 24 June 2016 implementing enhanced cooperation in the area of jurisdiction, applicable law and the recognition and enforcement of decisions in matters of matrimonial property regimes, OJ L 183, 8.7.2016.

[10] Council Regulation (EU) 2016/1104 of 24 June 2016 implementing enhanced cooperation in the area of jurisdiction, applicable law and the recognition and enforcement of decisions in matters of the property consequences of registered partnerships, OJ L 183, 8.7.2016.

[11] Cf. Anzenberger (2020a), pp. 143–144; Anzenberger (2020b), pp. 149, 154; cf. National report for Belgium, pp. 73–74.

[12] Anzenberger (2020a), pp. 220–222.

[13] Cf. Sect. 4.2.

enforcement regime.[14] This is due to the possibility of partial recognition and partial enforcement of enforcement titles.[15] A more complicated situation arises, however, where the *claim in question cannot easily be assigned to one single regulation*, e.g., where the payment of a sum of money has been agreed on, settling two different original claims (in the above example, claims arising from a bike accident and maintenance claims). In this case, literature suggests that the applicable regulation should depend on the 'main emphasis' of the settlement in each individual case.[16] If there is no clear main emphasis, some authors propose that the more specific regulation should apply,[17] which—according to this view—is methodically achieved by a 'generous interpretation' of the exceptions in Art. 1 para. 2 Brussels Ia-Regulation.[18] While these proposals can lead to satisfactory results in some cases, they can also raise demarcation problems in other cases. For example, there may be situations where it is not apparent which of the original claims forms the 'main emphasis' of the settlement. And there will be other situations where it is not clear which European regulation is more 'specific'. In the author's view, it would be more consistent to simply assume the emergence of a new civil claim (for the purposes of the Regulations on International Civil Procedure Law) in cases where the original claims are 'blended beyond recognition'.[19] This 'new' civil claim would then—in the absence of a specific legal nature—fall within the scope of application of the Brussels Ia-Regulation (cf. Art. 1 para. 1 Brussels Ia-Regulation). From the parties' point of view, this should not be problematic: if they wish to retain the enforcement rules provided for their original claims, they can structure the settlement according to their own ideas (and thus formulate the claims in a separable manner).

From the perspective of legal policy, this raises the question of the *necessity of such an artificial fragmentation*. The general reason for the existence of divergent procedural rules for various legal matters (both at a national and a European level) is that the societal values and interests involved in the clarification of facts can be different, depending on the subject of matter that needs to be investigated.[20] In some legal matters, for example, it may be desirable to have the court investigate circumstances *ex officio*, while in other matters, it may be preferable to place the responsibility for establishing the substantive truth in the hands of the parties. Also, displaying the substantive legal situation in a procedure may require different

[14] Brenn (2010), Article 58 EuGVVO, margin 5; Geimer et al. (2020), Article 59 EuGVVO, margin 9; Staudinger (2021), Article 59 Brüssel Ia-VO, margin 6.

[15] For the Brussels Ia-Regulation cf. Kodek (2014), Article 36 EuGVVO, margin 31; Leible (2021), Article 36 Brüssel Ia-VO, margin 14.

[16] Staudinger (2021), Article 59 Brüssel Ia-VO, margin 6.

[17] Mankowski (2021), Article 1 Brüssel Ia-VO, margin 79; Staudinger (2021), Article 59 Brüssel Ia-VO, margin 6.

[18] Mankowski (2021), Article 1 Brüssel Ia-VO, margin 79.

[19] Anzenberger (2020b), p. 155.

[20] Anzenberger (2020a), p. 218; Ballon (1980), pp. 45 et seq.

'technical' approaches, depending on the respective substantive law. In some legal matters—e.g., in inheritance matters—it may be necessary to involve several persons as parties to the proceedings, while questions in other fields of civil law may be better clarified in a two-party proceeding. In this respect, it is quite plausible that European Civil Procedure Law also provides for different rules for issues belonging to different substantive areas of law. However, there are good reasons for *questioning this sharp separation* of legal matters when concluding (and enforcing) a court settlement. In most European legal systems, the core of a court settlement is an agreement between the parties regarding rights or legal relationships,[21] which is approved or certified by a court in some way (cf. Sect. 2.2.2).[22] However, many aspects of a procedural system suddenly lose their justification when 'only' a court settlement is concluded (for example, protective considerations in favour of one party when determining jurisdiction). In Austria, for example, it is argued that a court settlement can also include claims belonging to different types of civil proceedings[23] and that the local jurisdiction regime can be disregarded when concluding a court settlement.[24] The same is true on a European level: since the procedural differences of the individual legal matters lose importance when the parties decide to conclude a court settlement, it would make sense to make the recognition and enforcement of court settlements *subject to a uniform regime* (for example, in one single European Regulation), regardless of the legal matter of (civil) rights and legal relationships laid down in the settlement. This would eliminate the divergences in the handling of court settlements in the various European Regulations and, at the same time, increase clarity and legal certainty for their cross-border circulation.

2.2 *Lack of a Precise Definition*

2.2.1 The Current Legal Situation in the European Regulations

Most of the European Regulations (in International Civil Procedure Law) not only contain explicit rules on the enforceability of court settlements but also provide a *definition* of this legal instrument: According to Art. 2 lit. b Brussels Ia-Regulation,

[21] National report for Belgium, p. 69; National report for Bulgaria, pp. 66–67; National report for Croatia, pp. 44–45; National report for Cyprus, p. 57; National report for the Netherlands, p. 39; National report for Germany, p. 118; National report for Poland, p. 62; National report for Slovenia, p. 87.

[22] National report for Belgium, p. 68; National report for Cyprus, p. 57; National report for Germany, p. 117; National report for Italy, pp. 49–50; National report for Lithuania, p. 32; National report for Spain, p. 59; National report for Sweden, p. 36; National report for Slovenia, p. 86; cf. National report for Croatia, p. 45.

[23] Anzenberger (2020a), pp. 220 et seq.; Fucik and Kloiber (2005), para 30 AußStrG, margin 1; Gitschthaler (2019b), para 30 AußStrG, margin 15.

[24] Anzenberger (2020a), p. 231; Fasching (1990), margin 1329; Gitschthaler (2019a), para 204–206 ZPO, margin 17; Kodek (2018), para 433 ZPO, margin 8.

for example, a court settlement is a 'settlement which has been approved by a court of a Member State or concluded before a court of a Member State in the course of proceedings'. The definitions in Art. 2 para. 1 subpara. 2 of the Regulation on Maintenance Obligations, Art. 3 para. 1 lit. h of the Regulation on Matters of Succession, Art. 4 para. 9 of the Regulation on a European Account Preservation Order,[25] Art. 3 para. 1 lit. e of the Regulation on Matrimonial Property Regimes and Art. 3 para. 1 lit. f of the Regulation on Property Consequences of Registered Partnerships are almost identical. However, no explicit definition (but a very similar understanding of court settlements) can be found in Art. 24 of the Enforcement Order Regulation. In the Brussels IIb-Regulation the term 'court settlement' is not used at all; instead, Art. 65 Brussels IIb-Regulation speaks of 'agreements on legal separation and divorce which have binding legal effect in the Member State of origin' and 'agreements in matters of parental responsibility which have binding legal effect and are enforceable in the Member State of origin'.

A closer look at those definitions shows that they are quite vague and rather suboptimal from a legislative point of view. Not only is the term being defined actually used in the definition (thereby creating a circular logic), but there are also no positive criteria for identifying what legal acts may be considered a court settlement.[26] Some answers to these deficiencies can at least be derived from the case law of the ECJ, according to which 'settlements in court are essentially contractual in that their terms depend first and foremost on the parties' intention'.[27] The *lack of a sharp definition* may not be a problem in many cases because the concept of a court settlement is well-known in most Member States (although its concrete form varies between the different Member States and can be controversial in some of them, cf. Sect. 2.2.2). In some Member States, however, there are legal acts whose classification as 'court settlement' (Art. 2 lit. b Brussels Ia-Regulation) or as 'judgment' (Art. 2 lit. a Brussels Ia-Regulation) is less obvious, for example in Belgium, where there is the 'amicable settlement' (minnelijke schikking) as well as the 'consent judgment' (akkoordvonnis), which can be reached via settlement, via mediation or via collaborative negotiations.[28]

Scientific literature has proposed several *possible 'demarcation lines'* that might be used to distinguish between a court settlement and a judgment. One such proposition uses a mere formal distinction, according to which it should depend on whether the act in question takes the form of a judgment or a decision,[29] in which

[25]Regulation (EU) No. 655/2014 of the European Parliament and of the Council of 15 May 2014 establishing a European Account Preservation Order procedure to facilitate cross-border debt recovery in civil and commercial matters, OJ L 189, 27.6.2014.

[26]Cf. Frische (2006), p. 137 on the same problem regarding the definition of a judgment.

[27]Case C-414/92, Solo Kleinmotoren GmbH v. Emilio Boch, 2.6.1994, ECLI:EU:C:1994:221.

[28]National report for Belgium, pp. 67–69.

[29]Von Hoffmann and Hau (1995), pp. 217, 218; Peiffer and Peiffer (2023), Article 59 VO [EU] Nr. 1215/2012, margin 6.

case it should not be considered a court settlement. Another criterion proposed in literature focuses on the functional role of the court, i.e., whether the court only documents the 'court settlement' and examines it in the light of certain minimum legal requirements or whether it takes a decision on the substance.[30] Finally, some authors suggest a distinction based on the effects of the act in question, where 'judgment-like' effects, such as a *res judicata*-effect, shall indicate that it is a judgment.[31] From the author's point of view, the most important factor for distinguishing a judgment and a court settlement is whether the legal act created is predominantly of a contractual nature (which also includes procedural contracts) or predominantly a sovereign decision.[32] This assessment takes into account both the formal form of the legal act and the functional role of the court.[33] The effects of the acts in question, however, do not constitute a suitable criterion for demarcation in the author's opinion, not only because the effects of judgments—as well as the ones of court settlements—can vary strongly in different Member States (and therefore there are no 'exclusive' effects that determine when to consider an act a 'judgment' or a 'court settlement'), but also because court settlements are perceived as 'judgment surrogates' in some legal systems, potentially generating the same legal effects as judgments.[34] Following this understanding, if the court of law takes a sovereign decision, then—as a rule of thumb—this legal act is to be considered a 'judgment' for the purposes of the Brussels Ia-Regulation, even if it was reached by consensus in the proceedings (for example, if one party admits the claim or if the parties can predetermine the facts on which the decision is based).

2.2.2 Common Core in the Member States?

When considering a possible definition of a court settlement on a European level, what comes to mind is to search for a *common core* in the various national legal systems. The national reports of this scientific research do indeed show that some characteristics are similar in all investigated Member States: The first noteworthy characteristic is that there has to be some sort of *agreement between the parties*: While—as one would expect—there are differences in the questions which substantive rights and legal relationships can be subject to a court settlement[35] (some

[30] Kropholler and von Hein (2011), Article 58 EuGVO, margin 1b.

[31] Peiffer and Peiffer (2023), Article 59 VO [EU] Nr. 1215/2012, margin 9; Loyal (2022), Article 2 Brüssel Ia-VO, margin 22.

[32] Kropholler and von Hein (2011), Article 58 EuGVO, margin 1a.

[33] Anzenberger (2020b), pp. 153–154.

[34] In Slovenia, for example, court settlements are considered to have a res judicata effect (National report for Slovenia, p. 89).

[35] Cf. National report for Bulgaria, pp. 67–68; National report for Croatia, p. 45; National report for Cyprus, p. 58; National report for Czech, p. 33; National report for Germany, p. 122; National report for Italy, p. 50; National report for Poland, p. 63; National report for Slovenia, p. 87; National report for Sweden, p. 36.

legislations, for example, prohibit settlements on parental rights or maintenance between former spouses,[36] on matters of personal status[37] or marriage itself[38]) or regarding the question whether there actually has to be a dispute between the parties in order to conclude a settlement,[39] it appears that all investigated legal systems require a *consensus between the parties on the content of certain rights or legal relationships*.[40] However, it is noteworthy that, in some legal systems, a court settlement can also be concluded by merely agreeing on the termination of the proceedings (as some authors in Germany[41] and also in Austria[42] claim). Now, one could argue that the termination of the proceedings ends the current 'procedural relationship' between the parties and that these settlements would fall under the 'common core' as described above. However, even if a common definition of the court settlement would restrict its content to an agreement 'on the merits' of a possible procedure (and therefore exclude national 'court settlements' that merely lead to the termination of a procedure), no real harm would be done: If the only effect of a 'court settlement' is the termination of an ongoing proceeding, there is no real need for a transfer of effects to other Member States (since even the omission of *lis pendens* would not be a 'direct' effect, but rather a 'reflex' of concluding a court settlement, which means, that there is no need to 'export' the effect of termination a proceeding to other Member States).

The second characteristic found in every Member State is the necessity of some sort of *involvement of a court* when concluding the court settlement.[43] Again, there are various possibilities on how a court can be involved (for example, already before an action was brought in[44] or during proceedings;[45] in the presence of the parties[46] or

[36] National report for Bulgaria, p. 68.

[37] National report for Czech, p. 33; National report for Spain, p. 59.

[38] National report for Spain, p. 59.

[39] National report for Bulgaria, p. 66.

[40] National report for Belgium, p. 69; National report for Bulgaria, pp. 66–67; National report for Croatia, pp. 44–45; National report for Cyprus, p. 57; National report for the Netherlands, p. 39; National report for Germany, p. 118; National report for Poland, p. 62; National report for Slovenia, p. 87.

[41] National report for Germany, p. 118; Henckel (1970), p. 39; Mende (1976), pp. 30 et seq.; Paulus (2015), para 794 ZPO, margin 12.

[42] Klicka (2015), para 204–206 ZPO, margin 9; Trenker (2020), pp. 299 et seq.; differently Anzenberger (2020a), p. 55.

[43] National report for Belgium, p. 68; National report for Cyprus, p. 57; National report for Germany, p. 117; National report for Italy, pp. 49–50; National report for Lithuania, p. 32; National report for Spain, p. 59; National report for Sweden, p. 36; National report for Slovenia, p. 86; cf. National report for Croatia, p. 45.

[44] National report for Croatia, p. 44; National report for Poland, p. 62; National report for Slovenia, p. 86.

[45] National report for Croatia, p. 44; National report for Poland, p. 62; National report for Spain, p. 58; National report for Slovenia, p. 86.

[46] National report for Bulgaria, p. 67; cf. Anzenberger (2020a), p. 361.

by a mere written contract submitted to the court;[47] or regarding the mediatory role of the court[48]), but there seems to be the *necessity of* some sort of *approval by the court* before a court settlement can be validly concluded. The role of the court needs to be marked very clearly, though, since the *line between 'mere' court settlements and 'actual' consent judgments* seems to be drawn quite differently (and maybe not always very sharply) in the investigated Member States;[49] some Member States don't even know the concept of a consent judgment (or only in the forms of a "recognition judgment" or 'waiver judgment'[50]). Therefore, for the purposes of the European Regulations, it seems necessary to create a sharper demarcation line between court settlements and judgments.

In *other aspects* (such as the question of whether there needs to be a current dispute to conclude a settlement[51]), there are quite some *divergencies* among different Member States. This is generally not really problematic since creating international provisions for the transfer of effects of legal instruments does not require a complete identity of the prerequisites and effects of the legal instruments in question. Instead, it seems sufficient to find the core elements that determine court settlements for the purposes of the regulations and mark down its concept in comparison to other legal instruments (like decisions or other enforceable instruments). Therefore, a definition should be rather broad in this context to facilitate the cross-border circulation of court settlements and make it an attractive option of amicable dispute resolution in cross-border cases. Nevertheless, for reasons of practicability and predictability, the definition needs to be precise enough to know when exactly the rules relevant to court settlements are to be applied. It should therefore contain elements of the two characteristics that were found *a common core in the European Member States*, being a *consensus between the parties on the content of rights or legal relationships*, as well as the *involvement of a court* (either because the court approved the settlement or because it was concluded there in the course of the proceeding), and provide a *clear demarcation line to other legal instruments* (especially judgments).

---

[47] Foerste (2023), para 278 ZPO, margins 16 et seq.; Prütting (2020), para 278 ZPO, margins 44 et seq.; Saenger (2023), para 278 ZPO, margins 21 et seq.

[48] Cf. National report for Slovenia, p. 87.

[49] Cf. National report for Cyprus, p. 57; National report for Lithuania, p. 32.

[50] Deixler-Hübner (2018), para 394 ZPO, margins 1 et seq. and para 395 ZPO, margins 1 et seq.

[51] In Germany, for instance, a civil settlement can be transformed into a court settlement (National report for Germany, p. 119), which indicates that a court settlement can be concluded even if there is no (more) dispute; in the Dutch and Spanish legal system, however, the core of a court settlement is a dispute between the parties (National report for the Netherlands, p. 39; National report for Spain, p. 58); in Austria, a praetorian settlement can be concluded before the start of a legal dispute with judicial mediation before a district court (Anzenberger 2020b, p. 152).

3 Issues Regarding the Conclusion of Court Settlements

3.1 International Jurisdiction

The question of *international jurisdiction for the conclusion of court settlements* is rarely addressed in scientific literature, which is probably due to the fact that it is not explicitly mentioned in the European Regulations and rarely causes problems in practice. Nevertheless, it can gain importance where *rights and legal relationships that are not a subject of the dispute* are also to be settled in a procedural settlement (for example, in a so-called 'general settlement', where all open disputes shall be settled) and where some of these rights and legal relationships would fall under the exclusive jurisdiction of another Member State (for example, according to Art. 24 Brussels Ia-Regulation). For the scope of the Brussels Ia-Regulation, according to the prevailing doctrine in Germany and Austria, the *regime of international jurisdiction does not apply to court settlements*,[52] which means that court settlements could be concluded in every Member State, even despite the 'contrary' exclusive jurisdiction of a specific Member State. When looking at the wording of the provisions on jurisdiction in Chapter II of the Brussels Ia-Regulation, it is noticeable that they not only refer to 'judgments' in the sense of Art. 2 lit. a of the Brussels Ia-Regulation but use more general terms, such as 'suing' (Art. 4 para. 1, Art. 7 and 11 Brussels Ia-Regulation), 'in matters relating to' (Art. 17 para. 1 Brussels Ia-Regulation) or 'proceedings' (Art. 24 Brussels Ia-Regulation),[53] which could indicate applicability to court settlements. However, the enforcement of court settlements may only be refused due to a violation of public policy (*ordre public*; Art. 59 in conjunction with Art. 58 para. 1 Brussels Ia-Regulation), but not because of violations of exclusive jurisdiction (in contrast to 'judgments' according to Art. 45 para. 1 lit. e Brussels Ia-Regulation). If the European legislator had wanted the rules on international jurisdiction (and especially on exclusive jurisdiction) to be applied to the conclusion of court settlements, he would most likely not have reduced the grounds for a refusal to an infringement of public policy.[54] This argument, as well as the lack of any necessity to protect the parties[55] (who voluntarily decide to settle amicably), do in fact speak in favour of leaving aside the rules on international jurisdiction of the Brussels Ia-Regulation when concluding a court settlement. The same arguments can be brought forward with respect to the other European

[52] Cf. Anzenberger (2020a), pp. 231–233; Geimer et al. (2020), Article 59 EuGVVO, margin 9; Hess (2021), Article 2 EuGVVO, margin 23; Peiffer and Peiffer (2023), Article 59 VO [EU] Nr. 1215/2012, margin 17; cf. for the mediation settlement Frauenberger-Pfeiler and Risak (2012), pp. 798, 801; differently Staudinger (2021), Article 59 EuGVVO, margin 8.

[53] Peiffer and Peiffer (2023), Article 59 VO [EU] Nr. 1215/2012, margin 17.

[54] Anzenberger (2020a), p. 232; Peiffer and Peiffer (2023), Article 59 VO [EU] Nr. 1215/2012, margin 17.

[55] Cf. Geimer (2000), pp. 366, 369; Peiffer and Peiffer (2023), Article 59 VO [EU] Nr. 1215/2012, margin 17.

Regulations as well: the grounds for refusal of enforcement of court settlements are very limited in all the Regulations (cf. Sect. 4.1), and the infringement of exclusive jurisdiction rules is not listed in any of them. Therefore, from the author's point of view, it is very convincing to *disregard the rules on international jurisdiction when concluding a court settlement* not only in the context of Brussels Ia-Regulation, but within the *scope of all European Regulations*.

3.2 Lis Pendens as an Obstacle to the Conclusion of a Settlement?

Another question that has received only little attention in legal literature is whether the European *lis pendens* also affects the conclusion of court settlements. This concerns in particular court settlements which are concluded outside of pending civil proceedings (for example, the Austrian praetorian court settlement according to para. 433 ZPO (Zivilprozessordnung[56]) or the mediation settlement according to para. 433a ZPO[57]). The admissibility of such a settlement despite *lis pendens* is—within the scope of application of the Brussels Ia-Regulation—supported by the wording of Art. 29 para. 1 Brussels Ia-Regulation, according to which the *lis pendens* shall affect *'proceedings involving the same cause of action and between the same parties are brought in the courts of different Member States'*. The 'mere' conclusion of a court settlement outside of a 'regular' civil proceeding can—from the author's point of view—not be considered a separate 'proceeding' in the sense of Art. 29 para. 1 Brussels Ia-Regulation (the same is true for the wording of Art. 30 para. 1 Brussels Ia-Regulation: *'Where related actions are pending'*). Also, according to Recital 21 Brussels Ia-Regulation, parallel proceedings should be avoided '*in the interests of the harmonious administration of justice*' in order to avoid irreconcilable decisions in the different Member States. From this viewpoint as well, it seems preferable to allow court settlements despite *lis pendens* because they do not burden the administration of justice, but rather—due to the quick and amicable resolution of the dispute—significantly relieve it and therefore free up resources. In addition, provisions on a *lis pendens* (at least in general) also serve to protect the parties from repeated simultaneous claims by the other party.[58] However, such a purpose is not necessary during the conclusion of a court settlement (since the parties deliberately decide to do so). This is why, for example, the prevailing doctrine in Austria assumes the admissibility of a settlement conclusion despite

---

[56] Civil Procedure Code.

[57] Cf. Anzenberger (2020a), p. 152.

[58] Eichel (2023), Article 29 Brüssel Ia-VO, margins 9–10; Gottwald (2022), Article 2 Brüssel Ia-VO, margin 2; Mayr (2020), Article 29 EuGVVO, margin 1.

the national *lis pendens* in other proceedings.[59] Overall, it is therefore convincing not to consider *lis pendens* an obstacle for the conclusion of a court settlement in another Member State.

4 Issues Regarding the Cross-Border Circulation of Court Settlements

4.1 Divergencies in the European Regulations Regarding Enforcement

Probably the most important (procedural) function of a court settlement in practice is its *role as an enforcement title*.[60] Therefore, it is not surprising that all the aforementioned regulations (cf. Sect. 2.1) contain provisions on its cross-border enforceability. However, the respective modalities of enforcement, as well as possibilities for the debtor to object enforcement, can strongly vary in the respective regulations. While a *declaration of enforceability* is no longer required within the scope of the Brussels Ia-Regulation, the Brussels IIb-Regulation and the Enforcement Order Regulation (Art. 59 Brussels Ia-Regulation; Art. 65 para. 2 Brussels IIb-Regulation; Art. 24 para. 2 of the Enforcement Order Regulation), the creditor still needs this formal act within the scope of the other regulations (cf. e.g., Art. 48 para. 1 in conjunction with Art. 28 of the Regulation on Maintenance Obligations; Art. 61 para. 1 in conjunction with Art. 43 of the Regulation on Matters of Succession; Art. 60 para. 1 of the Regulation on Matrimonial Property Regimes; Art. 60 para. 1 of the Regulation on Property Consequences of Registered Partnerships).

There are also major *differences regarding the grounds for refusal of enforcement*: While according to most regulations, the enforcement of court settlements can only be objected due to an *infringement of public policy* (Art. 59 in conjunction with Art. 58 para. 1 Brussels Ia-Regulation; Art. 61 para. 3 of the Regulation on Matters of Succession; Art. 60 para. 3 of the Regulation on Matrimonial Property Regimes and Art. 60 para. 3 of the Regulation on Property Consequences of Registered Partnerships), some other Regulations (at least 'formally'—due to the *reference technique* of these individual provisions) allow an objection due to the untimely service of the document initiating the proceedings (Art. 24 lit. b of the Regulation on Maintenance Obligations), the incompatibility with an earlier decision (Art. 24 lit. c

[59] Anzenberger (2020a), p. 262; Ballon et al. (2018), margin 438; Klicka (2015), para 204–206 ZPO, margin 10; Kodek (2018), para 433 ZPO, margin 14; Schneider (2019), para 30 AußStrG, margin 6.

[60] Anzenberger (2020a), p. 22; Ballon et al. (2018), margin 439; National report for Austria, p. 64; National report for Croatia, p. 44; National report for Germany, p. 122; National report for Italy, p. 49.

and d of the Regulation on Maintenance Obligations; Art. 68 para. 1 lit. b and c as well as para. 2 lit. c and d Brussels IIb-Regulation) or even other grounds (cf. Art. 68 para. 2 lit. b Brussels IIb-Regulation). With regard to these last-mentioned grounds for refusal, however, it is quite questionable whether they can really be raised against the enforcement of a court settlement: After all, it is not very plausible to invoke an infringement of the right to be heard when concluding a settlement. Moreover, the irreconcilability with earlier decisions is also quite unlikely to play a considerable role in many constellations (since a court settlement will often also have a novation effect). If, on the other hand, a court settlement has been confirmed as a *European Enforcement Order*, according to Art. 24 para. 2 of the Enforcement Order Regulation, its enforcement can no longer be challenged at all.[61]

These divergencies between the individual regulations can be explained historically[62] and are to be accepted under the current legal situation. *De lege ferenda*, however, a *standardization of the legal situation between the individual regulations* would be desirable, especially since these distinctions have no factual justification as far as court settlements are concerned. This would—at the same time—increase clarity and legal certainty for cross-border circulation of court settlements and overall increase their attractiveness as a means for amicable dispute resolution.

4.2 Necessity to Transfer Other Effects of Court Settlements?

It remains to be discussed how other effects of a court settlement are to be dealt with in cross-border situations. In some Member States court settlements have *a res judicata-effect* (e.g., in Slovenia;[63] this is also advocated by some voices in Austria[64]), an *effect of substituting formal requirements*[65] (meaning that they replace other formal requirements for the conclusion of certain contracts), or a *constitutive effect*[66] (even regarding legal relationships that are not actually subject to the party's substantive power of disposal). The cross-border transfer of the effects of a legal act traditionally happens via recognition.[67] So, if a court settlement is recognized in the other Member States, its effects (for example, a *res judicata*-effect) extend to the

[61] Adolphsen (2022), Article 24 EuVTVO, margin 8; Rechberger (2008), Article 24 EuVTVO, margin 6.

[62] Neumayr and Nunner-Krautgasser (2018), pp. 116 et seq.; Rechberger and Simotta (2017), margins 1286 et seq.

[63] National report for Slovenia, p. 88.

[64] Anzenberger (2020a), pp. 115–144.

[65] Anzenberger (2020a), pp. 107–115.

[66] Cf. Anzenberger (2020a), pp. 144–146.

[67] Rassi (2020), Article 36 EuGVVO, margin 2; Rechberger and Simotta (2017), margin 1291.

recognizing state.[68] Therefore, the question of the possible *recognition of court settlements* can be of great significance.

Within the scopes of the *Brussels IIb-Regulation* and the *Regulation on Maintenance Obligations*, court settlements are *explicitly recognizable* (Art. 65 Brussels IIb-Regulation and Art. 48 para. 1 of the Regulation on Maintenance Obligations),[69] so that not only the effect of enforceability but also all other settlement effects extend to the other Member States. According to the ECJ[70] as well as the prevailing doctrine,[71] however, this is not the case within the scope of the *Brussels Ia-Regulation*: This doctrine is based on the fact that court settlements do not constitute judgments according to Art. 2 lit. a Brussels Ia-Regulation, so that the provisions on recognition (explicitly referring to judgments) do not apply. This doctrine is also supported by the systematic argument that the enforceability of court settlements is regulated in Art. 59 of the Brussels Ia-Regulation and that there is no reference to the applicability of the provisions on recognition in Art. 58 of the Brussels Ia-Regulation. A similar situation can be found in the *Regulation on Matters of Succession*: Art. 61 of this Regulation only contains rules for the enforceability of court settlements, provisions on a (possible) recognition are missing. Therefore, one could investigate the suspicion that the lack of rules on recognition may have been unintentional: Recital 8 of the Regulation explicitly states that, in *'order to achieve those objectives, this Regulation should bring together provisions on jurisdiction, on applicable law, on* recognition[72] *or, as the case may be, acceptance, enforceability and enforcement of decisions, authentic instruments and court settlements and on the creation of a European Certificate of Succession'*. A similar wording can also be found in Recital 59 of this Regulation. In the author's opinion, the wording '*or, as the case may be, acceptance*' (which, according to the intention of the European legislator, should represent a kind of 'weakened recognition'[73]), however, expresses that not every type of transfer of effects is to be applied to every listed legal act (but only insofar as the Regulation expressly provides for it).[74] So, in an overall assessment of this wording, from the author's point of view, there is *no clear indication* that the European legislator *wanted to allow the recognition of court settlements* within the regime of the Regulation on Matters of Succession. These considerations can be transferred to the regimes of the *Regulation on Matrimonial Property* and the *Regulation on Property Consequences of Registered Partnerships*. In these two

[68] Cf. Hess (2021), Article 36 EuGVVO, margins 2–3; Kodek (2014), Article 36 EuGVVO, margin 32; Neumayr (2023), margin 3.945; Nunner-Krautgasser (2010), pp. 794, 797; Oberhammer (2018), pp. 323 et seq.

[69] Sengstschmid (2010), Article 46 EuEheKindVO, margins 13 et seq.

[70] Case C-414/92, Solo Kleinmotoren GmbH v. Emilio Boch, 2.6.1994, ECLI:EU:C:1994:221.

[71] Kodek (2014), Article 36 EuGVVO, margin 22; Neumayr (2023), margins 3.939 and 3.949; differentiating and in much detail Frische (2006), pp. 130 et seq.

[72] The emphasis was inserted by the author.

[73] Cf. Franzmann and Schwerin (2023), Article 59 EuErbVO, margins 7–8.

[74] Anzenberger (2020a), p. 143.

Regulations, there are no explicit rules on recognition either (cf. Art. 60 of the Regulation on Matrimonial Property and Art. 60 of the Regulation on Property Consequences of Registered Partnerships), and there is an almost identical wording in Recital 16 of the Regulation on Matrimonial Property and Recital 16 of the Regulation on Property Consequences of Registered Partnerships.

So again, the *'picture' is fragmented* across the different European Regulations. And again, this is problematic for several reasons: It is possible that one single court settlement falls within the scope of multiple European Regulations and therefore is subject to different recognition regimes, which entails the problems and legal uncertainties already laid down in Sect. 2.1. Also, the 'non-recognizability' of settlements within the scope of some of the regulations weakens the attractiveness of court settlements as such in cross-border constellations, which is diametrically opposed to the tendency of the European legislator to promote amicable dispute resolution (as can be noticed, for example, in the creation of the Mediation Directive,[75] the Directive on Consumer ADR[76] or the Regulation on Consumer Online Dispute Resolution[77]). Therefore, from a legislative point of view, consideration should be given to the possibility of *standardizing and expanding the options for the recognition* of court settlements across the European Regulations.

5 Summary

Despite its practical relevance, the legal framework on international aspects of court settlements is rather inhomogeneous. There is currently *no sharp definition* of court settlements in any of the European Regulations, which is problematic due to the diversity of amicable conflict resolution instruments in the individual Member States. A closer look at the provisions on *international jurisdiction* and *lis pendens* shows that the respective rules cannot apply to court settlements. The rules on *recognition and enforcement*, on the other hand, are scattered among the different regulations (with a questionable substantial justification) and are designed rather heterogeneously regarding the scope and the modalities of the extension of the effects. From a legislative point of view, it would therefore be desirable to *harmonize the law* on the one hand and to *clarify the rules in force* on the other hand for the area of court settlements.

[75] Directive 2008/52/EC of the European Parliament and of the Council of 21 May 2008 on certain aspects of mediation in civil and commercial matters, OJ L 136, 24.5.2008.

[76] Directive 2013/11/EU of the European Parliament and of the Council of 21 May 2013 on alternative dispute resolution for consumer disputes and amending Regulation (EC) No. 2006/2004 and Directive 2009/22/EC, OJ L 165, 18.6.2013.

[77] Regulation (EU) No. 524/2013 of the European Parliament and of the Council of 21 May 2013 on online dispute resolution for consumer disputes and amending Regulation (EC) No. 2006/2004 and Directive 2009/22/EC, OJ L 165, 18.6.2013.

References

Adolphsen J (2022) Article 24 EuVTVO. In: Rauscher T, Krüger W (eds) Münchener Kommentar zur Zivilprozessordnung mit Gerichtsverfassungsgesetz und Nebengesetzen, 6th edn. Verlag C. H.Beck, München

Anzenberger P (2020a) Der gerichtliche Vergleich. LexisNexis Verlag, Wien

Anzenberger P (2020b) The cross-border enforcement of court settlements within Brussels Ia Regulation: from a European and an Austrian perspective. LeXonomica 12(2):149–162

Ballon O (1980) Die Zulässigkeit des Rechtswegs. Duncker & Humblot, Berlin

Ballon O, Nunner-Krautgasser B, Schneider B (2018) Einführung in das Zivilprozessrecht, 13th edn. MANZ Verlag, Wien

Brenn C (2010) Article 58 EuGVVO. In: Fasching H, Konecny A (eds) Kommentar zu den Zivilprozessgesetzen, 2nd edn. MANZ Verlag, Wien

Deixler-Hübner A (2018) Para 394 ZPO. In: Fasching H, Konecny A (eds) Kommentar zu den Zivilprozessgesetzen, 3rd edn. MANZ Verlag, Wien

Eichel F (2023) Article 29 Brüssel Ia-VO. In: Vorwerk V, Wolf C (eds) Beck'scher Online Kommentar ZPO, 46th edn. Verlag C.H.Beck, München

Fasching H (1990) Lehrbuch des österreichischen Zivilprozessrechts: Lehr- und Handbuch für Studium und Praxis. MANZ Verlag, Wien

Foerste U (2023) Para 278 ZPO. In: Musielak H-J, Voit W (eds) Zivilprozessordnung mit Gerichtsverfassungsgesetz, 19th edn. Verlag Franz Vahlen, München

Franzmann T, Schwerin T (2023) Article 59 EuErbVO. In: Geimer R, Schütze R (eds) Internationaler Rechtsverkehr in Zivil- und Handelssachen. Verlag C.H.Beck, München

Frauenberger-Pfeiler U, Risak M (2012) Der prätorische Mediationsvergleich. ÖJZ 67(18):798–802

Frische T (2006) Verfahrenswirkungen und Rechtskraft gerichtlicher Vergleiche: Nationale Formen und ihre Anerkennung im internationalen Rechtsverkehr. C.F. Müller, Heidelberg

Fucik R, Kloiber B (2005) Außerstreitgesetz samt AußStr-BegleitG, WohnAußStrBeglG und den übrigen Reformgesetzen. MANZ Verlag, Wien

Garber T (2019) Article 46 Brüssel IIa-VO. In: Gitschthaler E, Höllwerth J (eds) Internationales Familienrecht, EU-Verordnungen und Haager Übereinkommen zum Ehe-, Partner- und Kindschaftsrecht. Verlag Österreich, Wien

Geimer R (2000) Freizügigkeit vollstreckbarer Urkunden im Europäischen Wirtschaftsraum. IPRax 20(5):366–369

Geimer R et al (2020) Article 59 EuGVVO. In: Geimer R, Schütze R (eds) Europäisches Zivilverfahrensrecht, Kommentar, 4th edn. Verlag C.H.Beck, München

Gitschthaler E (2019a) Para 204-206 ZPO. In: Rechberger W, Klicka T (eds) Kommentar zur ZPO, 5th edn. Verlag C.H.Beck, München

Gitschthaler E (2019b) Para 30 AußStrG. In: Gitschthaler E, Höllwerth J (eds) Kommentar zum Außerstreitgesetz. MANZ Verlag, Wien

Gottwald P (2022) Article 2 Brüssel Ia-VO. In: Rauscher T, Krüger W (eds) Münchener Kommentar zur Zivilprozessordnung mit Gerichtsverfassungsgesetz und Nebengesetzen, 6th edn. Verlag C.H.Beck, München

Henckel W (1970) Prozeßrecht und materielles Recht. Schwartz Verlag, Göttingen

Hess B (2021) Article 2 EuGVVO, Art. 36 EuGVVO. In: Schlosser P, Hess B (eds) EU-Zivilprozessrecht mit EuGVVO, EuMVVO, EuGFVO, EuZVO, EuBVO, EuKtPVO, 5th edn. Verlag C.H.Beck, München

Klicka T (2015) Para 204-206 ZPO. In: Konecny A, Fasching H (eds) Kommentar zu den Zivilprozessgesetzen, 3rd edn. MANZ Verlag, Wien

Kodek G (2014) Article 36 EuGVVO. In: Czernich D, Kodek G, Mayr P (eds) Europäisches Gerichtsstands- und Vollstreckungsrecht: Brüssel Ia-Verordnung [EuGVVO 2012] und Übereinkommen von Lugano 2007, 4th edn. LexisNexis Verlag, Wien

Kodek G (2018) Para 433 ZPO. In: Fasching H, Konecny A (eds) Kommentar zu den Zivilprozessgesetzen, 3rd edn. MANZ Verlag, Wien

Kropholler J, von Hein J (2011) Europäisches Zivilprozessrecht, Kommentar zu EuGVO, Lugano-Übereinkommen 2007, EuVTVO, EuMVVO und EuGFVO, 9th edn. Verlag Recht und Wirtschaft, Frankfurt am Main
Leible S (2021) Article 36 Brüssel Ia-VO. In: Rauscher T (ed) Europäisches Zivilprozess- und Kollisionsrecht EuZPO/EuIPR, 5th edn. Verlag Dr. Otto Schmidt, Köln
Loyal F (2022) Article 2 Brüssel Ia-VO. In: Wieczorek B, Schütze R (eds) Zivilprozessordnung und Nebengesetze, 5th edn. Walter de Gruyter, Berlin
Mankowski P (2021) Article 1 Brüssel Ia-VO. In: Rauscher T (ed) Europäisches Zivilprozess- und Kollisionsrecht EuZPO/EuIPR, 5th edn. Verlag Dr. Otto Schmidt, Köln
Mayr P (2020) Article 29 EuGVVO. In: Fasching H, Konecny A (eds) Kommentar zu den Zivilprozessgesetzen, 3rd edn. MANZ Verlag, Wien
Mende W (1976) Die in den Prozeßvergleich aufgenommene Klagerücknahme. Heymanns Verlag, Köln
Neumayr M (2023) Kap 3 Die Brüssel Ia-Verordnung XII. Anerkennung und Vollstreckung. In: Mayr P (ed) Handbuch des europäischen Zivilverfahrensrechts. MANZ Verlag, Wien
Neumayr M, Nunner-Krautgasser B (2018) Exekutionsrecht, 4th edn. MANZ Verlag, Wien
Nunner-Krautgasser B (2010) Die Anerkennung und Vollstreckung englischer freezing injunctions in Österreich. ÖBA 58(12):794–800
Oberhammer P (2018) Anerkennung ausländischer Entscheidungen und Instanzenzug. ecolex 29(4):323–326
Paulus C (2015) Para 794 ZPO. In: Wieczorek B, Schütze R (eds) Zivilprozessordnung und Nebengesetze, 4th edn. Walter de Gruyter, Berlin
Peiffer E, Peiffer M (2023) Article 59 EuGVVO. In: Geimer R, Schütze R (eds) Internationaler Rechtsverkehr in Zivil- und Handelssachen. Verlag C.H.Beck, München
Prütting H (2020) Para 278 ZPO. In: Rauscher T, Krüger W (eds) Münchener Kommentar zur Zivilprozessordnung mit Gerichtsverfassungsgesetz und Nebengesetzen, 6th edn. Verlag C.H. Beck, München
Rassi J (2020) Article 36 EuGVVO. In: Fasching H, Konecny A (eds) Kommentar zu den Zivilprozessgesetzen, 3rd edn. MANZ Verlag, Wien
Rechberger W (2008) Article 24 EuVTVO. In: Fasching H, Konecny A (eds) Kommentar zu den Zivilprozessgesetzen, 2nd edn. MANZ Verlag, Wien
Rechberger W, Simotta D (2017) Grundriss des österreichischen Zivilprozessrechts, Erkenntnisverfahren, 9th edn. MANZ Verlag, Wien
Saenger I (2023) Para 278 ZPO. In: Saenger I (ed) Zivilprozessordnung – Familienverfahren, Gerichtsverfassung, Europäisches Verfahrensrecht Handkommentar, 9th edn. Nomos Verlagsgesellschaft, Baden-Baden
Schneider B (2019) Para 30 AußStrG. In: Schneider B, Verweijen S (eds) AußStrG: Außerstreitgesetz Kommentar. Linde Verlag, Wien
Sengstschmid A (2010) Article 46 EuEheKindVO. In: Fasching H, Konecny A (eds) Kommentar zu den Zivilprozessgesetzen, 2nd edn. MANZ Verlag, Wien
Staudinger A (2021) Article 59 Brüssel Ia-VO. In: Rauscher T (ed) Europäisches Zivilprozess- und Kollisionsrecht EuZPO/EuIPR, 5th edn. Verlag Dr. Otto Schmidt, Köln
Trenker M (2020) Einvernehmliche Parteidisposition im Zivilprozess: Parteiautonomie im streitigen Erkenntnisverfahren. MANZ Verlag, Wien
von Hoffmann B, Hau W (1995) Deutscher Prozeßvergleich kein Anerkennungshindernis nach Art. 27 Nr. 3 EuGVÜ. IPRax 15(4):217–218
Wolfsteiner H (2020) Para 794 ZPO. In: Rauscher T, Krüger W (eds) Münchener Kommentar zur Zivilprozessordnung mit Gerichtsverfassungsgesetz und Nebengesetzen, 6th edn. Verlag C.H. Beck, München

Authentic Instruments

Piotr Rodziewicz

Abstract Subject of recognition and enforcement, apart from judgments and court settlements, may also be authentic instruments. Brussels I bis contains separate regulation devoted to authentic instruments, nevertheless, the provisions explicitly require the appropriate application of selected regulations concerning judgments to authentic instruments. It should also be emphasized that the regulations provide only for the enforceability of documents but are silent as to their recognition. This chapter presents provisions of Brussels I bis regulation on authentic instruments. Emphasis has been made to presentation definition of authentic instrument in Brussels I bis as well as qualification and description of characteristic features of certain national law authentic instruments from a perspective of authentic instrument definition under Brussels I bis. Significant part of chapter has been devoted to the recognition mechanism and enforceability of authentic instruments. In this regard, the similarities, and differences in terms of recognition and enforcement with court judgments have been presented. Chapter contains also analysis concerning grounds for refusal to enforcement authentic instruments.

1 Introduction

The principle of mutual trust constitutes the backbone of Brussels I bis Regulation.[1] Under Article 58 of the regulation, authentic instruments in civil and commercial matters issued in one European Union Member State can freely circulate in all Member States without the need for any special procedure. The abolition of *exequatur* with respect to authentic instruments allows authentic instruments that

[1] Regulation (EU) No. 1215/2012 of the European Parliament and of the Council of 12 December 2012 on jurisdiction and the recognition and enforcement of judgments in civil and commercial matters, OJ L 351, 20.12.2012. See Dymitruk et al. (2021), pp. 1–16.

P. Rodziewicz (✉)
University of Wroclaw, Faculty of Law, Administration and Economics, Wroclaw, Poland
e-mail: piotr.rodziewicz@uwr.edu.pl

V. Rijavec et al. (eds.), *Diversity of Enforcement Titles in the EU*, Ius Gentium: Comparative Perspectives on Law and Justice 111,
https://doi.org/10.1007/978-3-031-47108-7_15

are enforceable in their Member States of origin to be enforceable in other Member States without any declaration of enforceability. The regime of free circulation is grounded in the principles of equality between Member States and of mutual trust in the administration of justice.[2]

In most legal systems, authentic instruments are enforcement titles, which may entitle individuals to initiate enforcement proceedings that lead to compulsory performance. Authentic instruments are even more diverse than judgments: in principle, judgments may be issued only by a court; authentic documents may be issued by public entities that are not courts, non-public bodies that perform only specific public competences, or private entities that may be entitled to issue authentic documents under specific provisions.[3]

To date, European Union law has failed to harmonise the nature and manner that official documents are used. Although, illustratively, official documents are the product of national legal systems, it is the provisions on judicial cooperation in civil and commercial matters that perceive and indicate how they can be used from the perspective of the legal effects they incorporate in other Member States. Authentic instruments are essentially a product of the legal systems of continental Europe; as such, they do not exist in common law systems. Nevertheless, Member States, such as Sweden, form part of the civil law tradition of legal systems;[4] authentic instruments, however, do not constitute enforcement titles in Sweden, and even notarial deeds are not recognised under Swedish law.[5]

2 Definition of an Authentic Instrument

Brussels I bis Regulation introduces an autonomous definition of an authentic instrument that is applicable with regard to its enforcement in a state other than that of its origin. This definition is consistent with the understanding of an authentic instrument within the legal systems of Member States. The Brussels I Regulation contained no definition of an authentic instrument; this changed when Brussels I bis Regulation entered into force. The legal definition of an authentic instrument is contained in Article 2 I of Brussels I bis Regulation, which stipulates that ‘authentic instrument’ means a document that has been formally drawn up or registered as an authentic instrument in its Member State of origin. The authenticity of such a document relates both to the signature and to the content of the instrument, as well as those established by a public or other authority empowered for that purpose. The provision in question merely indicates the criteria for recognition of a specific document issued in accordance with the law of a particular Member State as an

[2]See Dymitruk et al. (2021), p. 2.

[3]See Dymitruk et al. (2021), p. 2.

[4]See Ortwein II (2003), pp. 405, 411.

[5]Bylander and Linton (2020).

authentic instrument. The cited definition is not entirely new, as it was first introduced in Article 4 paragraph 3 of Regulation (EC) No 805/2004 of the European Parliament and of the Council of 21 April 2004 creating a European Enforcement Order (EEO) for uncontested claims.[6] The only difference between the definition contained in the EEO regulation and that of Brussels I bis Regulation is that the EEO regulation provides that 'authentic instrument' covers arrangements relating to maintenance obligations concluded with or authenticated by administrative authorities. Maintenance obligations fall beyond the scope of Brussels I bis Regulation and are subject to Council Regulation (EC) No 4/2009 of 18 December 2008 on jurisdiction, applicable law, recognition and enforcement of decisions and cooperation in matters relating to maintenance obligations.[7] With this in mind, it is understandable that the definition of an authentic instrument used in Brussels I bis Regulation is limited in scope.

To analyse the elements that allow a document to be recognised as an authentic instrument, the instrument should first be issued by a public authority or official. In this respect, the judgment issued by the European Court of Justice (ECJ) in case C-260/97 Unibank A/S v. Flemming G. Christensen[8] on the basis of the Brussels Convention remains relevant. The ECJ held that an 'acknowledgment of indebtedness enforceable under the law of the State of origin whose authenticity has not been established by a public authority or other authority empowered for that purpose by that State does not constitute an authentic instrument within the meaning of Article 50 of the Brussels Convention'; in other words, for a document to be considered an authentic instrument, it must be authenticated by a public authority or an entity expressly authorised to do so. Such a public authority or official must also be empowered to authenticate instruments. Authentication must be performed using an authentication procedure, which follows from provisions concerning the issuing of authentic instruments. Documents must abide by the relevant rules on the formalities for drawing up and issuing authentic instruments. The legal effect establishing that a document provides conclusive proof of its content is a key element that allows documents to be recognised as authentic instruments.[9]

---

[6]Regulation (EC) No 805/2004 of the European Parliament and of the Council of 21 April 2004 creating a European Enforcement Order for uncontested claims, OJ L 143, 30.4.200. Jacek Gołaczyński (2015), para 4.

[7]Council Regulation (EC) No. 4/2009 of 18 December 2008 on jurisdiction, applicable law, recognition and enforcement of decisions and cooperation in matters relating to maintenance obligations, OJ L 7, 10.1.2009.

[8]Case C-260/97, Unibank A/S v. Flemming G. Christensen, 17.06.1999, ECLI:EU:C:1999:312.

[9]Council of the Notariats of the European Union: Comparative study on authentic instruments national provisions of private law, circulation, mutual recognition and enforcement, possible legislative initiative by the European Union (November 2008), https://www.europarl.europa.eu/RegData/etudes/STUD/2008/408329/IPOL-JURI_ET(2008)408329_EN.pdf.

3 Types and Overview of Authentic Instruments

National Reports demonstrate clearly that the most significant type of authentic instrument that constitutes an enforcement title is a notarial deed. In most Member States that have been the subject of research, notarial deeds fall within the definition of an authentic instrument in the Brussels I bis Regulation.[10] Moreover, in some Member States, such as Croatia, private deeds solemnised by notaries fall within the same definition.[11] Although public notaries are not public authorities, they are, nevertheless, empowered to draw up authentic instruments. The ECJ, in case C-42/92 Adrianus Thijssen v. Controledienst voor de verzekeringen,[12] as well as in case C-52/08 European Commission v. Portuguese Republic,[13] specified that the enforceability of an authentic instrument does not confer on a notary any powers relating to direct and specific participation in the exercise of official authority. The enforceability of a notarial deed depends on a debtor's consent to submit to possible compulsory enforcement without initiating prior proceedings. It follows that a notarial deed is unenforceable without the consent of the debtor. This necessitates discussion of other issues, such as whether the consent to submit to enforcement must be an element of a notarial deed constituting an enforcement title, and whether it is possible to deduce the necessity to include such an element within a notarial deed for the purposes of its enforcement in accordance with Brussels I bis Regulation. In some Member States, such as Sweden[14] and Cyprus,[15] notarial deeds are not recognised in national law as authentic instruments that may constitute enforcement titles.[16]

In some legal systems, private entities that do not exercise public authority were also once entitled to issue documents that could constitute grounds for enforcement. In Poland, according to Article 96 of the Banking Act of August 29, 1997, banks were entitled to issue bank enforcement titles until November 27, 2015. The Polish Constitutional Tribunal later found that granting special privileges to banks as private entities concerning facilitation of the pursuit of claims was incompatible with the Polish Constitution, and that Article 96 section 1 and Article 97 section 1 of the Banking Act of August 29, 1997 was inconsistent with Article 32 section 1 of the

[10] See Kola Tafaj (2020); Valdhans (2020); Rijavec et al (2020).

[11] See Kunštek et al (2020).

[12] Case C-42/92, Adrianus Thijssen v. Controledienst voor de verzekeringen, 13.07.1993, ECLI: EU:C:1993:304.

[13] Case C-52/08, European Commission v. Portuguese Republic, 14.05.2011, ECLI:EU:C:2011: 337.

[14] In Sweden, certain agreements regarding alimony obligations are directly enforceable by the Swedish Enforcement Authority (see Council of Bars and Law Societies of Europe 2011), maintenance obligations, however, remain beyond the scope of the research.

[15] See Christofi and Loizou (2022).

[16] Council of Bars and Law Societies of Europe (2011); Bylander and Linton (2020).

Polish Constitution.[17] The tribunal also found that the right of banks to issue bank enforcement titles constituted a violation of Article 32 section 1 of the Polish Constitution—namely the principle of equality in relation to the banks' customers. The conclusions of the tribunal are consistent with the ECJ's ruling in case C-260/97 Unibank A/S v. Flemming G. Christensen in their assertion that banks are not public authorities and do not exercise public powers in regard to bank enforcement titles.

The case discussed above is not an isolated one. In Bulgaria, agreement between parties for settlement of legal disputes through mediation that has been certified or registered by a public body falls within the definition of an authentic instrument.[18] With this in mind, the question of whether such settlements should be enforced on the basis of the Brussels I bis Regulation in a manner applicable to settlements or authentic instruments has arisen. It should be noted, however, that this discussion does not pertain to court settlements, but those concluded before a mediator that is approved by a public authority; therefore, such settlements fail to meet requirements of court settlement outlined in Article 2(b) of the Brussels I bis Regulation.

In Italy, authenticated private deeds pertaining to the obligations of sums of money contained therein, bills of exchange, and other debt instruments to which the law expressly attributes the same effects constitute enforcement titles.[19] This necessitates discussion on whether such documents constitute authentic instruments in the understanding of Brussels I bis Regulation. According to Article 474 of the Italian Code of Civil Procedure, private deeds created autonomously by the parties are extrajudicial titles. From the perspective of the enforcement of private deeds, bills of exchange, and other debt instruments, it must be determined whether documents drawn up by private entities can be treated as authentic instruments. The ECJ's ruling in case C-260/97 Unibank A/S v. Flemming G. Christensen shared the view that: 'an acknowledgment of indebtedness enforceable under the law of the State of origin whose authenticity has not been established by a public authority or other authority empowered for that purpose by that State does not constitute an authentic instrument within the meaning of Article 50 of the Brussels Convention'. Therefore, private deeds regarding the obligations of sums of money contained therein, bills of exchange, and other debt instruments, which are enforcement titles according to Italian law, can be enforced abroad as authentic instruments on the condition that they have been authenticated by a public authority;[20] such deeds will then fall within the scope of the definition of an authentic instrument in Brussels I bis Regulation, and may be enforced on the terms appropriate for authentic instruments.

The classification of a document as an authentic instrument largely depends on the law of its country of origin. This group of authentic instruments also comprises commercial contract policies in Spain ('pólizas de contratos mercantiles') signed by

[17] Republic of Poland Constitutional Tribunal, P 45/12, OTK-A 2015/4/46 (2015).

[18] See Naydenova (2022).

[19] See Kaczorowska et al (2022).

[20] See Fitchen (2020), p. 130.

the parties and by a registered trade broker.[21] Although lawyers and 'solicitadores' in Portugal have competence to authenticate documents, private documents may also be authorised and become authentic instruments.[22]

A non-court settlement that is concluded before or authenticated by a public authority may also qualify as an authentic instrument; thus, non-court settlements certified or registered by a public body other than a court fulfil the conditions for qualification as authentic instruments. For example, a mediation agreement in Spain (acuerdo de mediación), if raised to public deed, may qualify as an authentic instrument;[23] the same is true of a settlement agreement by mediation in Albania made in accordance with Article 22 of law number 10385, dated 24.02.2011 'On mediation for resolving disputes'.[24]

Another example of an authentic instrument that is enforceable under the Brussels I bis Regulation is a decision of the Lithuanian Labour Dispute Committee. The Labour Dispute Committee is a mandatory pretrial dispute settlement body that specialises in individual labour disputes. Decisions made by the committee are binding for the parties and enforceable.[25]

In some states, bailiffs are also entitled to issue authentic instruments. One example can be found in France, where the status of authentic instruments has been bestowed upon titles issued by bailiffs in cases of non-payments of cheques.[26]

In some states, particular types of securities constitute enforcement titles; these can, therefore, also be analysed as potential authentic instruments under the Brussels I bis Regulation. Under North Macedonian law, debenture bonds serve as authentic instruments.[27] In Spain, bearer or registered financial bonds ('títulos al portador') that represent past due obligations and coupons have the status of enforcement titles. This also applies to unexpired certificates ('certificados no caducados') issued by the entities responsible for accounting records regarding securities represented by book entries defined in the Securities Market Law.[28]

Irrespective of the authentic instruments presented, it is also necessary to highlight the countries in which internal law does not allow for authentic instruments, and those in which no regulation exists in this area.[29]

In practice, the notarial deed is by far the most common authentic instrument, as it is recognised in most legal systems of continental European states. The remaining authentic instruments constitute a highly diverse group of titles that may constitute a

---

[21] See Bores Lazo and Serrano Ron (2020).

[22] See Caramelo Gomes et al (2020).

[23] See Bores Lazo and Serrano Ron (2020).

[24] See Kola Tafaj (2020).

[25] See Lietuvos Profesinu Sajungu Konfederacija, Labour dispute committee, https://www.lpsk.lt/en/legislation/labour-dispute-committee/.

[26] See National report for France. Project EU-En4s — JUST-AG-2018/JUST-JCOO-AG-2018.

[27] See Zoroska Kamilovska and Rakočević (2020).

[28] See Bores Lazo and Serrano Ron (2020).

[29] See Christofi and Loizou (2022); Bylander and Linton (2020).

base for enforcement. In some countries, many authentic instruments exist that can constitute a base for execution (the best example of this is Spain[30]); other national legal systems do not recognise authentic instruments in domestic law. National law dictates the status of an instrument as an authentic one; thus, recognition of an authentic instrument on the basis of the Brussels I bis Regulation is secondary to its regulation in national law.

4 Recognition of Authentic Instruments

Although the Brussels I bis Regulation fails to provide a definition of 'recognition', one has been established in doctrine and case law. According to doctrine, recognition of an authentic instrument involves granting the same effectiveness that is accorded to it in its state of issue.[31]

The Brussels I bis Regulation establishes the principle of automatic recognition of foreign judgments. In reference to judgements, it provides that a judgment given in a Member State shall be recognised in other Member States without the need for any special procedure. The regulation does not extend this rule to authentic instruments; instead, it provides separate provisions on authentic instruments and settlements, which are contained in Chapter IV of the Brussels I bis Regulation (article 58 et seq.). According to Article 58 paragraph 1. the regulation covers only the enforcement of authentic instruments. This provision provides that an authentic instrument that is enforceable in its Member State of origin is enforceable in other Member States without the need for any declaration of enforceability. The European Union legislator has intentionally limited its regulation to the enforcement of authentic instruments. Its approach to authentic instruments is neither a uniform nor a coherent one. On the basis of other legal instruments pertaining to judicial cooperation in civil and commercial matters, authentic instruments are subject not only to enforcement, but also to recognition. Two prime examples of legal instruments that directly regulate the recognition of authentic instruments are Regulation (EU) No 650/2012[32] and Council Regulation (EU) 2019/1111.[33] The absence of provisions on the recognition of authentic instruments in the Brussels I bis Regulation does not influence the obligations flowing from authentic instruments, as their

[30] See Bores Lazo and Serrano Ron (2020).

[31] See Dymitruk et al. (2021), pp. 1–16.

[32] Regulation (EU) No. 650/2012 of the European Parliament and of the Council of 4 July 2012 on jurisdiction, applicable law, recognition and enforcement of decisions and acceptance and enforcement of authentic instruments in matters of succession and on the creation of a European Certificate of Succession, OJ L 201, 27.7.2012. See Article 59.

[33] Council Regulation (EU) 2019/1111 of 25 June 2019 on jurisdiction, the recognition and enforcement of decisions in matrimonial matters and the matters of parental responsibility, and on international child abduction, OJ L 178, 2.7.2019. See Article 65.

content is accepted.[34] Article 61 of the Brussels I bis Regulation abolishes any requirements pertaining to legalisation or other similar formalities required for documents issued in a Member State in the context of the regulation's scope of application. The abolition of legalisation and other equivalent requirements applies to each document issued in the context of the Brussels I bis Regulation. The expression, 'documents issued in a Member State in the context of this Regulation' shall be interpreted according to the view that is broadly shared in doctrine: that it includes authentic instruments.[35]

In conclusion, authentic instruments are ineligible for recognition in the Brussels I bis Regulation but are accepted. This entails a key effect in comparison with court judgments: the absence of regulation with regard to recognition means that the concept of mutual recognition cannot be transferred from judgements to authentic instruments; thus, authentic instruments do not produce a *res judicata* effect.[36]

5 Enforcement of Authentic Instruments

5.1 General Remarks

The Brussels I bis Regulation, not only forms the basis for enforcement of court judgments and court settlements, but also contains regulation on the enforcement of authentic instruments in Article 58. According to the regulation, an authentic instrument that is enforceable in its Member State of origin shall be enforceable in other Member States without the need for any declaration of enforceability. In the cases of judgments and of settlements, the Brussels I bis Regulation has abolished *exequatur.*[37] The mechanism, which is based on mutual confidence between Member States, also covers authentic instruments.[38] The condition of enforcement of an authentic instrument is enforceability in its Member State of origin.

As presented in doctrine, an assessment of the formal conditions of enforceability should verify whether an authentic document has fulfilled the formal requirements provided by its country of origin for a given authentic instrument; it should not be an assessment of the entirety of enforcement proceedings in that country.[39] An authentic instrument enforceable in its Member State of origin should be enforced under the same conditions as a domestic one.[40] Nevertheless, an authentic instrument that is going to be enforced should meet a series of formal requirements, which follows

[34] Vekas (2015), p. 984.

[35] Gołaczyński (2015), para 4.

[36] Fitchen and Kramer (2015), para 14.31.

[37] Martiny (2021), p. 142.

[38] See Schmon (2020), p. 20.

[39] Zatorska (2015).

[40] Kramer (2016), pp. 983–984.

from Article 60 of the Brussels I bis Regulation. Under this provision, the competent authority or court of the Member State of origin shall, at the request of any interested party, issue a certificate, in the format set out in Annex II, that contains a summary of the enforceable obligation recorded in the authentic instrument. The only formal conditions for the enforcement of an authentic instrument are its enforceability in the issuing country and the presentation of a certificate, which conforms to the conditions set out in Annex II, summarising the enforceable obligation that the authentic instrument records (and translation, if required).

Article 43 of Brussels I bis Regulation, in connection with Article 58 paragraph 1 of Brussels I bis Regulation seeks to protect debtors from entirely unexpected enforcement.[41] According to the provision, where enforcement is sought of an authentic instrument granted in another Member State, a certificate should be served on the person against whom enforcement is sought prior to the first enforcement measure. An authentic instrument must accompany such a certificate, if not already served on that person. A person against whom enforcement is sought who is domiciled in a Member State other than an authentic instrument's Member State of origin is entitled to request a translation of the authentic instrument to contest its enforcement if the authentic instrument is not written in, or accompanied by a translation into, either a language which he/she understands or the official language of the Member State in which he/she is domiciled. Where several official languages exist in a single Member State, the official language or one of the official languages of the place where he/she is domiciled may be used. This provision is intended to ensure protection for debtors: if a translation of an authentic instrument is requested, no measures of enforcement may be taken other than protective ones until that translation has been provided to the person against whom enforcement is sought.

An authentic instrument must meet conditions of authenticity in the Member State of origin, according to Article 58 par. 2 of the Brussels I bis Regulation. As presented above, in relation to the recognition of authentic instruments according to Article 61 of the Brussels I bis Regulation, any requirements pertaining to legalisation or other similar formalities have been abolished for the authentic instruments that are going to be the subject of enforcement under Brussels I bis Regulation.[42]

5.2 *Enforcement Refusal*

The Brussels I bis Regulation introduces only one base for refusal of enforcement of authentic instruments. According to Article 58 paragraph 1 of the Brussels I bis Regulation, enforcement of an authentic instrument may be refused only if such enforcement is manifestly contrary to public policy in the Member State of

[41] Fitchen (2020), p. 130.

[42] Gołaczyński (2015).

enforcement. As a result, the protection of the legal order of the state in which an authentic instrument is to be enforced has been adopted as the only ground for refusal of enforcement. Bases for rejection of the enforcement of authentic instruments conform to the current view expressed in paragraph 51 of the judgment of the Court of Justice of the European Union (CJEU) of 6.9.2012 in case C-619/10 Trade Agency Ltd v. Seramico Investments Ltd.[43] According to this finding, reliance on the public policy clause is admissible only where the recognition or enforcement of a judgment given in another Member State would unacceptably infringe the legal order of the requested Member State; in other words, that it would infringe on a fundamental principle. Such a breach should constitute a manifest failure to respect a rule of law regarded as essential to the legal order of the requested Member State, or a law recognised as fundamental in that legal order. As ruled in the judgment in Case C-7/98 Dieter Krombach v. André Bamberski, the court of an enforcement state cannot invoke the public policy clause in the case of a defendant domiciled in that state solely on the ground that the court of the issuing state has based its jurisdiction on the nationality of the victim. According to the decision of the Polish Supreme Court of 6 October 2011, V CSK 426/10,[44] the structural differences between notarial deeds drawn up in the Federal Republic of Germany containing an enforcement title ('die Zwangsvollstreckungsklausel'), regulated in Article 794.5 of the German Code of Civil Procedure (ZPO) and the notarial enforcement order provided for in the provisions of Article 777 paragraph 1 points 4 and 5 of the Polish Civil Procedure Code do not constitute grounds for considering that the execution of the German enforcement order in Poland would be contrary to the Polish legal order. This is an institution of procedural law known to both legal orders that has similar legal functions, i.e., enabling a creditor to obtain an enforcement order in a timely manner in the event of a failure to perform an obligation covered by such a title; minor procedural differences do not constitute a basis for the refusal of enforcement.

A basis for the refusal of enforcement of an authentic instrument in the Brussels I bis Regulation does not exclude application of the grounds for refusal under the national law of the requested Member State to the extent that has not led to an inconsistent base for refusal of an enforcement that follows from Article 58 paragraph 1 of the Brussels I bis Regulation. This follows from Article 41 paragraph. 2 of the Brussels I bis Regulation in connection with Article 58 paragraph 1 of the Brussels I bis Regulation.

[43]Case C-619/10, Trade Agency Ltd v. Seramico Investments Ltd, 06.09.2012, ECLI:EU:C:2012:531.

[44]Republic of Poland Supreme Court, V CSK 426/10, OSNC -ZD (2012).

6 Conclusion

Authentic instruments, as well as court judgments, are subject to automatic enforcement in other European Union Member States; thus, the *exequatur* procedure has been abolished with regard to authentic instruments, and they may constitute grounds for enforcement equal to judgments. In summary, the EU-En4s project has demonstrated that the notarial deed is the most common authentic instrument that may form a basis for enforcement in the Member States. In some countries, the catalogue of authentic instruments is more extensive; in others, authentic instruments generally do not appear in national law as a basis for enforcement. The Brussels I bis Regulation allows for the free and unlimited circulation of authentic instruments. Nevertheless, authentic instruments remain products of national law, which, for the purposes of their enforcement in another Member State, must be enforceable in the issuing state and conform to the definition of an authentic instrument under Article 2 (c) of the Brussels I bis Regulation. In light of the above, the question arises whether the *de lege ferenda* postulate can be formulated in an attempt to harmonise some authentic instruments in the European Union. From a practical perspective, it seems that attempts to harmonise regulation of notarial deeds in the Member States that may constitute a basis for the initiation of enforcement is particularly relevant.

References

Bores Lazo J, Serrano Ron I (2020) National report for Spain. Project EU-En4s — JUST-AG-2018/JUST-JCOO-AG-2018

Bylander E, Linton M (2020) National report for Sweden. Project EU-En4s — JUST-AG-2018/JUST-JCOO-AG-2018

Caramelo Gomes J, Marques Cebola C, Lucas E et al (2020) National report for Portugal. Project EU-En4s — JUST-AG-2018/JUST-JCOO-AG-2018

Christofi D, Loizou D (2022) National report for Cyprus. Project EU-En4s — JUST-AG-2018/JUST-JCOO-AG-2018

Council of Bars and Law Societies of Europe (2011) Comparative study on authentic acts and instruments with comparable status and effects according to national legislation within the EU, considering in particular the role of lawyers. https://www.ccbe.eu/NTCdocument/Report_Authentic_Act1_1302619714.pdf

Council of the Notariats of the European Union (2008) Comparative study on authentic instruments national provisions of private law, circulation, mutual recognition and enforcement, possible legislative initiative by the European Union. https://www.europarl.europa.eu/RegData/etudes/STUD/2008/408329/IPOL-JURI_ET(2008)408329_EN.pdf

Dymitruk M, Gołaczyński J, Kaczorowska M et al (2021) Differences between the recognition and enforcement of authentic instruments and the recognition and enforcement of judgments. Lexonomica 13(1):1–16

Fitchen J (2020) The private international law of authentic instruments. Hart Publishing

Fitchen J, Kramer X (2015) Authentic instruments and court settlements (Arts. 58-60). In: Dickinson A, Lein E (eds) The Brussels I Regulation Recast, pp 512–540

Gołaczyński J (ed) (2015) Jurysdykcja, uznawanie orzeczeń sądowych oraz ich wykonywanie w sprawach cywilnych i handlowych

Kaczorowska M, Voinich A, Previatello M (2022) National report for Italy. Project EU-En4s — JUST-AG-2018/JUST-JCOO-AG-2018
Kola Tafaj F (2020) National report for Albania. Project EU-En4s — JUST-AG-2018/JUST-JCOO-AG-2018
Kramer X (2015) In: Magnus U, Mankowski P (eds) Brussels I bis Regulation: Commentary. Otto Schmidt, Gologne, Germany, pp 982–988
Kramer X (2016) In: Magnus U, Mankowski P (eds) Brussels Ibis Regulation: Commentary. Otto Schmidt, Cologne, Germany, pp 982–988
Kunštek E, Kunda I, Mihelčić G et al (2020) National report for Croatia. Project EU-En4s — JUST-AG-2018/JUST-JCOO-AG-2018
Lietuvos Profesinu Sajungu Konfederacija, Labour dispute committee, https://www.lpsk.lt/en/legislation/labour-dispute-committee/
Martiny D (2021) The recognition and enforcement of court decisions between the EU and third state. In: Trunk A, Hatzimihai N (eds) EU civil procedure law and third countries. Nomos, pp 127–146
Naydenova D (2022) National report for Bulgaria. Project EU-En4s — JUST-AG-2018/JUST-JCOO-AG-2018
Ortwein B II (2003) The Swedish legal system: an introduction. Indiana Int Comp Law Rev 13(2): 405–445
Rijavec V, Baghrizabehi D, Drnovšek K et al (2020) National report for Slovenia. Project EU-En4s — JUST-AG-2018/JUST-JCOO-AG-2018
Schmon C (2020) The Interconnection of the EU Regulations Brussels I Recast and Rome I: Jurisdiction and Law
Valdhans J (2020) National report for Czech Republic. Project EU-En4s — JUST-AG-2018/JUST-JCOO-AG-2018
Zatorska J (2015) Komentarz do rozporządzenia nr 1215/2012 w sprawie jurysdykcji i uznawania orzeczeń sądowych oraz ich wykonywania w sprawach cywilnych i handlowych. https://sip.lex.pl/komentarze-i-publikacje/komentarze/komentarz-do-rozporzadzenia-nr-1215-2012-w-sprawie-jurysdykcji-i-587675212
Zoroska Kamilovska T, Rakočević M (2020) National report for North Macedonia. Project EU-En4s — JUST-AG-2018/JUST-JCOO-AG-2018
National report for France. Project EU-En4s — JUST-AG-2018/JUST-JCOO-AG-2018.

Part V
Other Cross-Border Considerations

Due Process and Cross-Border Enforcement in Lithuania and Portugal

Eugénio Pereira Lucas, Mykolas Kirkutis, Dalia Višinskytė, Remigijus Jokubauskas, and Darius Bolzanas

Abstract The chapter deals with the issues related to cross-border enforcement and due process in Lithuania and Portugal. It analyses how the concept of due process is defined by the national courts in both countries in cross-border civil cases and whether this interpretation is compatible with the case law of the European Court on Human Rights and Article 6 of the European Convention of Human Rights with establishes the general requirements of the right to a fair trial. Particularly the authors focus on the common problems of due process which arise in cross-border situation, such as service of documents, proper notification (summoning) of court hearings and equality of arms. The problems of service of documents arise when the national courts use methods of service of documents which results not in the direct service of documents to the addressee, but other persons. The authors found that pursuant to the national case law when assessing the appropriateness of service of documents in such cases, it must be determined whether the addressee was actually aware of the court proceeding initiated in a foreign country. Furthermore, the author analyze the application of public policy clause as the ground for non-recognition of judgments. The interpretation of the public policy clause by the national courts in Lithuania and Portugal is narrow. Lithuanian and Portuguese case law distinguish between procedural and substantive public policy. In practice procedural public policy is of great importance while substantive public policy does not play any considerable role. The authors found that the content of public policy is interpreted in accordance with the international principles of due process set out in the case law of the European Court on Human Rights and the case law of the Court of Justice of the European Union.

E. P. Lucas
Politécnico de Leiria, Leiria - IJP, Porto, Portugal
e-mail: eugenio.lucas@ipleiria.pt

M. Kirkutis · R. Jokubauskas (✉)
Mykolas Romeris University in Vilnius, Vilnius, Lithuania
e-mail: remigijus@jokubauskas.org

D. Višinskytė · D. Bolzanas
Mykolas Romeris University, Faculty of Law, Vilnus, Lithuania
e-mail: dalia.visinskyte@mids.ch

V. Rijavec et al. (eds.), *Diversity of Enforcement Titles in the EU*, Ius Gentium: Comparative Perspectives on Law and Justice 111,
https://doi.org/10.1007/978-3-031-47108-7_16

1 Introduction

A judgment of the court is an expression of state power. This power is normally limited to the territory of the state in which the judgment is rendered. Even today, enforcement of a foreign judgment in another state is still considered as an interference into the sovereignty of that state which is allowed under certain conditions intended to ensure that a foreign judgment can only be enforced if it is in accordance with the basic requirements of due process and public policy. However, social and economic reality requires states to accept judgments rendered in foreign states and ensure that such judgments are recognized and enforced.

Recognition and enforcement of foreign judgments means that their effects are extended from the Member State of origin to other states in which recognition (and enforcement) procedures are carried out and where they constitute a *res judicata* (final judgment) and preliminary ruling power. For a long time the enforcement of foreign judgments was based on the principle that a foreign judgment can be enforced in other states only after it has been recognized by the state in which the enforcement procedure is sought (so called *exequatur*). But this kind of enforcement procedure for foreign judgments in the European Union (with an economy based on a well-functioning domestic market and fundamental freedoms based on the free movement of persons, capital, goods and services) was not efficient. Therefore, with the adoption of the Brussels I bis Regulation, exequatur was abolished from European Union civil procedure law. Consequently, a judgment that becomes enforceable in the Member State of origin becomes enforceable in all other Member States and it should be enforced in accordance with the law of the executing State under the same conditions as a judgment given in the executing State. According to the case law of the Court of Justice of the European Union (thereinafter—CJEU), a foreign judgment must in principle have the same effects in the State in which recognition is sought as it does in the State of origin.[1]

Nevertheless, the Member States maintain sovereignty in the judicial sphere and grounds for non-recognition of foreign judgments remain in most European Union instruments related to civil and commercial matters. One of requirements for the acceptance of foreign judgments is their compatibility with the requirements of due process in the state of origin and failure to ensure this requirement may lead to a violation of the public policy of the state where enforcement is sought and the non-recognition of the judgment. Thus, the public policy exception aims to protect the sovereignty and the constitutional order of the state. This means, that public policy is a national concept (connected to the specific order of each Member State) which can change over time.[2] However, the Member States do not have absolute autonomy to determine the content of their public policy. Limits are placed on the

[1]Case C-456/11, Gothaer Allgemeine Versicherung AG and others v. Samskip GmbH, para 34, 15.11.2012, ECLI:EU:C:2012:719.

[2]Case C-41/74, Yvonne Van Duyn v. Home Office, para 18, 4.12.1974, ECLI:EU:C:1974:133.

content of public policy by the CJEU.[3] The issues related to the vagueness and problems of the application of public policy exception have been analyzed by various authors.[4]

Since Lithuania and Portugal are Member States of the European Union, the aim of this publication is to compare how the due process and public policy clause are applied in these countries. The interpretation of public policy is still closely connected with national regulations and fundamental principles of justice in the Member States which, consequently, could lead to different understandings of the content of public policy. The authors seek to assess whether these legal categories are understood in the same way in both the selected states, and what impact that has for the free movement of judgments in the European Union. It is important to understand whether the possibilities for enforcement of foreign judgments are the same in both Lithuania and Portugal, and if not to identify the main differences in this area.

2 Due Process in Lithuania

Due process is an important element in national and cross-border civil proceedings.[5] Failure to ensure due process in the proceedings in the Member State of origin may lead to ineffective enforcement proceedings in other Member States since the courts of those states may refuse to enforce a judgment if due process was not ensured.[6] Also, such a failure may lead to the liability of the Member State in proceedings in the European Court of Human Rights (hereinafter—ECtHR).

Due process in Lithuania is recognized as fundamental aspects of fair civil proceedings. Article 30 of the Constitution of the Republic of Lithuania ensures that a person whose constitutional rights or freedoms are violated has the right to apply to a court. Under Article 31 of the Constitution of the Republic of Lithuania, individuals are guaranteed the right to have their dispute heard by an independent and impartial tribunal in public. These are the fundamental provisions which establish access to the court and the main guarantees of the right to a fair trial.

---

[3]Case C-38/98, Régie nationale des usines Renault SA v Maxicar SpA and Orazio Formento, 11.05.2000, ECLI:EU:C:2000:225; Case C-7/98, Dieter Krombach v André Bamberski, 28.03.2000, ECLI:EU:C:2000:164, Case C-302/14, flyLAL-Lithuanian Airlines AS v Starptautiskā lidosta Rīga VAS and Air Baltic Corporation AS, 23.10.2014, ECLI:EU:C:2014:2319.

[4]Basedow (2021); Meyer (2022); Magnus Mankowski (2016); Dickinson et al. (2015).

[5]The Convention for the Protection of Human Rights and Fundamental Freedoms, Article 6(1); the Charter of Fundamental Rights of the European Union, Article 47; Regulation (EU) No 1215/2012 of the European Parliament and of the Council of 12 December 2012 on jurisdiction and the recognition and enforcement of judgments in civil and commercial matters (recast), Recital 38; Dickinson et al. (2015).

[6]The Brussels I bis Regulation, Article 45(1).

According to the Constitutional Court of Lithuania, due process is based on equality before the court, publicity, adversarial proceedings, the right to be heard in the court and other universally recognized democratic principles. In resolving a conflict, the court as a public authority renders a judgment (an act of justice). When hearing a dispute and rendering a judgment the court shall rely on procedural rules which should ensure that the procedural guarantee of the right to a fair trial for all the parties is respected. One of those rules requires the court to use clear and convincing reasons for its decision when determining the rights and obligations of a person. For a person who disagrees with a court's decision against him, the law guarantees the possibility of an appeal against that decision through the court hierarchy.[7] Thus, the requirement of due process is complex and involves a number of significant procedural guarantees which should be ensured.

A due process is also based on equality before the tribunal, publicity, adversarial proceedings, the right to be heard in court and other universally recognized democratic principles.[8] Justice is administered by applying special procedural forms whose purpose is to ensure the rights of a person in court proceedings, to facilitate the establishment of the real circumstances of a case and to make a fair decision. In civil proceedings, the principle of equality of persons before the court manifests itself as the principle of procedural equality. A dispute between equal parties to the proceedings, in which each of the parties to the proceedings has equal opportunities, constitutes the essence of civil proceedings.[9] Also, the court has emphasized that the procedural rights of the parties are equal. The rights of one party correspond to the rights of the other party. For example, the plaintiff has the right to bring an action, the defendant has the right to defend himself against that action by filing defences to the plaintiff's claim or by filing a counterclaim. It is important that the principle of equality of arms is observed at all stages of the proceedings, as the implementation of other procedural principles also depends on respect for the principle of equality.[10] Thus, when the court resolves a dispute, there is an assurance that all parties enjoy the guarantee of the constitutional right to due process (the person applying to the court and the person defending himself or herself from the claim). The court must provide them with equal and adequate opportunities to exercise the procedural rights established by law in defence of their rights and legitimate interests.

The case law of the ECtHR when interpreting the right to a fair trial is also relevant for the national understanding of due process. The right to a fair trial is inseparable from a person's right to be heard in court and includes the right to be aware of the claims against him and to file responses to them, and in order to exercise this right, the person must first be duly informed, in accordance with the procedure established by law, about the court proceedings that have been initiated and the content of procedural documents. The right to be informed of the proceedings and to

[7] Decision of the Constitutional Court of the Republic of Lithuania, 1.10.1997.

[8] *Ibid.*

[9] Decision of the Constitutional Court of the Republic of Lithuania, 18.04.1996.

[10] Decision of the Constitutional Court of the Republic of Lithuania, 19.12.1996.

be heard is an integral part of the right to a fair trial and civil proceedings must ensure the effective exercise of the right to a fair trial by both parties to the dispute.[11] In assessing whether the public authorities have ensured adequate protection of the rights of the individual, the ECtHR takes into account whether the public authorities have made all possible (best) efforts to locate the person involved in the proceedings. Another important criterion for a court to decide on a violation of the right to a fair trial is whether the person whose case has been heard in his or her absence has an available remedy at national level, i.e., whether he can effectively challenge the lawfulness of the proceedings in his absence.[12]

Following the guidance of the case law of the ECtHR, the Supreme Court of Lithuania has emphasized that a procedural situation where a decision is rendered in absentia without proper notification of the other party to the dispute is not permitted.[13] The court found that the right of a person to be informed about the proceedings and to be heard in court is an integral part of his right to due process, and that civil proceedings must ensure the effective and real exercise of the right to a fair trial by both parties to the dispute. Therefore, the rules of civil procedure must be interpreted and applied in such a way that the result achieved does not conflict with these principles. This case is important because according to Article 287 (1) of the Code of Civil Procedure of the Republic of Lithuania (hereinafter 'CCP') a person against whom a decision was rendered in absentia has the right to request a review of it within 20 days of the decision, and if more than 3 months have passed since the decision was rendered, the court is not entitled to renew the missed deadline. The Supreme Court reasonably deviated from mandatory regulation and gave priority to due process. This means that the principle of due process is more important than mandatory regulation and deviation from national mandatory regulation is justified when it is pursued to guarantee the person's right to a fair trial and due process.

Another important question may arise when the due process category is examined: the question whether the party to a dispute has equal guarantees in civil proceeding, especially when the case is re-examined, and he remains passive throughout the whole reopened proceeding. For example, in one case the applicant questioned the length of the trial, arguing that the retrial of the case had lasted for more than a year and a half during which the court had adjourned several hearings, and that the case had been reopened without any legal basis. The applicant alleged that during the retrial after he had clarified the claim, the defendant had not submitted any response which constituted a default judgment, but the court had not rendered the judgment in absentia and had substantially and unreasonably reopened the case tolerating the defendant's absence for no reason. In this case the appeal court recognized that courts must be active in correcting errors and that referring the case back to the court of first instance for re-examination must be reasonable and justified so that the case can be heard as soon as possible. However, the court also

[11] Nunes Dias. v. Portugal, no. 69829/01, Eur.Ct. H.R., 2003-IV.

[12] *Ibid.*

[13] Decision of the Supreme Court of Lithuania, 7.12.2012, no. 3K-3-551/2012.

noted that the circumstances relied on by the applicant did not presuppose the illegality of the proceedings and were not legally relevant to the question of the legality and merits of the judgment of the court of first instance.[14]

Also, the requirements of due process demand a guarantee that the parties can defend their rights effectively in civil proceedings. In one case a breach of due process was found because the court did not ensure that one of the parties to the dispute would be represented by a lawyer. The court of appeal found that due to the poor health of the applicant he should have been assisted by a qualified representative, and that his (the attorney's) absence was a breach of the principle of due process.[15] This means that the right to have a qualified representative is also an integral aspect of due process. Thus, the court must be satisfied that a party acting in the proceedings without a representative will be able to represent himself properly. If there are doubts about a party's abilities to defend himself properly, the court should ask the party if he would like to find a qualified representative and if the party wants to do this, court should allow enough time for such party to find an attorney.

Only certain forms of representation in court are in line with the principle of a fair trial. According to Article 56(1)(4) of the CCP, representatives of natural persons may, by court order, be persons with a higher university legal education, when they represent their close relatives or spouse (cohabitant). The mandatory nature of legal education is determined by the specific features of the institution of representation, which requires that the representative, even when representing a close relative or spouse, has special legal knowledge to ensure adequate protection of the rights and interests protected by law and the right to a fair trial.[16]

In the authors' opinion, due process also encompasses the court's actions. The court, as the entity governing the proceedings, must ensure fairness in the decision-making process. For example, in the case law of the Supreme Court of Lithuania, a lack of due process was also recognized when a procedural document (a response to a complaint) was not included in the case file prepared by the first instance court due to an error of the court clerk. The court found that the court of appeal violated not only the party's right to be heard, to submit arguments in response to a separate complaint, and to exercise other rights established by the CCP, but also the principle of equality of arms, thus violating one party's right to a fair trial.[17] Also, the court has an obligation to ensure the language guarantee is respected throughout the proceedings (Article 11 of the CCP). The proper implementation of the principles regulating the language of court proceedings also applies in relation to other principles of civil procedure—adversarial proceedings, oral procedure, procedural equality of arms, directness, right to be heard, and right to appeal as a condition of enforcement. However, a violation of the principles governing the language of court

[14]Decision of the Klaipėda Regional Court, 3.02.2017, no. 2A-119-459/2017.

[15]Decision of the Šiauliai Regional Court, 22.12.2014, no. 2S-1070-267/2014.

[16]Decision of the Supreme Court of Lithuania, 2.03.2019, no. e3K-3-181-219/2019.

[17]Decision of the Supreme Court of Lithuania, 8.07.2021, no. 3K-3-222-611/2021.

proceedings is a ground for the annulment of a court decision if an appeal or cassation appeal is based on this circumstance.

Another important aspect of due process is the right to know about the proceedings and to be able to prepare an effective defence. The importance of a proper notification of civil proceedings has also been recognized in case law as an aspect of due process. For example, regarding the peculiarities of the service of procedural documents on a legal person, the Supreme Court of Lithuania has stated that, before applying the fiction of service of documents established in Article 123(4) of the CCP, the court must take measures to serve procedural documents on legal persons at other addresses known to the court. In the case of a failure to serve a procedural document at the registered office of the legal person, the court must use other reasonable means available to it, such as sending documents to the addresses of other parties to the case, to the residence of the head of the administration of the legal person, electronic means of service, etc.[18] In another case, the court found that, in accordance with Article 123(4) of the CPC, a procedural document may be served: (1) on any other employee of the legal person at the place of service; (2) the head of the administration as a natural person; (3) a member of the management body as a natural person; (4) an adult family member of the head of the administration as a natural person; (5) an adult family member of a member of the management body as a natural person.[19] If it is not possible to serve a procedural document at the registered office of the legal person in the Register of Legal Entities, service on the head of the administration or members of the management body specified in the Register of Legal Entities as natural persons, as well as adult family members is considered appropriate.[20] Thus, according to the relevant case law, the service of a procedural document at the address of the residence of the head of administration of the legal person as a natural person is an appropriate procedural measure, taking into account the legal position of the head of the legal person.[21]

One of the difficulties in cross-border civil proceedings is service of documents. The problematic issues of cross-border services of documents and the application of Regulation No 1393/2007 on Service of documents[22] (hereinafter—Regulation No. 1393/2007) have also arisen in the case law of Lithuanian court. The problems of service of documents and due process have been addressed in legal literature.[23] One such problematic issue in cross-border service of documents and protection of due process is the right to know and understand about court proceedings in another

[18] Decision of the Supreme Court of Lithuania, 21.03.2019, no. e3K-7-16-313/2019.

[19] Decision of the Supreme Court of Lithuania, 17.03.2004, no. 3K-3-202/2004.

[20] Decision of the Supreme Court of Lithuania, 29.11.2012, no. 3K-3-534/2012.

[21] Decision of the Supreme Court of Lithuania, 6.04.2020, no. 3K-3-36-695/2020.

[22] Regulation (EC) No 1393/2007 of the European Parliament and of the Council of 13 November 2007 on the service in the Member States of judicial and extrajudicial documents in civil or commercial matters (service of documents), and repealing Council Regulation (EC) No 1348/2000 OJ L 324.

[23] Jokubauskas (2019); Jokubauskas et al. (2020); von Hein and Kruger (2021).

country. This element of due process requires that the defendant shall be aware of the proceedings instituted against him (her) and understand the subject matter of the dispute and thus have the possibility to prepare an effective defence. The right of the addressee to refuse to have a document served on him is linked with the essence of due process (fair trial).[24]

In one case[25] the Court of Appeal of Lithuania had to deal with the question whether the failure to translate the annexes of the claim into the defendants' native language violated their right to due process. In this case a pilot training school sued the defendants, Portuguese nationals who had trained to become pilots in this school, for debt for the provided services. The claim was translated into the defendants' native language (Portuguese), but the annexes to the claim were served on the defendants in English. Therefore, the defendants refused to accept the documents sent to them. In this case, the court considered the fact that the contract concluded by the parties was drafted in English and signed by the defendant. However, it was also established that the defendants had an English language proficiency test certificate for their professional exam, and in their resume it was stated that they knew English language very well. Thus, the court stated that the documents were served properly, and the defendant refused to accept them without a reason.

Also, the Lithuanian Court of Appeal recognized as improper service of documents a situation where the procedural documents were served through the Embassy of the Republic of Lithuania in the Kingdom of Spain. In this case the first instance court sent the claim and annexes to the addressee (a Lithuanian national) via diplomatic channels. Later the first instance court received a letter by fax from the Embassy of the Republic of Lithuania in the Kingdom of Spain informing ir that the procedural documents were sent to the defendant by registered mail, and that according to the postal data they were served, but the embassy did not receive the document (confirming the receipt of the documents) signed by the addressee.[26] The first instance court found that such service of documents was lawful and settled the case without the appearance of the defendant in court. After the decision was rendered, the defendant filed a claim to re-examine the case since he was not aware of it. The first instance court dismissed the request and the appeal against this decision was lodged with the appeal court. The Court of Appeal of Lithuania found that the first instance court failed to ensure that the defendant was informed properly about proceedings initiated against him and the first instance court failed to analyse whether the defendant was actually aware of the proceedings, since the ambassy merely noted that the documents were served without any proof of actual service.

The national case law of Lithuanian courts suggests that when assessing the appropriateness of service of documents in such cases, it must be determined whether the addressee was actually aware of the court proceeding initiated in a

[24] von Hein and Kruger (2021), p. 19.

[25] Decision of the Court of Appeal of Lithuania, 22.02.2018, no. e2-239-464/2018.

[26] Decision of the Court of Appeal of Lithuania, 15.03.2018, no. e2-329-302/2018.

foreign country.[27] Thus, it should be established whether a person against whom legal proceedings were initiated in a foreign country was informed about the proceedings at least once in a timely manner and in a way that allowed him to understand the essence of the claim.[28] Documents may not be always served on a person in accordance with all existing formal rules, but they should certainly be served in advance and in such a way that the defendant can effectively defend his rights in court. The purpose of such an interpretation is to deprive a party of the opportunity to abuse his procedural rights in such a way that he does not participate in the trial of the dispute in court on the grounds that his notification of the start of the proceedings had formal procedural defects.[29]

Due process in Lithuania is interpreted broadly to ensure the effective and efficient exercise of the rights and obligations of all parties involved in civil proceedings. The national courts consider the requirement of due process, because the breach of the due process principle may lead to an inability to enforce the resulting judgment in another Member State even if the international nature of the dispute does not exist at the time of the proceedings. One of the main problematic issues especially in cross-border cases is service of documents which is key for the fairness of the proceedings.

3 Due Process in Portugal

As in Lithuania due process is a fundamental aspect of fair civil proceedings in Portugal. Article 20 and 268 of the Portuguese Constitution (thereinafter—CRP) establish various aspects related to due process, namely access to law and effective judicial protection. Thus, in the Portuguese legal system, due process has a constitutional expression and not just a legal one. As a constitutional norm, due process has a constitutional supremacy that the infra-constitutional norms must be in accordance and with which the other constitutional norms must harmonize. These rules are directly applicable to all entities (public and private), according to article 20 of the CRP.

Due process incorporates the guarantee of access to law and justice as an expression of both procedural guarantees (procedural due process) and the prerogatives incorporated into substantive law (substantive due process).

The right to access to the court is guaranteed by a fair process, which includes the right to file an action, the right to process, the right to a decision and the right to the execution of the court decision. Due process of law in a procedural sense is not only a guarantee of means, but also a guarantee of results.

---

[27] Decision of Court of Appeal of Lithuania, 3.09.2012, no. 2T-20/2012.

[28] Decision of the The Supreme Court of Lithuania, 5.10.2009, no. 3K-3-375/2009.

[29] Decision of the Court of Appeal of Lithuania, 29.10.2013, no. 2T-57/2013.

Article 20 of the CRP guarantees that everyone has the right to access the law and the courts in order to defend those of their rights and interests that are protected by law, and that justice may not be denied to anyone due to lack of sufficient financial means.[30]

The CRP also guarantees that, according to the law, everyone has the right to legal information and advice, to legal counsel and to be accompanied by a lawyer before any authority,[31] and that the law shall define and ensure adequate protection of the secrecy of legal proceedings.[32]

It is equally established that everyone has the right to receive a decision in every case in which they are intervening, within a reasonable time limit and by means of fair process,[33] and for the purpose of defending their personal rights, freedoms and guarantees. In order to defend personal rights, freedoms and guarantees, the law assures to the citizens judicial procedures characterized by their swiftness and priority, in order to obtain effective and timely protection against threats or violations of these rights.[34]

The adversarial principle is fundamental to guarantee the effective participation of the parties in litigation, ensuring that they can participate in all stages of the process relevant to the final decision (facts, evidence, questions of law). As a rule, this principle prohibits the court from rendering decisions on grounds on which the parties have not had the opportunity to present their arguments. This principle is established in article 3 of the Code of Civil Procedure (hereinafter CPC).

Equally relevant is the principle of equality, which establishes the obligation that all parties must enjoy same rights, and any arbitrary discrimination is prohibited.

Thus, article 20 of the CRP establishes several interconnected, although distinct rights. These rights are the right of access to law, the right of access to the courts, the right to legal information and consultation, the right to legal aid, and the right to legal counsel.

The right to access to the court and to effective judicial protection is an essential guarantee of the protection of fundamental rights, being, therefore, inherent in the idea of the rule of law which is established in article 20 of the CRP and article 6 of the Treaty on European Union. In this regard, Gomes Canotilho and Vital Moreira state that "Due process as established in the Portuguese Constitution must be understood in a broad sense, not only as a fair process in its legislative conformation (. . .), but also as a process materially informed by substantive principles of justice in its various procedural moments".[35]

According to article 18 (1) of the CRP, the constitutional provisions concerning rights, freedoms and guarantees are directly applicable and thus the provisions of

[30] Constitution of the Portuguese Republic, 2.04.1976, Artile 20(1).

[31] Ibid., Article 20(2).

[32] Ibid., Article 20(3).

[33] Ibid., Article 20(4).

[34] Ibid., Article 20 (5).

[35] Canotilho and Moreira (2007), p. 415.

article 20 of the CRP on access to law and effective judicial protection, are also directly applicable. As these rules are of immediate execution, the judge must, if necessary, fill any legal gaps that may be encountered in the application process with these constitutional provisions.

But for its effective application this constitutionally guaranteed right requires implementation through legal institutions, requiring, therefore, that the State provides such institutions, in order to make available to citizens a judicial organization and a range of processes that guarantee the stipulated effective judicial protection.

As a result of these different rights, contradictory situations may be identified, such as the need to balance the relationship between the adversarial principle and the principle of a timely judicial protection (procedural celerity). This balancing exercise may lead to a limitation of the adversarial principle, which is not an absolute principle, and which must be interpreted in relation to other principles, namely the principle of a timely judicial protection.

Likewise, the principle of timely judicial protection cannot override the principle of material truth, or the principle of procedural equality, and the process may take longer to ensure these other principles.

The jurisprudence of the Portuguese Constitutional Court (hereinafter TC) relating to procedural due process has, as a rule, always been based on the object of extensive interpretation. Some examples of the relevant case law are presented below.

The TC recognizes that the right of access to law is distinct from, although connected to, the right of access to the courts, the right to legal information and consultation and the right to legal aid. All of these are seen as part of the essential content of the right to due process, and the TC requires the legislator to ensure the enjoyment of these rights.[36]

As to the right to legal counsel and to be accompanied by a lawyer before any authority, the TC considers it to be an essential element of the administration of justice and an essential element of the constitutional guarantee of access to law and to the courts,[37] and these rights are not restricted to Portuguese citizens but also extend to foreigners and stateless persons.[38]

The TC also considers that any procedural rules or procedures that imply an inadmissible reduction in the defendant's opportunities to conduct his defence should be considered illegitimate.[39]

---

[36] Judgment of the Constitutional Tribunal of Portugal, no. 661/94, https://www.tribunalconstitucional.pt/tc/acordaos/19940661.html.

[37] Ibid; Judgment of the Constitutional Tribunal of Portugal, no. 106/04, https://www.tribunalconstitucional.pt/tc/acordaos/20040106.html.

[38] Judgment of the Constitutional Tribunal of Portugal, no. 216/95, https://www.tribunalconstitucional.pt/tc/acordaos/19950216.html; Judgment of the Constitutional Tribunal of Portugal, no. 208/04, https://www.tribunalconstitucional.pt/tc/acordaos/20040208.html.

[39] Judgment of the Constitutional Tribunal of Portugal, no. 337/86, https://www.tribunalconstitucional.pt/tc/acordaos/19860337.html.

Regarding access to the appellate courts, the TC established that the limitations on appeal, for example, non-appealability due to the jurisdiction (e.g., article 678 of the CPC) does not affect the right to a fair trial, does not give rise to inequalities and does not configure discrimination because after all actions contained within a given jurisdiction receive the same treatment.[40]

Regarding the duration of the process, the extension of the limitation period, due to the lasting interruptive effect without justification, is understood by the TC that it constitutes a disproportionate procedural presupposition, in direct violation of the principle of due process of law.[41]

In an analysis of the substantive aspect of due process, the principle of proportionality is used as a mechanism to combat the abuse of governmental power.

The TC has repeatedly stated that the constitutional acceptance of the principle of proportionality was unchallenged, at least since 1982[42] and the TC has successively recognized the constitutional value of the principle of proportionality.[43]

According to Gomes Canotilho and Vital Moreira the principle of proportionality unfolds into three subprinciples: (a) principle of adequacy, that is, the legally foreseen restrictive measures must reveal themselves as an adequate means to the pursuit of the ends covered by the law (safeguarding other constitutionally protected rights or assets); (b) principle of enforceability, that is, the restrictive measures provided for in the law must prove necessary (became enforceable), because the purposes pursued by the law could not be obtained by other means less onerous for rights, freedoms and guarantees); (c) principle of proportionality in the strict sense, which means that the restrictive legal means and the ends obtained must be situated in a 'fair measure', preventing the adoption of restrictive legal measures that are disproportionate, excessive, in relation to the ends obtained.[44]

The TC concludes that the application of the principle of proportionality was initially restricted to the conformation of acts of public authorities and the protection of fundamental rights, but there was a subsequent and progressive extension of the

[40] Judgment of the Constitutional Tribunal of Portugal, no. 287/90, https://www.tribunalconstitucional.pt/tc/acordaos/19900287.html; Judgment of the Constitutional Tribunal of Portugal, no. 239/97, https://www.tribunalconstitucional.pt/tc/acordaos/19970239.html.

[41] Judgment of the Constitutional Tribunal of Portugal, no. 411/10, https://www.tribunalconstitucional.pt/tc/acordaos/20100411.html.

[42] Judgment of the Constitutional Tribunal of Portugal, no. 302/01, https://www.tribunalconstitucional.pt/tc/acordaos/20010302.html.

[43] Judgment of the Constitutional Tribunal of Portugal, no. 25/84, https://www.tribunalconstitucional.pt/tc/acordaos/19840025.html; Judgment of the Constitutional Tribunal of Portugal, no. 958/96, https://www.tribunalconstitucional.pt/tc/acordaos/19960958.html; Judgment of the Constitutional Tribunal of Portugal, no. 476/20, https://www.tribunalconstitucional.pt/tc/acordaos/20200476.html; Judgment of the Constitutional Tribunal of Portugal, no. 31/21, https://www.tribunalconstitucional.pt/tc/acordaos/20210031.html.

[44] Canotilho and Moreira (2007), p. 153.

relevance of such principle to other legal realities and can be applied in the field of legal-private relations.[45]

4 Public Policy in Lithuania

Public policy is generally considered to be a safeguard against gross injustice in the national courts of the Member States of the EU, allowing the application of European private law and national standards of fairness in an international context.[46] It is recognized that a public policy clause may also include a procedural aspect that protects the parties' right to due process. If the right to a fair trial was not respected in the process of rendering the judgment it might be the basis for non-recognition of the judgment and incompatibility with the public policy of the State in which recognition and enforcement is sought.[47]

In Lithuanian case law the distinction between procedural and material public policy is made. According to the relevant case law, the public policy exception is divided into procedural and substantive. Also, it has been constantly emphasized that the different interpretation and application of substantive law is not regarded as the violation of public policy. For instance, the fact that a national court deciding on the non-recognition of a judgment would apply a different rule of law to resolve a dispute between individuals in a different way is not a sufficient ground for not recognising a judgment given in another Member State. The fundamental problem with the substantive public policy clause, however, is its relationship to morality. It is generally argued that fundamental principles of morality can be attributed to a substantive public policy clause. However, the content of public order, and morality, is so vague and varied that their application requires special attention.[48]

Lithuanian case law recognizes that public policy may be invoked when the recognition or enforcement of a foreign judgment in the Republic of Lithuania would be incompatible with its legal system and would pose a risk to the fundamental principles of law. In such cases, the risk should arise from a manifest infringement of a rule of law which is considered to be fundamental in the legal system of the State in which the recognition and enforcement of the foreign judgment is questioned or which is considered to be fundamental in that legal system.[49] The notion of public policy is interpreted as international public policy which includes the fundamental principles of fair trial as well as the imperative norms of law which enshrine fundamental and universally recognized principles of

---

[45] Judgment of the Constitutional Tribunal of Portugal, no. 302/01, https://www.tribunalconstitucional.pt/tc/acordaos/20010302.html.

[46] Decision of the Supreme Court of Lithuania, 8.04.2015, no. 3K-3-197-611/2015.

[47] Decision of the Supreme Court of Lithuania, 6.05.2020, no. 3K-3-144-684/2020.

[48] Kirkutis and Višinskis (2021), p. 80.

[49] Decision of the Court of Appeal of Lithuania, 9.07.2013, no. 2T-49/2013.

law.[50] Thus, in Lithuanian case law public policy as a ground for non-recognition of foreign judgments is interpreted strictly.

The purpose of public order is to protect the basic, vital interests of the state and society. In other words, the concept of public policy includes the basic principles on which the legal system of the state, the functioning of the state and society are based.[51] Thus, public policy must be interpreted more narrowly than national public policy and include the imperative standards and principles adopted in international practice. Such violations of public order may be recognized in cases where it is established that the recognition and enforcement of a judgment of a foreign state would conflict with the fundamental principles of law and moral norms enshrined in the Constitution of the Republic of Lithuania and recognized at the international level.

When the application for non-recognition of a foreign judgment is submitted, the court assesses the compatibility of a foreign judgment with the public order of the Republic of Lithuania only by analyzing the compatibility of the foreign court judgment with the public order of the Republic of Lithuania and not of other states.[52] Compliance with the public order of the Republic of Lithuania shall be verified only by analyzing the impact of the consequences of the recognized foreign judgment to the public order of the Republic of Lithuania. Such analysis requires assessment whether enforcement of a foreign judgment would (not) violate the public order of the Republic of Lithuania.[53]

One of the aspects of public policy in Lithuania is fair commercial practice regarding amount of penalties (a fine or forfeit) in violation of a contract. This relates to the substantive aspects of public policy since such penalties are established in the civil law and are understood as a form of civil liability. The issue arises when the court in the foreign state established a significant amount of penalty against the party which breached the contract. In Lithuanian civil law such penalties should serve only are compensations to the minimum damage, but not punitive damages against the party which violated the contract. This rationale is based on the need to ensure that civil liability only has compensatory, but not the punitive function. For instance, the Court of Appeal of Lithuania acknowledged that the principle of fairness is a part of the public policy of international and Lithuanian law. Interpreting the provisions of Articles 1(2) and 1(5) of the Civil Code of the Republic of Lithuania and the institute of unjust enrichment (usury) of one of the parties, the court acknowledged that essential principles of economic and commercial activity are established in the Republic of Lithuania and civil law relations conditions and the attractiveness of fair business practices and a transparent business environment the size of the fines that have nothing to do with their purpose.[54] In another case the

[50] Decision of the Supreme Court of Lithuania, 7.03.2006, no. 3K-7-179/2006.

[51] Decision of the Supreme Court of Lithuania, 30.09.2008, no. 3K-3-443/2008.

[52] Decision of the Court of Appeal of Lithuania, 5.02.2020, no. 2T-18-943/2020.

[53] Jokubauskas et al. (2020), pp. 295–296.

[54] Decision of the Court of Appeal of Lithuania, 10.12 2013, no. 2T-75/2013.

Court of Appeal of Lithuania found that he amount of default interest imposed is not and cannot be considered a breach of public order. The court followed a similar interpretation of the law in other similar cases. The court held that an important factor was that the amount of default interest was determined by agreement between the parties, who were free to agree on the nature and amount of liability for non-performance of contractual obligations.[55] Therefore, the amount of default interest is not in itself a breach of public policy. It is also necessary to assess the entities and their ability to negotiate the terms of liability.

The substantive public policy also includes of the fundamental and basic values enshrined in the Constitution of the Republic of Lithuania, such as protection of private (family) life, the best interests of the child, as well as the basic principles of a fair trial. Public policy is also linked to the basic principles of private law relations, which prohibit the use of usury. Therefore, courts applying the public policy clause must be guided by the principles of freedom of contract and the will and value of the parties in concluding the contract.[56] International public policy which is relevant to legal relations extending beyond one state, is a much narrower system of mandatory legal norms that must be observed in all cases, even when a certain legal relationship is governed by the legal norms of a foreign state.[57]

To sum up, public policy as a ground for non-recognition of foreign judgments is interpreted more narrowly than national public policy. The public policy is divided into procedural and substantial. The content of public policy is interpreted in accordance with the international principles of due process set out in the case law of the ECtHR interpreting the provisions of the Convention and in the case law of the CJEU interpreting the related provisions of EU regulations in civil matters.

5 Public Policy in Portugal

As in Lithuania, in Portugal, the case law recognizes that public policy may be invoked when the recognition or enforcement of a foreign judgment in the Republic of Portugal would be incompatible with its legal system and would jeopardize fundamental principles of law. The main idea is that a foreign judgment shall not be recognized or enforced if such recognition is manifestly contrary to the public policy of Portugal.

The first problem that arises here is undoubtedly linked to the indeterminate nature of international public policy in the Portuguese legal system. In fact, we are facing an indeterminate concept and it is not possible (nor desirable) to proceed to its definition.[58]

---

[55] Jokubauskas et al. (2020), pp. 114–115.

[56] Kirkutis and Jokubauskas (2020), p. 200.

[57] Jokubauskas et al. (2020), pp. 114–120.

[58] de Lima and Varela (1987), pp. 69–251.

The concept of international public policy is not defined in the law or in international conventions. It results more from an assessment of the fundamental principles and content on which the legal, economic, political, social and ethical order of a given national community is based rather than from the existence of a written or common law.

With this constraint in Portugal, the international public policy concept is wider than the Portuguese public policy concept, and there is a greater tolerance for the rules of the foreign legal system in order to allow for the difference between the various international legal orders,[59] but always ensuring that the Portuguese judge has the means that will allow him/her to rule out the decision of a foreign State, when it violates the principle of international public policy.

Under the terms of Regulation (EU) No 1215/2012, each Member State of the European Union may refuse the recognition of a judgment if such recognition is manifestly contrary to public policy (ordre publique) in the Member State addressed.[60]

The Portuguese Supreme Court (hereinafter STJ) defines the concept of international public policy as being vague, fluid and imprecise and considers that it can be designated as an amalgamation of basic values and dominant conceptions of a social, ethical, political and economic nature expressed in principles and rules that the applicator must, at each historical moment, interpret and recognize.[61]

In practice, the application of this ground for refusal has been exceptional and, in principle, the foreign decisions there are more likely to run into this limitation would be the decisions issued under substantive laws of legal systems different from the Portuguese legal system, than in States with which they share the same historical influences, as well as fundamental principles, and social and economic contexts.

The STJ considers that the offense of public order can be a violation of certain groups of norms: (i) the substantive public order, when it involves the violation of principles and norms of substantive law or of private international law (e.g. mandatory norms on competition); or (ii) the procedural public order, when principles and norms of procedural law are violated (e.g. the right to a fair trial, the duty to justify decisions, the adversarial principle, the guarantee of the impartiality of the court).[62]

The Regulation (EC) No 44/2001 stated that a foreign judgment shall not be recognized such recognition is manifestly contrary to the public policy of the

---

[59] Moura Ramos (2002), pp. 248–249; de Magalhães Collaço (1959), p. 422.

[60] Article 45 (1) (a) in conjunction with Article 46 of Brussels I bis Regulation.

[61] Decision of the Portuguese Supreme Court, no. 1036/12.4YRLSB.S1, http://www.dgsi.pt/jstj.nsf/954f0ce6ad9dd8b980256b5f003fa814/5b7762ab568fa1b080257d7a005445ca?OpenDocument&Highlight=0,1036%2F12.4YRLSB.S1.

[62] Decision of the Portuguese Supreme Court, no. 736/14.9TVLSB.L1.S1, http://www.dgsi.pt/jstj.nsf/954f0ce6ad9dd8b980256b5f003fa814/dd62e71d5e970e6b802581160039d63b?OpenDocument.

enforcement State.[63] In 2010 the proposal of the Commission suggested introducing a uniform European standard for procedural public policy, but this ground for review has remained unchanged under the Regulation (EU) No 1215/2012.[64] Thus, the courts of the enforcement State will always have the right to apply their own national concept of public policy.

The limits of the national courts is inspired by the ECHR, namely its article 6 (1).[65] The case law of the European Court of Justice (hereinafter CJEU) does not define the cases whether the national court must refuse enforcement, but only whether a national court may refuse enforcement on a particular procedural ground, if the violated principle of national public policy has sufficient weight with regard to European standards, in particular under the standards of the ECHR. For example, the CJEU has accepted the refusal of enforcement in a case where the court of origin excluded the defendant from further participating in the proceedings and considered that that exclusion measure constituted a manifest and disproportionate infringement of the defendant's right to be heard,[66] or where the court of origin refused to hear the defendant's representative when the defendant did not appear in person.[67]

The international public policy of the Portuguese State is an exception to the acceptance of application of the substantive rules and sentences of foreign legal system that will have to be understood restrictively.[68]

6 Conclusions

Due process plays a central role in the process of fostering the process of cross-border enforcement in the European Union. It is enshrined in the Constitutions of Lithuania and Portugal and it is applied by the respective constitutional courts to guarantee the fundamental procedural rights of litigants. Thus, due process has a constitutional supremacy that the infra-constitutional norms must comply with and with which the other constitutional norms must harmonize.

At a European Union level the article 47 of the EU Charter of Fundamental Rights stipulates that everyone is entitled to a fair and public hearing within a reasonable time by an independent and impartial tribunal previously established by law (this principle is incorporated into the substance of EU law and applicable by the CJEU),

---

[63] Article 34(1), Regulation (EC) No 44/2001 of 22 December 2000, on jurisdiction and the recognition and enforcement of judgments in civil and commercial matters.

[64] Article 45(1)(a) of Brussels I bis Regulation.

[65] Case C-7/98, Dieter Krombach v André Bamberski, 28.03.2000, ECLI:EU:C:2000:164, paras 22–27.

[66] Case C-394/07, Marco Gambazzi v DaimlerChrysler Canada Inc. and CIBC Mellon Trust Company, 2.04.2009, ECLI:EU:C:2009:219.

[67] Case C-7/98, Dieter Krombach v André Bamberski, 28.03.2000, ECLI:EU:C:2000:164.

[68] de Lima Pinheiro (2015), p. 659.

and the article 6(1) of the ECHR. Since Lithuania and Portugal are the Member States, these provisions are also applicable in the national case law of these states.

Lithuanian and Portuguese case law, distinguish between procedural and substantive public policy. In practice procedural public policy is of great importance while substantive public policy does not play any considerable role.[69]

The objective of public policy is to protect the fundamental values of the forum State against results that violate fundamental principles and content on which the legal, economic, social and ethical order of a given national community, which may derive either from the application of foreign law or from the recognition or enforcement of foreign judgments. Normally, the national courts refer to the constitutional principles which are derived from their respective constitutions, and to the general principles of their own procedural systems.

What is considered public policy in a given State is based on its legal, economic, political, social and ethical structure, and may not be part of public policy in a State with a different system, especially in States of different legal systems. In the case law of Lithuania and Portugal there seems to be no significant differences. In this sense, the CJEU determined that Member States are free to establish the content of their respective public policy exceptions,[70] so the courts of the enforcement State will still be entitled to apply their own national concept of public policy.

References

Basedow J (2021) EU private law. Intersentia

Canotilho J, Moreira V (2007) Constituição da República Portuguesa Anotada, vol I, 4.ª edição revista. Coimbra Editora, Coimbra

de Lima Pinheiro L (2015) Direito Internacional Privado, vol I, Introdução e Direito dos Conflitos – Parte Geral. AAFDL Editora, Lisboa

de Lima P, Varela A (1987) Código Civil Anotado, vol I, 4.ª edição. Coimbra Editora, Coimbra

de Magalhães Collaço I (1959) Direito Internacional Privado, vol II. Associação Académica da Faculdade de Direito de Lisboa, Lisboa

Dickinson A, Lein E, James A (2015) The Brussels I Regulation Recast. Oxford University Press, Oxford

Hess B, Pfeiffer T (2011) Interpretation of the Public Policy Exception as Referred to in EU Instruments of Private International and Procedural Law, Study for European Parliament, Directorate general for Internal Policies. Policy Department C: Citizens' Rights and Constitutional Affairs. https://www.europarl.europa.eu/thinktank/en/document.html?reference=IPOL-JURI_ET%282011%29453189

Jokubauskas R (2019) Service of documents in cross-border civil cases. Jurisprudencija 26(1)

[69] Hess and Pfeiffer (2011), p. 152.

[70] Case C-7/98, Dieter Krombach v André Bamberski, 28.03.2000, ECLI:EU:C:2000:164, para 22; Case C-38/98, Régie nationale des usines Renault SA v Maxicar SpA and Orazio Formento, 11.05.2000, ECLI:EU:C:2000:225, para 27; Case C-420/07, Meletis Apostolides v David Charles Orams and Linda Elizabeth Orams, para 56, 28.04.2009, ECLI:EU:C:2009:271.

Jokubauskas R, Kirkutis M, Tamošiūnienė E et al (2020) Užsienio teismų spendimų pripažinimas ir leidimas vykdyti Lietuvos teismų praktikoje. Mykolas Romeris University

Kirkutis M, Jokubauskas R (2020) Viešosios tvarkos pažeidimas kaip užsienio teismų sprendimų nepripažinimo pagrindas Lietuvos teismų praktikoje. Jurisprudencija 27(1):187–201

Kirkutis M, Višinskis V (2021) Problems of recognition of foreign judgments and res judicata in European Union. Socrates 2(20):75–83

Magnus Mankowski M (2016) Brussels I bis Regulation – commentary, vol 1. De Gruyter

Meyer O (ed) (2022) Public policy and private international law. A comparative guide. Edward Elgar

Moura Ramos R (2002) Estudos de Direito Internacional Privado e de Direito Processual Civil Internacional. Coimbra Editora, Coimbra

von Hein J, Kruger T (eds) (2021) Informed choices in cross-border enforcement. Intersentia

Recognition and Enforcement of EU Enforcement Titles in Albania as '3rd Country' and *Vice-Versa*

Flutura Kola Tafaj

Abstract While it can be certainly said that the application of Brussels I bis Regulation guarantees free movement of EU civil and commercial judgments and authentic instruments within the EU Member States, the situation is different with non-EU judgments and authentic instruments, the recognition and/or enforcement of which would be subject to the non-harmonized national laws, that is, those in force in each Member State. This non-unified procedure of EU countries regarding the recognition and enforcement of civil and commercial judgments of third countries makes it possible that the same judgment can be recognized and implemented in one EU Member State and not be recognized in another EU Member State. This chapter is to provide a general overview of the process of recognition and enforcement of EU enforcement titles in Albania, comparing with the same process in the other EU countries for the non-EU judgments, aiming to highlight the problems and ways to improve the situation. Since the Albanian legislation for the recognition and execution of foreign judgments in Albania dates back to 1996, there is a need for an expanded interpretation in accordance with private international law. Therefore, this paper tries not only to identify the problems encountered but also to give an insight into their interpretation.

1 Introduction

Brussels I bis Regulation does not provide a definition of what is meant by 'recognition'. However, referring to the CJEU case law, 'recognition must have the result of conferring on judgments the authority and effectiveness accorded to them in the

F. K. Tafaj (✉)
University of Tirana, Faculty of Law, Tirana, Albania
e-mail: f.kola@kola-associates.com; flutura.tafaj@fdut.edu.al

V. Rijavec et al. (eds.), *Diversity of Enforcement Titles in the EU*, Ius Gentium: Comparative Perspectives on Law and Justice 111,
https://doi.org/10.1007/978-3-031-47108-7_17

State in which they were given'.[1] Based on this definition, the concept of 'recognition' is related to the judgments and not all kinds of enforcement titles. Enforcement titles are a broader concept that might also include (depending on the national legislation) different official acts, authentic instruments, etc. In most legal systems, authentic instruments are enforcement titles that may entitle one to initiate enforcement proceedings leading to compulsory performance. Authentic instruments are an even more diverse group of enforcement titles than judgments.[2]

While it can be certainly said that the application of Brussels I bis Regulation guarantees free movement of EU civil and commercial judgments and authentic instruments within the EU Member States, the situation is different with non-EU judgments and authentic instruments (including Albanian judgments), the recognition and/or enforcement of which would be subject to the non-harmonised national laws. While valid judgments are subject to both a recognition and an enforcement stage, authentic instruments are only subject to an enforcement stage (which is very similar to the enforcement of judgments; the only difference is the limited scope of grounds for refusal of recognition for authentic instruments).[3]

The recognition and enforcement of judgments of third States (ex. Albania) to the EU Member States remain subject to the national rules, that is, those in force in each Member State. Referring to the different national rules on recognition and/or enforcement in the EU Member States, there is not enough initiative for Albanian companies to have business transactions or other commercial activity with EU Member State companies because, in any kind of transaction, the Albanian company should consider how it is going to enforce a judgment in each particular EU Member State and cannot see the European Union as a common forum. This non-unified procedure of EU countries regarding the recognition and enforcement of civil and commercial judgments and authentic instruments of third countries makes it possible that the same judgment can be recognised and implemented in one EU Member State and not be recognised in another EU Member State or it may have different decisions on the same case because of the impossibility of application of *lis pendens*. Addressing all of these issues is the focus of this chapter.

[1]Court of Justice of the European Union (CJEU): C-456/11, Gothaer Allgemeine Versicherung AG, ERGO Versicherung AG, Versicherungskammer Bayern-Versicherungsanstalt des öffentlichen Rechts, Nürnberger Allgemeine Versicherungs-AG, Krones AG v Samskip GmbH, 15.11.2012, ECLI:EU:C:2012:719, para 34: 'As the Court has observed, referring to the Report of 27 September 1968 on the Convention on jurisdiction and the enforcement of judgments in civil and commercial matters, drawn up by Mr Jenard (OJ 1979 C 59, p. 1), recognition must "have the result of conferring on judgments the authority and effectiveness accorded to them in the State in which they were given" (C-145/86, Hoffmann/Krieg, para 10). Accordingly, a foreign judgment that has been recognised under Article 33 of Regulation No. 44/2001 must in principle have the same effects in the State in which recognition is sought as it does in the State of origin (see, to that effect, Hoffmann, para 11)'.

[2]Dymitruk et al. (2021), p. 2.

[3]Dymitruk et al. (2021), p. 13.

2 Recognition and Enforcement of EU Enforcement Titles in Albania, a Non-EU Country

2.1 The Concept of 'Enforcement Title' in the EU Member States

There is no general definition for enforcement titles in the EU Member States, granted by any EU Regulation. Each Member State typically provides a list of acts that are qualified as enforcement titles according to its laws. Exceptionally, the Netherlands provide two different lists for (i) domestic enforcement titles and (ii) foreign enforcement titles.[4] More or less, all Member States provide the same legal acts as enforcement titles. For example, the Austrian Enforcement Order provides that the enforcement titles can be roughly divided into (i) court titles (titles issued by an ordinary civil or criminal court); (ii) administrative titles and (iii) documents not issued by an administrative authority (e.g., enforceable notarial acts).[5] According to Belgian law, the enforceable titles are (i) court decisions, (ii) consent orders, (iii) arbitral awards, (iv) notarial acts and (v) administrative documents, which are enforceable by law. An example of an administrative document that is enforceable would be a title from the tax authority, more specifically, a tax assessment register.[6] According to Article 474 of the Italian Code of Civil Procedure, there are two types of enforcement titles: judicial and extra-judicial. Judicial titles include judgments, measures and deeds issued by a court during or at the end of court proceedings. Extra-judicial titles include debt instruments, public deeds and authenticated private deeds created autonomously by the parties.[7] In Slovenia, enforcement is uniformly governed by the Claim Enforcement and Security Act, and according to Articles 17 and 18 of this Act, an enforcement title is: 1. An enforceable court decision (a judgment; an arbitration award; a decree; a payment or another order from court or arbitration; a court settlement (concluded before a court)); 2. An enforceable notarial deed; and 3. Another enforceable decision or a document which is by law ratified and published international treaty or in the Republic of Slovenia directly applicable legal act of the EU specified as an enforcement title.[8]

[4] Sujecki (2020), pp. 6–7.

[5] Prodinger & Nunner-Krautgasser (2020), p. 7.

[6] Rys (2020), p. 11.

[7] Kaczorowska et al. (2022), p. 8.

[8] Rijavec et al. (2020), p. 6.

2.2 General Background on the Recognition of EU Judgments in Albania

The Republic of Albania does not provide for recognition and enforcement of foreign enforcement titles but only for recognition and enforcement of foreign judgments. In order to be enforceable in Albania, a foreign judgment must be subject to the procedure of recognition. In the absence of bilateral or multilateral agreements on recognition and enforcement of foreign judgments, the provisions of the Code of Civil Procedure (hereinafter 'CCP') are applicable, and the latter provides only for the recognition and enforcement of judgments.

Albania is not an EU Member State, and therefore Brussels I bis Regulation is not applicable. Albania has not ratified the Convention on Choice of Court Agreements (30 June 2005), which is applicable for recognition and enforcement of a judgment given by a court of a Contracting State designated in an exclusive choice of court agreement (Article 8), and therefore this Convention is inapplicable too. Albania has ratified the Hague Convention on the Recognition, and enforcement of foreign judgments in civil and commercial judgments concluded on 1 February 1971 (among four other countries[9]), but Article 21 of this Convention[10] requires concluding a Supplementary Agreement between States in order to make the Convention applicable. Albania has not concluded any Supplementary Agreement for that purpose, and therefore the Convention is not applicable. The Convention on the Recognition and Enforcement of foreign judgments in civil or commercial matters, concluded on 2 July 2019 (hereinafter 'Judgments Convention'), is not yet in force.[11]

With regard to the recognition and enforcement of civil and commercial judgments, Albania has signed bilateral agreements with some of the EU countries,[12] but as a matter of fact, practically, these bilateral agreements are almost ineffective, really obsolete, written in very poor language and in some cases incomprehensible. A literal interpretation of the provisions is not possible.[13] However, even those

---

[9] Cyprus, Kuwait, the Netherlands, Portugal.

[10] 'Decisions rendered in a Contracting State shall not be recognised or enforced in another Contracting State in accordance with the provisions of the preceding Articles unless the two States, being Parties to this Convention, have concluded a Supplementary Agreement to this effect.'

[11] Information retrieved on 14 October 2021 on the official website of the Hague Conference of Private International Law, https://www.hcch.net/en/instruments/conventions/authorities1/?cid=137.

[12] Agreement between the Republic of Albania and the Republic of Bulgaria on Mutual Legal Assistance in Civil Matters, ratified by Law No. 9348, dated 24.02.2005; Convention between the Republic of Albania and the Republic of Greece on Judicial Assistance in Civil and Criminal Matters, signed on 17.5.1993; Romania 'On Mutual Legal Assistance in Criminal and Family Civil Matters', Decree No. 3250, dated 17.04.1961, GZ No. 6/1962, p. 125; Hungary 'On Mutual Legal Assistance in Civil, Criminal and Family Matters', Decree No. 3119, dated 06.06.1960, GZ No. 3/1961, p. 75.

[13] Kola Tafaj (2019).

agreements provide only for recognition and enforcement of judgments. The bilateral agreement between the Republic of Albania and the Republic of Bulgaria on Mutual Legal Assistance in Civil Matters, ratified by Law No. 9348, dated 24.02.2005, exceptionally provides in Article 19 that the term 'judgment' capable of recognition and enforcement means final and interim judgments as well.

Therefore, we might state that the existing Albanian legal framework offers the opportunity to recognise and enforce only foreign civil and commercial judgments and no other enforcement titles issued outside Albania, such as authentic instruments.[14] Exceptionally, though, a court settlement is equivalent to an authentic instrument, according to Brussels I bis Regulation (Article 59 of Brussels I bis Regulation provides that a 'court settlement which is enforceable in the Member State of origin shall be enforced in the other Member States under the same conditions as authentic instruments'). Albanian courts recognise court settlements because, under Albanian procedural law, they are equivalent to any other final judgment, and as will be explained below regarding the meaning of a foreign judgment, for the purpose of recognition, the Albanian courts interpret 'judgment' according to the Albanian legislation and not that of the state of origin of the judgment.

Albanian courts do not apply the principle of reciprocity on the recognition and enforcement of foreign civil and commercial judgments. Whatever the state of origin of the foreign civil or commercial judgment, the Albanian courts only refuse to recognize a foreign judgment on the basis of the provisions of the CCP or any bilateral agreement: they do not take reciprocity into consideration. For example, although Austrian courts do not recognize Albanian judgments, the Albanian courts can freely recognize Austrian judgments if they meet the criteria of Article 394 through 396 of the CCP. Albanian courts also freely recognize German judgments,[15] despite the fact that German courts are doubtful concerning the application of reciprocity.[16]

Under the Albanian CCP, a foreign civil and commercial judgment can be enforced in Albania only after it is recognised by a decision of the Appeals Court,[17] which does not decide on the merits of the case,[18] but only reviews if there are grounds for refusal of recognition. The criteria are *prima face* the same as provided by the other EU countries and are applicable not only for civil and commercial judgments but even for judgments issued on family matters, like divorce, adoption etc. Under Article 394 of the Albanian CCP, a foreign civil or commercial judgment cannot be recognised in Albania when:

[14] Judgment of the Appeal Court of Tirana, No. 47, 17.06.2020, p. 3, para 7.

[15] Judgment of the Appeal Court of Durres, No. 27, 05.12.2005.

[16] See point 3 below.

[17] See Article 395 Albanian Code of Civil Procedure.

[18] See Article 397 Albanian Code of Civil Procedure.

a) The dispute cannot be in the jurisdiction of the court that has rendered the foreign judgment.
b) The defendant in absence was not duly notified about the claim on a regular basis in order to be given the possibility to be defended.
c) The Albanian court has rendered a different judgment on the same dispute, between the same parties, for the same cause.
d) The same dispute, submitted before the foreign judgment became final, is under examination before an Albanian court.
e) The foreign judgment has become final in violation of the legislation of its country of origin.
f) The foreign judgment does not comply with the basic principles of Albanian legislation.

In principle, the process of recognition of a foreign judgment by the Albanian court is not complicated, and the courts lean towards recognising them without unnecessary requirements. The grounds for refusing are mostly related to the notification of the defendant;[19] missing documents that prove that the judgment is final;[20] type of judgment (civil or administrative);[21] and the lack of jurisdiction of the court that has rendered the foreign judgment.[22]

Through the most recent amendments of the CCP, the party that successfully obtains recognition of a foreign judgment in the Court of Appeals, as the competent court to recognise foreign civil and commercial judgments, should not initiate a new process for the enforcement of the judgment. Pursuant to Article 511 (a) of the CCP, enforcement will be ordered by the court that authorised recognition by issuing an enforcement order in the enacting clause of the recognition decision. However, mostly from the practical point of view, the process of recognition by the Albanian courts raises some issues which need to be addressed.

2.3 Issues to Be Considered Related to the Recognition of Foreign Civil and Commercial Judgments in the Republic of Albania

Until a decade ago, there were some uncertainties regarding the court procedures for the recognition of foreign civil and commercial judgments. These uncertainties were generated by the terminology of the Albanian CCP, which literally provides that the court procedure for recognition of a foreign judgment is a procedure that should be heard without the party against whom enforcement is sought. However, the absence

[19] Judgment of the Appeal Court of Tirana, No. 288/15 Reg.; No. 7, 28.01.2019.

[20] Ibid.

[21] Judgment of the Appeal Court of Tirana, No. 30-2018-4659, 27.07.2018.

[22] Judgment of the Appeal Court of Tirana, No. 93, 20.07.2011.

of the party against whom the enforcement is sought makes it impossible for the court to investigate all legal barriers provided in Article 394 of the Albanian CCP (e.g., to prove that the party against whom the judgment was issued is regularly notified of the process). Therefore, the question of summoning of the person against whom the enforcement is sought, was addressed to the High Court of Albania, which in Unifying judgment, No. 6, dated 01.06.2011, unified the position, stating that the *party against whom enforcement is sought must be summoned to appear before the Appeal Court* in accordance with Article 193 of the CCP.[23]

With regard to the recognition and enforcement of foreign civil and commercial judgments, the Albanian courts tend to give the term 'judgment' a very narrow meaning compared to that given by the Brussels Regulation. For the purposes of Brussels I bis Regulation, 'judgment' means any judgment given by a court or tribunal of a Member State, whatever the judgment may be called, including a decree, order, decision or writ of execution, as well as a decision on the determination of costs or expenses by an officer of the court. For the purposes of Chapter III of Brussels I bis Regulation, a 'judgment' includes provisional measures ordered by a court or tribunal which by virtue of Brussels I bis Regulation has jurisdiction as to the substance of the matter. The Albanian court strictly interprets the meaning of the term 'judgment' according to Albanian law, without taking into consideration what other legislation is meant with this legal term, despite the fact that Article 394 (d) CCP provides that a foreign judgment will be recognised in the Republic of Albania if the foreign judgment has become final in violation of the legislation of its country of origin. The Tirana Appeal Court has refused to recognise a judgment of the Court of Rome of the Republic of Italy, reasoning, among other things, that the above judgment is more of an executive order than a judgment, and therefore, does not constitute a judgment as per the meaning of 'judgment' given in Article 306–319 of the Albanian CCP.[24]

Albanian courts do not recognise the foreign judgments on provisional measures[25] reasoning that according to Albanian law, they are not final judgments. The Tirana Court of Appeals has refused the recognition of a foreign judgment for provisional measures, reasoning that 'it has not become final according to the basic principles of Albanian legislation, provided in Article 394 (dh) CCP'.[26] The court could have reached the same conclusion, but the analysis had to be done on the basis of Article 394 (d) and not (dh), analysing whether or not the judgment of

[23] Article 193 CCP: 'Where the Court considers that the judicial proceedings should take place in the presence of a third party, which finds that it has interests in the case, the court shall call it as long as the order for setting the judicial hearing has not been issued, under Article 158/c of this Code. The secretary notifies him by writ.'

[24] Judgment of the Appeal Court of Tirana, No. 58, 11.04.2019, p. 14.

[25] Exceptionally, the Agreement between the Republic of Albania and the Republic of Bulgaria on Mutual Legal Assistance in Civil Matters, provides in Article 19 that the term 'judgment' capable of recognition and enforcement implies final and interim judgments as well.

[26] Judgment of the Appeal Court of Tirana, No. 34, 01.03.2012.

the court of the foreign state was final according to the legislation of the country of its origin and not according to Albanian legislation.

Even in decisions with a wider interpretation, the reference in the Albanian legislation is obvious. For example, regarding the request of an Italian company for the recognition of an Electronic Obligation Order, the Court of Appeals of Tirana accepted the request for the recognition of the judgment, reasoning that 'it is true that the CCP of the Republic of Albania does not recognise the procedure for issuing the Electronic Obligation Order, as it occurs in the EU countries, and as it is foreseen to be included in our Code, as a measure for effective trials, but the decision that resulted in the conclusion of this procedure has the character of a court judgment for the obligation of the debtor party to perform payment, as the fulfilment of the contractual obligation'.[27] In the author's opinion, for the purpose of interpreting the 'judgment', the second part of the above paragraph would be sufficient, without considering whether Albanian law regards the Order as a judgment or not, because Article 394 (d) of the CCP requires that the foreign judgment has become final according to its legislation. In such a case, if the court is satisfied that the judgment (in the form of an order, decision, judgment, etc.) has become final according to the legislation of the country of origin, then the impediment provided in Article 394 / (d) of the CCP would be surmounted.

Currently, the key point regarding the recognition of a judgment consists in the interpretation given by the Albanian courts to the legal obstacle for recognition provided in Article 394 (dh) CCP that provides: 'A foreign civil or commercial judgment cannot be recognised in Albania when ... (dh) the foreign judgment does not comply with the basic principles of the Albanian legislation'.

Unlike other EU countries[28] and Brussels I bis Regulation, the CCP does not provide as a barrier to the recognition of a foreign judgment, the situation when it is 'contrary to the public order', but instead envisages as a barrier the case when the foreign judgment 'does not comply with the basic principles of Albanian legislation'. This manner of formulating Article 394 (dh) of the CCP has generated serious issues regarding the recognition of foreign civil and commercial judgments in Albania. In judicial practice, it is noticed that, when foreign judgments involve concepts (or procedural aspects) of law that are unknown in the Albanian system, or when the Albanian system provides otherwise, the judgments risk not being recognised because the Albanian court reasons that under Article 394 (dh) of the ACPC, the judgment does not comply with the basic principles of the Albanian legislation. For example, the Appeal Court of Tirana refused to recognise a default judgment issued by a Macedonian court, reasoning (among other things) that this judgment does not comply with the basic principles of the Albanian legislation because the Albanian legislation does not provide for a default judgment.[29] In a

[27] Judgment of the Appeal Court of Tirana, No. 40, 23.02.2017.

[28] Article 64 of Italian Law 218/95, 31 May 1995; Spanish Law 29/2015, July 30, Of International Legal Cooperation In Civil Matters, BOE-A-2015-8564.

[29] Judgment of District Court of Tirana, No. 7, 28.01.2019.

recent case, an interested party had applied for the recognition of an adoption judgment (of an adult) handed down by an Italian court. The Vlora Court of Appeals considered that the recognition of such a judgment would be in contradiction with the Albanian legislation, which provides that adoption is allowed only for minors. For this reason, the Vlora Court of Appeals suspended the recognition process and referred the case to the Constitutional Court requesting the repeal of the Family Code norm that allows adoption only for minors. The Constitutional Court did not admit the case to a plenary session because the Court of Appeals had improperly initiated the incidental review.[30] Also, the Tirana Appeal Court repeatedly refused to recognise a foreign judgment on changing the surname of a minor because (i) this is contrary to Article 52 of the Albanian Family Code, which provides that: 'A child shall have the common surname of the parents. When the parents have different surnames, all children shall have the same surname, as specified by the agreement of the parents. If an agreement cannot be reached, the children shall have the surname of the father'. And (ii) Article 57/1(3) of Law, No. 1012, dated 11.5.2009 'On civil status', (amended) provides that: 'A request to change the name or surname should be made only once and only for reasons of inadequacy', and the foreign court had not given an explanation in that regard.[31]

In the author's opinion, the clause 'basic principle of the legislation' should be interpreted the same way as 'public legal order'. In this respect, the CJEU approach should be taken into consideration. In the case of Dieter Krombach and André Bamberski, CJEU reasoned that while it is not for the Court (CJEU) to define the content of the public policy of a Contracting State, it is nonetheless required to review the limits within which the courts of a Contracting State may have recourse to that concept for the purpose of refusing recognition to a judgment emanating from a court in another Contracting State. Recourse to the public-policy clause can be envisaged only where the recognition or enforcement of the judgment delivered in another Contracting State would be at variance to an unacceptable degree with the legal order of the State in which enforcement is sought, inasmuch as it infringes a fundamental principle. In order for the prohibition of any review of the foreign judgment as to its substance to be observed, the infringement would have to constitute a manifest breach of the rule of law regarded as essential in the legal order of the State in which enforcement is sought or of a right recognised as being fundamental within that legal order. Recourse to the public-policy clause must be regarded as being possible in exceptional cases where the guarantees laid down in the legislation of the State of origin and in the Convention itself have been insufficient to protect the defendant from a manifest breach of his right to defend himself

[30] Judgment of the Constitutional Court of Albania, No. 112, 07.10.2021.

[31] Judgment of the Appeal Court of Tirana, No. 90, 03.06.2019, p. 3; Judgment of the Appeal Court of Tirana, No. 97, 13.06.2019, p. 3.

before the court of origin, as recognised by the European Convention on Human Rights.[32]

In another case, regarding the recognition of a foreign judgment according to the Convention of 27 September 1968 on Jurisdiction and the Enforcement of Judgments in Civil and Commercial Matters, the CJEU reasoned that the court of the State in which enforcement is sought cannot refuse the recognition of a judgment emanating from another Contracting State solely on the ground that it considers that national or Community law was misapplied in that decision. On the contrary, it should be considered whether, in such cases, the system of legal remedies in each Contracting State, together with the preliminary ruling procedure provided for in Article 177 of the Treaty (now Article 267 TFEU), affords a sufficient guarantee to individuals.[33]

In the spirit of Brussels I bis Regulation (former Convention of 27 September 1968 on Jurisdiction and the Enforcement of Judgments in Civil and Commercial Matters) and of the jurisprudence of the CJEU regarding the limits of interpretation of 'public policy', the author would strongly suggest that the Albanian courts should apply Article 394 (dh) CCP in very exceptional cases when the infringement would have to constitute a manifest breach of a rule of law regarded as fundamental within that legal order.

Another controversial norm of the Albanian CCP regarding the recognition of foreign civil and commercial judgments is Article 394 (ç), according to which 'a foreign judgment will not be recognised in the Republic of Albania if a lawsuit that is filed before the foreign judgment has become final is being adjudicated by an Albanian court'. This provision makes it possible that one of the parties in the process in any EU court, feeling that it is losing a case in that court, will hurry to file the same case before Albanian courts prior to the foreign court issuing the final judgment. In this scenario, the foreign judgment risks failing to be recognised in Albania under Article 394 (ç) of the Albanian CCP. The author sees this provision, not as the legislator's intention, but as a wrong transposition of the analogous norm in the Italian Code of Civil Procedure, from which most of the Albanian CCP norms have been transposed. This provision would realise its aim of avoiding parallel proceedings (*lis pendens*) if were to provide, in a similar way to Article 64 of Italian Law 218/95, a rule specific to a foreign judgment issued by a Court of a country not governed by Regulation 1215/2012 or the Lugano Convention. According to Article 64 of that law, 'A foreign judgment shall be recognised in Italy when the following conditions are met: ... (f) No proceeding between the same parties for the same matter was started before an Italian court prior to the commencement of the foreign proceeding'. This provision would permit the proper implementation of international

[32]Case C-7/98, Dieter Krombach v André Bamberski, 28.03.2000, ECLI:EU:C:2000:164, paras 22–23; 37; 44–45; Case C-38/98, Régie nationale des usines Renault SA v Maxicar SpA and Orazio Formento, 11.05.2000, ECLI:EU:C:2000:225, paras 27–28.

[33]Case C-38/98, Régie nationale des usines Renault SA v Maxicar SpA and Orazio Formento, 11.05.2000, ECLI:EU:C:2000:225, para 33.

lis pendens and would avoid the possibility of abuse as mentioned above. However, with the recent amendments of the Albanian CCP through law 38/2017, the legislator has taken a big step in avoiding this possibility of misapplication. The new Article 38 (1) of the CCP provides:

> 1. When the same claim, between the same parties, with the same cause and subject of the lawsuit is being considered simultaneously by a court of a foreign country and the Albanian court, the latter may suspend the proceedings on this dispute when:
>
> The lawsuit was filed before in time in the court of a foreign country;
>
> The decision of the court of the foreign country can be recognised and/or enforced in the Republic of Albania;
>
> The Albanian court is satisfied that the suspension is necessary for the proper administration of justice.

Having this new provision, the interested party may request the suspension of the case that started abusively before the Albanian courts (while the case was being heard in the court of the foreign state), and the Albanian court may, based on Article 38 (1) of the CCP, suspend the proceeding. When the foreign judgment becomes final, the Albanian court terminates the proceeding at the request of the interested party. This new provision minimises the risk of misapplication of Article 394 (ç), but does not completely avoid the risk, because Article 38 of the Albanian CCP does not provide *lis pendens stricto sensu* (as per Article 28 of Brussel I bis Regulation), and does not provide the same for related actions as provided by Article 29 of Brussel I bis Regulation. Article 38 of the ACCP is very similar to Article 33 of the said Regulation, which provides a conditional international *lis pendens*, according to which the court may or may not suspend the proceeding. Therefore, if the Albanian courts do not suspend the proceeding, the barrier provided by article 394 (ç) can be used by the interested party to oppose the recognition of the foreign judgment.

With regard to the recognition of the judgments of EU Member States in Albania, the Albanian Private International Law should also be taken into consideration. Article 72 of this Law is very similar to Article 24 of Brussels I bis Regulation and stipulates the claims for which the Albanian court has exclusive jurisdiction. Therefore, in the case of an application for the recognition of a foreign judgment on a dispute falling within Article 72 of the Private International Law, the Albanian courts will not recognise this judgment because according to Article 394 (a) 'the judgment of a court of a foreign state does not become effective in Albania when, in conformity with the provisions in effect in the Republic of Albania, the dispute cannot fall within the competence (jurisdiction) of the court which has issued the judgment'.

3 Recognition and Enforcement of Albanian Enforcement Titles in EU Member States

The recognition and enforcement of the judgments of third States (e.g., Albania) in EU Member States remain subject to the national rules, that is, those in force in each Member State. Therefore, in the best-case scenario, the recognition and enforcement of Albanian judgments are subject to different and unpredictable rules from state to state, and, in the worst one, some states may not provide for the recognition and/or enforcement of Albanian civil and commercial judgments at all. In order to illustrate this inconsistency, some examples are provided.

In Germany, with regard to the recognition of civil and commercial non-EU judgments the following conventions may be applicable: (i) the Lugano Convention 2007 on Jurisdiction and the recognition and enforcement of judgments in civil and commercial matters between the European Community, Switzerland, Norway, Iceland and Denmark; (ii) the Hague Convention 2005 on choice of court agreements and (iii) numerous bilateral treaties on mutual recognition and enforcement of foreign judgments with several states are applicable. Albania is not a Contracting State of any of the above Conventions joined by Germany and has not concluded any bilateral treaty with Germany. Therefore, the recognition and enforcement of Albanian civil and commercial judgments in Germany will take place pursuant to sec. 328, 722 and 723 of the German Code of Civil Procedure ('ZPO'). One of the criteria for the recognition of a foreign judgment, according to section 328, is reciprocity.[34] There is no clear interpretation regarding the application of this principle by the German courts. Generally speaking, this requirement means that the recognition and enforcement of German judgments in the foreign country of origin must not be substantially more difficult than the recognition in Germany of a judgment from the foreign state. Whether this requirement is fulfilled must be determined on a country-by-country basis.[35] According to Albanian law, a German civil and commercial judgment will be recognised as any other foreign civil and commercial judgment under the provision of the CCP for the recognition and enforcement of foreign judgments, and there is no special requirement like reciprocity. As a matter of fact, the Albanian courts have recognised at least one German judgment.[36] The interested party was the company Gerling-Konzern Allgemeine Versicherungs-Aktiengesellschaft. Before the Durres Court of Appeal, this company requested the recognition of a final judgment of the Bamberg Regional Court of Germany dated 06.03.2003 and 16.10.2003 in the civil case Gerling-Konzern Allgemeine Versicherungs Aktiengesellschaft vs. Dyrrahsped Transport Spedition, Custom and Shipping Agency. The Durres Court of Appeal recognised the German judgment on

[34] This rule does not contravene the judgment is being recognised if the judgment concerns a non-pecuniary claim and if, according to the laws of Germany, no place of jurisdiction was established in Germany.

[35] Langen et al. (2018).

[36] Judgment of the Appeal Court of Durres, No. 27, 05.12.2005.

the basis of the provisions of the CCP (Articles 394–398) without taking into consideration *de facto* reciprocity.[37] According to the author's research of papers, books and discussions with a German professor of international private law,[38] there is no case law published in Germany (neither *pro* nor *contra* reciprocity between Germany and Albania). Most commentaries on the Civil Procedure Code, in the context of § 328 ZPO, contain a list of countries stating whether reciprocity exists or not. With regard to Albania, the uniform answer is in the negative, although some commentaries refer to a recent publication of Uka/Wietzorek in the journal IPRax 2011, mentioning that this may be doubtful.[39]

In Austria, the situation regarding the recognition and enforcement of the Albanian judgments is even worse. A foreign civil or commercial judgment issued by a Court of a country not governed by Regulation EU 1215/2012, the Lugano Convention or any bilateral agreement for that purpose (as in the case of Albanian judgments), will be recognised under the Austrian Code of Civil Procedure, the Austrian Jurisdiction Act and the Austrian Enforcement Act (AEA). Austrian case law is not binding but is strongly taken into consideration by the courts.[40] One of the basic mandatory requirements for the declaration of enforceability under Austrian law (Article 79) is reciprocity which should have been ensured between the country of origin and Austria either by bilateral or multilateral treaties or other regulations (e.g., regulations on reciprocity). In the case of Austria, unlike Germany, the legal notion of reciprocity must be stipulated either in an international treaty or in an Austrian regulation.[41] Albania has not signed any bilateral or multilateral agreements with Austria concerning the recognition and enforcement of foreign civil and commercial judgments, and therefore, Albanian judgments cannot be recognised and/or enforced in Austria.[42]

In Italy, according to Article 64 of Italian Law 218/95, a foreign judgment issued by a court of a country not governed by Regulation EU 44/2011 or the Lugano Convention is recognised in Italy when the following conditions are met:

a) The foreign Court had jurisdiction to issue the judgment, according to Italian rules on jurisdiction.

---

[37] Dyrrahsped Transport Spedition, Custom and Shipping Agency AL-Durres filed an appeal in the High Court against this decision only on procedural grounds related to the issue of whether this company should be summoned by the Durres Court of Appeal as a third party or not. The High Court, with its decision of 13.03.2008, dismissed the case on the ground that the Dyrrahsped Transport Spedition, Custom and Shipping Agency company AL-Durrës withdrew its appeal.

[38] Christa Jessel-Holst, Professor of Private International Law at the Max Planck Institute in Hamburg, Germany.

[39] Kola Tafaj (2019).

[40] Kitzberger and Weber (2021), p. 5, point 3.

[41] Ibid., p. 6, point 11.

[42] Kola Tafaj (2019).

b) The document instituting the proceedings was validly served on the other party, pursuant to the rules in force in the foreign jurisdiction, and there is no violation of the right of the party to defend its case.
c) The parties have appeared in the proceeding according to the laws of the foreign jurisdiction, or the failure to appear in court was declared by the court in accordance with its rules.
d) The judgment is *res judicata* according to the law of the country where the decision was issued.
e) There is no Italian judgment with the effect of *res judicata* relating to the same matter.
f) No proceeding between the same parties for the same matter was started before an Italian court prior to the commencement of the foreign proceeding.
g) The foreign judgment is not contrary to public order.

From the above, we can notice that the recognition and enforcement of Albanian judgments in the EU countries are unpredictable for the interested party because it will depend on the legal framework of each country. Consequently, it may result that the same judgment will be recognised in a certain country and not be recognised in another EU country, or its recognition may be rejected in different countries, but for different reasons. The following case law demonstrates the inconsistency and unpredictability of the recognition and/or enforcement of Albanian commercial and civil judgments abroad.

An Albanian judgment rendered in the case AlbaniaBEG Ambient Sh.p.k. v Enel S.p.A. was issued by the Tirana District Court in 2009, affirmed by the Tirana Court of Appeals in 2010, and in 2011 the High Court of Albania declined to entertain a further appeal. The winning party, AlbaniaBEG Ambient Sh.p.k (hereinafter 'ABA'), requested the recognition of this judgment in at least five states: New York in the United States;[43] the Netherlands, France, Ireland and Luxembourg. In these five states, ABA had to deal with five different legal frameworks concerning the recognition and enforcement of a foreign judgment, and the reasoning of the outcome was different from state to state. We are presenting the outcome in three of the European countries.

In 2016 ABA submitted a motion for the recognition and enforcement of the Albanian judgment against ENEL in Ireland. On 13 September 2018, the Irish Court of Appeal upheld the decision of the High Court in *Albaniabeg Ambient Shpk v Enel SpA and Enelpower SpA*, confirming that jurisdiction for the purposes of proceedings seeking to enforce a foreign judgment should not be exercised in favour of a plaintiff unless they can show it is likely that some practical benefit will accrue to them. To enforce a foreign judgment under Order 11, a plaintiff must generally establish: (1) that it has a good arguable case; (ii) that it is likely to obtain a practical benefit from the proceedings and (iii) that it satisfies the comparative cost and

[43] United States District Court: Albaniabeg Ambient Sh.p.k. v. Enel S.p.A., 169 F. Supp. 3d 523 (S.D.N.Y. 2016)

convenience requirements of Order 11, Rule 2.[44] In conclusion, the Irish court did not recognise the Albanian judgment because the plaintiff could not demonstrate that any solid or practical benefit would ensue if the judgment were to be recognised and enforced in Ireland.

In 2014, ABA submitted a motion to seek the recognition of the Albanian judgment in the Netherlands. By the judgment served on 29 June 2016, the Amsterdam District Court recognised the Albanian judgment in the Netherlands. Enel filed a notice of appeal against the Judgment on 29 June 2016. On 17 July 2018, the Amsterdam Court of Appeal ruled that the Albanian court judgment was substantively arbitrary and manifestly unreasonable in the approach that it took to calculation of damages and the lack of reasons for that approach and therefore could not be recognised in the Netherlands, as this would violate Dutch public order.[45] Due to a violation of public order in the Netherlands, the Albanian judgment could not be recognised on the basis of Article 431 (2) DCCP.

In 2012, ABA submitted a motion to recognise the same judgment in France in front of the Tribunal de Grande Instance in Paris. Enel challenged the suit. On 29 January 2018, the Tribunal de Grande Instance refused to recognise the Albanian judgment in France for lack of the requirements under French law for the purposes of granting exequatur. Among other issues, the Tribunal de Grande Instance ruled that: (i) the Albanian ruling conflicted with an existing decision, in this case, the arbitration ruling of 2002 and that (ii) the fact that ABA sought to obtain in Albania what it was not able to obtain in the Italian arbitration proceeding, resubmitting the same claim through ABA, represented fraud.[46] ABA appealed the ruling.[47]

Apart from the unpredictability and inconsistency in the recognition of Albanian judgments in EU countries, another issue brought up by the current EU legal framework relating to the recognition of non-EU judgments is the possibility of having two different judgments for the same case. This is because, if a lawsuit is filed initially in Albania, and the same, or another related one, is filed later in Austria, the Austrian court will not be able to suspend its proceedings because of those initiated previously in Albania in accordance with Articles 33 or 34 of Brussels I bis Regulation (conditional *lis pendens* with a third country), because either way, it will not meet one of the criteria that is: 'It is expected that the court of the third State will give a judgment capable of recognition and, where applicable, of enforcement in that Member State'. The impossibility of fulfilling this condition makes it possible for both Albanian and Austrian courts to conduct the same proceedings in parallel and potentially come up with two different judgments. The situation would be the

[44] See: Murphy-O'Connor and Carey (2018), p. 271.

[45] Gerechtshof Amsterdam, 200.196.175/01 en 200.201.407/01, 17.07.2018, ECLI:NL:GHAMS:2018:3008. See also Meerdink (2019). Upheld on appeal to the Hoge Raad, 20/00819, 16.07.2021, ECLI:NL:HR:2021:1170.

[46] TGI Paris, 29 janvier 2018, case No. 12/06059.

[47] See Enel Annual Report (2018), p. 351 https://www.enel.com/content/dam/enel-com/documenti/investitori/informazioni-finanziarie/2018/annuali/en/annual-report_2018.pdf.

same in the case of *res judicata*. Even when an Albanian judgment become *res judicata* in the Republic of Albania, nothing would prevent the interested party from filing the same lawsuit in Austria because the judgment would not be recognised there.

4 Recommendations

The unification of the legal frameworks for the recognition and enforcement of a non-EU judgment in the EU (and not only) is a guarantee and security for Albanian investors, as is the New York Convention 1958 for arbitral awards, because they know from the beginning what to expect in any possible future unpleasant case, without the need to go through the provisions of each national law where they want to recognise and enforce their judgments.

Apart from the accession of Albania to the EU, which will solve the issue within EU Member States but does not seem to be imminent, ratification of the Judgments Convention by Albania and the EU (without reservation) would definitely avoid the requirement of reciprocity (either *de facto* or *de jure*) and would unify the requirements for the recognition and/or enforcement of an Albanian judgment abroad and *vice-versa*. Under the Judgments Convention, Albanian judgments will be recognised and enforced (or refused to be recognised and enforced) in every future Contracting State under the same grounds and in every Contracting State. In this way, the recognition and enforcement of Albanian judgments (and any third country judgment) abroad will be predictable and consistent.

The ratification of the Hague Convention on Choice of Courts Agreements, which entered into force on 1 October 2015 in 28 States (Mexico and all Members of the European Union, except Denmark), would also partially help. This Convention would unify and simplify the recognition and enforcement of foreign judgments in the case of exclusive choice of court clauses. Therefore, non-EU countries, including Albania, should start considering becoming a party to such Conventions.

Last but not least, the abolition of exequatur within the EU Member States was based on the principle of mutual trust between the Member States and less time-consuming and costly proceedings. The question arises: Based on this principle, is it time to consider that not only 'A judgment given in a Member State which is enforceable in that Member State shall be enforceable in the other Member State without any declaration of enforceability required', but even: 'A judgment which is enforceable in that Member State shall be enforceable in the other Member State without any declaration of enforceability required'. For example, if one of the EU Member States court (German court) recognises/enforces an Albanian judgment according to its national law (in the absence of a common rule set/Convention), shall that judgment be later on enforceable in any other EU Member State?

References

Dymitruk M, Gołaczyński J, Kaczorowska M et al (2021) Difference between the recognition and enforcement of authentic instrument and the recognition and enforcement of judgment. LeXonomica 13(1):1–16

Enel Annual Report (2018). https://www.enel.com/content/dam/enel-com/documenti/investitori/informazioni-finanziarie/2018/annuali/en/annual-report_2018.pdf

Kaczorowska M, Voinich A, Previatello M (2022) National Report for Italy. JUST-AG-2018/JUST-JCOO-AG-2018

Kitzberger K, Weber S (2021) Austria. In: Browne O, Watret T, Blears Latham G (eds) Enforcement of foreign judgments 2022. Law Business Research Ltd. https://weber.co.at/wp-content/uploads/2021/11/2022_enforcement_of_foreign_judgements_austria.pdf

Kola Tafaj F (2019) The benefit of Albania by Multilateralism of Convention on the Recognition and Enforcement of Foreign Judgments in Civil and Commercial Matters ("Judgment Convention"). In: Proceeding of 16th Annual Regional PIL Conference: 'Matrimonial and registered partnership property regimes in EU Private International Law/HCCH Judgments Convention', Tirana: Onufri, 2019

Langen M, Klein A, Stier D (2018) Litigation: enforcement of foreign judgments in Germany. White&Case LPP. https://www.lexology.com/library/detail.aspx?g=f476bc5a-60f4-4f1a-9aad-22a5e11fb708

Meerdink E (2019) Netherlands. In: Taylor D (ed) The Dispute Resolution Review, 11th edn. Law Business Research Ltd, Great Britain, pp 342–361

Murphy-O'Connor J, Carey G (2018) Enforcement of Foreign Judgments in Ireland: Irish Court of Appeal Declines Jurisdiction to Recognise and Enforce a Non-EU/EFTA Judgment where no Apparent Practical Benefit would Accrue to the Appellant. International Corporate Rescue 15 (5):270–273. https://www.matheson.com/docs/default-source/practice-area-attachments/corporate-restructuring-and-insolvency/enforcement_of_foreign_judgments_in_ireland_-_irish_court_of_appeal_update.pdf?sfvrsn=f7f82d9a_2

Prodinger L, Nunner-Krautgasser B (2020) National Report for Austria. JUST-AG-2018/JUST-JCOO-AG-2018

Rijavec V, Baghrizabehi D, Drnovšek K et al (2020) National Report for Slovenia. JUST-AG-2018/JUST-JCOO-AG-2018

Rys M (2020) National Report for Belgium. Project EU-En4s — JUST-AG-2018/JUST-JCOO-AG-2018

Sujecki B (2020) National Report for the Netherlands. Project EU-En4s — JUST-AG-2018/JUST-JCOO-AG-2018